# The Pacific
# Northwest

## An Interpretive History

### Revised and Enlarged Edition

CARLOS ARNALDO SCHWANTES

UNIVERSITY OF NEBRASKA PRESS
LINCOLN AND LONDON

⊖ The paper in this book meets the minimum
requirements of American National Standard for
Information Sciences—Permanence of Paper for
Printed Library Materials, ANSI Z39.48-1984.

Library of Congress Cataloging-in-Publication Data
Schwantes, Carlos A., 1945–
The Pacific Northwest: an interpretive history /
Carlos Arnaldo Schwantes. – Rev. and enl. ed.
p.   cm.
Includes bibliographical references (p.    ) and index.
ISBN 0-8032-4225-5 (alk. paper). –
ISBN 0-8032-9228-7 (pbk.: alk. paper)
1. Northwest, Pacific–History.   I. Title.
F851.S34   1996
979.5–dc20   95-31650   CIP

The preparation of this book was funded by the
John Calhoun Smith Memorial Fund of the
University of Idaho and sponsored by the Institute
for Pacific Northwest Studies.

*Dedicated*
*to the memory of*
THOMAS M. BOWEN
(1952–1993)

Our region is a familiar place, where we know, to some extent, the lay of the land, the traits of the people and their resources, needs, and problems. —V. B. STANBERY quoted in Howard W. Odum and Harry Estill Moore, *American Regionalism* (1938)

There was a time not long ago when the Pacific Northwest might have qualified as one of the country's best kept secrets. Life in this far corner of the United States was an unpublicized pleasure that residents jealously guarded and people elsewhere usually associated with endless rain. But the weather may be one of the few things that has stayed the same. Change is coming to the coastal states of Washington, Oregon and neighboring Idaho, and it is not entirely welcome.—WILLIAM V. THOMAS in *American Regionalism: Our Economic, Cultural and Political Makeup* (1980)

Sixteen miles out of Seattle the eastward march of the city was stopped in its tracks by the foothills of the Cascades. Beyond Issaquah the black cliffs of the forest began, and the social character of the road abruptly changed, as the last of the VW's melted into the last of the white condo blocks. Until now I'd been in the fast lane; no longer. Mud-slathered pickups with jumbo tires charged past the Dodge wearing angry slogans on their tailgates: JOBS BEFORE OWLS. SUPPORT THE TIMBER INDUSTRY. SAVE A LOGGER—SHOOT AN OWL. Behind the glass of a cab window, a Zippo lighter flashed in the gloaming.—JONATHAN RABAN in "The Next Last Frontier," *Harper's* (August 1993)

# Contents

# Contents

Contents

# Illustrations

# Preface to the Revised Edition

For me the study of Pacific Northwest history has become an intensely personal experience, especially so during the five years since completing the first edition of this book. I wanted to examine personally the ruts of the Oregon Trail in eastern Wyoming or rendezvous with memories of Captain George Vancouver as he charted some little-known cove in Puget Sound or return to a remote canyon in northern Idaho where striking metal miners battled mine-owners a century ago. I cannot go back *in time*, but I can seek inspiration by going to *a place* of historical significance. This grass-roots approach to history is all a bit crazy, perhaps, but it is certainly worth the effort if somehow I can translate these personal encounters into a new and better edition of *The Pacific Northwest: An Interpretive History*.

Today I would gladly describe myself as a field historian, one who pursues his craft with equal facility in the archives or while tramping through the woods with a camera and notebook. I think I understand better now why a high school vocational aptitude test predicted a career for me in forestry. Certainly I felt completely at ease in the woods on an August morning in 1992 when with camera in hand I waited for dawn to backlight the crest of the Bitterroot divide between Idaho and Montana. Accompanying me to the ridge top, although most of them were still asleep in their tents, were two dozen students from the University of Idaho taking a week to retrace the footsteps of early explorers in the mountains above the Lochsa and Clearwater rivers. Perhaps as children some of these students had been intrigued by the brown and white signs posted along the federal highway below to mark the route of Lewis and Clark; perhaps some had been hooked by tales of discovery and exploration in the mandatory fourth grade class in Idaho history. In much the same way I hoped to use the study of Lewis and Clark to interest them in new approaches to the larger history of the Pacific Northwest.

In the second edition of *The Pacific Northwest* I seek to take readers on similar journeys of discovery. To that end I have rewritten and updated many sections of the original book as well as added several new chapters on topics previously mentioned only briefly or not at all. I have asked new questions of the historical record and wrestled again with several old ones that defy simple explanations. Numerous titles have been added to the Suggestions for Further Reading.

I confess that I myself did not grow up studying Pacific Northwest history. Most of what I recall from grade school history classes back in Indiana are the tales of pioneers hacking homesteads out of the woods and building corduroy roads across a marshy landscape. In its own way it was fascinating history. My introduction to Pacific Northwest history came only much later, initially from the Lewis and Clark interpretive signs posted along the roads of Montana and Idaho as I drove west in 1969 from Ann Arbor, Michigan, to my new home near Walla Walla, Washington. That historic community was an excellent place to initiate an ongoing love affair with the region's past.

Twenty-five years later, and after having lived also in Eugene, Seattle, Victoria, and now Moscow, Idaho, I find myself still immersed in study of the region's past; but also I am increasingly drawn to pondering its future in terms of the profound economic and social changes that have recently overtaken the Pacific Northwest or will almost certainly do so in the near future. Thus the new edition of *The Pacific Northwest* seeks to look both ways, past and future, as it appraises life in the Far Corner of North America.

In addition to the people who helped me earlier, I wish to thank several individuals who contributed to this new edition: William S. Greever, University of Idaho; Julie Roy Jeffrey, Goucher College; Thomas McClintock, Oregon State University; Larry J. Weathers, Pacific County Historical Society and Museum, South Bend; Barbara Johns, Tacoma Art Museum; Payton Smith, Seattle attorney; Carol Zabilski, *Pacific Northwest Quarterly*; Rocky Barker, Idaho Falls *Post-Register* and one of the most astute environmental reporters of the entire region; Kenton Bird, graduate student in American Studies at Washington State University; and Rob McIntyre, graduate student in music at the University of Idaho, and the students in my Pacific Northwest history classes. I am especially indebted to former president Elisabeth

Zinser of the University of Idaho for her continuing support and encouragement, to president and former provost Thomas O. Bell, and Dean Kurt O. Olsson.

I dedicated the first edition of *The Pacific Northwest* to Professor Robert E. Burke of the University of Washington, who continues to be a valued friend and mentor. I want to dedicate the second edition to another good friend, Tom Bowen, an orthopedic surgeon in my hometown of Moscow who was killed only a week before I completed the revised manuscript in December 1993. A master of high-tech medicine, Tom was felled a day after his forty-first birthday by that most primitive of foes, a lodge pole pine that had long stood unnoticed beside the road that wound down to his Whitewater Ranch on Idaho's Salmon River, but which in a moment was toppled by a gust of wind or the weight of fresh-fallen snow onto the unsuspecting passer-by. I know that Tom passionately loved the beautiful but lonely and unforgiving backcountry of central Idaho, even as he loved his family: his wife Patti, my former student, and their children Joe, Ben, Alyssa, Kelsey, David, and Sarah. Maybe there was some larger meaning in this freak accident, but I cannot see it. It was a tragedy pure and simple, but one mitigated by hope and happy memories. A happy memory never wears out from frequent use.

# Preface to the First Edition

This book presents a short interpretive history of the Pacific Northwest. It seeks main themes, paints with broad strokes, and engages in what one of my colleagues calls responsible reductionism. Capsule biographies of representative figures introduce each of the five parts and are intended to capture a sense of the past.

Some readers may wonder whether the hinterland theme introduced in chapter 1 is appropriate to describe the Pacific Northwest. For geographers a hinterland is an area that lies behind a seaport or seaboard and supplies the bulk of its exports. *Hinterland* as used in this book has a broader though still legitimate meaning: it describes a region that until the Second World War was remote from the continent's main centers of economic and political power and until recent times was often tributary to more developed cities and regions.

Readers may also question why I did not spend more time on one topic or another or why I profiled Tom McCall, for instance, instead of some other figure to introduce the modern Pacific Northwest. The choice of what material to emphasize represents an author's value judgment tempered by suggestions from colleagues and by the availability of previously published histories.

Alas, for the Pacific Northwest, much still remains to be written about events after the Second World War and, indeed, about many other aspects of the region's history. A number of these gaps result from what can be labeled the heroic nature–heroic men approach to Pacific Northwest history. Its persistent theme is that because nature assumed heroic proportions in the far Northwest, heroic men were needed to tame or subdue it. A classic photographic image is that of loggers reposing full-length in an undercut they have just made in a giant Douglas fir or cedar. Perhaps because such images are so common, both popular and scholarly histories tend to emphasize the "heroic" accomplishments of outstanding men—or sometimes a group of men—but only occasionally those of women.

Typically, the women who find their way into the region's history texts are those who individually or collectively fit the heroic image—pioneer women of the Oregon Trail or Rosie the Riveter and her sisters in the region's war industries. Individual women who may fit the heroic mold include Sacagawea and the Oregon suffragist Abigail Scott Duniway.

Numerous other classes of Northwest women—like farmers' and miners' wives—generally have not made it into prominent regional histories. Even now a great deal remains to be written about them. Their important contributions to the household economy have typically been eclipsed by the image of their men driving thirty-mule powered combines over the rolling wheat fields of eastern Washington or blasting for silver ore far below the surface of Idaho's panhandle.[1]

The heroic nature–heroic men approach has also had the effect of stunting research and writing on the region in the twentieth century, particularly after 1920. In the minds of many people, Pacific Northwest history after the First World War is pale and unappealing compared with the heroic phase that centers on subduing wild and unpredictable nature. Whether conscious of that tendency or not, scholars and publishers tend to reinforce it by their choice of subjects to present to the public—and the public in turn by what it buys. I can only hope that this brief interpretive account will encourage readers to write a good deal more about slighted or ignored aspects of Pacific Northwest history.

For their suggestions and other forms of help I am indebted to a fine group of historians, anthropologists, librarians, and archivists: William R. Swagerty, Roderick Sprague, Terry Abraham, and Barry Rigby, my colleagues at the University of Idaho; Mary Reed of the Latah County Historical Society; Lewis Saum and Vernon Carstensen of the University of Washington; Alfred Runte, Seattle historian; Lawrence Dodd of Whitman College; Richard

1. A book that promises to stimulate further work in this area is Karen J. Blair, ed., *Women in Pacific Northwest History: An Anthology* (Seattle: University of Washington Press, 1988).

M. Brown and Keith Richard of the University of Oregon; David H. Stratton, George Frykman, and Lawrence Stark of Washington State University; Merle Wells, Judith Austin, Larry Jones, and Elizabeth Jacox of the Idaho State Historical Society; Edward Nolan of the Eastern Washington State Historical Society; Paul Spitzer, historian of the Boeing Company; Nancy Gale Compau of the Spokane Public Library, Laurie Filson of Oregon State University; Susan Seyl of the Oregon Historical Society; Richard Engeman and Carla Rickerson of the University of Washington's Pacific Northwest Collection; Elaine Miller of the Washington State Historical Society, and Carolyn Marr of the Museum of History and Industry, Seattle. I am indebted also to the many students who took my Pacific Northwest history classes and helped to shape my thinking about this region.

For the time they spent reading the entire manuscript, I owe special thanks to Robert E. Burke, University of Washington; G. Thomas Edwards, Whitman College; William G. Robbins, Oregon State University; and Siegfried Rolland, University of Idaho. In fact, by encouraging me to move to the University of Idaho, Sig became the godfather of the entire project. Also present at the creation were the National Endowment for the Humanities and Walter Nugent of the University of Notre Dame. It was in Walt's 1984 NEH-sponsored Seminar for College Teachers that I found the courage to undertake this work.

To W. Kent Hackmann, chairman of the Department of History at the University of Idaho; Galen O. Rowe, dean of the College of Letters and Science; and Arthur R. Gittins, former dean of the Graduate School, I am grateful for the support they gave to the research and writing. Of course, I alone am responsible for any errors of fact or judgment in the chapters that follow.

The Pacific Northwest

# CHAPTER I

# A Sense of Place:
# The Essential Pacific Northwest

*

First impression! As I found her so will I always think of Seattle. As young and eager. Life still the great unexplored; living still the great adventure. With no old past to stop and worship; no dead men's bones to reckon with; no traditions chained to her ankles. She lives in new-lumbered houses and seems to despise old timber that has lost its fragrance. Older cities forget that they were once—trees. In those cities they love old "musky, tusky" houses where the regicides once hid or Paul Revere stopped and supped a cup of tea. But in Seattle, it is as though the trees had change to house shapes, still keeping the essence and benediction of earth-contact.—*Seattle, Her Faults & Her Virtues* (ca. 1925)

*

Any search for commonly agreed upon boundaries for the Pacific Northwest will prove fruitless. Countless miles of borders divide and subdivide the region's variegated landscape into counties, cities, national parks and monuments, national and state forests, and even soil conservation districts, yet the regional perimeter, except along the Pacific Ocean, remains as indistinct as a fog-shrouded promontory. State and local boundaries are precisely defined by law, and often they are quite dramatic: Hells Canyon forms what may be the most spectacular border in the United States, separating Oregon and Idaho. One hundred thirty miles long and in places 7,700 feet deep, one-third of a mile deeper than Grand Canyon, the remote gorge compresses the Snake River into a maelstrom of white water. Far less visible but nonetheless still marked by signs posted along Oregon and Idaho highways is the

45th parallel, the line of latitude equidistant from the Equator and North Pole. It thus seems all the more ironic that the single boundary not defined in any meaningful way is that of the Pacific Northwest itself. Nowhere does an official roadside marker welcome people to the region.

The fact is that Pacific Northwesterners themselves cannot agree upon their region's bounds. In addition to the generally accepted core states of Washington and Oregon, some people would include western Montana and even northern California and British Columbia within the region. Idaho presents the greatest challenge to easy classification because some residents perceive their state as oriented toward Oregon, Washington, and the Pacific Rim, while others consider it part of the intermountain West that includes Montana and Utah. A popular quip in geographically divided Idaho is that the state has three capitals: Spokane for the northern half, Salt Lake City for the southern half, and Boise for everywhere else. Some scholars classify Oregon and Washington within the Far West or Pacific states and Idaho within the Mountain states, or they separate the lush, green Douglas-fir country of Oregon and Washington west of the Cascade mountains from the high, often arid interior.

Ultimately, anyone studying regions of the United States must decide where to draw their boundaries, and this book extends the perimeter of the Pacific Northwest to encompass the three states of Oregon, Washington, and Idaho. That simple arrangement may seem somewhat arbitrary, but it conforms reasonably well to the logic of geography, economics, and history that together constitute common ground for places as different as metropolitan Seattle and the sparsely populated rangelands of eastern Oregon and central Idaho.

A region can best be defined by discontinuities that mark its borders and by the geographical, political, economic, social, and cultural bonds that give it some sense of internal unity or community. The discontinuities that mark the perimeter of the Pacific Northwest and give it the general shape of a parallelogram are the Pacific Ocean, the Klamath (Siskiyou) Mountains and Great Basin desert, and the Rocky Mountains, and the Canadian border, one political and three natural boundaries. At its maximum reach, the Pacific Northwest extends 480 miles north to south and 680 miles east to west.

Several unifying forces operate within this 250,000-square-mile region: the Columbia River and its numerous tributaries, networks of transportation and communication, patterns of trade and commerce, and a special sense of place derived from history and geography. These integrative forces

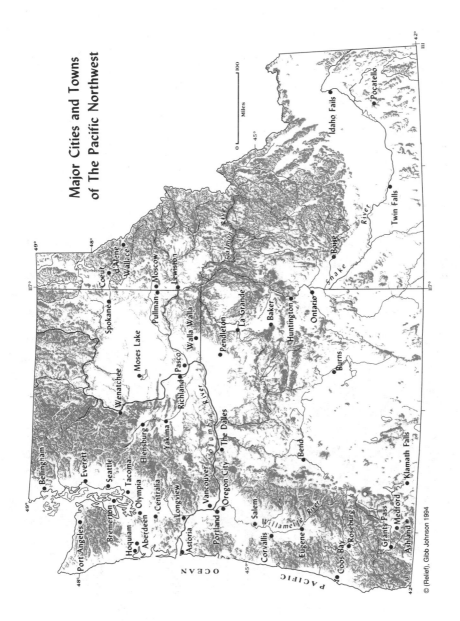

# Major Cities and Towns
# of The Pacific Northwest

Miles

© (Relief), Gibb Johnson 1994

3

lessen internal divisions caused by mountain ranges, distance, state boundaries, and differing economic activities and political and religious cultures.

An understanding of the main currents of Pacific Northwest history begins with an appreciation of the region's geographic setting, one of the most diverse natural landscapes in North America. It continues with an awareness that, for the better part of its recorded history, life in the Pacific Northwest revolved around supplying the world with raw materials—furs and skins, logs and lumber, wheat and a variety of agricultural commodities, fish and other seafoods, and precious and base metals.

Yet no matter how valuable its natural resources were to succeeding generations of entrepreneurs, the Pacific Northwest remained geographically remote from the continent's centers of economic and political power. That remoteness, combined with its historic role as supplier of raw materials, defined the Pacific Northwest as a colonial hinterland. Even at the dawn of the twenty-first century, large portions of the region still grapple with the economic and social consequences of decades of hinterland status; and though the metropolitan centers of Seattle and Portland can no longer

1. Vista House at Crown Point overlooks the western
entrance to the Columbia River gorge. "The scenery
combines all that is picturesque and beautiful in mountain, stream, forest, cataract and cascade," boasted a
1904 guidebook issued by the Oregon Railroad and Navigation Company to describe its water-level route
through this vital gateway. Courtesy Oregon Historical
Society, ORHI 3865.

JOHN MUIR ON THE JUXTAPOSITION OF PORTLAND AND MOUNT HOOD

The heights back of Portland command one of the best general views of the forests and also of the most famous of the great mountains both of Oregon and Washington. Mount Hood is in full view, with the summits of Mounts Jefferson, St. Helens, Adams and Rainier in the distance. The City of Portland is at our feet, covering a large area along both banks of the Willamette, and with its fine streets, schools, churches, mills, shipping, parks and gardens makes a telling picture of busy, aspiring civilization in the midst of the green wilderness in which it is planted. . . .

Never shall I forget my first glorious view of Mount Hood one calm evening in July, 'though I had seen it many times before this. I was then sauntering with a friend across the new Willamette bridge between Portland and East Portland, for the sake of the river views, which are here very fine in the tranquil summer weather. . . . I was not conscious of anything occurring on the outer rim of the landscape. Forest, mountain and sky were forgotten; when my companion suddenly directed my attention to the eastward shouting, "Oh, look! look!" in so loud and excited a tone of voice that passers-by, sauntering like ourselves, were startled and looked over the bridge as if expecting to see some boat upset. Looking across the forests over which the mellow light of the sunset was streaming, I soon discovered the source of my friend's excitement. There stood Mount Hood in all the glory of the Alpen glow looming immensely high, beaming with intelligence, and so impressive that one was overawed as if suddenly brought before some superior Being newly arrived from the sky. . . .—John Muir, "Mt. Hood from Portland," *Pacific Monthly* 7 (May 1902): 213–14

be classified as hinterlands of the United States, part of their special appeal to residents and tourists alike derives from continuing ties to the region's own extensive outback, a relationship made visible in both cities by the spectacular and seemingly unspoiled natural backdrop formed by snow-capped mountains nearby.

NATURALLY NORTHWEST

What special qualities define the Pacific Northwest? What makes Pacific Northwesterners' sense of place distinct from that of Californians, southerners, or New Englanders? One simple and obvious answer is the environment, the region's spectacular natural setting—the stunning juxtaposition of mountains and water that characterize its coastline and Columbia River gorge; the vastness of its interior, a land of sagebrush plains and empty spaces. Residents occasionally refer to the region as "God's Country," and the opening stanza of "America the Beautiful" could well describe its mountain peaks and amber waves of grain.

Fundamental to a Pacific Northwesterner's sense of place is the awareness that much of the region remains uninhabited or only lightly populated. A person trapped in rush-hour traffic on one of Seattle's floating bridges may not believe that claim, yet the population of the entire Pacific Northwest was only 8.7 million in 1990—approximately equal to that of Los Angeles County. But residents of the region are spread out over an area the size of the six New England states and New York, Pennsylvania, Delaware, Maryland, Virginia, and North Carolina. Oregon alone encompasses more area than the United Kingdom of Great Britain and Northern Ireland.

To describe the Pacific Northwest as lightly populated is technically correct but very misleading. The region's residents tend to gather like bees into a few urban hives. More than half of Washington's population lives in a handful of counties that border the east side of Puget Sound and embrace the cities of Seattle, Tacoma, Olympia, Everett, Bellingham, and Bellevue. A second population center is Spokane on the state's eastern edge.

Two-thirds of Oregon's population is concentrated in the Willamette Valley, which extends a hundred miles from Portland south to Eugene. Of Oregon's eleven cities with populations of thirty thousand or more, only Medford lies outside the Willamette Valley. Idaho has always been more rural than the other two states, yet two separate urban complexes centering on Boise and Pocatello contain half its population. Idaho has only three cities of thirty thousand or more, and all are situated on the Snake River plain in the southern part of the state. Washington, with twenty-three cities of thirty thousand or more, is the most urbanized of the three states. The percentage of population living in urban areas—communities with twenty-five hundred or more residents—varies from 76 in Washington to 71 in Oregon and 57 in Idaho. The national average in 1990 was 75 percent.

Because of the tendency of Pacific Northwesterners to cluster in a few urban areas, the population density of King County, Washington—site of the region's most populous city, Seattle, with slightly more than half a million residents—is 708 people per square mile. Yet several sprawling counties in eastern Washington have fewer than 4 people per square mile. A dozen counties in eastern Oregon and central Idaho are even more lightly populated.

This settlement pattern means that even urban residents of the Pacific Northwest experience a strong sense of their natural setting. The composite city stretching from Everett to Olympia—sometimes referred to as Pugetopolis—is ninety miles long but narrow enough to afford boaters and fishermen easy access to the open waters of Puget Sound in one direction and backpackers, skiers, and hunters convenient escape to the Cascade mountains in the other. From the shores of Puget Sound to the ski slopes at Snoqualmie Pass is little more than an hour's drive, about the same time it takes Portlanders to reach Timberline Lodge on Mount Hood.

It is even easier to maintain visual contact with the region's spectacular natural setting. On a clear spring day after a winter of leaden skies and intermittent drizzle, many a resident of Seattle or Portland draws fresh inspiration from the sight of Mount Rainier or Mount Hood floating majestically on the horizon. A person can travel the length of Puget Sound or the Willamette Valley and never lose sight of the Cascades or the Coast Ranges. Portland, in fact, has municipal regulations that protect "view corridors" through the central city. The heart of Portland is not a building but rather an outdoor gathering place: Pioneer Courthouse Square, a one-block, open-air plaza located in the center of the shopping district.

Contact with the natural setting is easier still in Idaho, which, except for the Snake River plain, is one vast sea of mountains and foothills dotted with a few modest islands of farmland such as the Camas Prairie and the Palouse in the northern panhandle. One wit suggested that if its vertical surfaces could be rolled flat, Idaho would become the largest state in the union. But Idaho without its mountains is inconceivable. The rugged, nearly inaccessible terrain of much of the state—especially the Bitterroot and Sawtooth ranges—is one reason why Idaho life will for the foreseeable future be oriented to outdoor activities.

The landforms of the Pacific Northwest are not matters of just geology and real estate but also of aesthetics and culture. The most repetitive theme in the region's literature is the interaction of people and their natural environment; much of the region's history is played out against a backdrop of dramatic landforms. Not surprisingly, Pacific Northwesterners commonly translated their sense of place into a belief that natural environment determined the types of people who settled Oregon, Washington, and Idaho. Rugged mountains and gargantuan trees called forth strong-willed, self-reliant individuals to match them, or so Northwesterners have often claimed.

Even if this romantic notion was impossible to prove, it remained central to the thinking of generations of settlers and helps to explain why so many newcomers defined progress as taming nature through exploitation of the region's abundant natural resources. Perceptions of abundance still shape public discussions of how best to treat the region's land, timber, and water resources.

7

MOUNTAIN SHADOWS: PACIFIC NORTHWEST GEOGRAPHY

In a sense, the entire Pacific Northwest can be described as lying in the mountains' shadow. Few areas are so situated that mountains are not readily visible, and even those anomalous places still experience the influence of mountain ranges on regional weather patterns, vegetation, and economic activities.

At many points along the Pacific Coast of Oregon and Washington, mountains touch the sea. The Coast ranges extend from northern California to the Olympic Peninsula of Washington and average about fifty miles in width. For most of the distance their peaks seldom top three thousand feet, and in southwestern Washington they flatten into a series of low rises called the Willapa Hills. Farther north, the land again rises dramatically to form the Olympic Mountains, topped by Mount Olympus at eighty-two hundred feet above sea level.

Lying between the coastal mountains and the Cascade range is an alluvial plain about 350 miles long and 50 miles wide that forms the Puget Sound–Willamette lowlands. Separating the northern from the southern portion of the plain are gentle hills located about halfway between Olympia and Vancouver, Washington. The Puget Sound–Willamette lowlands constitute the heart of the Pacific Northwest. Here are located two state capitals and a concentration of cities, colleges and universities, television and radio stations, corporate headquarters, banks, and manufacturing establishments greater than anywhere else in the region. Despite its essentially urban character, this alluvial plain still supports a thriving and diverse agricultural industry.

The Cascade mountains extend from northern California into southern British Columbia and vary in width from more than one hundred miles at the Canadian border to less than fifty miles at the California border. Numerous lava flows surmounted by large and small volcanic peaks characterize the range. The most famous of these volcanoes is Mount Saint Helens, which erupted violently in 1980 but since has been relatively quiet. The Cascades also include several dormant volcanoes, a few of which have erupted within the past two centuries. Other well-known Cascade peaks are Lassen and Shasta in California, Hood in Oregon, and Rainier, Adams, and Baker in Washington. Rainier at 14,410 feet is the highest mountain in the Pacific Northwest and is topped in the forty-eight contiguous states only by Mount Whitney (14,494 feet) in California's Sierra Nevadas and by Mount Elbert (14,433 feet) and two sister peaks in the central Colorado Rockies.

### MOUNT SAINT HELENS

Mount Saint Helens once was the loveliest of Cascade peaks. At 8:32 on the Sunday morning of 18 May 1980 it stunned the nation and the world when it blasted away its crown with a force five hundred times greater than the atomic bomb dropped on Hiroshima in 1945. Speeding at up to 120 miles per hour, a whirlwind of heat, ash, and debris denuded two hundred square miles of heavily forested land within a fifteen-mile arc to the north. All told, the blast killed nearly sixty people, an estimated fifteen hundred elk, five thousand black-tailed deer, two hundred black bears, and hundreds of thousands of birds and fish. Massive mudflows down the Toutle and Cowlitz valleys filled the Columbia River's main channel and raised it from a depth of 40 feet to a mere 14 feet. This brought shipping to an abrupt halt.

A dense boiling cloud rose from the crater and deposited several inches of ash on portions of eastern Washington and northern Idaho, leaving its traces even on the East Coast and giving rise to a wry comment: "Don't come to Washington this year; Washington will come to you." On that Sunday in May and for several days following, the predominant mood in the Pacific Northwest was one of apprehension and fear. Some residents wondered whether this eruption was a prelude to something worse. Perhaps Mount Baker would erupt next. Perhaps the ash was poisonous or radioactive. Yet after cleanup crews reopened streets and highways in eastern Washington, life returned to normal. Nonetheless, the Pacific Northwest Regional Commission published a pamphlet called "Exploding the Myth: The Pacific Northwest Remains Beautiful" to counteract any erroneous impressions in other parts of the United States.

Mount Saint Helens was not the only Cascade volcano to erupt in the twentieth century. In 1914–17, Mount Lassen vented steam, ash, and lava. During the nineteenth century, several peaks including Hood, Saint Helens, and Rainier put on eruptive displays. None, however, was as violent as the May 1980 blast or the even more spectacular one half a dozen millennia earlier when Oregon's Mount Mazama exploded with a force forty-two times greater than that of the Saint Helens eruption.

When filled with water from rain and melting snow, a caldera nearly two thousand feet deep and six miles wide formed the natural wonder of Crater Lake, famed for its breathtaking indigo blue water.

Mount Saint Helens and its immediate vicinity became a national volcanic monument in 1983. Nature is still at work healing the scars caused by the eruption. The event reminds Pacific Northwesterners what it means to live in the mountains' shadow, especially when some of those mountains turn out to be dormant—rather than extinct—volcanoes.

But Mount Rainier appears far more spectacular than the others because it rises abruptly from the coastal plain and towers above lesser peaks. Its massive slopes support twenty-seven named glaciers, the single largest mountain glacier system in the lower forty-eight states and the source of several Northwest rivers. The Cascade Range includes three national parks and the Mount Saint Helens National Volcanic Monument.

At the eastern edge of the Pacific Northwest stand the Rocky Mountains, an uplifted area that includes numerous ranges like the Bitterroots, which form the Idaho-Montana border. Local chains like the Wallowas of northeastern Oregon or the rugged Klamath Mountains that straddle the Oregon-California border add variety to the region's landscape.

The common impression that the Pacific Northwest is a land of evergreens, ocean mist, and snowcapped peaks contrasts with reality: much of the region's surface is treeless and arid. First-time visitors to the dry areas are often surprised witnesses to the ways mountains and elevation influence rainfall. Most of the world's arid regions result from a planetwide system of air currents, but those of the Pacific Northwest result from mountain rain shadows.

The Cascades, the Rockies, and other ranges influence weather as part of a complex process that begins over the Pacific Ocean. As prevailing northwesterly winds sweep across its surface during the winter months, they become laden with moisture later lost crossing the land. The marine air enables much of the region to enjoy relatively mild winters. Portland, Oregon, for example, experiences far less snow and less frequent subzero weather than St. Paul, Minnesota, or Portland, Maine, cities that lie farther south. During the winter months, much of the region is covered with marine air and layers of clouds that restrict the total hours of sunshine. Northern Idaho, for instance, though located more than three hundred miles from the ocean, receives only about 50 percent of the maximum sunshine available in winter because of the marine climate.

As moist air from the Pacific rises to cross the coastal mountains, atmospheric pressure decreases, the air cools, and like a squeezed sponge the clouds release some of their moisture in the form of rain or snow. In parts of the Olympic Peninsula an annual rainfall of 120 to 140 inches is common, and some years it can top 180 inches, or the equivalent of two billion gallons of water for each square mile of forest. The result is a veritable evergreen jungle of moss-festooned forest giants like the Sitka spruce and Douglas fir, all softly illuminated by sunlight filtered through layers of vaporous clouds. The Hoh, Queets, Quinault, and Bogachiel valleys of the Olympic Peninsula are probably the best extant examples of the Northwest rain forest, a soggy ecosystem found no other place on earth.

In the Puget Sound–Willamette lowlands the average annual rainfall is about the same as that in New York City or New Orleans (thirty to fifty

2. Two loggers strike a pose that once epitomized the
Pacific Northwest's timber-dependent economy. Courtesy Forest History Society.

inches), but because the precipitation so often occurs as drizzle, the winter
rain seems interminable and the weather dreary. In Portland and Seattle it
rains an average of 150 days each year.

Wet winters and relatively dry summers characterize much of the Pacific
Northwest, just the reverse of the weather pattern of the Great Plains and
Rocky Mountains. People in Portland and Seattle must water their lawns
during the summer, and August is a time of forest-fire danger. The relationship between temperature on land and sea explains this phenomenon: during winter the land is cooler than the sea; during summer the reverse is true.
Summertime air increases in temperature as it moves from sea to land and
thus is able to retain more of the moisture it collected from the Pacific.

Regardless of the season, when clouds from the Pacific Ocean sweep up the face of the Cascades, they reach higher, cooler elevations than in the Coast ranges. Snowfall on some peaks during the winter months may total three hundred inches and on occasion may exceed one thousand inches annually. Paradise Inn, located at the fifty-four-hundred-foot level on the south slope of Mount Rainier, recorded a total of 93.5 feet of snow during the winter of 1971–72.

The clouds lose much of their remaining moisture by the time they pass two dozen miles beyond the summit of the Cascades. Farther down the eastern slope the land becomes noticeably drier, and the moisture-loving Douglas firs and tangled undergrowth that thrive on the west side give way to ponderosa pines and eventually to the grasses and sagebrush that survive where annual rainfall averages ten inches or less.

The lowest precipitation occurs in the central and eastern portions of both Washington and Oregon and in southern Idaho—a highly varied landscape of hills, eroded slopes, rugged mountains, flat plains, and sandy deserts, all underlain with basalt, a volcanic rock. Precipitation increases gradually as one travels across eastern Washington to the Idaho panhandle, from an annual average of six inches along the Columbia River in central Washington to twenty-one inches at Pullman, 140 miles east and 1,300 feet higher.

Famed for its fertile soil, the Palouse country that surrounds Pullman and overlaps a portion of the Washington-Idaho border is one of the most productive wheat-growing regions in the United States, yet immediately north and west of the Palouse lie the channeled scablands, a series of dry canyons called coulees, where the soil is thin and the country is suitable mainly for grazing cattle. From the Palouse to the Rockies, annual precipitation increases until it almost equals that in parts of the Puget Sound–Willamette lowlands, enabling stands of western white pine, red cedar, and Douglas fir to thrive in the Idaho panhandle. Commercial forests account for 65 percent of the total land area of northern Idaho and 70 percent of Oregon and Washington west of the Cascades, but only 30 percent of those two states east of the Cascades.

Much of the annual precipitation eventually returns to the Pacific Ocean to repeat the cycle, but not before it generates electric power and irrigates arid lands. If water from rain or snow does not evaporate or sink into the soil, it reaches the Columbia River and reenters the Pacific near Astoria, Oregon. Primary exceptions to this pattern are local rivers and streams that drain into Puget Sound or directly into the ocean from the Coast ranges.

On a map of the Pacific Northwest, the Columbia River and its tributaries resemble a giant gnarled oak tree resting on its side with its topmost branches reaching as far inland as southern British Columbia, western Montana, and northwestern Wyoming. From its source in the Canadian Rockies, the Columbia River extends a distance of 1,270 miles to the Pacific Ocean and drains 258,000 square miles, an area larger than France, Belgium, and the Netherlands combined. More than any other physical feature it knits the disparate elements of the Pacific Northwest together, crossing desert, high plains, wheat fields, cattle ranges, and grassland as it threads its way between mountains to reach the sea. Over the years the Columbia River has been a vital transportation link and highway of history, a source of irrigation water and hydroelectric power, a cause for environmental concern, and dramatic regional symbol.

Joining the Columbia just north of the Canadian border is the Pend Oreille River, which drains far northern Idaho and western Montana. The Columbia's largest tributary, the Snake River, joins it near Pasco, where the trunk of the growing river twists south and then abruptly west. Originating a thousand miles east near Yellowstone National Park, the Snake is itself one of the major rivers of the United States. After cutting through the plains of southern Idaho, where a portion of its water irrigates six million acres of farmland, the Snake plunges into Hells Canyon, the deepest gorge in North America. The chutes and rapids here terrorized explorers and completely blocked river communication between northern and southern Idaho. The Deschutes and John Day rivers enter the Columbia east of the Cascades after draining the sparsely populated land of central Oregon. A hundred miles from the sea, the Willamette River, having served the needs of Portland, Salem, and Eugene, joins the Columbia's massive trunk.

The Columbia River flows through four mountain ranges, pours more water into the ocean than any other river in North America except for the Saint Lawrence, Mississippi, and Mackenzie, and exceeds every river on the continent in the generation of hydroelectric power. In fact, its waters contain an estimated 40 percent of the nation's total hydroelectric potential. Except for a 50-mile stretch bordering the Hanford Nuclear Reservation in central Washington, the Columbia has been engineered into a chain of lakes formed by dams that stretch from Bonneville Dam to the Canadian border. Through a series of eight locks, towboats and barges can climb the Columbia and Snake rivers to reach Lewiston, Idaho's only seaport, located 460 miles inland and more than seven hundred feet above sea level.

The Columbia River was an avenue of trade and commerce and knitted together the Pacific Northwest even before the coming of Euro-Americans. For Indian people as well as for newcomers, the Columbia counteracted the divisive influence of mountains, especially the Cascade Range, a wall breached only by the Columbia and one other river, the Klamath, in southern Oregon.

There can be little doubt that the Cascades once hindered easy communication and transportation in Oregon and Washington and that the mountains bordering the Salmon River divided Idaho—and still do during the season when snowdrifts and avalanches block the passes and grades. Today, in the legislatures of all three states, opinions frequently divide along these mountain barriers.

Even so, the divisive quality of the region's mountain ranges has probably been overstated. The sight of Mount Rainier or Mount Hood inspires people regardless of whether they live east or west of the Cascades. The Cascade Range forms a backdrop for residents of Seattle and of Ellensburg on the opposite side and is equally a part of a sense of place in both communities. Central Idaho's rugged Salmon River country affords the same recreational opportunities to hunters, fishermen, and backpackers whether they live in Lewiston to the north or Boise to the south.

Mountains contribute to the irregularity of natural and manmade landscapes in the Pacific Northwest. Unlike the prairie states, where rectangular fields of corn and soybeans extend to the horizon, the far Northwest gives the appearance of being rough and unfinished. Except for state and international boundaries and city streets, straight lines are uncommon features of the landscape. The region's coastline is irregular and its land is uplifted into jagged peaks and sinuous hills that give the Palouse country in July and August the appearance of a swelling ocean of wheat. To become accustomed to the Pacific Northwest climate and landscape—to become accustomed to life in the mountains' shadow—is crucial to developing a sense of place.

AN AMERICAN HINTERLAND?

Patches of clear-cut forest land and abandoned sawmills, closed mines and forsaken fish canneries were increasingly common features of the Pacific Northwest landscape in the late twentieth century. A sense of place, it seems, must also come to terms with economic activity, or lack thereof.

The region's role as supplier of raw materials gave economic life in the Pacific Northwest some special contours. Even before contact with European and American traders in the late eighteenth century, Native Americans had established among themselves elaborate trade networks based on the use of natural resources like fish and roots. Beginning in the 1780s with the trade in furs and skins, Pacific Northwest commodities played important supporting roles in the metropolitan-dominated economic systems of Europe and North America, although the region itself remained a colonial hinterland for the next two centuries and thus was economically vulnerable to forces beyond its control. For several generations the region rode an economic roller coaster that alternated crazily between boom and bust, and no one seemed able to get off.

As recently as the 1980s—despite the existence of urban centers as large as Seattle and Portland and the great aircraft manufacturing plants of Boeing —it was still appropriate to describe the Pacific Northwest as a hinterland, at least the bulk of it outside metropolitan areas. Two Pacific Northwests had emerged, economically speaking: the relatively prosperous high-technology, manufacturing, and exporting businesses centering on Seattle and Portland, and the traditional extractive industries of the less populated areas. Difficulties in the latter sector inevitably affected the entire region in the form of diminished tax revenues and underfunding of state services and institutions; and during the mid-1980s there were troubles aplenty in mining, agriculture, and timber. Other imponderables such as freight rates and the cheap electricity needed to lure new businesses and industries or to keep the existing ones competitive in distant national and international markets continued to influence the region's economic future.

Hinterland status also shaped the Pacific Northwest past. Certain features of the region's early history bear more resemblance to the natural resources frontier of Canada than to the commercial and agricultural settlements of the eastern United States. The Pacific Northwest was integrated into the fur trade centering on Montreal and the Saint Lawrence Valley and later the Hudson's Bay region well before it developed close economic and social ties with the United States. Reorientation of the region did not occur until after American missionaries arrived in the late 1830s, and a substantial number of settlers from the Ohio and Missouri valleys came the following decade.

When Oregon achieved territorial status in the late 1840s, two generations had passed since the opening battles of the Revolutionary War, thirty states had entered the Union, eleven men had served as president of the United States, Harvard College was already two hundred years old, and the population of New York City was rapidly approaching seven hundred thousand. In the late 1840s about ten thousand non-Indian people lived in the entire Oregon Territory, which included not only the future states of Oregon, Washington, and Idaho, but also western Montana and a portion of western Wyoming. The territory's most populous non-Indian community was Oregon City, with fewer than a thousand residents. Nearby Portland had even fewer residents, and the future cities of Seattle, Tacoma, Spokane, and Boise did not exist.

The northwestern corner of the United States, in short, was both geographically remote from the East Coast and chronologically distant from the mainstream of American history. But rather than be merely a backwater of American history, the Pacific Northwest followed a separate watercourse toward regional development. The following chapters chart its main features.

# Part I

# Isolation and Empire

# Profile: The Third Voyage of Captain James Cook

The fur of these animals, as mentioned in the Russian accounts, is certainly softer and finer than that of any others we know of; and therefore the discovery of this part of the continent of North America, where so valuable an article of commerce may be met with, cannot be a matter of indifference.
—James Cook and James King, *A Voyage to the Pacific Ocean* (1784)

Geographical isolation fundamentally shaped the course of Pacific Northwest history. Far longer than most temperate areas of the world the Northwest remained beyond the reach of Europe and the rest of North America. The region's geographical isolation in turn contributed to a pronounced time lag in its historical development. The frontier seemed to linger longer, and social and economic changes that evolved over a period of decades elsewhere often were telescoped into a much briefer span of time in the Northwest or skipped entirely.

The year 1776 offers a good promontory from which to observe the region's chronological isolation. In Philadelphia, thirteen American colonies formally declared their independence from Great Britain on July 4 and set forth on an uncharted political course. Only eight days later the distinguished explorer Captain James Cook sailed from Plymouth, England, on his third great voyage of discovery. That venture, which had important consequences for the Pacific Northwest, neatly coincided with the course of the American Revolution: the expedition's two ships—but not Cook—returned home in 1780, four years and three months after setting sail.

James Cook was the most famous navigator of his day. The son of a Scottish farm laborer who had settled in Yorkshire, he was appreciated as a youth to a grocer and a dry goods merchant. At the age of eighteen he was apprenticed to the owner of a fleet of coal-carrying ships, and a career at sea followed. Cook became a military man and student of science, a careful and conscientious captain in the Royal Navy, an explorer of new lands for the British Empire, and a dispeller of geographical myths.

In his day Cook was recognized foremost for his efforts to improve the health and save the lives of men at sea. He promoted the use of sauerkraut and lemon and orange syrups to cure scurvy—a disease characterized by lethargy and anemia, bleeding gums, loss of teeth, stiffness of joints, and slow healing of wounds. This medical advance made lengthy voyages practicable. Upon returning from his second voyage, Cook was elected a Fellow of the prestigious Royal Society and received its highest award for his work of preserving the health of his crew on long voyages.

A tall and unpretentious man, he was forty-seven years old at the start of his third voyage. Having been around the world twice—once in each direction—he intended to retire when he completed his second voyage in 1775. But the lure of solving one of the world's most tantalizing geographical mysteries and the opportunity to collect a handsome financial reward for doing so caused Cook to set forth once again, leaving at home his thirty-eight-year-old wife, Elizabeth, eight months pregnant.

Cook's mission, as stated in sealed instructions from the British Admiralty, was to find the fabled Northwest Passage. That quest was so important in the eyes of the English-speaking world that Benjamin Franklin, confident that the explorer would soon be sailing through the long-sought waterway, issued an order prohibiting the fledgling American navy from interfering with "that most celebrated navigator and discoverer, Captain Cook." Although Americans were in the midst of war with Britain, they should treat Cook and his crewmen "with all civility and kindness, affording them as common friends to mankind."

The nation that discovered the Northwest Passage would achieve a shortcut through North America to the markets of Asia. In other words, that nation stood to gain immense riches and power. The belief that such a passage really existed rested on a combination of hope, myth, and geographical possibility. Since the time of Columbus, explorers from several European nations had sought in vain for an entrance from the Atlantic. The British Parliament offered the discoverer a £20,000 prize in 1745—perhaps $500,000 in today's money—and extended the offer to include ships of the

3. Captain James Cook (1728–79). Courtesy Museum of
History and Industry, Seattle, 11863.

Royal Navy in 1775. Cook was to seek the Pacific entrance to the passage, a quest that would take him to the last of the world's temperate coastlines to be brought into close association with Europe.

Cook was no stranger to the Pacific. During two previous voyages of discovery, he had traveled to the exotic lands of the South Pacific, even to the Antarctic Circle. On his third voyage he sailed first to the Cape of Good

Hope, then west to Australia, New Zealand, and islands he had previously visited in the South Pacific. He even had the good fortune to discover a new group of islands that he named after his patron, the Earl of Sandwich. We know them today as the Hawaiian Islands.

Nearly two years after leaving England, Cook reached the Pacific Northwest coast in early March 1778. A reception of hail, sleet, fog, and howling winds prompted him to name the first landmark Cape Foulweather, a promontory that juts into the ocean a few miles north of present Newport, Oregon. His was not the first expedition to reach these shores, but European contact before Cook had been sporadic, the work of discovery and exploration haphazard, and national claims to the area exceedingly vague.

Two hundred years earlier, in 1579, a fellow Englishman, Francis Drake, had sailed northward along the Pacific coast perhaps as far as Oregon or even British Columbia. He described the area as one of "most vile, thicke, and stinking fogges," named it Nova Albion, claimed it for England, and left. His territorial claim was ambiguous, because even today there is no agreement about how far north he sailed. After Drake, the Pacific Northwest remained largely unknown to the European world, and Russian and Spanish expeditions along the coast in the mid-1700s did but little to change that. Moving northward from Mexico, the Spanish knew more than any other Europeans about the Pacific coast, but they endeavored to keep their records secret. Their discoveries, as far as the rest of Europe was concerned, were scarcely discoveries at all.

Cook's expedition was methodical in a way no previous voyage to North Pacific waters had been. The admiralty instructed him to reach the west coast of North America at about forty-five degrees north latitude to avoid provoking an international incident with the Spanish, who, with expeditions launched from their base in Mexico, had established imperial claims to the lands south of that line. From that point, Cook was to proceed north but not explore the coast in detail until he reached sixty-five degrees. If he found the Northwest Passage he was to sail east through it. In addition, he was to remain alert for a northeast passage navigable across the top of Russia.

Cook's instructions also made clear the scientific nature of his third voyage. He was to make a careful record of the natural resources of the region and to take possession of unclaimed lands for the king of England—unclaimed, that is, by nations such as Russia and Spain, because the presence of the native peoples was of little consequence in European eyes.

As his two ships, *Resolution* and *Discovery*, sailed north through troublesome and dangerous waters, Cook remained well offshore and thus missed discovering both the mouth of the Columbia River and the Strait of Juan de Fuca, the gateway to Puget Sound. But he did enter Nootka Sound, an exceptionally fine anchorage on the west coast of Vancouver Island, which he mistook for the North American mainland. There he made contact with the native peoples of the coast. Juan Pérez, a Spaniard, was the first European to visit the area when his expedition anchored just outside the entrance to Nootka Sound in August 1774 to barter pieces of metal, iridescent shells, and beads for sea otter robes.

During the month Cook's expedition remained at Nootka to repair its ships, officers compiled detailed accounts of Northwest Coast Indian life. Crew members exchanged trinkets with the Indians for the luxuriant pelts of the sea otter, some of which they used for shipboard bedding. The sea otter pelts acquired in almost casual fashion later proved a surprisingly valuable treasure.

The *Resolution* and *Discovery* continued north along the coast of Alaska and the Aleutian chain and entered the Arctic Ocean in May. By midsummer the expedition had advanced beyond seventy degrees north latitude when an impenetrable wall of ice blocked its way and threatened to crush the ships against the shore. Forced to retreat, the explorers turned south to spend the winter in Hawaii, reaching the islands late in 1778.

The Hawaiians were friendly and accommodating hosts, but they had a passion for anything they could pry loose from Cook's ships, especially iron goods, even down to the long nails that fastened protective sheathing to the ship's hull. Finally, when Cook could tolerate the stealing no longer, he and an armed guard went ashore at Kealakekua Bay on 14 February 1779, in an attempt to recover a stolen boat or secure a hostage. The Hawaiians became enraged when they heard that another party of crewmen had killed a chief. They hurled stones at the English, who responded by firing into the crowd. When Cook's men paused to reload their weapons, the Hawaiians rushed forward with knives and clubs, killing five expedition members, including Cook.

The survivors sailed north once again, but the Arctic ice defeated their quest for the Northwest Passage. As they headed for home along the China coast, they made the fortuitous discovery that sea otter pelts from Nootka Sound were worth a fortune in Canton. Crewmen came close to mutiny because of their eagerness to return for more pelts, but their officers prevailed and the two ships sailed for England.

Captain Cook's third voyage failed to locate the Northwest Passage—a route that indeed existed, as the Norwegian explorer Roald Amundsen proved in 1906, but it was so ice choked as to have little practical value. Cook's expedition nonetheless added new lands to the British Empire and new knowledge about the North Pacific Coast. Publication of the expedition's official records in 1784 gave the Pacific Northwest for the first time a clearly defined place in European imperial and commercial systems. But even before that date, news about the expedition had set in motion a commercial rush to exploit the fur resources of the Northwest Coast. In short, Cook's ships initiated the region's role as a resource-rich hinterland open to exploitation by more developed parts of the world.

Cook's third voyage clearly illustrates the geographical and historical remoteness of the Pacific Northwest from Europe and the settlements on the eastern seaboard of America. For the English-speaking world, the Pacific Northwest remained a blank sheet of paper at a time when American history had already recorded the battles of Lexington and Concord and the Declaration of Independence.

Cook's third voyage served as a training school for mariners who would subsequently return to the Pacific Northwest, some as captains of fur trading vessels and others as explorers. Best known among the explorers who sailed with Cook was George Vancouver, who during a voyage of discovery for the British government in the early 1790s described and mapped many sites on Puget Sound—including the body of water itself, named for his lieutenant, Peter Puget. Another crewman of note was John Ledyard, an American, who in 1783 published an account of the voyage and encouraged fellow countrymen to pursue the North Pacific–China trade.

Most important, Cook's third voyage ended the previous pattern of sporadic and haphazard European contact with the Pacific Northwest and its native peoples. As an increasing number of fur traders from several nations cruised the coastal waters, it became obvious that a new era had dawned, one that was especially ominous for the Northwest's first inhabitants: the Indians.

# CHAPTER 2

# The First Pacific
# Northwesterners

*

As has been said of Columbus on the eastern shore of the Americas, Cook in
the west "did not discover a new world; he established contact between two
worlds, both already old."—Robin Fisher quoted in *Captain James Cook
and His Times* (1979)

*

Captain James Cook's third expedition had its main encounter with native
peoples of the North Pacific at Nootka Sound. During a month's layover in
April 1778 to repair their ships, Cook and his officers prepared detailed
reports of the Nootkas' physical appearance, customs, material culture, and
trading preferences.

It was apparent to Europeans that the Nootka Indians physically resembled Asians or Polynesians. They were short and stocky, with round and full
faces and high cheekbones. Long black hair hung down over their shoulders.
"The women are nearly of the same size, colour, and form, with the men,
from whom it is not easy to distinguish them, as they possess no natural
delicacies sufficient to render their persons agreeable," penned one European, revealing his cultural biases. This, however, did not keep the crewmen from making wistful remarks about the sexual reticence of native
women. Some women eventually did spend their nights aboard ship with
the men, though probably not on the *Resolution* commanded by Cook.
Being anxious to avoid the spread of venereal disease from Europeans to
native populations, he had forbidden such contacts. Those women were
probably slaves. Indian men likely had arranged their services in exchange
for items of trade.

4. A Nootka village in 1778. Courtesy Historical Photograph Collections, Washington State University Libraries, 70-0072.

The Nootkas practiced elaborate ceremonial rituals. When Cook first
entered the sound, the Indians paddled around his ships, throwing feathers
and red ocher on the water. Although the ritual signified peaceful intentions, the uncomprehending Europeans might just as well have mistaken it
for a sign of hostility. The Nootkas' subsequent encounters included singing, dancing, and displays of wealth. Europeans missed much of the significance of those rituals, interpreting them as simple buffoonery or silly tricks.

The main source of Nootka sustenance was the sea. From it the Indians
skimmed an abundance of fish and other marine life. Cured kelp stems
made strong fishing lines, and the plant's hollow bulbs served as convenient
containers for whale oil. The Nootkas were quite proficient in the use of
oceangoing canoes, but unlike the Vikings or Polynesians, they were not
really deep-sea navigators. They sailed along the coast and disliked ventur-
ing beyond the sight of land.

Europeans observed that the Nootkas lived in extended wooden buildings—longhouses some twenty to forty feet wide and fifty to one hundred
feet long. Overlapping red-cedar planks attached to a permanent frame were
easily removed and transported to another homesite. The Nootkas typically
had three homes: one facing the sea for the summer fishing season, another

in a sheltered cove for the winter, and a third upriver at the site of the salmon runs.

From all indications, the Nootkas were eager to trade sea otter pelts for metal objects. Cook noted that they were already familiar with iron and wanted metal blades of any sort. He learned too that they could be sharp traders. On one occasion they deceived his men by selling them containers of oil partly filled with water.

Despite the fact that each culture found aspects of the other that were strange, there is no indication that the Nootkas regarded Europeans as superior to or more powerful than themselves. At that time neither group dominated the other; their trading relations were for the most part friendly. Cook's third voyage thus represented a harbinger of more extensive contacts to come, not an end to the Indian way of life.

What Cook and his officers observed of the Nootkas was in varying degrees true of the physical appearance and culture of other Northwest Coast Indian groups. The Nootkas were only one group that anthropologists classify within the Northwest Coast cultural area. Within the Pacific Northwest, scholars identify two other great cultural areas: Plateau and Great Basin. Each of those included a variety of subgroups commonly called tribes (although some were only extended families) that shared traits and styles of life, though not necessarily a common language. In all, there were about 125 different tribes speaking more than fifty languages. The boundaries of the three cultural areas are indistinct, and today are the subject of scholarly disagreement, as are many other aspects of Indian culture.

Much of the complexity of Indian life was lost on Euro-Americans, who tended to lump together disparate families and villages under tribal designations. On the eve of white contact, the Nez Perces of the Plateau cultural area, for instance, numbered approximately four thousand people scattered among 130 bands and villages, some associating more closely with neighboring peoples than with other Nez Perce Indians. Euro-Americans also misspelled and invented Indian names, an obvious case being Nez Perce, a French derivation. The name Kalapuyan, applied to the Indians of Oregon's Willamette Valley, was spelled more than thirty ways. Those differences incorporated into treaties between Indians and whites led to years of confusion. Euro-Americans also had difficulty grasping the fact that many Indian cultures had no set territorial boundaries. Tribes had concepts of territory, but their idea of the "ownership" of village, hunting, and berry-picking sites was very different from that of Euro-Americans. In traditional times, land was sacred to the natives, something never to be actually owned, although human occupants might serve as its guardians or custodians. Herein too lay the seeds of misunderstanding and conflict when Indians signed treaties with whites.

### INDIANS OF THE COAST

Indians of the Northwest Coast cultural area occupied a narrow fringe of North America extending from southern Alaska to northern California. Mild climate, heavy rainfall, lush forests, an abundance of food and leisure time, a rich and varied material culture, and homesites on sheltered bays and harbors characterized their habitat. Physically isolated by mountain ranges from other native peoples, their orientation was toward the sea and the protected coves where their villages were located.

In their isolation they developed a common dependence upon marine resources, canoe navigation, and a material culture that emphasized woodworking. They were among the finest woodworkers in the world. Despite their common characteristics, Indians of the Coast cultural area were divided one from another by the rugged land and the barriers posed by language and locally oriented forms of society and government. Their primary social and political unit was the extended family, represented in certain tribes beginning in the nineteenth century by freestanding totem poles—essentially family crests.

Among the Indians of the North Pacific Coast, moving south from the panhandle of present-day Alaska, were the Tlingits (who consisted of fourteen subdivisions), the Haidas of the Queen Charlotte Islands, the Tsimshians, Kwakiutls, Bella Coolas, and the Nootkas, all of British Columbia, and the Coast Salish people, who inhabited the land from southern British Columbia to the Oregon coast south of the Columbia River. Among the Coast Salish were the Makahs, Quinaults, and Puyallups. Stretching south from Coos Bay, Oregon, were independent Athapascan-speaking villages and bands like the Tolowas and Chetcos. In the midst of several broad language groupings lived enclaves of linguistically diverse peoples like the Penutian-speaking Chinooks of the lower Columbia River.

The Coast peoples were hunters and gatherers. The land and sea around them was so rich in food that they did not need to cultivate crops. Their only domesticated animals were dogs, used mainly for deer hunting or for fibers: one woolly breed of dogs was kept in pens and sheared twice a year. Anthropologists once considered cultures so heavily dependent upon naturally occurring products for their sustenance to be primitive in comparison to those based on agriculture, yet therein lay an anomaly. The environment

28

5. The Makahs, who lived on the northwestern tip of the Olympic Peninsula, were famed for their skill as whalers. Courtesy Special Collections Division, University of Washington Libraries, A. Curtis 19229.

yielded such a surplus of natural resources that Coast Indians had no trouble feeding themselves and finding enough leisure time to improve and elaborate their material culture and to conduct a lively trade. At the same time they developed a highly stratified and class-conscious social structure atypical of other North American maritime hunting and gathering groups.

The economy and life-style of Coast Indians centered on the resources of the sea. Hunting marine mammals was economically important and enhanced the prestige of the participants. Most spectacular of all were the whale hunts of the Nootkas and the Makahs, the latter inhabiting part of the Olympic Peninsula. Land mammals were more difficult to exploit, and therefore Coast peoples practiced hunting only to a limited extent.

But life in the Coast culture area was hardly idyllic. Warfare aimed at driving out or exterminating another lineage or family was an established practice in the northern portion of the region. Peoples to the south carried on feuds much more limited in violence and extent. After a successful attack, the northern warriors sometimes beheaded their victims, brought the heads home, and impaled them atop tall poles in front of their villages. Only the Tlingits practiced scalping.

Several groups practiced slavery, though more for symbolic than for economic reasons. Slaves were primarily war captives and retained no rights. Tlingit chiefs, for example, were reported to have crushed slaves to death beneath enormous posts set up at a house-building ceremony. On the arrival of a visiting chief, the Kwakiutls sometimes killed slaves on the beach in order to use their bodies as rollers for the visitor's canoe. Such conspicuous displays of wealth enhanced the group's prestige. It should be noted here that trade rivalries might distort perceptions of native savagery: the Nootkas apparently exploited European dread of cannibalism to sully the reputation of nearby peoples and thus gain competitive advantages in the contest for fur wealth.

Ceremonies of various types were a significant part of daily life, especially during the winter months. Summer was a time for work; the rainy, blustery days of winter were reserved for ceremonial performances. Indians did not separate material objects from things of the spirit. Consequently, food gathering, especially of salmon, a dietary staple of Coast peoples, involved some of their most important religious ceremonies. It was believed that salmon represented a race of supernatural beings who dwelled in a great house beneath the sea. When a salmon died, its spirit returned to its place of origin, and thus it behooved humans not to offend the salmon people by the careless disposal of their bones. If the bones were properly returned to the water, the being resumed a humanlike form without discomfort and could repeat the trip next season. All Northwest Coast peoples had long lists of taboos and prohibitions designed to maintain good relations with the salmon people. Although it may have been inadvertent, in that way they displayed a superlative ecological wisdom.

The Kwakiutls, Nootkas, and others also practiced a world-renewal ceremonial cycle. Performances were spectacular, with sensational stage effects unsurpassed among Indians of North America. Many of their masks had movable parts; tunnels and trap doors allowed actors "miraculously" to appear and disappear; lines of hollow kelp stems concealed under the floor enabled performers to project their voices from unexpected places.

Anthropologists have studied the potlatch more than any other ceremony. In its many variations and elaborations, the potlatch was a feature of Indian culture from southern Alaska to the Oregon coast. The elaborate,

THE CHINOOK JARGON

The first Pacific Northwesterners spoke a bewildering variety of languages and dialects that were as mutually unintelligible as English and Japanese. In western Washington the prevailing tongue was Coast Salish. Chinookan dialects were spoken in Oregon from the mouth of the Columbia to Tillamook Bay and east to the Cascades, but the Tillamooks belonged to the Coast Salish–speaking people. The interior tribes spoke languages derived from the Algonquin language stock and the Salish, Sahaptian, and Numic families.

The Chinook jargon facilitated communication among Indians as well as with Euro-Americans. A simply structured hybrid language that by the 1830s had expanded to include approximately seven hundred words of Indian, English, and French origin, augmented by signs, the Chinook jargon proved remarkably adept at embracing additional words to describe new trade goods. But it was poorly suited to Euro-American attempts to explain complex matters like land holding and religion.

One unhappy result was a series of treaties negotiated between whites and Indians, the language and meaning of which are still a matter of legal dispute.

Here are some examples of Chinook jargon:

| | |
|---|---|
| Boston | American |
| Hi-ack | Make haste, hurry |
| Cultus | Trifling, common |
| Mem'e-lose | Dead |
| Muck'a-muck | Food, to eat |
| Pot'latch | Give, or gift |
| Skoo'kum | Strong |
| Til-li-cum | People/Tribe/ Friends |
| Kleutch'man | Woman |
| Ty-ee' | Chief |
| Too-tooche' | Breasts, milk |
| Too-tooche' gleece | Butter |
| Gleece | Grease |
| Pire | Fire |
| Gleece-pire | Candle |

—terms from James G. Swan, *The Northwest Coast, or, Three Years' Residence in Washington Territory* (1857; reprint, New York: Harper & Row, 1961): 415–22

competitive potlatch that prevailed among the northern peoples received the most comment. In this classic encounter, two powerful rivals might give away and destroy valuable trade goods and money during the course of the contest. Ostensibly the occasion might be a young person's coming of age, a marriage, or a funeral, but the destruction of property also signified that a person was so powerful and rich that material goods were of no consequence to him. The potlatch served to unite people, because each member of the host's lineage or extended family was expected to contribute to the extent of his or her ability.

The oratory, elaborate form, and disposal or destruction of enormous accumulations of wealth scandalized outside observers and sparked controversy among anthropologists. Some scholars viewed the potlatch as a way to redistribute the wealth. Others thought that it addressed the great religious issues of life renewal or was part of a class struggle by traditional chiefs to maintain their hereditary power. Canadian missionaries promoted legislation in 1884 that made giving or assisting in a potlatch dance a misdemeanor punishable by up to six months in prison. That law remained on the books until 1951.

The word *potlatch* comes from the Chinook jargon, a trade language that enabled Indians of the Northwest Coast to overcome communication difficulties. The Chinookan peoples—the Clatsops, Cathlamets, Skilloots, and others whose homeland lay along the lower Columbia River—occupied a strategic position as middlemen in the trade between Indians to the north and south and between those of the Coast and the Plateau cultural areas. They traded slaves captured in California to the Nootkas for canoes and other products. Through Chinookan traders, prized shells from the west coast of Vancouver Island reached Indians of the interior.

Often classified with Indians of the Northwest Coast cultural area are those who inhabited Oregon's inland valleys: Kalapuyans and Molallas of the Willamette Valley and various independent groups that whites popularly referred to as Rogue River Indians. Those peoples, far more than the natives living along the coast proper, added nuts, roots, and game to their diet.

### INDIANS OF THE PLATEAU

Like the Indians of the Coast, those of the Plateau cultural area are grouped by anthropologists into numerous tribes, bands, and families. As distinct entities, they divided roughly according to river valleys and watersheds and occupied an area extending from the Cascades to the Rockies and from central Idaho to central British Columbia. Living along the upper reaches of the Columbia were the Kalispels (whom French-speaking trappers called Pend d'Oreilles), Kutenais, Coeur d'Alenes (so named by French-Canadian fur traders but called "Skitswish" in their own Salish language), Flatheads, Colvilles, Sanpoils, Okinagans, and Spokanes. In the Columbia basin country lived the Yakimas, Klikitats, Umatillas, Walla Wallas, Palooses, and Nez Perces (so named by fur traders though they did not pierce the septum of their noses and were known in their own Sahaptian tongue as Ne-Mee-Poo, "the people"). The Klamaths and Modocs lived in south-central Oregon. As a rule, the tribes living in the northern portion of the region spoke Salish languages and dialects and those in the central and south spoke various Sahaptian tongues.

When Euro-American fur traders and explorers reached the Plateau cultural area in the early years of the nineteenth century, Indians lived in small, semipermanent fishing settlements along major streams and tributaries. Each settlement was usually an autonomous unit with its own leaders, most of whom had gained their standing through democratic methods of selection rather than by heredity. On occasion, villages or bands (groups of villages associated voluntarily by common bonds) came together to trade, fish, hunt, gather roots in a communal harvest, socialize, or wage limited warfare against a common enemy. Because whites only poorly understood that decentralized arrangement, they eventually forced the notion of a single tribal chief upon the Indians. Prior to Euro-American intrusion, the Nez Perces had a permanent governing council, a political organization that could speak for all of them, but they had no head chief empowered to sign away their lands in treaties.

The economy of the Plateau Indians was based on hunting and gathering. Their diet was rich in salmon, which made annual runs up all the major rivers of the interior. Depending upon the season, the Plateau people engaged in various types of food-gathering and -preserving activities. During the salmon run of May and June they used scoops, nets, spears, and other devices to catch the fish, which they dried and ground into a nutritious meal for later use and for trade. From June to September, the Nez Perces lived in temporary camps on the camas grounds where they harvested and prepared the starchy bulbs for winter food. Camas, second in importance only to fish in their diet, resembled small onions and were eaten cooked or raw. The annual gathering of the camas was a time when members of different Nez Perce bands got to know one another. Indians of the Plateau also dug several other kinds of vegetables, including wild turnip, bitterroot, and biscuit root, harvested berries in season, and hunted deer, elk, mountain sheep, and other game. Some natives even hunted bison, which appear to have lived on the Columbia plateau in limited numbers until the 1770s and on the Snake River plain in southern Idaho until the early 1800s.

Plateau Indians had home territories, but they traveled more often and over longer distances than did Coast Indians because of the dispersed nature of their food supply. Most Plateau people had a casual attitude toward community property, although the Nez Perce and Coeur d'Alene peoples fiercely protected their territory. They regarded intruders on their hunting and gathering grounds as trespassers. When the Nez Perces experienced conflict it was usually with their closest neighbors to the north, the Coeur d'Alene and Spokane peoples. But their oldest and most bitter enemies were the Shoshonean-speaking people to the south. Nez Perce occasionally taunted

Indian Groups
of The Pacific Northwest

© (Relief), Glbb Johnson 1994

34

the Shoshonis and drew them into ambushes in the canyons of the Salmon and Snake rivers, and the Shoshonis made daring raids into Nez Perce territory. Each side generally observed a truce during the busy summer months.

Before the coming of the horse and extensive contact with tipi-dwelling Plains Indians, Plateau Indians spent their winters in protected valleys housed in circular earthen-roofed lodges built partly underground. During the summer they moved to cooler elevations and lived in rough pole lodges covered with mats of tule or cattail. Plateau peoples were ideally situated to borrow and give freely through contact with their neighbors, especially after they acquired horses in the early 1700s. Before the horse, they had traveled entirely by foot or water.

The horse had an impact on Indian society and culture not unlike that of the automobile on twentieth-century America. The Nez Perces used horses to make regular trips to the Great Plains to hunt bison and exchange trade goods. Through contact with natives there they adopted such innovations as skin tipis, buckskin clothing, and feathered headdresses for festive occasions. Their diet also changed after the coming of the horse; fish, which had constituted approximately 80 percent of the Nez Perce diet, increasingly gave way to buffalo, elk, deer, and antelope.

The Nez Perces first obtained horses from the Shoshoni Indians of the Great Basin around 1730; the latter had acquired them from the Comanches of the southern plains, who in turn got them from Spaniards who had introduced horses in the New World. Large horse herds flourished on the rich natural grasses of the plateau, and the natives of the region became adept horsemen. Although Plateau Indians did not place the same value on acquisitiveness and material possessions as their contemporaries on the coast, they considered a man with many horses to be rich. Some Oregon headmen had as many as five thousand horses apiece. The Nez Perces traded surplus horses to other tribes and later to Euro-American fur traders.

### INDIANS OF THE GREAT BASIN

Few regions of the present United States were more inhospitable to human habitation than the lands of the Great Basin, the high desert country of southern Idaho, eastern Oregon, Nevada, and Utah. Indians of the Great Basin spent much of the year foraging for food in small and dispersed groups, although several families might come together for a communal rabbit drive or to dig for camas bulbs. It was common for Shoshonis to name their subgroups after the food most abundant in their customary dwelling grounds:

6. A "Sheepeater" band of Shoshoni as photographed by
William H. Jackson around 1871. Courtesy Smithso-
nian Institution, 1713.

thus among the Shoshonis were groups whose names translated as "seed
eaters," or "fish eaters," or "mountain-sheep eaters."

The Shoshonis dwelled in southeastern Idaho, while to their west and
south lived the Northern Paiutes. Living among the Shoshonis were the
Bannocks (who called themselves Panakwate but which Euro-Americans
heard as "Panak" or "Bannack"), a small band of northern Paiutes who
moved from southeastern Oregon into Shoshoni territory. Collectively
these were known as the Snake Indians, a name apparently derived from
claims that they frightened Plains natives with sticks having snakes painted
on them.

Given the meager resources available in the Great Basin, a land of dry
soil, low rainfall, and high evaporation, the Shoshoni-Bannocks were relatively well-off, utilizing salmon, game animals, birds, and edible plants of
the Boise and Salmon river drainage systems in their diet. Salmon ascended
the Snake River as far as Salmon Falls in early summer, and bison were
common in parts of southern Idaho until the 1830s.

36

The Shoshonis, like the Nez Perces, acquired numerous horses after 1700 and used them to travel to the Great Plains, where they hunted buffalo and traded with the tribes living there. Curiously, although the Shoshonis were the first of the northern tribes to obtain horses, they were one of the last to acquire firearms. Thus, when their neighbors the Blackfeet, Cheyennes, Arapahos, and Utes acquired guns, they harassed the Shoshonis and sought to drive them back into the mountains and restrict their mobility. Perhaps one reason why first contacts between Euro-Americans and the people of the Snake River plain were so peaceable was that Indians needed help in defending themselves against marauding Blackfeet, who claimed a vast western domain as their own.

The Northern Paiutes inhabited much of what is now southwestern Idaho, southeastern Oregon, and northern Nevada. It was an arid domain where even in the best of times the small scattered Paiute bands lacking permanent villages and complex social organization spent their time traveling by foot from one oasis to another in a never-ending search for water, firewood, and food. Although individual bands occasionally cooperated with each other, there was no tribal unity. Usually only a few families remained together for any length of time, for there simply was not a large enough supply of rabbits, birds, mice, grasshoppers, lizards, pine nuts, and other food items to feed many people. They developed a nutritious flour compounded from seeds and roasted pine nuts and crafted woven baskets to store and transport their food. The Northern Paiutes did not practice agriculture, although they developed rudimentary forms of irrigation in order to increase the yield of natural vegetation.

Because the Northern Paiutes used digging sticks to unearth roots, Euro-Americans referred to them contemptuously as Digger Indians. Although they represented the best human adaptation to extremes of heat and cold and the desiccation of a desert environment, the Northern Paiutes remained the least favored materially of North America's native peoples.

Indians of the Great Basin held an annual intertribal rendezvous near the confluence of the Boise and Snake rivers. Here they celebrated the opening of the fishing season and traded with one another. Nez Perce visitors from the north came to trade their fine ponies; Indians of the Columbia River might swap prized shells from the Pacific Coast for the buffalo hides and dried meat brought by the Shoshoni. The Paiutes offered arrowheads fashioned from obsidian.

An even more important intertribal gathering took place at the Grand Dalles of the Columbia River, the home territory of the Wishrams, Wascos, and other peoples. It was the most important point of contact between Coast and Plateau cultures. Here was the cosmopolitan center of Northwest Indian life, site of great month-long trade fairs analogous to those held in medieval Europe, a time for trading, dancing, ceremonial displays, games, gambling, and even marriages. The Wishrams and Wascos sometimes hosted several thousand visitors who came to trade dried salmon meal, bison robes, and slaves from the interior for canoes, marine shells and shell beads, and fish oil from the coast. The development of complex patterns of exchange enabled Indian trade goods from the Pacific Northwest to reach as far as Alaska, southern California, and Missouri.

### THEIR NUMBERS THINNED

Two speculative questions should be asked about the first inhabitants of the Pacific Northwest: where did they originate and what was their population at the beginning of sustained European contact? Once it was believed that the Coast culture was essentially an extension of that of Asia. Anthropologists now argue that it was derived from that of ancient Eskimos and spread through the interior to the coast. Although no definitive answer is yet possible, it has been documented that Indian civilization on Washington's northwestern coast has existed continuously for nearly six thousand years, and some scholars estimate that human habitation of the Pacific Northwest dates back twelve thousand years.

Equally speculative are the estimates of Northwest Indian population before the coming of Euro-Americans. There may have been a hundred thousand natives or two or three times that number. It does make a difference, because unless some idea of the original Indian population is known, it is impossible to assess the Euro-American impact on the first Pacific Northwesterners. This much is certain: the advent of an ongoing relationship with Euro-Americans brought about a significant reduction in the Indian population.

That Euro-Americans ultimately prevailed over Indians was less a matter of warfare than of disease. It was neither the guns of the whites nor their whiskey that really decimated the Indian population, but their germs. Violent clashes between Euro-Americans and Indians have attracted the attention of historians, but far more deadly than bullets were the invisible killers—smallpox, malaria, measles, and influenza—germs to which Indians had no natural immunity. As a result of epidemics of both identifiable and unknown origin, the biologically vulnerable Indian population declined rapidly after the 1780s.

In some cases, disease spread from Euro-Americans to nearby tribes and then to distant people who had never seen a white person. A smallpox epidemic struck the Nez Perces in 1781–82 when white traders unintentionally introduced the disease into eastern tribes, and it spread across the Great Plains to devastate the Nez Perces and other residents of the Plateau.

Near the mouth of the Columbia River, Ross Cox noted in 1814 that "about thirty years before this period, the smallpox had committed dreadful ravages among these Indians, the vestiges of which are still visible on the countenances of the elderly men and women." He noted that Canadian and American traders blamed one another for introducing the disease. "The unfortunate Indians when in the height of the fever, would plunge into a river, which generally caused instant death; and thousands of the miserable wretches by suicide anticipated its fatal termination."[1]

Various diseases commonly labeled "fever and ague" (probably a virulent form of influenza) wiped out whole villages of Chinooks on the lower Columbia River and Kalapuyans in the Willamette Valley between 1829 and 1833. Over a three-year period the Chinook population declined to one-tenth its former size, and riverbanks were strewn with the unburied dead. "The depopulation here has been truly fearful," observed the physician John Kirk Townsend in his eyewitness account of the lower Columbia River in 1834. "A gentleman told me, that only four years ago, as he wandered near what had formerly been a thickly peopled village, he counted no less than sixteen dead, men and women, lying unburied and festering in the sun in front of their habitations. Within the houses all were sick; not one had escaped the contagion; upwards of a hundred individuals, men, women, and children, were writhing in agony on the floors of the houses, with no one to render them any assistance."[2]

How different the subsequent history of the Pacific Northwest might have been had there been twice as many Indians living in the region at the time of European contact, or had the Indians not been so susceptible to European diseases, or had the Europeans contracted a deadly plague from the Indians. By the time missionaries and settlers came to the Pacific Northwest in the 1830s, disease already had reduced the region's Indian population to a fragment of its former size.

The demographic disaster had a profound impact on Indian morale and

1. Ross Cox, *Adventures on the Columbia River, Including the Narrative of a Residence of Six Years on the Western Side of the Rocky Mountains* (London: H. Colburn and R. Bentley, 1832), 1:312–13.

2. John Kirk Townsend, *Across the Rockies to the Columbia* (1839; abridged reprint, Lincoln: University of Nebraska Press, 1978), 222–24.

7. This Russell Lee photograph from September 1941
shows Native American fishermen at Celilo Falls on
the Columbia River. Slack water created by The Dalles
Dam in 1957 flooded the historic fishery. Courtesy Library of Congress, USF34-70154-D.

spiritual life, in many cases taking away their warlike habits and making
them fearful of Euro-Americans. John Kirk Townsend observed that, in
areas where Euro-Americans once had to arm themselves for protection, the
Indians "are as submissive as children."

The Black Death that ravaged Europe in the mid-1300s wiped out about
one-third of its population and contributed to profound changes of all types.
The far greater death rate among Native Americans weakened social structures and traditions, demoralized survivors, and thus opened the way for
new forms of religion that might offer solace and future protection from
such calamities.

CHAPTER 3

# Encounters with a
# Distant Land

*

Nothing can be more iniquitous than the rule which Civilized Governments have established, of taking Possession of the Countries of every People, who may be more rude and barbarous than themselves.—Alexander
Walker in *An Account of a Voyage to the North West Coast of America in
1785 and 1786* (1982)

*

Almost every placename on a map of the Pacific Northwest has a story
behind it. Some of the stories are biographical; some are capsule histories.
Names like Snoqualmie Pass and Moses Lake; the counties of Snohomish,
Skagit, Yakima, Walla Walla, Tillamook, Clackamas, Nez Perce, and Shoshone, and the communities of Spokane, Yakima, Coos Bay, Klamath Falls,
and Pocatello recall the first Pacific Northwesterners. Another set of names,
those of Puget Sound, Vancouver Island, Mounts Rainier and Saint Helens,
the Strait of Juan de Fuca, the San Juan Islands, and the Columbia River,
remind of still another aspect of Pacific Northwest history: the era of the
North Pacific maritime frontier.

During the span of a generation or two—from the 1740s to the 1790s—
seafarers from Europe and the United States dispelled the fog of geographic
ignorance that had previously shielded the North Pacific coast from outsiders. This was the world's last temperate zone coastline to yield its secrets
to Euro-Americans. By the end of the 1790s, explorers had effectively con-
signed a practicable Northwest Passage to the dustbin of theoretical geography. At the same time, those voyages provided cartographers with detailed

information on the coasts of Oregon and Washington, the lower Columbia River, the Strait of Juan de Fuca, and Puget Sound. During those same years, seaborne traders from several nations developed a profitable commerce in the region's furs and skins.

Motivating explorers and traders from Russia, Spain, Great Britain, France, and the United States were the three C's of empire: *curiosity, conquest,* and *commerce*. Rarely were those three forces separate from one another. Curiosity is perhaps too weak a term to describe the intense intellectual passion of the Age of Enlightenment. Yet Europeans and Americans of the 1700s were curious about the world as never before, relentlessly pushing back boundaries of ignorance whether they ran through the heavens, under a microscope, or along the shores of the Pacific Ocean.

### EMPIRE BUILDERS

Spain was the preeminent power in the Pacific basin for nearly three centuries after 1493. In that year Pope Alexander VI issued a proclamation giving all New World lands not held by a Christian ruler to Spain and Portugal and treating the Pacific Ocean as if it were a Spanish lake. Spain concentrated its attention on the Pacific coast south from Mexico and on equatorial trade routes linking its American empire and the Philippines. Interlopers like the Englishman Francis Drake had penetrated its waters and plundered Spanish ships, but their activities scarcely posed any immediate territorial threat to Spain.

From time to time, Spain dispatched exploratory voyages along the west coast of North America, and on occasion her mariners were blown off course and shipwrecked, according to the tales of Northwest Coast Indians. But Spain showed little interest in a region that seemed so pitifully lacking in either economic resources or good harbors. Only Russian exploration in the mid-1700s aroused Spain from her imperial lethargy. When Russian explorers and traders started probing south through the seas off Siberia and Alaska, reaping a valuable harvest in furs and skins along the way, Spain finally cast a concerned look northward.

In the search for furs, the Russians had apparently established a modest presence in the far eastern reaches of Asia as early as 1648, but sustained Russian interest in the waters off North America began only in the latter years of the reign of Czar Peter the Great. Because no one had yet discovered whether Asia and North America might be joined together at some northern latitude, Peter dispatched an expedition from the Russian capital at Saint Petersburg in 1719 to learn more about the relationship between the

8. One of the hazards of exploration: Vancouver's ship,
the *Discovery*, grounded on the rocks in Queen
Charlotte's Sound in 1792. On a high tide and a calm
ocean, the ship floated free a few hours later without apparent damage. Courtesy Library of Congress.

two continents. Four years later, after an overland crossing of more than ten
thousand miles, the explorers returned without a conclusive answer. Peter
did not give up, and on his deathbed he planned another expedition.

His widow and successor, Catherine I, shared his interest in exploration;
within weeks after ascending the throne in 1725, she dispatched an expedition commanded by Vitus Bering, a Danish captain in the Russian navy.
Bering returned five years later and reported that the two continents were
not joined. Catherine soon sent Bering on a second and far more elaborate
and ambitious assignment, partly scientific and partly to extend Russian
sovereignty into the Pacific. The main body of this five-hundred-person
expedition—soldiers, surveyors, interpreters, painters, and secretaries in addition to a large library of scientific books—departed in 1733 and made its
way slowly across Siberia to the Pacific. After constructing two ships, the
Russians explored the coast of Alaska in 1741. Misfortune overtook Bering,
marooning him on a cold, forbidding island where he and many crewmen

perished, but not before extending the empire of the czar to the North American continent.

Aleksei Chirikov, commander of the expedition's other ship, fared better. The survivors straggled back to Saint Petersburg, the last of them arriving in 1749, sixteen years after they first set out. Although many lives were lost, Bering's expedition established that it was possible to travel from Asia to North America by water and that the North Pacific region was rich in furs. A profitable commerce might be developed.

During the next fifty years other Russians followed Bering and Chirikov, expanding the trade in sea otter and other furs. Outstanding among them was Grigorii Shelikhov who established the first permanent Russian settlement in North America in 1784 at Three Saints Bay on Kodiak Island. That was, in fact, the first permanent settlement of Euro-Americans anywhere on the North Pacific. Shelikhov envisioned a string of posts extending hundreds of miles south along the coast, each settlement a mark of Russian possession. Of even greater importance was Aleksandr Baranov, a businessman who headed the monopolistic Russian-American Company, founded in 1799, and made it a major economic force in the North Pacific. His headquarters at New Archangel (Sitka) was one of the first nonnative communities in the region. Under Baranov, the Russian company established a presence as far south as Fort Ross (short for Russia) near Cape Mendocino north of San Francisco.

Although much of the Russians' activity was shrouded in secrecy, including the extent of their fur trade, their expansion into the North Pacific did not go unnoticed in other capitals of Europe. First to challenge the Russians was Spain, which undertook land and sea expeditions northward from Mexico into California in 1769 and 1770 and established permanent settlements there to blunt intrusion into an area already considered its own. Juan Pérez led an expedition in 1774 that sailed slightly north of the Queen Charlotte Islands before scurvy forced it to turn back.

On the return voyage, the Spanish anchored in the vicinity of Nootka Sound, which Pérez called San Lorenzo. Twenty-one canoes carrying nearly 150 Nootka villagers made contact with the Spanish and exchanged gifts. Some bolder Indians boarded the *Santiago* and took silver spoons that Cook's expedition noted four years later. The Spanish studied the natural setting and its inhabitants, but Pérez failed to make any charts or take formal possession of the region.

The following year a Spanish expedition under the command of Juan Francisco de la Bodega y Quadra sailed north along the Pacific coast and reached fifty-eight degrees north before scurvy forced it to retreat. On the

THE SCOURGE OF SCURVY

On long voyages to the Pacific Northwest, seamen faced health hazards that ranged from fleas and lice (especially common on sea otter pelts) to malaria and dysentery; but the worst of their unwelcome companions was scurvy. A nutritional deficiency caused by lack of vitamin C, this "dreadful distemper" made crewmen miserable and could eventually kill them. Before Captain Cook, one-half and occasionally two-thirds of a ship's crew might die of scurvy and other sicknesses. Scurvy occasionally caused ailing seamen to desert and expeditions to be aborted. Yet on his long second voyage around the world, Cook lost but one man to sickness.

Sufferers might restore their health by eating fresh food rich in antiscorbutics (scurvy preventatives), such as wild celery, parsley, and onions, and spruce beer or tea. Even tender stinging nettles could be added to the soup pot to counteract the disease. Cook experimented with a variety of remedies, including carrot marmalade, soda water, sauerkraut, lemons, and oranges. Cook's Spanish counterpart, Alejandro Malaspina, likewise sought to deal with the scourge of scurvy by serving his sailors gazpacho, made from tomatoes, peppers, garlic, vinegar, and olive oil.

In 1795 the Royal Navy stocked its ships with citrus fruits (lime juice), thus giving rise to the nickname "limeys" for British sailors. Within five years the scourge of scurvy had disappeared from His Majesty's ships. The term "vitamin C" came into use more than a century later, in 1921.

return voyage an associate, Bruno de Heceta or Hezeta (pronounced *Ey-they-ta*), detected the powerful current of the Columbia River pushing against the *Santiago*, causing him to believe "it may be the mouth of some great river or some passage to another sea." His men were so weak from scurvy that Heceta decided against crossing the great river's treacherous bar and instead continued south. Because of the secretive nature of Spanish exploration, he declined to broadcast his findings. Credit for the important discovery thus goes to the American Robert Gray, who in 1792 sailed a short distance up the Columbia and confirmed what Heceta had suspected.

In 1776, the year James Cook began his third voyage, the Spanish founded the first Euro-American settlement on San Francisco bay, a tiny community destined to become the most important city on America's West Coast. Another major Spanish expedition followed in 1779 under the command of Ignacio de Arteaga. It probed as far north as 59°52′, where Mount Saint Elias loomed in the distance. At this point, which Bering sighted from a different direction in 1741, the empires of Russia and Spain made tentative contact. Arteaga's ships continued slightly farther north before turning south, adding on paper a large area to the far-flung Spanish empire.

But as Russians pushed south and Spaniards north, the British under

James Cook wedged themselves in between the two expanding empires at Nootka, creating the potential for a major international clash. The British intrusion intensified interest in profiting from the region's furs, or "soft gold" as some have labeled it. That development was the first of many extractive endeavors that have dominated the Pacific Northwest economy.

MARITIME FUR TRADE

Cook's men understood that the Russians had turned a profit in furs, but they did not realize the full economic potential of the trade until they reached Canton, where they sold twenty worse-for-wear animal skins for an exorbitant price even in today's money. And the Chinese besieged Cook's men for still more.

The object of their attention was the lustrous pelt of the sea otter, a rich jet-black glossy fur with shimmery silvery undertones. One of Cook's contemporaries remarked that "excepting a beautiful woman and a lovely infant" the pelts were among the most attractive natural objects. Sea otters occasionally weighed eighty pounds and attained a length of nearly four feet, making them a much larger creature than the smaller land otter. They fed in relatively shallow water, searching the bottom for abalone and occasionally preying on squid, octopus, and sea urchins. Their breeding grounds covered a six-thousand-mile arc from Japan's northernmost islands through the Aleutian Islands southward along the Northwest Coast to California. Almost wholly aquatic, sea otters came ashore only in severe storms. The bonds between parents and offspring were so strong that trappers seized the young to lure the adults to their death.

After Cook's expedition discovered this new source of fortune, the first trader to reach the Northwest Coast was James Hanna, who sailed from the port of Macao on the China coast in 1785. At Nootka Sound he traded iron bars for furs and skins, which he sold a year later in Canton for twenty thousand Spanish dollars, a handsome profit. Hanna hastened back to Nootka only to find that two other ships had taken nearly all the furs the natives had to offer. Hanna was forced to search farther north along the coast. Such were hazards the of the trade.

During the remainder of the 1780s, Nootka was a busy place as European and American trading ships made ports of call. In a typical transaction, the Indians exchanged sea otter pelts for such trade goods as sheets of copper, heavy blue cloth, or muskets, powder, and shot. Inventive traders are also known to have swapped a ship's curtains, anchor, crockery, and even a

Japanese flag for furs or fresh food. Prices varied over time, so that the cost of a sea otter's skin inflated from one to five muskets during the late nineteenth century. In China, Euro-Americans traded the pelts for tea, porcelain, silk, and similar items that commanded high prices in Europe or on the Atlantic seaboard.

Even as Nootka Sound became the most important anchorage for fur traders on the North Pacific Coast, imperial claims to the region remained unresolved. Although Juan Pérez had anchored off Nootka's entrance, the secretive Spaniards published no account of his activities. Cook, during his month there, made no effort to take formal possession of the area because he heard vague reports of Spanish visitors and assumed that they had already claimed it for their king.

The matter of conflicting imperial claims finally led to an international incident in 1789 known as the Nootka Sound controversy. In that year the Russians were a well-established presence in the North Pacific; Spain laid claim to Nootka and the entire western coast of North America; Great Britain challenged that notion; and the United States, seeking new markets to replace those lost by separation from Great Britain, showed increased interest in the Pacific fur trade. A French scientific expedition under Jean-François de Galaup, Count La Pérouse, also had explored the area between 1786 and 1788, but that effort ended disastrously when a severe tropical storm wrecked the expedition. No clues ever came to light about possible survivors, including La Pérouse. Fortunately, his scientific observations had been sent back to Paris from previous stops and were published in four volumes. The La Pérouse tragedy, coupled with the outbreak of the French revolution a short time later, discouraged follow-up voyages. In short, despite their vastness, the North Pacific waters had become too small to accommodate the territorial and economic ambitions of rival nations.

The British sea captain John Meares visited Nootka in 1788. With the permission of a local chief, Meares erected a modest trading post that he expected would one day form the center of a North Pacific trading system, but it was not to be. The structure was apparently dismantled when Meares departed a few months later, yet the British later used its brief existence to strengthen their territorial claims to the area. In mid-1789, a Spanish expedition, finding no sign of British settlement, took formal possession of Nootka for His Catholic Majesty, the King of Spain, and erected a fort. When a British ship commanded by Captain James Colnett arrived a short time later and proposed to construct a trading post, Don Estéban José Martínez informed Colnett that he commanded a garrison at Nootka in the name of the Spanish king. Colnett responded with a British counterclaim based on Cook's discoveries.

Suspecting a British plot to acquire Nootka, Martínez seized the British vessels, arrested Colnett and his crew, and sent them to Mexico for trial. News of the high-handed action, embellished and distorted into a major Spanish insult to the British, created a furor in England. Rival empires stood at the brink of war.

Despite Nootka's remoteness, the conflict between Britain and Spain nearly engulfed the infant United States. The administration of President George Washington debated the possibility that British troops might try to conquer Spanish Louisiana by marching across America's sparsely populated Ohio country from bases in Canada. The crisis at Nootka thus sparked the first cabinet-level foreign policy debate in the United States under the new Constitution of 1787.

How European nations established claims to these lands lay at the heart of the controversy. For three centuries Spain, backed by the Pope's 1493 edict, had done so through a symbolic act of taking possession. The ritual consisted of going ashore, planting a cross with an appropriate inscription, reciting a religious litany, and burying a bottle containing a written version of the act of possession beneath a pile of stones at the foot of the cross. With the Malaspina expedition of 1789–94, Spain adopted a new practice of establishing sovereignty through a limited act of possession, mapping the claim, and publishing the results of any new discoveries. Indeed, because the English had published a record of Cook's third voyage, they were thus able to establish a more convincing claim to Nootka than the Spanish. Native peoples, incidentally, at first counted for little in this Eurocentric notion of sovereignty. Even when whites negotiated treaties with the Indians, the concept of transferring title to the land remained alien to the Indian view of the world.

England and Spain averted war over Nootka when they signed a convention in 1790 limiting Spain's dominions to discoveries secured by treaties and immemorial possession and compensating the English for damages done them at Nootka. The actual limits to Spanish claims were not set, however, and Spain maintained a presence at Nootka for five more years until a second Nootka convention resolved the controversy. Distracted by affairs in Europe and unable to discredit the territorial claims of its rival, Spain yielded Nootka to the English. The decline of the Spanish empire accelerated during the next two decades. Having lost interest in the Pacific Northwest, Spain ceded to the United States all claims to the region north of the 42nd parallel by signing the Adams-Onís Treaty of 1819.

An agreement with the United States in 1824 and with Britain in 1825 extinguished Russian claims to the lands south of 54°40′ (today the southernmost tip of the Alaska panhandle). That left Americans and Britons in joint possession of the Oregon country, their condominium arrangement modeled after the joint British and Spanish occupation of Nootka Sound in the early 1790s. As for Nootka Sound, the decline of the maritime fur trade left it isolated. Today it remains one of North America's backwaters, reachable only by boat or plane.

### EXPLORATION

As seafarers exploited the natural resources of North Pacific waters in the 1780s and 1790s, they continued to explore its islands, bays, and inlets. Voyages of discovery up the Strait of Juan de Fuca provide a vivid illustration of the process of knowledge accumulation. It is ironic that the man who gave his name to that body of water did so by a simple feat: telling what most authorities regard as a big lie.

A Greek named Apostolos Valerianos, commonly called Juan de Fuca, claimed to have made a voyage for Spain in 1592 that took him north from Mexico along the Pacific coast to a point between forty-seven and forty-eight degrees latitude. In a region he described as being rich in gold, silver, and pearls, he discovered the Strait of Anian, the Spanish designation for the fabled Northwest Passage. For twenty days he sailed through the strait, he said, reached the North Atlantic, and then backtracked to Mexico. By the early 1600s the curious tale had found its way into histories and maps of the North Pacific.

On his northern voyage, James Cook looked in vain for de Fuca's fabled strait and acidly commented, "We saw nothing like it, nor is there the least possibility that ever any such thing existed." In the fog he missed seeing the body of water that separates Vancouver Island and the Olympic Peninsula, a twenty-mile-wide strait opening remarkably near where de Fuca claimed to have crossed the continent.

An Englishman, Captain Charles Barkley, apparently made the first indisputable European discovery of the Strait of Juan de Fuca in 1787. He made no attempt to penetrate its hundred-mile length, but a year later John Meares sent in a company of explorers who he later claimed took possession of its shores for Great Britain.

Further British and Spanish explorations followed, until in 1792 Captain George Vancouver sailed through the strait and around the island that today bears his name. For two months, his men explored the great inland sea that Vancouver called Puget Sound. To the principal bays, inlets, and

49

THE MALASPINA EXPEDITION

To the three C's of empire might be added a fourth: competition. When Alejandro Malaspina, a Spanish naval officer, sought imperial approval for an around-the-world scientific expedition, he cited the exploits of Cook and La Pérouse and urged Spain to do as Britain and France had. Receiving all necessary official assistance, the Malaspina expedition departed Spain for the New World in 1789 and after two years reached the waters off Alaska's Yakutat Bay. The Spaniards remained among the Tlingits for nine days, compiling extensive written and visual records and collecting artifacts. The expedition continued its scientific activities for two weeks at Nootka and then cruised south along the coasts of Washington and Oregon, delineating various headlands with some exactness.

Ethnographic records were vital to the scientific part of the expedition, but the Spaniards also made hydrographic and oceanic charts to aid commercial navigation in these remote waters, and they assessed the political intent of other nations in the North Pacific. The discovery of the fabled Strait of Anian, which persistent Spaniards believed might yet be found, and the strengthening of Spain's pretensions to exclusive sovereignty in the Pacific Northwest and the entire Pacific Ocean were two added objects of the Malaspina expedition. In that regard the mission failed, but it provided the world with a wealth of North Pacific Coast artifacts and observations of native lifestyles.

other physical features, he assigned names that in many cases still identify them: Admiralty Inlet, Dungeness, Port Orchard, Port Discovery, Possession Sound, Restoration Point, Deception Pass, Bellingham Bay, Whidbey and Vashon islands, and the Gulf of Georgia. Vancouver also named Mounts Baker and Rainier. Hood Canal and Mount Rainier were named after two of Vancouver's friends in the British admiralty who never sailed in Pacific waters.

The last of the great eighteenth-century discoveries along the Pacific coast of Oregon and Washington was made by an American, Captain Robert Gray, whose ship, the *Columbia*, became the first U.S. vessel to circumnavigate the globe when she returned to Boston harbor in 1790. A swarm of American fur traders and whalers followed Gray's lead, making the long voyage from New England ports, rounding Cape Horn, and fanning out into all parts of the Pacific.

Gray was a trader who came late to the North Pacific. Like all latecomers to any frontier, he found the field of opportunity considerably narrowed. Undiscouraged, he returned to the North Pacific in 1791 to trade for pelts. In the process, Gray discovered the harbor on the coast of Washington that bears his name and, in May 1792, the majestic river he named for his ship:

Columbia's River, a spelling soon modified to a more familiar form. Although Gray's men explored only a short distance upstream and Gray never returned to the river, he laid the foundation for a U.S. claim to the area by depositing a rough chart of the lower river with the Spanish governor at Nootka, thereby duly notifying European powers of the American discovery.

Following Gray, Vancouver's expedition reached the mouth of the Columbia in October 1792. His lieutenant, William Broughton, surveyed a hundred miles up the river to a site near present Vancouver, Washington, and made the first detailed chart of the waterway. Broughton contended that Gray never actually entered the river itself but only the sound at its mouth. That assertion was the basis for a British claim to the river, although when Broughton's charts were published in 1798 they retained the name Gray gave to the great waterway.

It was during the era of maritime exploration that Euro-Americans first attempted to establish a permanent settlement within the present confines of the Pacific Northwest. This was at Neah Bay, a heavily wooded place on the Strait of Juan de Fuca, where a Spanish-Mexican expedition led by Salvador Fidalgo established the colony of Nuñez Gaona in late May 1792. Disembarking the *Princesa*, crewmen felled trees to construct a blacksmith's shop, bakery, barracks, a small fort with six mounted guns, and corrals for their cattle. The Spaniards also planted several vegetable gardens.

Even as their tiny settlement expanded, the newcomers kept a longboat on the beach in case an Indian attack made it necessary to flee to their frigate anchored offshore. When Indians killed an expedition member working alone in the woods, an enraged Fidalgo fired on two canoes, killing all the occupants except for a boy and girl. This rash act brought him a reprimand from his superiors, including the Spanish king.

Various other problems with the Neah Bay location, including a poor anchorage and the occasionally severe winds that swept across the Strait of Juan de Fuca, caused Spain to abandon the four-month-old settlement in late September. Among the legacies of the Neah Bay and Nootka Sound settlements are the first cattle, pigs, goats, and other livestock introduced into the region, and the first tomatoes, onions, garlic, turnips, radishes, corn, and cabbage. With its seventy seamen and thirteen soldiers, Nuñez Gaona was the oldest non-Indian settlement in the Pacific Northwest. Nearly two decades passed before Euro-Americans again attempted to establish a base in the Pacific Northwest.

There would be no more discoveries of major consequence on the North

Pacific Coast after the 1790s, but the unknown lands of the interior were another matter. No Euro-Americans knew what lay east of the Cascade mountains, nor did they know the course of the Columbia River. Here were more curiosities, more possibilities for commerce, and more lands to claim. In 1793, even as Vancouver undertook to dispel the last wisps of mystery surrounding de Fuca's Northwest Passage, Alexander Mackenzie and a party of fur traders from the opposite side of North America crossed the Continental Divide and approached the very waters Vancouver was mapping. The two just missed making contact.

The peak years of the maritime fur trade lasted from the 1790s until the War of 1812, and during that time Americans had edged out the British. Overtrapping took such a toll on profits that, by the first decade of the nineteenth century, the future clearly belonged to fur empires spanning the continent by land. Other Pacific Northwest placenames—Lewiston, Clarkston, Astoria, and Boise—recall that era.

# CHAPTER 4

# Continental Dreams and
# Fur Empires

*

The progress of discovery contributes not a little to the enlightenment of mankind; for mercantile interest stimulates curiosity and adventure, and combines with them to enlarge the circle of knowledge.—Alexander Ross, *Adventures of the First Settlers on the Oregon or Columbia River, 1810–1813* (1849)

*

Pacific Northwesterners honor the names of Lewis and Clark above all others. Cities and counties, rivers and peaks, streets and schools, all testify to the importance of the two explorers who have long symbolized the westering impulse in American life.

### THE CORPS OF DISCOVERY

The overland expedition led by Meriwether Lewis and William Clark reached the Oregon coast in late 1805, twenty-seven years after James Cook. Although the two ventures differed in obvious ways, they had certain common features: both were military expeditions; both sketched in details on the map of North America; and both spurred the commerce in furs. Publication of official and unofficial records of each expedition stimulated the curiosity and commercial ambitions of those who followed.

Like Cook, Lewis and Clark sought a Northwest Passage. Their quest was for an easy portage through the mountains that separated the head of navigation on the Missouri River and that of a river draining into the Pa-

---

HONORING LEWIS AND CLARK

| | |
|---|---|
| Lewiston, Idaho | Clark Fork River (in Montana and northern Idaho) |
| Clarkston, Washington | |
| Lewis County, Idaho* | Lewis and Clark River (Oregon) |
| Lewis County, Washington | Lewis and Clark State Recreation Area, Washington |
| Clark County, Washington | Lewis and Clark Trail State Recreation Area (Washington) |
| Lewis-Clark State College (in Lewiston, Idaho) | |
| | Lewis and Clark State Park (Oregon) |
| Lewis and Clark College (in Portland, Oregon) | Lewis and Clark Exposition (Portland, 1905) |
| Fort Lewis, Washington | |

*But not Clark County, Idaho, named for Sam Clark, a pioneer settler.

---

cific. Such a passage did not exist, but until Lewis and Clark proved that, the dream fired the imagination of Thomas Jefferson. As early as 1786, when he was minister to France and dined frequently in Paris with John Ledyard, a Connecticut adventurer who visited the Pacific Northwest as a member of Cook's third voyage, Jefferson enthusiastically embraced the idea of exploring the West. Thus from Cook to Ledyard to Jefferson, curiosity about the unknown Northwest passed from one generation to inspire the next.

What most spurred Jefferson was the 1801 publication of Alexander Mackenzie's *Voyages from Montreal* with its powerful declaration of British intent to secure the fur commerce of the Columbia River. Lewis and Clark may have carried this book with them to the Pacific Ocean; Lewis was certainly familiar with it. Jefferson, who read Mackenzie's book during the summer of 1802 at his Monticello home, where he had gone to escape the heat and humidity of Washington, must have pondered Mackenzie's affirmation: "By opening this intercourse between the Atlantic and Pacific Oceans, and forming regular establishments through the interior, and at both extremes, as well as along the coasts and island, the entire command of the fur trade of North America might be obtained, from latitude 48. north to the pole, except that portion of it which the Russians have in the Pacific."[1]

---

1. Alexander Mackenzie, *Voyages from Montreal, on the River St. Laurence, Through the Continent of North America to the Frozen and Pacific Oceans* (London: T. Cadell, 1801), 411.

Jefferson's response would be an overland expedition modeled after the great exploratory voyages of Cook and Vancouver. He would encourage expansion of a St. Louis–based trade system across the American West in an effort to block a rival British-Canadian system based in Montreal and the Saint Lawrence River valley.

In January 1803, less than two years after he became president and only a short time before the United States completed purchase of the sprawling Louisiana Territory that doubled the nation's size, Jefferson sent Congress a secret message requesting an appropriation of $2,500 to finance an expedition up the Missouri River and thence to the Pacific Ocean. The president spoke of the need to extend the external commerce of the United States and to learn more about the unknown lands of North America. Curiosity and commerce were thus inextricably part of the Lewis and Clark expedition, and not mere idle curiosity, but carefully planned scientific reconnaissance. Jefferson, it must be noted, had no explicit territorial ambitions in the far Northwest, although the expedition's accomplishments would bolster future United States claims to the area.

The Corps of Discovery commenced the main phase of its historic journey from a winter camp near St. Louis on 14 May 1804. Jefferson selected his private secretary, Captain Meriwether Lewis, to command the expedition. With the president's approval, Lewis invited his old friend William Clark to be coleader. Although Clark was commissioned only a second lieutenant because of bureaucratic myopia within the War Department, Lewis kept that fact secret and treated him as a captain, in every respect his equal.

Lewis was thirty years old in 1804 and had for most of his life been a soldier. Clark was thirty-four years old and a soldier, but unlike Lewis, he had seen considerable Indian fighting. The two captains complemented one another well: Lewis, the better educated, functioned as businessman and scientific specialist; Clark served as engineer, geographer, and master of frontier lore. Lewis usually left daily management of the boats to Clark, who was also more diplomatic in dealing with Indians. In addition to Lewis and Clark, the corps included twenty-seven young unmarried soldiers, a mixed-blood hunter named George Drouillard, and Clark's black slave, York.

The corps ascended the lower Missouri River in a fifty-five-foot keelboat and two pirogues or large dugout canoes. Traveling about fifteen miles each day, they reached the villages of the Mandan and Hidatsa Indians about fifty miles north of present Bismarck, North Dakota, in late October. There they

9. Meriwether Lewis (1774–1809). Courtesy Library of Congress.

10. William Clark (1770–1838). Courtesy Library of
Congress.

spent the winter in temporary quarters called Fort Mandan. From here one group of soldiers returned the following spring with the expedition's first year's records and scientific specimens. The main body of the Lewis and Clark expedition continued west up the Missouri, endured a month-long portage around the several great falls of the river, and finally reached the base of the "shining mountains" in late August.

Lewis and Clark had anticipated a relatively easy portage across the Rockies to the navigable headwaters of the Columbia River. Instead, when they reached the continental divide at Lemhi Pass they gazed west upon range after range of mountains that stretched as far as their eyes could see. When they attempted to follow the Salmon River through the mountains of future Idaho, its wild waters forced them back. The explorers then turned north, and in the company of their recently acquired Shoshoni guide, Old Toby, struggled across the Bitterroot Mountains. From Lolo Pass (southwest of present Missoula), instead of crossing to the ridge top and following a traditional Indian route, the Lolo Trail, Toby led them down an old fishing trail to the headwaters of the Clearwater River. With their food almost gone and game practically nonexistent, the Corps of Discovery had no choice but to kill and roast one of their colts. Sergeant Patrick Gass called the horse meat "good eating."

To return to the main trail the Corps of Discovery struggled up a ridge so steep that some of the horses gave out, others slipped and were injured, and one rolled down the mountainside, smashing Clark's field desk which it carried, although the animal itself somehow escaped injury. The explorers finally reached the top, where at an elevation of more than 7,000 feet they slogged west through a snowstorm unanticipated in mid-September. Thirty-three cold, wet, and hungry people were reduced to making a meal of a few pheasants and another of their colts. For nine days they struggled across the Bitterroot Range, "this horrible mountainous desert," as Gass described it in his journal.[2] Clark complained that he had never been so wet or cold in his life: "indeed I was at one time fearful my feet would freeze in the thin mockersons which I wore. . . ."

Their situation grew so desperate that on 18 September they "dined," in Lewis's words, on a few canisters of dehydrated soup, an unpalatable army experimental ration Lewis had obtained in Philadelphia, a little bear's oil, and about twenty pounds of candles. Hunger and fatigue nearly broke the

2. Patrick Gass, *Gass's Journal of the Lewis and Clark Expedition* (1811; reprint, Chicago: A. C. McClurg, 1904), 142.

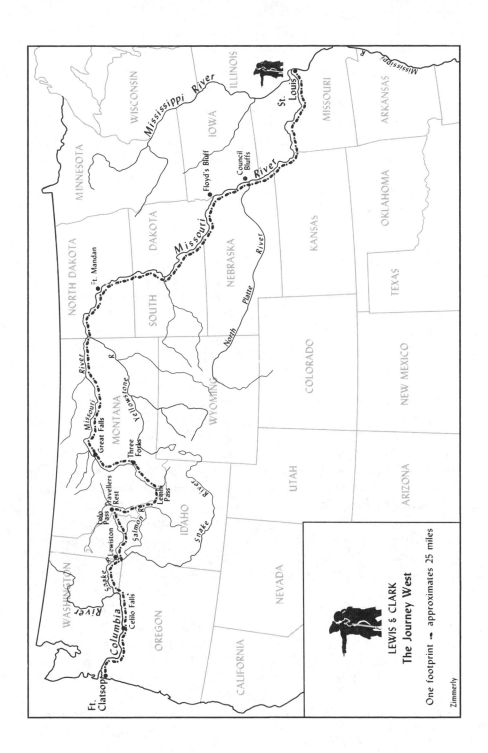

LEWIS & CLARK
The Journey West

One footprint ⋅—⋅ approximates 25 miles

Zimmerly

men's spirits. Several of them became ill with dysentery and broke out in skin sores. Never would the expedition come so close to failure as it did in the snows of the Bitterroot Mountains.

Clark took a party of six hunters and scouted ahead of the main troop for game. Two days later Clark's advance guard descended to the Weippe Prairie and made its first contact with the Nez Perce. Having endured several days of near starvation, the explorers indulged in such a hearty meal of salmon, buffalo, berries, and roots that Clark confessed in his journal, "I find myself verry unwell all the evening from eateing fish & roots too freely."

The Corps of Discovery survived its ordeal in the Bitterroots only to suffer severe and lingering bouts of gastritis that afflicted several members, including Lewis and Clark. After entrusting their horses to the Nez Perce and constructing five dugout canoes on a riverbank near present-day Oro-fino, Idaho, the explorers continued down the Clearwater, Snake, and Co-lumbia rivers. When on 7 November 1805 the corps neared the long-sought waters of the Pacific, Clark rejoiced in his notebook, "Great joy in camp we are in *View* of the Ocian, this great Pacific Octean which we been So long anxious to See. and the roreing or noise made by the waves brakeing on the rockey Shores (as I suppose) may be heard distinctly."[3] So intent was Clark on reaching his long-sought goal that his imagination apparently got the best of him here, for he mistook an estuary of the Columbia River for the Pacific Ocean, which the Corps of Discovery did not reach until a few days later. After ten storm-plagued days in camp on the north shore, the expedi-tion relocated across the river to a more favorable site. On 8 December the men began to build a small stockade on the Netul (now Lewis and Clark River) and named it Fort Clatsop after the nearest Indian tribe.

After enduring an exceedingly damp and disagreeable winter (only twelve days were free of rain) and failing to secure a hoped-for ship home, the Lewis and Clark expedition headed east on 23 March 1806. They faced the daunting prospect of having to retrace their steps across the Bitterroot Mountains. Deep snow blocked their way until late June. The explorers returned to the mouth of Lolo Creek in midsummer, and there the corps divided temporarily into two parties. Lewis took nine men across country to the falls of the Missouri, while Clark and the others explored a more roundabout passage along the Yellowstone River. The two captains and their troops were reunited on 12 August below the confluence of the Mis-

3. Gary Moulton, ed., *The Journals of the Lewis & Clark Expedition* (Lincoln: Univer-sity of Nebraska Press, 1988), 5:209, 223; 6:33.

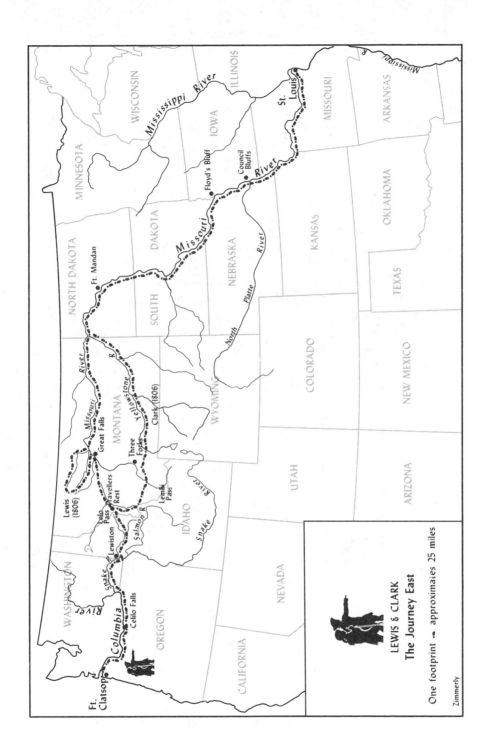

LEWIS & CLARK
The Journey East

One footprint ⚊ approximates 25 miles

Zimmerly

souri and Yellowstone rivers in eastern Montana. Six weeks later, on 23 September 1806, they returned to St. Louis, where they were greeted with great rejoicing.

During the twenty-eight-month odyssey, the expedition traveled more than eight thousand miles, and, remarkably, only one man lost his life. Sergeant Charles Floyd died of "biliose chorlick"—probably a ruptured appendix—on the journey up the Missouri River. The only violent encounter occurred when Indians attempted to steal the explorers' horses in the Blackfeet country of north-central Montana. In the ensuing scuffle one Indian was stabbed to death and another shot through the abdomen.

Lewis and Clark accomplished much more than simply adding a noteworthy chapter to the history of exploration. Most obviously, they revealed that the far Northwest was rich with beaver and other fur-bearing animals, and this information lured a generation of trappers and traders to the new land. Their journals, which rank among the treasures of the nation's written history, contain drawings, maps, and artifacts that added greatly to knowledge about terrain, native peoples, and the flora and fauna of the West. They bolstered America's future claims to a part of the world that was remote but hardly ignored. From a global perspective, the Lewis and Clark expedition represented only one more act in an ongoing imperial and commercial drama, but it was one that more than any other captivated scholars and fired the imagination of ordinary American citizens (and of British and Canadian trade rivals as well).

THE NOR'WESTERS

The fur trade, so entwined with the early history of the Pacific Northwest, was the first large-scale corporate enterprise in North America. Great profits were to be made selling the warm, beautiful, and fashionable furs. During Europe's Middle Ages, only the nobility and clergy had the right to wear furs such as ermine and sable, but in the eighteenth century a rising middle class also sought such luxuries. Growing demand and the discovery of fur-bearing animals in the New World coincided with a declining supply from Russia and Scandinavia. Thus, the whims of fashion made it worthwhile for trappers to "risk their skins for a skin," as it was popularly phrased. The most significant of the various furs and skins during the continental phase of the trade was beaver. Fashion-conscious gentlemen favored its slick fur for their tall, broad-brimmed stovepipe hats. The hat-making industry

Accompanying Lewis and Clark when they resumed their progress west from Fort Mandan in early April 1805 were an interpreter, Toussaint Charbonneau, his young Shoshoni woman, Sacagawea, and their baby, Jean Baptiste, affectionately nicknamed "Pomp" by Clark. No one associated with the expedition has been more thoroughly romanticized than Sacagawea. Over the years, many disagreements about her life have resulted as authors have made extravagant claims for Sacagawea as expedition guide and American heroine.

Not one shred of evidence exists of a romantic bond between Sacagawea and Clark, as some novelists have imagined. Nor was Sacagawea the expedition's guide in any usual sense of the word. Only once or twice did she provide guide services, such as in late July and early August 1805 when she recognized important topographical features indicating that the expedition had entered Shoshoni territory. Although she did not accompany Lewis's advance party when it made contact with her people, Sacagawea did help the party secure pack horses from her brother (or cousin), Chief Cameawait, for the arduous climb ahead.

Lewis once wrote of Sacagawea, "If she has enough to eat and a few trinkets I believe she would be perfectly content anywhere." This is perhaps too harsh an assessment because Sacagawea did have a role as translator. Moreover, her physical presence and that of her child evidently reassured Indians that the Lewis and Clark expedition was not a war party. Sacagawea died 20 December 1812 at Fort Manuel in present South Dakota; Clark became the guardian for her son and educated him.[4]

alone used one hundred thousand beaver pelts each year to supply fine headwear to European aristocrats and a rising commercial class.

Oldest and most prominent of the fur companies in North America was the Hudson's Bay Company chartered by King Charles II in 1670, but beginning in the 1780s it faced a vigorous young rival in the newly formed North West Company of Montreal. The new firm's corporate motto was Perseverance, an apt description of the force that drove Nor'westers steadily westward to the Pacific when the Hudson's Bay monopoly blocked them from North America's choicest hunting and trapping grounds. A generation of Nor'westers—some explorers, some canny businessmen, some expert managers, and some combining all three qualities—boldly probed the continent's western passes and rivers to establish the first permanent European outposts among the native peoples of the Pacific Northwest.

4. For further information on the controversies surrounding Sacagawea, see James P. Ronda, *Lewis and Clark among the Indians* (Lincoln: University of Nebraska Press, 1984), 256–59.

For fifteen years prior to Lewis and Clark, Alexander Mackenzie spear-headed efforts to expand the North West Company's fur-trading network. In 1789 he led a party of Nor'westers down the great Canadian river later named for him, but to his disappointment he discovered that it emptied into the frozen Arctic Ocean, not the Pacific. That failure dampened the enthusiasm of the North West Company for Mackenzie's explorations, but he succeeded in becoming the first Euro-American to cross the breadth of North America, reaching the Pacific Ocean near present Bella Coola, British Columbia, in 1793. Though the route proved commercially futile, Mackenzie continued to nurture his dream of British territorial sovereignty and economic power extending from sea to sea. For those feats of exploration he was later knighted.

Aware that rival agents of Great Britain, France, and Spain had already penetrated the western wilderness, Thomas Jefferson responded with the Lewis and Clark expedition. But even before the two captains could suggest ways to redirect the fur trade of the far Northwest south into the United States, preliminary reports from the expedition further stimulated exploratory and trade activity by the North West Company on the Pacific slope. In 1805–1806, before Lewis and Clark returned to St. Louis, Simon Fraser, a twenty-nine-year-old Nor'wester, conducted extensive exploration of the region that became British Columbia. In the area then called New Caledonia, he established two of the North West Company's first three trading posts west of the Continental Divide. Fraser also in 1808 traced the wild currents of a river mistakenly thought to be the Columbia. That river now bears his name. The realization that the difficult and dangerous Fraser River was useless as a highway for furs, together with information from the Lewis and Clark expedition, caused the North West Company to shift its attention southward.

David Thompson, a trader, surveyor, map maker, and gifted explorer for the North West Company, responded to Lewis and Clark in 1807 with the first of several journeys that led him through a labyrinth of mountains and valleys that comprised the upper reaches of the Columbia River system in British Columbia, Idaho, and Montana. His travels culminated in 1811 with a descent of the Columbia to its mouth, where he was disappointed to find that American rivals had already established a crude fort. Thompson is remembered for his explorations and for the several important fur posts he established, including Spokane House, located northwest of the present city of Spokane, and Kullyspell House on the shore of Lake Pend d'Oreille.

ASTOR AND THE AMERICANS

Even as Thompson and his fellow Nor'westers extended the reach of Montreal's fur merchants, the first American traders probed the Rocky Mountains from another direction. When Lewis and Clark neared the Mandan villages on their return journey to St. Louis, they released Private John Colter, who headed west to search the upper Yellowstone country and the Teton Valley of eastern Idaho for beaver. Also released early was George Drouillard. Both men eventually ended up as employees of the merchant and trader Manuel Lisa. Excited by information gathered by Lewis and Clark, Lisa dispatched parties of traders up the Missouri River from his St. Louis base.

Andrew Henry, Lisa's partner in the Missouri Fur Company, and a group of trappers entered what is now southeastern Idaho after a battle with the Blackfeet forced them to cross over the Rocky Mountains in search of less dangerous country. In 1810, on a fork of the Snake River near modern Saint Anthony, they built a temporary winter post called Fort Henry. Although it amounted to little more than a few log cabins and a dugout, Fort Henry was the first American fur post west of the Rocky Mountains. After the trappers broke camp the following spring and spread out through the Rocky Mountain country, one of their parties met another group of American traders and trappers heading west. These were the Astorians.

John Jacob Astor, a businessman whose interest in the far Northwest was stimulated by reports of the region's natural wealth, laid plans for a vast new business empire. A stout, arrogant immigrant who came to the United States from Germany in 1784, Astor had been involved in the fur trade of the upper Great Lakes. But after learning about the "soft gold" farther west, he organized the American Fur Company in 1808 to exploit fur-bearing animals on a grand scale. Two years later he created a subsidiary, the Pacific Fur Company, to tap the riches of the Oregon country, a move that was in defiance of British claims to the area.

Astor supplied money for the new enterprise, while Canadian and U.S. associates served as partners and managed operations in the field. From a post he proposed to build near the mouth of the Columbia River, his traders and trappers would fan out across the Northwest to collect the furs they would ship to markets in China. Astor also viewed his Pacific Fur Company as a U.S. response to British-Canadian challengers.

To turn his dream into reality, Astor dispatched overland and naval expe-

ditions to the North Pacific coast. Heading the overland party was Astor's
field agent, Wilson Price Hunt, a twenty-seven-year-old St. Louis fur merchant who was greatly interested in exploration but woefully inexperienced
for an undertaking of this complexity. Assisting him was Donald MacKenzie, formerly of the rival North West Company. The Hunt party departed
Saint Louis in October 1810, a month after the seafaring Astorians left New
York.

Assigned to reconnoiter an overland route and to seek sites for a string of
trading posts extending from the Missouri to Columbia rivers, members of
the Hunt party—consisting of a small group of company officials and about
fifty employees—were plagued by blunders, Indians, and scheming rivals.
The Astorians meandered needlessly and endured hunger, thirst, sickness,
and death.

On the high plain above the Snake River in southern Idaho, the Astorians
trudged across a "dreary waste, without verdure; and where there was neither fountain, nor pool, nor running stream. The men now began to experience the torments of thirst, aggravated by their usual diet of dried fish. The
thirst of some of the Canadian voyageurs became so insupportable as to
drive them to the most revolting means of allaying it [by drinking their own
urine]. For twenty five miles did they toil on across this dismal desert, and
laid themselves down at night, parched and disconsolate beside their worm
wood fires; looking forward to still greater suffering on the following day.
Fortunately it began to rain in the night to their infinite relief; the water
soon collected in puddles and afforded them delicious draughts." The words
of Washington Irving, who penned this vivid account of the Astorians'
trouble-plagued journey, left no doubt as to why the French Canadians described the Snake River as the "accursed mad river."

An advance guard reached the log palisades of Fort Astoria in January
1812 and others straggled in during the next several days and weeks. Along
the Columbia River in eastern Oregon, Astorians later located two lost
partners, Ramsay Crooks and John Day, whom the Indians had stripped
naked and left stranded without even flint to build a fire. Day apparently
went insane before he died a few years later. Hunt's overlanders found no
practical route between the Missouri and the Columbia, but their arrival
reinforced the modest American presence in the Pacific Northwest.

Seagoing members of Astor's enterprise fared no better. Loaded with
thirty-three young Scots and Canadians, trade goods, and materials to erect
a fortified post, the *Tonquin* sailed from New York City in September 1810
and made its way around Cape Horn to the Columbia River. The eight-

11. *Tonquin* crossing the bar of the Columbia River, 25
May 1811. Courtesy Library of Congress.

month, twenty-two-thousand-mile voyage was an ill-starred affair, filled
with bickering and feuding between the irascible Captain Jonathan Thorn
on one side and his crew and passengers on the other. Even as they prepared
to enter the Columbia River, Thorn's stubbornness cost eight crewmen
their lives when he ordered them out in small boats to seek a passable
channel through the treacherous waters of the bar. "Farewell my friends, we
will perhaps meet again in the next world," was one departing officer's
tragically accurate prediction of his fate. The needless deaths cast a pall over
the entire enterprise as the ship battled its way to a protected cove on the
south bank of the river where in late March 1811 passengers and supplies
were unloaded and Fort Astoria took shape.

Astor hoped to use the *Tonquin* to transport furs to China, but that was
not to be. What actually happened to the *Tonquin* after it left Astoria to
trade with the inhabitants of Nootka Sound may never be known, but according to the ship's native interpreter who escaped harm, the tyrannical
Captain Thorn so antagonized the Indians—on one occasion rubbing a head-
man's face with a fur in a trade dispute—that they rushed aboard the vessel,
overwhelmed the crew of 23 to 26 hands, and killed nearly every one. However, a few sailors reached the hold, where they touched off several tons of

black powder, blowing themselves, nearly two hundred Nootkas, and Astor's little ship of horrors to bits.

The Astorians fanned out from the mouth of the Columbia in several directions to explore and exploit the fur resources of the Northwest. They built Fort Okanogan (the first American structure in the future state of Washington), Fort Spokane (next door to the North West Company's Spokane House), and posts on the Clearwater and Boise rivers. A seven-man party led by Robert Stuart returned overland from Fort Astoria to New York in mid-1812. By traveling slightly south of the route followed by Hunt, the Stuart party discovered South Pass, an easy crossing through the Rockies and a key part of the future Oregon Trail. But dramatic changes in the fur trade after the War of 1812 caused Americans to ignore or forget this geographical information.

British and American fur traders engaged in a lively competition in the Oregon country that ended prematurely with the outbreak of the War of 1812. News of the conflict reached Astoria early in 1813, and after months of indecision, the Americans agreed under duress to sell out to their British competitors at a substantial loss. However, in December 1813, before the sale was finalized, the commander of a British warship occupied the post and renamed it Fort George, giving the British empire its first post on the North Pacific coast.

The Treaty of Ghent (1814) settled the war by restoring all territory taken during the conflict, including that lost by the Astorians. Americans thus reasserted their claims to the region, even as Spain pulled back to the present Oregon-California border in 1819 and Russia to north of the 54°40′ line in 1825. That left Great Britain and the United States alone to settle the future of the Oregon country. Conventions in 1818 and 1827 failed to produce agreement. Thus the Pacific Northwest remained "free and open" to residents of both nations until 1846, when Great Britain and the United States divided the Oregon country along the 49th parallel, the present international boundary. The brief presence of the Astorians in the Pacific Northwest thus proved highly significant, although Jefferson's hope of linking far western trade to a St. Louis–based commercial system went unrealized.

CONTESTED TERRAIN

Following the War of 1812, it appeared that the North West Company would dominate the fur trade of the Oregon country. Astor declined to reenter the contest on the Columbia—where he had never made a profit—and instead retreated to the upper Missouri and Rocky Mountain country.

Here he carefully nurtured his fortune. Abandoning the fur trade in 1834, Astor increased his riches by investing in Manhattan real estate, becoming the richest man in America and the nation's first millionaire.

Plagued by dwindling revenues, the North West Company entered several hitherto unexploited areas of the Pacific Northwest in search of furs. It erected Fort Nez Perces (later named Fort Walla Walla) at the confluence of the Columbia and Walla Walla rivers in 1818 and from there dispatched trapping parties into the Snake River country. The Snake brigades became an annual event, and Donald Mackenzie, formerly of Hunt's overland party of Astorians, returned to the ranks of the Nor'westers after the Astoria venture fizzled and led the company's first three expeditions into the Snake country. A great bear of a man whose inexhaustible fund of energy earned him the nickname "Perpetual Motion," he established the pattern for all future expeditions. Departing from customary practices, the Snake brigades sought no trade with the Indians but instead lived off the land and trapped for themselves.

In another of their business practices, however, the Nor'westers continued an arrangement initiated by Astorians: furs from the company's Columbia Department moved westward to the Pacific Coast instead of overland to the East. By arrangement with American shipowners, the "soft gold" traveled from Fort George to markets in China. This mutually beneficial arrangement was a response to the East India Company's trading monopoly, which froze other British but not American traders out of China. It lasted until the company's charter was modified in the early 1830s.

For the company that had done so much to open the interior of Oregon, the year 1821 proved fateful: the North West Company of Montreal was forcibly absorbed by its old rival, the Hudson's Bay Company—a firm of such ancient lineage that some claimed that its initials meant "Here Before Christ." The rising incidence of violence between employees of the rival outfits in the Great Lakes and Hudson's Bay region was chiefly responsible for the merger. To halt the brawling, kidnapping, hijacking, dueling, and other forms of mayhem, the British colonial secretary forced union with the Hudson's Bay Company upon the younger rival. The enlarged Hudson's Bay Company (the "Honourable Company") thus acquired the operations, organizational structures, and personnel of the North West Company. The resulting empire stretched from the Atlantic to the Pacific and north to the Arctic and encompassed millions of square miles, thousands of employees, and hundreds of establishments.

The size and complexity of this new domain prompted Hudson's Bay

Company leaders to reassess their operations, particularly whether they should continue the fur trade in the Oregon country. Prior to acquisition of the North West Company, the older outfit had shown little interest in this distant land. Overland communication was long, difficult, and costly; moreover, to evaluate the far Northwest's economic potential, Hudson's Bay directors had little more than dismal ledger accounts and rumors. The beaver pelts of the North Pacific, for example, were not as luxuriant as those taken in the colder Hudson's Bay region, and the trade consequently did not turn as great a profit. Some directors suggested abandoning the distant Northwest, but a majority considered such a step premature.

George Simpson, a thirty-four-year-old Scot recently named governor of the Northern Department of Rupert's Land, to which the Columbia District was subordinate, undertook a quick field inspection in 1824. His recommendations on how best to streamline operations and nurture trade in the Pacific Northwest had a far-reaching influence. Simpson, who abhorred waste and inefficiency, believed that company employees, when not actively engaged in trading, should be kept busy in farming, fishing, or some other profitable activity. Such diversification would lessen the dependency on furs for profits, for he hoped to open foreign markets to grain, beef, butter, fish, and wood from the Columbia River country.

Simpson ordered the regional headquarters relocated from Fort George to a new site a hundred miles upstream that was more strategically situated and offered far better agricultural possibilities (Fort George was reduced to secondary importance after 1828). There on the north bank of the Columbia River rose Fort Vancouver, the site of today's Vancouver, Washington. Fort Vancouver was likely to remain on British soil should the jointly occupied Oregon country be divided along the Columbia River, but it also formed a key link in a truly global system of commerce extending from Asia across North America to Great Britain.

To carry out his plans, Simpson appointed Dr. John McLoughlin as chief factor for the Columbia District. A man of dominant and vivid personality, the thirty-nine-year-old McLoughlin (pronounced McLocklin) left a lasting imprint on Pacific Northwest history. He was born in Quebec in 1784 and at the age of fourteen was apprenticed to a physician. After four years he earned a license to practice medicine and surgery. Young Dr. McLoughlin entered the service of the North West Company, first as an assistant to the regular physician and later as a trader east of the Rockies.

Little is known of McLoughlin's personal life: he was of mixed Irish, Scottish, and French-Canadian ancestry and became a Roman Catholic late

12. Dr. John McLoughlin (1784–1857), the "Father of
Oregon," photographed late in life. Courtesy Oregon
Historical Society, ORHI 251.

in life. He married the half-Swiss, half-Indian widow of a fur trader who bore him four children in addition to the four she brought to the marriage from her first husband. McLoughlin was a man of striking appearance, standing six feet, four inches tall, raw boned, well proportioned, and strong. His eyes were piercing; a flowing mane of prematurely white hair hung down over his massive shoulders. Local Indians called him the White Headed Eagle. McLoughlin ruled the sprawling Columbia District from 1824 until 1846. Given the tenuous nature of British and American authority in that region, this single Hudson's Bay Company official wielded great power. Together McLoughlin and the Hudson's Bay Company maintained an extraordinary presence in a remote, frontier domain.

### BUILDING AN EMPIRE ON THE COLUMBIA

Chief Factor McLoughlin was headquartered at Fort Vancouver, which functioned as the nerve center of a vast and complex commercial system based not only on furs but also on a lively trade in deer hides, prized shells, gold dust, and the products of farm, forest, and stream. Here was a small, almost self-sufficient European community that included a hospital, thirty to fifty small houses where employees (*engagés*) lived with their Indian wives; storehouses for furs, trading goods, and grain; and workshops where blacksmithing, carpentry, barrel making, and other activities were carried on. Approximately twenty-two major buildings, including the imposing residence of the chief factor and a jail, were located within the main stockade. Outside this enclosure lived many employees—the boatmen, artisans, and general laborers—in an area known as "the village," a collection of some thirty to fifty wooden buildings spread across the plain, including a school and several churches.

Nearby was a sawmill that provided lumber for building construction and repairs. The company also operated a shipyard, two gristmills, two dairies, an orchard, and a farm of several hundred acres where employees planted crops and raised herds of cattle and other domestic animals. Ships from distant ports called at Fort Vancouver bringing news, books, and periodicals to stock the post's library.

An unusually cosmopolitan population collected around Fort Vancouver: Delaware and Iroquois Indians from the East, local Chinooks, Hawaiians, mixed-blood Métis from the prairies, French Canadians, and Scotsmen, and presiding over them all was the imperious John McLoughlin, harsh, brooding, and given to occasional temperamental outbursts. More than profit and loss were involved in a Hudson's Bay post: each enclave was a visible link in a truly imperial system joining London with the vast Pacific Northwest.

In its effort to reinforce British territorial claims in the Oregon country, the Hudson's Bay Company formed a subsidiary in 1839, the Puget's Sound Agricultural Company, to carry on commercial farming at Fort Nisqually south of present-day Tacoma. Fort Nisqually and Cowlitz Farm, sixty miles farther south, raised 4,530 sheep and 1,000 cattle in 1841 and substantial crops of wheat, oats, barley, peas, and potatoes. Fort Colville, about halfway up the Columbia River, specialized in grain production. Some of the food was necessary to support the fur trade, but various Hudson's Bay farms also supplied food to Alaska, enabling the Russian-American company to dispose of its costly agricultural outpost in California in the early 1840s to John Sutter (later made famous by the gold rush). All that was lacking to make the Hudson's Bay Company farms a long-term success was settlers who were willing to remain subject to the paternalism of the company.

## WHAT CURSED COUNTRY

George Simpson's reorganization plan included stepped-up efforts to bar American rivals from the Snake River country. Until the early 1830s, the Hudson's Bay Company continued the fur brigades initiated by Nor'westers and in the process added to knowledge of that remote and inhospitable region. The jumping-off point moved to various locations, but one thing never changed: life in the Snake country was always dangerous. Finan McDonald, a veteran of the old Northwest Company and leader of the 1823 expedition into the Snake country, lost six men in a fatal encounter with Indians. An unnerved McDonald thanked God when he reached home safely and prophesied that he would return to the Snake country only when the beaver there grew skins of gold.

Alexander Ross, head of the Snake brigade in 1824, inadvertently opened a new chapter in the history of the fur trade when members of his party met seven St. Louis–based trappers near present-day Blackfoot, Idaho. This chance encounter with Jedediah Smith and six other Americans surprised the Hudson's Bay Company men. During the decade that had elapsed since Astor's ill-starred Pacific coast venture, few Americans entered the Oregon Country, although as the result of the 1818 convention, they possessed as much right as the British to trap its streams.

Unaccountably, Ross bragged to Smith and the Americans that during

73

the previous four years the Hudson's Bay Company had taken eighty thousand beaver pelts from the region. That was a great exaggeration, but it whetted Smith's desire to pursue such riches for himself. The persistent Americans even accompanied the Hudson's Bay men back to that year's base of operations at Flathead Post on the Clark Fork River, much to the displeasure of Ross's superior, George Simpson, who had already resolved to replace him as head of the Snake brigades. Only a short time earlier Simpson had blasted Ross as "a self-sufficient, empty-headed man" whose "reports are so full of bombast and marvelous nonsense that it is impossible to get at any information that can be depended on from him." When Ross allowed the rival Americans to accompany him deep into territory the Hudson's Bay Company considered its own, he seemed to confirm Simpson's acerbic judgment.[5]

Replacing Ross was Peter Skene Ogden, who led the Snake brigades for five years beginning in late 1824. This burly, ruthless veteran of the old North West Company was well qualified to carry out an order from Simpson to trap the animals of the Snake country to the point of extinction. Ogden was to turn the area into a "fur desert" to implement a "scorched-earth" policy that would keep Americans out of the Columbia River region and thereby bolster British territorial claims in anticipation of the day when an international boundary would divide the Oregon country.

Ogden had not entered the fur trade out of economic necessity. He grew up in a rich and respected Montreal family and could have lived a comfortable life pursuing a legal career in the Saint Lawrence Valley. Ogden, however, had an innate love of adventure and while still in his teens entered the rough and tumble world of the fur trade. Like his predecessor, "Perpetual Motion" MacKenzie, Ogden was man of phenomenal physical energy. He explored an enormous amount of Great Basin country new to Euro-Americans, and not without reason is the city of Ogden, Utah, named for him.

In the words of one associate, Ogden was a humorous, honest, eccentric, law-defying "terror of the Indians."[6] The latter point was surely an exaggeration, for he enjoyed uncommonly good relations with Native Americans. Ogden even took as his common-law wife an Indian, Julia Rivet, who was his equal in wilderness survival skills and resourcefulness. She and their young children accompanied him on several of his six expeditions into the interior West.

5. As quoted in John S. Galbraith, *The Hudson's Bay Company as an Imperial Factor, 1821–1869* (Berkeley: University of California Press, 1957), 88.
6. As quoted in Galbraith, *The Hudson's Bay Company as an Imperial Factor*, 90.

In the vast and dangerous Snake country, the Hudson's Bay Company risked encounters both with hostile Indians and American competitors. When Ogden reached the Henry's Fork area of eastern Idaho in 1825, he found thirty American mountain men already there ahead of him, busily trapping whatever beaver remained. To Ogden's chagrin, several of the self-employed trappers attached to his expedition soon defected to the Americans.

During an expedition in 1826, several of Ogden's men suddenly became ill while trapping along the Raft River. One man dropped unconscious near his traps, and others complained of severe pain in the head and limbs. Soon half the brigade was too weak to move. Ogden attributed the mysterious affliction to their eating tainted beaver meat and used himself as a guinea pig in a successful effort to confirm his diagnosis. He thereupon prescribed for himself the same remedy he gave his men: pepper mixed with gunpowder and water. Whatever the medicine's value, the Snake brigade was soon back on its feet. Ogden concluded that the beaver had eaten poisonous water hemlock that grew in abundance along the Raft River. In the Snake country, nature added many other torments—driving sleet, deep snow, bitter winds, and a barren landscape, the conditions that prompted Ogden to exclaim: "What cursed Country is this."

### COMPANY MEN AND MOUNTAIN MEN

Missouri businessman General William Henry Ashley launched a new phase of American activity in the far Northwest when he dispatched his first expedition of fur traders up the Missouri River in 1822. Most of Ashley's men were not salaried employees like the *engagés* who signed contracts to work as boatmen or trappers for the Hudson's Bay Company, but instead were free trappers or "mountain men," colorful individuals like Jedediah Smith and Jim Bridger whose explorations acquainted Euro-Americans with vast areas of the West. The twenty-four-year-old Smith, with the aid of friendly Crow Indians, rediscovered South Pass through the Rocky Mountains in 1824 and two years later led an exploring expedition across the Mojave Desert into California. His was the first American party to travel overland through the Southwest.

No group of westerners has ever been more thoroughly romanticized than the mountain men, who were often portrayed as knights-errant clearing the way for American civilization in the West. Their familiarity with the land certainly furthered knowledge of western geography. Yet the typical American trapper, although often portrayed as a free-spirited individual

75

who enjoyed the freedom of the hills, was in fact a person who lived a tenuous life of privation. He endured often unprofitable hunts and occasional harassment by Indians. Whether as an independent trapper or as an employee of one of the St. Louis–based fur companies, the American mountain man was often at the mercy of poorly capitalized merchants who were inclined to strike sharp bargains. As a result, he seldom felt loyalty to an employer nor did he enjoy the security of a large organization in dealing with the Indians.

American trappers incurred the wrath of Indians far more often than did employees of the Hudson's Bay Company. During the two trading seasons from 1824 to 1826, Indians killed a total of thirty-two Americans in the Snake country, and though the Hudson's Bay Company was not immune to the danger of attack, its loss of life was substantially less. Occasionally one party of American trappers committed an outrage against Indians, who in turn wreaked vengeance on the next mountain man to come along. Indians who might not hesitate to attack a small band of American trappers would likely think twice before attacking parties associated with the powerful Hudson's Bay Company.

General Ashley popularized the "rendezvous system," a scheme dating from 1825 that replaced permanent trading posts and thereby saved money. The trappers associated with Ashley and his successors in the Rocky Mountain Fur Company and similar enterprises, along with their Indian allies, gathered at an appointed place each summer to trade pelts for a year's supply of goods sent west from St. Louis by pack animals and wagons. This arrangement dominated the Rocky Mountain fur trade until 1840, when the last major rendezvous was held.

The typical rendezvous was a combination fair, circus, and rodeo with opportunity for feasting, drinking, carousing, and contests of skill. Although often held on the Green River in future Wyoming, in 1829 and 1832 it took place in Pierre's Hole, on the east side of the Grand Tetons in present-day Idaho. The Pierre's Hole rendezvous of 1832 began in the usual way: approximately 200 mountain men—some associated with the Rocky Mountain Fur Company, some with John Jacob Astor's American Fur Company, and some independents—came together with about two hundred lodges of Nez Percé, Flathead, Shoshoni, and Bannock Indians to await the annual supply caravan from St. Louis. But on 18 July the gathering erupted into the Battle of Pierre's Hole when a large band of Blackfeet entered the campsite. Old quarrels caused a Flathead warrior to shoot fatally an approaching Blackfeet chief and thus spark a general melee. When the fight ended, as many as ten Blackfeet, seven Nez Perce, and six trappers lay dead. The surviving Blackfeet escaped to take revenge on trappers and their Indian allies in the Upper Missouri country for several more years.

John McLoughlin estimated that between 1832 and 1838 there were from five hundred to six hundred Americans annually in the Snake country. That figure, however, exaggerated their influence in the far Northwest because most Americans remained in the Rocky Mountain country on the region's eastern fringes. Although American trappers in the Rocky Mountains greatly outnumbered the men of the Snake brigades—perhaps they even outnumbered the entire Hudson's Bay Company work force in the Pacific Northwest—they represented more of a nuisance to the "Honourable Company" than a significant competitive threat. The Hudson's Bay Company retained the advantage of greater capital, better organization, more knowledge of the terrain, and better relations with the Indians than did the average American mountain man.

NATHANIEL WYETH: THE ICE MAN AND FORT HALL

None of the handful American fur traders who ventured west from the Rocky Mountains to the Columbia River was successful. For five years beginning in 1832, Boston ice merchant Nathaniel Wyeth attempted to revive the old dream of John Jacob Astor by establishing a fur trading business on the lower Columbia River. After repeated failures there, he expanded his economic horizons to include the Rocky Mountain country where he obtained a contract to supply trade goods to the 1834 fur rendezvous to be held that year on the Green River.

When Wyeth finally reached the rendezvous site he found that St. Louis suppliers had arrived first and stolen his customers. His contract was unenforceable, so he was stuck with a large supply of merchandise a thousand miles or more from the nearest market. Wyeth's best alternative was to build a trading post on a site north of present-day Pocatello, Idaho. On 5 August 1834, when the fort was enclosed after a month of construction, Wyeth named it for a senior partner in his enterprise and ordered a celebration. The next morning a homemade American flag was raised over Fort Hall and saluted. Stocked with bacon, flour, beans, whisky, and other goods, the post was ready to cater to fur traders and Indians.

Unfortunately for Wyeth, his fortunes continued to sag. The Hudson's Bay Company responded to the commercial invasion of its Snake country domain by subsidizing the operation of Fort Boise, which was built in August 1834 near the confluence of the Snake and Boise rivers and close to an annual Indian rendezvous. Wyeth returned to Boston and reentered the ice

# Fur Trading Posts

Fort Colville (1825)

Fort Okanogan (1811)

Kullyspell House (1809)

Fort Spokane (1812)

Spokane House (1810)

Fort Nez Perces (1818) (Later Fort Walla Walla)

Fort Nisqually (1833)

Cowlitz Farm (1839)

Fort Vancouver (1824)

Fort Astoria (1811) (Later Fort George)

Fort Henry (1810)

Fort Boise (1834)

Fort Hall (1834)

PACIFIC OCEAN

Miles

0        100

© (Relief), Gibb Johnson 1994

78

business in 1836. Two years later he sold Fort Hall to the Hudson's Bay Company, which now regained its near monopoly in the region's fur trade. Despite his hard luck and lack of commercial success in the Pacific Northwest, Wyeth had stirred popular interest in the distant region by bringing the first American missionaries and scientists to the territory in 1834.

The two Hudson's Bay forts ended the need for the Snake brigades. In addition, Fort Hall began supplying goods to the growing stream of travelers along the Oregon Trail and even gained some unexpected customers with the arrival of the first party of Mormons in the Salt Lake Valley in 1847. The American emigrants were good customers, but they were also agents of change. The desire of overland travelers for meat made it more profitable for Indians and independent trappers around Fort Hall to hunt antelope than beaver; and by 1850 the former Mormon customers now stocked stores of their own and undersold the Hudson's Bay Company post. The loss of profit, the changing nature of the fur trade, and growing Indian unrest in the Snake River country together caused the Hudson's Bay Company to abandon Fort Boise in 1855 and Fort Hall in 1856.

The fur trade era in the Pacific Northwest lasted about sixty years—from the 1780s until the late 1840s. A generation of fur traders and trappers revealed to the world some of nature's treasures in the distant land, yet their contribution to settlement of the region was at best indirect. They knew only too well that population growth and commerce in furs were incompatible. Wherever the farmer appeared, fur trappers and traders retreated into an ever-shrinking domain. Changing fashion, notably the switch from top hats made from beaver pelts to those of silk, as well as over-trapping took a toll on profits. A few Pacific Northwesterners found trapping to be a profitable activity even in the late twentieth century, but by then the age typified by great fur companies, the rendezvous, and the mountain men was long past.

The fur trade era inaugurated the role of the Pacific Northwest as a colony whose natural resources were ripe for outsiders to exploit. The first Pacific Northwesterners typically used only those resources that were part of their diet or material culture. As a consequence, their impact on the environment was minimal. But the cultural practices of the Euro-Americans prevailed, and in subsequent decades their attitudes justified ruthless exploitation of the region's mineral and timber wealth. Hence, the era of the fur trade revealed economic attitudes and patterns that were to be replicated in the future and with far greater impact upon the region's natural environment.

# Part II
# The Pioneers' Northwest

# Profile:
# The Whitman Tragedy at Waiilatpu

*

They are an exceedingly proud, haughty and insolent people. . . . We feed them far more than any of our associates do their people, yet they will not be satisfied. Notwithstanding all this there are many redeeming qualities in them, else we should have been discouraged long ago. We are more and more encouraged the longer we stay.—Narcissa Whitman describing mission life among the Cayuse to her mother, Clarissa Prentiss, 2 May 1840.

*

Narcissa Prentiss was an idealist. Had she lived a century and a half later she might have joined the Peace Corps or done volunteer service in Appalachia or an inner-city clinic. In the 1830s she was willing to leave her family and comfortable home in upstate New York to become a Christian missionary among Indians living beyond the Rocky Mountains. Only one thing blocked her way: the pious young Presbyterian was single, and the American Board of Commissioners for Foreign Missions rarely sent an unmarried female on an errand into the wilderness.

Her marriage to Marcus Whitman in February 1836 removed that impediment. Narcissa and Marcus actually knew little about each other when they exchanged their vows, but strengthening the bond of romantic love was their shared desire for mission service. The bride was an attractive woman, twenty-seven years old, endowed with a fine singing voice and strong religious convictions. The groom was thirty-three years old, a devout Presbyterian and handsome physician possessed by a desire to become a medical missionary. Like Narcissa, he had offered himself to the American

83

Board and been turned down, in his case because of a history of illness. But that proved only a temporary setback, because the board reversed itself, and Whitman journeyed west in 1835 as an assistant to Samuel Parker, an autocratic, egotistical minister. The pair traveled with the annual fur trade caravan to the Green River valley in western Wyoming, site of that year's rendezvous and an excellent place to learn about the Indians who lived farther west.

Fur traders, a hard-boiled lot by any standard, did not welcome the men of God and subjected them to derision and name-calling. Whitman nonetheless won their respect when he contained a cholera outbreak and removed a three-inch iron arrowhead that had lodged for months in Jim Bridger's back. Thus began a friendship that continued until Whitman's death twelve years later. At the rendezvous, the Nez Perces and Flatheads appeared genuinely happy to have Christian missionaries in their midst. Parker traveled ahead to select suitable sites for their work, while Whitman returned home to raise money and recruits—and to marry Narcissa Prentiss, to whom he had hastily proposed before his western trip.

April 1836 found the newlyweds hurrying west across the Great Plains to overtake the annual fur caravan. Three Nez Perces, two hired men, William H. Gray, and Henry and Eliza Spalding accompanied the Whitmans. The American Board had selected Gray to serve as mechanic and carpenter and Spalding as a minister. Marcus may not have been acquainted with the thirty-three-year-old Presbyterian cleric before that spring, but Narcissa knew him well. Born out of wedlock, Spalding had endured an unhappy childhood and matured into an embittered, suspicious, and quick-tempered man. At Franklin Academy in New York, he fell in love with a fellow student, Narcissa Prentiss, or at least he thought she would make a suitably religious wife. Spalding apparently proposed to her, but in vain; he then turned to Eliza Hart. Spalding's past created tensions between the Whitmans and Spaldings during the long journey to Oregon and subsequently disrupted their missionary labors.

The sojourners celebrated the Fourth of July crossing the Continental Divide at South Pass and arrived at the Green River rendezvous two days later. From that point Hudson's Bay Company traders guided them to their destination. Just east of Fort Hall, a broken axle forced Spalding to convert his flimsy wagon into a two-wheeled cart. The contraption bumped over the Snake River plain as far as Fort Boise before the missionaries discarded it, much to the relief of Narcissa, who considered it an encumbrance. Yet, no wheeled vehicle had traveled that far west before, a fact that would not be lost on would-be emigrants back east.

The missionaries pressed ahead on horseback, crossing the Blue Mountains to reach Fort Walla Walla and finally Fort Vancouver, where on 12 September 1836 Chief Factor John McLoughlin received them with great courtesy. The journey had lasted 207 days and covered more than three thousand miles. Narcissa and Eliza became the first white women to cross North America from coast to coast. Despite the difficulties, no one suffered greatly; Narcissa, in fact, arrived at Fort Vancouver three months pregnant. What the Whitmans and Spaldings accomplished, other families were inspired to duplicate.

But what about Samuel Parker, who was to have prepared the way for Whitman and his recruits? He sailed for home before they arrived. In his midfifties and feeling his age, Parker gave up the venture and spent his time writing a descriptive book about Oregon. For their part, Marcus Whitman and Henry Spalding journeyed back up the Columbia to evaluate suitable mission sites, while their wives remained at Fort Vancouver. Life at the fort dazzled Narcissa, who called it "the New York of the Pacific Ocean" in one of her letters home.

Whitman located an especially fertile and attractive site for his mission station on the Walla Walla River, twenty-five miles upstream from the Columbia and near the tree-covered slopes of the Blue Mountains. As long as anyone could remember, the Cayuse Indians had built their lodges in the same area. They called the site Waiilatpu, meaning "Place of the Rye Grass."

Whitman's choice disappointed the Nez Perces who had expected both missionaries to settle among them. They reminded Whitman that the Nez Perces did not have the same difficulty with whites as the Cayuses did, and they prophesied that the missionaries would soon see the differences. McLoughlin, too, warned Whitman that he would encounter trouble with the Cayuses.

A band of Nez Perce Indians escorted Whitman and Spalding another 110 miles inland to their principal village on Lapwai Creek, a short distance upstream from its junction with the Clearwater River, where Lewis and Clark had passed thirty-one years earlier. At Lapwai ("Butterfly Valley") the Spaldings built a house and school. Convinced that white encroachments would inevitably destroy the game hunted by the Nez Perces, Spalding sought to convert them to farming and for that purpose acquired seeds and simple tools. Spalding was responsible for both the first irrigation project in Idaho and the first publishing venture in the Pacific Northwest. But fellow missionaries publicly criticized the Spaldings for devoting more time to educating the Nez Perces in matters of agriculture and home economics than in religion.

The Whitmans' first two years at Waiilatpu were pleasant enough. They worked with vigor to build their station and gain the confidence of the proud Cayuse people. Adding sparkle to their lives was the birth of a daughter, Alice Clarissa, the first child born of U.S. citizens in the Pacific Northwest. Among their visitors during these early years were Hudson's Bay Company men, American mountain men, and the first trickle of settlers traveling overland to Oregon. With the help of able-bodied Hawaiians, Marcus sawed lumber from the Blue Mountains, milled grain, and slowly erected a complex of buildings. The Whitmans learned the Nez Perce language, which the Cayuses understood, and attempted to teach the Cayuses the rudiments of writing, agriculture, and Christianity. To round out his busy days, the doctor ministered to the physical needs of whites and Indians.

Ministering to the Cayuses was always challenging and often frustrating. The common goal of Protestant missionaries was not only to Christianize Indians but also to "civilize" them. That meant destroying Indian culture. The Whitmans thus hoped to convert the Cayuses to farming, an activity wholly alien to their hunting and gathering way of life but one better suited to missionary education and conversion. Unlike the Spaldings, who hoped to postpone extensive contact between whites and Indians, the Whitmans were located on the main trail to Oregon and saw no hope for Indians unless they assimilated the ways of white settlers.

The cultures of the Cayuse people and the Whitmans conflicted in many ways. Cayuses viewed the manual labor of tending fields as beneath their dignity; they practiced polygamy and wondered why Whitman had only one wife; and they helped themselves to crops raised at the station. Marcus, though, regarded this as stealing and punished them for it. When mission personnel put emetics in melons to discourage the Cayuses from taking them, the Indians wondered about people who would poison the fruits of the earth.

On one occasion an angry Cayuse claimed that the land belonged to them and demanded to know what the Whitmans had paid for it. Marcus pointed out that the Cayuses had seemed eager to have missionaries settle in their midst; moreover, he resisted giving anything for the land because he feared that he would forever be paying tribute to the tribe. As tensions increased, there were occasional acts of Indian vandalism, like breaking windows at the mission house.

With mounting frustration and cultural misunderstanding came personal tragedy: little Alice Clarissa Whitman drowned in the Walla Walla River that flowed just a few feet beyond the door of her home. She was twenty-seven months old. The child's death weighed heavily on the once ebullient Narcissa: she became depressed, developed a growing dislike of the "filthy" Indians, and doubted her own fitness for frontier missionary service. Growing up in a small and culturally homogenous town in rural New York had poorly prepared her to deal with the Indians' alien way of life. Her tendency to judge others by her own cultural standards prevented Narcissa from finding much to admire in native peoples. Her health deteriorated, and when her husband was gone for nearly a year to plead the mission's case to the American Board, fear and loneliness nearly overcame her.

The increasing awareness that she would not likely bear another child caused Narcissa to welcome the children of others into her "little family." First there was the two-year-old daughter of the mountain man Joe Meek and an Indian woman, followed by another mixed-blood child of the fur trade, six-year-old Mary Ann Bridger, and then a mixed-blood boy. She added the seven Sager children, orphaned in 1844 when their parents became sick and died on the journey west. The growing number of children seem to restore happiness to Narcissa's life, even if she ignored the Indians whom she had originally come to serve.

Because of reports of feuding among the Whitmans, Spaldings, and other American Board missionaries, and, even worse, because the missionaries had made few converts among the Indians, the American Board ordered Waiilatpu and Lapwai closed, the Whitmans transferred to Tshimakain (a mission established in 1838 just northwest of present Spokane), and the Spaldings eastward. When word of the decision reached Waiilatpu, the impetuous Marcus Whitman and an associate rode east during the fall and winter of 1842 to persuade the board to change its mind.

Crossing the Rocky Mountains during winter was a remarkable feat of endurance. That accomplishment coupled with his later "martyrdom" provided the basis for the legend that Marcus Whitman saved Oregon for the United States. One admirer even claimed that Whitman stopped at the White House, where he persuaded President John Tyler to wrest Oregon from the grasping British. Whitman's trip was successful in that the American Board reversed itself and permitted the mission stations to remain open.

Culture conflict between whites and Cayuses worsened. When Marcus returned in 1843, the first large contingent of white immigrants to Oregon accompanied him. Numbering nearly nine hundred, they drove their wagons overland from Missouri as far as the Columbia River. The Indians, not without reason, believed that Whitman had gone east to gather reinforcements of American farmers and soldiers.

The Cayuses viewed the changes with apprehension, knowing well the fate of Indian people elsewhere. Nearly five thousand whites crossed the Blue Mountains on their way to the Willamette Valley in 1847. Although the main trail bypassed Waiilatpu after 1844, those who were sick and destitute turned their wagons north to the mission, bringing with them their alien culture and an epidemic of measles and dysentery. An estimated 50 percent of the Cayuses died in less than two months. With rising anger, they noted that white children treated by Whitman usually recovered, but not Indian children. The Cayuses thus came to perceive the white doctor as killing Indians through some form of witchcraft; their tradition called for the death of such a malevolent person. On a cold, foggy day—29 November 1847—shortly after the last wagon departed, the Cayuses attacked the mission station at Waiilatpu.

Two of their leaders, Tiloukaikt and Tomahas, entered the compound, and while Tiloukaikt distracted Marcus by deliberately provoking him into an argument, Tomahas killed the unsuspecting missionary with tomahawk blows to the head. The Indians also killed Narcissa and eleven others and destroyed the mission buildings. A few whites escaped, but the rest were taken captive.

When word of the tragedy reached Fort Vancouver, an outraged Hudson's Bay Company dispatched tough, wiry Peter Skene Ogden and a party of sixteen men to rescue survivors and impress upon surrounding Indians the wisdom of remaining neutral should war break out between whites and the Cayuses. The Negotiators exchanged blankets, shirts, tobacco, handkerchiefs, muskets, flints, and several hundred musket balls for forty-seven survivors. Meanwhile, friendly Nez Perces delivered the Spaldings and their party from Lapwai. The events of 1847 concluded a chapter in the history of Protestant missions.

Shortly after the dawn of a new year, when survivors were safely out of the Walla Walla Valley, the first "Indian war" in Pacific Northwest history erupted between the Cayuses and a volunteer force of five hundred riflemen from the Willamette Valley. After eluding their pursuers for two years, the Cayuse surrendered five tribesmen, including Tiloukaikt and Tomahas, to

13. A lurid depiction of the death of Marcus Whitman.
No likenesses of Marcus Whitman (1802–47) and Narcissa Whitman (1808–47) have ever been positively
identified. Courtesy Oregon Historical Society, ORHI
1644.

save the rest of their people from suffering and destruction. Taken west to
Oregon City, they were given the formality of a trial and hanged in mid-
1850.

Joseph Meek, the United States marshal, used his Indian hatchet to cut
the rope and drop the five Cayuses to their death. The former mountain
man never forgave the Cayuses when his daughter Helen sickened and died
following the massacre. It was Meek who had carried news of the tragedy
and petitions from Willamette Valley settlers to Washington, D.C., in 1848,
a move that spurred Congress to create the territory of Oregon, the first
territorial government west of the Rocky Mountains.

After the massacre, the Spaldings settled in the Willamette Valley where
Henry became a farmer and Indian agent before returning to Lapwai as a
teacher in 1863. He resumed his missionary work following reappointment
by the American Board eight years later.

Until his death in 1874, Spalding carried in his mind the notion that rival
Catholic missionaries had masterminded the Cayuse attack on the Protes-
tant Whitmans. From the time he reached the safety of the Willamette
Valley, he thundered against the murderous conspiracy hatched by the Ro-

man Catholic hierarchy and the Hudson's Bay Company, and he so fanned the flames of religious prejudice that Catholics feared that their churches and schools in the region would be burned. So insistent were Spalding's accusations that even some of his fellow Protestants thought he was insane. When Eliza Spalding died in 1851, he had carved on her headstone: "She always felt that the Jesuit Missionaries were the leading cause of the massacre."

Ironically, the first outsider to reach Waiilatpu after the massacre was a Catholic priest, J. B. A. Brouillet, who performed the burial service. Considering the bloody circumstances, it was the decent and honorable thing to do, but Spalding never forgave him.

The tragic story of the Whitmans eventually generated an enormous body of writing that has nearly overshadowed the rest of Pacific Northwest history, transformed Marcus and Narcissa from well-meaning missionaries into long-suffering and sacrificing saints, and for years sustained the legend that Marcus Whitman saved Oregon. Despite these excesses, the episode highlights several significant features of the region's pioneer era. It vividly illustrates the potential for conflict, cultural and otherwise, between white settlers and native peoples, and between missionaries of differing faiths and backgrounds.

The Whitman story reveals, too, an inevitable tension between the missionary ideal of saving Indian souls for the heavenly promised land and the day-to-day reality of providing sustenance to white newcomers and even fostering their settlement of the earthly promised land in Oregon. In the latter work, the Whitmans, Spaldings, and their associates were far more successful than in the former. During its missionary activity from 1836 to 1847, only twenty-one Indians were baptized into the First Presbyterian Church of Oregon (six adults and fifteen children). During that same time the Whitman mission served as an important beacon guiding several thousand emigrant whites bound for fertile lands in the Willamette Valley.

Today Waiilatpu is the Whitman Mission National Historic Site, and Lapwai is part of the Nez Perce National Historical Park. Honoring the Whitman name are a liberal arts college in Walla Walla and Washington's leading wheat-producing county. The term Cayuse is seldom heard, however. Tribal descendants have been incorporated into the Confederated Tribes of the Umatilla comprising the Umatillas, Cayuses, and Walla Wallas, who live on a small reservation east of Pendleton, Oregon.

CHAPTER 5

# Bound for the Promised Land

*

It is a great undertaking to leave comfortable homes for greater advantages than our State possesses, in Oregon. There is a toilsome journey before them. Long and tiresome it will be. True there will be many circumstances that will render portions of it interesting; still it will be tiresome and at times must come among the emigrants feelings of anxiety for the end.
—*David Newsom: The Western Observer, 1805–1882* (from his comments for 3 April 1851)

*

A major stimulus to missionary activity in the Pacific Northwest was the practice of some Indian tribes of flattening their babies' foreheads. And therein lies a mystery. Why did the practice evoke a powerful response only in the 1830s? Euro-Americans had known about it for years. Lewis and Clark described forehead flattening among the Chinook people of the lower Columbia River in 1805–1806, where head flattening distinguished the free born from the slaves (round-heads) and outsiders. What new set of circumstances aroused the missionary impulse among Euro-Americans thirty years later?

One factor was growing popular enthusiasm for the Oregon country. Hall Jackson Kelley, a well-educated but eccentric Boston schoolteacher, became obsessed with colonizing the remote region with white settlements, and by the 1820s he was the leading advocate of immigration. To his single-minded crusade he sacrificed home, family, and position. Kelley was initially little more than an armchair theorist because he knew of Oregon only through reading the journals of Lewis and Clark and talking to seamen and hunters. But that did not stop him from extolling its virtues in countless speeches, pamphlets, circulars, and petitions. Many people with whom he came in contact regarded him as "a little touched," whereas to others he was merely a bore.

In a memorial to Congress in 1828, Kelley described Oregon as "the most valuable of all the unoccupied parts of the earth." The following year he organized the American Society for Encouraging the Settlement of the Oregon Territory, but his plan to lead a party of settlers to Oregon soon collapsed. Undiscouraged, Kelley remained an Oregon booster until the 1850s, but only once, in 1832, did he actually visit his promised land. After an adventure-filled overland trek that took him across Mexico and through California to Fort Vancouver, the Hudson's Bay Company gave him a reception that could best be described as frigid: he was mistaken for a horse thief wanted in California. The conviction that the Hudson's Bay Company persecuted him only heightened Kelley's interest in wresting the lands of the Pacific Northwest from Britain.

Other enthusiasts for the region included Virginia congressman John Floyd, who spoke eloquently of Oregon though he had never been there. The same was true of Senators Thomas Hart Benton and Lewis F. Linn of Missouri, who kindled further interest in the region. Collectively, Oregon's boosters were responsible for a flood of books, newspapers, and lectures that portrayed the region as paradise on earth. There were skeptics, of course, but their words of caution were not compelling to most Americans.

Coinciding with the promotional enthusiasm—Oregon fever—was a quickening of the Protestant conscience as a result of the revivalism promoted by Charles G. Finney and other evangelists beginning in the mid-1820s. An incident that occurred in 1831 provided the specific impetus to missionary activity in the far Northwest: an Indian delegation consisting of three Nez Perces and one Flathead journeyed to St. Louis seeking William Clark, superintendent of Indian affairs and a tribal hero since the days of the Lewis and Clark expedition. Conversing only in sign language, they requested the "book" and the "black robes" for their people. They may have meant the Holy Bible and the Jesuits, but it is equally possible that they wanted a portion of the white man's power that appeared to reside in his printing and religion.

Christianity was certainly not new to the Pacific Northwest. Roman Catholic voyageurs from Quebec pursued the fur trade among the region's Indians, and some married native women. In this way they transmitted elements of Christianity to the Indians. The Hudson's Bay Company in 1825 sent the sons of Spokane and Kutenai leaders to an Anglican mission school at the settlement of Red River in present Manitoba. Their return four years later encouraged other Indian fathers to send their sons away to pursue similar courses of study. Best known of the mission-educated young men was Spokan Garry, who, armed with a King James Bible and an Anglican Book of Common Prayer, ministered to the Indians of the plateau. Influenced by Flathead contacts, the Nez Perces were curious enough—or impressed enough by the possibility of tapping into a source of the whites' power—to send representatives to St. Louis to learn more.

Word of their arrival spread from pulpit to pulpit, accompanied in the Methodist *Christian Advocate and Journal* by a drawing of one Indian's profile, his malformed forehead sloping back from his eyebrows to a peak above his ears. All of this electrified the Protestant world, which remained blissfully ignorant of the fact that the heads of the Indians who visited St. Louis were shaped normally. When the call went forth for all good Protestants to help the poor, misguided, deformed Indians, the response was immediate.

### THE MISSIONARY ERA

First to answer the prickings of conscience was Jason Lee, a young Methodist minister. Fortunately for Lee, Nathaniel Wyeth had returned to Boston with two Indians, one of whom was a Nez Perce with a congenitally malformed head. Wyeth did not disabuse Lee of his belief that the native was a genuine Flathead, and in fact Wyeth allowed Lee to display the two Indians at fund-raising meetings throughout the East.

Jason Lee, his nephew Daniel, and a few associates traveled overland to Oregon with Wyeth and his party in 1834. When they arrived at Fort Vancouver, the missionaries took John McLoughlin's advice to remain in the Willamette Valley instead of traveling to the remote and wild country of the Flatheads in western Montana, their original destination. With McLoughlin's help, Lee established his mission on the banks of the Willamette River about ten miles north of present Salem. The site was near French Prairie, a small settlement of French Canadians, many with Indian wives, who had retired to agricultural pursuits after serving the Hudson's Bay Company.

The Indians of the Willamette Valley, including some Chinook with deformed heads, were broken and dispirited as a result of the great malaria epidemic of 1829–33. Lewis and Clark had estimated their number at ten thousand, but disease had reduced their population to a mere fraction by the

1830s. Lee did his best for them—maintaining a mission school and conducting religious services—but he gave most of his attention to letters and trips to the East extolling the new promised land and further fanning the flames of Oregon fever. He returned from the East Coast in 1840 with a shipload of fifty-one New Englanders—called The Great Reinforcement—and used funds from church donations to help establish pioneer settlements at The Dalles and other locations. In that way Lee succeeded in creating a modest American counter-presence to the Hudson's Bay Company, which, ironically, had encouraged him in the first place. The Methodist's Mission Society in New York dismissed Lee in 1844 on the grounds that his efforts had grown too secular.

The second major Protestant venture in the Pacific Northwest commenced in 1836 when the American Board of Commissioners for Foreign Missions, an ecumenical coordinating body for Congregationalist, Presbyterian, and Dutch Reformed believers, sponsored the Whitman and Spalding party. The American Board also operated a mission called Tsimakain among the Spokanes. It was headed by Elkanah and Mary Walker and Cushing and Myra Eells, New England Congregationalists who lived there from 1839 to 1848. A fourth American Board mission operated from 1839 to 1841 among the Nez Perces at Kamiah, sixty miles up the Clearwater River from Lapwai. Asa Bowen Smith and his wife Sarah maintained the post. Smith, who was always more the scholar and linguist than either frontiersman or missionary, selected the site because it lay close to the heart of Nez Perce country, where he hoped to learn the native tongue in its purest form. He eventually compiled a Nez Perce dictionary and grammar.

Like Lee's activity in the Willamette Valley, the work of the Whitmans, Spaldings, Walkers, Eellses, and Smiths was replete with irony. While seeking to help Indians develop what Euro-Americans regarded as a better way of life, the missions divided native peoples into Christian and non-Christian factions, and the coming of white settlers brought disease and disruption to the lives of Indians living near the missions.

Missionaries inevitably faced problems of how best to work with Indians. Should they induce a nomadic hunting and gathering people to become farmers in order to settle them around a mission station? Should they instruct Indians in English or in their native tongue? Could stations be self-supporting and still allow missionaries enough time for religious work?

Spalding attempted to resolved these dilemmas by urging the Nez Perce to abandon their migratory ways and adopt the agrarian lifestyle he considered better suited to their survival in a world ever more dominated by Euro-

Americans. Some Nez Perce did abandon the annual buffalo hunt in 1837 in order to raise potatoes and other crops. Spalding soon had a blacksmith shop and gristmill in operation, and in 1839 he imported a small printing press from Hawaii on which he was able to publish the gospel of John and other materials in the Nez Perce language. A water-powered saw mill and flour mill followed in 1840.

This technology could be seen as evidence of steady progress, but in his attempts to Christianize the Nez Perce, Spalding experienced many setbacks and frustrations. Unconverted young men sometimes used his fence rails for firewood or danced around the mission school to the amusement of students and the annoyance of Spalding. Yet if he chastised the troublemakers they might retaliate by cutting the tail off one of the mission cows, or worse.

Another of Spalding's problems was that the missionaries themselves did not get along well with one another. His fellow missionary on the Clearwater, Asa Bowen Smith, was highly critical of Spalding's attempts to turn Nez Perce Christians into farmers and ridiculed his views in letters to American Board superiors back east. Smith's acerbic tongue alienated other missionaries as well and may have been one reason why he built his mission at so remote a site as Kamiah.

Smith's numerous complaints together with a lack of spiritual success finally caused the financially strapped mission board to order the Whitmans to take over the Lapwai post and both the Spaldings and Smiths to return to the East. Only Marcus Whitman's dramatic personal appeal in 1842 caused the board to change its mind. When the Lapwai mission was abandoned following the 1847 Whitman tragedy, the Spaldings had 44 acres under cultivation, and 164 horses, cattle, and hogs—far more livestock than converts to show for eleven years of activity.

The era of Roman Catholic missions in the Pacific Northwest dates from 1838, when two Franciscan priests from Canada, Francis Norbert Blanchet and Modeste Demers, responded to a call from French-Canadian employees of the Hudson's Bay Company who had retired to farms along the Willamette River. The Hudson's Bay Company supplied canoes and provisions to Blanchet and Demers during the long and difficult overland journey. The bishop of Quebec instructed them "to regain from barbarism and its disorders, the savage tribes scattered over that country" and to extend their help "to the poor Christians who have adopted the customs of the savages and live in license and forgetfulness of their duties."

Blanchet and Demers established the first Roman Catholic mission in the Pacific Northwest on the Cowlitz River north of Fort Vancouver, and another on the Willamette not far from Jason Lee's post. The priests, having neither wives or families to bring with them, did not have an interest in fostering settlement, unlike Protestants. Blanchet remained in the Pacific Northwest becoming archbishop in 1846. He died in 1883.

Roman Catholic missions continued with Pierre Jean De Smet, a Jesuit missionary from Belgium who journeyed from St. Louis to the Oregon country in 1840 with an American fur trading caravan. A man of charm and unusual endurance, De Smet became a skilled negotiator between Indians and whites as well as a tireless advocate of missionary activity. During his lifetime he supposedly traveled 180,000 miles, making sixteen trips to Europe to promote Indian missions.

During his six-year term in the Pacific Northwest, De Smet and his fellow Jesuits Anthony Ravalli, Nicolas Point, and others established several missions in the Rocky Mountains, including the Mission of the Sacred Heart among the Coeur d' Alenes on the banks of the Saint Joseph River (now the St. Joe River) in 1842. Periodic flooding required that the post be relocated to a site on higher ground in 1846, where two years later Anthony Ravalli began building a permanent church.

To construct the Greek Revival style structure, Ravalli used only a broad ax, an auger, some ropes and pulleys, a penknife, and the labor of unskilled Indians. Catholic priests, including the frail Father Joseph M. Cataldo (whose name became most closely identified with the structure), labored at the Sacred Heart Mission from 1846 to 1877, converting Indians to the new religion and an agricultural way of life. In time two-thirds of the Coeur d'Alene Indians were baptized into the Catholic Church.

These outposts of Christianity existed for varying lengths of time at more than thirty sites in the early Pacific Northwest. There were six Methodist mission sites, four American Board, some two dozen Roman Catholic, and one Mormon (Church of Jesus Christ of Latter-day Saints). In response to a call from Brigham Young, 27 Mormon missionaries made a four-hundred-mile trek north from Salt Lake City in May 1855 to settle among the Bannocks and Shoshonis on a remote fork of the Salmon River. There they built a fort of planks and mud and named it Lemhi after a king in the Book of Mormon. The Salmon River mission grew to 136 people, but it was not a long-term success and was abandoned three years later on orders from Young during a time of rising tension and violence between Mormons and Indians and the U.S. Army. Fort Lemhi was never reestablished.

Catholics and Protestants have historically differed on many tenets of

14. F. Jay Haynes photographed the Coeur d'Alene or
Cataldo Mission in 1884. It is currently Idaho's oldest
standing building. Courtesy Haynes Foundation Collection, Montana Historical Society, H-1392.

Christian faith, even as Protestant denominations and sects differed among
themselves. These differences and lack of true knowledge of other faiths fed
dislike and distrust in the Pacific Northwest. The Methodists, for example,
resented the intrusion of other Protestants into their Northwest domain,
but Protestants were of like mind in believing that Roman Catholic popery
represented the greatest of dangers. Unlike the Protestant missionaries,
who were Americans and blatantly ethnocentric, the Catholics tended to be
immigrants and thus strangers in the land themselves. No doubt Protestants regarded them with suspicion because of nationalism as much as
because of religious differences: for many non-Catholics, the Catholics
seemed allied with the Hudson's Bay Company and a British future for the

Pacific Northwest. Members of one Catholic order, the Jesuits, appeared especially sinister to Protestants, who shuddered at tales of Jesuit plots and intrigue. A literature of horror arose to exploit that fear—much as happened during other eras when Americans developed exaggerated fears of organizations and beliefs they did not understand. Marcus Whitman wrote home in 1842, "Romanism stalks abroad on our right hand and on our left, and with daring effrontery boasts that she is to possess the land. I ask, must it be so?"

Catholics in turn were suspicious of Protestants, believing that, while they pretended to spread their faith, their true mission was to foster trade and commerce. Catholics feared that the Protestants' authoritarian approach toward Indians, particularly their lack of sensitivity to native cultures, fostered conflict between Euro-Americans and Indians. Protestants responded that Catholic accommodation to native traditions like polygamy and shamanism showed too great a willingness to compromise with sin in all its blackness. They feared, too, that Jesuits encouraged Indians to massacre Protestants. This conviction haunted the mind of Henry Spalding after the Whitman massacre, and Protestants frequently accused Jesuits of masterminding the subsequent Indian wars in the interior Northwest. Indians, not surprisingly, factionalized into Christians and traditionalists, Protestants and Catholics.

Giant illustrated charts, or ladders, used to teach Indians the right path to salvation were a graphic depiction of the intense rivalry between Catholic and Protestant missionaries. Measuring up to six feet long, the charts were essentially historical maps of the road to salvation; they usually began with Creation and extended through the Christian era to the time of modern Indian missions. One Catholic ladder showed Protestants as tortured pilgrims falling into hell. Eliza Spalding created a Protestant version in which she reversed the roles: Catholics, including mitered bishops, were portrayed as pitching headlong into the flames.

The heyday of the mission era lasted not even two decades (1834–48) and merged into the advent of pioneer settlers traveling by land and sea to Oregon. In the work of Christianizing Indians, the missionary record was at best mixed. The missionaries' ideals were lofty, their motivation generally sprang from the best of human qualities, but in too many cases the results of their efforts reflected an inability to surmount cultural and religious biases. However history may judge their successes and shortcomings, the missionaries did play a role in better defining the Pacific Northwest in Euro-American minds and thereby helped to encourage pioneer settlement of a distant corner of North America.

### THE ROAD WEST

The words "Oregon Trail" invariably conjure images of pioneer families plodding west by covered wagon. Along the route to the Pacific, emigrants faced the dangers of violent winds, floods, quicksand, buffalo stampedes, disease, and, on rare occasions, Indian attack. By some accounts, 10 percent of the travelers perished along the way, mainly from disease and accident. The arduous, two-thousand-mile trek to Oregon, which represented the longest overland journey that American settlers attempted, became a defining moment in the lives of a generation of Pacific Northwest pioneers.

The Oregon Trail extended to the Willamette Valley from several jumping-off places along the Missouri River—the favorite site prior to 1850 being Independence, Missouri, located on the river's great bend near present Kansas City. Council Bluffs, Iowa, became a favorite starting point after 1850. On a map the trail resembled a badly frayed rope, with strands originating in several locations and alternate routes unraveling at intervals. Winding across future Wyoming and Idaho, the Oregon Trail traversed some of the most inhospitable terrain in North America. Until the building of Fort Hall in 1834 there was not so much as a cabin along the route, and even ten years later the situation had improved only slightly.

The Oregon Trail originated with a series of accidental discoveries by Robert Stuart's Astorians returning east from the Columbia River in 1812 and by the mountain man Jedediah Smith, who after 1824 publicized South Pass (in future Wyoming) as an easy crossing of the Rockies. Narcissa Whitman and Eliza Spalding's journey in 1836 provided a precedent for family travel over the trail. Their party's flimsy, two-wheeled cart made it as far west as Fort Boise; within a few years Oregon-bound pioneers would drive heavy wagons to the Columbia River and eventually all the way to the Willamette Valley.

The first family to move to Oregon for the express purpose of establishing a home arrived in 1840. The party used wagons as far west as Fort Hall. A larger group of twenty-four headed west from Independence in 1841. That same year the Bartleson-Bidwell company became the first party of emigrants to trace the overland route to California.

More than a hundred persons and eighteen wagons rolled west in 1842 under the guidance of Dr. Elijah White, a former Methodist missionary assigned as an Indian subagent for Oregon. The White party was the first to form a typical wagon train in which families predominated. That year thus marked the beginning of the familiar saga of covered wagon migration to

Oregon. The White party also brought Marcus Whitman the news that the American Board planned to abandon the mission at Waiilatpu. After his famous winter ride east, Whitman returned to Oregon in 1843 with the largest party of emigrants to that time. This group was also the first to get its wagons intact to the Columbia River. Called the Great Migration, it consisted of nearly nine hundred emigrants in a hundred wagons accompanied by as many as seven hundred head of oxen and cattle.

The number of emigrants journeying overland to Oregon reached nearly fifteen hundred, and the following year grew to twenty-five hundred. Those pioneers traveled not in one great caravan but in several smaller groups. Migration became an annual event, with an estimated four thousand emigrants heading west along the trail in 1847. Between 1840 and 1860, some fifty-three thousand people completed the journey by wagon, on horseback, or pulling handcarts from jumping-off points along the Missouri River to Oregon. The Oregon Trail remained the major highway to the Pacific Northwest until a railroad line paralleling its route through southern Idaho was completed in 1884. The trail also occasionally served as a route for cattle and sheep drives east.

## LIFE ON THE OREGON TRAIL

During the early years a typical overland journey required seven months. Starting in April, emigrants made their way slowly west from the Missouri Valley across the Great Plains. At the Platte River, they traveled upstream until the river forked to become the North Platte and then the Sweetwater. Beyond South Pass they continued to the Green River, then west to the Hudson's Bay Company oasis at Fort Hall. From there Oregon-bound travelers crossed the Snake River plain to the Hudson Bay Company's Fort Boise, then on to the Grande Ronde Valley, the Blue Mountains, and the Whitman mission. Finally, they followed the south bank of the Columbia River to The Dalles. From that point they usually portaged downriver to the Willamette Valley, reaching their destination in October.

The emigrants timed their departure from the Missouri Valley so that livestock could feed off the lush grasses of the Great Plains at their peak. Compared to what followed, the physical obstacles posed by the Great Plains proved relatively unimportant. Although each mile was hard-won, few parts of the trail were less hospitable than the dusty, blistering, and seemingly endless stretch across the Snake River plain. Emigrant parties reached the plain during the hottest part of summer, having already endured

# Route of The Oregon Trail

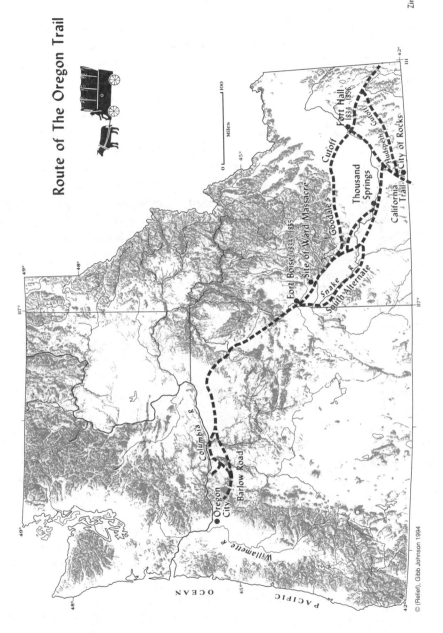

Zimmerly

© (Relief), Gibb Johnson 1994

nearly 1,300 miles on the trail. Animals and humans were tired and thirsty, but the cool waters of the Snake River lay far below the canyon's rim, so tantalizing and yet so impossible to reach. Moreover, the sharp-edged basalt lacerated the hooves of draft animals. Early travelers seldom penned favorable descriptions of the land they scorned as nothing more than desolate sagebrush flats and sand, a maze of ravines and treeless hills. Here game was scarce and for mile after wearying mile, wagon wheels churned up prodigious clouds of alkali dust. During the heyday of the trail, from 1840 to 1860, few if any emigrants stopped short of the Willamette Valley to establish a permanent home on the Snake River plain. Euro-Americans would seldom attempt to settle there until irrigation transformed the land.

Travelers toiled across the arid plains of the Snake River country, pushed up the Grande Ronde Valley, crossed the Blue Mountains, and paused only briefly at the Whitman Mission. They usually continued along the treeless plateau south of the Columbia River to the maelstrom of white water called the Grand Dalles (now The Dalles). A final difficulty lay at the very edge of the promised land. In the shadow of Mount Hood, where the Columbia River had cut a deep gorge through the Cascade mountains—and where today's motorist speeds along an interstate highway blasted from cliffs that crowd the water's edge—pioneers were forced to abandon their wagons and take to the water in crude, poorly constructed rafts and barges to complete the eighty-mile trip from the Grand Dalles to the Willamette Valley. For unskilled navigators, the journey by raft through the Columbia's turbulent waters was exceedingly dangerous. Self-built rafts often disintegrated in midstream or became engulfed in giant whirlpools. The loss of goods or life was always tragic, but especially so near the destination.

Beginning in 1846 some Oregon argonauts used Sam Barlow's toll road, a welcome but crude, difficult, and expensive alternative to the river. The Barlow Road ran 110 miles from the Grand Dalles along the southern slope of Mount Hood to Oregon City in the Willamette Valley. At Laurel Hill pioneers used rope snubs and tree drags to lower their wagons and oxen down a 60 percent grade. For many years it was strictly a one-way road west, the incline being too steep to use in the opposite direction. Despite the difficulties, travelers paid Barlow tolls of five dollars per wagon and one dollar for each head of livestock. A small number of argonauts branched off the main trail just west of the Blue Mountains and headed up the Yakima Valley, over the Cascades at Naches Pass, and down into the fertile valleys of western Washington; some followed the Applegate cutoff across southern Oregon.

The Oregon Trail has been called the world's longest graveyard, with one body, on average, buried about every eighty yards. People lost their lives to swollen rivers, quicksand, rattlesnakes, and accidents; children were occasionally crushed by wagon wheels or stepped on by oxen. However, the number one killer on the trail was disease: influenza, severe dysentery, and Asian cholera so devastating that a person might be healthy at dawn and dead before nightfall. A major cause of disease on the trail, ironically, was the argonauts' own polluted environment. People occasionally left animal carcasses to rot by the trail or buried their dead in shallow, hastily dug graves that were easily opened by wolves and other wild animals. A party of travelers might dig a shallow well for drinking water, allow the party and their stock to pollute it, and then move on, leaving the water hole for the next unwary travelers to slake their thirst.

Emigrant trains represented temporary communities on the trail. Members organized themselves into semimilitary units and elected slates of officers. The earlier in the history of the trail the migration occurred, the more complex the organization might be. Once they left Missouri or Iowa, emigrants were beyond the pale of law; hence, they usually adopted rules and regulations specifying punishments for crime. One code decreed that every man was to carry a Bible and other religious books with him, "as we hope not to degenerate into a state of barbarism." Harmony was the ideal, but tension and friction inevitably arose, sometimes necessitating reorganization or division of the train into several parties.

The chief expense of getting to Oregon was for transportation—oxen, wagon, and gear—which cost close to $400. Wagons had to be constructed with great care to endure the rigors of the trail. Only well-seasoned hardwood could withstand great extremes of temperature and humidity. Into a space that usually measured no more than four feet wide by twelve feet long went the dietary essentials of wheat flour (about 200 pounds per person), corn meal, hard tack, and about a bushel of dried fruit per adult to prevent scurvy. Bacon could be kept from going rancid by packing it in a bed of bran. Salt, sugar, coffee, and tea were so precious that they were often stored in double cloth sacks. After packing the bare necessities, pioneers added their farm implements. Leftover space might contain a few books, some extra clothing, or perhaps a little furniture. But the total must not weigh too much, because it was foolhardy to overburden and exhaust the team of six mules or four yoke of oxen upon which survival depended.

No consensus ever emerged on the best draft animals. Oxen were cheaper than mules and less likely to stampede or to be stolen by Indians. Mules, other argued, were faster and stayed healthy on scarce feed. In the end, the bulk of emigrants relied on young oxen, which men drove by walking along side them, cracking a long bull whip. Usually trailing along was a cow or two, their milk especially desirable for children. Any of the day's leftover milk could be churned into butter. Along the trail there were catfish in the prairie streams and trout in the mountains. In many places the buffalo were plentiful, and their meat could be cut into thin strips and hung on the sides of the wagons' canvas tops to dry in the hot summer sun.

Men and women shared responsibilities on the trail. Women prepared breakfast while the men and older boys hitched up the draft animals, a task that took about half an hour. Men usually drove, although one traveler recalled meeting a train of eleven wagons in 1852 all driven by women. As a result of a cholera epidemic, not one man had remained alive in the entire train. Overlanders averaged about fifteen miles a day. Sometimes they arranged their wagons in parallel fashion so as to travel relatively free of the dust of those ahead, or they might rotate their positions in line. At night, they arranged their wagons in a circle to form a corral for their animals and a temporary fort should Indians attack.

In truth, most emigrants got to Oregon with little or no difficulty from Indians, and not even all Indian attacks were what they were purported to be. White highwaymen masquerading as Indians occasionally preyed on overlanders. Thievery and not murder constituted the major threat posed by Indians; counterbalancing this picture were numerous cases in which Indians provided Oregon-bound pioneers with information, food, equipment, horses, survival skills, and other forms of assistance. Statistics indicate that the most likely site for an Indian attack was on the Snake River plain. Here some bloody incidents were recorded, one of the worst being the massacre of the Alexander Ward party on the Boise River in 1854. Only two young boys who hid out in the underbrush survived out of a party of twenty-three overlanders. The last major conflict with Indians on the trail occurred in 1862.

As encounters with Indians suggest, the Oregon Trail experience changed over time. The trail itself evolved, so that the experience for travelers headed west in 1845 was not exactly the same as for those who followed a decade later. The way west was never easy, but as new cutoffs were discovered and developed, the average number of days required to make the journey decreased, from 169 during the years 1841–48 to 128 during the 1850s. In the early years, parties employed special guides. Later groups seldom required their services because the way to Oregon had become so well known. By the

15. An emigrant train crossing the Great Plains in 1857. Indian attacks were the overlanders' primary fear, yet in actuality they seldom occurred. The majority of early travelers saw few Indians along the trail and in the 1850s and 1860s could take some comfort in forts the War Department built along the route. Only in the mid-1850s, when Indians began to worry about en- croachments on their lands, did they become hostile and aggressive, especially in the region beyond South Pass. Courtesy Library of Congress, USZ262-741.

1850s, as private trading posts and army forts sprang up alongside the trail, talk of leaving civilization behind to go west was no longer appropriate.

After 1848 the character of travel east of Fort Hall changed, too, with the addition of many gold seekers bound for California. Immigrants to Califor- nia and Oregon followed the same route to Fort Hall. Beyond there, the California trail branched to the southwest. A common belief among Oregon pioneers was that the less respectable overlanders sought quick fortune in the gold fields of California, while conservative, orderly, family-oriented folk sought Oregon. That feeling was clearly captured in an Oregon anecdote about a fork in the trail where "a pile of gold-bearing quartz marked the road to California; the other road had a sign bearing the words 'To Oregon.' Those who could read took the trail to Oregon." Whether the anecdote is true or not, clearly the society that developed in the Willamette Valley after the 1840s was different from that in California. The agrarian, family-oriented values that the firstcomers brought with them to Oregon were communicated to potential settlers through letters and pamphlets, and those who were attracted by such things tended to reinforce the community's values.

### PERSPECTIVES ON THE OREGON ODYSSEY

One alternative to the Oregon Trail was the 11,000-mile-long voyage around Cape Horn, an experience different from but seldom easier than the overland odyssey. Usually it took six to eight months to sail down the Eastern seaboard, around South America, and up to the Columbia River. Ships often made intermediate stops at Rio de Janeiro, Valparaíso, and Honolulu, which from a navigation standpoint was a logical port of call because the winds and currents that swung away from the South American continent carried mariners far out into the Pacific Ocean; it was easier to sail to Hawaii with the wind and current than hug the coast and fight the often fierce headwinds. Nonetheless, after California's 1848 gold rush, San Francisco tended to replace Honolulu as a waystation on the voyage to Oregon.

The storms off Cape Horn were fierce, and both crew and passengers approached the area with trepidation. The bar of the Columbia River presented another challenge to captains, who had to calculate the combined effect of wind, water, tide, and the always dangerous and shifting sands. Before 1847 there was no official pilot service across the bar. Between 1839 and 1859, sixteen ships wrecked at the mouth of the Columbia.

Food was always a problem on long voyages. Ships stocked many of the same staple items as found on wagons of the overland route: flour, hardtack, corn meal, molasses, coffee, and dried fruit. Lack of refrigeration excluded most fresh fruits and vegetables. Instead, ships typically carried a menagerie of pigs, chickens, and ducks for food, and sometimes a cow or goat for milk. Occasionally passengers or crew caught fresh fish for the dinner table. Drinking water was a problem: even when stored in watertight compartments below deck it often became tainted by saltwater seepage and the warmth of the sun.

To pass time during the long and tedious voyages, passengers sometimes played games of chess and backgammon or fished from the ship. A few of them succumbed to boredom and too much alcohol. Tropical diseases also took a toll on passengers. Malaria and yellow fever were major problems on

HAWAIIANS IN THE PACIFIC NORTHWEST

For many years after Captain Cook's third voyage, the Hawaiian Islands were a regular stopping place and winter harbor for ships headed to the North Pacific coast. In the late 1780s English merchant-adventurers initiated the use of Hawaiians—known in the Pacific Northwest as Owyhees, Kanakas, or Sandwich Islanders—to work as seamen and laborers in the expanding fur trade. John Jacob Astor's ill-fated ship, the *Tonquin*, brought twenty-four Owyhees to the lower Columbia River, and subsequent vessels increased their numbers in the Northwest to about three hundred by 1825. When H. H. Hunt built a sawmill twenty miles upriver from Astoria, he made an agreement with King Kamehameha to acquire the labor of five Hawaiians for $5 a month each plus salmon and potatoes for food.

The Hudson's Bay Company employed Hawaiians as sawmill workers, agricultural laborers, and voyageurs and seamen. Placenames still recall their presence. When Indians killed two Hawaiians accompanying a Hudson's Bay Company fur brigade near the present Oregon-Idaho border, Peter Skene Ogden named the nearby river Owyhee in their memory.

Another important source of employment for Hawaiians in the Pacific Northwest were the Protestant missionaries. On one occasion a Hawaiian intervened to protect the life of Henry Spalding, who had become engaged in a bitter argument with an Indian. Reporting to his superiors from his mission at Kamiah, Asa Bowen Smith lamented the lack of reliable native labor, claiming that "4 Indians would not be worth so much as one Hawaiian."

When American settlers moved to Oregon in large numbers in the 1840s, most of them treated Hawaiians with the same prejudice they demonstrated toward Chinese, Indians, and blacks. Denied citizenship and property rights, the early Hawaiians of the Pacific Northwest returned to their islands in the 1850s.

one other alternative to the overland route to Oregon: the portage through the steamy jungles of Panama or Nicaragua. Given the risks of other options, it is not surprising that prior to 1850 most people bound for Oregon preferred the long trail overland. Until that year, when the ships of the Pacific Mail Steamship Company inaugurated three monthly trips between Portland and San Francisco, oceangoing vessels arrived in the Pacific Northwest only on an irregular basis.

Why did people undertake the long overland journey to Oregon? Their motives were varied, and no doubt many emigrants would have been hard pressed to explain their real reasons for moving west. Some hoped to improve their health; others relished the challenge and excitement of starting a new life out West or wanted simply to escape the virulent passions that surrounded the issues of race and slavery. Recordsetting floods in Missouri,

16. Erecting a log cabin in rural Idaho. Courtesy Idaho
State Historical Society, 60-72-43.

Iowa, and Illinois in 1836, 1844, and 1849 inundated and destroyed farms, and the receding waters left sickness in their wake, causing desperate people to seek alternatives. Finally, hard times gripped the Midwest after the Panic of 1837 caused many of the region's farmers to sink hopelessly into debt. In this atmosphere "Oregon fever" sparked lively debates in countless courthouses, crossroads stores, and homes. Standing out most clearly in these discussions was the desire for economic improvement. In an agrarian society that measured wealth in terms of landholdings, the belief that Oregon contained an abundance of fertile land easily acquired under federal laws was compelling. Not surprisingly, many Oregon-bound pioneers were impoverished farm families from the Ohio and Missouri valleys.

The great trek to Oregon was a never-to-be forgotten experience for all who completed it. It was unlike anything they had done before or would likely do again. Memories of the trail experience were preserved in the letters and diaries of the original travelers and are still kept vivid through reenactments of wagon train journeys and displays in visitor centers. Probably the most spectacular displays are found at the Bureau of Land Management's $10 million Oregon Trail Interpretive Center located outside Baker City, Oregon. Opened in 1992, it offers depictions of everyday life on the trail and a panoramic view of still visible wagon ruts from the summit of

Flagstaff Hill. From this hard-won promontory, Oregon argonauts had once paused to scan the beautiful valley below them, ponder the awesome flanks of the Blue Mountains in the distance ahead, and anticipate the long-sought promised land.

Whether they were fully conscious of it or not, the traders and trappers, missionaries, overland trail pioneers, and other Euro-Americans who came to the Pacific Northwest in search of furs, lost souls, or farms contributed at least informally to defining the land that became the Pacific Northwest. The U.S. government reentered the process in the late 1830s and 1840s when it launched the first official exploratory expeditions since Lewis and Clark. Soon a new generation of maps, descriptive documents, and artwork provided federal officials and a curious public an image of the far Northwest more precise than ever before. This information influenced both the diplomacy and the grass-roots governments that rearranged the region's political landscape.

CHAPTER 6

# Oregon Country: Rearranging the Political Landscape

*

Already we are sending numerous emigrants every year across the Rocky mountains; and we are sending them there without the protection of law, and without the restraints of civil government. We have left them, hitherto, to the unlimited control of their own passions. We must send them laws and a regular form of government.—Senator James Buchanan of Pennsylvania, Speech, 12 March 1844

*

Some of the most profound changes in Pacific Northwest history occurred during the 1840s. When the decade dawned, the Oregon country had no political boundaries and no effective government apart from the influence of Hudson's Bay Company officials and the American missionaries. Ten years later, an international boundary divided the country along the 49th parallel, and the Hudson's Bay Company had shifted its main operation to the British side of the border. Chief Factor John McLoughlin, long-time patriarch of the Oregon country, retired in early 1846 to land he owned near Oregon City, and three years later the Hudson's Bay Company moved its departmental headquarters north to Fort Victoria on Vancouver Island.

Thousands of land-hungry settlers supplanted fur traders and missionaries as the most representative non-Indian group in the new Northwest. They brought permanent changes to the Willamette Valley and other areas when they laid out farms, towns, and a network of roads. They organized a government for themselves in 1843 and five years later pressured Congress into creating the Oregon Territory. Finally, the Whitman tragedy of 1847 initiated a change that no one wanted: three decades of periodic warfare between Indians and whites. Those conflicts, too, contributed to rearranging the region's political landscape.

## PIONEER SETTLEMENTS

For many an overlander, the first year in Oregon proved nearly as difficult as life on the trail. Very few of the early emigrants were rich, and many arrived in extreme poverty, having lost their belongings to the remorseless Columbia River. To survive the first winter, they purchased goods on credit from the Hudson's Bay Company or sought temporary employment in one of its many enterprises. People already in residence aided the newcomers, partly because of a genuine desire to assist and partly because they realized that good public order depended on their charity.

That first winter newcomers lodged in the homes of relatives or friends or resorted to bunking in local schools and meeting houses. For some pioneers, only a cold, damp campsite was available. The Pacific Northwest's earliest Euro-American settlers lived in a variety of simple structures that ranged from teepees, willow huts, and tents to log cabins and adobe buildings. Lumber sawed by hand at the rate of $8 to $12 a day made frame buildings of any type an expensive luxury. Many pioneers fashioned their dwellings from logs hand-hewn on two sides and chinked with mud or moss. The floor was packed earth, and because glass was so scarce they used stretched cotton cloth or deer skins for windows. A large iron stove or fireplace provided warmth.

Willamette Valley settlers hastened to lay the foundations for economic survival as well. In wheat the pioneer Euro-Americans discovered a good "poor man's crop" that required little operating capital and usually returned a good profit from the first year. Indeed, wheat was the only major crop durable enough to be sold outside the West Coast before refrigerated railroad cars made it possible (in the late 1880s) to ship fruit to the East.

The discovery of gold in California in 1848 attracted some adventurers from the Willamette Valley to the diggings; at the same time, the new California market stimulated commercial agriculture in the Pacific Northwest. The price of wheat climbed from one dollar to six dollars a bushel, and a steady stream of ships sailed up the Columbia River to load wheat for California. Oregon in 1850 produced a total of 208,000 bushels of wheat, mostly in the Willamette Valley. Farmers were not the only ones to benefit from the region's first economic boom; mill operators, tradesmen, and professionals prospered as well.

Oregon City in 1844 became the first incorporated U.S. municipality

17. Front Street south of Morrison in Portland in 1852.
Courtesy Oregon Historical Society, ORHI 5490.

west of the Rocky Mountains. Located at the falls of the Willamette a few miles upriver from present-day Portland, Oregon City was the capital of the Oregon Territory from 1849 to 1852. It became Oregon's largest settlement by 1850, when its 933 residents accounted for almost one-tenth of the territory's non-Indian population. Blessed with a growing population and abundant water power to run its two flour mills and five sawmills, Oregon City's prosperity seemed assured. But Portland soon overshadowed it.

Situated near the confluence of the Willamette and Columbia rivers, Portland enjoyed a favorable location during an age when commerce moved by river and ocean. Its wharves formed the heart of a transportation network that expanded along waterways and trails into the Columbia plateau and up the Willamette Valley. The city's trade ultimately extended to San Francisco and the world beyond. In its first decade, Portland established itself as Oregon's center of commerce and population and the economic capital of the Northwest hinterland. Domination of water transportation gave the growing city an advantage it maintained even after the arrival of railroads and the growth of population centers in Idaho's mining regions and on Puget Sound. Only Seattle, which got off to a slow start in 1852, eventually surpassed Portland in population and regional importance—although the latter assertion remains a matter of heated debate and the basis for an ongoing urban rivalry.

Even as emigrants planted their first communities in the Oregon country, a pressing need arose to clarify matters of law and government. Early land claimants in the Willamette Valley wanted to protect their property, and by the mid-1840s there was an equally pressing need to define the international boundary between British and American territory in the Pacific Northwest.

### GRASS-ROOTS GOVERNMENT

In 1818 and again in 1827, Great Britain and the United States agreed to occupy the Oregon country jointly. As a result of that unusual arrangement, British residents were subject to the authority of the Hudson's Bay Company, the agency officially responsible for enforcing British civil and criminal law in several remote parts of North America. In cases of criminal misconduct, the accused were transported to the nearest permanent British settlement for trial in a regular court. The company ruled effectively, and as a result, there was no legacy of western badmen and outlaws in its domain.

By contrast, the Americans in the Oregon country were beyond the limits of the United States government and its laws. Moreover, Congress, having more important concerns, seemed in no hurry to remedy that arrangement despite settlers' petitions urging establishment of a territory there to protect property and insure public morality. The alternative—submission to Hudson's Bay Company rule—was anathema to a people who often perceived the British enterprise as a grasping monopolistic octopus. The American settlers debated whether it would be better to form an independent government or wait until the United States acted.

For Americans, settlement preceded establishment of effective government. When only a handful of non-Indians lived in the Oregon country, government was of little consequence. But new circumstances arising in the early 1840s forced pioneers to fashion a government for themselves. Following a time-honored American tradition of compact writing and constitution making, early Oregonians simply took matters of law and order into their own hands.

The process of creating a government and laws took place over a period of several months, even years, though it initially it amounted to nothing more

113

than a series of ad hoc responses to specific problems that confronted pioneers. First they faced a legal dilemma: Ewing Young, a trapper and cattleman who had amassed a substantial estate in the Willamette Valley, died without leaving a will or apparent heirs. To dispose of his property, a committee of settlers met after his funeral in 1841. They appointed a missionary, Ira Babcock, as temporary judge to probate Young's estate using New York laws as a model.

The settlers took another halting step toward creation of a full-fledged government in February and March 1843 when they met to discuss wild animal attacks on their livestock. They established an executive committee to administer a rudimentary system of tax collection and disburse funds for a wolf bounty. The so-called Wolf Meetings are credited with setting the stage for the formal creation of a provisional government two months later.

Approximately one hundred American and French-Canadian settlers met at Champoeg in May 1843 "to take into consideration the propriety for taking measures for civil and military protection of this colony." By a slender majority they voted to organize a provisional government. Most French Canadians dissented for fear that organization was but a step toward incorporation into American territory, and McLoughlin refused to recognize the new government's legitimacy, thus heightening anti-British, anti–Hudson's Bay Company sentiment in the American community.

The homespun government that Americans fashioned during the spring and summer of 1843 was a patchwork that embodied familiar traditions and materials readily at hand. Working from the one law book in their possession, which contained Iowa territorial laws and a trilogy of hallowed documents—the Declaration of Independence, the Constitution, and the Northwest Ordinance of 1787—settlers framed a constitution that provided for an executive committee of three men and a system of voluntary taxation. The following summer, when a wave of newcomers made its influence felt, settlers revised the constitution to provide a single executive and compulsory taxation. They also prohibited alcoholic beverages and excluded black settlers. Despite its obvious shortcomings, Oregon's grass-roots government lasted until Congress approved a territorial government in 1848.

MANIFEST DESTINY: FIFTY-FOUR FORTY OR FIGHT

Even as Oregon pioneers fashioned their provisional government, they weighed momentous changes of another sort. During the mid-1840s an expansionist mood termed Manifest Destiny gripped the United States as never before. An influential and growing number of citizens asserted that it was the nation's God-given destiny to expand to the limits of the continent.

For three decades—from the end of the War of 1812 to the conclusion of the Oregon Treaty in 1846—American opinion remained divided on the worth of the far Northwest. Counterbalancing the rhapsodies of Thomas Hart Benton, Hall Jackson Kelley, and other Oregon boosters were the assertions of skeptics and naysayers, like the New York newspaper that described the hinterland as fit only for a penal colony.

As the time approached to define the international boundary through the Pacific Northwest, additional information about the geography and natural resources of the distant region reached the President and members of Congress from renewed investigation of the land and resources of the West. Later known as the Great Reconnaissance, this phase of exploratory activity lasted nearly three decades and resulted in many volumes of documents and a rich scientific and artistic legacy that would shape official thinking about the remote corner of the continent.

The tentative beginning of this new era of western reconnaissance dates from 1832, when Captain Benjamin Louis Eulalie de Bonneville, a French-born officer in the U.S. Army, ostensibly took a leave of absence from the army and became a fur trader for the next four years. Many historians now believe he was in reality spying out the promised land, searching for a route across the Rocky Mountains to California. If so—and the proof is elusive—Bonneville was the first American since Lewis and Clark to undertake official exploration of the far Northwest.

On one of these trips, he traced a route from western Missouri to the rugged Salmon River country, where he established winter quarters in 1832. The next spring the Bonneville party retreated to the annual fur traders' rendezvous at the Green River, then headed west again across the Snake River plain, eventually reaching Fort Walla Walla and the Columbia Valley in 1834. It was Bonneville who demonstrated the feasibility of taking loaded wagons across the continental divide at South Pass, about seven thousand feet above sea level but with easy gradients, and gained information that later proved valuable in shaping U.S. policy toward the Oregon country.

During the 1840s the federal government unequivocally reentered the business of exploring the far Northwest: from the west, members of a navy expedition probed the waters of Puget Sound and up the Columbia and Snake rivers as far as the Spaldings' mission station at Lapwai. From the east came army explorers led by John C. Frémont.

Most personnel in the army's elite Corps of Topographical Engineers (though not Frémont himself) were West Point graduates trained in such skills as engineering and map making. They brought a new degree of sophistication to the exploration of the West. The army commissioned Frémont to map and survey the trail to Oregon. He and thirty-nine men set out from Independence, Missouri, in May 1843 on their "secret" mission to Oregon. The party pushed past the British outpost of Fort Hall, across the Snake River plain, and west along the Columbia River to Fort Vancouver; backtracking a bit, the expedition then headed south through the high desert country east of the Cascade Range.

Frémont was the first explorer to recognize and name the Great Basin that encompassed parts of southern Idaho, Utah, and Nevada. His cartographer Charles Preuss completed a detailed map of the Oregon Trail. The Preuss map was a veritable gold mine of information that gave would-be emigrants precise distances and information on landmarks, river crossings, and Indian tribes. When Frémont presented his report to Congress it created a sensation and was widely printed and distributed. It helped that Frémont was married to Jessie Benton, daughter of the influential Missouri Senator Thomas Hart Benton, a key spokesman for development of the Oregon Country.

Less influential with prominent members of Congress but nonetheless important to the diplomatic negotiations was the navy expedition led by Charles Wilkes. From 1838 to 1842 the United States Exploring Expedition, or Wilkes expedition, made a voyage of discovery around the world. The ships arrived off the coast of Oregon in 1841. Lieutenant Wilkes and the expedition crew members named more than 250 landmarks in what is now Washington. From lower Puget Sound, survey groups and scientist explored and mapped the interior of the Oregon country.

In mid-July 1841, while on a Wilkes mission to explore the Columbia River with three civilian scientists aboard, the *Peacock* ran afoul of the notorious bar at the mouth and broke apart in the pounding surf. None of the 133 lives aboard were lost, but the loss of the sloop of war was more than an embarrassment for her captain, Lieutenant William L. Hudson. When Wilkes reported his discoveries to Congress, the fate of the *Peacock* dramatized the importance of Puget Sound as the only truly valuable harbor in the Pacific Northwest. "Mere description," recalled Wilkes, "can give little idea of the terrors of the bar of the Columbia. All who have seen it have spoken of the wildness of the scene, and the incessant roar of the waters, representing it as one of the most fearful sights that can possibly meet the eye of the sailor." On the other hand, Wilkes lauded the splendor and safety of Puget

18. Taking the measure of a new land: the Wilkes Expedition in the Oregon Country in 1841. Courtesy Library
of Congress.

Sound: "Nothing can exceed the beauty of these waters, and their safety."
He asserted that no country in the world possessed a waterway equal to it.
Because of its reconnaissance, the Wilkes expedition would play a crucial
role in determination of an international boundary that gave the United
States both the Columbia River and Puget Sound.

On several occasions during the era of joint occupation, United States
and British negotiators considered ways to divide the Oregon country. But
nothing decisive happened until 1844 when the Democratic party nomi-
nated James K. Polk as president on an expansionist platform calling for the
"re-annexation of Texas and the re-occupation of Oregon"—not just the
Willamette Valley but the entire Oregon country, in defiance of British
counterclaims. The next year U.S. expansionists took up the cry, "Fifty-four
Forty or Fight," a provocative reference to the northernmost boundary of
the disputed territory. The Pacific Northwest soon occupied center stage in
a complex diplomatic drama, the outcome of which was by no means certain.

In his inaugural address in 1845, Polk declared that American title to
Oregon was "clear and unquestionable." A few months later, however, Polk

proposed to the British that Oregon be divided at the 49th parallel, a location U.S. negotiators had favored in earlier talks. When the British balked at accepting that boundary—preferring instead to run the boundary down the Columbia River from the 49th parallel to the sea—the president resumed his belligerent stance. He informed Congress that he was no longer willing to compromise and asserted that both national honor and interest were at stake in Oregon.

Only the most ardent expansionists seriously believed that the United States had a legitimate claim to the entire Oregon country. In the Willamette Valley and other lands south of the Columbia River, Americans predominated by virtue of occupation, but north of the Columbia their presence was negligible. In that area lived hundreds of Hudson's Bay Company employees and their families, all British subjects, but only a handful of United States citizens. Still farther north—in the area between the 49th parallel and the 54°40′ line—there were no Americans. Thus, the focal point of the dispute was the territory north and west of the Columbia River, which forms about two-thirds the present state of Washington.

According to the historian Norman Graebner, the United States was unyielding in its claims to the Puget Sound country because the nation was actually battling for a commercial position on the Pacific coast. Unlike the Atlantic seaboard, the Pacific coast from Baja California to the Strait of Juan de Fuca lacked good harbors. California was still part of Mexico, and the dangerous conditions described by Wilkes diminished the commercial value of the Columbia River. Only Puget Sound, therefore, offered the United States a gateway to the Pacific and the ports of Asia. For reasons of commerce and the less tangible matters of national pride and destiny, the United States stubbornly maintained its claim to Puget Sound despite the modest number of its citizens north of the Columbia River.

Congressional debate on the boundary issue dragged on until the spring of 1846, when the United States invited Great Britain to reopen negotiations. At that time a cabinet crisis and other internal problems bedeviled the British. Moreover, it no longer seemed vital to retain the lower Columbia River in order to protect Hudson's Bay Company interests because in 1845 the company had announced plans to move its regional headquarters to Vancouver Island. As a result of those developments, the British government was in a far more conciliatory mood than earlier.

In the end, Polk got less than he publicly demanded but avoided serious trouble with Britain at a time when the United States was edging toward war with Mexico. The Senate ratified the treaty in June 1846: the agreement divided the Oregon country by extending the international boundary along the 49th parallel from the crest of the Rocky Mountains to middle of the Strait of Georgia. From there the line dipped south and west through the Strait of Juan de Fuca to leave southern Vancouver Island and Fort Victoria in British hands. The Hudson's Bay Company retained the right to navigate the Columbia River south of the 49th parallel, and it was promised protection for its posts and lands in American territory.

Thomas Hart Benton no doubt spoke for many Oregon boosters when he predicted that the commercial advantages of the Pacific Northwest "will be greater—far greater than any equal portion of the Atlantic States." Only the matter of a poorly defined water boundary southeast of Vancouver Island caused further trouble between the United States and Great Britain. The so-called Pig War, an incident of comic opera proportions, erupted in 1859 on tiny San Juan Island, one of several islands claimed by both countries. At issue was a pig belonging to an employee of the Hudson's Bay Company that had strayed into an American settler's potato patch and was shot. That unneighborly display touched off a noisy dispute between British and American residents and elicited some posturing by troops from both nations and loose talk about avenging national honor. Fortunately, common sense prevailed, and the fifty-six-square-mile island remained under joint military occupation until arbitration by the emperor of Germany finally fixed the international boundary in 1872. The settlement gave the United States title to the contested islands and the British withdrew.

OREGON: THE ROAD TO STATEHOOD

The formal settlement of the boundary issue had little immediate impact on Americans living in Oregon. Until the Whitman tragedy of late 1847 dramatized their isolation, they continued to be treated as Uncle Sam's stepchildren. After the bloodshed at Waiilatpu, the provisional government sent former mountain man Joseph Meek to plead its case in the national capital. Arriving in St. Louis in May 1848 after crossing half a continent in the dead of winter, he announced himself as "Envoy Extraordinary and Minister Plenipotentiary from the Republic of Oregon to the Court of the United States." Newspapers played up Meek's dramatic odyssey and helped publicize the cause he represented; some even suggested that, had the federal government done its duty in Oregon, blood might never have been spilled at Waiilatpu.

Congress created the territory of Oregon the following August. President

Polk named Meek—who also happened to be a relative of the president's wife—marshal and Joseph Lane of Indiana, a loyal Democrat and a hero of the Mexican War, governor of the new territory. Traveling by sea the pair arrived in Oregon on 2 March 1849, and with appropriate fanfare, Lane proclaimed the existence of a new territory the following day. A few months later, U.S. Army troops established bases alongside the Hudson's Bay Company posts at Fort Vancouver and Fort Nisqually, and U.S. mail service began.

Oregonians soon realized that territorial status was not all they hoped it would be. The proud framers of their own government and laws now found themselves treated very much like colonials. That lowly status was hardly unique to Oregonians: residents of all territories remained second-class citizens for an indeterminate time prior to statehood. According to the federal Constitution, Congress retained supreme power over all territories. It could, for example, determine the length of territorial legislative sessions and the number of legislators, and it might veto their enactments. Congress could also freely alter any territorial boundaries. As in any colonial system, the potential for tyranny was great, but Uncle Sam generally remained too indifferent to territorial affairs to guide them with a firm hand. He was, nonetheless, generous enough to pay most territorial expenses.

Federal power functioned most directly through officers appointed in Washington, D. C., and residing in each territory. Those officials included a governor, a secretary, three or more justices, and any lesser functionaries to administer local federal offices. An "organic act" modeled after the Northwest Ordinance of 1787 provided a general framework for territorial government. Over time, specific features of America's colonial system changed to permit a certain amount of improvisation by both the federal government and individual territories.

As a result of America's far-flung colonial system, outsiders could easily mismanage a territory; presidential appointees might be wholly insensitive to local needs and feelings. Inexperience, administrative difficulties, low pay, frontier discomforts, and changes of presidents contributed to a high rate of turnover among territorial officers. Richard D. Gholson, one of Washington's fourteen territorial governors, left so little impression that no portrait of him is known to exist. There were, of course, those who left quite a mark, including the first territorial governors of Oregon and Washington, Joseph Lane and Isaac Stevens.

Each territory selected a delegate to represent it in Congress. Although he lacked a vote and the other formal powers of a congressman, the delegate

### THE DONATION LAND CLAIM ACT OF 1850

In rearranging the landscape of the new Northwest geographically as well as politically, few congressional enactments had greater impact than the Donation Land Claim Act of 1850. This measure recognized the generous claims established under Oregon's provisional government and set up a system for acquiring additional land. According to this early-day homestead act, each white male citizen eighteen years of age or older was entitled to 320 acres of land if single; if he married by 1 December 1851, his wife could hold an additional 320 acres in her own right. A person had only to reside on the land and cultivate it for four years. In the eyes of congressional supporters, this act and its subsequent revisions rewarded settlers who had helped the United States win a very generous boundary settlement as well as encouraged further immigration to the nation's far corner.

The effects of the first large-scale disposition of land in the Pacific Northwest were far-reaching. During its five-year existence, eight thousand claimants acquired nearly three million acres. By far the largest number of donation land claims was located in the Willamette Valley. Because claims were supposed to be square in shape—or if not square, then oblong—the act superimposed a recognizable pattern on the face of the land.

Likewise, it superimposed a racial and ethnic pattern on pioneer Oregon. The act stimulated white immigration and settlement, but its provisions excluded blacks and Hawaiians. Prior to 1850, Hawaiians had constituted a substantial portion of the region's work force, but most of them eventually returned to the islands. Moreover, the land was given away free to white settlers before Indian title to it was extinguished. Finally, because a white family could acquire a 640-acre tract of farmland—the size of many a Southern plantation—the Donation Land Claim Act contributed to a debate over slavery that increasingly agitated Oregon politics during the 1850s.

functioned as publicist, lobbyist, agent of the territory and its officers, and major dispenser of Uncle Sam's political plums. Lane, who resigned as Oregon's governor before Polk's Whig successor could replace him, was repeatedly elected the territory's delegate to Congress in the 1850s. He became a powerful figure in Oregon and in national Democratic party politics.

The decade of territorial government was for Oregon a time of political acrimony. Residents fought over where to locate the capital, Salem winning over Oregon City and Corvallis; and Democratic and Whig cliques battled over political appointments in venomous verbal duels that enlivened early-day journalism. Oregon voted three times—in 1854, 1855, and 1856—against statehood, only to vote overwhelmingly for it in 1857. Underlying much of the controversy and seemingly contradictory political behavior was the issue of race. Oregonians were responding to the great national issue of the day: slavery.

For nearly two decades, debate over slavery agitated politics in the Pacific Northwest despite the region's remoteness from slave states. The reason was that Oregon's first white settlers brought their cultural baggage with them, and for those moving from Missouri and other states of the Mississippi and Ohio valleys, that included a strong set of opinions about blacks and slavery.

Many pioneer settlers were antiblack but differed over whether slavery should be permitted in their territory. It was hardly an irrelevant question: the generous grants permitted under the Donation Land Claim Act together with a mild climate made the Willamette Valley well suited for slave labor, or so some residents asserted. A few Oregonians actually owned slaves despite their prohibition by the territorial organic act.

Other Oregonians feared that slavery would enable the rich to dominate the poor and thus re-create the caste system that many an immigrant farmer from Missouri or Kentucky had sought to escape. Oregon's majority party, the Democrats, included many advocates of slavery, most notably Joseph Lane. The Supreme Court's *Dred Scott* decision in early 1857, which disallowed territorial but not state legislation regarding slavery, may have been the prime reason Oregonians switched their position on statehood between 1856 and 1857. The *Dred Scott* case strengthened the hand of those who argued that statehood was necessary to protect Oregon's special concerns regarding race and slavery.

In August 1857 the writers of a proposed state constitution assembled in Salem, the territorial capital, which at that time had a population of almost a thousand residents, nearly two-thirds of them male. Among the sixty delegates were thirty farmers, nineteen lawyers, three mechanics, three ministers, two physicians, an editor, a printer, and a surveyor. Together they fashioned a document that codified the overland pioneers' essentially pastoral vision of a good society. Conservative in outlook, they used as models the constitutions of several older states, mainly those of the Old Northwest (and especially Indiana), the states where eighty-two percent of the delegates had lived before moving to Oregon.

In a special election held the following November, Oregonians approved the proposed constitution by a vote of 7,195 to 3,195; casting two additional ballots at the same time, they rejected slavery by a three to one margin and excluded free blacks and mulattos by an eight to one margin. Oregon thus became the first U.S. state to exclude African Americans other than by ordinary statutory law. In mid-March 1859, the *Brother Jonathan* sailed into Portland bringing news that on 14 February President James Buchanan had

19. California Street in early Jacksonville, Oregon.
Courtesy Oregon Historical Society, ORHI 83080.

approved the Oregon admission bill passed by Congress. After enduring a decade of territorial status, Oregon became the nation's thirty-third state.

Residents of Washington and Idaho would wait another thirty years before following Oregon's lead, when their states became the forty-second and forty-third in 1889 and 1890, respectively. As the time lag suggests, Washington and Idaho were more accurately the children of mother Oregon than her siblings; they belonged to the next generation of states. Though clearly different in so many ways, Washington and Idaho would evolve as two troubled territories whose fates were inextricably linked by common treaty troubles and gold fever.

# CHAPTER 7

# Growing Pains: New Territories, Gold Fever, and a Civil War

\*

In the spring of 1861 came the mad rush up the Columbia, simultaneous with the booming of cannon on the coast of South Carolina. The Civil War was on in the East, and a new golden era had opened in the West.—William Armistead Goulder, *Reminiscences: Incidents of the Life of a Pioneer in Oregon and Idaho* (1909)

\*

During the decades of the 1850s and 1860s, Oregon became a state and two new territories emerged in the Pacific Northwest. Especially for Washington and Idaho, this was a time of severe growing pains created by a bedeviling combination of problems that ranged from social instability to rudimentary governments poorly equipped to deal with new challenges, and added to this mix was the lure of new wealth awaiting diligent agrarians and gold-seekers alike. Finally, overshadowing all local matters in the early 1860s was the Civil War, which threatened the nation's very existence.

### TREATY TROUBLES AND GOLD FEVER IN WASHINGTON TERRITORY

The Oregon Territory encompassed an enormous geographical area—approximately 350,000 square miles—that was never truly unified. People in the scattered and isolated settlements north of the Columbia River, in what was then termed Northern Oregon, believed that Willamette Valley farmers dominated territorial affairs and neglected the interests of others. Settlers met at Cowlitz Landing in August 1851 and at Monticello (now part of

Longview) in November 1852 to petition Congress to grant them the status of a separate territory called Columbia. Oregon's delegate Joseph Lane introduced a bill to that effect the following month and skillfully steered it through the House of Representatives.

When a New Jersey congressman asked Lane how many people lived in Northern Oregon, he responded that its population equaled that of Oregon Territory when it was created in 1848. Lane was evasive because he did not want to reveal that the proposed territory contained only about three thousand non-Indian residents, a number generally considered too small to form a territory. When on another occasion a representative suggested substituting the name of the nation's first president for Columbia, Lane quickly responded, "I shall never object to that name." He sensed that honoring the much revered George Washington would give Congress an additional reason to vote for the bill. The legislators and the president approved creation of the sprawling, if underpopulated, new territory in March 1853.

Washington's early legislature spent most of its time granting special acts or privileges, creating new counties, chartering railroads that were never built, authorizing construction of bridges and ferries, and chartering all kinds of social organizations—temperance, literary, and music associations and fraternal lodges. The legislators also granted divorces until the judiciary assumed that function in 1866.

Washington's first governor was Isaac I. Stevens, a young Massachusetts native and officer in the Corps of Engineers during the recent war with Mexico. Afflicted by a mild form of dwarfism that gave him a large head and short, stubby legs, Stevens seemed driven by a limitless supply of energy to surmount his physical difficulties and prove himself. At West Point he graduated at the head of his class in 1839. He combined the roles of governor, Indian agent, and chief of a national railroad survey project to further his dream of building an empire of white settlers in the Pacific Northwest.

To that end, Stevens concluded a series of heavy-handed treaty negotiations with the Indians of Washington (which then included western Montana and northern Idaho) that effectively redefined the land. He traveled from Puget Sound to the Rocky Mountains in 1854 and 1855, intimidating and cajoling Indian people into signing away most of their land in exchange for a variety of goods and promises. Occasionally he used the medium of the imprecise Chinook jargon to explain complex land transactions, and where necessary he appointed "chiefs" and "subchiefs" to sign for their people.

To the impatient young governor, Washington's seventeen thousand Indians were children whose culture was of little value. He intended to open

20. When Governor Isaac Stevens (1818–62) convened
the May 1855 council in the Walla Walla Valley, he addressed the native leaders arranged before him in concentric circles. Eastern Washington State Historical
Society, Spokane WA, L86-1264.

most of his domain to white settlement by concentrating the natives on
reservations and teaching them how to farm. Quite simply, the governor
and many others never questioned the necessity of removing Indians from
the path of white civilization, although Stevens did hope that it could be
accomplished peaceably through negotiation.

It proved far easier to confine Indians of the coast to small reservations
encompassing their traditional homes and fishing grounds than to pen up
the seminomadic groups of the interior. Stevens met with tribal spokesmen
of the Plateau peoples at a great council in May and June 1855 in the Walla
Walla Valley, about six miles from the remains of the old Whitman mission,
and secured one of the earliest treaties negotiated between whites and Indians of the Pacific Northwest. The gathering, attended by approximately
five thousand Nez Perces, Yakimas, Cayuses, Walla Wallas, Umatillas, and
other Indians, was far from harmonious. But Stevens's policy prevailed,
especially after he allotted the two largest and most powerful tribes, the

Yakimas and Nez Perces, sizable reservations encompassing much of their traditional hunting and gathering ground. The smaller tribes reluctantly acquiesced to the new arrangement.

Stevens forced Indians to relinquish title to the land in exchange for the retention of fishing rights and for various federal allowances or annuities along with instructions and tools for farming, the latter even though much of the land was poorly suited for agriculture. In return for three reservations and several promises, Indian leaders signed away forty-five thousand square miles of land. Despite the haste of the negotiations, four years would pass before Stevens's Walla Walla treaties would win Senate approval.

All over the Pacific Northwest, the oft repeated process of treaty making had tragic consequences for the Indians. Trouble arose from a number of sources: Indians utterly unacquainted with agriculture found the transition from a hunting and gathering way of life difficult; greedy federal agents occasionally pilfered or redirected supplies intended for the Indians; and white miners and settlers continued to encroach on Indian lands. Forced onto ever shrinking holdings, some bands accepted their new status only reluctantly.

It is hard to imagine that Euro-Americans did not fully comprehend what they were doing when they redefined the land of the Pacific Northwest through their treaties: Governor and U.S. Senator W. J. McConnell used strong language to describe the process in his 1913 memoir-history of Idaho: "As the crickets and jack rabbits sometimes over-run and destroy the crops in these valleys today, without asking leave, so we of the Anglo-Saxon race in those days over-ran and destroyed the hunting grounds of the original owners, and without asking leave took forcible possession thereof. Not having the time to spare from our other pursuits to sufficiently punish the Indians for presuming to bar our progress, we appealed to the government to support us in holding the country we had entered."[1]

Native Americans greatly resented the results of the treaty making, and warfare erupted on both sides of the Cascade Range in the mid 1850s. Some treaty provisions dealing with Indian fishing rights remained unaccepted by whites for more than a century. Meanwhile, Stevens won election in 1857 as Washington's delegate to Congress and, like his friend and fellow delegate, Joseph Lane of Oregon, plunged into national Democratic party affairs.

When Oregon became a state in 1859, the immense but sparsely settled eastern segment of the former territory was attached to Washington, thus

---

1. W. J. McConnell, *Early History of Idaho* (Caldwell: Caxton, 1913), 120.

creating a geographical monstrosity that stretched from the Olympic Peninsula to the Rocky Mountains and included Idaho and the far western portions of Montana and Wyoming. The great distance that separated its capital at Olympia, on the southern edge of Puget Sound, from several new
mining settlements in the interior complicated the governing of Washington Territory. The situation grew immeasurably worse with the discovery
of precious metals in the interior.

Gold! That single word lured thousands of fortune seekers into the remote eastern portion of Washington later to become Idaho. The mining
excitement that would play so crucial role in the early history of both territories dated from August 1860 when Elias Davidson Pierce and twelve
men left the village of Walla Walla and traveled quietly and illegally across
the Nez Perce reservation. Not long after the illicit prospectors found some
promising diggings on Oro Fino Creek, word of the discovery leaked out and
the Clearwater rush was on. This was not the first major gold discovery in
Pacific Northwest history—prospectors had discovered gold in southern
Oregon in the early 1850s and in north-central Washington later in the
decade—but none of the other discoveries would result in so dramatic a shift
of population away from the coast into the interior, nor would they have
longer-lasting political consequences than the new stampede to the northern Rocky Mountains.

By midsummer 1861, a jerry-built collection of tents and nondescript
structures fashioned from hand-hewn logs and whipsawed lumber grandilo-
quently called itself Pierce City. Any why not? The booming community
was now the seat of the most populous county in Washington Territory.
Soon a second collection of stores, hotels, and saloons took the name Oro
Fino City. Located about three miles from Pierce, Oro Fino City boasted
of six restaurants, two hotels, two bakeries, four meat markets, twenty
whisky shops, ten gambling saloons, a watchmaker, a bookshop, a barber
shop, three doctors' offices—about seventy-five buildings in all.

During the high-water season, an army of gold seekers traveled by steamboat up the Columbia and Snake rivers from Portland to Lewiston, where
they obtained saddle and pack animals to push on into the interior. Some
miners walked to the diggings. Provisions were packed into the Clearwater
country from booming Walla Walla or bought from the Nez Perce, who
began trading with the miners shortly after the first prospectors arrived.
Indian farmers living along the fertile bottom lands of the Clearwater,
Snake, and Salmon rivers provided eggs, corn, and cattle to the newcomers.

A local army officer refused to let Lewiston merchants erect permanent structures because this was still Nez Perce land, but so many newcomers arrived each day that stopping them proved hopeless. In fact, Lewiston and the mining camps of Pierce City, Oro Fino, Elk City, Florence, and Warrens were all located on Nez Perce land. Despite the obvious injustice done to them, the Indians did not retaliate with violence, as sometimes happened in other parts of the West. The Nez Perces desired to maintain peaceable relations with Euro-Americans.

Early Lewiston, like most Northwest mining towns in their initial stages, amounted to little more than a collection of tents. One popular type of building was made by erecting poles upon which rafters were set. The sides, ends, and roof were covered with brown muslin. There were no windows, and the doors were frames of small poles covered with the same type of cloth. More than 120 fabric structures of this type lined the streets of Lewiston during the Clearwater mining rush of the early 1860s. Because they quickly became frayed and weather-beaten, people called the place "rag town." Sunlight brightened the interior during the day, and candles and lamps illuminated both the interior and the street at night. Residents needed no streetlights.

Many of the first goldseekers were depression-ridden farmers from Oregon's Willamette Valley who left for the Clearwater diggings despite the protests of Portland newspapers, which considered the sudden relocation irresponsible. The ranks of miners included churchmen, merchants, laborers, and lawyers, virtually anyone capable of handling a pick and shovel. The argonauts came from all over the United States as well as from Mexico, Canada, Great Britain, Italy, France, China, and the Hawaiian Islands. The typical miner wore a beard and had a look in his eyes that contemporaries described only as "gold crazed." In this group a gray haired man was a rarity, though many of the gold seekers were already veterans of earlier mining rushes to California, British Columbia, and Colorado.

Express companies transported some $3 million worth of gold dust down the Columbia River in 1861. Gold dust was legal tender, and every miner carried some in a buckskin pouch. Bankers, merchants, and hotelmen kept a pair of small brass scales handy to weigh the precious metal. Gold dust was generally worth $16 an ounce, but less than that in some districts. A scoundrel occasionally tried to mix heavy yellow sand with the dust to cheat the unwary. Because at this time banks were practically unknown, frugal miners sometimes buried gold dust in baking powder cans in or about their cabins.

Food prices varied. In Oro Fino City in 1861 the cost of such staples as

21. This panoramic view of Lewiston, Washington Territory, in 1862, shows it to be a town still fashioned mostly of tents. Courtesy Oregon Historical Society, ORHI 485.

bacon, beans, and sugar averaged four times higher than in Portland. During the winter of 1861–62, some Oro Fino residents packed in potatoes on their backs through fifteen to twenty miles of deep snow. Uncooked potatoes sliced up and soaked in vinegar provided a remedy for the dreaded disease of scurvy.

Inevitably some prospectors reached the diggings too late to claim the choicest ground. Their continued search for the elusive yellow metal led them south, where they discovered rich placers at Elk City and Florence in the rugged and remote Salmon River country, and still farther south into the Boise Basin, where they discovered gold on Grimes Creek in August 1862.

*Arrastres* and stamp mills in the Boise Basin seldom stopped as they methodically ground the gold-bearing quartz to powder. At the peak of the excitement, sawmills ran day and night, and lumber was purchased to build houses or sluice boxes as fast as it could be carried off. Collections of small buildings fashioned from rough lumber that took the names of Centerville, Placerville, Idaho City, and Pioneer went up as if by magic. The Boise Basin yielded $20 million worth of gold by 1866.

Never mind the damage to the environment—excitement was in the air. The miners were participants in a giant lottery, and none could predict who would find the elusive pockets of gold that would make a poor man a king. The arrival of pack trains laden with all sorts of merchandise enlivened the miners' days. On the streets the braying of mules mixed with fiddle music

from the saloons and the hammering of carpenters. The din of hammers and saws occasionally grew so loud that it interrupted conversations.

Within three years of its founding in 1862, Idaho City boasted opera and theater houses, music stores, tailor shops, breweries, bowling alleys, bakeries, and other urban amenities, not to mention the numerous saloons found in every mining camp. Idaho City in the summer of 1863 had 6,275 residents, 5,691 of them male. For a brief time the population of Idaho City exceeded even that of Portland. Occasionally an early settler simply dug a home in a dry hillside and hastily roofed it over with pine boughs that were then covered with dirt. It was not uncommon for several families to live together in one rude shelter. Miners' dugouts and log cabins lined every gulch and ravine in the Boise Basin in 1863, but as the number of sawmills increased, buildings of sawed lumber became more common.

In the mining country, as was true in earlier booms in California and elsewhere, towns sprang up like mushrooms and faded just as fast as miners stampeded to new diggings. Thousands of disappointed gold seekers followed each new excitement. An estimated eight thousand people were in Florence in late June 1862; two weeks later six thousand of them had departed. Oro Fino City was soon abandoned, and the place burned to the ground in August 1867. A few of the mining towns, notably Pierce and Idaho City, survived in scaled-down form; most communities of this type did not.

A boom of dizzying proportions also energized Walla Walla, quickly

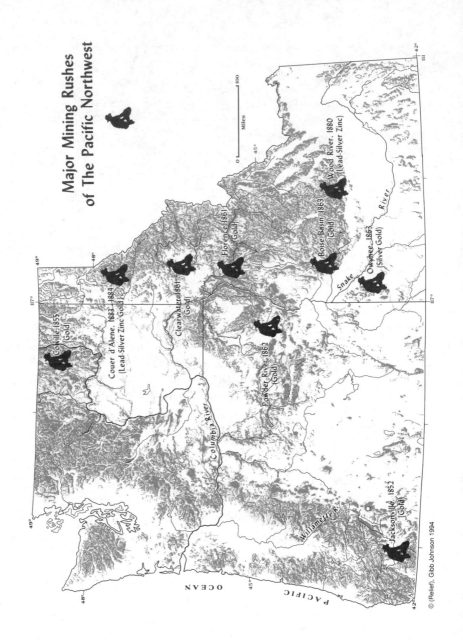

Major Mining Rushes
of The Pacific Northwest

Colville, 1855
(Gold)

Couer d'Alene, 1883–1884
(Lead-Silver Zinc Gold)

Clearwater, 1861
(Gold)

Florence, 1861
(Gold)

Wood River, 1880
(Lead-Silver Zinc)

Boise Basin, 1863
(Gold)

Owyhee, 1863
(Silver Gold)

Powder River, 1862
(Gold)

Jacksonville, 1852
(Gold)

Snake River

Columbia River

Willamette R.

PACIFIC OCEAN

Miles

© (Relief), Gibb Johnson 1994

132

transforming it from a village clustered around a newly established military post into the largest city in Washington Territory. Walla Walla became the main supply center for mining camps located on the Clearwater and Boise rivers, in western Montana, and even as far north as the diggings in British Columbia's Kootenay region. Long trains of mules and horses laden with supplies for distant mining camps filled Walla Walla's streets, and stage-coaches arrived and departed every day. From this hub Major Pinckney Lugenbeel set forth in 1863 to locate a new military base called Fort Boise to help protect travelers on the Oregon Trail (and around which the modern city of Boise grew); and it was also from Walla Walla that Lieutenant John Mullan completed a 624-mile-long road east to Fort Benton to link steamboat navigation on the Missouri and Columbia rivers and provide a faster route for the movement of soldiers and mining supplies. For miners from all over the inland Pacific Northwest, Walla Walla became a winter haven and their hard-won fortunes fair game for the merchants who ran the city's numerous saloons, hotels, restaurants, and stores.

During the 1870s and 1880s, Walla Walla further evolved into a prosperous agricultural center and its mining-derived wealth became a source of investment capital throughout the inland Northwest. Only with the building of two transcontinental railroads in the early 1880s, both of which relegated Walla Walla to feeder lines, would its population fall behind that of Spokane and Seattle.

Besides creating considerable excitement and much personal wealth, the Pacific Northwest mining boom of the 1860s infused the U.S. economy with badly needed gold during the Civil War. Discovery of still more gold in the portion of Washington Territory that is now western Montana and rapid population growth in the interior also resulted in the creation of new territories.

### THE TRIALS OF IDAHO TERRITORY

When as a result of the mining booms of the early 1860s Walla Walla emerged as the largest population center in Washington and transportation hub of the interior, Olympia residents regarded the upstart as a potentially dangerous rival that might replace their Puget Sound community as territorial capital. Backers of Olympia, in short, were only too glad to have Congress combine Washington's remote mining regions into a sprawling new territory, called Idaho (despite a last minute attempt to name it Montana), on 4 March 1863.

At first the boundaries of Idaho Territory extended far beyond the eastern limits of the old Oregon country to encompass present Idaho, Montana, and all but the southwestern corner of Wyoming, an area one-quarter larger than Texas. Within this immense space lay a hodgepodge of mining camps and towns so scattered that scarcely a trail connected them all. Legislators from the upper Missouri River area found it nearly impossible to reach the capital at Lewiston, and territorial officials faced a similar challenge when they sought to administer the vast domain. Except from the perspective of Olympia's boosters who wanted only to jettison their territory's eastern counties in order to create a more compact Washington that would not jeopardize the status of their town as capital, Idaho's boundaries made little sense.

It should not be too surprising that, when members of Idaho's first legislature finally assembled in Lewiston in December 1863, they unanimously petitioned Congress to divide the territory to make it easier to govern. Yet even after the creation of Montana Territory in May 1864 greatly diminished Idaho's size, it still encompassed a large portion of future Wyoming west of the Continental Divide. Alas, Congress was not yet done tinkering with the shape of Idaho: federal lawmakers shrank Idaho to its present shape in July 1868 by carving away the southeastern portion of Idaho, which later became part of Yellowstone Park, all of the Grand Tetons, and a portion of the oil- and coal-rich Green River country, an area that could today be pumping tourist and energy dollars into the Gem State's treasury instead of Wyoming's. Even after Idaho's boundaries contracted to their present contorted limits, the territory remained geographically and culturally divided, perhaps the most awkwardly constituted of the fifty states.

Idaho's early territorial years can only be described as a time of trouble. Not only was the territory too big to govern effectively, especially when communication and transportation were so poor, but the nonresident administrators appointed by a distant government in Washington, D. C., commanded so little respect in Idaho that they were often derided as "carpetbaggers." Financial woes made the situation even worse. Normally Congress provided most of the funds needed to run its western territories, but at the time of Idaho's creation the nation was split by a bloody and costly Civil War. Fighting for its very survival, the Union had little money to spare. Add gold fever and epidemic gambling and liquor consumption to the problems caused by distance and poor administration, and all the ingredients for turmoil were present.

Abraham Lincoln appointed an old friend, William H. Wallace, as Idaho's first territorial governor. When the new governor traveled to Idaho from Washington, D.C., he went by sea to San Francisco and Portland, crossing the Isthmus of Panama. It required a total of four months to reach the territory. Wallace served less than a year—from March 1863 until January 1864—before getting himself elected to Congress and thereby more than doubling his annual salary to $6,000.

Caleb Lyon, a faithful Republican appointed by President Lincoln as the territory's second governor, had a reputation as a New York art and literature critic. Being something of a dandy, he never fit in with the rough-and-tumble miners of Idaho and was ill suited to govern the raw territory. Because he insisted on styling himself as Caleb Lyon of Lyonsdale, Idaho pioneers twitted him as "Cale of the Dale." It is said of Lyon that he came into office in a storm and left it in a cyclone.

Only a few months after he arrived in the territory, Lyon added his signature to legislation moving the capital from Lewiston to Boise and thereby embroiled himself in a bitter conflict. Arguing that the move was illegal, Lewiston got a local judge to enjoin temporarily the transfer of the territorial seal and archives. Lyon evaded a summons to appear in court when he slipped out of town by feigning a duck hunting trip that took him down the Snake River to the safe haven of Washington. In Lewiston an infuriated populace denounced Lyon, and the sheriff assigned an armed guard of six local citizens to keep Boise partisans from stealing the seal and archives, as they attempted to do in late 1864. Meanwhile, the egotistical and ambitious Lyon quietly departed for the more promising environment of the national capital. For two months Idaho had no governor at all.

The acting governor, territorial secretary Clinton Dewitt Smith, took eight months to reach Idaho when Plains Indians blocked overland travel and forced him to detour by way of the Isthmus of Panama. Smith became embroiled in the ongoing capital controversy when he managed to slip the seal and archives out of Lewiston to Boise, but after only seven months on the job he drank himself to death. Meanwhile, the Boise County treasurer embezzled $4,000 in revenues he had collected for the territory, nearly bankrupting it. The next de facto governor, Horace Gilson, was a thief who quietly looted the treasury of $41,000 before absconding to Hong Kong and Paris.

As for Caleb Lyon, after an eleven-month absence he unexpectedly returned in 1865 to finish his term. To Lyon's credit, he did try to curb settlers from attacking Indians and he negotiated what he regarded as an important treaty with the Shoshonis (but which the U.S. Senate never got around to ratifying). His Indian policy was to make Lyon even less popular with white

22. Caleb Lyon (1822–75) of Lyonsdale, New York,
Idaho Territory's eccentric second governor. Courtesy
Idaho State Historical Society, 544.

residents: J. S. Reynolds of the *Idaho Statesman* warned in 1865 that nothing less than a "military escort could preserve him from violence, if not
from death."[2]

2. As quoted in Merle W. Wells, "Caleb Lyon's Indian Policy," *Pacific Northwest
Quarterly* 61 (October 1970); 200.

When he left for good the following year, Lyon was suspected of having stolen $46,000 in Indian funds that he was responsible for distributing as Idaho's superintendent of Indian affairs. He lamely claimed that he was trying to return the money to Washington, but while en route on a sleeping car, a thief had stolen it from under his pillow. Some of Lyon's successors added additional chapters to this tale of incompetence.

During twenty-seven years of the territorial era, sixteen men were appointed and confirmed as Idaho's governor. Four of them failed to take office, and six remained in the territory less than a year, some only a few days. Thomas Bennett, who was governor from 1 November 1871 until 4 December 1875, was absent twenty-three months of his term. Only eight men served terms of a year or more. Because governors were so frequently absent, territorial secretaries served as acting governors during eight of twenty-seven years. Such lengthy absences did not decrease significantly until 1885, when an Idaho resident, Edward Augustus Stevenson, was appointed governor.

The territorial phase of government and politics lasted nearly three decades and had few redeeming features. Idaho seemed forever to totter on the brink of insolvency or administrative incompetence, and larcenous carpetbag governors helped themselves to public funds. But that was only part of the problem. Among the other types of crime that plagued early Idaho were jumping good claims, salting poor claims, passing bogus gold, crooked games of chance, theft, and gunplay resulting in mayhem.

Perhaps because of its sprawling size and the uncertain nature of its government, early Idaho territory was beset by occasional outbursts of violence. Most shocking of the early violent episodes was the grisly murder of Lloyd Magruder in 1863 on the Nez Perce Trail that connected Lewiston and the Virginia City diggings beyond the Bitterroots. Hill Beachey, a friend of Magruder, tracked the four highwaymen and had them extradited from California to Idaho. After a short trial, three of the four men were hanged, though not before Idaho discovered it actually had no criminal law.

In 1863, when Congress established Idaho, it failed to provide for a criminal or civil code. And because the new territory encompassed lands taken from the jurisdictions of Washington, Dakota, Utah, and Nebraska, it was not sufficient simply to consider that the laws of Washington Territory still applied, as some people did. In 1866 the territorial supreme court freed two convicted murderers when it declared that Idaho had no criminal law from 4 March 1863 until 4 January 1864, the date when the territory's original laws were adopted. Despite this technicality, few if any Idahoans regretted the "illegal" hanging of the murderers of Lloyd Magruder. But this case did not end early Idaho's law-and-order difficulties.

Living in the mining camps were men like "Cherokee Bob," "Dutch Fred," and "Boone Helm"; the names of these fugitives from justice in other states and territories became synonymous with lawlessness. When government officials proved unable to deal with such pressing crimes as horse stealing, highway robbery, and the passing of bogus gold dust, vigilance committees arose in Payette, Lewiston, and nearly a dozen other communities to deal with the worst of the troublemakers.

In remote Virginia City, in the portion of Idaho soon to become Montana, a rising tide of lawlessness caused angry and frustrated citizens to conclude that Sheriff Henry Plummer secretly headed a gang of thieves called "The Innocents." During Plummer's eight months as sheriff, The Innocents were claimed to have murdered no less than 102 people and robbed countless others. In January 1864 angry vigilantes hanged Plummer and two associates. Occasionally the vigilance committees left the body of an evildoer hanging from a tree as a warning to others tempted to break the law.

Another of Idaho's sources of discord resulted from its peculiar pattern of settlement. Unlike neighboring states (except Nevada), it was settled largely by emigrants from other parts of the West, not from the East or Midwest, and a notable number came north from Utah. Even as mining booms attracted people to the diggings in the northern and western parts of Idaho, members of the Church of Jesus Christ of Latter-day Saints, commonly called Mormons or Latter-day Saints, migrated north from the Salt Lake Valley to establish agrarian settlements in Idaho. The contrast between the pietistic agrarian Mormon settlements and "get-rich-quick" mining camps was stark, creating a cultural as well as geographic division that endured for decades.

The first Mormon pioneers traveled west in 1847 from Illinois to the Great Salt Lake to build a Zion free of the religious persecution they had previously encountered. They likened their migration to "the gathering" of ancient Israel, and some seventy thousand church members undertook the trek to the Great Basin between 1847 and 1869. Some of the poorer Saints lugged their belongings on handcarts. Their leader, Brigham Young, envisioned the proliferation of Mormon communities throughout the Rocky Mountain west. Beginning with Salt Lake City, church members were encouraged to establish more than three hundred communities from southern California to Canada. Thus on 14 April 1860, a band of thirteen colonists founded Franklin, Idaho's first town. Not many years passed before Mormons constituted the largest single religious group in the Gem State.

23. Brigham Young (1801–77), inspiration behind numerous Mormon settlements in early Idaho. Courtesy Church Archives, The Church of Jesus Christ of Latterday Saints.

Mormon settlements in the Pacific Northwest tended to develop along similar lines. Each was to be a self-contained community that centered on family and religion. Church authorities presided over a highly organized society. Colonists united to construct schools, meeting houses, irrigation canals, roads, and bridges. Mormon settlements could be identified by their wide streets, landmark tabernacles and other church structures, and general air of prosperity. Homesteads clustered closely about the church and fields lay on the outskirts. Faith, morals, crops, and irrigation were all regarded as matters of community concern.

No state or territory outside Utah has a larger percentage of Mormons in its population than Idaho; and nowhere in the United States did the Mormon and non-Mormon populations divide as sharply as they did in Idaho. Therein lay the seeds of a future anti-Mormon crusade. In the near term, however, it was the division between Union and pro-Confederate factions during and after the Civil War that most complicated matters in the Pacific Northwest.

### THE CIVIL WAR ERA

From a national perspective, the crucial issues of the 1860s were the causes and consequences of the Civil War. The war remains the bloodiest conflict in American history, and although few of the sixty-four thousand residents of the Pacific Northwest participated directly, they became involved nonetheless. If nothing else, Civil War events gave residents much to think and talk about. They suffered a fright when the Confederate raider *Shenandoah* was rumored to be cruising off the coast.

The rapidly changing fortunes of Joseph Lane mirrored the passions and disagreements that animated Civil War politics in the Pacific Northwest. Although he was once immensely popular, Lane's unyielding proslavery, pro-Southern stand alienated many Oregonians. In the 1860 election he ran for vice-president with John C. Breckenridge on a Democratic ticket devoted to those principles. Their loss to Lincoln and the Republicans brought an end both to Lane's political career and to Democratic party dominance of Oregon. The region's first territorial governor returned to the Pacific Northwest an outcast; in several communities, residents hanged Lane in effigy. From that time until he died in 1881 on his homestead near Roseburg, Lane had no political influence.

While most Pacific Northwesterners remained loyal to the Union cause, Southern sympathizers talked openly of seceding to form a Pacific republic. The idea of an independent nation had been discussed for several years, but the Civil War made its advocates so bold that the legislatures of Oregon and Washington Territory passed resolutions repudiating such a creation.

Idaho's first legislature adopted a strong anti-slavery resolution, yet supporters of the South were so numerous in its mining camps that Idaho was in many ways a Confederate territory. Although Idaho was a long way from the battlefields of the East and South, Civil War tensions still threatened to destroy it. During 1863 large wagon trains rolled west from Missouri and Arkansas and brought to Idaho entire families desperate to escape the warfare that threatened to destroy their home states. Emigration from the border states not only swelled the ranks of Southern sympathizers but also brought prospective brides to the overwhelmingly male territory. The appeal of mining camp bonanzas made Idaho a haven for draft-dodging fortune seekers from both sides. Because those men might loathe military service yet loyally support their respective causes, their presence made for lively discussions and flag-waving demonstrations that led to an occasional mining camp brawl.

Almost every American in Idaho's mining camps had a friend or relative in one of the Union or Confederate armies. Thus they anxiously awaited the arrival of the stagecoach and with it the latest newspapers. Because there were never enough copies for everyone, little groups formed around the fortunate individuals to learn the latest news from the battlefields around Atlanta or Richmond. If the Confederacy was victorious, jubilant men publicly cheered for Jefferson Davis and the Rebel cause. They filled the saloons, all clamoring for "booze" and predicting speedy recognition of the Confederacy by foreign governments. With news of Union triumphs, Yankee supporters cheered Abraham Lincoln and gathered in the saloons to toast success by singing "We'll Rally 'Round the Flag, Boys" or some other Northern song. Occasionally the two sides spilled into the streets, where they battled one another with their fists.

The U.S. Army had stationed units in the Pacific Northwest since the late 1840s, primarily to protect travelers on the Oregon Trail and to enforce treaties with the Indians. Civil War tensions between Republicans and pro-Southern Democrats prompted the federal government to establish a series of new army posts in the Pacific Northwest. In addition, the Union stationed troops at Columbia Barracks (Fort Vancouver), Fort Steilacoom, Fort Walla Walla, and several lesser posts. When most of the regulars were called east, volunteers from the Pacific Northwest and California manned those posts.

Several soldiers who distinguished themselves on eastern battlefields were well known to Pacific Northwesterners. In the Union army were Major General Isaac Stevens, who fought to stop Stonewall Jackson's advance and died at Chantilly in northern Virginia in 1862, and Oregon's first Republican senator, Colonel Edward D. Baker, killed at the Battle of Ball's Bluff on the Potomac River in 1861. As a young captain, the Union general George B. McClellan had led a party surveying a road across the Cascades. General Ulysses S. Grant served at Fort Vancouver in 1853, and General Philip Sheridan was there in 1855. General George Pickett, who served as a commander on San Juan Island, joined the Confederate army and was immortalized in "Pickett's Charge" at Gettysburg.

### BOUNDARIES IN PERSPECTIVE

For Pacific Northwesterners the three decades from 1840 to 1870 were a time for establishing boundaries. Not just the obvious ones like those that separated American from British territory, or Oregon from Washington, or one person's farm or mining claim from another's, but boundaries of mind and spirit as well. Territorial and state laws, constitutions, and organic acts attempted to define the often imprecise boundaries between permissible and impermissible conduct. Even the outcome of the Civil War set more precise constitutional limits on state power than existed before.

Boundaries between personal success and failure were perhaps harder to draw, although frontier society was inclined to err on the side of generosity. Certainly if fashioning three territories and one state, platting cities and planting farms, raising crops and numerous children, laying out roads and putting down roots were tokens of success, then the pioneer generation of Pacific Northwesterners had reason to be proud of its successes.

But there was also that other boundary, the rigidly confining one that white settlers drew between themselves and others—the Indians, blacks, and Asians. Although whites might minimize its existence, that boundary appeared in their thinking, codes of law, and newly redrawn maps. Exclusion on the basis of race was only one of the gaping holes in the social fabric of the early Pacific Northwest.

# CHAPTER 8

# Holes in the Social Fabric

\*

Men come and go like the waves of the sea. A tear, a tomanawos [medicine man], a dirge, and they are gone from our longing eyes forever. Even the white man, whose God walked and talked with him as friend to friend, is not exempt from the common destiny. We may be brothers after all. We shall see.—Words of Chief Seattle, 1854, as quoted in the Seattle *Sunday Star*, 5 November 1887

\*

The social fabric that the Pacific Northwest's first Euro-American settlers wove together was for the most part sturdy and serviceable, embodying their vision of a good society. But as might be expected of any homespun effort, the result was not without its flaws. Most conspicuous were the several holes and a ragged fringe symbolizing treatment of those people that the dominant groups excluded or confined to the margin. Indians, blacks, Asians, Mormons, women, and others were at various times victims of blatantly discriminatory laws and activities. Complicating matters was the fact that on occasion the victim became victimizer, as when ancient quarrels between Indians led one group to cooperate with whites against another, or when Indians attacked and killed approximately fifty Chinese miners in southern Idaho in 1866. Yet, the discerning observer can also find instances of goodwill and social harmony and examples of individuals who successfully shaped their lives despite prejudice or legal impediment.

One of the most profound changes of the 1840s was a noticeable alteration of the region's racial composition. During the years of the fur trade, there had been much intermixing of Caucasian, Indian, and Polynesian peoples. Fur company personnel—Scots, French Canadians, and Iroquois Indians coming overland from the East—frequently were joined by Plains Cree and Plains Ojibwa (Chippewa) wives, or they married women from western tribes. The wife of John McLoughlin was of Swiss and Ojibwa ancestry; Peter Skene Ogden twice married Indian women.

The racial blends in the old Oregon country included French-Indian, Scots-Indian, Hawaiian-Indian, French-Hawaiian, Iroquois–western Indian, and an occasional black-Indian, because African Americans sometimes jumped ship or came overland. Although that was a unique population pool, beginning in the 1840s the great migration of people of northern and western European ancestry overwhelmed it and gave the region the predominant racial and cultural characteristics it retains to this day. The exceptions proved only temporary, as in 1870 when the census recorded that 25 percent of Idaho's population was Chinese, a figure never again equaled in a Northwest state by any racial minority. Various discriminatory taxes and land laws—including the Oregon Donation Land Claim Act of 1850, which excluded blacks and Hawaiians from its provisions—mirrored the pioneers' racial views. The Washington legislature in 1861 forbade intermarriage between whites and Indians, thus halting a long-standing practice. Oregon in 1866 prohibited intermarriage between whites and blacks, Chinese, Hawaiians, or anyone more than one-quarter black or more than one-half Indian. Idaho enacted similar legislation.

### PHASES OF INDIAN-WHITE RELATIONS

Indian-white relations in the Pacific Northwest passed through four overlapping phases. The first, a time of generally peaceable contacts between equals, dated from early maritime exploration until the Whitman tragedy of 1847. For the traders and trappers, Indians often provided a labor force and served as sources of supply in a complex economic system. Petty misunderstandings occasionally erupted, and some led to violence. Euro-American diseases also afflicted native society, but during that first phase, there was no sustained effort to drive out the newcomers or dispossess Indians of their land.

The second phase, involving three decades of conflict, lasted from the Cayuse War of 1848 until 1879, when the U.S. Army routed a band of Shoshonis known as Sheepeaters. By that date most of the region's Native Americans were confined to reservations. During the third phase, Indians became a colonized and beleaguered people, confined to shrinking and increasingly undesirable land. Finally, after first promoting the reservation system in an effort to keep Indians and whites separate and thus minimize conflict, Congress changed its mind and passed the General Allotment Act (or Dawes Severalty Act) in 1887. The new measure attacked traditional tribal customs of collective property relations by encouraging Indians to become agrarians and assimilate into white society. Indians, of course, were not consulted before the proposal became law.

Although the Dawes Act was intended as a reform measure, it diminished reservation lands across the United States by nearly two-thirds between 1887 and 1934 by periodically opening major portions of the natives' land base to white settlement. Each of the 638 remaining Coeur d'Alene Indians of northern Idaho, for example, received 160 acres under the Dawes Act. At the same time, however, the federal government opened three-fourths of their former reservation to white homesteaders. The state of Idaho purchased a scenic portion of Coeur d'Alene lands from the federal government, and as Lake Chatcolet it became the Pacific Northwest's first major state park.

There were also periodic land rushes: a pistol shot at high noon on 18 November 1895 opened the Nez Perce reservation to the white homesteaders who scrambled to claim 3,000 pieces of real estate. The tribe received a cash settlement of $1.6 million divided into five installments for their alienated land. Today the Nez Perce retain only a fraction of the acreage that comprised their reservation in 1863. The basic flaw of the Dawes Act, apart from failing to recognize the value of Indian culture, was that it did not consider the needs of young people born to Indians. Framers of the Dawes Act apparently assumed that Indians would only decline in number.

Indian people sometimes received token compensation for the loss of land, and sometimes they received nothing but unfulfilled promises. During this phase, most whites viewed Indians as a broken people, a casualty of the onward rush of progress; as the author of one of the region's local histories phrased it in 1903, "When the indomitable Anglo-Saxon race began following the course of destiny to the westward the doom of the thriftless aboriginal peoples was sealed. . . . The day of a grander development for the vast, prodigious west, teeming with the crude elements of wealth production, had at last dawned. The night of savagery was over."[1] For Indians the night had only begun.

The fourth phase of Indian-white relations was a time of contradiction

---

1. *An Illustrated History of North Idaho* (Chicago: Western Historical Publishing, 1903), 44.

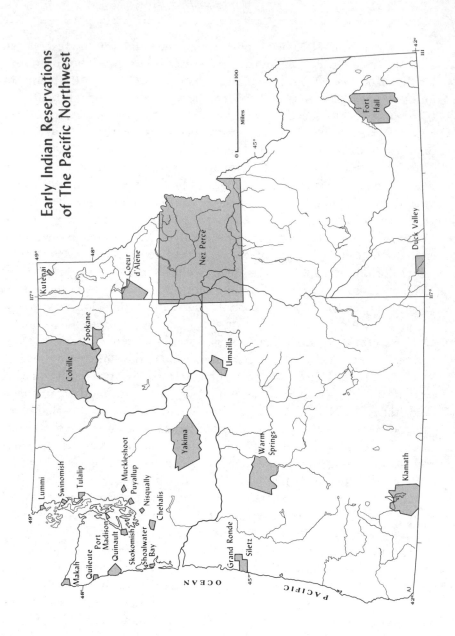

Early Indian Reservations
of The Pacific Northwest

and of reluctant white recognition of Indian rights coupled with the Indians' growing pride in their own heritage. That phase began when Congress granted U.S. citizenship to Indian people in 1924, and it continued with the Indian Reorganization Act (known as the Indian New Deal) of 1934. The latter attempted to prevent further shrinkage of reservations and even to obtain some land for landless bands. And yet the fourth phase still saw Congress in 1954 terminate federal aid granted by treaty to the Klamaths and some Oregon coastal Indians and sell their remaining tribal land. Indians increasingly asserted their rights during the 1960s and 1970s, and the national government made some effort to turn federal programs on the reservations over to Indian control. At that time, courts recognized Indian fishing claims in cases that represented long-delayed responses to three crucial decades of conflict between Indians and whites.

### THREE DECADES OF INDIAN-WHITE CONFLICT

Two things above all else lay at the root of Indian-white violence between 1847 and 1879: land and precious metals. Whites were greedy for both, and too often that meant their crossing, digging up, or appropriating Indian lands. A contributing cause was the failure of two cultures to comprehend one another.

Nothing preoccupied the first generation of white settlers in the Pacific Northwest more than land—buying and selling, dividing and developing. Many newcomers of the 1840s and 1850s were family-oriented agrarians who, unlike the fur traders and trappers of years past, perceived nothing of an economic or social partner in the Indian. They believed that the nomadic natives, being scarcely more civilized than deer and other wild creatures, should yield the land to agriculturists who would settle and cultivate it. Violence was inevitable under those circumstances.

One result of the Pacific Northwest's first Indian war in 1848 was that Oregonians retained an enduring memory of the "Whitman Massacre" and a spirit of bitterness that left neither sympathy for the fate of native peoples nor respect for Indian claims to the land. Between 1851 and 1868 the Indians of Oregon were forced onto ever-shrinking reservation lands.

Anson Dart, Oregon Territory's first superintendent of Indian affairs, initially considered relocating Indians living west of the Cascades onto remote and semiarid lands to the east, but people whose culture was rooted in the lush green country of the coast and Willamette Valley balked at the move, even as Indians living east of the Cascades feared the importation of diseases unfamiliar to them. But efforts to obtain reservation land west of the Cascades ran afoul of the Oregon Donation Land Claim Act, which sanctioned homesteading without regard for the legal obligation to extinguish Indian title to the land. Dart finally located a few remote parcels not yet encumbered by white claims.

Serious trouble erupted in the Rogue River country in 1851 when gold seekers and agrarians entered the land occupied by native bands collectively known as the Rogue River Indians. The Table Rock Treaty of 1853 set aside a temporary reservation to quell the conflict. Although the treaty served as a model for subsequent ones, it failed in its immediate aim, because friction between Indian and gold seeker worsened and blew up into full-scale war in 1855.

In that year also, warfare erupted in Washington Territory shortly following the treaty negotiations hastily conducted by governor and Indian agent Isaac I. Stevens. The discovery of gold on the upper Columbia River in 1855 brought whites trooping across Yakima lands. When the Indians rose in violent protest, Stevens declared martial law and temporarily closed the area to white settlement. Although General John E. Wool, commander of the U.S. Army in the Pacific Northwest, believed that the governors of Oregon and Washington had wronged the natives, it became his duty as a good soldier to subdue both the Rogue River and Yakima Indians. Oregon volunteers and army regulars decisively crushed the Rogue River peoples in 1856 and exiled them to a new reservation in the Coast ranges. Trouble with the Yakimas ended temporarily that same year with the defeat of Chief Kamiakin. In one of several hostile incidents that took place during the last half of the decade, Indians attacked the village of Seattle in early 1856.

East of the Cascades, Indian resentment burst forth in renewed conflict in 1858 when most tribes of the Columbia basin, with the conspicuous exception of the Nez Perces, united to resist white encroachments. In that struggle, Colonel Edward Steptoe and 156 army soldiers marched north from Fort Walla Walla into the land of the Spokanes. Near Rosalia, a combined force of Spokanes, Yakimas, Coeur d'Alenes, and Palooses dealt the army a humiliating defeat. To avenge the army's honor, Colonel George Wright returned with nearly six hundred well-armed regulars. He proved a ruthless adversary, using new long-range rifles and slaughtering seven hundred Indian horses to demoralize his enemy. Wright then marched grimly through Indian country, preemptorily hanging a total of twenty-four chiefs and others considered guilty of fomenting what was then termed the Yakima War.

No more wars erupted in Washington (except in the portion that later became Idaho), and Indian-white conflict in Oregon remained confined to local incidents east of the Cascade mountains until the Modoc War flared up just south of the Oregon-California border in 1872. Once again the main cause was white land hunger, this time in a remote part of the region where settlers wanted a Modoc band removed and confined to a nearby reservation with a much larger number of Klamaths, their ancient enemies. In the ensuing struggle, a handful of Modocs, well camouflaged in a rugged area known as the Lava Beds, kept hundreds of soldiers at bay. The army suffered 120 casualties including the respected General Edward Canby, who was murdered under a flag of truce: during peace negotiations, the Modoc leader Keintpoos, called Captain Jack by whites, suddenly drew a pistol from beneath his coat and shot Canby in the face. The death of the Civil War hero and the highest ranking officer ever killed in conflict with Indians stunned the nation and outraged the army, fueling its determination to subdue the Modocs.

The six-month struggle ended with an army victory and the surrender of Captain Jack, who along with three other Modocs was subsequently tried and hanged at Fort Klamath for murder. In a grotesque turn of events, their heads were shipped to the army medical museum in Washington, D. C. One hundred fifty-five Modoc prisoners of war, one-third of whom were children, were exiled to Indian Territory (Oklahoma).

Some of the most vicious fighting occurred in Idaho, during the Battle of Bear River in 1863, when Colonel Patrick E. Connor and California volunteers sent to protect settlers at Franklin surprised and virtually annihilated a band of Shoshone men, women, and children. During the wild struggle, which pitted modern military weaponry against Indian bows and arrows, tomahawks, and muskets, the California volunteers suffered 22 deaths, while Connor's official tally listed 224 Indian casualties. Utah citizens who visited the battlefield the next day counted 368 slain Indians, including nearly 90 women and children. It ranks with the worst slaughters of Indians in the American West, but because it occurred during the time of such Civil War battles as Fredericksburg and Stone's River, the Battle of Bear River received little newspaper attention.

Far better-known, despite fewer casualties, is the so-called Nez Perce War of 1877. Two decades earlier, the Nez Perces had acceded to one of Stevens's 1855 treaties confining them to a large reservation. But in 1863, after trespassing whites discovered gold within its boundaries, some Indian leaders consented to a much shrunken reservation bordering the Clearwater

River east of Lewiston. About one-third of the Nez Perce (the "nontreaty" group) disavowed the agreement that cut their reservation from 7.7 million acres to about one-tenth of that amount. They continued to make their homes elsewhere. White Bird's band of Nez Perce remained on the lower Salmon River south of the new reservation, and those of Chief Joseph's band lived west of the Snake River in Oregon's majestic Wallowa Valley.

Hin-mah-too-yah-lat-kekht ("Thunder Traveling to Loftier Mountain Heights"), young Chief Joseph, inherited his father's leadership role in 1871. Young Joseph insisted from the first that his four hundred people in the Wallowa Valley were not bound by the treaty of 1863 because his father had never signed it. The federal government initially agreed, and President Ulysses S. Grant ordered part of the valley set aside as a reservation in 1873. But after protests from land-hungry whites, the government changed its mind, and two years later it insisted that Joseph and his people move to the reservation on the Clearwater River. With the Wallowa Valley opened to white settlement at the same time, the nontreaty Nez Perces appeared to have little choice but to obey the government's ultimatum. In mid-May 1877, General Oliver O. Howard gave them thirty days to leave the valley, to cross Hells Canyon and the Snake River, dangerously swollen by spring runoff, and to settle on the reservation. The Indians began relocating when on 13 and 14 June three young warriors from White Bird's band, brooding upon an injustice by local whites, killed four settlers. War inevitably followed.

The events of mid-1877 cannot actually be described as warfare. Six hundred Indian men, women, and children, together with a herd of more than two thousand horses, made a desperate flight across the Bitterroot Mountains to the plains of Montana, where they hoped to find safety among their friends the Crows. Failing that they planned to seek sanctuary in Canada. Theirs was less a retreat than a flight to safety, a tragic odyssey in which they were pursued by Howard and his soldiers. Curiously, the commander of the army's Department of the Columbia and a one-armed Civil War hero, Oliver O. Howard was a friend of freed blacks and was known as the "Christian" or "praying" general because he delivered sermons to the garrisons he inspected.

At the Battle of the Big Hole River, 9 and 10 August, the Nez Perces lost thirty warriors and forty other men, women, and children. The army suffered twenty-nine killed and forty wounded. The desperate Nez Perces headed south, winding through Yellowstone Park where their presence frightened and scattered tourists, and then north toward the international border.

On 30 September in the Bears Paw Mountains just forty miles short of their goal, the Nez Perce were overtaken by Colonel Nelson Miles and 383 troopers from Fort Keogh. The cavalrymen, who were still smarting from the Custer disaster the previous year, attacked almost immediately. In the ensuing battle, 53 officers and enlisted men were killed or wounded; the Indians lost 22 men, women, and children. At times the soldiers seemed dazed by the Indian defenders, but after a day of intense fighting followed by five days of siege in bitterly cold weather, the army prevailed.

Joseph gave up the flight on 4 October. In words recorded by Howard's aide, he concluded a brief speech with the now famous promise, "Hear me, my chiefs! I am tired. My heart is sick and sad. From where the sun now stands I will fight no more forever."[2] After an eleven hundred–mile odyssey punctuated by eighteen engagements, including four major battles, the flight was over. In the end a total of 418 Nez Perce were taken captive: 87 men, 184 women, and 147 children. Approximately a hundred more Nez Perces escaped and fled across country in the hope of still reaching Canada. Some made it, but others died of exposure or hunger or were murdered by Indians of other tribes.

The prisoners were exiled to Oklahoma and not allowed to return to the Pacific Northwest until 1885. The trip home was not a joyous one. Increasing tensions marked the seven-day journey by rail: at Pocatello a military escort had to be secured before the train could proceed on across Idaho. Because of continuing ill will in the Clearwater Valley, Joseph and a band of 150 followers settled on the Colville Reservation in north-central Washington, where Joseph died in 1904. The conflict of 1877 cost the federal government $930,000 and the lives of approximately 180 whites, mostly soldiers, and 120 Indians (65 men and 55 women and children), and it drastically curtailed the freedom of the Nez Perces. Joseph was more politician than military leader, but when whites glorified his military genius, it made his pursuers' difficulties seem more plausible.

Friction with settlers provoked an uprising of Bannocks in south-central Idaho and eastern Oregon in 1878. After several engagements, General Howard drove the fugitives back onto their reservation. A year later the last resisters, a few families of Sheepeaters, surrendered to Howard's persistent troops and were moved onto the Fort Hall Reservation. The government soon diminished the size of the reservation by three-fourths when it opened

2. An in-depth study of the controversy surrounding Joseph's famous "surrender" speech in the Bears Paw Mountains is Harvo Aoki, "Chief Joseph's Words," *Idaho Yesterdays* 33 (fall 1989): 16–21.

24. Chief Joseph (1840–1904), made famous by the
"war" of 1877. This photograph was made in 1903.
Courtesy Historical Photograph Collections, Washington State University Libraries, 70-0149.

the best land to white settlement. The newcomers built a town, which they named for the prominent Shoshoni leader, Pocatello. If nothing else, whites could always afford to be magnanimous in the naming of their settlements.

The United States government had placed most Indians of the Northwest on reservations by 1880. Ostensibly this arrangement had been accomplished through treaty making between sovereign and independent nations, but it was actually through disease, intimidation, corruption, and sheer force of numbers that whites established a clear boundary between themselves and Indians and left a gaping hole in the social fabric.

BLACKS AND ASIANS

Unlike the Indians who were driven onto reservations, blacks and Asians had no prior claim to the land. Racism, cultural biases, and a host of vague fears explain the discrimination they encountered, not white land hunger.

Probably the first black to reach the Pacific Northwest was one of Robert Gray's seamen killed by Indians near present-day Tillamook, Oregon. Blacks were among the pioneers who emigrated to Oregon in the 1840s. Some came as free persons and some as slaves. One notable black pioneer was George Washington Bush, who fought with Andrew Jackson to defeat the British in the Battle of New Orleans (1815). When his home state of Missouri later passed a law barring free blacks from residence, the legislature made an exception for the popular Bush, who became an affluent cattleman.

In 1844, at the age of sixty, Bush financed a racially integrated party of overlanders to Oregon, purchasing six wagons for the trip. But during the course of the long overland journey, news reached the party that Oregon had recently enacted a law barring blacks from settling there; thus the Bush family and several close white friends (a total of about thirty people) headed north to land near present Olympia where they believed they were sufficiently isolated to escape harassment. They thus became the first Americans to settle north of the Columbia River, an area soon designated by Oregon's provisional government as Vancouver County. Here arose the agricultural settlement of Bush Prairie.

When controversy seemed likely over the ownership of Bush's land because of the "whites only" provision of the Oregon Donation Land Claim Act, Congress responded positively in 1855 to a request by Bush's neighbors to pass a special resolution giving him legal title to his original homestead. By 1860 Bush had amassed approximately eight hundred acres, and before he died four years later he had become a leading spokesman for Washington agriculture. One of his sons, William Owen Bush, was elected to the territorial legislature in 1889.

Bush's initially chilly reception stemmed from the fact that Oregon's white pioneers of the 1840s brought with them the fears and prejudices common in the border states from which many originated. Despite their distance from the South, Oregonians participated in an acrimonious public debate over slavery and related issues for two decades. Oregon settlers who met at Champoeg in 1843 adopted a measure prohibiting slavery, a ban restated the following year when their provisional government required slaveholders to free their slaves, though with the added requirement that all blacks must leave the territory within three years. Any black who violated the law was to be whipped, a punishment to be repeated after six months if he or she still refused to leave.

The provisional government seemed determined to emphasize that free blacks, as well as slaves, were not welcome in the region. The immediate cause of the punitive measure was not a growing number of blacks in Oregon, because the 1850 census recorded only 207 in the entire territory. Many whites disliked blacks and simply wanted to create a new society free of the racial tensions they had experienced back in the border states. Whites also became alarmed when a black man who had married an Indian threatened to incite his wife's people to war.

The provisional government restricted the rights to vote and hold public office to free white males, whereas the Donation Land Act excluded blacks from its largesse. The laws of Oregon Territory and later the state constitution included similar antiblack provisions. Although federal constitutional amendments after the Civil War overturned those provisions, the state of Oregon did not formally remove the antiblack clause from its constitution until 1926; it did not ratify the Fifteenth Amendment to the United States Constitution until 1959, eighty-nine years after that measure had granted blacks the right to vote. Even in the early days, however, Oregon seldom enforced its discriminatory provisions.

The black population of Oregon numbered 128 in 1860. It included farmers, miners, barbers, cooks, blacksmiths, and common laborers. Some blacks worked as domestics for white families, and a few were slaves. Blacks preferred to form subcommunities in urban areas rather than endure the greater hostility common in rural districts. But the city of Portland assigned black and mulatto children to a segregated school that opened in 1867. By 1900, Portland's 775 blacks constituted about 65 percent of the total African American population in Oregon.

25. At the main gate of Fort Sherman, Idaho, a black soldier stands at parade rest in the 1890s. The site of the
base, which lasted from 1878 to 1900, is now overgrown
by urban Coeur d'Alene. During the unprecedented forest fires of August 1910, President William Howard Taft
dispatched two companies of African American soldiers
from Fort George Wright in Spokane to help contain the
conflagration in northern Idaho. Some of the troops
were no strangers to the region, having previously been
dispatched to the Coeur d'Alene mining district during
an outbreak of industrial violence in 1899. Courtesy
Museum of North Idaho, Fish-1-57.

Seattle's black population grew from a single resident in 1860 to 406 in
1900, though the slowly growing African American community remained
overwhelmingly male through the 1880s. Prior to 1890 blacks lived throughout the city, working mainly as barbers, cooks, waiters, railroad porters, and
unskilled laborers in the construction industry; some of the women held
service jobs, working mainly as maids. It was during the 1890s that Seattle
residents of all races began to regroup into income-graded neighborhoods:
wealthy and middle class residents (mainly whites) relocated on the hills,

while the poorer people of all races remained behind on the less desirable flatlands along the harbor.

The number of African Americans in the Pacific Northwest increased only gradually; as late as 1930, they accounted for just .3 percent of the region's total population, yet as small as their numbers were, Oregon's two thousand blacks in the 1920s became targets (along with Catholics and Jews) of the state's powerful Ku Klux Klan movement. Black residents of Seattle and Portland nonetheless gained mutual support from the churches, social clubs, and civic organizations their pioneers had founded.

Among early Asian residents of the Pacific Northwest, the Chinese were by far the most numerous. They had been driven from China by land shortages, overpopulation, famines, natural disasters, and the Taiping Rebellion of 1850–64. They began arriving as individuals or in groups shortly after 1860, and although they could be found in numerous occupations, mining and railroad construction attracted the greatest numbers. In 1870 more than half of Idaho's 6,579 miners were Chinese. Approximately seven hundred Chinese lived in Silver City in 1874 at the peak of mining activity. There they maintained a Masonic lodge, two temples (commonly called Joss Houses), four stores, three or four restaurants, two laundries, and five gambling establishments.

The region's Chinese reflected many different backgrounds, but to most whites they remained only objects of prejudice, violence, and various special taxes and property-holding restrictions. Washington's territorial legislature levied a quarterly tax of $6 on each Chinese in 1864; two years later Idaho's lawmakers approved a tax of $5 per month on foreign miners. They defined all Chinese—from gardeners to laundrymen—as miners and permitted the local sheriff to seize property and sell it at auction on three hour's notice if the tax was not promptly paid. The common expression "Why, he hasn't a Chinaman's chance" summed up well the prevailing prejudice. James O'Meara, editor of the *Idaho World* of Idaho City reflected popular hostility when he warned in his paper in 1865: "The Chinamen are coming. Lord deliver us from the locusts of Egypt, they devour all men before them."

Because Chinese miners were willing to work claims with great patience and accept a small return for their efforts, whites universally regarded their presence in the diggings as a certain sign that a mining region had passed its peak. The belief that Chinese had accumulated great quantities of gold through their frugality led to one of the most vicious massacres in Pacific Northwest history. In that incident a gang of "cowboys" shot or hacked to death thirty-one Chinese miners. The site was north of Hells Canyon, the

## "NO CHINAMEN NEED APPLY"

The following editorial appeared in a Wallace, Idaho, newspaper during the height of the region's anti-Chinese agitation:

John Chinaman got into the California mines, into many other mines, but he must not think of attempting a visit into those of northern Idaho. If he insists on coming, however, let him bring a roast hog, plenty of fire crackers and colored paper, and all the essentials of a first class Chinese funeral. He need not bother to bring the corpse. It will be in readiness. Ta! Ta! John!"—*Coeur d'Alene Sun*, 22 March 1884

---

year was 1887, and the probable motive was robbery. Prior to their slaying, victims were tortured in an apparent attempt to learn where they had hidden a supposed cache of gold. Only the death count in the slaughter of approximately fifty Chinese miners by Paiute Indians in 1866 exceeded this toll.

On the railroads, trouble arose when white workers feared that the importation of a potentially unlimited supply of cheap labor threatened their jobs. When hard times hit the Pacific Northwest in the mid-1880s, unemployed white workers participated in several crusades to drive the Chinese from the region. The agitation led to anti-Chinese violence in Tacoma and Seattle, martial law, and the dispatching of federal troops to quell the disorder.

White workers who had rallied behind banners proclaiming "The Chinese must Go!" were confident that the law would hesitate to punish them because they enjoyed both the support of public opinion and the implied consent of lawmakers on Capitol Hill: in 1882 Congress had passed the Chinese Exclusion Act (partially at the instigation of organized labor) to suspend immigration of Chinese workers until 1892. It also made all Chinese ineligible for citizenship and barred them from working in certain industries, such as mining. But that was not enough, as violence on Puget Sound and various forms of anti-Chinese activity elsewhere proved. In Pierce City, Idaho, vigilantes lynched five Chinese who they believed were responsible for the murder of a white merchant. The Chinese were hanged from a pole lashed between two pine trees. No perpetrator of anti-Chinese violence in the mid-1880s was ever punished.

The region's Chinese population declined slightly during the 1890s, while the number of Japanese residents climbed dramatically. The exit of Chinese from the railroad, lumber, and canning industries opened a door for Japanese immigrants, typically young males who arrived without families.

26. These Chinese were engaged in hydraulic mining in
Idaho's Rocky Bar region around 1900. Courtesy Idaho
State Historical Society, 76-119.2/a.

In 1887, only a year after Seattle's anti-Chinese riot, 200 Japanese men
arrived to work in the canneries and logging camps of Puget Sound. More
soon arrived to operate stores, restaurants, and lodging houses to meet the
needs of Japanese laborers. Seattle's Japanese population increased from 125
in 1890 to 3,000 in 1900. By the early twentieth century, a distinct international district had formed south of Seattle's downtown area. Because that
was where the black community also coalesced, various racial groups were
sometimes allied and sometimes pitted against one another. The Japanese
constituted Seattle's largest ethnic minority until World War II.

Outside Seattle, Japanese laborers were employed on the Oregon Short
Line in southern Idaho as early as 1892 and by the end of the decade had
become a common sight all along the line from Nampa to Pocatello. In the
first decade of the twentieth century many Japanese men found work in
Idaho's expanding sugar beet industry. These and other menial jobs typically served as stepping stones to various forms of self-employment. Some
Japanese became successful truck gardeners and others prosperous mer-

chants in the region's larger cities. Even so, they experienced much the same racial animosity as the Chinese.

In addition to violence directed against Chinese, an anti-Hindu (East Indian) riot erupted in Bellingham and an anti-Japanese riot occurred in Vancouver, British Columbia, in 1907. Those were only the major outbursts. Until after the Second World War, hostility to Asians remained a prominent feature of Pacific Northwest life. At one time it was common for restaurants to post signs reassuring white customers that they employed no Chinese help.

## THE ANTI-MORMON CRUSADE

Coexisting with racial prejudice in the Pacific Northwest was a virulent strain of religious intolerance in Idaho. After establishing early settlements in southeastern Idaho in the 1860s, Mormon pioneers pushed farther north into the upper Snake River Valley, although these settlements (unlike those along the Utah border) were not church sponsored. Mormons steadily increased in number until by 1877 Idaho had thirty-one distinct Mormon settlements and, by 1890, about twenty-five thousand Mormon residents. Mormons constituted about one-quarter of Idaho's total population at that time and perhaps as many as one-half of all its churchgoers. It was a religious division unique in American history.

As they grew in population and influence in southeastern Idaho, the Mormons were caught up in the sectional political rivalries that wracked the territory. Their growing numbers gave Mormons power at the polls, especially when they tended to vote as a bloc for Democratic candidates, nearly always the victorious side in Idaho before the 1880s. Because of the voting pattern, losers charged that Mormons took their orders from Salt Lake City and had no real interest in Idaho matters.

The Mormon sense of group solidarity and their religious and dietary customs caused outsiders, or "Gentiles," to regard them with suspicion. Being a "peculiar people," a Biblical term the Latter-day Saints applied to themselves, inevitably seemed to breed persecution. Some Gentiles considered Mormon devotion to church to be un-American, while others undoubtedly coveted the fertile Mormon farmsteads.

Above all, however, it was their belief that males had the right to marry more than one wife, a practice referred to as polygamy, that made Mormons convenient targets for hostile Gentiles. In fact, probably no more than 3 percent of Idaho's Mormons actually engaged in plural marriage.

More than anyone else, it was Fred T. Dubois who shaped the vague anti-

27. This anti-Mormon cartoon appeared in full color in the *West Shore*, a Portland booster publication. Dating from the late 1880s, it depicts Idaho as an avenging angel casting Mormonism into a a fiery pit. Courtesy Special Collections Division, University of Washington Libraries, uw 6321.

Mormon resentments into a powerful political movement. After attending Yale College, Dubois moved to Idaho in 1880 where four years later he became a United States marshal. When Congress passed the Edmunds Act in 1882, which barred polygamists from voting, holding office, or serving as jurors in cases involving plural marriage, it handed Dubois a powerful weapon to use against Mormons. Interested in more than simply harassing polygamists, Marshal Dubois sought to undermine the Idaho Democratic party by associating it with Mormons and then to elevate himself to a prominent position among territorial Republicans.

Dubois was successful in his quest: anti-Mormons in the legislature created the Idaho Test Oath, a stringent measure that could be used to force a person to testify under oath whether he belonged to the Mormon church or believed in its doctrines. A person did not have to be a practicing polygamist but only belong to an organization that sanctioned polygamy in order to be disenfranchised. After the Test Oath Act became law in 1885, Mormons fought it all the way to the United States Supreme Court and lost.

As Republicans grew in power, Dubois rode the wave of anti-Mormon sentiment to Capitol Hill, where as territorial delegate he worked to get Idaho admitted as a state. Framers added provisions of the Test Oath Act to the Idaho constitution, and voters overwhelmingly ratified it.

In September 1890 the church's president urged all Latter-day Saints to comply with civil laws regarding marriage, but this did not prevent Idaho's first legislature from barring Mormons from the polls. The 1893 legislature removed most of the anti-Mormon restrictions. As for Dubois, he became one of Idaho's United States Senators before taking himself and the anti-Mormon cause into the Democratic party in 1900, thereby enlivening Idaho politics during the early years of the twentieth century. By that time the state legislature had restored the franchise to Mormons, some of whom now voted against their old tormentor; others, in an ironic twist, became his political associates.

Some Idahoans wanted to disenfranchise Mormons because they continued to sanction plural marriage in heaven, but the state's judiciary ruled that so long as Mormons complied with civil law, Idaho could not extend its jurisdiction into the hereafter. In 1982 voters removed the anti-Mormon test oath from Idaho's constitution.

## THE FIGHT FOR FEMALE SUFFRAGE

At the time of the Civil War, the population of the Pacific Northwest, like that of most frontier regions, was decidedly male. In Washington Territory

| Denomination | Washington | Idaho | Oregon | Utah |
|---|---|---|---|---|
| Roman Catholic | | | | |
| Presbyterian | | | | |
| Methodist | | | | |
| Baptist | | | | |
| Disciples | | | | |
| Lutheran | | | | |
| Congregational | | | | |
| Episcopal | | | | |
| Latter-Day Saints | | | | |
| Adventist | | | | |
| Eastern Orthodox | | | | |
| United | | | | |
| Friends | | | | |
| Evangelical | | | | |
| All others | | | | |

Percentage of Communicants, 1910, by Denomination

(Each symbol approximates 5 percent)

men outnumbered females nine to one, a ratio that prompted Governor William Pickering to have three hundred single women transported from Boston to provide wives for his male constituents. Asa Mercer followed in Pickering's footsteps and brought another boatload of women to Seattle.

Despite the attention they received as prospective brides, Northwest women experienced various forms of discrimination, none more hotly contested than their ineligibility to vote. The region's suffrage crusade dates from 1871 when the prominent national activist Susan B. Anthony toured the Pacific Northwest in the company of Portland's Abigail Scott Duniway. The indefatigable Duniway continued the crusade for several more decades and justly deserves to be remembered as the mother of female suffrage in the Pacific Northwest. In addition to caring for a semi-invalid husband, raising six children, and publishing one of the region's leading reform papers, the *New Northwest* (1871–87), she crisscrossed the region numerous times to lecture on women's rights.

Duniway and her allies enjoyed some successes, as in 1878 when the Oregon legislature passed a law giving married women the right to own, sell, or will property and to keep their wages, and in 1881 when Washington passed a similar law. Two years later the territorial legislature extended the vote to women. One Washington pioneer, Phoebe Goodell Judson, recalled "I took my turn on petit and grand jury, served on election boards, walked in perfect harmony to the polls by the side of my staunch Democratic husband, and voted the Republican ticket—not feeling any more out of my sphere than when assisting my husband to develop the resources of our country."[3]

But Judson, Duniway, and their sisters were doomed to disappointment and years of frustration when Washington's territorial supreme court voided female suffrage in 1887 on a technicality. The legislature restored it a few months later, but in the bizarre Nevada Bloomer case of 1888, named for a saloonkeeper's wife who was the principal figure in a challenge mounted by liquor interests, the territorial supreme court again overturned the measure. During the next decade, Washington voters twice defeated female suffrage measures. Still the crusaders persisted, firm in their conviction that once women had the vote, economic and other rights could be obtained.

A breakthrough came in 1896 when, after a quiet and inexpensive campaign managed mostly by local women, Idaho overwhelmingly approved a

3. Phoebe Goodell Judson, *A Pioneer's Search for an Ideal Home* (1925; reprint, Lincoln: University of Nebraska Press, 1984), 277.

28. Abigail Scott Duniway (1834–1915), tireless advocate of women's rights. Courtesy Oregon Historical Society, ORHI 47215.

constitutional amendment making it the first Pacific Northwest state to
enfranchise women.[4] All but Custer County voted for the amendment.
Ironically, the lone dissenter was the county Abigail Duniway had called
home for several years. Her mocking and ridicule apparently had a tendency
to alienate people of both genders. Three women won seats in the Idaho

4. The Idaho territorial legislature in 1871 fell one vote short of providing for female
suffrage.

House of Representatives in 1898 and a token number of other offices. As they soon discovered, the right to vote did not mean that women gained real political power.

Fourteen years passed before Washington followed Idaho's lead: Emma Smith DeVoe, a friend of Duniway's, headed a campaign that won women the franchise in 1910 by a 2-to-1 margin. Duniway herself lived long enough to see Oregon's all-male electorate narrowly approve woman suffrage in 1912.

A combination of several fears explains why voting rights for women involved such a long struggle. Liquor interests were afraid that women would vote as a bloc to outlaw saloons and alcoholic beverages. In fact, some suffragists claimed credit for laws that made gambling illegal and closed saloons on Sunday. Democrats feared that women tended to vote Republican. Some over-chivalrous males thought it best to protect women from the rough-and-tumble crowds that hung around polls on election day. Finally, some women feared that engaging in the practice of voting would reduce their feminine charms. In Duniway's case, she also faced a formidable foe in her own brother, Harvey Scott, the influential publisher of the Portland *Oregonian*.

### SOCIAL RELATIONS IN PERSPECTIVE

In many ways the holes in the Northwest's social fabric reflected national trends. Religious and racial strife were facts of life from Boston to Birmingham, with intergroup harmony seemingly reaching a low point in the United States during the 1890s and improving only slowly until the 1950s and 1960s.

From the perspective of the late twentieth century, the region's social fabric appears considerably stronger than it did in the 1870s and 1880s. Intergroup relations have changed for the better. Racial and religious equality is now a matter of law, although it is sometimes ignored in practice, and the region's various racial and ethnic minorities have made significant strides in becoming an integral part of Northwest society. In 1993, for example, Seattle's overwhelmingly white electorate reelected Norm Rice, one of the nation's key black mayors, to a second consecutive term. Voters had previously elected black mayors in several other cities, including Spokane, Pasco, and Pocatello, where Les Purce became Idaho's first black mayor and later the first black to head the state's Democratic party.

But various problems persist, and old prejudices occasionally take new and subtle forms. Idaho's governor between 1977 and 1987 was John V. Evans, the first Mormon to be elected as the state's chief executive.[5] At first glance, it would appear that anti-Mormon prejudice no longer agitated Idaho political life. But look again. When Evans ran for governor on the Democratic ticket in 1978, his Republican opponent was also a Mormon, and Mormonism became the chief, if unspoken, issue of the campaign. Terms like "Mormon conspiracy" appeared in the press. Because his opponent was more clearly identified with the Mormon church, Evans benefited from conservative and Republican voters who crossed over to vote Democratic. Latent anti-Mormonism remained alive in Idaho.

Anti-Indian prejudice reared its head in Washington in 1984 in the guise of Initiative 456, which sought to diminish Indian fishing rights. Although the measure was denounced as racist, voters narrowly approved it. Some would argue that measures like Initiative 456 signified that the Pacific Northwest was growing more conservative and less tolerant of diversity after half a century of movement in the other direction.

5. Another Mormon, Arnold Williams, moved up to that office in 1945, having first been elected lieutenant governor on the Democratic ticket. He was defeated for reelection in 1946.

# Part III

# From Frontier to Urban-Industrial Society

# Profile: Henry Villard and
# the Last Spike

In this country, at this day, railroads are not a mere convenience to local population, but a vast machinery for the building up of empires.—Governor Marshall F. Moore to the Legislative Assembly of Washington Territory, 9 December 1862

At remote Gold Creek in Montana Territory several hundred guests gathered to celebrate the completion of a railroad joining the Great Lakes with Portland and Puget Sound. The date was 8 September 1883. Fourteen years earlier at Promontory, Utah, the driving of a symbolic gold spike had joined Central Pacific and Union Pacific tracks to form America's first transcontinental railroad. The Northern Pacific Railroad through Montana completed a second transcontinental line. Henry Villard, a handsome, genial man in his midfifties, presided over the celebration.

As head of the Northern Pacific, Villard believed that his company's triumph over nature and economic adversity merited international attention. He invited to the last spike ceremony several hundred politicians, bankers, railroad officials, investors, and journalists, many from Great Britain and Germany, countries that had given Villard substantial financial support.

To begin their journey, Villard's guests from the East Coast and Europe traveled to St. Paul, a city that celebrated the last spike in a manner that future generations reserved for astronauts and Olympic champions. A parade nearly twenty miles long and including approximately twenty thousand marchers moved through the city's lavishly decorated streets. Not to be outclassed by its neighbor and rival, Minneapolis staged a parade that entertained an estimated hundred thousand onlookers. From Minnesota the guests headed west across the prairies in four well-provisioned special trains. A fifth train left Portland carrying dignitaries from the Pacific Coast; cities and towns along the way scheduled additional festivities.

The last spike celebration took place approximately sixty miles west of Helena, near the confluence of the Clark Fork River and Gold Creek. The promoters erected a sign that read "Lake Superior 1,198 miles/Puget Sound 847 miles." A newly built wooden pavilion decorated with pine boughs, bunting, and the flags of Germany, Great Britain, and the United States stood nearby. It was capable of seating nearly a thousand people.

Milling about the platform and reviewing stand were the financial barons of three nations all dressed in the accoutrements that symbolized power in America's Gilded Age, while huddled nearby in a small and somewhat sullen group were Crow Indians, citizens of a shrinking hinterland already doomed to experience great and lasting changes. During the previous summer on the plains of eastern Montana, hunters had waited in vain for the great herds of buffalo that annually ranged south from Canada in search of food. Of the millions of shaggy beasts that roamed the Great Plains just a decade earlier, only a few hundred remained in the northern West the year of Villard's final spike ceremony. During 1882 the Northern Pacific had hauled 200,000 hides out of Montana and Dakota.

Wherever railroad tracks went, the old West confronted the new, but seldom so dramatically as at Gold Creek. Everything about Gold Creek was symbolic; that was Villard's intent. Yet some of the day's symbolism was subtle and ironic, and none more so than the various forms of juxtaposition so clearly visible to invited guests. For one moment the old West of Indians, trappers, and pioneers stood face to face with the new West of high finance, nationwide markets, and rapid advances in communication and transportation.

At 3 P.M. Villard signaled for the ceremony to begin, and a brass band opened with the "Star-Spangled Banner" and other popular selections. Villard then summarized the history of the Northern Pacific. The day's featured speaker, the former secretary of state William Evarts, next addressed the guests. A local paper observed that his oration was "impressive" but its weightier passages "bored to death" the Montana portion of his audience. Numerous other dignitaries extolled the glory and importance of the Northern Pacific's achievement.

After the speechmaking, everyone adjourned to the right-of-way to watch rival construction teams lay the last twelve-hundred feet of track. The final spike and sledgehammer were specially wired so as to telegraph each blow to company officials waiting in Portland, St. Paul, and New York. Their receivers recorded a last click at 5:18 P.M., signaling that America's second transcontinental railroad was at last a reality. Following a lavish banquet, Villard's guests continued to the West Coast, where still more celebrations and welcomes awaited them.

The final spike festivities proved a great promotional success for the Northern Pacific and signified the dawn of a new era for Pacific Northwesterners. The newness lay not in the railroad itself—local lines had existed in the region since the late 1850s—but in the direct and convenient connection it provided to the East.

The new link was several decades in the making. Because of America's expanding trade with China during the 1840s, the New York merchant Asa Whitney proposed a transcontinental railroad to Congress in late 1845. His motives were not entirely economic; he wanted also to promote settlement and believed that "Nature's God had made this for the grand highway to Civilize and Christianize all mankind."[1] Although he was an eloquent speaker well-armed with statistics and a variety of arguments, Whitney's dream evoked mainly sneers and ridicule. Congress remained unmoved, but like earlier dreams of a Northwest Passage or an easy portage across the Rockies, his idea won enthusiastic backers. More than any other person, Whitney added serious discussion of a transcontinental railroad to the public agenda at a time when even conceptualizing such a link represented a bold feat of imagination. American railroads had barely advanced beyond the experimental stage by 1850, and only a handful were longer than 150 miles.

Formidable as technological problems might be for an industry still in its infancy, there were also matters of finance. Who should pay for the massive project? The West was a debtor region; it contained few residents with capital sufficient to build local railroads much less national ones. The region was unlikely to attract the necessary funds from hard-headed eastern financiers. Unlike the situation in the East where railroad lines connected preexisting population centers and markets, western lines had to extend across hundreds and even thousands of miles of rugged and lightly popu-

1. Eugene V. Smalley, *History of the Northern Pacific Railroad* (New York: G. P. Putnam's Sons, 1883), 65.

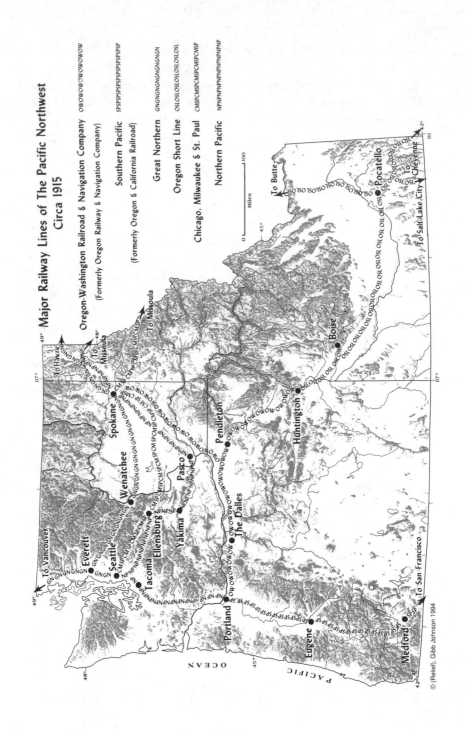

Major Railway Lines of The Pacific Northwest
Circa 1915

Oregon-Washington Railroad & Navigation Company  OWOWOWOWOWOWOW
(Formerly Oregon Railway & Navigation Company)

Southern Pacific  SPSPSPSPSPSPSPSPSPSP
(Formerly Oregon & California Railroad)

Great Northern  GNGNGNGNGNGNGN

Oregon Short Line  OSLOSLOSLOSLOSLOSLOSL

Chicago, Milwaukee & St. Paul  CMSPCMSPCMSPCMSP

Northern Pacific  NPNPNPNPNPNPNPNPNP

© (Relief), Gibb Johnson 1994

lated country. They would have to generate passenger and freight revenue by running from nowhere in particular to nowhere at all. In other words, the railroads of the West would have to create new towns and markets and foster settlement of countless miles of farmland by promising investors a share of future wealth, a task that sobered even the most optimistic westerner. In the West, moreover, the labor needed for construction was high priced and difficult to obtain. Clearly, in the mid-nineteenth century only the federal government had the resources to support a transcontinental railroad.

The imaginative Whitney petitioned Congress to grant him a sixty-mile-wide strip of land along the right-of-way of a proposed railway line from the Great Lakes to the lower Columbia River. He would sell the land—an area larger than the state of Illinois—to finance construction. Congress refused, but Whitney's northern transcontinental scheme elicited proposals from other regions, each with its special plan and route for reaching the Pacific.

In the early 1850s, Congress finally authorized the United States Army to conduct five transcontinental railway surveys to find a feasible route to the Pacific. The northern survey, under the direction of Isaac I. Stevens, worked its way west from St. Paul, while his subordinate, Lieutenant George B. McClellan, explored the Cascade Range for suitable passes. The government published the surveys between 1856 and 1861, but only in 1862—after the Civil War broke the regional deadlock over the best route—did Congress authorize loans and grants of land to subsidize construction of a railway along a central route. Sixty-one separate railroads received federal land grants totaling 131,350,534 acres before Congress terminated the program in 1871.

Congress chartered the Northern Pacific Railroad in 1864. The staggering cost of the Civil War prevented it from providing a cash subsidy for each mile of track laid, but it authorized instead the largest land grant ever offered to an American railroad, a sixty-million-acre swath of land the size of New England. On a map the Northern Pacific grant resembled an elongated checkerboard of alternating one-mile squares of government and railroad land extending from Lake Superior to the Pacific Ocean. It varied in width from forty miles in Minnesota and Oregon to eighty miles in the territories. The government deeded the odd sections to the railroad upon completion of each twenty-five miles of line.

This land grant, it must be noted, came with certain strings attached; ultimately the Northern Pacific forfeited some of the land through noncompliance with the terms of the grant. It actually received a total of a little more than thirty-nine million acres, an area still twice as great as any other railroad received. The grant obligated it to provide reduced rates on federal shipments such as mail until 1946. Even so, the Northern Pacific's successor, the Burlington Northern Railroad, was one of the largest nongovernment landholders in the United States.

As generous as the original Northern Pacific land grant was, the lack of a cash subsidy created severe financial difficulties and hampered construction. The company further labored under the twin burdens of having no sizable population centers to serve and the popular belief that the north country was too cold to permit successful railroading and settlement.

One person who did come to believe in the Northern Pacific project was the noted Civil War financier Jay Cooke, who joined wholeheartedly in the venture after learning everything he could about the subject. His hired promoters so insistently proclaimed that the Northern Pacific country possessed a mild climate and other agreeable features that the region came to be popularly caricatured as "Jay Cooke's Banana Belt." With Cooke's prestigious Philadelphia firm acting as financial agent, money at last flowed in.

Groundbreaking took place near Duluth in 1870, and two years later the line had opened for business as far west as the Red River valley separating Minnesota and Dakota Territory. But not long after the tracks reached Bismarck, Cooke's firm failed, precipitating the panic of 1873. During the hard times that lasted most of the decade, construction halted and the Northern Pacific sank into bankruptcy.

Surely many Pacific Northwesterners must have wondered if they would live long enough to see the Northern Pacific completed. At the time of its financial collapse, the railroad consisted of two poorly built lines separated by more than 1,500 miles of mountain and prairie: the eastern section extended 450 miles from Lake Superior to the Missouri River, the western section a little over 100 miles from Tacoma to Kalama, a village on the north bank of the Columbia River. From that point, passengers and freight were ferried to Portland. Lack of additional construction in the mid-1870s caused frustrated citizens of Seattle and eastern Washington to propose building their own Seattle and Walla Walla Railroad across the Cascade Range through Snoqualmie Pass. As for Asa Whitney, the man who spent his personal fortune trying to promote the idea of a transcontinental railroad west from Lake Superior, he died in poverty in 1872, well before his vision became reality.

When prosperity returned toward the end of the 1870s, the reorganized Northern Pacific under the leadership of its president, Frederick Billings, again pushed construction forward. But not until Henry Villard gained control of the company in 1881 did the line at last realize its transcontinental destiny. Given the Northern Pacific's twenty-year ordeal, Villard had a right to celebrate its completion.

Like the early history of his railroad, Villard's life was a chronicle of triumphs and bitter disappointments. Born in German Palatine in 1835 as Ferdinand Heinrich Gustav Hilgard, he immigrated to the United States eighteen years later after a disagreement with his tyrannical father. He adopted the name Villard to prevent his demanding father from learning of his whereabouts and forcibly returning him to Germany and service in the army. Penniless and an academic failure, he struggled to support himself as a common laborer.

Young Henry only gradually emerged from the German community, breaking free from a succession of menial jobs around the Midwest by working first as a reporter for German-American newspapers and then for the English-language press. He covered the Lincoln-Douglas debates, the 1860 presidential election, and the Civil War. Villard married Fannie Garrison, the daughter of the well-known abolitionist William Lloyd Garrison. The ambitious young journalist also found time to study law and railroad promotion and finance.

Villard pushed himself so hard that he suffered a physical breakdown and was forced to seek relief in the spas of Europe. There a group of worried Germans who had invested in American railroads selected him as their overseas agent, a move that soon made him a rich man.

By the end of the decade, Villard had formed the Oregon Railway and Navigation Company and extended its tracks along the south bank of the Columbia River from Portland to a junction with the Northern Pacific near present-day Pasco, Washington. Bringing rail service to the expanding agricultural districts of the interior Northwest proved exceedingly profitable, but Villard still sought both a reliable connection to the East and a way to prevent a Puget Sound community from rivaling Portland. In an act of incredible financial daring, he raised $8 million to enable his company to buy the Northern Pacific in the famous "Blind Pool" in 1881. On the strength of his reputation alone, investors put their money into a project about which they knew nothing.

When Northern Pacific rails finally met at Gold Creek, Villard controlled a vast transportation empire and stood at the peak of his career. A few months later, cost overruns and other money crises caused by his haste to finish the line tested the limits of his financial genius. During the next

29. F. Jay Haynes photographed Henry Villard (1835–
1900) at Mammoth Hotel, Yellowstone National Park,
in June 1889. Villard poses with a cane. Courtesy
Haynes Foundation Collection, Montana Historical Society, H-1991.

decade Villard experienced a dizzying series of reverses. His physician
warned him that stress could cause his physical collapse at any time. In
January 1884 Villard resigned from the Northern Pacific, citing "nervous
prostration" as the primary reason. He regained a seat on the company's
board of directors three years later and served as its chairman from 1889 to
1893 when the railroad went bankrupt during the depression of the 1890s.
The one-time financial baron died in 1900, though not without leaving
behind his signature across the Pacific Northwest. It was a signature written not just in iron and steel rails but also in the form of books, laboratory
equipment, and other aid he gave the University of Oregon and the University of Washington during their years of financial struggle.

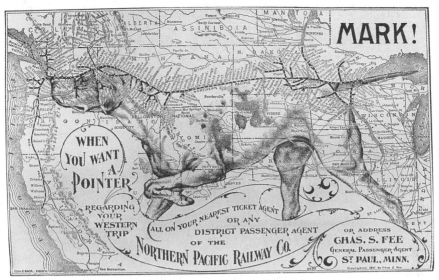

30. "When you want a Pointer." A turn-of-the century
map advertising the route of the Northern Pacific Railway. Courtesy Spokane Public Library.

This, in short, was the meaning of Villard's final spike at Gold Creek: a
journey that once required three to five months now took only five or six
days. For investors and homeseekers from distant regions and for residents of
the Pacific Northwest, an era of isolation had ended. Newcomers traveling
by rail poured into the region—especially into Washington—at a rate un-
imaginable only a decade earlier. Cities and farms transformed the landscape, and large-scale business enterprises and organized labor attained a
prominence and power not possessed before. The Oregon of the pioneer "is a
thing of the past," observed the Portland *Oregonian* after the final spike
ceremony. "The transcontinental railroad has annihilated time and space,
and at our door stands a train that is composed of cars loaded through from
ocean to ocean. A new Oregon springs up to-day, and we must prepare for it."

Thus, in September 1883, when his financial downfall lay yet in the
future, a major builder of the new Northwest felt entitled to savor the good
times, banquets, parades, bunting, flags, and accolades of his peers. Still,
there were a few discordant notes, mainly from the unfortunate villages
that Villard's twin ribbons of steel bypassed and thereby excluded from the
new mainstream of Northwest life.

After Gold Creek, several additional transcontinental lines were completed to the Pacific coast, each extending numerous branches into the

Northwest's mining, timber, and agricultural regions. However, no decade would rival the 1880s for the miles of track laid across the region. If the boundary-setting, government-creating decade of the 1840s featured the most important transitions in the region's history, then the railroad-building decade of the 1880s surely followed a close second.

# CHAPTER 9

# Metropolitan Corridors:
# Forging New Transportation Links

*

Give us a railroad! Though it be a rawhide one with open passenger cars and a sheet iron boiler; anything on wheels drawn by an iron horse! But give us a railroad.—Francis Cook, *Territory of Washington,* quoting the Walla Walla *Watchman* (1880)

*

Indians, fur traders, and missionaries had much in common in matters of transportation: their three basic modes of travel were by foot, water, and horse. To those the pioneer settlers added carts and wagons drawn by a variety of animals, but all such forms of transportation remained essentially private. Common carriers—enterprises specializing wholly in transporting goods and passengers with services available to any user—arrived in the Pacific Northwest only in the mid-1840s and did not become large-scale operations until the mining booms of the 1860s stimulated such enterprises. Thereafter, common carriers employing a variety of conveyances, from packtrains, stagecoaches, freight wagons, steamboats, and sailing ships to railroad freight and passenger trains, tied the region together and integrated it with the larger world. Without the construction of a railway network it would be impossible to account for the rapid commercial and urban growth that the Northwest experienced after the mid-1880s.

### EARLY TRAVEL BY WATER AND LAND

Inland rivers and valleys together with the Pacific Ocean and the many tidal estuaries along the coast formed the earliest and easiest avenues of com-

179

munication and transportation. Because travel by water had its limits, a generation of fur traders and explorers, drawing in many cases upon knowledge supplied by local Indians, mapped out and blazed supplemental trails and roads. Overland travelers and government surveyors elaborated on this information, and railroad and highway builders later chose to follow some of the same routes. One such example is the old Oregon Trail across southern Idaho and through the Columbia gorge now traversed by the Union Pacific Railroad and Interstate 84.

Trails and crude territorial and military roads, often amounting to little more than footpaths, threaded their way across the Pacific Northwest before the coming of the railroads. One of those was the Mullan Road, perhaps second only to the Oregon Trail as a route of historical significance. That military highway, intended as a northern alternative to the Oregon Trail, owed its origin to the railroad-surveying project headed by Isaac I. Stevens, who designated Lieutenant John Mullan and thirteen men to gather data on winter weather in the Rocky Mountains. In 1854, after Congress appropriated $30,000 to survey a military road from Fort Benton, at the upper limit of steamboat navigation on the Missouri River, to Fort Walla Walla, Mullan was appointed to head the project. Construction did not begin until 1859, after Congress had appropriated another $100,000 and Indian warfare on the Columbia plateau ceased. The 624-mile-long route opened in August 1862, but even before its completion, an army unit covered the distance in fifty-seven days.

Except for this troop of soldiers, the route never fulfilled its destiny as a military route. Compared to twentieth-century highways, the Mullan Road was primitive: its grades were steep and in some places impassable in wet weather. Although it was billed as a wagon road, in the rugged Bitterroot and Coeur d'Alene mountains, it frequently amounted to little more than a pack trail. The quieting of Indian-white conflict in eastern Washington diminished its value as a military route, but it remained strategically important during the Civil War and helped to facilitate the flow of commerce to the gold camps of the northern Rocky Mountains. Immigrant parties occasionally used it on their way west to open new agricultural lands on the Columbia plain.

By 1866 some twenty thousand people and an unknown number of animals (including at least seven camels used by packers on a trial basis) had passed over the Mullan Road, most of them going from west to east, primarily from Missoula to Fort Benton. Packers occasionally used the route during the mining rushes of the 1860s, as did cattlemen who drove livestock west to the Columbia River during the years of the open range in the 1870s and 1880s. But spring flooding and lack of Congressional funds for maintenance inevitably took their toll. The road fell into disrepair. Not until the federal highway program of the 1920s was the route effectively utilized as a transcontinental highway. Today Interstate 90 closely follows Mullan's route across the Idaho panhandle.

Steamboats plying Pacific Northwest waters formed an integral part of the region's expanding transportation network. The *Beaver*, a diminutive paddle boat constructed in England for the Hudson's Bay Company and delivered to John McLoughlin at Fort Vancouver in 1836, was the first steamboat in the Northwest. Among the *Beaver*'s many tasks was supplying Russian Alaska. After more than fifty years of service, the steamer ran aground in British Columbia and sank.

The sidewheeler *Columbia*, which commenced regular service between Astoria and Portland in 1850, was the first steamship to ply the Columbia as a common carrier. Half a dozen steamships soon joined her on interior waters, and their number greatly increased after the gold discoveries of the 1860s.

Transportation up the Columbia and Willamette rivers from Portland was no simple matter. The falls at Oregon City required passengers and freight traveling to and from Eugene City and other upper Willamette landings to portage at that point. Even more formidable obstacles interrupted navigation on the Columbia. The construction of a wooden, mule-powered tramway at the Cascades during the late 1850s provided a short, easy portage for passengers and freight. Farther upriver, near Dalles City (now The Dalles), a longer portage line replaced a crude wagon road in 1863. The tracks of the first true railroad in the Pacific Northwest climbed eleven miles past the rapids to slack water above Celilo Falls. Steamboat service to the interior Northwest above Celilo commenced in 1858 with the sternwheeler *Colonel Wright*.

During the 1860s mining rush to Idaho, steamboats carried gold seekers up the Columbia River as far as Umatilla and Wallula, jumping-off points for interior camps, and if the Snake River was running high enough, all the way through to Lewiston, trailhead for the northern mines. They carried prospectors and gamblers, and boatloads of axes, shovels, tents, mining equipment, foodstuffs, and whiskey; downstream they carried passengers and the yellow dust that was the cause of all the activity. For ship owners it was an exceedingly lucrative business.

From landings on the Columbia River, pack and saddle trains hauled

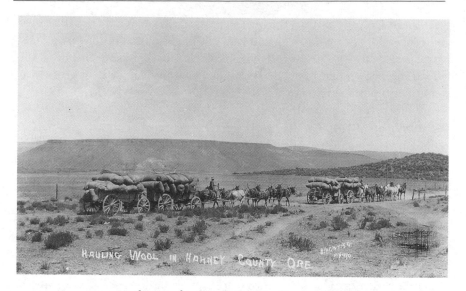

31. Hauling wool in Harney County, Oregon. Courtesy
Special Collections Division, University of Washington
Libraries, UW 4380.

passengers and freight overland to eastern Oregon and Boise Basin mining
towns. A single train might include as many as a hundred animals, each
carrying 250 to 400 pounds of freight. It took thirteen days to cover the three
hundred miles from Umatilla to Boise City, which soon became the transportation hub of southern Idaho. Some eager goldseekers simply strapped
packs to their backs and hit the trail for the long hike overland. This most
elementary form of transportation was referred to as "Foot and Walker's
Transportation Line." Eventually freight wagons and stagecoaches dominated the route as roads improved. It was a succession of transportation
technology common in other parts of the Pacific Northwest as well.

### THE RISE OF COMMON CARRIERS

Because isolation was the fate of immigrant settlers, inauguration of regular
mail, passenger, and freight service, however crude and inefficient, was
welcomed as a sign of liberation and progress. Probably the first common
carrier in the old Oregon country was an ox-powered stage that began twice-
weekly operation between Oregon City and the Tualatin plain in 1846. It
promised to operate "rain or no rain—mud or no mud—load or no load—but

not without pay." Other primitive stagecoach lines soon followed. By 1857 a Concord coach was able to complete the fifty-mile run from Portland to Salem in a single day.

Of all forms of early transportation none seemed more ubiquitous than the stagecoach. How much it once meant to hear the cry, "Stage!" In isolated camps and villages the one great event of the day was the arrival of the stage with its load of mail and passengers. Like the locomotive engineer of a later era, the stage driver was a popular and respected man.

Travel by stage was never without its trials. Early roads were often little more than dirt paths, and rain could turn long stretches into knee-deep quagmires. One traveler remembered a driver ordering, "First class passengers, keep your seats. Second class passengers, get out and walk. Third class passengers, get behind and push." In dry weather the dust spread over passengers like the waves of the sea. The alkali made their skin sore and rough and burned their eyes and noses. Still more alarming were the roads that wound down steep hillsides. Stages made periodic stops at stations to change drivers and give passengers a chance to eat. Carrie Strahorn in her book *Fifteen Thousand Miles by Stage* (1911) recalled a station on the Snake River plain where over the door hung this sign: "Hotel de Starvation, 1,000 miles from hay and grain, seventy miles from wood, fifteen miles from water, but only twelve inches from hell." Unmarried men usually kept these houses. A typical meal of bread, beans, bacon, and black coffee cost $1.00.

The California Stage Company, one of the largest organizations of its kind in the United States, established direct and regular service between Portland and Sacramento in 1860. The seven-hundred-mile journey required six days. Convenient connections linked Sacramento to the growing metropolis of San Francisco and to St. Louis. A variety of stagecoach outfits hauled passengers and mail between Oregon and California until completion of a railway line in 1887. Several other outfits offered express and light package service, most notably Wells, Fargo and Company of San Francisco, which utilized a far-flung network of stagecoach and freight lines in the 1860s and 1870s to serve mining regions in the interior Northwest.

In the evolution of the Pacific Northwest's early common carriers, no one wielded more influence than Ben Holladay, the stagecoach king, who sought to create a far-reaching transportation monopoly. Few businessmen exemplified better than Holladay the ruthless, uninhibited spirit of freewheeling capitalism during the latter decades of the nineteenth century. Holladay's specialty was the ruthless elimination of competition: he was even reputed to have staged "Indian" attacks in an effort to drive rival stage operators out of business. This swashbuckling financial adventurer would treat Oregonians to a spectacle the likes of which old-timers had never seen before.

Holladay's was the classic rags-to-riches story: born in a log cabin in Kentucky in 1819, at the height of his power in the 1860s and 1870s he maintained mansions in Washington, D.C.; New York City and White Plains, New York; and Portland and Seaside, Oregon. Disdained by many as a semiliterate, boorish man, Holladay entertained lavishly as he sought to expand his political and economic influence. To some observers he embodied the vulgar new materialism that was debasing American life; to others, he was typical of an enterprising new breed of westerners.

Before coming to Oregon in 1868, Holladay had already organized a far-flung empire of stagecoach and freight wagon lines, river boats and coastal steamers, and won for himself the popular titles of "Stagecoach King" and "Napoleon of the West." He laid the foundation for his transportation empire in 1862 when he gained control of stagecoach and freight wagon lines that, with the aid of federal mail contracts, extended from Salt Lake City to the booming mining camps and supply centers of Boise City, Walla Walla, and Virginia City, Montana. His stagecoach network reached its greatest extent in early 1866 when the Holladay Overland Mail & Express Company stretched west along 5,000 miles of roads between the Missouri River port of Atchison, Kansas, to the steamboat landing at The Dalles, Oregon. This arrangement eliminated the need for Pacific Northwesterners to travel to the East by way of California.

Faced with financial reverses as a result of Indian attacks and other problems, Holladay sold his stagecoach empire to Wells, Fargo in 1866. Two years later, he moved from California to Oregon where he used the financial muscle created by sale of his staging business to win control of Willamette Valley railroads from local businessmen. By investing in a company operating ships along the Pacific coast from Alaska to Mexico he was further able to expand his influence over various railroad and steamship properties in Oregon; he also devised a scheme to vastly increase his already considerable fortune by gaining control of a large and valuable grant of land that Congress had given Oregon to subsidize construction of a railway line along the Willamette Valley. To win the coveted land grant, Holladay unblushingly corrupted the Oregon legislature by subsidizing newspapers, hiring lawyers, and distributing money and special favors to purchase politicians. Holladay, who bragged openly of his control of the press and his influence over Oregon politics, introduced the Pacific Northwest to an era of corruption aptly labeled "the great barbecue."

In the Willamette Valley he organized the Oregon and California Railroad and issued millions of dollars' worth of bonds that were purchased by English and German investors—people who knew little about Holladay or the railroad. He was able to extend Oregon and California tracks south from Portland as far as Roseburg before hard times by 1873 halted construction and eventually cost Holladay control of his transportation empire.

Holladay dominated Oregon politics and transportation for nearly a decade, yet his great business enterprise rested upon a surprisingly shaky foundation. He was forever rearranging his holdings by creating or merging subsidiaries. His steamship and railroad interests were interlocked in a bewildering arrangement of double pledging their securities to creditors. The result, observed Henry Villard, the man who finally beat him at this game, was that although Holladay's creditors were among the shrewdest and most experienced bankers in Europe, they allowed themselves to be caught in the web of his financial machinations.

The aggressive Holladay finally overreached himself. The panic of 1873 left his companies destitute and unable to pay interest to bondholders. To untangle the snarl, German bondholders dispatched Villard to Oregon in 1874 as their agent to see what might be salvaged from their American misadventure. Villard and his backers gradually tightened the financial noose on Holladay until in April 1876 they acquired complete control of his properties and vanquished the erstwhile transportation king. Holladay retired and lived in Portland until his death in 1887. He died at the age of sixty-eight, having lost fame and good health along with his fortune. More than one hundred lawsuits punctuated his final years.

When Villard gained control of the Oregon and California Railroad and other Holladay properties in 1876, he also acquired his predecessor's dreams of empire. Using Holladay's rail and river monopoly in the Willamette Valley as his financial base, Villard gained a similar position in the Columbia Valley when he acquired the Oregon Steam Navigation Company for $5 million in 1879.

The group of local capitalists who organized the Oregon Steam Navigation Company in 1860 dominated traffic on the Columbia River and reaped a fortune during the inland gold rush. After only six months in operation, the Oregon Steam Navigation Company declared a twenty percent dividend, and that was only a promising beginning for what soon emerged as one of the Pacific Northwest's premier business enterprises. The line of freight wagons at its Portland docks was so great that it remained unbroken day and night, seven days a week.

By 1865 the Oregon Steam Navigation Company operated a fleet of nearly thirty passenger and freight steamboats, thirteen schooners, and four barges on the Columbia River alone. One Oregon Steam Navigation boat on the middle river was the new sidewheeler *Idaho*. It dominated the thirty-eight-mile run between the Cascades and The Dalles and was probably the source of the name of the modern state of Idaho.

The reach of the Oregon Steam Navigation Company extended south along the Willamette River and east as far as the middle Snake River in southern Idaho and the Clark Fork River in western Montana. By 1867 it was possible to ship goods from Portland to Helena, Montana, in only seven days. The Oregon Steam Navigation Company competed for the trade of the inland Northwest with merchants from California and Missouri.

In the eyes of many Northwesterners, however, high profits combined with monopoly power on the Columbia and Willamette rivers to make the Oregon Steam Navigation company an object of envy and hatred for two decades after 1860. The big three businessmen who dominated the "financial wonder of its day" became very rich. One of them, Simeon G. Reed, went on to invest in various enterprises, including mines in northern Idaho and livestock breeding, and thereby vastly enlarged his wealth. His widow willed $3 million toward the founding of Reed College, which opened in Portland in 1911.

After Villard acquired the Oregon Steam Navigation Company in 1879, he reorganized it as the Oregon Railway and Navigation Company. As its new name indicated, the new firm operated steamboats and extended a network of railway lines from Portland to tap the agricultural riches of the Walla Walla Valley and other interior points. Like its predecessor, the Oregon Railway and Navigation Company made huge profits serving the inland Northwest, though its primary cargo had shifted from mining supplies and gold dust to golden grain from the wheatfields of the Walla Walla Valley and Palouse country.

Of all the transportation advances that Pacific Northwesterners witnessed during the nineteenth century, the railroad was the most revolutionary, although it did not completely displace steamboats and stagecoaches for many years. Until the advent of motorized vehicles in the early twentieth century, stages continued to supplement rail service in remote areas. The completion of the Cascades canal in 1896 and The Dalles–Celilo canal in 1915 opened the main body of the Columbia to through navigation, and yet river transportation remained in the shadow of the railroads until the

32. The *Spokane* and *Lewiston* were two of the steam-
boats that provided transportation up the Columbia and
Snake rivers as far inland as Lewiston, Idaho. Courtesy
Spokane Public Library.

federal government completed a series of dams and locks on the Columbia
and Snake rivers in the 1960s and 1970s. After that, railroads actually found
themselves at a rate disadvantage with barge lines for grain traffic from the
interior Northwest as far east as Montana, where grain traveled by truck to
Snake River ports.

### RAILROAD BUILDING: LOCAL AND TRANSCONTINENTAL

The Pacific Northwest's earliest railroads served local needs, such as por-
taging passengers and freight around the falls of the Columbia or moving
wheat from the breadbasket of the Walla Walla Valley to a steamboat landing at Wallula on the Columbia River. The Walla Walla and Columbia River
Railroad, a thirty-two-mile-long narrow-gauge line that Dr. Dorsey S. Baker
completed in 1875, illustrates how a pioneer entrepreneur could marshal
local resources to build a short, low-cost railway.

Undaunted by naysayers and finally able to obtain some local financial backing, Baker was in his late forties and an established physician, merchant, and banker when he took up the new career of railroad builder. Construction began in 1871 with several gangs of Chinese laborers grading the line. Other workmen floated logs down the Yakima River to a small sawmill at "Slabtown," an eddy on the Columbia River just north of Wallula, which was capable of turning out a mile of track material a week. To keep expenses low, Baker used regular T-shaped rails only on the curves; he substituted wooden rails topped with lengths of strap iron on the straight sections.

This home-grown enterprise was variously called Dr. Baker's Road, the strap iron road, and the rawhide road, the latter a derisive name arising from a confused and erroneous notion that the cost-conscious Baker utilized strap leather instead of iron. One retelling of that myth in a national journal even claimed that during a particularly hard winter, wolves desperate for food ate the rawhide and temporarily severed Walla Walla's link to the outside world. In fact, wooden rails were not unusual in the far Northwest. Before Baker launched the Walla Walla and Columbia River Railroad he had already seen them used successfully on portage lines in the Columbia Gorge.

The truth is that by charging only half of what teamsters formerly received, the Walla Walla and Columbia River Railroad reaped staggering profits that helped to make Baker a very rich man. In 1879 Baker sold six-sevenths of his railroad to the Oregon Railway and Navigation Company, and the new owners immediately removed the strap iron and upgraded the track. They widened the line from three-feet to standard-gauge in 1881 in preparation for a through route to Portland. Baker, meanwhile, invested his growing fortune in other frontier enterprises, including what is now the Baker-Boyer National Bank in Walla Walla. In the end, the real joke was on those who declined to invest in Dr. Baker's "rawhide" moneymaking machine.

During the 1880s, tracklaying went forward throughout the region at a furious pace. When Villard's overextended holding company collapsed in 1884 and the Northern Pacific and Oregon Railway and Navigation Company fell into separate hands, the two companies raced to build a latticework of competing yet often unprofitable lines across the agricultural lands of the Palouse.

Having lost direct access to Portland when its ally turned competitor, the Northern Pacific extended its own main line from the Columbia River up the Yakima Valley and over the Cascade mountains to Tacoma. After boring through the mountains under Stampede Pass in what was at that time the second-longest tunnel in the United States, the line opened in 1887; the Northern Pacific thus offered service to Tacoma, Seattle, and Portland entirely over its own rails. As Portland backers feared, the Stampede Pass line funneled a substantial portion of interior grain to Puget Sound ports.

The Union Pacific, a partner in building the first transcontinental railroad, emerged as the Northern Pacific's major competitor when it took steps to tap the resources of the Pacific Northwest. With that goal in mind, a subsidiary company, the Oregon Short Line, completed a railroad across southern Idaho in 1884. True to its name, the Oregon Short Line provided a shortcut between the Union Pacific main line in Wyoming and Huntington, Oregon, where it met the tracks of the Oregon Railway and Navigation Company, now of the Union Pacific.

Despite the wealth of the Oregon Railway and Navigation Company, the sprawling Union Pacific system formed at best a rickety, overextended financial structure that collapsed during the hard times of the 1890s. Only after the financier Edward H. Harriman acquired and reorganized the company in 1897 did it become what it remains today, one of the most financially secure railroads in the United States.

Through rail service from the Pacific Northwest to California commenced in late 1887 following a final spike ceremony at Ashland, Oregon. Charles Crocker, the head of the Southern Pacific, reminded observers at the Ashland ceremony that the line now linked Portland and New Orleans to create the longest railway system in the world. For years the Southern Pacific was also the largest nongovernment employer west of the Mississippi River and, as a result of the sizable land grant acquired through the Oregon and California Railroad, became one of America's largest private landholders.

In late 1885 the Canadian Pacific Railway completed a line between Montreal and Vancouver; a connection to Seattle opened in 1891. Two years later the Great Northern Railway quietly finished a line from Seattle to St. Paul. Last spike ceremonies by that time no longer had any publicity value. In June 1893, the same month the Great Northern completed its transcontinental line, a financial panic convulsed Wall Street and precipitated the worst depression in American history prior to the hard times of the 1930s.

Although local and regional lines continued to be built until the First World War and at least some construction continued until the early 1930s, the depression of 1893–97 brought to a close the greatest era of railroad building in Pacific Northwest history. Last to join the ranks of northern transcontinentals was the Chicago, Milwaukee, and St. Paul Railway, which extended its track from the Midwest to Puget Sound in 1909. That line should never have been built, and the railroad's subsequent financial troubles highlighted major changes that overtook American transportation during the second decade of the twentieth century.

The Milwaukee Road, as it became popularly known, was a prosperous midwestern carrier before it decided to tap the commerce of the Pacific Northwest. Some financial analysts questioned the wisdom of that decision, and later events made them wise prophets. The completion of the Panama Canal in 1914 took a far larger bite from the transcontinental freight business than railroads expected. By 1928 the canal carried 20 percent of the lumber marketed in the United States and almost half the production of the Pacific Northwest.

Automobile and truck competition that first grew worrisome during the 1920s was similarly unanticipated when the Milwaukee Road built its Pacific extension. Moreover, between 1916 and 1920 the railroad took the bold step of electrifying much of its line from central Montana to Puget Sound. That technological marvel, representing the world's most extensive railroad electrification project at that time, excited the imaginations of jaded railroad travelers, science fiction writers, and regional promoters. The latter group especially appreciated how well the innovative railroad advertised the Northwest's abundance of "white coal," or hydroelectric power.

In the end, the hoped-for savings from electrification never offset the enormous cost of installation and thus contributed to the railroad's growing financial woes. The Milwaukee Road entered receivership in 1925, the first of three bouts of bankruptcy, and in 1981 it abandoned service west of Montana.

Of the entrepreneurs associated with the Northwest's great era of railway building, no one better merited the title of Empire Builder than James J. Hill,

33. Milwaukee Road operated luxury passenger trains between Chicago and Seattle and Tacoma from 1911 to 1961. Like all passenger trains, the *Olympian* of this 1931 advertisement not only defined what travelers saw of the Pacific Northwest but also when they saw it. Railroads usually arranged the schedules of premier passenger trains to cross flatlands by night and mountains by day, thereby reinforcing a common prejudice that plains were boring and mountains picturesque. Courtesy Milwaukee Road Collection, Milwaukee Public Library.

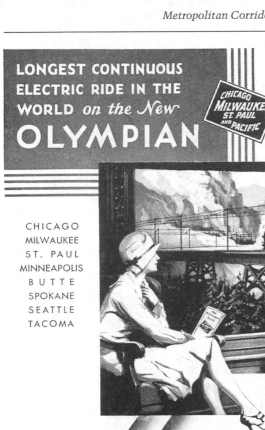

34. The vigorous "Empire Builder," James J. Hill (1838–
1916), in the familiar stance of an evangelist for Pacific
Northwest development. Here he is photographed at
the Stearns County, Minnesota, Fair, in 1914. When he
spoke at the opening-day ceremonies of Seattle's
Alaska-Yukon-Pacific Exposition five years earlier, Hill
had compared the growth of the West after completion
of the transcontinental railroads to "that which follows
the application of water to your soils." Courtesy James
Jerome Hill Reference Library.

a businessman with diverse interests in the Pacific Northwest. The Canadian-born Hill began his business career modestly enough as a shipping clerk in St. Paul, Minnesota. While he was still in his twenties, he started his own warehouse and express business. In 1878, shortly before turning forty, he acquired a decrepit railway line, the St. Paul and Pacific. From that modest acorn grew a mighty oak, the Great Northern, financially the strongest of all the northern transcontinentals.

Unlike the Northern Pacific and Union Pacific, the Great Northern worked its way west almost entirely on a pay-as-you-go basis, constructing branch lines and encouraging agricultural settlement rather than depending on government land grants. So soundly was the Great Northern financed that it weathered the depression of the 1890s while scores of other lines, including the Northern Pacific, went bankrupt. Hill outmaneuvered Edward Harriman of the Union Pacific in 1901 in a battle for control of the Northern Pacific and also acquired the Chicago, Burlington, and Quincy to gain entrance to Chicago.

When the various "Hill Lines" attempted to consolidate under the control of a holding company—the Northern Securities Company—the United States Supreme Court blocked the move in 1904. But that setback did not stop Hill from expanding his empire in other ways by purchasing or building new lines to link Spokane and Portland and battling Harriman for access to central Oregon. "Give me enough Swedes and whiskey and I'll build a railroad to Hell," Hill is reputed to have said. The Empire Builder died in 1916, but the tracks of the Great Northern railroad pushed on to reach northern California in 1931.

A latter-day monument to Hill was the Burlington Northern Railroad, formed in 1970 from the trunk lines that seventy years earlier he had unsuccessfully attempted to combine under the Northern Securities banner. Since 1971, Amtrak has operated a daily passenger train between Chicago and Seattle called the Empire Builder, a name inherited from the Great Northern. In the early years of Amtrak operation, a portrait of James J. Hill occupied its accustomed place in the dining car.

### THE RAILROAD-MADE PACIFIC NORTHWEST

Wherever Pacific Northwest railroads ran their tracks, they left names on the land. "Some official put an inky finger on the map. 'There,' he said, 'is a good place for a city. Call it Smith's Coulee, after our master-mechanic.'" In his account of the naming of Smith's Coulee, the Pulitzer Prize–winning journalist Ray Stannard Baker sought to explain to easterners the encompassing role railroads played in western life. Although Smith's Coulee existed only in his imagination, Baker accurately described a process repeated countless times across the new Northwest.[1]

In eastern Washington are the towns of Oakesdale, named for Thomas F. Oakes, general manager of the Northern Pacific Railroad; Prescott and Endicott, for C. H. Prescott and William Endicott Jr., two directors of Henry Villard's Oregon and Transcontinental holding company; and Starbuck, for General W. H. Starbuck, a "Nantucket Yankee" associated with the Oregon Railway and Navigation Company, who gave the town its first church bell. The town of Pullman was named for the sleeping car magnate George Mortimer Pullman, apparently in hopes that he would make a generous bequest to his namesake community. In fact, according to local legend, Pullman donated the munificent sum of $50. In Idaho, the town of Burley recalls a long-time official of the Oregon Short Line, while Avery was named for the son of William Rockefeller, a director of the Chicago, Milwaukee and St. Paul Railway.

When tracks of the Washington, Idaho and Montana Railway headed east from Palouse, Washington, into the white pine country of the Idaho panhandle, they came first to new milltown of Potlatch (meaning "great feast") and then to Princeton. The next town was called Harvard. This set a pattern for naming the rest of the town sites: Yale, Stanford, Vassar, Cornell, Purdue, and Wellesley. Most were chosen by young college men who surveyed the right of way and supervised construction. Despite the impressive appellations, few of the places ever amounted to more than lonely railroad sidings.

H. R. Williams, a vice president of the Milwaukee Road, named thirty-two stations across the state of Washington according to a formula that required each placename to be reasonably short, easily spelled, pleasant sounding, and unlikely to cause confusion when telegraphed in Morse code. Among his choices were Othello, after the Shakespeare play; Horlick, after a brand of malted milk; Warden, after a major stockholder; and Vassar, after the women's college (and obviously a popular name among males of the time).

Pacific Northwesterners developed a love-hate relationship with the railroad companies. They welcomed new lines to their communities, believing that rail connections guaranteed permanence, growth, and prosperity; they sulked when railroads passed them by. Would-be cities on Puget Sound

---

1. Ray Stannard Baker, "Destiny and the Western Railroad," *Century Magazine* 75 (April 1908): 893.

fought bitterly with one another in the early 1870s to be designated the terminus of the Northern Pacific. The new town of Tacoma won the prize, but its rival, Seattle, refused to concede, although the Northern Pacific initially relegated it to the end of a branch line. The future of Seattle looked considerably brighter after Hill selected the city as the Pacific terminus for his Great Northern.

After the fall of 1883 and the completion of a through line to the East, the coming of rails to a Pacific Northwest community meant major changes. Their routes functioning as metropolitan corridors, railroads linked the towns and villages of America's hinterland to Wall Street and Capitol Hill. Railroads not only opened the door to a nationwide market for local products—especially for bulky items like wheat and timber—but also increased competition for local merchants and redefined spatial relationships. If prices on main street were too high, citizens of once isolated communities like Klamath Falls and Coeur d'Alene needed only to thumb through catalogs and order merchandise from distant supply houses like Montgomery Ward or Sears Roebuck in Chicago and have it shipped west by rail. Travel on business or to visit friends and relatives became easy, and if one went first class in one of the ornate sleeping cars, the journey might actually be pleasurable.

But this new freedom had its price. Sometimes the price was relatively insignificant, as when railroads adopted standard time zones in 1883 and individual communities chose to abandon the multitude of local standards formerly used. For travelers it meant arranging their lives according to a railroad timetable.

Sometimes the price was much greater. Except in Pacific Coast ports, westerners were much more dependent upon railroads than most people living east of the Mississippi. After all, many western communities were children of the steel rail, and the timber, mineral, and agricultural industries of the interior Northwest looked to rail transportation for survival. Railroads made commercial agriculture the lifeblood of the Palouse, but they did not always respond to farmers' needs: in the early 1890s when farmers were unable to secure enough boxcars to haul their unusually heavy harvest of grain to market, they protested loudly. Farmers across the Pacific Northwest learned similar lessons in dependence.

Railroad power required residents of Washington's Yakima Valley to make a series of abrupt and traumatic adjustments. When the Northern Pacific Railroad first proposed to route its Cascade Branch through the area in the mid-1880s, the five hundred residents of Yakima City were confident

RAILROADS AND WESTERN SETTLEMENT

Railroads avidly promoted settlement of their huge tracts of western land through sales campaigns both in North America and in Europe. Their advertisements appeared in thousands of newspapers, and they distributed millions of elaborate, often multicolored promotional brochures in English, German, Norwegian, and other languages. The Northern Pacific published its own promotional magazine, and its timetables carefully explained to travelers how to acquire a homestead in the new Northwest. Railroads regularly ran homeseekers' specials and hauled immigrant families and their belongings at reduced rates.

Agents met immigrants at dockside in New York and other East Coast ports and helped them travel west to settle on lands the company had reserved for certain nationalities. That arrangement is one reason why Germans, Scandinavians, and Russians tended to cluster in distinct rural settlements scattered from the Dakotas to Washington.

The selling price of the railroad land generally ranged from $1.25 to $20.00 an acre, depending on its perceived value, but with frequent cash discounts. The companies also instituted a variety of low down payment plans to speed settlement and generate much-needed traffic.

Despite their apparent beneficence, railroads were often the targets of complaint. In eastern Washington, the slow rate at which the Northern Pacific proceeded with the management of its land grant caused early settlers to fear that they might be evicted or forced to pay exorbitant fees to gain legal title to their holdings.

that their community would prosper. Yakima City's growing population and its location at a constricted part of the valley where tracklayers had no choice but to pass through the town seemingly guaranteed that the Northern Pacific would select the site for its station and yards. But the railroad ran its tracks straight through Yakima City without erecting so much as a toolshed and chose instead to build an entirely new town on railroad land a few miles away. On a sagebrush plain the Northern Pacific laid out a settlement called North Yakima.

A wail of protest went up from residents of Yakima City but to no avail. Northern Pacific officials dismissed the proposed station site there as marshy and unsuited for building, although some people claimed the railroad had earlier failed to extort free land for its right-of-way and station and was now exacting its revenge. Regardless of the circumstances, Yakima City residents looked on helplessly as Northern Pacific trains steamed through their town without stopping.

North Yakima dated from 4 February 1885. Its city plan reserved space for the new capitol of Washington, which many observers expected to be moved soon from Olympia to a more central location. The Northern Pacific also provided that any businessman who wanted to relocate from Yakima City could have a new building site free. As a result many stores and business structures were moved intact on rollers to North Yakima. The local bank continued to operate as usual as it crept along to the new location.

Some residents of Yakima City stubbornly fought back, however, and one of them threatened to use a few cans of nitroglycerine to destroy railroad facilities. That was perhaps not an idle threat, for someone did bomb the office of the *Yakima Signal* as the newspaper inched its way to the new town. Finally, in order to defuse the threat of violence, the railroad agreed to pay transportation costs for anyone who wished to relocate, not just for merchants, but hostility to what many people perceived as an unprecedented display of railroad power lingered. An editorial cartoon in the *Seattle Press* in October 1887 showed a Northern Pacific official riding a train through tumbledown Yakima City and thumbing his nose, while just ahead lay a prosperous North Yakima. Antirailroad agitation formed the basis for several political protest movements in the Yakima Valley during the next two decades.

By early 1918 when North Yakima officially shortened its name to Yakima and became the metropolis of a prosperous agricultural valley, the original Yakima City was long gone. But what happened there thirty years earlier illustrated how westerners not yet a generation removed from pioneer life were forced to make rapid and often painful adjustments to the new America created by transcontinental railroads. The Yakima episode was one vivid example of the type of transformation that the region's railroads could demand.

A railroad could also bless or blight a community through freight rates. In an era lacking effective government regulation of economic matters, the only restraints on railroad rates were competition and the willingness of customers to pay. Citizens of Spokane battled that harsh truth for years. They complained that railroads charged more to ship goods from supply houses in Chicago to Spokane than to Pacific coast ports like Seattle and Portland, four hundred miles farther west. In fact, Spokane residents paid freight charges equal to hauling goods to tidewater then back again to Spokane.

Suppose, for example, a Spokane resident ordered something from Sears Roebuck in Chicago in 1897. The cost to ship a hundred pounds of freight first class from Chicago to Seattle or Portland was $2.40, but from Chicago to Spokane the rate was $3.60, or 50 percent more. The reason for this

35. The Oregon Railroad and Navigation Company was
only one of several Pacific Northwest railroads that operated farm demonstration trains to teach farmers how
to improve their crops and livestock. Courtesy Oregon
Historical Society, ORHI 76643.

difference, claimed the railroads, was competition from waterborne carriers, which landlocked Spokane lacked. That rate difference translated into
a higher price in Spokane for everything from seeds and soap to bicycles and
underwear.

Spokane residents battled for the lower or "terminal" rates for years.
When the Interstate Commerce Commission issued an order in Spokane's
favor in 1911, its citizens celebrated in the streets with bells, whistles,
horns, and dancing. But their joy was premature, because the railroads appealed to the United States Commerce Court, and a lengthy legal contest
followed. Not until 1914 did Spokane win its rate fight. And yet, ironically,
in much of eastern Washington and northern Idaho, the rate structure had
favored Spokane over other locales and helped it become a major supply
center.

Railroad stations once functioned as centers of community life, civic showplaces, and portals to all other destinations along the metropolitan corridor. As late as 1919, when commercial radio had yet to make its debut, the best way to follow World Series action—other than to attend the game— was at the depot, where a kindly telegrapher might post each inning's score as it came in on the wire.

Given the fact that railroads were by far America's biggest business, whatever they did had an impact on citizens' lives in the new West. During their heyday from the 1870s until the late 1920s, railroads could not remain outside the public arena even had they wanted to. Their many activities furnished the basis for praise and condemnation, community prosperity and ruin. Their vast landholdings placed them second only to the federal government as agencies of settlement and development.

From the railway age to the present time, no private enterprise—not even the oil companies in the automobile age—occupied a position of similar power and influence. Thus, the story of the Pacific Northwest's railway era is inextricably linked to industrial expansion (most notably the dramatic growth of the region's timber industry), urban development, large-scale im- migration, and political reform movements.

CHAPTER 10

# The Stumps of Enterprise: A Natural Resource–Based Economy

*

Young men equipped with no fancy notions, but with plenty of every day sense, practical experience in some special business or profession, well founded integrity of character, and endowed with enterprise and push, whether with capital or not, rarely make a mistake by coming to the new State of Washington, and a great majority of them achieve much greater success than they could hope for in the East.—Charles T. Conover, "Should Young Men Go West." *Washington Magazine* (1890)

*

Tree stumps symbolized prosperity to nineteenth-century Pacific Northwesterners, because felling trees was often associated with activities that connoted growth and progress. From the forests, builders hacked townsites where blackened stumps still smoldered in the center of newly graded streets; massive stumps once stood at the very doors of Tacoma's best hotels; and enterprising settlers occasionally fashioned snug homes from hollow stumps. Not without reason was early Portland nicknamed Stumptown. The rail baron James J. Hill once quipped to a group of Northwest businessmen that he had seen only four stumps on Puget Sound without a town name attached.

In the early twentieth century, when the lumber industry was the Pacific Northwest's largest employer and economic mainstay, few people questioned whether acres of stumps were ugly or wasteful. Harvesting the region's "limitless" forests was popularly equated only with money and jobs, prosperity and growth. During the "cut and run" era, it mattered little if loggers saved time by sawing trees fifteen feet above ground and left stumps containing thousands of board feet of perfectly good lumber. Beginning with the maritime fur trade, a key feature of the regional economy was dependence on harvesting or extracting nature's wealth. As a result, the history of the Pacific Northwest includes many examples of economic instability and the plunder of natural and human resources.

During the first four decades of the nineteenth century, the region's economic life centered on the trade in skins and furs. Then came an era of commercial agriculture, tidewater sawmills, fish canning, and periodic mining booms. The region's rapid growth during the final two decades of the nineteenth century rested upon an economic foundation that can be summarized in a few monosyllables: wood, fish, grain, and ore. To those basic commodities could be added cattle, sheep, fruit, and coal.

In the early 1880s—the formative decade of the region's modern economic history—much of the Pacific Northwest's future wealth could be described only as potential or undiscovered. At that time the forests blanketing western portions of Oregon and Washington and the Idaho panhandle, apart from the trees at tidewater where lumber could be easily transported to market by sea, had little economic value. Major coalfields in the Cascades and the great mineral bonanza of Idaho's Coeur d'Alene region remained yet undiscovered, and the full agricultural potential of the semiarid interior was not yet apparent. It would take the transforming power of irrigation and a growing network of railway lines to make the sage-covered lands of the Yakima Valley yield an abundance of fruit and those of southern Idaho grow the state's famed potatoes.

### FISHING THE FRONTIER

Commerce in skins and furs undoubtedly ranks as the oldest market activity in the Pacific Northwest, but what ranks second? Forestry? Agriculture? Fisheries? It could be any of those. Each was associated in some way with the Hudson's Bay Company, which, if not always a pioneer, was the first significant developer of the region's agriculture, timber, and marine resources. As early as the 1820s, remote company posts on the Columbia River sold fish to London buyers.

For many years the most important product of the region's fisheries was salmon. Five varieties of salmon were caught along the entire Pacific watershed, especially in Puget Sound and the lower Columbia River. Salmon are anadromous; that is, they spawn in fresh water and spend most of their adult life in the ocean, ranging over thousands of miles. After approximately five years they return home to spawn, sometimes in remote tributaries of the Columbia River a thousand miles or more from the sea, although in recent decades the building of dams has narrowed the fish's inland range.

Over the years, the region's commercial fisheries were by no means limited to salmon. Money was to be made in oysters, clams, shrimp, halibut, and dozens of other edible forms of marine life, not to mention production of fish oil, fertilizer, and algae. Salmon, however, ranked first in commercial value, and the image of millions of them returning upstream, driven by some mysterious instinct to leap rapids and low waterfalls, caused the fish to become as closely identified with the wild Northwest as cod was with New England.

The modern salmon industry of the Pacific Coast originated when Hapgood, Hume, and Company established a small cannery on the Sacramento River in 1864. Two years later the Hume brothers opened a cannery on the lower Columbia River, and that first year they produced 6,000 cases each holding 48 one-pound cans of Chinook salmon, for a total value of $64,000. Profits were spectacular because canned salmon was popular in the East, Great Britain, and other areas as a cheap, nourishing working-class food. From that modest beginning, more than fifty canneries were built along the banks of the Columbia River and its tributaries by 1883, and numerous others dotted the banks of coastal rivers of Oregon and Puget Sound. Astoria, located near the mouth of the Columbia River, became a center of canning operations. The Columbia River salmon catch peaked in 1895 with 635,000 cases, but by that time Puget Sound's cannery output was still larger. Cannery operations on the Sound dated from 1877 and peaked in 1913 with 2.5 million cases. Alaska's salmon canning industry, which had a later beginning, eventually eclipsed that of both Oregon and Washington.

Fishermen were predominantly Scandinavians and Finns, who logged or farmed in the off-season. Many cannery workers were Chinese. Canning was at first a slow, messy business with individual tins requiring careful soldering by hand. Beginning in 1903, however, a revolutionary machine called the Iron Chink dramatically thinned the ranks of cannery workers by doing the work of fifty men. By means of rotating knives and brushes, this machine automatically decapitated and cleaned fish at the rate of one per second. Another change occurred at the turn of the century when numerous small canneries formed cooperatives such as the Columbia River Packers Association to market their products more efficiently and to stabilize profits.

RUDYARD KIPLING ON CANNING

The steamer halted at a rude wooden warehouse built on piles in a lonely reach of the [Columbia] river, and sent in the fish. I followed them up a scale-strewn, fishy incline that led to the cannery. The crazy building was quivering with the machinery on its floors, and a glittering bank of tin-scraps twenty feet high showed where the waste was thrown after the cans had been punched. Only Chinamen were employed on the work, and they looked like blood-besmeared yellow devils, as they crossed the rifts of sun-light that lay upon the floor. When our consignment arrived, the wooden boxes broke of themselves as they were dumped down under a jet of water, and the salmon burst out in a stream of quick-silver. A Chinaman jerked up a twenty-pounder, beheaded and detailed it with two swift strokes of a knife, flicked out its internal arrangements with a third, and cast it into a bloody dyed tank. The headless fish leaped from under his hands as though they were facing a rapid. Other Chinamen pulled them from the vat and thrust them under a thing like a chaffcutter, which, descending, hewed them into unseemly red gobbets fit for the can. More Chinamen with yellow, crooked fingers, jammed the stuff into the cans, which slid down some marvelous machine forthwith, soldering their own tops as they passed. Each can was hastily tested for flaws, and then sunk, with a hundred companions, into a vat of boiling water, there to be half cooked in a few minutes. The cans bulged slightly after the operation, and were therefore slidden along by the trolley-ful to men with needles and soldering irons, who vented them, and soldered the aperture. Except for the label, the "finest Columbia salmon" was ready for the market.—Observation by Rudyard Kipling in 1889 and published in *American Notes* (1899): 59–60

Cutthroat competition and unsound practices, like stringing traps and nets across river mouths so that few adult fish survived to spawn, character-ized commercial fishing almost from the beginning. At times such an ar-mada of fishing craft jammed the lower Columbia that it seemed a person could walk across the river on their decks.

Early on, cannery operators on the Columbia River expressed concern about yearly fluctuations in salmon runs. The Washington legislature de-clared a closed season in 1877; Oregon responded the following year with two weak conservation measures, one regulating the size of openings in gill nets to allow smaller fish to escape, the other prohibiting fishing during certain hours of the week. Neither Oregon nor Washington vigorously en-forced early conservation measures. Over the decades a bewildering accre-tion of laws and regulations—such as those outlawing traps, explosives, and drugs—attempted to protect commercial fishermen from themselves. Quite simply, they possessed technology too efficient to insure their industry's long-term survival.

36. Commercial fishwheels on the Columbia River near
Beacon Rock. After a tour of the area in 1889, Rudyard
Kipling described a typical fishwheel as "infernal arrangement of wire gauze compartments worked by the
current and moved out from a barge in shore to scoop
up the salmon as he races up the river." The fishwheels
are long gone today, but Beacon Rock is a Washington
state park. Courtesy Minnesota Historical Society,
54222.

Hydroelectric dams created another set of problems. Grand Coulee Dam,
which has no fish ladders barred salmon from eleven hundred linear miles
of streams in Washington, Idaho, and British Columbia when it was completed in 1941. Each additional dam on the Columbia and Snake rivers
added nitrogen to water below the spillways. When absorbed into the blood-
stream of fish, nitrogen creates a fatal condition known as the bends. At
times 95 percent of the smolts or young salmon died during their hazard-
filled trip to the sea, primarily as a result of the bends or being chewed up by
turbines in the dams.

The Northwest Power Act of 1980 proposed to restore fish populations
damaged by hydroelectric development. Whether it can actually do so by

artificial propagation remains to be seen. The region's first hatchery was established on the Clackamas River near Portland in 1877. But even with numerous additional hatcheries during the twentieth century, anadromous fish still face many life threats, including the lack of genetic diversity that makes salmon vulnerable to diseases that occasionally kill millions of them while still in the hatchery. Some experts maintain that hatchery-raised salmon lack the superior taste and survival skills of wild salmon.

### THE GROWING IMPORTANCE OF AGRICULTURE

Agriculture in the Pacific Northwest was clearly different from that practiced in the Midwest and border states where the region's first Euro-American settlers originated. The image of pioneers clearing wilderness to create a self-sufficient family farm is common in American history. But that is not an accurate portrait of events in the Pacific Northwest, where both commercial and subsistence agriculture existed simultaneously almost from the beginning. Even before pioneer families of the Willamette Valley first raised grain and livestock to meet their personal needs, Hudson's Bay Company farms supplied food to its own employees as well as to settlers in Russian Alaska.

In 1846, when wheat first became a major crop in the Oregon country, the provisional government declared wheat legal tender and pegged its value at one dollar per bushel. During the California gold rush, the price of Willamette Valley wheat soared to six dollars per bushel, and more than fifty ships entered the Columbia seeking cargoes of grain. Mining booms closer to home during the 1850s and 1860s further stimulated the growth of commercial agriculture.

Wheat and oats, cattle and sheep became the chief commercial products of farm and ranch, but conspicuously missing were the extensive fields of corn and the large herds of swine so typical of agriculture in the Mississippi and Ohio valleys. Corn, that great staple of American agriculture for two centuries, did not thrive in the Willamette Valley: the weather west of the Cascades was too dry during the summer growing season and the nights were too cool. The problem perplexed many an early settler.

Moreover, instead of a continuous expanse of farmland like that stretching across the Midwest from eastern Ohio to central Nebraska, agricultural regions of the Pacific Northwest resembled islands separated from one another by forests, mountains, and vast prairies of sagebrush and native grasses. The Willamette Valley, which received enough moisture to make farming relatively easy for emigrants from the Midwest, was the first of these islands to be settled. Twenty years later, in the early 1860s, the technique of dryland farming to conserve soil moisture transformed the semiarid Walla Walla Valley into an agricultural cornucopia. Its farmers raised substantial quantities of grain and cattle to feed the mining population of Idaho.

Another island of agriculture emerged on the well-watered land east of Puget Sound, which became famed for dairying and truck gardens. Farming techniques perfected in the Walla Walla Valley enabled fields of wheat to spread to other parts of the inland Northwest, relentlessly replacing native grasses on the uplands of eastern Oregon and the rolling hills of the Palouse to create the main breadbasket of the Northwest.

Last to be put to the plow was semiarid land that needed extensive irrigation to yield crops: the Snake River plain of southern Idaho around the turn of the century and the Columbia basin of central Washington beginning in the 1950s. Irrigation first played a significant role in Northwest agriculture during the two decades after 1890. As a result of irrigation, wheat and potato production boomed in southern Idaho, and orchards blossomed in numerous locations once considered too dry for grain or fruit.

"Famous Potatoes!" Because of that slogan on automobile license plates, the potato has become as closely identified with Idaho as dairy products are with Wisconsin. In the 1920s the Gem State still ranked far behind Maine as a potato producer. But in the contest for national supremacy, Idaho's big Russett Burbank spuds eventually stood eye to eye with Maine's, and the easterners blinked first. Idaho gained the title of the nation's number one potato producer in the late 1950s. The growing popularity of french fries in the fast food restaurants that proliferated in recent decades made the Idaho potato one of the most sought-after food items in America.

Even so, no agricultural commodity bulked larger in the Northwest economy than wheat. By 1910 it represented 44.5 percent of the value of all of Washington crops, and Whitman County was declared the richest county per capita in the United States. Wheat was raised mainly in Washington's southeastern quarter, which as early as 1889 accounted for 93 percent of the state's total. Idaho and Oregon also grew wheat, but their production never equaled that of Washington.

Agriculture became a big business and the annual grain harvest in August or September an important and colorful event. Reapers and combines drawn by dozens of horses or mules, smoking and puffing steam-powered threshing machines, and an army of itinerant laborers all contributed to the

37. A typical harvest scene in eastern Oregon at the
turn of the century. The work required an army of
hands: team drivers, field pitchers, stationary steam en
gineers and firemen, separator men, threshers, and laborers who cut, threshed, and sacked wheat. Courtesy
Oregon Historical Society, ORHI 35719.

sense of drama. Gasoline-powered tractors and combines increased in number after 1914 until, by the mid-1930s, mules and horses had largely disappeared from the harvest scene. The amount of labor required to harvest the
crops likewise changed. Approximately 75 horses and 30 men were required
to harvest 1,000 bushels of wheat a day in 1914; now a single operator riding
in an air-conditioned and computer-controlled combine and a couple of
truck drivers can harvest 2,500 to 3,500 bushels a day. As a result, the army
of casual laborers once common in grain-producing areas has disappeared.

In the early days, when the nimble fingers of itinerant harvesters had
sewn up the last sacks of grain, steamboats hauled the interior crop down
the Snake and Columbia rivers to docks in Portland, where much of it
continued by sailing ship to markets as distant as London. It was no small
feat to transport wheat from the Palouse plateau down the rimrock to the
Snake River landings two thousand feet below. The job required aerial
trams, incline railways, special pipelines, and a variety of other innovative
devices.

The development of an extensive network of railroads during the 1880s

A WOMAN'S VIEW OF THE HARVEST

There was another side to the harvest that Annie Pike Greenwood recalled with obvious distaste:

"There is never a moment of stopping for us two women. We can hear the hum of the machine, and through the living-room window, where the table is set the length of the room, we can see the monster spewing forth the ivory straw, which the sun tips with silver glitterings like Christmas-tree tinsel. A cloud of dust, like smoke, hangs over everything.

We do not talk, we two women. We must rush, *rush*, RUSH! There is no such pressure on the men out-of-doors as there is on the women in the kitchen. Everything must be ready on the very dot of time when the threshing-machine stops with a great silence. Probably the earth would change its orbit, and a few planets crash, if it should ever occur that the threshing meal was not exactly ready when the first tableful of men was ready for it. . . .

The best part of threshing is the very tip of the tail of the last day, when you see the monster and its attendant dragon crawling down the road to another farm. You can never know what it is to be really light-hearted and free until you have endured the galley-slavery of a week or two of cooking for threshers."—Annie Pike Greenwood, *We Sagebrush Folk* (1934), 177ff.

made it possible for the first time to ship carloads of wheat from the inland Northwest to the wharves of Seattle and Tacoma. An increasing amount of grain went by railway boxcars to ports on Puget Sound, diminishing Portland's hegemony over the grain trade. Even so, much of the wheat still traveled to market in sacks until rising prices during World War II encouraged growers to switch from burlap bags to the less expensive bulk loading methods still used today.

The soft white winter wheat that predominates in the Pacific Northwest is best suited for cake and pastry flour. By the late twentieth century its main market was Asia, where it was used mainly for noodles. As early as the mid-1970s, Japan imported 85 percent of all Northwest wheat.

The agricultural product that ranked second only to grain in its contribution to the Northwest economy was livestock. The region's cattle industry originated from stock raised at several Hudson's Bay Company posts and at mission stations or from animals driven to the Pacific Northwest over the Oregon Trail or from California and Texas. Cattle raising first emerged as a large-scale enterprise in the interior Northwest during the mining boom of the 1860s when the high cost of meat encouraged some disillusioned miners to become stock raisers. One early Idaho entrepreneur, William Byron, imported five hundred head of cattle from Washington Territory in the spring of 1864 and butchered them to feed the miners of the Boise Basin.

Byron and others soon discovered that cattle thrived on the bunchgrass and edible varieties of sage that covered the Snake River plain. More cattle soon arrived from Texas, Nebraska, and California. With rangeland open to all, seemingly all it took to launch a profitable business was a few cows and a branding iron. Stockmen also raised horses to supply draft animals for the growing number of stage and freight lines.

By the 1870s some herds numbered as many as twenty to thirty thousand animals. Cattlemen held roundup twice a year. In the spring they concentrated on branding and marking bull calves, in the fall on sorting out fat beef for market. To help with this arduous work the largest ranchers employed hundreds of young men as cowboys, about three hands for every thousand animals. The Pacific Northwest's first cowboys were often called "vaqueros," and as late as the 1880s the foremen of large ranches on the Snake River plain were "major domos." A number of early ranching terms and many of the region's first cowboys were of Hispanic origin: both had migrated north from Texas and the American Southwest.

Capital from California and Nevada enabled several of the region's cattle kings to achieve prominence during the heyday of the open range. One of the most notable was Peter French of southeastern Oregon. Early in the 1880s he organized the French-Glenn Livestock Company, an empire that controlled a hundred thousand acres of land. Like his counterparts in Texas, French raised thousands of head of cattle and hired cowboys to manage them. A dominating personality who feuded with the homesteaders encroaching on his range, French died in 1897 when a settler gunned him down.

Railroads and the introduction of stock cars and refrigerated cars during the last years of the nineteenth century opened up markets as distant as Chicago for Northwest beef, but the new mode of transportation also brought an army of homesteaders to acquire prime grazing land for their farms. Their insistence that cattlemen confine their herds to privately owned and fenced-in land, together with a series of harsh winters that decimated the herds during the 1880s, hastened the end of the open range.

Sheep arrived in the Pacific Northwest by a variety of means, notably through the agricultural activities of the Hudson's Bay Company. Marcus Whitman imported sheep from Hawaii to his mission station and taught Indians how to herd them. From California, herders drove several thousand sheep north to the Willamette Valley, more came over the Oregon Trail, and some prized specimens arrived by boat from as far away as England, Australia, and New Zealand. During the past century, Idaho frequently ranked as the nation's leading producer of lambs and sheep.

Sheep thrived best on the grasslands of the interior, but there they en-

38. A flock of sheep gathers beside the Columbia River
ferry at Lyle, Washington. Courtesy Oregon Historical
Society, Gi 181.

countered opposition from cattlemen. To cattlemen, the sheepmen were
interlopers whose woolly beasts destroyed the range for cattle. Confrontations took place in various legal arenas as well as on remote parts of the
range, where scattered incidents of vandalism and violence were meant to
discourage sheepmen.

Strife culminated in 1896 with the murder of two sheepherders in an
isolated area southeast of present-day Twin Falls, Idaho. "Diamondfield"
Jack Davis was arrested for the crime. The employee of a large cattle company, he was found guilty on the basis of largely circumstantial evidence
and sentenced to hang. The celebrated case aroused intense feeling among
the cattlemen who proclaimed his innocence and the sheepmen who favored execution. In 1899 Davis survived a dramatic last-minute reprieve
from the gallows and was pardoned in 1902. This episode did not end the
conflict, however. Several episodes of sheep shooting occurred in central
Oregon at the turn of the century.

The economic value of sheep lay in their lambs, mutton, and wool, the latter finding its way to the region's mills after 1857. In that year the first textile mill west of the Mississippi opened in Salem. Five more woolen mills were in operation in the Willamette Valley by 1866. By the turn of the century, Pendleton had become one of the leading wool-processing centers in the United States. Today the town's name is synonymous with the quality clothing and blankets produced by the Pendleton Woolen Mills, a company that dates from 1909, although most of its plants are now located in places other than Pendleton.

The region's first orchard was located at Fort Vancouver. Twenty years later, in 1847, Henderson Luelling established a nursery in Milwaukie, near Portland. He had carried both seedlings and grafted trees over the Oregon Trail in boxes fitted inside a covered wagon. By the early 1850s, enterprising Oregonians sold fruit to California miners. In one year alone in the early 1860s, 3.5 million pounds of Oregon apples reached San Francisco. After completion of a northern transcontinental railroad and the development of refrigerated cars, Northwest fruit traveled to eastern markets. During the next two decades, orchards became an important source of supplemental income to farmers in several parts of the region.

Large-scale commercial orchards became common between 1905 and 1915. Oregon's Hood River and Rogue River valleys and the irrigated lands of Washington's Yakima, Wenatchee, and Okanogan valleys emerged as major producers of apples, pears, prunes, and cherries. In 1908, during a phenomenon known as "apple fever," Washington growers planted at least one million apple trees. By 1917 the state stood first in the nation in apple production.

During the boom years it seemed easier to develop new and better varieties of fruit than to market them or control the growers' tendency to overproduce. The result was a business that oscillated between good times and bad. During the apple glut of the 1920s, Northwest orchardists ripped out millions of fruit trees. In an effort to improve their marketing, orchardists formed cooperative organizations such as the Hood River Apple Growers Union, which developed a brand name, Diamond Brand, for its products. There was also the problem of weather: when in 1919 a disastrous freeze killed many apple trees in the Hood River Valley, growers started replacing them with pear trees, which today account for three-quarters of the valley's fruit production.

The region's beet sugar industry is another story of boom-and-bust. Begun by Mormon pioneers in Utah, it became a big business in the early twentieth century when the Northwest's first beet sugar factory opened near Idaho Falls in 1903. This plant subsequently became part of the Utah-Idaho Sugar Company. When soft drink manufacturers increased their use of corn sweeteners during the 1970s, they dealt the beet sugar industry a severe blow.

Engaged in what was almost an agricultural sideshow during the first three decades of the twentieth century were the region's stump farmers, a hearty but inevitably impoverished lot who had enough energy and optimism to spend countless hours blasting and pulling out stumps in an attempt to convert infertile patches of logged-off land into pastures and fields. Unscrupulous promoters lured many an unsuspecting person to that backbreaking way of life.

### DIGGING FOR DOLLARS

The development of commercial agriculture in the Pacific Northwest owed much to mining booms that created the first sizable local and regional markets for the products of farm and ranch. The great era of western mineral bonanzas lasted fifty years—from the discovery of gold in California in 1848 to the Klondike rush of 1898. As an important economic activity in the Pacific Northwest, mining dates from the early 1850s, when prospectors discovered gold in several southern Oregon locales (notably Jacksonville) and in north-central Washington near Fort Colville. A major find occurred on the Fraser River in 1858 and briefly rivaled the bonanza in California. The great number of Americans streaming across the international boundary so worried James Douglas, governor of Vancouver Island, that he preemptorily extended British authority to the mainland and thereby set the stage for the creation of British Columbia. The Fraser River rush was the first of many mining booms that lured Americans north of the international boundary to seek their fortunes.

More of the precious yellow metal was discovered in eastern Oregon, Idaho, and Montana during the 1860s. These mining rushes were responsible for creation of Idaho and Montana Territories and the growth of communities like Walla Walla and Boise. But after the gold fever of the 1860s subsided, the Pacific Northwest's mining industry experienced a long and disappointing decade during the 1870s without any significant new finds.

In 1872 Congress passed a law to give prospectors priority to use and buy federal lands once they located valuable mineral deposits on them. The law dangled the promise of unencumbered riches and cheap land to hasten development of the West's natural resources. But the 1872 law, critics later charged, gave the mining industry many advantages at taxpayer expense while leaving the land scarred and polluted. It remains a source of controversy today.

Whether spurred by the new mining law or not, boom times returned in 1880 with a lead-silver rush to Idaho's Wood River Valley (now the Sun Valley area) that was reminiscent of the Boise Basin excitement twenty years earlier. The Wood River boom was only the beginning of a new era of prosperity. When prospectors discovered yet another bonanza on a fork of the Coeur d'Alene River in northern Idaho, they set in motion one of the region's biggest mining stampedes. The new rush occurred during the winter and spring of 1883–84 when five thousand gold seekers each scrambled to reach the diggings first. Buoyed by the hope of sudden riches, they braved twenty-foot-deep snowdrifts in the passes by using toboggans and snowshoes, the only transportation available until the snow melted some months later.

The first mineral to be discovered in the remote creek beds was gold, which miners at first recovered using relatively simple and inexpensive placer methods. Many of those who staked claims were farmers from the nearby Palouse country. But by the time Noah Kellogg, an unemployed carpenter, discovered silver on the south fork of the Coeur d'Alene River in 1885, the character of the bonanza had already begun to change dramatically as mining rapidly became more complex and expensive. Silver, unlike the gold discovered earlier, was not to be recovered by agrarians who worked their claims after the harvest.

A prospector could remove gold from gravel deposits in creek beds using such simple tools as a shovel, pick, and pan, or a rocker or sluice box constructed from wood near at hand. Panning was used mainly for sampling deposits; it was simply too time consuming compared to other, more efficient technologies. The exact method of placer operation depended more than anything else on the availability of water: where it was plentiful, sluices were preferred; rockers worked best where water had to be used sparingly.

More expensive methods of surface mining required water cannons called monitors. Another example of advanced mining technology was the dredge, essentially a floating sluice box equipped with a digging apparatus, but large dredges were far too expensive for the average miner to purchase. Lode or hard rock mining, which involved tunneling into the earth and hauling out gold-bearing rock by the ton to refine a few ounces of the precious yellow metal, compounded the problems of complex technology and high cost. Silver, unlike gold, never occurred naturally in pure form and thus could be recovered only through lode mining, which required large sums of money to develop the mines, build milling and smelting facilities, and extend railway lines.

As a result of large-scale industrial mining, the Coeur d'Alene region quickly became the domain of giant mining enterprises whose hired miners held a status not unlike that of contemporary factory hands in the East. The miners were dependent upon employers for wages and lived in isolated communities that bore a remarkable resemblance to the drab, grimy industrial villages of Pennsylvania and eastern Ohio. Hand drilling and blasting with black powder was laborious, slow, and dangerous. While innovations like dynamite and the pneumatic drill made work easier, they also posed serious health hazards. Early versions of the pneumatic drill spewed out such thick clouds of silicosis-causing dust that they were termed "widow-makers."

One of Idaho's silver mines, the Sunshine near Kellogg, would ultimately yield more of the white metal than all the mines of Nevada's famed Comstock Lode. When in 1985 the billionth ounce of silver was mined in the valley, the Coeur d'Alene district claimed the largest recorded silver production in the world. Nonetheless, most of the capital required to develop these great metal mines and most of the dividends they paid would pass into the hands of investors from outside the district. Almost from the beginning, Spokane became the main supply point for the Coeur d'Alene mines and their dominant urban center. Strengthening this relationship was a combination of boat and railway links between the growing Washington metropolis and the dozen or more mining towns of the Idaho panhandle.

All three Northwest states produced copper but never in the quantity discovered under Butte, Montana, in the 1880s. As Butte evolved into one of the greatest mining camps on earth, it exerted a major influence on industrial relations in the Coeur d'Alenes. Marcus Daly, an Irish immigrant, purchased what he thought was a silver mine in 1878 for $30,000; the Anaconda subsequently developed into one of the largest and most valuable copper mines in the world, supplying a metal for which demand grew with the dawn of the electric age. The recovery of copper, like silver, involved lode mining, expensive reduction works, and a large force of hired miners and other hands. And if anything, industrial mining gave Butte an even grimmer physical appearance than that of the Coeur d'Alene towns. A frequent by-product of large-scale silver and copper mining was the industrial violence that made Butte and the Coeur d'Alene mining district bywords for labor disputes and bloodshed.

Besides metals and a variety of valuable industrial minerals like sand, salt, gravel, and phosphate, the Pacific Northwest contained deposits of coal. Modest-scale mines opened on Oregon's Coos Bay in 1853, and the coal sold profitably in California. During the 1870s and 1880s, much larger mines opened in the Washington Cascades. Sizable operations located in the foothills east of Seattle and Tacoma and west of Ellensburg employed several hundred men and supplied coal for railroads and home heating in markets as distant as San Francisco. Washington coal mines remained important until shortly after the First World War when they, and their Coos Bay and Vancouver Island counterparts, found it impossible to compete successfully with California oil. Oil, in fact, remains one important mineral not found in commercial quantities in the Pacific Northwest, although some geologists are still hopeful of finding deposits off the Oregon coast or under the basalt of the Columbia plateau.

## TALL TIMBER COUNTRY

An estimated seventy million acres of commercial forest land once blanketed the Pacific Northwest. Douglas fir, spruce, hemlock, and cedar were the predominant species west of the Cascade Range; ponderosa pine was dominant on the eastern slopes, and western white pine in the panhandle of Idaho. No economic activity is today more closely identified in the popular mind with the Pacific Northwest than logging and sawmilling, and for good reason. In 1910, when Washington was the nation's number one lumber-producing state, 63 percent of its wageworkers depended upon the forest products industry for jobs. That number remained well above 50 percent for many years.

Harvesting the vast timber wealth of the Pacific Northwest originally resembled mining more than agriculture. Here was a natural resource only to be exploited, with little thought given to conservation or sustained yields. First to consider the commercial possibilities of Northwest timber was the multifaceted Hudson's Bay Company, which erected the region's initial sawmill in 1827 near Fort Vancouver. After expanding its operations, the mill shipped lumber as far as the Hawaiian Islands. Many early facilities were crude and hand operated, but an increasing number were powered by water or steam. As early as 1850 a steam-driven mill operated in Portland, and by the following year Oregon City had five mills, all driven by water.

Devastating fires in San Francisco created demand for timber to rebuild the city. In response, several milltowns on Puget Sound were founded about 1852–53, where the waters never froze and thick forest lined the shores. In

39. A Washington lumber camp. Such places flourished
in the early twentieth century, with most of them located either on river banks or deep in the woods alongside the tracks of logging railroads built by timber
companies. As the forest was cut, the camps moved too.
Courtesy Special Collections Division, University of
Washington Libraries, UW 1765.

1853, F. C. Talbot and his partner, Andrew Jackson Pope, two young Maine
natives who had gone to California during the gold rush and entered the
timber business there, selected a site on Puget Sound to build a large steam-
powered sawmill. Called Port Gamble, the development physically resembled a New England mill village and was the first of several company towns
to dot the shores of Puget Sound. Pope and Talbot chose the site because
miles of virgin timber stretched back from the shoreline, and a natural deepwater anchorage protected ships from Pacific storms. By year's end, additional entrepreneurs had followed Pope and Talbot's lead, and during the
next several years, Port Blakely, Port Ludlow, and other company towns
kept busy meeting the lumber needs of San Francisco, Hawaii, and Asia. At

one time the Puget Sound lumber fleet numbered approximately 150 vessels.

Until the early 1880s logging was confined mainly to the water's edge, where the "cargo mills" of Puget Sound, Grays Harbor, the lower Columbia River, and Coos Bay served far-flung markets. The orientation of the industry was toward San Francisco, the largest consumer of timber products on the West Coast and home to several businessmen who reaped fortunes from cheap and easily acquired timberlands of the Pacific Northwest. The completion of the Northern Pacific line offered access to markets east of the Rocky Mountains, but the key to success remained railroad rates low enough to allow Pacific Northwest lumber to compete successfully with lumber from the Great Lakes and the South. That did not happen until after the turn of the century. Until then, the railroad boom of the 1880s and early 1890s created a local market for ties, bridge timbers, and building materials for stations and other trackside structures.

Loggers moving to the Pacific Northwest encountered problems unknown in the forests of the Great Lakes states. The uneven terrain and gargantuan size of Northwest trees—Douglas firs sometimes stood more than three hundred feet tall and western red cedar occasionally grew fifteen feet in diameter—made logs difficult to transport to the mills, especially through the mud and snow of winter. One technique was to construct a corduroy roadway of logs partially sunk into the earth, grease them, and use oxen to skid timber across them to the mills at tidewater. When cheap drinking establishments appeared alongside the mills, the expression "skid road" acquired a dual meaning, the more enduring of which was corrupted into today's "skid row." Another technique for getting logs to the mill was to float them down the mountainsides in long water-filled troughs called flumes. A third method was to float logs down a river, sometimes with the aid of splash dams that temporarily raised the water level on remote tributaries.

The development of special narrow-gauge logging railroads in the 1880s opened up hitherto inaccessible stands of trees at a time when timber near tidewater was becoming depleted. Eventually, thousands of miles of such lines snaked through the woods; virtually every county in Oregon had at least one logging railroad by 1910. The development of heavy-duty trucks made logging railroads rarities by the end of the Second World War.

The railroad was only one of many technological innovations to change the nature of the timber industry. Until the 1880s, trees were felled with axes and cut or "bucked" into standard lengths with crosscut saws com-

217

monly called Swede fiddles or misery whips. When loggers in the California redwoods discovered that they could use saws to fell trees, the new technique spread quickly up the coast in the 1880s. The two-man crosscut saw became the logger's principal tool. Next came the steam donkey—a stationary steam engine invented by John Dolbeer in 1881 to yard logs to a railroad siding or to a waterway.

High-lead logging dates from the years 1905–10, and it further speeded operations during the next forty years. A high-climber used a special belt and spiked boots to muscle his way some two hundred feet up the side of a spar tree; then he chopped off the top (which itself could be as large as an entire tree in the Midwest or East) and attached the heavy pulleys and cables used to haul logs clear of stumps and debris to a landing. Like so many innovations, the high-lead technique increased the opportunity for mishap and helped make logging one of the most dangerous occupations in the United States.

Innovation also changed the nature of sawmilling, where circular saws gave way to band saws after 1876. Such saws decreased waste and increased by ten times the amount of lumber a mill could cut in a day. Drying kilns helped shorten the time it took to prepare the lumber for market. The new technology—especially the steam donkeys and logging railway—was expensive, however, and gave a competitive edge to individuals and corporations already having accumulated enough money to buy and operate it. Small firms (commonly called gyppo outfits after the 1930s) were increasingly forced to operate in the shadow of industrial giants.

The great age of Pacific Northwest timber production dawned at the turn of the century, when timbermen from the Great Lakes states looked west to replace their dwindling sources of supply. A harbinger of change occurred in 1888 when a group of Minnesota businessmen purchased eighty thousand acres of Pacific Northwest timberland and founded the St. Paul and Tacoma Lumber Company. This firm opened the region's largest sawmill in Tacoma to produce for local needs, the cargo trade, and markets in the East. Directors of the company expected to receive the cheap railroad rates necessary for Puget Sound timber to compete successfully in markets east of the Rocky Mountains. But their dreams were not fully realized until more than a decade later, when another Minnesota timber baron turned his attention to the forests of the far Northwest.

He was Frederick Weyerhaeuser, a businessman who had already reaped a fortune from the forests of Wisconsin and Minnesota during the post–Civil War era and who came to dominate the Pacific Northwest timber industry after 1900. Weyerhaeuser's Summit Avenue neighbor in St. Paul was the railroad magnate James J. Hill, who badly needed capital for a financial transaction involving one of his railroads. Accordingly, Hill offered Weyerhaeuser and associates nine hundred thousand acres of the Northern Pacific Railroad land grant—mostly Douglas fir forest—for six dollars an acre. It was one of the largest private land transfers in American history.

Although the land Weyerhaeuser acquired from Hill in 1900 later seemed like a colossal bargain, many of the timberman's friends initially regarded it as an exceedingly speculative purchase. Could Northwest lumber compete successfully with lumber from the South? Perhaps not in 1900, but Weyerhaeuser was looking to the future, and because they trusted his judgment, many lesser capitalists soon joined the "great rush" to buy Pacific Northwest timberland. Sawmills went up by the hundreds. In eastern Washington and northern Idaho alone, more than three hundred sawmills were producing lumber by 1909. Lake Coeur d'Alene resembled an enormous millpond as log booms lined its shore. Construction of a giant mill in 1905 gave rise to the company town of Potlatch and typified the trend to bigness overtaking the industry. A construction boom in the Dakotas and the massive rebuilding after the San Francisco earthquake and fire of 1906 stimulated production of Pacific Northwest timber. During that year, mills ran extra shifts to meet the demand in California.

Weyerhaeuser's involvement in the Northwest timber industry took many forms because of the decentralized nature of his financial empire, one that once totaled more than ninety affiliated companies. The Weyerhaeuser family had substantial investments in nine Idaho timber firms, including Boise Payette (now Boise Cascade) and Potlatch, and in this way was instrumental in fostering the timber business in the western white pine forests of the state's panhandle. Prior to Weyerhaeuser involvement, the forests of this rugged and difficult country had little commercial value.

In the early twentieth century, Weyerhaeuser and its affiliated companies owned 26 percent of all timberlands in Washington and nearly 20 percent of those in Oregon. The Weyerhaeuser Timber Company constructed the world's largest sawmill in Everett, Washington, in 1914.

Between 1898 and 1914, Oregon and Idaho tripled their timber production. Shortly before the San Francisco earthquake, Washington became America's leading lumber-producing state, a title it retained for all but one year from 1905 to 1938 when Oregon surpassed it. Oregon trailed Washington for so many years because its stands of timber were less accessible than those that crowded the shores of Puget Sound. From the beginning,

40. In the 1890s, "cigar rafts" transported logs from the lower Columbia River to sawmills as far south as San Diego, California. These seagoing monsters were sometimes more than five hundred feet long with fifty or more tons of log chain. Occasionally one broke up under tow through heavy seas. A few exporters even towed some log rafts to Japan in the early twentieth century. Courtesy Oregon Historical Society, ORHI 11436.

Washington's timber industry also included larger, more heavily capitalized units than those in Oregon or Idaho.

Ruinous competition, overproduction, market chaos, and dependence on railroad rates to compete in distant markets plagued the lumber business. Firms often had to continue operations regardless of the price of lumber simply to cover fixed costs like timberland taxes and investments in equipment. The resulting glut inevitably forced down prices and wages and brought on militant labor activity. Operators formed the West Coast Lumbermen's Association in 1911 to establish industry-wide standards and marketing practices, but the problem of chronic instability endured.

Two technological innovations helped mitigate the industry's financial instability. One was the discovery in 1909 of the sulfate or Kraft process to transform commercially worthless wood like western hemlock into newsprint. For many lumbermen it was like finding a whole new forest. The Northwest's paper industry dates from the construction of a mill at Oregon City in 1866 that used rags and straw, but it did not become significant until the erection of several sulfate- and sulfite-process pulp and paper mills in the 1920s. In time the Pacific Northwest became a leading producer of pulp and paper in the United States. A second innovation was plywood, developed in 1904 at a box and barrel factory near Portland, but that industry did not become commercially important until the mid-1920s. The development of plywood made it possible to recover millions of board feet of wood, once thought lost to forest fires.

An integral part of the Pacific Northwest timber story are the national forest reserves dating from 1891 when Congress permitted President Benjamin Harrison to set aside federal timberland. The measure drew little attention at the time. His successor, Grover Cleveland, added still more land, creating a total of 28 reservations on 41 million acres, but no one equaled the zeal of Theodore Roosevelt who vastly enlarged the national forests. In fact, the name "National Forest" dates from 1907 and the Roosevelt administration.

Roosevelt's zeal for national forests did not go uncontested. To many residents of the Pacific Northwest, the president's move appeared to be an ill-conceived attempt to atone for the nation's profligate past by controlling its remaining forest lands instead of continuing to sell or give them away to private interests. In a region with millions of acres of federal lands waiting to be exploited, the conservation ethic imposed by Uncle Sam seemed certain to lock up resources and stunt growth. A secondary consideration was states' rights: some Pacific Northwesterners believed that individual states, not the federal government, should manage public lands within their boundaries. Others, however, feared that individual states would only give away more land to private interests.

Among Roosevelt's critics was Idaho's Weldon R. Heyburn, who after his election to the U.S. Senate in 1903 became chief spokesman for opponents of the forest reservation system. He considered the reserves a threat to the sovereignty of Idaho and at one point protested to Roosevelt that they paralyzed the state's economic growth. Heyburn headed a successful fight in the

Senate in 1908 to forbid any further expansion of national forests in Oregon, Washington, and Idaho. But the wily Roosevelt set aside seventeen million additional acres of national forest reserves *before* he signed the restrictive measure. Heyburn continued his war on the national forests until his death in 1912. Today there are thirty-four national forests in the Pacific Northwest comprising more than 44 million acres.

## A BOOM-AND-BUST ECONOMY

From early times, the fisheries, farms, ranches, mines, and mills of the far Northwest produced much more than the region's small population could consume. International markets thus played a vital role in the region's economy and were the primary cause of its instability. As early as 1868, a British ship left Portland with a cargo of Northwest wheat for the London market. Ten years later, eighty-one ships transported Northwest grain to markets in Europe, Asia, and Australia. In the early twentieth century, both the Great Northern and Northern Pacific railroads operated steamship lines that linked Pacific Northwest producers to Asian markets. The region was likewise heavily dependent on distant markets within the United States. San Francisco, St. Paul, and other financial centers supplied much of the capital necessary to develop Northwest resources.

Individual states, most notably Idaho, represented extreme cases of economic dependency. In 1900, some 93 percent of Idaho employees engaged in stock raising produced for markets beyond the state. That figure was 97 percent for the gold and silver industry, 90 percent in the lead and zinc industry; and 67 percent in lumber and logging. By contrast, only about 10 percent of Idaho workers engaged in general and crop agriculture produced for markets outside the state.

The Pacific Northwest, in short, was vulnerable to fluctuations in the national and international economy. At times the region's economy careened along like a roller coaster, as it alternated between phases of boom-and-bust. In no industry did the ride seem wilder than in lumber. Competition was keen—not only among Northwest firms, but also between companies in the Northwest and those in other regions, most notably the South. Because of the high cost of rail transportation, only the very best Northwest lumber could compete with Southern lumber in the Midwest market.

It was not easy for the Pacific Northwest to overcome its role as a producer of raw materials or semifinished items like dimensional lumber. Wage earners engaged in manufacturing constituted only 4.2 percent of

41. C. E. Watkins photographed the Oswego Iron
Works, located near Portland, in 1867. Courtesy Oregon
Historical Society, ORHI 21593.

Oregon's population in 1900. The figures for Washington and Idaho were 6.6 and 0.9 percent. Not until the United States entered the First World War in 1917 did manufacturing other than of wood products become a significant component of the region's economy.

Prior to the growth of the shipbuilding industry during World War I, the region's largest manufacturing establishments were those that milled wheat into flour and wood into dimensional lumber. Until the Second World War, flour milling ranked second to lumber among all manufacturing industries in the Pacific Northwest. Smaller establishments canned fish, wove woolen fabric, or produced a variety of specialized wood products such as shingles, doors, molding, and furniture. Other companies produced some of the tools used in the region's extractive industries. Foundries, woodworking shops, tanneries, meat-packers, bakeries, and breweries were among the important small-scale manufacturers.

Overoptimistic businessmen erected an iron works seven miles south of

Portland in 1866 and a year later shipped fifty tons of iron to San Francisco. The plant at Lake Oswego was abandoned in 1894 because of the uncertain market and the low quality of local iron ore and coal. Peter Kirk, an experienced ironmaster from England, and a group of eastern investors attempted to build a steel mill near Seattle in the early 1890s, but the venture failed even before the mill was completed. Kirk's project lacked raw materials and a suitable market. The most dramatic struggle to develop a profitable iron and steel industry in the Pacific Northwest took place in Irondale, near Port Townsend, from 1881 to 1919. The venture ultimately failed because steel mills in Pittsburgh and other eastern centers of production sold their product cheaper in Washington than any local mill could. Eastern manufacturing and transportation advantages would for many years after 1900 overwhelm would-be competitors in the Pacific Northwest. Irondale, in fact, represented the last attempt to develop an iron and steel industry on the West Coast until the Second World War.

Even with the growth of large-scale manufacturing outside the forest products industry after 1917, the Pacific Northwest was unable to escape the boom-and-bust cycles. Several times during the twentieth century, residents had to learn anew the unpleasant facts of economic life in a hinterland.

CHAPTER II

# A Quickening Pace of Life:
# Immigration and Urban Growth

*

I saw Tacoma in 1887, and again in 1889 and 1890, and the growth of the city in this short time was such that in both cases I could hardly recognize the place. It seemed as if some fairy had visited the town and changed every black stump into a four-story brick building by touching it with her wand. The cause of this sudden "spurt" was the completion of the Cascade Division of the Northern Pacific Railroad, and the Stampede Tunnel, which opened up the vast coal-fields along this road, and made the Pacific Coast cities independent of Pennsylvania coal.—Henry T. Finck, *The Pacific Coast Scenic Tour* (1890): 220.

*

During the ten years following completion of a northern transcontinental railroad in 1883, the Pacific Northwest experienced a rate of growth seldom equaled in other regions of the United States. A person who visited Seattle in 1880 and returned in 1893 would barely recognize the place. The straggling village of wooden structures and dirt streets had blossomed into a metropolis of brick and stone, its thoroughfares bustling with trade and commerce. There were substantial business blocks, pretentious residences, churches, schools, a university, and social organizations—all symbolizing economic achievement and cultural refinement—electric lights, gasworks, and factories and plants manufacturing everything from soda water and cigars to furniture and stump pullers. An expanding network of streetcar lines encouraged the growth of new neighborhoods at the city's edge.

The region experienced some temporary setbacks, as occurred when a

GROWTH DURING THE 1880S

(SELECTED STATISTICS)

|  | *1880* | *1890* | *Percentage Increase* |
|---|---|---|---|
| Population: |  |  |  |
| Idaho | 32,610 | 84,385 | 158.8 |
| Oregon | 174,768 | 313,767 | 79.5 |
| Washington | 75,116 | 349,390 | 365.1 |
| Miles of Railroad (single track): |  |  |  |
| Idaho | 206 | 945 | 358.7 |
| Oregon | 347 | 1,433 | 313.0 |
| Washington | 212 | 1,775 | 737.3 |
| TOTAL | 765 | 4,153 | 442.9 |
| True Value of Real and Personal Property | $245,000,000 | $1,558,991,511 | 536.3 |
| Capital in Manufacturing | $10,191,768 | $77,732,470 | 662.7 |
| Average No. Acres in Farms | 5,951,931 | 12,391,344 | 108.2 |
| Agricultural Production: |  |  |  |
| Bushels of wheat | 9,941,921 | 26,760,959 | 169.2 |
| Pounds of wool | 7,234,796 | 13,658,945 | 88.8 |

short but severe depression sparked social turmoil in the mid-1880s or when fires ravaged Seattle, Spokane, and Ellensburg in 1889. The fire in June of that year reduced to rubble more than thirty blocks of downtown Seattle; the damage totaled as much as $20 million. Certainly not all statistics registered increases. The commercial value of the output of Oregon's fish canneries fell 57 percent between 1880 and 1889 and cost two thousand workers their jobs, but a huge increase in the value of the output of Washington fish canneries offset that loss. Certain statistics considered accurate barometers of regional development climbed impressively during succeeding decades, but so many statistics registered gains during the 1880s that Pacific Northwesterners perceived the decade as a time of unprecedented growth and of fundamental changes in a number of social and economic relationships.

Some of these changes are not easily quantified. Thousands of newcomers who arrived after the completion of the Northern Pacific in 1883 left an especially enduring impression upon the character of Washington Territory. Their numbers undermined the power and influence of the pioneer generation and gave Puget Sound and Washington an unsettled, sometimes rambunctious political character. Because a much lower percentage of newcomers settled in Oregon, they were more easily absorbed into existing society; the established communities of pioneer families in Portland and Salem thus maintained their dominance in a conservative state. Moreover, Oregon remained essentially a state of home-owned enterprises during the 1880s, while Washington and Idaho grew increasingly dependent upon outside capital to develop their natural resources.

PATTERNS OF IMMIGRATION AND SETTLEMENT

Who were the new arrivals and why did they come? Until completion of a northern transcontinental railroad, the Pacific Northwest remained isolated from America's main population centers. Getting to the Northwest required a long and arduous journey. Additional impediments to settlement were the slow pace of federal land surveys and conflict with the Indians. Finally, there was the problem of ignorance of the region's natural resources. An Olympia editor complained in 1857, "Our territory is not yet fairly known."

Twenty years later every community with faith in its future seemed to have acquired a promoter. In fact, the region's chambers of commerce, local immigration boards, private associations, and railroad and steamship companies were the primary inspiration for the immigration boom of the 1880s. State and territorial governments seemed content to let those agencies shoulder primary responsibility for advertising the region's resources.

Newcomers arrived mainly from other parts of the United States, notably the Middle West. Even so, in 1900 Washington included a higher percentage of foreign-born residents than did the United States as a whole. In that year, 22 percent of Washington's population was foreign born, 16 percent of Oregon's, and 15 percent of Idaho's; the average for the United States was 14 percent. Even more revealing, 47 percent of Washington's residents had at least one foreign-born parent; the national average was 34 percent. The foreign-born population of Portland ranged from 25 to 36 percent between 1860 and 1880, with people who had at least one foreign-born parent numbering as high as 50 percent.

Among the region's foreign born, immigrants from Scandinavia (Norway, Sweden, Iceland, and Denmark), Great Britain, Canada, and Germany were by far the most numerous. These were the so-called old immigrants. The "new immigrants" from southern and eastern Europe did not arrive in significant numbers until the opening decade of the twentieth century. The character of Asian immigration changed as the number of Chinese decreased relative to the number of Japanese people, whose numbers increased noticeably after 1900.

Some immigrant groups arrived as families, and some largely comprised single males. An unbalanced ratio between genders was typical of many early racial, ethnic, and religious groups. Washington's Chinese and Japanese residents in 1900 numbered 8,982 men and 264 women. Portland's Jewish community, which dated from the late 1850s, counted among its first arrivals a preponderance of young, single men, nearly all of them German born or of German parentage.

It was widely believed that many newcomers were Scandinavians. Indeed, Scandinavians began arriving on Puget Sound in large numbers during the 1880s—often after having first settled in Minnesota or Wisconsin. More Swedes and Norwegians settled in Washington in proportion to the already resident population than in any other state. Scandinavians constituted 25 percent of Washington's foreign-born population by 1910, but Norwegians and Swedes never accounted for more than 7 or 8 percent of the state's total population, and the Danish population remained much smaller than that.

Not all new arrivals were Europeans or Asians. The first group of Mexicans in the Pacific Northwest after the fur trade era were mule packers who dominated overland trade routes between northern California and southern Oregon when the mining frontier moved to the Rogue River area in 1851. These packers also served the U.S. Army during the Rogue River War of 1855. Experienced Mexican miners from the state of Sonora were among the thousands of fortune seekers who reached the inland Northwest during the gold rush of the early 1860s. Among the Hispanic miners were also Mexicans from California, Chileans, and Peruvians. One of the important technologies imported from Sonora, where mining antedated that in the American West by more than a century, was the *arrastre*, a large but inexpensive stone device for crushing quartz to remove the gold. After the inland mining rushes of the 1860s, Mexican gold miners, mule packers, and cowboys remained part of Pacific Northwest life for many more years.

Beginning in the early twentieth century, an increasing number of Mexican and Mexican American migrants supplied field labor in the region's expanding agricultural industry. Labor agents recruited whole families of workers from Colorado and Wyoming to tend sugar beet fields in the Pacific

RACE AND ETHNICITY IN THE PACIFIC NORTHWEST, 1880–1910

|  | 1880 | 1890 | 1900 | 1910 |
|---|---|---|---|---|
| Blacks | 865 | 2,989 | 3,912 | 8,201 |
| Native Americans | 6,239 | 20,375 | 19,216 | 19,575 |
| Chinese | 16,004 | 14,807 | 15,493 | 10,931 |
| Japanese | 3 | 385 | 9,409 | 17,710 |
| Irish | 6,883 | 14,607 | 13,135 | 16,957 |
| English | 6,143 | 18,660 | 20,087 | 32,411 |
| German | 7,982 | 29,813 | 33,145 | 52,395 |
| Scandinavian | 4,651 | 32,192 | 40,882 | 98,933 |

Note: The Indian population in 1880 includes only people not living on reservations.

Northwest, so that by the summer of 1919 there were several thousand sugar beet workers in southeastern Idaho of Mexican or Mexican American ancestry. The backbreaking hand labor of thinning sugar beets sometimes lasted from four in the morning until nine at night, and not until the 1950s would mechanization come to the fields. Other Mexicans found better paying jobs in railroad construction and track maintenance, but agriculture remained the primary employer of Hispanic labor.

Patterns of immigration and settlement were not random. Many Greeks who migrated to Idaho clustered in Pocatello, where they formed a predominantly male subcommunity supplying labor to the Oregon Short Line railroad and the metal mines of Utah. Puget Sound tended to attract Swedes and Norwegians because its climate, topography, and job opportunities reminded them of home. Letters from first arrivals helped attract fellow nationals to a particular location, as did ties of family and neighborhood. The foreign-language press played a similar role. At one time, Swedish, Norwegian, Italian, Japanese, and German newspapers were published in Seattle; a Finnish paper was published in Astoria, and a German in Portland. Chinese- and Japanese-language papers in the Northwest date from the 1890s.

For similar reasons, immigrants gravitated to certain occupations and industries: Swedes to lumber and logging, Norwegians and Finns to fishing, Danes to dairying, Irish to construction and mining, Italians to agriculture, Greeks to railroad labor. The Japanese found employment in any one of several manual occupations, including railroad construction, logging and lumbering, fishing, and farming—which typically served them as way stations to entrepreneurship.

Portland's pioneer Jewish community was drawn to merchandising. As early as the 1860s, Jews achieved prominence in the city's retail trade and emerged as a significant influence in community life. Among the most noteworthy of the city's Jewish merchants was Bernard Goldsmith, a jeweler and wholesale merchant who arrived in Portland in 1861, having already become a wealthy man in California. Eight years later Goldsmith was elected to the first of two terms as mayor. The story was much the same in Seattle, a destination of Jewish immigrants from Germany, Poland, and Russia between 1880 and 1914. Members of this Ashkenazic group made up the bulk of Seattle's four thousand Jews in 1910. Since the early twentieth century Seattle also recorded the third-largest concentration of Sephardic (Spanish) Jews in the United States.

A number of distinctive ethnic communities appeared in the Pacific Northwest. Large numbers of Basques who had emigrated from the Iberian Peninsula to California and Nevada, came north to southern Idaho and the Yakima Valley between 1890 and the mid-1920s. Contrary to popular belief, not all Basques were sheepherders. Many congregated in Boise, which became the nation's leading Basque center, and from there they ventured into mining or hired themselves out to construct irrigation canals and dams. As was the case in any community where members of one nationality collected, the Basque community developed its own hotels and boarding-houses. It established a mutual aid society in 1908 to assist people out of work, sick, or temporarily in need of money. They also had a Basque Roman Catholic church.

In all such communities, ethnic groups shared their language, foods, and customs, and in that way they found shelter from the nativist prejudice all too common at the time. Among Northwest Jews, the B'nai B'rith fostered intergroup aid. Modeled after fraternal organizations like the Free and Accepted Masons and the International Order of Odd Fellows and established first in Portland in 1866, the B'nai B'rith provided a sense of fraternity and filled a need in a society that even denied Jews insurance coverage.

Not all such enclaves were located in large cities. In eastern Washington, German farmers established small settlements in the 1880s and soon attracted numerous compatriots. Italians formed a prosperous agricultural community in the Walla Walla Valley that in later years became famous for its produce, especially sweet onions. Though distinct ethnic enclaves tended to disappear as children and grandchildren were assimilated into the

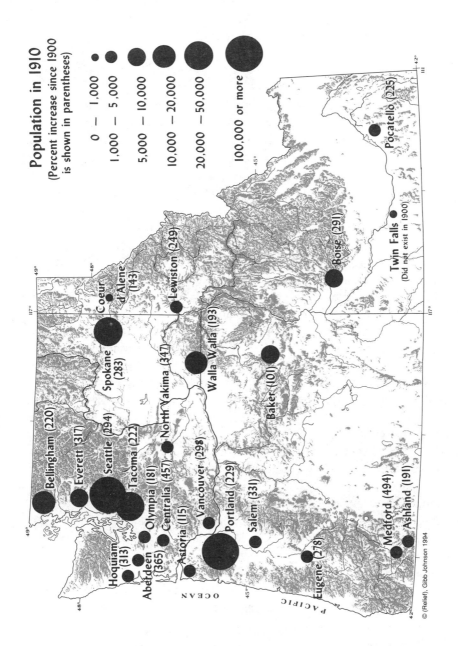

Population in 1910
(Percent increase since 1900
is shown in parentheses)

0 — 1,000
1,000 — 5,000
5,000 — 10,000
10,000 — 20,000
20,000 —50,000
100,000 or more

Pocatello (225)

Boise (291)

Twin Falls
(Did not exist in 1900)

Coeur
d'Alene
(143)

Lewiston (249)

Spokane
(283)

North Yakima (347)

Walla Walla (193)

Baker (101)

Bellingham (220)

Everett (317)

Seattle (294)

Tacoma (222)

Olympia (181)

Centralia (457)

Vancouver (298)

Portland (229)

Salem (331)

Hoquiam
(313)

Abetdeen
(365)

Astoria (115)

Eugene (278)

Medford (494)

Ashland (191)

PACIFIC OCEAN

© (Relief), Glbb Johnson 1994

231

larger community, in Seattle and other cities, international districts remain viable.

Early towns in the Pacific Northwest were invariably fashioned from a similar array of businesses, such as general stores, livery stables, and saloons. Banks, however, were scarce. The first agricultural settlements seldom required cash, and when a miner wanted to stash his gold he sometimes turned to a trustworthy storekeeper who kept it in his safe. Over time some of the merchants evolved into bona fide bankers. A successful town also needed a newspaper to recite its virtues and a hotel or boardinghouse to provide a place to stay for newcomers, businessmen, and speculators.

Saloons were numerous in all but the Mormon settlements of the interior. Especially popular in early mining camps, the saloon functioned as poor man's club and community social center. There were often no restrictions on the vending of liquor, and whisky was the favorite drink, taken straight and at a gulp. Among the familiar names for whiskey were "tangleleg," "lightning," and "tarantula-juice"; one popular name for saloons was "The Bank," an appropriate title considering that so much of the miners' hard-earned capital ended up there. Many of these establishments employed talented musicians at high salaries and engaged "hurdy-gurdy girls" to dance with all comers at fifty cents per dance. With drinks for self and a partner at fifty cents, each dance cost a dollar. Other popular forms of recreation on the mining frontier consisted of gambling, dancing, and the theater. Almost every mining town in Idaho had a "Bella Union" saloon, a "What Cheer" hotel, or a "California" theater.

The general store, filled to the ceiling with all manner of hardware and food, and redolent with the pungent odors of everything from turpentine to cinnamon, was another popular gathering place in any small town, especially so when it also housed the local post office. Storefront advertising typically included the barber's red and white pole, the jeweler's oversize watch, and the tobacconist's wooden Indian. The various businesses lined a main street and together with churches and schools formed the heart of a community. Until the advent of large national enterprises like James Cash Penney's Golden Rule Stores in the early twentieth century, all of these establishments were locally owned. Larger communities had department stores that were lined from floor to ceiling with wood and glass cases displaying everything from hats and corsets to dresses and gloves. One of the lures of the "big city" was the large emporium of commerce that dazzled the eyes of country folk.

42. An island on the land: Aberdeen, Washington, as
photographed by Charles Pratsch in 1889. The settlement dates from 1884 when a sawmill was erected and
the town site platted. By the early twentieth century,
Aberdeen together with Hoquiam, its sister city on
Gray's Harbor, formed a major center for logging and
sawmilling. Courtesy Historical Photograph Collections, Washington State University Libraries, Pratsch
35.

During 1880s and 1890s, as never before, urban centers both large and
small proliferated across the Pacific Northwest. An expanding network of
railroads fostered the growth of numerous village trading centers from
which farmers and ranchers shipped their products to urban markets; many
such places arose along the tracks at regular intervals so that agrarians could
reach town to transact business and return home to their farms and ranches

the same day. Railroad builders' division points and repair shops also spurred the growth of towns. Ultimately, railroads encouraged the growth of a few large metropolitan centers by extending their reach into the hinterlands to link together city and country in the Pacific Northwest and integrate them both into a national hierarchy of municipalities and markets.

Boosted by the expanding network of tracks and agricultural and mineral bonanzas, the population of the Pacific Northwest increased by 165 percent during the growth decade of the 1880s. It is significant that by far the largest part of this increase occurred in urban areas, and most notably in Portland, Seattle, Tacoma, and Spokane. In 1890, those four communities were the only ones in the region having more than eight thousand inhabitants. By 1910 the same four cities included nearly one-third of the entire population of Oregon, Washington, and Idaho.

The noted English writer Rudyard Kipling visited the Pacific Northwest during the extraordinary urban growth of the 1880s and found Tacoma "staggering under a boom of the boomiest." He passed down "ungraded streets that ended abruptly in a fifteen-foot drop and a nest of brambles; along pavements that beginning in pine-plank ended in the living tree." Kipling observed a massive brick and stone foundation awaiting the erection of an opera house and, everywhere, the blackened stumps of trees. "The real-estate agents were selling house-lots on unmade streets miles away for thousands of dollars." On Tacoma's muddy streets "men were babbling about money, town lots, and again money."

Kipling's traveling companion from California observed, "They are all mad here, all mad. A man nearly pulled a gun on me because I didn't agree with him that Tacoma was going to whip San Francisco on the strength of carrots and potatoes. I asked him to tell me what the town produced, and I couldn't get anything out of him except those two darned vegetables." Kipling's response was to take a steamer to British Columbia "to draw breath."[1] Another English visitor during the late 1880s, James Bryce, found Seattle and Tacoma feverish to create instant civilizations.

Every city on the Pacific Coast aspired to become the metropolis of the West. The more aggressive ones skirmished with real and imagined rivals, using weapons that ranged from climate and crime statistics to a barrage of promotional pamphlets. Urban rivalries were deadly serious contests fueled by money, optimism, and the conviction that only growth insured perma-

1. Rudyard Kipling, *From Sea to Sea and Other Sketches* (Garden City, New York: Doubleday, Page, 1925), 2:90–93.

URBAN GROWTH, 1880–1920

(RESIDENTS IN COMMUNITIES OF 2,500 OR MORE)

| | 1880 | 1890 | 1900 | 1910 | 1920 |
|---|---|---|---|---|---|
| *Number* | | | | | |
| Boise | 1,899 | 2,311 | 5,957 | 17,358 | 21,393 |
| Portland | 17,577 | 46,385 | 90,426 | 207,214 | 258,288 |
| Seattle | 3,553 | 42,837 | 80,871 | 237,174 | 315,312 |
| Spokane | 350 | 19,922 | 36,848 | 104,402 | 104,437 |
| Tacoma | 1,098 | 36,006 | 37,714 | 83,743 | 96,965 |
| Walla Walla | 3,588 | 4,709 | 10,049 | 19,364 | 15,503 |
| *Percent* | | | | | |
| Idaho | 0 | 0 | 6.2 | 21.5 | 27.6 |
| Oregon | 14.9 | 27.7 | 32.1 | 45.6 | 49.8 |
| Washington | 9.3 | 35.6 | 40.7 | 53.1 | 54.8 |

nence, stability, and profit. At stake were real estate values, railroad and steamship connections, and community pride.

Tacoma's population at the beginning of the decade stood at 1,098, and at the time of Kipling's 1889 visit approached 36,000, an increase of more than 3,000 percent. At the start of the decade, Walla Walla still ranked as the territory's most populous town, but by 1890 that title belonged to Seattle, which had grown by an impressive 1,000 percent to more than 42,000 residents. Still more spectacular was Spokane's 6,000 percent increase. Portland's 164 percent increase seemed almost leisurely by comparison.

Aggressive urban growth continued into the twentieth century. "The Eastern visitor finds the cities of the Northwestern coast brimful of life, color, significance, picturesque interest; and though the forces which have combined in their making are somewhat similar, each has a distinct character and individuality," noted the visiting journalist Ray Stannard Baker in 1903. "They have the rather unusual capacity of doing big things and talking about them lustily at the same time. It is the cry of the street corners: 'Just watch us grow. See us getting to the front.' "[2]

2. Ray Stannard Baker, "The Great Northwest," *Century Magazine* 65 (March 1903): 658.

THE BIG FOUR CITIES PLUS BOISE

Portland was the city that gravity built. It enjoyed the natural advantage of a location that enabled it to dominate the commerce of both the Willamette and Columbia rivers.

Situated on the west bank of the Willamette twelve miles upriver from its junction with the Columbia, Portland dates from 1843. Because of its favorable location, Portland was the one community in the Pacific Northwest that evolved into a city *before* the coming of transcontinental railroads. In its early years it had several rivals, the most formidable one being Oregon City and its growing complex of mills at the falls of the Willamette. But Portland possessed a superior deepwater anchorage, an advantage that proved decisive after 1848 in securing trade between the Willamette Valley farms and California's goldfields. Its wharves were piled with cargoes of lumber, wheat, fruit, and other farm products leaving the Pacific Northwest for distant markets.

Portland recorded a population of eight hundred in 1850 and was incorporated the following year. Several other milestones marked the community's progress toward metropolitan status. Ladd and Tilton became the Northwest's first bank in 1859 and a financial bulwark of the Oregon country. Five years later, William S. Ladd and Henry W. Corbett opened a telegraph line to California, and on March 5, 1864, the *Oregonian* printed a special edition of news from the East that was only twenty hours old.

Growing trade with the booming gold camps of the upper Columbia region brought Portland prosperity. During the Clearwater rush of 1862, more than ten thousand people traveled to and from the mines in Portland-based steamboats; that number grew to thirty-six thousand in 1864. Freight on the river increased in addition. New wharves had to be built to handle all the traffic. Portland's role as hub of a steamboat monopoly and, later, of Henry Villard's railroad empire further enhanced the city's status. Gold and wheat made Portland rich and smug by the late 1870s, a place untroubled by booms or depressions, unhurried, and not a little complacent in its role as the region's premier metropolis.

But Portland was not a city wholly devoted to material pursuits. In the 1860s it could boast of several churches, a library, a music store, and several newspapers. After a fire in 1873 leveled thirty blocks, substantial brick and stone structures replaced its original wooden buildings. Cities of the Pacific Northwest had a mindless way of imitating their eastern counterparts by platting a monotonous grid of streets without regard for aesthetics or ter-

43. Portland's busy harbor at the turn of the century.
Courtesy Oregon Historical Society, ORHI 44893.

rain. Despite this, Portland became a city noted for its physical dignity and charm, as well as its God-fearing respectability.

As the egalitarianism of frontier days gave way to a more structured society, Portland developed an aristocracy dominated by the Ladds, Corbetts, Failings, and other first families. Yet even in this self-proclaimed enclave of New England on the Willamette, society's villas, chateaus, and castles were forced to coexist with the 30 houses of prostitution and 110 saloons recorded in the 1880 census. A bridge spanned the Willamette River by 1890, and electric streetcars clanged down city streets that reached away from both banks of the river. Three years later, one of the first electric interurban lines in the United States connected Portland to neighboring Oregon City. Electric railways contributed to the growth of numerous satellite communities in Portland's orbit and thus initiated what a later generation would label suburbia and urban sprawl.

Tacoma, which during the 1870s seemed likely to emerge as Portland's main rival, had its beginnings in 1852 around a small sawmill built on the shore of Commencement Bay at the southern end of Puget Sound. The original settlement became Old Tacoma when in 1873 the Northern Pacific selected a site three miles east for its terminus and platted a new Tacoma on the lowlands. The town grew rapidly as factories and wharves fringed the shore and building commenced on the tideflats. Dozens of steam- and sailing ships carried wheat, coal, and lumber from Tacoma's docks to distant markets.

The epithet City of Destiny seemed entirely appropriate when in 1888 Tacoma became the site of the world's largest lumber mill. A host of other sawmills and wood products factories soon followed, but the great depression of the 1890s hit Tacoma especially hard and shattered its dream. By 1900 the city's fate was clearly not to become the dominant metropolis on Puget Sound, though it might legitimately claim to be the lumber capital of America. Destiny, so it seemed, favored Tacoma's archrival to the north.

The growth of Seattle lagged dramatically behind that of Portland and remained barely ahead of Tacoma's until the 1890s. The first settlement inside the present urban boundary of Seattle was at Alki Point in 1851, but this proved such a poor location that settlers moved across Elliott Bay the following year to the foot of what is now Yesler Way. In 1853 the first steam-powered sawmill on Puget Sound formed the nucleus around which modern Seattle took shape.

From the waterfront Seattle gradually marched up steep slopes to the east. Early residents who could afford to do so preferred to build their homes on ridges and hilltops that afforded pleasing vistas of the Olympic Mountains to the west and Lake Washington and the Cascades to the east. In time, railroads filled the almost unused tideflats with their tracks and terminals; spur tracks to each wharf brought freight cars alongside cargo ships.

In its quest for urban greatness, Seattle faced a formidable obstacle because the Northern Pacific favored Tacoma. For a time the railroad relegated Seattle to a branch line known locally as the orphan road. Seattle's will to succeed was so strong that contemporaries labeled its special type of frontier boosterism the Seattle Spirit. The city's promotional efforts paid a handsome dividend in the form of the Great Northern Railway that James J. Hill completed from St. Paul in 1893. From Seattle, Hill extended his reach across the Pacific by acquiring a steamship line.

Between 1898 and 1910 Seattle enjoyed its greatest growth, becoming a cosmopolitan metropolis during that short span of time. Just after the turn of the century, Seattle embarked upon one of the most ambitious civil engineering programs in American history, one that literally moved mountains to reshape the downtown area and gave a new dimension to the Seattle Spirit.

During the course of three decades, sixty regrade projects sluiced some

44. Ernest Ingersoll, who visited Seattle in 1884, reported in *Harper's New Monthly Magazine* that as yet everything was in a "scattered, half-baked condition. The town has grown too fast to look well or healthy. Everybody has been in so great haste to get there and get a roof over his head that he has not minded much how it looked or pulled many stumps out of his door-yard." F. Jay Haynes took this photograph of Yesler Way in the spring of 1890 when the city was rebuilding after the previous summer's fire destroyed thirty blocks of downtown buildings. Courtesy Haynes Foundation Collection, Montana Historical Society, H-2255.

50 million tons of earth into Elliott Bay and adjacent mud flats. The most remarkable of those projects was the Denny Regrade. Begun in 1898 and completed in 1930, it removed a hill that blocked the northward expansion of the city's business district, creating thirty-seven blocks of level building land and shaping a new harbor in the bay. Seattle's numerous railroad connections and a tireless campaign of self-promotion helped it to far outdistance Tacoma in population by 1900 and to overtake Portland for first place in the 1910 census.

Unlike Portland and the cities of Puget Sound, Spokane lacked the natural advantages of a port. Except for the falls of the Spokane River, it pos-

WHEN CRIME BECAME AN INDICATOR OF PROGRESS

"Week before last some stranger from Port Blakely, while crossing the bridge over the marsh at the south end of town [Seattle], about ten o'clock at night, was knocked down and robbed of some thirty dollars in coin which he had with him. We mention this now on account of not having heard of it in time for our last issue, and to appraise our readers of the fact that there are men lying around loose here who are in need, and are disposed to make a slung shot raid on the belated stranger whenever a favorable opportunity presents itself. It is anything but an agreeable state of affairs, it is reprehensible, and all that sort of thing; still it is nothing more than what occurs in every city, and may be considered, in fact, a sure indication of activity and progress in our midst."—*Seattle Post-Intelligencer*, 18 September 1871, 3

sessed no discernible assets prior to the coming of railroads. Dating from the building of a small sawmill at the falls in 1871, Spokane grew only slowly until the boom of the 1880s. When the community incorporated in 1881, the year the Northern Pacific reached town, its thousand residents could hardly have imagined that within ten years their pastoral village would evolve into a regional railroad hub, with lines radiating south to tap the agricultural riches of the Palouse and east to Idaho's mines and forests. Additional railway lines built by the local entrepreneur D. C. Corbin linked Spokane to the mining wealth of southern British Columbia, and as a result, the town was in closer touch with Canadian affairs than most other American cities were.

Boise was clearly not in the same league as the big four cities of Oregon and Washington; nonetheless, it has ranked as the most populous community in Idaho since 1880. Boise resembled Spokane more than the cities of the coast for obvious reasons: both were landlocked, both profited from nearby discoveries of precious minerals, and both became hubs of agricultural empires.

Boise was platted in 1863 following the discovery of gold in nearby mountains. That year the U.S. Army erected Fort Boise. From here the army could protect travelers on the Oregon Trail and be ready to restrain Rebel sympathizers should they create trouble in nearby mining camps. Apart from the new military post and the mining boom in its hinterland, Boise City's chief assets were an abundance of fertile land and a milder climate than that of the mining towns of the Boise Basin. When the town was selected territorial capital in 1864, Boise's population was 1,658, which included an influx of pro-Confederate refugees from Missouri.

Mining activity declined in the late 1860s, but Boise gained a look of

45. This view of Spokane was taken in 1906 from atop
the county courthouse. By the turn of the century,
Spokane clearly dominated economic and social life in
the large area of eastern Washington and northern Idaho
that the city's promoters liked to call the Inland Empire. Courtesy Spokane Public Library.

permanence as trees grew from the sagebrush plains. It became a city of
families, unlike the typical mining camp, and it profited from the growth
of agriculture. In 1870, for example, when there were only 414 farms in all
of Idaho Territory, 65 percent of them were located in the Boise area. The
population of Boise increased to 2,311 by 1890, and that number would
more than double during the final decade of the nineteenth century as a
result of a boom in irrigated farmland in the Boise Valley. Although bypassed by the Oregon Short Line Railroad and relegated to the end of a spur
track from 1887 until the mid-1920s, when the Union Pacific finally routed
a line through the city, Boise suffered no worse transportation handicaps
than other place in the inland Northwest.

By 1910 the Pacific Northwest's major metropolitan centers had already
assumed the roles they were to play for the remainder of the twentieth

46. Looking east down Boise's Main Street, ca. 1915.
The Idanha Hotel is the turreted building in the center
of the photograph. Courtesy Idaho State Historical Society: 73–11.3.

century, and the same was true for a myriad of the small, often single-industry towns that served as lumber, farm, mine, or railroad centers. Astoria became synonymous with fishing and canning; Everett, Aberdeen, and Klamath Falls with forest products; Hood River with fruit; Colfax, Pomeroy, and Ritzville with wheat; Shaniko with sheep; and Wallace with metal mining.

The turn-of-the-century decades were probably the golden age for many agricultural towns, especially the county seats. During the years from 1889 to 1910, the population of Dayton, seat of Washington's Columbia County, grew from 996 to 2,589, while that of Colfax, seat of nearby Whitman County, quintupled from 444 to 2,783. Contributing to their prosperity was a growing farm population that depended on county seats for legal services and merchandise. Even the smaller rural villages grew and prospered until the agricultural depression of 1920–21 and the advent of widespread automobile travel later in the decade, both of which wrought changes that benefited larger trade centers like the county seats. But not for long, because the

47. F. Jay Haynes photographed the booming town of
Murraysville (now Murray), Idaho, in 1884. The hub of
the Coeur d'Alene mining district was a half-mile-long
street of huts, shacks, and tents. Such communities
were typically organized with such great rapidity that
there were few women and almost no children. Courtesy Haynes Foundation Collection, Montana Historical Society, H-1380.

same automobile technology soon made it possible for rural folk to conduct
business in still larger regional centers like Spokane. In a sense, there was a
settling and then an unsettling of major agricultural regions of the Pacific
Northwest during the first half of the twentieth century. Beginning in the
late 1980s, however, the prevailing population trend seemed to reverse once

again as an increasing number of people moved to rural and small-town areas in search of refuge from big-city problems.

Mining towns, even more than rural villages, were highly susceptible to boom-and-bust cycles. Idaho City boasted six thousand residents in 1864 and outranked Portland for a year or two as the region's largest population center. Idaho City had only three hundred residents in 1980, but that fact alone made it one of the more fortunate of former mining communities. Not all ghost towns were connected with mining. Shaniko and Hardman, located in central Oregon, declined as a result of changes in transporting sheep to market. In one-industry company towns like Potlatch, the closure of the local sawmill made survival a matter of prolonged struggle. In the case of Valsetz, Oregon, the closing of the mill meant sudden death for the Boise Cascade community: the company literally bulldozed it into oblivion in the early 1980s.

Today the number of vanished villages and towns across the Pacific Northwest would probably total in the thousands. Every one of them, like every abandoned mine and farmhouse and every derelict sawmill and factory, testifies to profound social and economic changes that have periodically swept across the Pacific Northwest during the past century. Once-lively towns also faded with changes in transportation technology, as when railroads supplanted river transportation or when railroads consolidated their division points and shops following the transition from steam to diesel locomotives in the 1950s and 1960s, or earlier when enclosed automobiles and all-weather roads enabled rural residents to shop farther from their homes at the expense of local trade centers.

OUTDOOR LIFE

Even in the largest, most rapidly growing metropolitan centers, Pacific Northwesterners maintained close ties with their natural setting. In both city and country, a defining characteristic of everyday life was (and still is) the popularity of outdoor activities. During the late nineteenth century, various occupations once associated mainly with economic gain or personal survival, such as hunting and fishing, evolved into popular sports. A hundred years later the list of favorite outdoor activities had expanded to include backpacking, whitewater rafting, downhill and cross-country skiing, golf, sailing, and swimming. Over the years the continuing love affair with outdoor activities has added up to considerable money, and the amount continues to grow.

It was in the late 1870s that hunting and trapping for sport first attracted

---

THE RISE OF TOURISM AND GAME CONSERVATION

In the late 1880s the Northern Pacific Railroad ended special carload rates on wild animal meat traveling from Lake Pend d' Oreille, in northern Idaho, to eastern markets. After hauling tons of buffalo hides and meat from the Great Plains, the railroad became a convert to conservation when it realized that tourism was a much more profitable and enduring business than the wholesale slaughter and ultimate extinction of the West's game animals.

General passenger agent Charles S. Fee noted that "to a very considerable portion of the traveling public, the game and fish of the region traversed by the Northern Pacific Railroad con-stitute its chief attraction. This large and ever increasing class of travelers are well-to-do people who have money to spend, and are thus desirable patrons of the road. Any course which will decrease the supply of the game which they seek will tend to reduce the travel over the road by this class, who will go where they believe game to be most abundant. For this reason, if for no other, the Northern Pacific desires to preserve, by every means in its power, the game which is so great an attraction to a large class of travelers."— *Forest and Stream* as quoted in *Wonderland Junior* (1888), 21

---

widespread attention on the west slope of Washington's Cascade Range. This gave "exciting and profitable employment to quite a number of persons, some of them old trappers from the Rocky Mountains, and from various other trapping grounds of the country, tough, rugged, often morose and hardened by exposure."[3] As the number of urban dwellers in the region grew, hunting and fishing only increased in popularity because the out-of-doors remained so accessible even to residents of metropolitan centers like Portland and Seattle.

Beginning in the 1880s wealthy tourists from the East might hire a private railway car built expressly to transport hunting and fishing parties to the Pacific Northwest. The Northern Pacific furnished one such car complete with cook and porter and would park it on sidings along its right of way for up to six weeks. Railroads would also play a prominent role in promoting enjoyment of the region's natural beauty through tourism.

The Pacific Northwest was slow to attract many tourists from outside the region. Even after through passenger trains reached Portland from St. Paul on a daily basis in 1883, most sojourners from the East still preferred the attractions of California and Colorado because of the extra time and money required to travel to the far Northwest. Nonetheless, as early as 1886 the Union Pacific Railway issued a booklet called *Inter-Mountain*

3. John K. Campbell, "Trapping and Hunting in the Cascades," *Washington Magazine* 2 (November 1890): 250–53.

*Resorts* that called attention to Salt Lake City, Ogden Hot Springs, Yellowstone National Park, and three southern Idaho destinations: Soda Springs, Shoshone Falls, and Guyer Hot Springs. These places offered tourists the chance to ponder curiosities of nature or society (whether Mormons or Indians) or the opportunity to improve physical and mental health, two forces driving tourism in the late nineteenth century. Hot springs were by far the most ubiquitous of early western tourist attractions. Health considerations figured prominently in advertisements for the Pacific Northwest's many hot springs, which remained popular with tourists from the 1880s through the 1920s.

The national parks of the Pacific Northwest became favorite tourist destinations after transcontinental railroads realized their potential for generating passenger revenues. The Northern Pacific was fortunate that the nation's first national park, Yellowstone (established in 1872), could easily be reached by stage from its mainline at Livingston, Montana. A fifty-four-mile branch line from Livingston finally reached Gardiner on the park's northern boundary in 1903, and from there it was only five miles by stage to Mammoth Hot Springs Hotel. The Northern Pacific could not keep so lucrative a source of passenger traffic to itself. The rival Union Pacific opened its own line through Idaho to the west entrance in 1908 to capitalize on the growing popularity of the nation's oldest national park. The Union Pacific considered building a grand hotel in Yellowstone Park but dropped the idea in the early 1920s when statistics showed that by then nearly two-thirds of all visitors arrived by private automobile, weakening the link between railroads and national parks.

If the Northern Pacific and Union Pacific became synonymous with Yellowstone National Park, Southern Pacific advertisements sought to promote Crater Lake National Park as a tourist destination. The Southern Pacific started conducting tours to Crater Lake from its tracks at Medford after the park was created in 1902. In much the same way the Great Northern Railway became synonymous with Glacier National Park.

Railroad promotion of national parks was at first aimed at wealthy Americans who had both time and money for an extended stay. The word "vacation" was not yet part of the vocabulary of Pacific Northwesterners, and paid vacations for the masses were still largely unknown when the new century dawned. Most vacations were for the wives and children of well-to-do businessmen in the region's growing urban centers. But another form of tourism—railroad, trolley, and steamboat excursion travel—evolved to cater to a less affluent crowd.

48. Crater Lake, Oregon's only national park, was created by Congress in 1902. A party of prospectors reached the natural wonder in 1853. Courtesy Oregon Historical Society, ORHI 48833.

Seattle and Tacoma residents could easily cruise Puget Sound aboard a commercial steamboat or cross over to the still pristine Olympic Peninsula. Completion of the Tacoma Eastern Railroad in the early twentieth century put the meadows of Mount Rainier within easy reach of Puget Sound residents. The railroad ran passenger trains fifty-five miles from Tacoma to Ashford where a good wagon road and stage lines enabled tourists to reach Longmire Springs at the base of Mount Rainier. Two hotels and mineral springs were located there.

Portland residents, like those of Seattle, Tacoma, and other cities of the Pacific Northwest, were well situated to take advantage of outdoor recreation made easily accessible by excursion trains and boats. One popular option was to take a steamboat down the Columbia from Portland to Megler, across the river from Astoria, and from there travel by narrow-gauge

NATIONAL PARKS IN THE PACIFIC NORTHWEST

| | Location | Size in 1982 (Acres) | Date Created |
|---|---|---|---|
| Yellowstone | Wyoming/Montana/Idaho | 2,219,823 | 1872 |
| Mount Rainier | Washington | 235,404 | 1899 |
| Crater Lake | Oregon | 160,290 | 1902 |
| Glacier | Montana | 1,013,595 | 1910 |
| Olympic | Washington | 914,579 | 1938 |
| North Cascades | Washington | 504,781 | 1968 |

passenger train to resort villages on the Washington coast. Closer at hand were Mount Hood and the Columbia River Gorge. From the railroad station at Hood River a daily stagecoach wound along the forty-mile-long road to Cloud Cap Inn, a quaint structure built of fir logs in 1889 at the base of Eliot Glacier on the north shoulder of Mount Hood between 6,500 and 7,000 feet. "Ladies intending to go on the glacier or climb the mountain should provide stout ankle boots and short woolen skirts. Tourists cannot be too strongly urged to take this trip," the Union Pacific advised in 1892.[4]

The Spokane, Portland and Seattle Railway in mid-1916 offered numerous "Sunday Picnic" fares from Portland to points along the Columbia River Gorge. Prices for a round trip ranged from $1.25 to $1.50. For $39.10 the railroad also offered special twenty-five-ride tickets to points as far inland as White Salmon, Washington, jumping-off point for alpine tours to Mount Adams, 12,307 feet high. One option for excursionists was to go one way by train and return aboard the steamboats *Bailey Gatzert* or *Dalles City* of the Dalles, Portland and Astoria Navigation Company. On the opposite bank of the river, a Union Pacific subsidiary promoted "Bonneville on the Columbia River," a picnic grove that in 1911 boasted a dance pavilion, refreshment stand, children's attractions, baseball diamond, trout fishing in the nearby Columbia River, and camping sites. Located only ninety minutes east of Portland by train, it was a favorite site for group picnics.

The coming of electric streetcars and interurban railroads at the turn of the century offered still other low-cost recreation opportunities to city residents. The Spokane and Inland Empire Railroad owned a minor league baseball team in Spokane and used its games to generate passenger business.

4. *Oregon and Washington Sights and Scenes via the Union Pacific* (Omaha: Union Pacific Railroad, 1892), 19. The inn ceased to function commercially in the 1920s.

More typical was the streetcar company that for the price of a nickel or two would whisk patrons to a bucolic setting that featured a picnic grove, small dance pavilion, and a few amusements and concession stands.

Trolley car parks were promoted as places where Sunday schools, fraternal societies, and other associations could meet together. "The real excuse for the existence of any park is that it offers opportunity for out-of-door pleasures which would otherwise be denied to the vast majority of our urban population." It did not hurt that "electric parks" and other recreation facilities boosted passenger traffic on trolley and interurban railways, particularly on weekends when ridership might otherwise be low.

"Artificial amusement parks" would to a large extent supersede picnic groves and other "natural" attractions by World War I. The former type dated back to the Midway at the 1893 Chicago World's Fair and during the following decade evolved into the "electric park," with its brightly illuminated grounds to dazzle the eyes with incandescent lamps. Invariably, a variety of thrilling rides—among them the Helter Skelter and Shoot the Chutes—provided the main lure of such parks. "Speed is almost as important a factor in amusing the million as is the carnival spirit," advised one park operator. "We as a nation are always moving, we are always in a hurry, we are never without momentum."[5]

In Portland the masses hurried to an amusement park called The Oaks that opened on a tree-covered sand spit in the Willamette River in 1907 and was soon billed as "Oregon's Coney Island." The first season, open-sided trolley cars carried 300,000 visitors, many of them families bearing small children and bulging picnic baskets. The Seattle Electric Company owned and managed both Madrona and Leschi parks on Lake Washington. They became city property when Seattle acquired the streetcar company. Adjacent to Seattle's Madrona Park was White City Amusement Park; Luna Park featured similar recreation in West Seattle near Alki Point.

Yet another popular attraction fostered by trolley companies were large and elaborate natatoriums. Ostensibly these were indoor swimming pools but many evolved into amusement parks. The Nat operated by Spokane United Railways in 1924 featured an array of standard concessions: merry-go-round, Ferris wheel, electric bumper cars, penny arcade, shooting gallery, and refreshment stands.

True trolley car tourism arrived in the early twentieth century when

5. Quotations on trolley companies and recreation facilities come from C. W. Parker, "Amusement Parks," *Electric Traction* 13 (April 1917): 255, and Frederick Thompson, "Amusing the Million," *Everybody's Magazine* 16 (September 1908): 386.

electric interurban lines developed distant recreation getaways for city dwellers. When it came to developing the local tourist trade—as distinct from a Sunday school outing to a park—the region's most innovative interurban company was the Spokane and Inland Empire Railroad. One of its several attractions was the dancing, dining, and swimming facility located at Liberty Lake, a body of water nestled in the mountains about seventeen miles east of Spokane. After the interurban opened a branch there in 1907, the Liberty Lake resort became so popular that the electric line built a hotel to accommodate visitors who wished to spend the night.

Still farther out was Coeur d' Alene, long a popular tourist destination, where steam trains and later electric cars from Spokane linked up with excursion boats for a trip across the lake and up the "shadowy" St. Joe River, a trip of some two hundred miles. Occasionally a small party of campers might be put ashore for an extended stay. A reporter in the 1890s observed that one such group brought along all sorts of gear, including a cow, which greatly amused shipboard passengers when it was pushed into the lake to swim to the campsite.

Especially after the end of the First World War in 1918, steam railroad excursions and interurban resorts both proved extremely vulnerable to a new breed called the "tin can" tourists, the cost-conscious travelers who toured the West in increasing numbers in their own automobiles. The automobile made family travel inexpensive for the masses and heralded an egalitarian era of tourism that blurred the tie between railroads and national parks and virtually erased that between trolley companies and amusement parks.

In popular forms of outdoor recreation, no less than in city building or countryside development, the pace of change in the Pacific Northwest noticeably quickened during the expansive years of the 1880s. Not even the severe economic depression of the following decade could moderate for long the supercharged rate of growth as mirrored in dramatically transformed skylines and rural landscapes. From the 1880s until the eve of the First World War the region was in many ways literally created anew.

# CHAPTER 12

# A Time of Testing: Omnibus States and the Excesses of the 1890s

*

I admire the East, but I do not love it; I love the South, but I do not admire it; and the West, I neither love nor admire, though it entertains me immensely.
—Sue Harry Clagett, "Sectional Traits of Americans," *West Shore* (1886)

*

The twelve years from 1888 to 1900 were marked by a series of unusual events that severely tested the political institutions of Oregon and her two new sister states, Washington and Idaho. Nationwide economic collapse during the early 1890s and popular protests on a scale never before witnessed in the Pacific Northwest severely stressed constitutions, courts, and laws.

In the spring of 1894, armies of unemployed men stole freight trains in Oregon, Idaho, and several other parts of the West in a desperate attempt to reach Capitol Hill and present themselves to Congress as a living petition for jobs. The U.S. Army halted them only after several dramatic chases. The few protesters who completed the journey failed to sway lawmakers, but their bizarre odyssey held newspaper headlines captive for more than a month. Some readers found the saga entertaining, but the unusual protest frightened many more Americans who wondered what it portended. Likewise, the meteoric rise of the Populist party as a vehicle for protest disconcerted many observers. All was not gloom and doom, however: the Klondike gold rush of 1897 wrote an exciting finish to the nineteenth-century Northwest, and in the end the region handily survived the stresses of the 1890s and emerged better prepared to address the complex demands of life in a new century.

## THE POLITICS OF PAROCHIALISM

Despite momentous issues raised by the great population influx of the 1880s, state and territorial legislatures conducted business as usual. Democratic and Republican politicians jockeyed for positions of power, occasionally joined in looting the public domain or the treasury, and promised voters to keep taxes low. Legislators seldom raised their sights above the pursuit of narrow, partisan, and material ends.

The prevailing philosophy of government was laissez faire, noninterference in economic matters. That mindset, together with bribes and other favors that railroads distributed to legislators, enabled corporations to dodge meaningful regulation. Businessmen like Ben Holladay, who bribed the Oregon legislature to obtain a land grant for his Oregon and California Railroad, served as role models encouraging public chicanery. The corrupt activities of Oregon's Senator John Hipple Mitchell underscored Mark Twain's quip that the United States had no distinctively native American criminal class except Congress. Mitchell's opponents accused him of declaring, "Whatever is Ben Holladay's politics is my politics, and whatever Ben Holladay wants, I want."

Neither Republicans nor Democrats completely dominated Northwest politics during that era. Oregon Republicans carried every presidential election between 1872 and 1908, but the Democrats provided a spirited opposition. The two parties traded the governor's chair five times between 1859 and 1895. After 1880, however, the Republicans retained control of the Oregon House of Representatives until 1935 and the state senate until 1957.

Idaho and Washington were not eligible to vote for a president until 1892, and territorial officeholders were appointed by presidents who, except for Grover Cleveland, were all Republicans. Republicans held a solid advantage over Democrats in Washington legislative elections, but Democrats held the edge in Idaho until Republicans succeeded in disenfranchising the Mormons in the mid-1880s.

Reformers seldom intruded into the political process before the 1890s. One of those infrequent insurgencies occurred in 1874 when Oregon voters elected independents to the state legislature, which subsequently passed laws regulating railroad freight rates and fares.

### THE OMNIBUS STATES PLUS IDAHO

A favorite topic of public discussion in Idaho and Washington during the 1870s and 1880s was statehood. Residents chafed at what they perceived to be a condition of vassalage—taxation without representation, no voice in the selection of territorial administrators, no settled public policy, and absentee governors who abused their veto power.

In 1889 thirty years had elapsed since Oregon achieved statehood. No new state had been admitted since Colorado in 1876, although Washington, Idaho, and several other territories considered themselves sufficiently ready.

The road to statehood for Washington had several potential pitfalls. Some residents fretted that the anti-Chinese agitation of the mid-1880s hurt their efforts because it gave Congress the impression that Washington was too immature for statehood. Others feared that when the territory enfranchised women it set a bad precedent, for no state had done so.

In the case of Idaho, it is a wonder that the territory survived intact until statehood. No less than four sessions of its legislature petitioned Congress to annex the panhandle either to Washington or Montana. Northern Idaho participated in a constitutional convention in Walla Walla in 1878, and the area was included in Washington's statehood plans for more than a decade. Dismemberment seemed imminent in the mid-1880s when Senator William M. Stewart of Nevada suggested that Congress attach northern Idaho to Washington. This step was but a prelude, many believed, to giving the remainder to Nevada, a state with serious economic problems because of the moribund condition of its all-important mining industry.

Both houses of Congress approved the plan in 1887, but Grover Cleveland had killed the bill with a pocket veto because of protests by Idaho's territorial governor, Edward A. Stevenson. Losing the panhandle was one thing, but the possibility of being swallowed up by a "rotten borough" like Nevada was apparently quite another. To placate the angry and frustrated northerners, the legislature voted in 1889 to locate Idaho's proposed university in the panhandle town of Moscow.

In the end, statehood for Idaho and Washington was delayed not so much by local matters as by a political impasse on Capitol Hill. Congress ignored petitions for statehood from the territories of the Northwest because the Democrats, who at various times controlled either the Senate or House, did not want to admit states that were likely to vote Republican. The logjam was not broken until Republicans captured the White House and both houses of Congress in 1888. In the lame-duck session of 1889, outgoing Democrats dropped their delaying tactics, apparently hoping to reap some last-minute favor for supporting statehood.

President Cleveland signed the omnibus bill and thus set in motion the admission process for Washington, Montana, and the two Dakotas. The

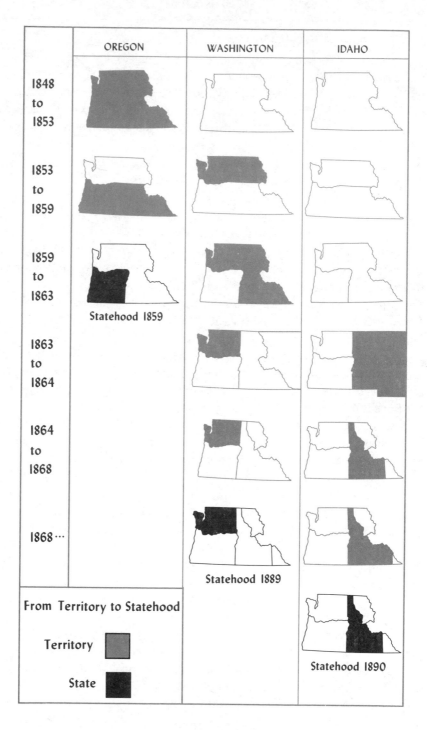

| | OREGON | WASHINGTON | IDAHO |
|---|---|---|---|
| 1848 to 1853 | | | |
| 1853 to 1859 | | | |
| 1859 to 1863 | Statehood 1859 | | |
| 1863 to 1864 | | | |
| 1864 to 1868 | | | |
| 1868 ··· | | Statehood 1889 | Statehood 1890 |

From Territory to Statehood

Territory

State

254

measure, commonly known as an enabling act, required prospective states to pledge themselves to a republican form of government, racial equality in matters of civil rights, religious toleration, assumption of federal debts, and maintenance of public schools free from sectarian control.

The omnibus bill conspicuously slighted Idaho and Wyoming, although powerful senators urged both to prepare for statehood anyway. As Oregon had done earlier, so Idaho in 1889 proceeded without formal congressional approval to hold a special convention and draft a constitution. In that way, Idaho came to be classified with the omnibus states.

### CONSTITUTIONAL CONVENTIONS

The framers of Washington's constitution who assembled in Olympia on 4 July 1889 represented a cross section of society. They included, among others, thirteen farmers, six merchants, six physicians, five bankers, twenty-one lawyers, one fisherman, three teachers, a preacher, a mining engineer, and two loggers. There were forty-three Republicans, twenty-nine Democrats, and three independents.

The Olympia gathering was not the territory's first exercise in constitution making. A reform-minded group of fifteen delegates had drafted a constitution in Walla Walla in 1878, but that effort failed to secure congressional approval. This time would be different.

Also meeting on 4 July 1889 were the seventy men who had gathered in Boise to write a state constitution for Idaho. They had come in response to a proclamation issued by Governor Stevenson (and reaffirmed by his successor, George L. Shoup) and had been selected by counties on a nonpartisan basis. In actuality, Republicans held a slight edge. The occupations represented in the group were similar to those in the Olympia gathering. Everything about the Idaho convention represented an act of faith: the Boise citizens who underwrote its expenses hoped to be reimbursed by the first state legislature.

State constitutions have a way of encapsulating the spirit and concerns of an era. Just as Oregon's constitution mirrored the hopes and fears of a pre–Civil War generation grappling with matters of race and slavery, so the constitutions that Washington and Idaho adopted thirty years later addressed the concerns of the first generation of Pacific Northwesterners of how to grapple with life in an increasingly complex urban and industrial America. In both Olympia and Boise, convention delegates who idealized the simple world of their pioneer forebears wrestled with the unsettling new problems of how states should deal with corporate power, industrial violence, and dismemberment and death in the workplace.

As the older states had done earlier, both Idaho and Washington framed their constitutions from a variety of documents already at hand. Washington borrowed from the constitutions of Oregon and California, the abortive Walla Walla constitution of 1878, and a model constitution proposed by W. Lair Hill, former editor of the Portland *Oregonian* and a specialist in constitutional law.

The Idaho and Washington documents were also modeled after the Constitution of the United States and included similar guarantees of individual liberty. Both provided for bicameral legislatures. They defined the structure and scope of government. They also addressed concerns unique to each age and place: tidelands in Washington; water rights, livestock, and the Mormon franchise in Idaho.

Civil rights proved to be problematic. Washington affirmed the state's duty to provide education for all children within its borders "without distinction or preference on account of race, color, caste, or sex." Yet its constitution denied Chinese the right to hold real property or mining claims. Idaho's fundamental law denied aliens the privilege of working for the state or any municipality, and it disqualified from voting all bigamists, polygamists, Chinese or persons of Mongolian descent, and Indians who were not taxed or who had not severed their tribal relations. Despite a provision proclaiming freedom of religion, the Idaho Constitution also denied Mormons the right to vote.

In matters of administration, the number of state executive officers elected by voters varied from seven in Idaho to eleven in Washington. Washington's constitution gave its governor an item veto to apply to all measures; in Idaho the item veto applied to appropriations only.

As often happened at state constitutional conventions, delegates strayed from the task of enunciating broad and fundamental principles of government. Instead, they provided uninspired codes of laws that addressed matters better left to future lawmakers. Idaho's constitution set a ceiling on state salaries, a measure that made little sense in the face of inflation in later years. Reflecting a strong agrarian bias, convention writers in both states added precise and detailed controls of corporate enterprise, especially of railroads. In the end Washington's constitution consisted of 25 articles subdivided into 245 sections, totaling approximately 30,000 words. That was seven times longer than the federal Constitution.

THE HOPES AND FEARS OF A GENERATION

Each section of the new state constitutions had some history behind it, but perhaps none was more curious than the background to Article I, Section 24 of the Washington Constitution: "The right of the individual citizen to bear arms in defense of himself, or the State, shall not be impaired, but nothing in this section shall be construed as authorizing individuals or corporations to organize, maintain, or employ an armed body of men." The first part of that section derived from the Bill of Rights, but the words that prohibited private armies addressed a problem of special concern to Washingtonians: on several occasions during the 1880s, employers had hired armies of private detectives to break strikes and eliminate unions in the isolated coal camps of the Cascade mountains.

An early draft of the constitution prohibited all private detective agencies from operating within the state. Although a majority of the delegates balked at supporting such a sweeping condemnation, they finally accepted a watered-down measure that prohibited private armies. Because subsequent legislatures hesitated to implement the measure, however, labor-management disputes continued to convulse the coal camps during the early 1890s. One consequence was the rise of populism, the most successful third-party movement in the state's history.

The Washington constitution makers also rejected a measure that would have provided for safety inspection of mines and given miners an eight-hour workday. Some delegates undoubtedly opposed the eight-hour-day concept as a matter of principle, while others likely believed that such specific matters should be left to future legislatures. In their rejection of this measure, the delegates evidently were determined to avoid framing a code of laws, a distinction they clearly failed to make in other sections. In the Idaho convention, a delegate seeking to include similar protections for labor in that state alluded to the prevailing agrarian bias in both conventions when he declared, "A great many who will vote against anything for the laboring classes will certainly support anything for the benefit of horses and cattle."

The debate over female suffrage offers another example of how constitution making mirrored the concerns of a generation. Although women had been unable to vote for delegates to the Washington constitutional convention, suffrage advocates made their presence felt. Their petitions flooded the gathering. But the assembly feared that a female suffrage provision jeopardized the constitution's chances of being ratified by the all-male electorate.

One delegate stated that he personally favored woman suffrage but, when acting in a representative capacity, had to vote against it. He preferred to leave the entire question to future legislatures. George Turner, a delegate who as a member of the territorial supreme court had played a major role in denying women the right to vote, made a lengthy speech urging that the people of the state rather than the legislature determine the question. The delegates finally added woman suffrage to a list of special issues for voters to consider separate from ratification of the new constitution.

Supporters also raised the issue of female suffrage in Boise, where Abigail Scott Duniway, an Idaho rancher at the time, made an appeal to the delegates. Idaho did not grant women the vote until six years after statehood.

STATEHOOD ACHIEVED

In a special election on 2 October 1889, Washington approved its state constitution by a vote of 40,152 to 11,879. At the same time, the female suffrage amendment lost by 35,527 to 16,613. The defeat meant that Washington women could vote in school elections (Article VI, Section 2), but—like Indians not taxed, males under twenty-one, people who did not meet the residency requirements, and all "idiots, insane persons, and persons convicted of infamous crime"—they were not enfranchised to vote in other elections. Voters also rejected a prohibition amendment by 31,487 to 19,546. In the contest for state capital, Olympia beat its chief rivals Ellensburg and North Yakima. And in the same election, Republicans swept to victory, capturing all of the state's executive offices, all but one of the thirty-five senate seats, and seventy of the seventy-nine house seats.

On 11 November 1889 Washington officially became a state. The news reached Olympia in the form of a telegram from Secretary of State James G. Blaine to governor-elect Elisha P. Ferry. Since the wire arrived collect, the governor had to pay sixty-one cents to read the words: "The President [Benjamin Harrison] signed the proclamation declaring Washington to be a state in the union at five o'clock and twenty seven minutes this afternoon." Bells were rung in impromptu celebrations all over Washington; bugles blared and drums rolled as village blacksmiths hammered out loud salutes by exploding charges of black powder on their anvils and men fired revolvers in the air.

Seven days later, Ferry, a former territorial governor (1872–80), was inaugurated as the new chief executive. The first state legislature selected Republicans from opposite sides of the Cascades to serve as United States senators: John B. Allen of Walla Walla and Watson C. Squire of Seattle.

Idaho's constitution was submitted to the voters on 5 November 1889, who ratified it by 12,398 to 1,775. Congress narrowly approved the document despite its anti-Mormon provision and Idaho's lack of an enabling act. Idaho became the nation's forty-third state on 3 July 1890. George L. Shoup, who served as the last territorial governor, was elected the new state's first chief executive.

As a result of intricate maneuvering dictated by state sectionalism, Idaho's first legislative session had the dubious distinction of needing to select *four* U.S. senators during its brief term (three of whom were actually seated).[1] In yet another concession to sectionalism, the constitution confirmed that Boise would keep the capitol and Moscow the state university, and it required the Idaho Supreme Court to hold sessions in Lewiston as well as Boise in order to diminish geographic obstacles to litigation.

Wyoming joined the union one week after Idaho. For the first time in the nation's history, a line of states stretched from coast to coast. During no previous twelve-month period had Congress added so many new states. For each of them the commencement exercise was now over, and a new era had begun. In Idaho and Washington, as in Oregon earlier, the first months and years of statehood were devoted to perfecting the machinery of administration and creating or adjusting state institutions to meet a host of new circumstances.

Idaho, for instance, granted women the right to vote in 1896 and was thereafter cited as a positive example in suffrage campaigns in other parts of the United States (only three other states, Wyoming, Colorado, and Utah, allowed women to vote at that time). Idaho's neighbors Washington and Oregon extended the franchise to women only in 1910 and 1912, respectively. This was a curious departure from the usual pattern in which Idaho usually lagged behind the two other Pacific Northwest states in enacting reform legislation.

Constitutions provided few guidelines on administrative matters, and thus as a result of piecemeal legislation, each state eventually possessed a bureaucracy composed of an overlapping welter of commissions, committees, bureaus, offices, agencies, and examining boards. As the system became increasingly cumbersome, people demanded reform.

Almost every legislature did some tinkering, yet over the years the law

---

1. See Margaret Lauterbach, "A Plentitude of Senators," *Idaho Yesterdays* 21 (fall 1977): 2–8, for a discussion of this strange episode.

NEW STATEHOOD

Children cry for it.

49. This early twentieth-century newspaper cartoon
suggests that the inland Northwest still dreamed of separate statehood, or, at least, that promoters of Spokane
as capital of the "Inland Empire" still did. Courtesy
Spokane Public Library.

makers established still more boards and commissions to study ways to improve state government. Idaho attempted to streamline the work of thirty-three boards, bureaus, and commissions and to consolidate eighty-seven state agencies into nine departments in 1919. Washington pursued a similar course in 1921, and Oregon did likewise in 1949. Administrative reorganization inevitably proved a complex and not always satisfying feat.

### 1890S BOOM AND BUST

Washington and Idaho barely had time to savor statehood before the Pacific Northwest experienced a period of devastating hard times. After nearly a decade of rapid growth, economic adversity "stole in like a thief" in mid-1893. The June financial panic that began on the East Coast severely shook the Northwest, and many of its financial institutions collapsed. Five banks failed in Spokane and fourteen in Tacoma. Across the United States, nearly five hundred banks and sixteen thousand businesses had failed by the end of 1893. Three of the nation's five transcontinental railroads, including both the Union Pacific and Northern Pacific lines serving the Pacific Northwest, went bankrupt.

Unemployment on a scale never before experienced compounded the nation's anguish. In a celebrated open letter to President Grover Cleveland, Oregon's Governor Sylvester Pennoyer complained that two-thirds of the workers in his state were without jobs. Actually, no one could be certain of the exact number of unemployed because neither the federal government nor many states kept such statistics. On Puget Sound, an equally unknown number of jobless workers huddled in driftwood shanties and subsisted on wild berries and clams. Their plight gave an ironic twist to the words of a song then popular among settlers in western Washington:

> And now that I'm used to the climate,
> I think that if man ever found
> A spot to live easy and happy,
> That Eden is on Puget Sound.
>
> No longer the slave of ambition
> I laugh at the world and its shams,
> As I think of my pleasant condition,
> Surrounded by acres of clams.[2]

2. "The Old Settler," from *Barton's Legislative Hand-Book and Manual, 1893–1894* (Olympia: State Printing, 1893), 154–55.

Some of the jobless claimed to have eaten so many clams that they could feel the tide rise and fall in their stomachs. But the great depression of the 1890s was hardly a subject for humor.

Even workers fortunate enough to keep their jobs often had their wages cut by 20 percent or more. Prices dropped, too, but that news was of little comfort to farmers. As the price of wheat fell to new lows, some Palouse agrarians allegedly committed suicide when faced with collection demands from implement dealers who were themselves often facing ruin. One of the Northwest's more spectacular bankruptcies was that of the McConnell-Maguire Company of Moscow, Idaho's largest mercantile firm; the principal stockholder at the time of the crash was no less a figure than the state's governor, William J. McConnell. In Boise the situation grew truly dark when the mayor turned off all but eight of the street lights to economize. Residents complained that thieves took advantage of the darkness.

Pacific Northwesterners were not worried only by thievery and insolvency. In cities of the West Coast, unemployed workers banded together in industrial armies and attempted to take their grievances en masse to Capitol Hill, getting there by commandeered freight trains if necessary—all in a desperate effort to present Congress with their demand for jobs. One army of two hundred jobless men made its way east from Portland. Its ranks included unemployed railroaders, because the desperate men commandeered a train in Montpelier, Idaho, and were steaming furiously toward Rock Springs, Wyoming, when the U.S. Army overtook them.

Troops brought the prisoners to Boise for trial. Most of them ended up spending a few months in a makeshift prison erected along the Snake River where the tracks of the Oregon Short line enter the state from the west. Following on the heels of the industrial army (or Coxey movement) was the Pullman Strike, the first nationwide walkout by railroad workers, which disrupted rail service in much of the Northwest.

Workingmen embittered by the loss of jobs or life savings in a failed bank and farmers and small businessmen who found it impossible to borrow needed money wanted more than ever to change the system that ruined them. Hard times thus set the stage for insurgent politics.

### POPULIST PROTESTS: SILVER TO THE RESCUE

During the decade of the 1890s, the People's or Populist party attracted considerable attention by serving as a rallying point for the spreading unrest. The Populists, in fact, would enjoy greater support in the Pacific Northwest than any other third party in the region's history.

LIKE BLOWING OUT A CANDLE

Q. [Representative John C. Bell] Mining is your chief industry?

A. [T. N. Barnard, photographer in Wallace, Idaho] Yes; it is our only industry.

Q. All other vocations depend upon the success of the miners?

A. Exactly.

Q. If the mines shut down, it is like blowing out a candle, practically?

A. It is, I think, on the same principle.

—*Report of the Industrial Commission on the Relations and Conditions of Capital and Labor Employed in the Mining Industry* 12 (1901): 415

In the election of 1890, the Republican party scored many successes in all three states. But Idaho broke ranks in 1892, when 55 percent of its voters supported the Populist candidate General James B. Weaver in the state's first presidential election. The new party subsequently emerged as an influential force in several counties and in the legislature. Washington voters in 1896 elected a Populist governor and a legislature dominated by reformers.

Populism especially appealed to voters who believed that during the post–Civil War decades a combination of evil economic forces had disinherited them: "The fruits of the toil of millions are boldly stolen to build up colossal fortunes for a few, unprecedented in the history of mankind; and the possessors of these, in turn, despise the republic and endanger liberty," thundered the party's famous Omaha platform of 1892. Populists in all three Pacific Northwest states advocated an assortment of reforms, among them government ownership of railroad, telegraph, and telephone lines, laws to prevent abuses of corporate power and influence, a graduated income tax on the rich, and several inflationary measures including the free and unlimited coinage of silver by the federal treasury.

Although the new party became most prominent after the onset of hard times in mid-1893, it actually originated well before that time. Unfortunately, the roots of Pacific Northwest populism are by no means easy to trace. The movement in Washington and Oregon appears to date from the troubled aftermath of anti-Chinese agitation in the mid-1880s, when supporters of expulsion redirected their protests from the streets to the ballot box. In the gubernatorial election of 1886, Oregon voters elected Sylvester Pennoyer, a Harvard-educated lawyer and Democrat who had skillfully harnessed anti-Chinese sentiment to propel his campaign. Pennoyer and other elected reformers rewarded their supporters with several modest prolabor measures. In Washington, an anti-Chinese party won control of Seattle's municipal government in mid-1886 and then formed a territory-wide organization. The return of prosperity before the fall elections destroyed the reform party at the polls, but the movement bequeathed its twenty-six-plank platform to the Populists of the 1890s.

When several veteran members of the Knights of Labor, a popular workers' organization that had spearheaded the anti-Chinese crusade, joined with members of the Farmers' Alliance, a prominent agrarian reform group, to organize the People's party in Yakima in July 1891, they resurrected the 1886 protest platform virtually plank by plank. The tangled roots of populism in Oregon could likewise be traced to the Knights of Labor and the Farmers' Alliance as well as to several short-lived reform parties sponsored by prohibitionists. Governor Pennoyer himself converted to populism in the early 1890s.

The pattern was much the same in Idaho, where Knights of Labor and members of the Farmers' Alliance joined forces to organize the People's party there in mid-1892. The party's initial platform included an anti-Chinese plank to placate organized labor, but Sinophobia had far less influence on the course of Idaho populism than did a price slump and labor unrest in the state's vital silver mining industry. From the first, Idaho Populists advocated the free and unlimited coinage of silver, an inflationary measure supported by mineowners and workers who believed that it would bolster their sagging industry.

Opposing supporters of silver were creditors, typically the eastern-based bankers and insurance executives who favored the gold standard and loathed the inflationary silver standard as a dishonest way to pay off debts. The battle of the standards was a complex matter, but in Idaho it was often restated as the simple conviction that what was good for the silver industry was good for Idaho. This in turn translated into widespread support for the Populist party and a prosilver wing of the Republican party.

Among evidence of the almost universal appeal of the silver issue was the fact that in the 1892 election Idaho Democrats rejected their party's presidential nominee, Grover Cleveland, and endorsed the Populist candidate, James Weaver, and the cause of free silver. Cleveland, who sought reelection on the Democratic party's pro-gold platform, received exactly two votes in Idaho, *both of them write-ins*. Adding stature and legitimacy to the Populist cause was the conversion of William H. Clagett, a northern Idaho lawyer who had chaired the state constitutional convention in 1889.

Although Idaho's Populist party originated in the southern half of the state, its emphasis on free silver quickly attracted a substantial following in the Coeur d'Alene mining district. Across the state line in Spokane—a city that depended heavily upon the output of Idaho metal mines for its economic health—and farther south in the grain belt of the Palouse region, it seemed that talk of free silver was on everyone's lips. In Whitman county, where nearly half the farmers were in debt—about twice the national average—the price of wheat had declined dramatically after 1890. Wheat that cost thirty-two cents a bushel to produce sold for twenty-three cents in 1894, and coming due were mortgages that had been contracted when grain prices were 50 to 75 percent higher. It is little wonder that the Palouse country contained many fanatic devotees of free silver and populism. "Free silver" had become the most prominent plank in the Populist party's national platform by 1896 and commanded the widest support.

After the financial disaster of 1893, many Pacific Northwesterners translated their anxieties into Populist votes, while others shunned the party and blamed it for popular excesses such as the contagion of train-stealing associated with the Coxey movement. Oregon rejected a bid by its two-term governor, Sylvester Pennoyer, to win a U.S. Senate seat as a Populist in 1894. Many Oregonians considered Pennoyer too sympathetic to protesters when he refused to order state troops to recapture a train stolen near Portland.

On the other hand, Washington voters sent twenty-three Populist legislators to Olympia in 1894 and all but eliminated the Democratic party in the state. Two years later, reform-minded Populists, Democrats, and Silver Republicans held simultaneous conventions in Ellensburg, each party writing its own platform but dividing up state offices according to a prearranged formula. The tactic worked. Fusionists captured the state legislature and elected John R. Rogers, a former Knights of Labor member and reform journalist, to the governor's office.

In the 1896 presidential election, Washington and Idaho voters supported William Jennings Bryan, the candidate of both the Democratic and Populist parties and an advocate of free silver, while Oregon went narrowly for William McKinley, the victorious Republican. In Idaho Bryan captured two-thirds of the state's vote and a coalition of Populists, Silver Republicans, and Democrats (whose national party platform now embraced the cause of free silver) seemed likely to dominate the legislature. Frank Steunenberg, a Populist-Democrat, captured the governor's office.

The 1896 election victories, however, proved to be a poor predictor of the Populist party's future. The Washington legislature of 1897 greatly disappointed the reformers. Although the insurgents had overwhelming numerical strength, members of the reform coalition did little except to battle one another. The legislature passed several specialized measures that organized labor supported, but it failed to secure a railway regulatory commission favored by farmers, and it referred the controversial issue of female suffrage to the voters (who defeated it). Olympia's entrenched railroad lobbies took advantage of the reformers' disunity and confusion. When the session ended, the Populists had little to be proud of and found themselves fighting for survival.

In the Oregon legislature of 1897, on the other hand, a handful of Populists held the balance of power between two factions of Republicans. Skillful maneuvering by William S. U'Ren and Jonathan Bourne Jr., a wealthy and ambitious silver Republican, prevented the legislature from organizing and thus catering to the corrupt political machine of U.S. Senator John H. Mitchell. The "Hold-up Session" proved a good argument for direct legislation to diminish the power of the professional politicians.

In all three states, bickering between fusionists, who advocated compromise and a close working arrangement with major political parties, and a middle-of-the-road faction, which urged the Populist party to pursue its own interests, hastened the decline of populism in the Northwest. The return of prosperity in mid-1897 further damaged the movement. In the 1898 election, even Spokane went Republican after supporting the Populist cause for half a decade. In elections between 1900 and 1902, Northwest voters effectively buried what was left of the once promising Populist movement under a series of quiet but impressive Republican landslides.

In a flourish of political independence that was to become a hallmark of Northwest politics during the twentieth century, Washington voters re-elected the popular John R. Rogers, a Populist turned Democrat, to a second term as governor in 1900. A few months later, Rogers died of pneumonia. Republicans did not lose another statewide race until 1912, and they remained the stronger of Washington's two major parties until the depression of the early 1930s. In much the same way, Republicans maintained a dominant position in the Oregon legislature, although they occasionally alternated with reform-minded Democrats for control of the governor's office.

Idaho voters clung stubbornly to the free-silver cause until turning overwhelmingly Republican in the 1902 election. Of the one hundred twenty contests for statewide offices held between 1902 and 1930, Republicans won all but nine. Only during the interval 1917–18 did Democrats control the legislature, and only two men succeeded in breaking the Republican hammerlock on the governor's office. They were James H. Hawley (1911–13) and Moses Alexander (1915–19).

Although the Populist party disintegrated, it left an unfinished agenda

| | | | |
|---|---|---|---|
| VOTING FOR PRESIDENT | | | |
| [BY ELECTORAL VOTE] | | | |

| Election | Idaho | Oregon | Washington |
|---|---|---|---|
| 1892 | P | 1 P; 3 R | R |
| 1896 | D | R | D |
| 1900 | D | R | R |
| 1904 | R | R | R |
| 1908 | R | R | R |
| 1912 | D | D | PR |
| 1916 | D | R | D |
| 1920 | R | R | R |
| 1924 | R | R | R |
| 1928 | R | R | R |
| 1932 | D | D | D |
| 1936 | D | D | D |
| 1940 | D | D | D |
| 1944 | D | D | D |
| 1948 | D | D | D |
| 1952 | R | R | R |
| 1956 | R | R | R |
| 1960 | R | R | R |
| 1964 | D | D | D |
| 1968 | R | R | D |
| 1972 | R | R | R |
| 1976 | R | R | R |
| 1980 | R | R | R |
| 1984 | R | R | R |
| 1988 | R | D | D |
| 1992 | R | D | D |

(D) Democrat; (R) Republican; (P) Populist; (PR) Progressive

and some uncommonly dedicated reformers. Some former Populists joined other insurgent movements. Ernest Lister, a labor leader and Populist officeholder in the administration of John R. Rogers, became a Democrat and was elected governor of Washington in 1912 and again in 1916. At that time, Democrats demonstrated no strong commitment to change, but Lister proved receptive to the counsel of reformers.

Also picking up where Populists left off was the next generation of insurgents—men and women who were active in the Republican party's progressive wing or who gravitated to one of the region's radical movements. An alternative that increased in popularity after 1917 was nonpartisan politics. Guiding that movement was the Nonpartisan League, an insurgency that originated two years earlier in North Dakota and spread to the Pacific Northwest, where it rekindled old Populist loathing for monopolies and the corrupt power brokers who often dominated Democratic and Republican politics.

### THE KLONDIKE RUSH

The events of 17 July 1897 were like the sunburst that follows a violent storm. In a single day—or so it seemed to Pacific Northwesterners—the gloom and pessimism caused by four years of economic depression and social and political turmoil vanished. It all happened when the Alaskan steamer *Portland* nosed into Seattle's Elliott Bay and brought confirmation of an incredible gold discovery in the Yukon. Five thousand onlookers jammed Schwabacher's Dock that morning as passengers held up sacks stuffed tight with thousands of dollars' worth of the yellow metal that disarmed even the most stubborn skeptics. Headlines in the Seattle *Post-Intelligencer* proclaimed the fantastic news:

Gold! Gold! Gold! Gold!
Sixty-Eight Rich Men on the Steamer Portland
Stacks of Yellow Metal
Some Have $5,000, Many Have More, and
a Few Bring Out $100,000 Each
The Steamer Carries $700,000

Within days, parlors and pool halls from Puget Sound to Massachusetts Bay buzzed with talk of finding fortunes in Canada's fabulous Klondike. Merely thinking about the precious metal revived hopes and dreams battered by years of monetary crises, widespread unemployment, and popular unrest. Pacific Northwest merchants, eager to capitalize on the Klondike trade by mining the miners' pocketbooks, intensified their longstanding commercial and urban rivalries.

After news of the fabulous Klondike bonanza reached Seattle, the city successfully promoted itself as the chief gateway to Alaska. A special Klondike edition of the *Post-Intelligencer* reached every corner of the nation: seventy thousand copies went to postmasters, fifteen thousand to transcontinental railroads, six thousand to public libraries, and four thousand to

50. Local mining rushes continued to occur in the Pacific Northwest after the Klondike stampede, but none ever had the widespread impact of that last great bonanza. One of the smaller rushes was to Idaho's remote Thunder Mountain district at the turn of the century, where Hawley and Puckett's law office opened for business in a tent. The Boise *Statesman* reported in March 1903 that the town of Roosevelt had "one hotel, three restaurants, three stores, three saloons, and a second-hand store, also a laundry . . . . About 180 men and 9 women spent the winter in Roosevelt. There are no children in camp." Courtesy Idaho State Historical Society, 60-73.30.

mayors. This public relations feat not only fostered a building boom that effectively doubled the city's population shortly before the turn of the century, it also linked Seattle and Alaska in the public mind for decades to come. Vancouver, Portland, San Francisco, and Tacoma became also-rans in the contest to capture the trade of Alaska. In fact, Alaska became for all practical purposes a colony of Seattle, so closely were the fortunes of the two entwined.

One million people, or so it was claimed, made plans to go to the Klondike; about a hundred thousand actually set out for the diggings. Most of the gold seekers of 1897–98 chose Seattle as their jumping-off point because of the vigorous promotional campaign and the city's obvious geographical advantages. Seattle's hotels overflowed with people waiting for ships to sail north. Most of the city's police force joined the wild exodus, even as the city experienced a rising tide of bunko artists, prostitutes, and gamblers on their way to the goldfields. One man staked his future on magazines, shipping bundles of them north in hopes that each copy could be sold for up to $10 to reading-starved miners. Horses and mules and dogs were shipped out in great numbers; no household's pet dog was safe. Some of the thousands of people headed north even took along gunny sacks to carry the gold nuggets they expected to scoop up by the handfuls.

For the Pacific Northwest, the rush to the Klondike was but a prelude to a renewal of dramatic economic growth. Astute land speculators, industrialists, financiers, railroad barons, and others realized that economic revival made the vast natural resources of Oregon, Washington, and Idaho every bit as attractive as those in the remote Klondike.

Pacific Northwesterners had barely recovered from the initial Klondike excitement when war broke out between the United States and Spain in 1898. Though the formal conflict lasted only a few months, rebellion in the Philippines continued for two more years. Cities of the Pacific Northwest experienced the excitement of visiting battleships and the prosperity that came from provisioning and transporting troops to the Philippines. Following this came new trade opportunities with China, Japan, and other nations of Asia. "Many of the events, it is true, notably the opening of the door to the far East, are mostly promissory assets," noted a prominent commentator in 1903, "and yet their prophecy of a golden future has not been without its profound effect on the growth of the Pacific cities and the attraction of energetic men of money."[3] It was this kind of optimism that long animated those who envisioned a prosperous and dynamic Pacific Northwest.

3. Ray Stannard Baker, "The Great Northwest," *Century Magazine* 65 (March 1903): 653.

CHAPTER 13

# Removing the Rough Edges:
# Society, Education, and Culture

\*

Other sections of the United States can mention their literature as a body, with respect. . . . The Northwest—Oregon, Washington, Idaho, Montana—has produced a vast quantity of bilge, so vast, indeed, that the few books which are entitled to respect are totally lost in the general and seemingly interminable avalanche of tripe.—James Stevens and H. L. Davis, *Status Rerum* (1927)

\*

Euro-American settlement of the Pacific Northwest involved far more than the frenzied pursuit of material gain, although at times it did seem that the work of surveying boundaries, platting towns, grading streets, staking mining claims, felling trees, cultivating fields, and promoting railway lines took priority over all else. But accompanying those basic economic activities was the important work of removing the rough edges from pioneer society. Many Pacific Northwesterners desired schools, churches, clubs, and a sense of order and cleanliness to give their upstart communities a settled air and to dispel the notion lurking, they feared, in eastern minds that life in the Northwest was crude and wholly materialistic. As recently established as the region's urban settlements were in the 1870s and 1880s, their culturally minded residents eagerly sought to organize music, literary, and art societies.

Schools were a special source of community pride, and Oregon, Washington, and Idaho funded public, nonsectarian educational institutions from pioneer days. Together with private and church schools, they contrib-

CIVILIZING INFLUENCES

The lack of women for wives is one of the most serious obstacles to the growth of [Washington] Territory. In the mills and logging camps of the Sound, and on farms and ranches of the interior, are several thousand hardy, industrious, able-bodied young men without wives or any present prospect of obtaining them. These men earn liberal wages, and having no families, in too many instances squander the earnings of months, during a few weeks of dissipation in the saloons and hells of the larger towns. Most of them, if they could procure "bonny and buxom" helpmeets, would build houses, create pleasant homes, fill the school houses with tidy bright eyed children, and become the permanent residents of towns and villages, thus giving new life and vitality to the commonwealth, while vastly increasing their own happiness.—Olympia *Tribune*, 9 September 1871

uted to the low rate of illiteracy long a positive feature of Pacific Northwest life.

Libraries and other forms of adult education were established at an early date. The Hudson's Bay Company once supplied its posts with reading material from England, and by the 1880s it was common for fraternal organizations and union halls to maintain reading rooms stocked with newspapers, magazines, and books. The free public libraries that appeared during the 1880s and 1890s were aptly described as the "people's university."

Newspapers, theaters, lyceums, and churches functioned as popular sources of adult education. Especially during the 1880s and 1890s, reform clubs proliferated to debate temperance, government ownership, and other controversial ideas. A growing array of women's clubs contributed to the social, literary, and moral uplift of frontier settlements—often through the establishment of public libraries and reading rooms, parks, and art exhibitions, or promotion of a variety of progressive laws, from pure food measures and the abolition of child labor to anti-gambling statutes and laws improving the status of women. The transformation of a frontier society was not lost on promoters, who lured a new generation of settlers to the Northwest by advertising its cultural and social amenities alongside its economic opportunities.

### SOCIETY WITH A CAPITAL *S*

The last thing many a Northwestern urbanite wanted was to be viewed as an uncouth country bumpkin by easterners. To avoid that humiliation, the wealthy acquired social pretensions that often became more eastern than those of the East itself, especially in Portland, the Northwest's first metropolis and home of its oldest moneyed elite. Large fortunes had already been amassed through a variety of pioneer enterprises by the 1880s, and the city's nouveau riche yielded nothing to their counterparts in Boston or New York in the ostentatious display of wealth. Their residences were overornamented monuments to conspicuous consumption, palatial showplaces that sometimes encompassed entire city blocks. Proper deportment and fashionable attire imported from Paris were serious matters, and socializing often took the form of elegant costume balls and formal dinners impeccably served. No other city in the region ever fully duplicated Portland's ability to appear far more prim and proper than its short history might warrant.

Despite the attention given to civility and decorum, the region's rough-hewn pioneer heritage was by no means forgotten. Especially in Oregon, where an association of early settlers evolved into the state's historical society in 1898, the "cult" of the pioneer ancestor became nothing less than a regional version of the Daughters of the American Revolution. With an unmistakably elitist bias, early-day historical societies placed far more emphasis on society with a capital *S* and genealogical research than on history. At times their aim seemed to be preservation of the records and memories of the pioneers and their descendants for the purpose of distinguishing them from lesser Northwesterners, those who arrived during a later era or who lived in one of the region's less imposing neighborhoods or in its many relatively unsophisticated rural districts.

Even within Portland, however, there existed an infamous and embarrassing section that reminded people of the city's nearness to the resources frontier, a section that had everything an itinerant logger or miner might spend his money on—shooting galleries, penny arcades, fortunetellers, herb doctors, and saloons like Erickson's, which occupied a full block, had a bar six hundred feet long, and was equipped to serve one thousand drinking men at a time. Here an orchestra of female musicians gowned in pink performed on a platform protected by a brass rail charged with enough electricity to short-circuit any tipsy, love-struck male.

That rambunctious young Northwest attracted much attention: it was the stuff of cheap blood-and-thunder novels and a sustainer of the illusion that America's frontier regions were seedbeds of democracy and egalitarianism. Yet, in every Northwest community that survived to maturity, economic and social stratification appeared early, and residents found themselves striving to reconcile the supposed openness of pioneer society with the formation of elitist organizations modeled after those in the East.

Carrie Strahorn recalled that in early Hailey, Idaho, "after the first year or two of joining hands with everybody in a social way there was a secret meeting of some of the elite to separate the gambling and saloon element from social functions. Every circular sent out, and invitations also, were signed 'By Order of the Committee,' so no one knew who was at the bottom of the movement, but from that time on, parties were as select as anywhere in the United States, and no gentleman appeared at a dinner or other social affair except in the conventional dress suit."[1]

SCHOOL DAYS

Builders of a new civilization in the Northwest valued education. Missionaries of various denominations considered education an integral part of their religious program, and at their stations they established schools for Indians and non-Indians alike. Even after the creation of publicly funded school systems, parochial and private grammar schools remained common in important towns in Oregon and Washington at least until the turn of the century. Nonetheless, tax-supported school systems arose in every western territory because not all early settlers were satisfied with the alternatives.

The type of public educational system that evolved in Oregon and Washington was patterned after that of New England. The Oregon School Law of 1849 emphasized free education and locally controlled school districts, a permanent school fund, certification of teachers in an effort to impose professional standards, and religious freedom of teachers and pupils. But when the constitution of 1859 embodied the free public school principle, critics charged that the state was too sparsely settled to fund a quality alternative to parochial and private schools. Therefore, it was not until 1872 that a functioning public elementary school program was actually in place. Since that time, the only substantive change has been to make elementary education compulsory.

The growth of public elementary schools was equally slow in Washington Territory. The Organic Act of 1853 provided that two sections of each township be reserved to fund the schools. A year later the territorial legislature authorized local public schools, but the territory's small and scattered population retarded their growth for nearly twenty years. Washington took an important step forward in 1895 with enactment of the so-called Barefoot School Boy Law that initiated the principle of state support

1. Carrie Adell Strahorn, *Fifteen Thousand Miles by Stage* (1911; reprint, Lincoln: University of Nebraska Press, 1988), 2:49–50.

274

for local school districts. That law allowed the state to levy a tax sufficient to provide for the education of each child of school age.

Schooling was a matter of slight importance in the boom-and-bust mining communities that typified early Idaho. After all, the camps were populated largely by single males who wondered why they should be taxed to pay for a school when in all probability they would live somewhere else next season. In the more stable agrarian settlements populated by families, education was viewed in a different light. Schools were required for the future well-being of the community; they fostered learning, culture, and patriotism and were widely considered necessary to attract additional settlers.

Mormons opened Idaho's first non-Indian school in the fall of 1860. From 1864, when the legislature established a public school system for the territory, until the 1880s, the typical Idaho school was a one-room structure in a mining camp, and the term rarely lasted longer than three months. The public school in Boise was housed in an old brick building so crowded that students attended only half-day sessions. Though poorly funded and physically inadequate, schools functioned as centers of community social life. They frequently hosted dances and box suppers, literary societies, picnics, and debates.

While most Pacific Northwesterners eventually accepted the idea of tax-supported elementary schools—and, in fact, Washingtonians at one time led every other state in per capita spending for education—the idea of public high schools was slow to win popular support. Especially in Oregon, their establishment was attacked repeatedly by influential people like Harvey Scott, the editor of the Portland *Oregonian* and a firm believer that high schools would serve only as havens for "drones," a luxury certain to undermine self-reliance and individualism. Other Oregonians agreed that the public need not be taxed to provide anything beyond elementary-level studies in reading, writing, spelling, arithmetic, history, and geography. School boards contested the issue on a district-by-district basis until the Oregon legislature created a statewide system of high school education in 1901. High schools in Washington date from Dayton in 1880 and Seattle in 1883. There were six high schools in Washington by 1889–90.

The region's colleges and universities were never subject to the same debate as its high schools, although the first tax-supported institutions of higher education amounted to more symbol than substance. Several of them traced their roots to private or denominational academies, which in the case of Oregon antedated all public colleges and universities. Willamette University in Salem traces its history to the founding of the Oregon

51. The growing importance of sports: the Sprague High
School track team and coach in Davenport, Wash-
ington, about 1908. Courtesy Eastern Washington State
Historical Society, Spokane WA, L85-261.4.

Institute in 1842, giving it claim to the title of the oldest college or university in the Pacific Northwest, and Pacific University in Forest Grove dates
from 1849. The Willamette Valley was in fact a veritable nursery of small
church-related colleges.

The region's first college or university funded by public money was the
University of Washington, which opened in Seattle in 1861 and was made
possible when Congress a few years earlier had given Washington and Oregon two townships (or 46,000 acres) each to support higher education. In its
first year thirty pupils enrolled in the primary department, thirteen in the

grammar school, seven in the preparatory department, and one in the college freshman class. All "departments" were taught by a faculty of one, Asa Shinn Mercer, who also served as acting president. The university operated only a few months each year and, before statehood, received at best meager funding.

Attempts to establish the University of Oregon encountered considerable opposition from those who felt that the Willamette Valley's several denominational academies and colleges provided the state adequate facilities for higher education. For several years after the state university opened in Eugene in 1876, the critics seemed justified. Only seven students graduated in 1881 and only four in 1885.

The University of Idaho dates from 1889, although it did not formally open its doors until 1892. Teaching commenced in Moscow in the unfinished and unfurnished wing of a building that stood in the midst of a plowed field. The first president supervised a faculty of one, who had no books or apparatus of any kind and not a single student on the college level. Some 30 of the 133 students in attendance at the lower levels that first year could barely write their names, and only 6 were of college caliber, a reflection perhaps of the fact that only three accredited high schools existed in Idaho.

The curricula of Northwest colleges and universities were patterned after those of East Coast institutions. They emphasized Greek and Latin classics and the natural sciences. Toward the end of the nineteenth century, they included classes in the liberal arts, and in some schools it became possible to substitute French and English for classical languages. Even more dramatic changes occurred on the campuses of the region's three land-grant universities.

A land-grant institution, according to the provisions of the Morrill Act of 1862, received some federal support in exchange for providing military training to its male students and maintaining a curriculum that emphasized "practical" training in agriculture, home economics, and engineering. The region's three land-grant institutions are Washington State University, founded in 1890 in Pullman; Oregon State University in Corvallis, which evolved in 1886 from a Methodist institute into Oregon State Agricultural College; and the University of Idaho. Each state also operated normal schools, or teachers' colleges, generally in small towns.

The region's private and public colleges and universities bore many resemblances. All passed through what could be labeled a heroic phase of development, a time of low enrollments and meager and uncertain funding, a time that required extraordinary dedication of faculty and administrators. Whitman College, which by the mid-1990s possessed a multi-million-dollar endowment, nearly closed a century earlier for lack of money and owes its survival to the Herculean labors of Stephen B. L. Penrose, who served as president from 1894 to 1934.

On all campuses, public and private, the morals and deportment of students and faculty were once a matter of close administrative concern and scrutiny. Students at the University of Washington in 1863 were forbidden to attend saloons, theaters, and balls and were required to assemble at the university's chapel on Sunday afternoons "to study the Scriptures as a Bible Class."

In those strenuous years of college and university education, instructors were expected to teach a variety of disciplines. The head of the Departments of Physical Science and Natural History at the University of Washington alone taught classes in physics, chemistry, physiology, botany, zoology, biology, mineralogy, and geology.

### ADULT EDUCATION IN A PIONEER SOCIETY

In an age informed and entertained by television, radio, and the movies, it is difficult to understand the importance of newspapers and periodicals as social and educational vehicles in pioneer societies. It was a poor community, indeed, that could not boast of at least one newspaper, and over the years the number of newspapers in the region certainly totaled in the thousands. Before radio achieved prominence in the late 1920s, no form of adult education was more influential than the press.

The press, in fact, formed the most broadly based educational influence in the community. It both mirrored and shaped local society and played a vital role in town-building and adult education. Newspapers and personal letters connected early Pacific Northwest mining communities with the outside world. In their eagerness for news, miners in remote inland camps sometimes paid as much as $2.50 for a single newspaper from California.

The region's first newspaper was the *Oregon Spectator*, a biweekly venture that began publication in Oregon City in 1846. Settlers who organized the Oregon Lyceum to promote science, temperance, morality, and the general intelligence were among its sponsors. The first newspaper in the region north of the Columbia River was the *Columbian*, launched in Olympia in 1852. Ten years later the rush of miners into the Clearwater region provided subscribers for Idaho's first newspaper, the *Golden Age* of Lewiston. The oldest continuously published Idaho newspaper is the *Idaho Statesman* of Boise, which dates from 1864.

---

"The publisher of the *Union*, one R. M. Smith, is known to be a murderer, a thief, a bigamist, a pimp, and with the knowledge of these facts the public will know what credit to attach to statements that appear in the paper he controls. The fellow is incapable of writing a sentence of good English, and to make up for his deficiency he has in his employ a notorious shyster and dead beat, named Ross, who is his equal in infamy, and is a ready tool to do his dirty work."—*Walla Walla Statesman*, 28 August 1875

---

Anyone with a modest amount of cash or a patron, a modicum of education and technical know-how, and a passion to say something could start a newspaper. A pioneer newspaper was an intensely partisan and personal operation, vastly different from the bland standardized fare typical of today's corporate-dominated press. Editors advocated controversial and unpopular causes and published embarrassing news about individual citizens' manners and morals, items almost certainly libelous today. They blasted rival editors with all the invective at their command; in Idaho City one such attack was titled, "A Dirty Dog's Vomit." These verbal excesses came to be known throughout the Pacific Northwest as the "Oregon Style" of journalism.

Personal threats from irate readers, some of whom were not satisfied merely with words, occasionally quickened the life of an editor. During the Civil War, Southern sympathizers in Lewiston took such violent exception to the views expressed by the Republican editor of the *Golden Age* that on several occasions they riddled with bullets the Union flag flying above his office. Readers expected a newspaper editor above all else to function as a community booster who promoted local attractions and damned all rivals. The worst thing an editor could do was to transfer his press and allegiance to a rival community.

In addition to community-oriented newspapers, the Pacific Northwest nurtured a host of specialty publications. Some were voices of literary criticism or church news; a good many others were protest journals promoting various causes. One of several oddities was a spiritualist publication that alternated each month under the titles the *World's Advance-Thought* and the *Universal Republic*. Each issue contained a "Soul-Communion Time-Table" that fixed a specific day and a time for residents of the leading cities of the world to hold collective soul-communion to invoke "the blessings of universal peace and higher spiritual light." The region's first literary journal, the *Oregon Literary Vidette*, began publication in 1879. A year earlier the region's first labor paper, the *Labor Gazette*, appeared in Portland. During the depression years of the 1890s, dozens of short-lived newspapers championed the cause of labor, populism, socialism, anarchism, spiritualism, and a host of other "isms and osophies." Although most publications were in English, the Pacific Northwest press included a lively foreign-language contingent.

The mortality rate among the Pacific Northwest's early newspapers was extremely high. Operating on high hopes and a shoestring budget, few survived longer than a year or two. Yet, from the several thousand newspapers and periodicals published in the Pacific Northwest, a few prominent editors and papers emerged.

The most influential voice in Oregon for nearly forty years belonged to Harvey W. Scott, editor of the Portland *Oregonian*. When he joined the paper in 1865, fifteen years after its founding, the *Oregonian* was an inconspicuous publication. Scott eventually acquired a part interest in it and well before his death in 1910 made it into the leading journal in the Pacific Northwest. As one of the region's first college graduates, Scott had a compulsion to educate his readers. His editorial columns preached the conservative doctrine of nineteenth-century individualism and untrammeled frontier opportunity. It was the kind of paper that Oregonians embraced or hated but could not ignore. Few men wielded more power in late-nineteenth-century Oregon than the remarkable editor who molded public opinion for many years.

The Spokane *Spokesman-Review* was the leading paper in the interior region of eastern Washington and northern Idaho. It originated as the weekly *Review* in 1883 when Spokane was a mere hamlet. Aided by the Coeur d'Alene mineral bonanza later that year, the paper evolved and grew until, by the turn of the century, it attained a circulation of more than forty thousand and covered a vast territory that stretched from Oregon to British Columbia and from the Cascades to the Rockies. Its Yale-educated publisher, William Hutchinson Cowles, was a young journalist who left the Chicago *Tribune* to come west in 1891; he became sole owner of the paper in 1894. Cowles gave its pages a progressive, reform-minded tone until the 1920s, when he steered it in an ever more conservative direction. The *Spokesman-Review* by the mid-1980s had become the flagship of the Cowles family media empire that included two Spokane newspapers, a television station, two radio stations, and extensive real estate interests.

Seattle was home to numerous newspaper ventures, including the *Union-Record*, which from 1918 to 1928 was one of the few daily labor journals published in the United States. By the turn of the century, two general interest papers had emerged from a crowded field: the *Post-Intelligencer* and the *Times*, the latter originally a sensation-seeking journal edited and published by the bombastic Colonel Alden J. Blethen, who acquired it in 1896.

The region's first African-American newspaper was the Seattle *Standard*, founded in 1892 by Britain Oxedine, a former North Carolina state legislator; but the paper lasted less than a year because the city's black population of 286 was too small to support it. Far more successful was the Seattle *Republican*, edited and published by Horace Cayton Sr. from 1894 to 1917. Cayton, who was born a slave in Mississippi, graduated from Alcorn College in that state in 1885 and soon moved to Seattle, where he worked as a reporter for the *Post-Intelligencer*. Various successful real estate ventures enabled him to bankroll the *Republican*.

Two years after launching the newspaper, Cayton married Susie Sumner Revels, daughter of Hiram R. Revels of Mississippi, the first black U.S. senator (1870–71). Susie Cayton worked as a reporter for the *Republican* and occasionally wrote its editorials. By 1910 the paper had ten thousand readers, not all of them black, and had become an influential voice in support of Washington's Republican party. At various times, Tacoma, Portland, and Spokane also supported local black newspapers.

Another popular vehicle for adult education was the Chautauqua, a cultural uplift movement that originated in upstate New York and was named for the lake on which it was headquartered. The typical Chautauqua resembled a frontier camp meeting crossed with a college lecture. It drew together both urban and rural folk. For several years after 1889, the annual Chautauqua was a popular event on Washington's Vashon Island and after 1895 in Gladstone Park near Portland, where the third-largest encampment in the United States was held. Six thousand people came to the 78-acre park in 1896 to hear William Jennings Bryan speak on the "Prince of Peace."

An equally remarkable Chautauqua was held each summer in the early twentieth century on the shore of Idaho's Spirit Lake. People came to this idyllic setting from all parts of the inland Northwest to hear lectures and participate in discussions of current social problems and world affairs. The Spirit Lake Chautauqua was hailed by supporters as an "important step toward the social and educational advancement of the Inland Empire." Behind the movement were prominent regional businessmen, but the speakers included nationally famous labor and religious leaders. Not all Chautauquas, however, took the form of mass assemblies. Little Kendrick, Idaho, boasted of a Chautauqua circle as early as 1892; its membership consisted of five women and the local minister.

## CULTURES POPULAR AND UNPOPULAR

When British author and critic Oscar Wilde toured the West in 1883, he found that citizens' enthusiasm for the arts generally outran their cultivation. When, for instance, he read the autobiography of Renaissance sculptor and goldsmith Benvenuto Cellini aloud to an audience of Leadville, Colorado, miners, they loved it so much that they reproved Wilde for neglecting to bring Cellini along with him on tour. When Wilde explained that Cellini had been dead for some time, one miner questioned, "Who shot him?" The rough-hewn listeners later escorted Wilde to a "dancing saloon where I saw the only rational method of art criticism I have ever come across. Over the piano was a printed notice: 'Please do not shoot the pianist. He is doing his best.' "[2] The supercilious Wilde would certainly have found much the same situation in the Pacific Northwest, where popular culture flourished in many forms.

Music of various types was available in the typical mining town of the 1860s. Both vocal and instrumental selections were popular. The sounds of an accordion, banjo, flute, or violin came from many a saloon, some of which doubled as concert halls. Itinerant professional musicians traveled from one town to another, giving performances and occasionally helping local talent form its own orchestras and brass bands. One mining town orchestra that was a popular feature at public dances included in its 1864 repertoire fourteen waltzes, eleven polkas, five reels, four jigs, and five operatic and three minstrel numbers. The one-time mining supply center of Walla Walla, Washington, today claims to have the oldest continuing symphony orchestra west of the Mississippi River.

Professional and amateur theater companies of varying quality also brought drama to the remotest parts of the region. In 1864, only shortly after the first Mormon settlers established homes in Paris, Idaho, a group of them produced the play *William Tell* in a log cabin. Amateur drama companies formed in numerous other Mormon communities: local actors made the scenery and carried it with them as they toured the small towns of southeastern Idaho. It was not at all unusual for church organizations along with schools and newspapers to foster community cultural development, though some forms of popular culture were unlikely to be endorsed by religious folk of any denomination.

Professional theatrical performances in the interior mining camps of the

2. Oscar Wilde, *Impressions of America*, in *The Writings of Oscar Wilde* (London: Keller-Farmer Co., 1907), 258–60.

1860s were often boisterous affairs at which patrons let loose a lot of animal passion in the form of whistling and stomping of feet, especially after the intermission, which they spent in the adjacent bar. Many such performances took place in an opera house, a name applied to a variety of forums and one of the most controversial purveyors of public entertainment. Opera houses were often home to productions staged by itinerant Shakespeare companies, while others featured balalaika players, dancing dogs, and a mixed assortment of melodramatic offerings, including lewd ones such as the popular and scandalous *Black Crook*, in which actresses wore tights and exposed their legs.

Especially notorious were the box houses of the larger cities, so called because the balcony was partitioned off into curtained boxes from which the patrons and their guests could view the show without being seen themselves. In such establishments vaudeville entertainment—a type of diversion consisting of specialty acts—functioned merely as an adjunct to the sale of liquor and sex.

In some box houses the female entertainers performed on the stage until midnight, then visited patrons in the boxes while another company presented further melodrama on stage. During the 1890s the forces of morality declared war on the box houses, and in Tacoma they passed a law excluding women from variety theaters. The Washington legislature in 1905 outlawed the employment of women in places where intoxicating drinks were sold.

Vaudeville shows that had been "cleaned up" for family entertainment were offered occasionally in regular theaters by the same troupes who performed in the saloons and box houses. John F. Cordray, who came to the West Coast in 1888, was the first person to operate a vaudeville theater successfully without the attraction of liquor. Neither did his theaters tolerate profane or boisterous language or rowdy characters.

John Considine, a box house operator in Seattle, started the first legitimate, popular-priced vaudeville chain in the world. At one time he and a partner operated twenty-one houses in the Pacific Northwest. Nonetheless, the advent of radio and talking motion pictures in the 1920s doomed vaudeville. Considine's rival was Alexander Pantages, a Greek immigrant who parlayed the unpretentious movie theater he opened in Seattle in 1902 into a multimillion-dollar chain of playhouses, one of the largest in the United States.

Like the stage productions that once toured the Pacific Northwest with forgettable names like "Three Weeks of Marriage" and "The Deuce Is in Him," a good many of the region's early novels and poems possessed few

52. Seattle's Third Avenue Theater in the early twentieth century. The building, which was torn down in 1907, had a thousand seats and two stages, one featuring polite fare and another for bawdier farce and melodrama. Courtesy Special Collections Division, University of Washington Libraries, A. Curtis 929.

enduring qualities apart from their historic value. Repeating a pattern common in older regions, the early literature of the Pacific Northwest evolved from explorers' books of travel, diaries, and letters, to histories and polemical tracts by missionaries and pioneer settlers, and finally to novels, poetry, and other products of the imagination. Most works in the latter category fell into the local color genre in which authors employed elegantly descriptive yet trite language to tell an emotionally unsophisticated story in a regional setting. Because their theme was invariably the environment and the human response to it, authors filled their works with babbling brooks, murmuring rivers, whispering pines, and other hackneyed tributes to the region's stunning natural setting, but they seldom incorporated genuine elements of folk life and art.

Among the exceptions were Joaquin Miller and Charles Erskine Scott Wood. Though not natives of the region, they were the only early Northwest literary figures to achieve an enduring national reputation. Miller, born in Indiana as Cincinnatus Hiner Miller, had his first book of poetry published in Oregon in 1868. Entitled *Specimines*, it attracted little attention in the state. Only after the colorful Miller left the Pacific Northwest did his writing capture the fancy of English and American literary society.

Few Pacific Northwesterners possessed more complex personalities or lived more diverse lives than Charles Erskine Scott Wood, who, like Miller, was something of a frontier original. Wood was born in Pennsylvania in 1852 and died in 1944; an officer who participated in the campaign against Chief Joseph, he was also a Portland lawyer who later became a prolific writer of short stories, books, and poems, a painter, humanitarian, and anarchist. His most popular work was *Heavenly Discourse* (1927); his most important was *Poet in the Desert* (1915). In it Wood juxtaposed human cruelty and nature's beneficence as experienced in the eastern Oregon desert, and he did it without slipping into the romanticization of nature so typical of early Northwest writing.

The earliest novel written and published in the Pacific Northwest was Margaret Jewett Bailey's thinly disguised autobiography, *The Grains; or, Passages in the Life of Ruth Rover* (1854). The book is at times flawed with the sentimentalism of the era, but it is of historical value for its unique and incisive perspective on the frontier era. The best selling of pre-1900 Northwest novels was Frederick Homer Balch's *Bridge of the Gods* (1890), a saccharine period piece about Indian life that went through twenty-nine editions between 1890 and 1935; it is still in print. Like other early works of Northwest fiction, it was far more imitative than innovative.

As was then typical in the rest of the United States, most early novelists in the Northwest were women.[3] The suffragist Abigail Scott Duniway wrote several volumes of fiction, the most notable being *Captain Gray's Company* (1859), the tale of a mother and two children who leave home to make the long trip to Oregon. It includes several autobiographical sections but possesses little literary merit. Also in the matriarchal literary tradition were Ella R. Higginson, poet and short story writer, and Eva Emery Dye, who wrote a series of novels glamorizing the pioneer tradition. Her best-known work was *McLoughlin and Old Oregon* (1900).

3. Also in this category was Frances Fuller Victor, a gifted historian who ghostwrote the volumes on Oregon and the Pacific Northwest Coast for Hubert Howe Bancroft's western history series.

Mary Hallock Foote (1847–1938) was the first prominent writer to use Idaho as a setting, although she was often critical of what she observed. She came to the West with her husband, a civil engineer, and resided in Idaho from 1883 to 1893. Beginning with *The Chosen Valley* (1892), Foote wrote and illustrated a series of highly autobiographical novels and short stories about the mining and irrigation frontiers, though most of them were superficial and romantic. Her *Coeur d'Alene* (1894) viciously criticized the striking miners; it was filled with heroes and villains but no real understanding of the conflict.

It was the decidedly parochial character of the first seventy-five years of Pacific Northwest fiction and poetry that caused James Stevens and Harold Lenoir Davis to issue their 1927 manifesto, *Status Rerum*,[4] blasting so much of it as bilge. *Status Rerum* represented a youthful outburst against the literary establishment for works that failed to reflect accurately the historical and social milieu of the region. Stevens, who wrote *Paul Bunyan* (1925), and Davis, who won the Pulitzer Prize for his novel *Honey in the Horn* (1935), were two of the region's best writers. The honors that later came to Davis for *Honey in the Horn*, which one critic described as a story of the homestead era in Oregon that "deflowers the sweeter legend of the heroic pioneers, seeing them as average humans and none too civilized in speech and customs,"[5] were evidence of the significant changes that awaited Northwest literature after it escaped its early romantic infatuation with the region's natural setting. *Status Rerum* thus stands as a watershed in Northwest literary development.

Reasons for the character of early Northwest literature are several. The Montana historian and journalist Joseph Kinsey Howard observed at a Northwest writers' conference in 1946 that it was difficult for pioneers to devote much time to literary pursuits until the house was built, the harvest was in, and the fire laid. Other explanations centered on the region's physical and intellectual distance from the literary circles of Boston and New York or on its small population, which restricted the sale of works of genuine merit. In other words, the early literary output of the Pacific Northwest reflected its status as a cultural hinterland. Despite the limitations cited in the 1946 conference, Northwest literature reflected a region's determined effort to remove its rough edges.

4. It was aptly subtitled *A Manifesto upon the Present Condition of Northwestern Literature: Containing Several Near Libelous Utterances upon Persons in the Public Eye.*
5. *Oregon: End of the Trail*, WPA Guide (Portland: Binfords and Mort, 1940), 114.

# CHAPTER 14

# Envisioning a New Northwest

*

"It is the same everywhere, from the Mississippi to the Pacific. Men seem to live in the future rather than in the present: not that they fail to work while it is called to-day, but that they see the country not merely as it is, but as it will be, twenty, fifty, a hundred years hence, when the seedlings shall have grown to forest trees."—James Bryce, *The American Commonwealth* (1893)

*

During the years bracketed by the completion of the Northern Pacific Railroad in 1883 and U.S. entry in the First World War in 1917, the Pacific Northwest moved inexorably into a postfrontier world. That transition was not always smooth or peaceable. The generation of men and women who came to the West in covered wagons and sailing ships passed from the scene. They had been committed to building a new society in the wilderness; those who followed them were also builders—of cities, transcontinental railroad lines, irrigation works, schools and colleges, and state constitutions.

Economic depression and social dislocation occurred in the mid-1880s and again from 1893 to 1897 to punctuate these years; but after prosperity returned in the late 1890s, the Pacific Northwest exuded a newfound air of confidence that took concrete form in two world's fairs, new skylines for cities, and an expanding number of prosperous-looking farms and ranches. Especially prominent during those ebullient decades, as observed by the journalist Ray Stannard Baker, was the contest by rival chambers of commerce to gather plums: "a plum, in the Western sense, is a new railroad, a new coaling station, a new manufacturing plant; it falls to the most energetic shaking."[1]

Baker added in 1903 that in the Pacific Northwest "everything seems to have happened within the last ten years; events which would be of epoch-making importance in any country at any time have here crowded one upon another with wanton prodigality, so that the Northwesterner, plumped down in the whirl of great things, can himself hardly grasp their full significance, contenting himself with confused superlatives." Between 1897 and 1912 the Pacific Northwest experienced its largest population increase prior to the Second World War and enjoyed one of the most prosperous periods in its history. During the heady time of rapid growth and change the promoters' long-envisioned New Northwest at last became a reality.

### PROMOTING THE PANORAMAS OF PROMISE

Governor Edward S. Salomon of Washington complained in 1871 that "numerous reports have been written and published on the resources of this Territory, many of which have been too highly colored. People, misled by the representations, have come here with great expectations and found themselves sadly disappointed. Our Territory offers inducements enough to settlers, and it is entirely unnecessary to state anything but the truth."[2]

Salomon was wrong: truth alone was not enough. The Pacific Northwest at that time was of little interest to most Americans; already a generation had passed since the era of "Oregon Fever" and the rush of covered wagons to the Willamette Valley. Of the four million people who emigrated to the West Coast between 1850 and 1910, the vast majority went to California. Boosters were needed to sell the Great Northwest to people who might otherwise gravitate naturally to the Golden State. Salesmanship was especially vital before completion of the Northern Pacific line in 1883 made overland travel by train to the nation's Far Corner relatively easy.

The popular image of the turn-of-the-century Pacific Northwest was created by individual boosters, real estate agents, newspaper editors, private immigration societies, chambers of commerce (often called commercial clubs), various "improvement companies," and especially the railroads. All

1. Ray Stannard Baker, "The Great Northwest." *Century Magazine* 65 (March 1903): 656.

2. Charles M. Gates, ed., *Messages of the Governors of the Territory of Washington to the Legislative Assembly, 1854–1889* (Seattle: University of Washington Press, 1940), 167.

had a common desire to attract settlers and investors in order to promote economic growth and guarantee a prosperous future. Their come-on was timeless: "Real Estate is the foundation of all wealth, as well as the backbone of the universe. The golden opportunity of becoming the Rothschild of Seattle is now within your grasp. Why delay?" asked one eager promoter of land near suburban Green Lake in 1888.

Various promotional publications conveyed the message that the Pacific Northwest was a land of boundless resources and get-rich-quick opportunities. The coal deposits of Washington, they typically boasted, were the largest in the United States, the soil of the Willamette Valley was literally inexhaustible, and crop failures were virtually unknown. One pamphlet claimed that it would "scarcely be possible to exaggerate the extent and value of the forests of the Pacific Northwest." Promoters portrayed the region as a healthseekers' paradise, filled with hot springs and mineral baths, the nights "cool and conducive to sound slumber." To this heaven they urged any person with ambition and determination to migrate.

Timber companies in the early twentieth century became promoters in order to dispose of their growing acres of logged-off lands to prospective farmers. Thousands of acres of "virgin logged-off land" of proved fertility awaited development, or so claimed one Potlatch Lumber Company brochure, *Fertile Logged-Off Lands of Latah County, Idaho*. This was only one of hundreds, perhaps even thousands, of different promotional pamphlets designed to sell the Great Northwest. Each envisioned the region not as it was but as it must someday become. "One is simply amazed at the vast amount of money, energy, patience, and persistence there is devoted to setting forth the resources, advantages, capabilities, and wonders of this part of the continent," observed one visitor to the West in 1888.[3]

Advertising, incidentally, was not limited to printed materials. It also took the form of oratory and elaborate displays at fairs and expositions, including the great national ones held in Philadelphia in 1876 and Chicago in 1893. The Union Pacific Railroad in the mid-1880s hired an immigration agent to entice prospective settlers with samples of potatoes and apples grown in the territory it served.

Unlike in Great Britain or the eastern half of the United States, where railroad lines slipped easily into the existing landscape, the trunk lines in

---

3. Emma Adams, *To and Fro, Up and Down in Southern California, Oregon and Washington, with Sketches in Arizona, New Mexico and British Columbia* (Cincinnati: Cranston & Stowe, 1888), 375.

# PUBLIC ATTENTION
### Is now largely directed to the
## VAST NEW REGIONS
#### Opened for Settlement by the completion of the
# NORTHERN PACIFIC RAILROAD
### Through MINNESOTA, NORTH DAKOTA, MONTANA, NORTHERN IDAHO, WASHINGTON and OREGON,
#### The widely known and prosperous
# Northern Pacific Country

The important Geographical Divisions traversed by this New **TRANS-CONTINENTAL LINE,** possess unusually large and varied Natural Resources.

**THERE ARE** New Towns growing into important trade centers, and there is a steady advance in the values of all property.

**THERE ARE** Large unoccupied areas of FERTILE LANDS especially adapted to Wheat Growing and General Farming.

**THERE ARE** EXTENSIVE GRAZING RANGES, the best in the United States for Stock Raising.

**THERE ARE** RICH MINERAL DISTRICTS to be developed and HEAVY BODIES OF TIMBER for lumbering purposes.

**THERE ARE** Navigable Rivers, Lakes and larger waters and innumerable water powers ready to be utilized.

**THERE ARE** Profitable Fisheries on the Rivers, Lakes and Puget Sound. The fish are of great commercial value.

**THERE ARE** Exceptionally good opportunities for Merchants, Manufacturers, Professional Men, Mechanics and Traders to engage in business.

## The Diversified Resources of this Grand Region
ready to be developed into innumerable paying industries, will put in use much capital **AND REQUIRE A LARGE NUMBER OF OPERATORS AND WORKING MEN.**

# THERE IS AMPLE ROOM
### *In this Great Belt of Productive and Prosperous Country*
# For Millions of Settlers

To secure **COMFORTABLE HOMES** and become **INDEPENDENT.**
Each State and Territory traversed by the **NORTHERN PACIFIC** possesses abundant resources to support a compact population. The countries are well watered, the soil is rich and productive, while the climate is superior in the qualities which assure healthful and pleasant living, is favorable for the production of crops, and usually more propitious than elsewhere found for the growth of wheat, oats, rye, barley, fruits and the vegetables.

**FREE!** For Maps and Publications, SENT FREE OF CHARGE, and for all information relating to Lands and the Northern Pacific Country, apply to or address,

PAUL SCHULZE, Gen'l Land Ag't,     R. J. WEMYSS, Gen'l Land Ag't,
    PORTLAND, OREGON.       ST. PAUL, MINN.
P. B. GROAT, Gen'l Emigration Ag't.   or,   CHAS. B. LAMBORN, Land Commissioner,
    ST. PAUL, MINN.       ST. PAUL, MINN.

the sparsely settled and largely undeveloped Pacific Northwest played a pivotal role in envisioning the modern landscape through their promotional activities. "Built upon faith in a virgin country, with a restless, expansive, ambitious people, the road is ever solicitous for development, being wholly unable to look upon its plains and mountains except with the eye of the prophetic imagination," or so Ray Stannard Baker described the process.[4]

Transcontinental railroads spent fortunes to advertise the region to prospective tourists and settlers. They distributed millions of pamphlets in the United States and Europe and established free information bureaus. In the process of advertising the New Northwest, railroads served not merely as carriers of passengers and freight but also as transmitters of visual information to people who knew little or nothing about the nation's far Northwest. Baker grasped this fact early in the twentieth century when he naively suggested to a railroad agent that his company might be interested in development. "Why," responded the official, "the West is purely a railroad enterprise. We started it in our publicity department." The remark contained more than the usual grain of truth, thought Baker, who added that "the West was inevitable but the railroad was the instrument of its fate."[5]

As early as the 1870s the Northern Pacific line, needing to convert its immense landed domain into cash to finance construction, became for a time the region's most important promoter and colonizing agent. The company's land department scattered agents throughout the United States and Europe: in 1883 the Northern Pacific had 831 active local agents in the United Kingdom alone. They distributed Pacific Northwest brochures at agricultural shows, fairs, and weekly stock and grain markets. Another 124 agents were busy on the continent recruiting immigrants from Norway, Sweden, Denmark, the Netherlands, Switzerland, and Germany. More than six hundred thousand copies of Northern Pacific publications were distributed in English, Norwegian, Swedish, Danish, Dutch, German, and Finnish. The apparent payoff was the flood of new settlers into areas tributary to the Northern Pacific in the 1880s.

---

4. Ray Stannard Baker, "Destiny and the Western Railroad," *Century Magazine* 75 (April 1908): 892–94.
5. Baker, "Destiny and the Western Railroad," 892–94.

---

53. In this advertisement from 1884, the Northern Pacific Railroad called public attention to its vast land holdings. Courtesy Eastern Washington State Historical Society, Spokane WA, L84-418.2.

Railroad promotion of the New Northwest only intensified in the early twentieth century. In 1902 the Great Northern had thirty-four agents at work in the country east of Chicago. They confined their activity to rural areas and typically gave illustrated lectures in country school houses. They used lantern slides and produce samples to excite interest in the New Northwest. Agents also visited fairs and circuses and slipped bundles of Great Northern literature under the seats of farmers' wagons. The various forms of promotional activity probably peaked from 1922 to 1925, when the nation's premier advertising agency, J. Walter Thompson, conducted a million dollar campaign for the Hill railroads to sell the wealth and resources of the Pacific Northwest to a nation ignorant of its Far Corner. This was probably the most elaborate and systematic advertising campaign of the region, and there would be nothing like it ever again.

The *Pacific Monthly*, a Portland-based magazine, illustrated the relationship among various parts of the promotion process by following the conversion of one Illinois farmer. He learned through the local newspaper that new promotional brochures were available at the railroad station; next he noticed the booklets in the depot window and got one of each. "The family sat up an hour late that night reading the pamphlets and looking at the colored pictures." Stories that told of unprecedented opportunities on the Pacific coast seemed too good to be true, they concluded, but lessening their doubts was a young man who gave an illustrated lecture a few nights later on Land Opportunities in Oregon.[6]

In the years after 1900, railroad promotional pamphlets evolved into works of art designed to appeal to prospective settlers from a variety of backgrounds. Stewart Holbrook, a popular observer of Pacific Northwest life, said of the booster pamphlets he read as a young Bostonian that they "somehow left the impression that one could have a decent living in Oregon and Washington simply by eating the gorgeous scenery." Indeed, many brochures featured varieties of luscious fruits on their covers in vivid color.

Railroads paid professional promoters to collect statistics and weave them into compelling pamphlets. Carrie Strahorn, who accompanied her husband Robert on many of his fact gathering trips for the Union Pacific Railroad, described the process: "We spent some weeks on Wood River [in Idaho] gathering statistics which Pard [her husband] wove into entertaining narrative, clothing it in attractive garb that it might coquette with restless

6. Randall R. Howard, "Following the Colonists," *Pacific Monthly* 23 (May 1910): 520–21.

spirits in the far East who were waiting for an enchantress to lure them to the great mysterious West."[7]

If statistics could effectively lessen popular doubts about the honesty of regional boosters, so too could photographs. The Great Northern published a turn-of-the-century brochure called *Photographs Tell the Truth: Pictures of the Great Northwest* which emphasized that the illustrations "are reproductions of photographs, and are therefore absolutely truthful. They give, in a very pleasing way, a perfect picture of the homes and farms of the most attractive part of Uncle Sam's big farm."

Railroads and chambers of commerce had a seemingly insatiable appetite for photographs that showed bountiful crops, unsurpassed scenery, modern cities, and scenes of industry and technology to illustrate their many promotional brochures. Their purpose was to emphasize how beautiful, modern, or progressive the New Northwest was, and hence why it was desirable as a home, place of business, tourist destination, and field for investment. No doubt many millions of people scanned the various brochures and broadsides that portrayed life in the Pacific Northwest essentially in terms of an advertiser's idealized civilization. Boosters sought to inspire newcomers to find personal success and happiness in the larger-than-life-size landscape of the Pacific Northwest, to fashion a "New Empire" for themselves and their children. The future of the region could be whatever people of perception and ambition willed it to be.

Spurred by the booming market in images that could sell the New Northwest, commercial photographers hastened to capture diverse aspects of life in the rapidly changing region. Logging scenes were the specialty of the Kinsey brothers, Darius and Clark; hardrock mining found two of its most faithful chroniclers in T. N. Barnard and Nellie Stockbridge of Wallace, Idaho; crewmen of the tall ships on Puget Sound often posed for the camera of Wilhelm Hester. None of the region's lensmen seemed more energetic or wide-ranging than Asahel Curtis of Seattle, who left a legacy of more than sixty thousand images documenting the region's turn-of-the-century decades of growth and rapid change. He made countless trips to record the region's natural beauty and document its urban development and agricultural expansion. In the process he preserved on film beautiful informal portraits of such representative types as loggers, coal miners, harvest hands, and cannery operatives.

7. Carrie Adell Strahorn, *Fifteen Thousand Miles by Stage* (1911; reprint, Lincoln: University of Nebraska Press, 1988), 2:45.

CAPTURING THE PACIFIC NORTHWEST ON FILM

After the California gold rush, photographers followed the mining frontier north to Oregon's Rogue River country in the early 1850s. Among the best known of the Pacific Northwest's pioneer lensmen was Peter Britt of Jacksonville, a Swiss native who arrived in 1852 and remained an active photographer until the end of the century. Photography during the 1850s and 1860s was a difficult and demanding trade that involved preparing a large wet-plate negative, often working in the confined space of a portable darkroom to apply a light-sensitive colloid to a clean glass plate, and then properly exposing the exceedingly slow film without benefit of a mechanical shutter or light meter. Yet in the hands of a master, the results could be astonishingly good: in 1867, the San Francisco–based Carleton E. Watkins created mammoth albumen prints of Oregon and the Columbia River that are still prized today. During the 1880s a new dry plate process simplified this work, and in 1888 George Eastman introduced the Kodak hand-held camera, which used rolls of flexible film. This remarkable innovation created the world of "snap shots" for amateurs.

The twenty years after 1900 were probably the golden age of black-and-white commercial photography, which numbered among its most prominent practitioners Fred Kiser and Benjamin Gifford of Portland, Asahel Curtis of Seattle, and Frank Palmer of Spokane. Not all of them were in the cities: Japanese-born Frank Matsura meticulously documented life in the remote Okanogan region of north-central Washington in the early 1900s. There were hundreds more commercial photographers across the Pacific Northwest, and tens of thousands of their images survive in various university and historical society archives.

If Pacific Northwesterners were publicly critical of regional boosters it was because their pamphlets aroused unrealistic expectations. Labor leaders in Oregon in the mid-1880s worried that "tons of lying pamphlets" only served to lure thousands of people west to flood local job markets and depress wages. Organized labor worked hard in 1886 to elect as governor Sylvester Pennoyer, who had as one of his top priorities the abolition of Oregon's State Board of Immigration. Pennoyer wondered aloud in his 1887 inaugural address (apparently oblivious to the Oregon Trail), "If the early pioneers of forty or fifty years ago could find Oregon without a trail through the forests or over the deserts, immigrants that desire to come here now can undoubtedly find their way." When legislators agreed and denied the Immigration Board further funding, a group of Portland entrepreneurs took over its functions, thereby probably confirming labor's suspicions that publicity benefited businessmen more than workers.

Outright deception inevitably appeared in some pamphlets. Other claims, if not actually dishonest, struck some observers as outlandish and worthy only of ridicule. Frances Fuller Victor, riding on a train through eastern Washington in the early 1890s, was amused by a promoter's injunction to "Keep Your Eye on Pasco!" "When you arrive," Victor wrote, "you look about for anything on which to keep your eye, which being blown full of sand refuses to risk more than the briefest glimpse afterwards." She noted that promoters claimed irrigation would redeem the sandy sagebrush waste around the hamlet, "but in the interim, keeping one's eyes on Pasco is a painful experience."[8]

How many settlers and tourists the pamphlets and exhibits actually attracted to the Pacific Northwest will never be known, though without question the publicists influenced many people with their vision of a dynamic and prosperous Pacific Northwest. Inevitably some would-be residents were disappointed to learn that publicists occasionally stretched the truth. Other people, however, accepted the challenge of starting life in the new settlements and relished their role as twentieth-century pioneers. When, for example, the name "Magic Valley" came into general use in the late 1930s in south-central Idaho, it was an apt description of the transformation wrought both by promotional pamphlets and irrigation.

### THE TRANSFORMING POWER OF WATER AND FIRE

Like many other commercial photographers of his day, Asahel Curtis returned time and again to photograph the Pacific Northwest's expanding landscape of irrigated farms and orchards in an effort to illustrate one particularly vivid transformation taking place at the turn of the century. The Curtis images emphasize that, at the same time the region's cities experienced rapid and seemingly uncontrolled population growth, another stream of people headed for the farmlands of the Northwest. In fact, the region's urban growth prior to the First World War did not come at the expense of rural depopulation. When irrigation opened new lands to settlement, cities and towns typically spearheaded agricultural development of the surrounding countryside and formed local markets for farmers.

Large-scale settlement of irrigated lands in the twentieth century marked the final phase of a process that began when immigrants first plodded west along the trail to Oregon. The 1850 census listed 1,164 farms in the Oregon country, almost all of them located in the Willamette Valley. The Donation

8. Frances Fuller Victor, *Atlantis Arisen; or Talks of a Tourist about Oregon and Washington* (Philadelphia: J. B. Lippincott, 1891), 351–52.

54. Doing a land office business: an army of would-be
homesteaders hopes to acquire a farm in the La Grande,
Oregon, area shortly after the turn of the century. Courtesy Idaho State Historical Society, 74-2.31.

Land Claim Act of 1850 conveyed virtually all the farmland in the valley to
settlers during the next five years.

Congress passed several additional measures ostensibly designed to encourage settlement of federal land, but the laws were clumsily written and
poorly suited to the western environment. The Homestead Act of 1862
offered 160-acre plots to settlers but extended them no credit to buy the
equipment necessary to start farming, provided no water, and offered no
services. In fact, the fertile and well-watered Willamette Valley was one of
the few areas of the region where 160-acre plots approximated the optimum
size for farms; however, settlers had already claimed its lands under the
Donation Land Claim Act. Elsewhere, especially in the semiarid country of
the interior, the traditional 160-acre homestead made little sense. Fewer
than twenty thousand claims were filed in Oregon and Washington during
the 1860s and 1870s under the provisions of the Homestead Act.

The Desert Land Act of 1877 granted 640 acres to a person willing to
irrigate it for three years. But the irrigation requirement proved prohibi-
tively expensive for individual farmers, especially when so much of the
Northwest's interior was remote from rivers and lakes. The Timber and

Stone Act of 1878 resulted in timber barons—not farmers—acquiring substantial holdings. Timbermen paid sailors, hoboes, and even their own employees to stake claims that eventually enlarged the company's domain. One Washington firm acquired a total of 100,000 acres in this way. Many would-be agrarians, in short, found it far more difficult to acquire suitable federal land than they expected. By the turn of the century, people who still dreamed of acquiring a farm from Uncle Sam placed their faith in the power of irrigation to transform the region's countless parched acres into desert gardens.

The Whitmans and Spaldings had pioneered the use of irrigation to raise crops at their missions. Mormons in Utah solved many thorny problems involving water rights and engineering and exported their expertise to pioneer settlements in southern Idaho. Early methods of irrigation varied greatly, from simply diverting water onto an open field to building extensive networks of ditches and canals. Inevitably, too, irrigation involved a certain amount of trial and error, of engineering guesswork that might leave a ditch unable to meet the water needs of people living along its banks. Often lacking survey instruments, early canal builders sometimes used frying pans or gun barrels to determine the necessary fall. Following the survey work they excavated the land with plows, scrapers, and shovels. In this manner small-scale irrigation projects went forward, though not always successfully. Construction of irrigation systems proceeded slowly in the 1860s and 1870s, picked up speed in the 1880s, and accelerated dramatically throughout the region during the late 1890s.

As irrigation in the Pacific Northwest matured, it passed through four somewhat overlapping stages: first were individual irrigators, then corporate enterprise, government aid to private enterprise, and finally large-scale federal reclamation. Following in the steps of farmers who built simple ditches either individually or cooperatively, as many Mormon pioneers did, to serve local and limited needs came private canal companies offering to irrigate substantially larger areas. Some companies were headquartered as far away as New York. All too often, however, private funds alone proved inadequate to do a proper job. Congress passed the Carey Act in 1894 to encourage state and private cooperation, and eight years later it created the Reclamation Service, offering western agrarians what amounted to a generous federal welfare program.

By the turn of the century, Idaho ranked first in irrigated land, Oregon second, and Washington a distant third. Idaho, in fact, became a national showcase for the Carey Act and eventually contained three-fifths of all land irrigated under its provisions. This measure encouraged reclamation by giving each western state a million acres of land if it found a way to irrigate them, either with private or public funds. The Twin Falls project, one of twenty-three Carey Act–funded projects in Idaho, exemplified what the Carey Act might accomplish. The largest private irrigation project in America also gave birth to the community of Twin Falls, an infant agricultural boomtown by 1905. As impressive as such achievements were, the total amount of western land irrigated under the Carey Act equaled only two average-size agricultural counties in Illinois. The state of Washington irrigated nothing under that law.

The Carey Act was designed to keep federal participation to a minimum. That policy changed with passage of the Newlands Act of 1902, which created the United States Reclamation Service (Bureau of Reclamation after 1923) to supervise a number of new dam and canal projects and complete defunct older ones like the New York Canal near Boise. The Minidoka project, which received its first water in 1909, was one of two large reclamation projects allotted to Idaho, and it made possible not only the reclamation of thousands of acres of farmland but also the building of a host of new agricultural communities. The completion of the 349-foot-high Arrowrock Dam in 1915—the world's tallest until 1932—gave the Boise Valley a surplus of water for the first time and permitted the creation of 1,167 new irrigated farms comprising 67,454 acres.

Large-scale irrigation on the Snake River plain (the location of roughly two-thirds of Idaho's irrigated land) helped push agriculture past mining and timber as the state's chief economic asset. By 1990 approximately three million acres were under cultivation on the Snake River plain, with the massive circular sprinkler systems developed after World War II being used to supplement older canal methods. Today, other irrigated lands in the Pacific Northwest include the Yakima, Wenatchee, and Okanogan valleys, the Columbia Basin project in central Washington, and scattered areas in eastern Oregon.

Reclamation was never simply a matter of economics and engineering, just as irrigation canals were never merely sources of water. Canals and their life-giving water created a special kind of oasis settlement that combined the complexity and dependency of urban life with a rural environment. Promoters often described such communities as perfect Gardens of Eden—one booster claimed that while clouds may fail to bring rain, "the canal never fails"—but such places were also highly vulnerable. The social and economic well-being of dwellers on reclaimed lands depended to a large

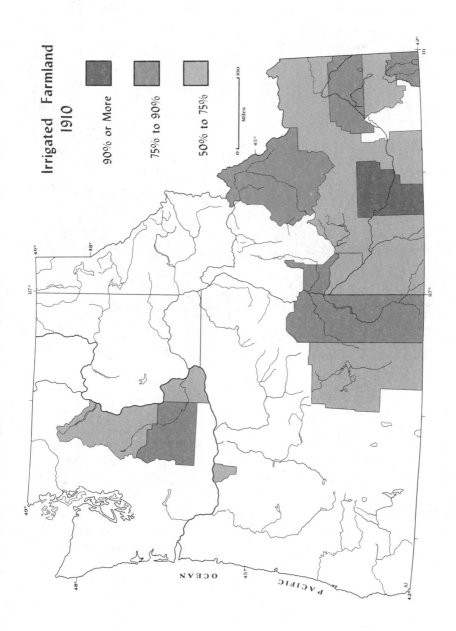

Irrigated Farmland
1910

90% or More

75% to 90%

50% to 75%

Miles
0        100

PACIFIC    OCEAN

55. Irrigation frontier: on a isolated stretch of the Snake
River plain in 1899, a construction crew working on the
Last Chance Ditch pitched its camp. Courtesy Idaho
State Historical Society, 79-95.37.

degree on federal money, power, bureaucracy, the technological expertise of
the few, and occasionally the caprice of nature. Such was irrigation's dark
underside.

An irrigator might spend countless hours uprooting and burning sagebrush to transform arid land into fields of potatoes and sugar beets, only to
have a drought reduce the amount of water available and cause crops to
wither and die. Unscrupulous or inexpert operators who failed to deliver the
amount of water they promised occasionally victimized irrigators. During
the 1920s the total amount of irrigated farmland in Washington actually
declined by thirty thousand acres. Some people simply walked away from
their parched crops and desiccated hopes; many irrigators in southern Idaho
channeled their anger into the Progressive party that sprang up there in the
early 1920s.

Framers of the Carey and Newlands acts had confidently expected that

IRRIGATION AS A WAY OF LIFE

Annie Pike Greenwood, who with her husband sought to farm the Snake River plain in the early twentieth century, reflected on the vulnerability as well as potential for conflict in an irrigation community when she wrote, "Water among us sagebrush folks was money. When a man stole your water, he committed grand larceny, no matter how much he himself might feel his crime mitigated by the hymns he sang to Jesus a-Sunday. Water in the sage-brush country is not free, as the rain from heaven. Both the just and the unjust have to pay for it, or it is shut off, though the Water Company is not hard-boiled about it, so far as I know. If your head-gate is stuffed with weeds or gunny-sacks, it may mean the loss of all the money you can make that year, for your crop will die."—Annie Pike Greenwood, *We Sagebrush Folk* (1934), 380

thousands of new 160-acre farms would be carved from the sage. Because the Newlands Act made it easy for a U.S. citizen to acquire irrigated land, it was hailed as a triumph of democracy. But in most areas of the West, it was common for irrigation projects to favor very large operators. During a time of low farm prices in the mid-1920s, it was estimated that settlers on the Minidoka project needed $500 in capital to succeed. Because few had that much money, over 40 percent of Minidoka's farmers ended up as the tenants of wealthy landowners.

Irrigation districts were eventually supposed to repay the cost of reclamation; few ever did. The Newlands Act thus functioned all too often as a grandiose welfare program that proclaimed the virtues of family-sized farms while making millionaires of some western agrarians who managed to amass large holdings. A final irony was in the word "reclamation," a term which implied that land was being returned to its original state of productivity and contained no hint that some land was best left as found.

Even as irrigation water transformed the arid lands, massive fires that swept through the forests of the Bitterroot Mountains in 1910 left an indelible impression of another sort on Pacific Northwesterners and an imprint on the landscape still visible today. Driven by hurricane force winds, the two-day conflagration that began on 20 August brought heavy smoke and darkness at noon. For a time it seemed as if spontaneous combustion would completely consume the tinder-dry woods where only a quarter-inch of rain had fallen since early June. Flames leaped three hundred feet high and appeared to mow down large stands of trees like a scythe cutting dry grass. The 1910 blaze consumed mining and railroad structures, homesteads, and even

56. Five years after the great fire of 1910, the Milwaukee
Lumber Company used logging railroads to remove
burned timber from the badly scarred hillsides of northern Idaho. Courtesy Idaho State Historical Society,
72-139.6.

whole communities. Women and children were hastily evacuated from Wallace before the flames roared in and incinerated a third of the town. After the
fire ruined Wallace's water system, the mayor permitted saloons to remain
open on Sunday because beer replaced drinking water (a substitution no
doubt cheered by many residents of the hard-drinking mining center).

The several thousand forest fires of 1910 blackened 3.3 million acres in
the four Northwest states. Smoke drifted as far east as Boston, and President
William Howard Taft dispatched two companies of black troops from Fort
George Wright in Spokane to help man the fire lines. At Avery they were
stationed at the doors of each coach of a special evacuation train to keep
order and, if cut off by fire, to escort all women and children into the nearby
river for their safety. The fire fighters of 1910 typically hiked twenty-five to
thirty miles a day to battle a blaze mainly with shovels and axes. Seventy-

two firefighters died. Salvage from the two-million-acre burn took years; some cedar charred in 1910 was still being sold in the late 1970s.

One result of the 1910 blaze was to emphasize fire protection as a major function of the Forest Service: previously there had been few lookouts and the detection of forest fires depended mainly on intermittent patrols. The change, however, did not prevent the great Tillamook Burn of 1933, when more than 300,000 acres of Douglas fir timber, equivalent to about two-thirds of the nation's annual output that year, was charred or sent eight miles into the atmosphere as smoke. After 1940, a campaign of public education designed to keep Washington and other timber-producing states green supplemented state and federal fire prevention measures, although in recent years another school of thought has held that fires are natural and should be allowed to burn for the health of the forest.

In any case, the transforming power of fire was not limited to the forests. Fire plagued the Northwest's urban dwellers from the beginning days of pioneer settlement. Because the chief building material was wood, it was used for everything from sidewalks and bridges to log cabins and false-front store buildings and barns. Most early government buildings were also fashioned from wood. Unfortunately, wooden structures illuminated by candles or oil lamps were highly vulnerable to fire which ravaged some communities almost on an annual basis. The booming mining community of Idaho City, for instance, suffered four disastrous fires between 1865 and 1871. The fire of 1865 left an estimated seven thousand people homeless, and that of May 1867 consumed 440 buildings. Fire also consumed the entire business district of Goldendale, Washington, in 1888. Some nineteenth-century communities responded to the threat of fire by placing barrels of water at intervals along the main streets, while others installed hydrants and water mains. Volunteer fire companies offered both protection and a popular social outlet.

Wooden communities were prone to destruction by fire, and in time they also came to symbolize to many Pacific Northwesterners an unprogressive urban environment. It became increasingly common after a devastating fire for cities and towns to replace wooden business structures with brick and stone ones in an effort to fireproof the community and give it the appearance of a prosperous modern city. Both Seattle and Spokane, after the great fires of 1889 destroyed the initial, mainly wooden cities, rebuilt with marble, granite, sandstone, and brick, and in the process added height to their downtown structures to set themselves apart from the single-story wooden villages of the hinterlands.

57. Among the forces shaping a new Northwest were
natural disasters like the flood that smashed through
Heppner, Oregon, following a cloudburst on 14 June
1903. It was all over in thirty minutes, but during that
time 225 people died, nearly all of them from battering
from the debris, not from drowning. That was about
one-quarter of Heppner's population. Violent storms are
not common in the Pacific Northwest, although on Columbus Day 1962 a hurricane slammed into western
Oregon without warning, uprooting trees, wrecking
buildings, setting houseboats afloat, and downing hundreds of miles of power lines. Winds at Seattle's Space
Needle were clocked at 83 miles per hour, while at
Hebo on the Oregon Coast they registered 170 miles per
hour. The freak storm killed forty-eight people in the
three West Coast states. Courtesy Oregon Historical
Society, ORHI 1445.

## THE BUILT ENVIRONMENT:
### SYMBOLS OF PROSPERITY AND REFINEMENT

The rural landscape of the Pacific Northwest, especially in the vicinity of a
sawmill, logging camp, or cannery, often had a slovenly appearance; likewise, most early settlements were ramshackle affairs, thrown together in a
hurry from available building materials. Some pioneer dwellings in Wash-

ington were mere huts carved from the stumps of giant cedar trees. More common was the ubiquitous log cabin. It was the common-denominator structure of most early settlements, revealing little about the owner's wealth or status. Sawmills, however, were among the first businesses in pioneer communities, and as soon as milled lumber became available, framed structures often replaced log cabins.

By the 1870s, as society became more stable and the first crude settlements began to achieve the patina that comes with age and affluence, "style" became an important feature of housing as local carpenters learned to adapt plans popular in the East. Imposing Italianate and Queen Anne style residences soon appeared in many communities, along with humble workers' cottages. It often appeared that more was better for the wealthy, who embellished their dwellings with turrets, towers, brackets, cupolas, and verandas; a parlor crammed with all kinds of ornaments became a symbol of prosperity and refinement. Every rural community had at least one or two pretentious mansions.

In larger cities, neighborhoods of more or less uniform home design emerged, as happened on Seattle's Queen Anne Hill. The division between haves and have-nots grew starker and much more visible than during pioneer days as simple frame cottages huddled together near the commercial sections of cities and in company towns such as Black Diamond, Washington. Many of the region's single working men lived in large boarding houses and residential hotels.

Styles in homes changed over the years. Fashionable residences in the early twentieth century shunned the popular styles of previous decades. The middle class trended away from embellishment toward simple craftsman homes, with the bungalow becoming such a popular variation that it dominated whole neighborhoods in the region's major cities.

Large and elegant residences lined fashionable thoroughfares. During the first decade of the twentieth century, some of the region's very wealthy also moved to secluded residential retreats beyond the city limits. William Boeing and other Seattle business magnates built vast estates in the Highlands north of the city in a rolling forested enclave. People with money erected vacation retreats on the Oregon coast, on Puget Sound islands, and along mountain lakes.

By the turn of the century, affluent Northwesterners were increasingly turning to professional architects to design their residences and public structures. Frank Lloyd Wright brought his Prairie style houses to Seattle in the early twentieth century, whereas the popular Spokane architect Kirtland Cutter favored a Swiss-style chalet design to create rustic but elegant structures well suited to the region's mountain and lake environment. He also designed ostentatious English country homes for wealthy families in the Spokane area.

The Pacific Northwest's built environment eventually included examples of a variety of architectural gems that ranged from the Mission style of the Union Pacific station in Boise to the Queen Anne style of Spokane's Brown Addition. Few if any structures, however, were more elaborate than Boise's Moorish-revival Natatorium, which opened to the public in 1892 and housed a 125-foot-long pool, dining room, club room, tea room, and bath. The Pacific Northwest's built environment included not only business blocks, railroad stations, court houses, and residences, but also landscape architecture. One of the nation's most prestigious landscape firms, the Olmsted Brothers of Brookline, Massachusetts, whose founder, Frederick Law Olmsted, had earlier designed New York's Central Park, applied its considerable talents in the landscape designs for many of the Pacific Northwest's urban parks, college and university campuses, and private residences.

Few examples of the region's built environment were more ostentatious than the Maryhill mansion that the prominent but eccentric businessman Sam Hill erected on a high and treeless promontory overlooking the Columbia River. Near Columbus (now Maryhill), Washington, a place where "the sunshine of the East meets the rain of the West," he purchased seven thousand acres of land in 1907 and there proposed to build a Quaker agricultural community that he dreamed would mature into a large city.

Hill's vision was that of a Pacific Northwest booster, but his cultural model was imported from Europe. His mansion, solidly constructed of poured concrete for fire protection, was in the style of a French chateau; nearby, he erected a concrete replica of England's Stonehenge as a World War I memorial. Hill filled his castle on the Columbia with Rodin sculptures, which became the centerpiece of a massive collection of nineteenth-century French Art. He even persuaded Queen Marie of Romania, the granddaughter of Queen Victoria of England and of Czar Alexander II of Russia, to travel to remote Maryhill in 1926 to dedicate his still-unfinished museum.

## A GROWING REGIONAL SELF-CONFIDENCE

During the first decade of the twentieth century, Portland and Seattle each hosted a world's fair. Portland's Lewis and Clark Exposition of 1905 drew

58. F. Jay Haynes photographed the Park Hotel in Centralia, Washington, in August 1890. The following month in an article that appeared in the *Washington Magazine*, J. K. Campbell complained: "The fact that most people eat all their food at restaurants and live in rooms or board at hotels, robs social life of that sacredness which is so endearing. The home town life of a western family is of a very unsatisfactory kind. Home to them is merely a place to sleep in, and not even that at all times. Home has a different meaning out west to what it has in most civilized places." Courtesy Haynes Foundation Collection, Montana Historical Society, H-2083.

59. The Court of Honor at Seattle's Alaska-Yukon-Pacific Exposition in 1909. The fountain remains a landmark on the University of Washington campus. Courtesy Special Collections Division, University of Washington Libraries, UW 1473.

about three million visitors and Seattle's Alaska-Yukon-Pacific Exposition of 1909 almost four million. At each fair a variety of popular entertainment enlivened the midway (the Trail in Portland and the Paystreak in Seattle), but the events also served to commemorate historic occasions and to boost the region. Portland's extravaganza commemorated one hundred years of regional growth since the Lewis and Clark expedition; the Seattle fair highlighted the accomplishments of the decade that followed the famous Klondike gold rush.

Will H. Parry, chairman of the ways and means and finance committee of the Seattle exposition, called it "merely a gigantic piece of advertising" for the Pacific Northwest. One correspondent who attended the Seattle fair observed, "This summer's show is essentially a bid to settlers, and invitation to home-seekers, and an advertisement for Eastern capital to come West and help develop the natural resources which offer wealth on every hand." There were dozens of promotional booths, each with its incessant chant "Boost, Boost, Boost." Massive electric letters told visitors "You'll like Tacoma," while nearby a billboard responded, "Yakima is Better."[9] Promoters designed the fairs to attract the attention of the eastern United States and Europe, and both were harbingers of the mass culture of the later twentieth century that would include movies, radio, and eventually television.

Each extravaganza represented a coming-of-age party for a city and a region, a time to reflect on the past and wax eloquent about the future. It became common for residents to speak of the Lewis and Clark Exposition as the division between the old and new Oregon, whereas the Alaska-Yukon-Pacific Exposition fixed in the popular mind a special connection between Seattle and Alaska.

During the opening years of the twentieth century, every major city developed a new skyline. Stimulated by the Lewis and Clark Exposition, the city of Portland embarked on a building boom that gave it a vertical dimension. In Boise, completion in 1901 of the Idanha Hotel, an elegant structure suggesting a six-story-high French chateau, initiated a building trend that created the appearance of a modern metropolis. Boise, with its many tree-lined streets, liked to promote itself as "the Athens of the desert," a phrase first used by attorney Clarence Darrow in 1906. From 1912 to 1930, however, no new tall buildings were built in Boise and the emphasis shifted from the city's skyline to its homes. A network of streetcar and electric interurban lines made it possible for Boise, as for every one of the region's major cities, to expand outward to encompass new suburban neighborhoods.

The City Beautiful movement, which swept the nation after Chicago's 1893 World's Fair and was widely regarded as a sign of modernity, left its mark on the cities of the Pacific Northwest. The Olmsted Brothers provided Seattle and Spokane with plans for city parks and graceful boulevards. The Olmsteds likewise drafted Portland's first city plan in 1903. The Greater Portland plan of 1911 envisioned a Paris on the Pacific. Like the ambitious Bogue plan announced the same year for Seattle, it offered boulevards, a civic center, and harbor improvements as antidotes to the disorderly growth of the past. Whatever their functional aspects, the Seattle and Portland plans emphasized civic beauty, but both became entangled in local politics, and only fragments of each plan were ever implemented.

9. R. S. Jones, "What the Visitor Sees at the Seattle Fair," *American Review of Reviews* 40 (July 1909): 65–68.

In some cases, envisioning a New Northwest meant planning for entirely new towns, such as New Plymouth in Idaho and Longview in Washington. When the irrigation colony of New Plymouth was launched in 1895 by the Payette Valley Irrigation and Water Power company, it was intended, in the words of its cofounder William E. Smythe, "to represent a high social and industrial ideal." Many New Plymouth colonists were professionals from Chicago and the urban Midwest. Their dream was to make the town self-sufficient through the development and operation of small diversified farm plots that produced for local and the Eastern markets. In this way the founders of New Plymouth hoped to give agrarians the advantages of town life while preventing the isolation all too common in a rural environment.

Even more ambitious was the plan for Longview, which attracted considerable attention before it became a reality in the 1920s. Large advertisements in popular national magazines proclaimed the opportunities and advantages to be found in the new industrial city arising on the lower Columbia River. R. A. Long, whose Southern-based lumber company sought new forests to conquer after World War I, purchased a total of twenty-two thousand acres in Washington in 1922 on which to develop an ideal city to house workers and prevent haphazard development around his vast new mill complex.

Long's dream community was loosely patterned after the Country Club district of Kansas City, where the Long-Bell Lumber company had its headquarters. Both developments featured streets and boulevards to accommodate automobile traffic, an extensive park system, and zoned residences, a relatively new development in municipal planning. In addition to the usual retail area and a distinct wholesale district, light industrial district, small apartment district, and civic center, there were income-graded residential districts. This was clearly to be a model city, not a typical milltown, that Long hoped would attract a high-quality, family-oriented class of worker.

With a vision similar to that of the city planners, Oregon engineer Samuel C. Lancaster designed the new Columbia River Highway, a route that was to be beautiful as well as functional. When Oregon opened the first section to traffic in 1915, the highway's spectacular engineering and aesthetic appeal attracted world attention. The first major paved highway in the Pacific Northwest also made automobile travel possible from Portland through the Columbia Gorge to eastern Oregon.

New industries, like beet sugar in Idaho, first developed in the 1890s by the Mormons of Utah, spurred economic growth in the Snake River country. With the erection of Idaho's first large beet sugar factory near Idaho Falls in 1903, the region gained a new cash crop. Boosters pointed with pride to the

60. The planned city of Longview, Washington, as it appeared about 1925. By 1990, Longview had become a community of 31,499 residents, but it never fulfilled the dream of those who envisioned it to be a model city. Courtesy Oregon Historical Society, CN 018740.

growing number of acres under irrigation (the number in Idaho doubled from 1.2 million in 1900 to 2.2 million in 1910), to the completion of the world's tallest dam on the Boise River in 1915, and to a growing amount of hydroelectric power. Some regional boosters claimed that the Pacific Northwest possessed one-third of the hydroelectric power likely to be generated in the United States. Spokane boosters predicted that "white coal" and the city's extensive railroad connections would make it a great national manufacturing center. Developers of even greater vision talked of the prosperity that growing trans-Pacific commerce would bring to the Pacific Northwest.

That was not entirely wishful thinking, because a variety of statistical indicators offered reason to view the future with confidence. From 1900 to 1910 the population of Oregon increased by two-thirds, while that of both Idaho and Washington more than doubled. A total of 2.1 million people were living in the Pacific Northwest in 1910. The region's manufacturing output and payrolls doubled between 1900 and 1914, the year the Panama Canal opened, and gave regional boosters additional reasons to think that an era of growth was only beginning.

By the eve of World War I, the people of the Pacific Northwest had many reasons to be proud of their region. Boosters could point to numerous schools and libraries, literary, debating, and music societies, professional organizations, and intellectual and artistic achievements as evidence that the region had succeeded in removing many rough edges from a society shaped by its recent frontier past and its natural resource–based present. The appearance in 1905 of the first professional history of the region, *A History of the Pacific Northwest* by University of Oregon professor Joseph Schafer, represented an expression of maturing regional self-confidence every bit as significant as the formation of some new association to market the region's fruit or timber or a new statistic recording a growing market for Northwest wheat in Asia.

But the regional self-confidence that was so much a part of envisioning a New Northwest proved a fragile thing, and all it took to shatter the euphoric mood was the economic downturn that began in 1912 and grew progressively worse over the next two years. It became apparent that the Pacific Northwest's prospects had been overstated and that it had not escaped the stranglehold of an extractive economy. With the loss of confidence and vision, festering social and economic problems of years past assumed a more menacing appearance, and the wartime years of 1914 to 1921 were neither happy nor settled.

# Part IV

# Progress and Its Discontents

# Profile: The World of
# May Arkwright Hutton

*

Some of the atrocities practiced on the prisoners in this improvised prison at Kellogg, Idaho, by old "General Bulldozium," Governor "Stepanfetchit" and his man "Friday," at the instigation of the Standard Oil Company and the silver and lead barons of the Coeur d'Alenes, are scarcely fit for polite ears. Read them, you curled darlings of wealth, you trifling puppets of society.—May Arkwright Hutton, *The Coeur D'Alenes; or, A Tale of the Modern Inquisition in Idaho* (1900)

*

Talk of gold and a sense of adventure brought May Arkwright to northern Idaho. Like thousands of others in 1883, the twenty-three-year-old from Ohio was lured to the mining country by advertisements proclaiming: "Nuggets weighing $50, $100, $200 of gold free for the picking up; it fairly glistens." But May had barely reached the Coeur d'Alenes before the transition from placer to lode mining gave the region an industrial character, with most miners now working for wages. The legitimate moneymaking opportunities open to women in such an economy were at best limited.

For the plain-faced and heavy-set May Arkwright, hardship was nothing new. Born out of wedlock and abandoned by her father, she spent her youth caring for an aged and blind grandfather. She became an accomplished cook by the age of ten. In the Coeur d'Alenes May earned a meager living feeding hungry miners at her boardinghouse. A diligent worker and a supporter of union labor, she got along well in the rough mining camp society of Kellogg

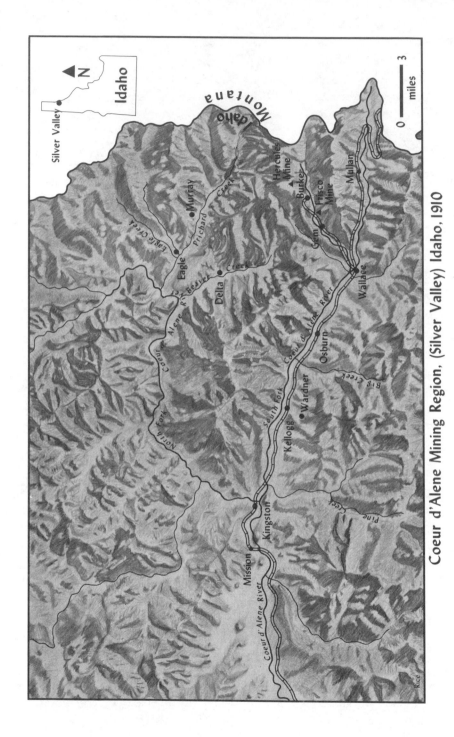

Coeur d'Alene Mining Region, (Silver Valley) Idaho, 1910

and Wardner. Her good food and love of life won the hearts of the miners, and of a railroader, Levi W. "Al" Hutton, whom she married in 1887.

May Arkwright Hutton had an inquisitive mind. She spent her spare time reading political tracts that fired her passion for justice and inspired her to fight for organized labor and female suffrage. In her unpolished and flamboyant way, she championed the underdog. In 1899 that meant getting her husband out of the hated "bull pen," the primitive stockade filled with men imprisoned in the latest mining war that convulsed the Coeur d'Alene region.

Two major episodes of industrial violence wracked the new state of Idaho during the decade of the 1890s, one in 1892 and another in 1899. Mine-owners battled on one side; unionized miners, on the other. First in the town of Wardner in 1887, and then in Gem, Burke, and Mullan, hard-rock miners had secretly formed unions in response to their need for economic protection and fraternity. Unions provided camaraderie, hospital care for the sick or injured, and money for a decent burial. Union halls typically had an assembly room large enough to handle a crowd of two hundred or more and served as centers of community life—places where workers could gather for dances, picnics, public lectures, and boxing matches.

But miners' unions were more than fraternal lodges and community centers; they were also organizations fighting for decent wages and hours, for safety regulations to minimize the dangers of a cave-in or poisonous air, and for an end to company stores and boardinghouses, two vivid reminders of the mineowners' paternalism and power. In a larger sense, the miners' unions fought for the right to exist at a time when management regarded them as threats to its nearly absolute control of the workplace.

At about the same time as the miners organized, the most powerful mineowners in the Coeur d'Alenes formed a protective association. A variety of problems beset the owners, chiefly the falling price of silver and rising railroad rates, but their new association soon emerged as a vehicle to checkmate union labor. Mineowners employed a variety of effective weapons: they cut wages, and when workers struck, they hired spies and armed guards, fired union members, and substituted nonunion or scab labor imported from outside the region.

In late 1891 the owners hired a Pinkerton detective, Charles A. Siringo, to spy on union meetings. He succeeded beyond his employers' wildest dreams. Adopting the alias C. Leon Allison, Siringo took a job at the Gem Mine, joined the local miners' union, and proved to be one of its most earnest members. His fellow workers soon elected him recording secretary, a position that for seven months gained him access to the union's innermost secrets. At night under cover of darkness, he regularly walked the three miles from Gem to Wallace to mail his reports to the mineowners.

When the mineowners discharged union members in midwinter and replaced them with scabs protected by armed guards, Siringo's spying proved vital. On several occasions his advance warnings enabled the owners to thwart union plans to stop scabs from entering the region. Suspicious union members finally unmasked Siringo, who eluded an angry mob when he dropped through a hole previously sawed in the floor of his rooming house and crawled under the board sidewalk to a nearby creek and freedom. But his treachery angered miners and triggered their violent retaliation against the owners.

The culminating act in the tense six-month drama began in the town of Gem on 11 July 1892 with the exchange of gunshots between union members and guards barricaded in the Frisco Mine's ore-processing mill. The fight spread to the Gem Mine. Sporadic shots continued for hours, then suddenly a roar shook the valley. Dynamiters had launched a bundle of explosives down a pipe that carried water into the Frisco mill. The blast demolished the structure, and falling timbers killed one worker and injured several others. The guards and scabs promptly surrendered, as did those at other mines and mills farther down the canyon. Miners disarmed the scabs and marched them to trains to ship them out of the valley. In the wake of the violence, six men were dead (three on each side), and more than a dozen were injured. But unrest had not ended.

At the Bunker Hill and Sullivan complex near Wardner, six hundred armed men seized a $250,000 concentrator and threatened to destroy it if the company—the most influential in the region—did not discharge its scabs. The manager agreed, and soon all the strikebreakers had left the Coeur d'Alenes. Someone tacked a broom onto the last boxcar to signify a clean sweep.

With the scabs gone, union miners celebrated their victory. But their jubilation was premature. Because of the violence, Governor Norman Willey declared martial law. State and federal troops soon arrived to put down the insurrection and protect scab workers. Union men, who had hoped never to see the strikebreakers again, were "crestfallen and sullen."

Charles Siringo, who had observed the violence from a concealed viewpoint in the hills, guided the soldiers as they rounded up hundreds of people. One witness predicted that "in two days the Coeur d'Alenes will be a vast military prison for the miners' union." That prophecy came true when authorities collected three hundred men in a vast dragnet—and not just union workers, but justices of the peace, lawyers, merchants, saloonkeepers—anyone sympathetic to the union and a few who were not.

Troops herded the prisoners into the two bull pens at Wallace and Wardner, where many of them were confined for nearly two months awaiting a hearing. At first most of the men considered their arrest a joke; they laughed and sang and enjoyed a supper prepared by the ladies. But as the weeks passed, they complained loudly, and tempers grew short. On one occasion when Siringo went into the prison yard to identify a certain person, the anger of the captives flared into a near riot. Only the cocked pistol Siringo held in his hand and the armed soldiers prevented bloodshed. Sanitary conditions became unbearable in the summer heat, and even those outside the Wallace stockade complained of "the most noxious odors" pervading the town.

In nearby Spokane, laboring people rallied in a show of support for the imprisoned miners. Nearly a thousand people met in the city's Haymarket Square in late July to hear speeches and music and to give donations for the prisoners. "The representatives of organized labor in Spokane have gone crazy," complained the Spokane *Review*, which supported the mineowners.

The state finally transported twenty-five union leaders to Boise for trial. Siringo was there to testify, and one of his targets was Ed Boyce, a muscular young Irish immigrant and an officer of the Wardner Miners' Union. Boyce was subsequently sentenced to spend six more months in prison. During his stint in jail, he and his fellow union members laid plans for a bigger and more effective organization, the Western Federation of Miners, a union that soon included not only Coeur d'Alene miners but also workers in Montana, British Columbia, and other mining districts in the West.

In the short run, though, the future looked bleak for organized miners. Their union had proved no match for the combined might of the owners and the military. The scabs and armed guards were soon back on the job as if nothing had happened. Boyce returned home to find himself blacklisted, unable to obtain work in any major mine. But his imprisonment ultimately proved a blessing in disguise: to many people he was a hero, and north Idaho voters sent him back to Boise in 1894—this time as a state senator. And two years later fellow miners elected him president of the Western Federation of Miners.

As head of the new union, Boyce was a fire-breathing militant. He injected life into the shaky organization, expanded its influence throughout the West, and urged it down the road to socialism. His experiences in the bull pen, the Boise prison, and even the Idaho legislature made him cynical about power and politics and the miners' chances of ever obtaining justice. "Every union," he advised, "should have a rifle club." In the war between the classes, Boyce was determined to win next time.

Next time arrived in 1899. Unlike Boyce, May and Al Hutton had managed to avoid trouble in 1892, and they certainly did not go looking for it in 1899. Al's job as a railway engineer was normally uneventful: for ten hours a day he steamed up and down a Northern Pacific feeder line, setting out empty cars at one mine, picking up loaded ones at another. But a gun in his back interrupted Al's routine on Saturday, 29 April 1899.

"Get this thing going," ordered the miner who prodded him with the weapon. A second man covered the fireman. Behind the engine other men swarmed onto boxcars. Al eased his train slowly down the tracks that threaded the narrow canyon from Burke to Gem. "Stop at the Frisco powder house," his captor ordered. There Al's nonpaying passengers broke into the locked building and loaded almost two tons of explosives onto the little freight, transforming it into the "Dynamite Express," a train bound for history if not glory.

Along the way to Wallace and Wardner, Al paused to pick up more passengers as ordered. Soon almost a thousand riders—nearly half of them masked and armed with rifles—had crowded aboard. They were headed for Wardner to teach the mighty Bunker Hill and Sullivan Company a lesson. Following the violence of 1892, the Western Federation of Miners had successfully persuaded most of the large mines in the Coeur d'Alenes to pay union-scale wages, but not the Bunker Hill and Sullivan. Its managers claimed that low profits had forced them to cut costs and to use only nonunion labor. Union members attempted to infiltrate the company's work force, but Bunker Hill and Sullivan invariably identified and discharged them. Tensions mounted until the day the miners commandeered Al Hutton's train.

When the Dynamite Express approached the Bunker Hill and Sullivan complex, company guards fled along with the superintendent and manager —a wise move considering the odds. The workers burned the company's office and boardinghouse and placed three thousand pounds of dynamite around the concentrator's support pilings. At 2:26 P.M., seconds after the last stick was in place, someone—probably a miner—lit the fuse. Three explosions reduced the costly structure to matchsticks. Miners rejoiced and congratulated themselves on their victory in the "Second Battle of Bunker Hill," a reference to the revolutionary war battle. The deed done, the miners

61. A violent explosion on 29 April 1899, reduced the Bunker Hill & Sullivan concentrator to kindling and opened another chapter in the lengthy war between labor and management in the Coeur d'Alene mining region. Courtesy Barnard-Stockbridge Collection, University of Idaho Library, Moscow ID, 8-X13.

ordered Al Hutton to take them home. Next morning, most of them reported for work as usual. But one young miner prophesied correctly, "You can't steal railroad trains, dynamite mines, and burn villages without some reaction."

Telegraph lines sped news of the violence to Idaho's governor, Frank Steunenberg. A man who emphasized the common touch—he refused to wear a necktie to any state function—Steunenberg had once been a member of a printers' union. With the backing of labor he was elected governor in 1896 and again in 1898. But he could not condone what had happened in the Coeur d'Alenes. He promised to "punish and totally eradicate from this community a class of criminals who for years have been committing murders and other crimes in open violation of law."

Because the Idaho militia was then stationed in the Philippines in the aftermath of the Spanish-American War, Steunenberg wired for federal troops and declared the Coeur d'Alene region to be in a state of insurrection.[1] Leaders of the Western Federation of Miners hastily left the area, but most rank-and-file members calmly awaited their fate.

Brigadier General Henry Clay Merriam and almost eight hundred blue-jacketed troops arrived by special train on 3 May, and the general promptly ordered every miner herded into the bull pen—between six hundred and seven hundred people. One of the prisoners was Al Hutton. He protested his innocence, but his wife protested even more vigorously. She visited the pen daily, smuggling in food when possible. She was popular with the prisoners, but the soldiers resented her rough and abusive manner and became hostile and obscene. But after two weeks she finally got her husband released, apparently when she appealed to the fraternal spirit of his fellow Masons.

But May Hutton was not through with the bull pen or the authorities. With a pen dipped in rhetorical acid, she wrote a libelous novel entitled *The Coeur d'Alenes; or, A Tale of the Modern Inquisition in Idaho.* In it she referred to the Mine Owners' Protective Association as the Mushroom Mining Men's Association and to Frank Steunenberg as Governor Stepanfetchit. One of the heroes of her lurid tale was Ed Boyce, the militant president of the Western Federation of Miners and a friend of the Huttons.

Circumstances connected Boyce and the Huttons in several ways. After Al's release from the bull pen, the railroad refused to rehire him because a coroner's jury had labeled him "a willing tool of the rioters." From then on he devoted his working hours to a small, seemingly unproductive mine— the Hercules—in which he and May had invested their savings of a few hundred dollars. Boyce acquired an interest in the same mine in 1901 when he married Eleanor Day, a sister of the man who had sold the Huttons their share of the property.

In many ways life in the Coeur d'Alenes in the 1890s was one big gamble: workers gambled with their lives every day in the mines; investors gambled with their dollars. For common folk, investing in a mine was a serious matter but as chancy as playing a slot machine today. The pull of a handle or the turn of a shovel might spell the difference between poverty and wealth. If Lady Luck smiled, the pay-off could be enormous, and in 1901 she smiled on the Hercules. Shortly after Boyce married, the mine developed into one

---

1. Martial law continued until the end of his term, and no miner was allowed to work at any mine in the district without a state permit. Permits were denied to those unable to prove they had not participated in the Bunker Hill bombing.

62. The Hercules Mine in Burke, Idaho, in 1901. May Arkwright Hutton (1860–1916) is pictured on the tracks; Levi W. Hutton is at the far right. Courtesy Barnard-Stockbridge Collection, University of Idaho Library, Moscow ID, 8-x145.

of the great Coeur d'Alene bonanzas. The Huttons were rich; the Boyces were rich.

The transformation of Ed Boyce was dramatic. He resigned as head of the Western Federation of Miners in 1902, reportedly because of ill health, and retired to Portland, where he lived another forty years. To give Boyce something to do, his wife and her family purchased the stately Portland Hotel, a genteel establishment in the heart of the city's financial district. Boyce managed it well, and for more than two decades members of the Portland business community favored its dining room, apparently unconcerned that its manager had once declared war on capitalists like them. The onetime militant had mellowed; gone was talk of violence and socialism. Improbable as it seemed, the former president of the Western Federation of Miners became president of the Oregon Hotel Association.

As for the Huttons, their small investment in the Hercules made them millionaires. They bought a big house in Wallace and entertained lavishly. In 1906 they moved to a mansion in Spokane and invested in real estate there. They had maids and a chauffeur-driven car, and May Hutton even tried to buy up and destroy all remaining copies of her embarrassingly amateurish novel. Yet despite all the changes in her life, she never lost her flamboyant style or her sympathy for the disadvantaged. She continued to campaign vigorously for woman suffrage and supported orphanages and day-care centers. In 1912 she became the first woman ever elected to the Democratic National Convention. Some people say May forgot her friends in organized labor after she became rich. That charge is false, because when she died in 1915, she left $5,000 to help build a labor temple in Spokane. Seventy years later, in 1985, along with William Boeing, Bing Crosby, and others, May Arkwright Hutton was named to the Washington State Hall of Fame.

One associate of the Huttons in the Hercules venture who failed to share in the big bonanza was Harry Orchard, a strange and violent man who wrote a bloody postscript to the Coeur d'Alene mining wars. It was Orchard who claimed to have touched off the blast that destroyed the Bunker Hill and Sullivan concentrator, but like many of his boasts, that assertion remains suspect. He apparently lost his share of the Hercules in 1898 or 1899 to settle a debt, although in a moralizing mood he later claimed that "women, gambling, and whisky got it all."

In late 1905 Orchard made headlines across America when he planted a bomb that killed Steunenberg at his home in Caldwell. For that crime, the state convicted Orchard and sentenced him to spend the rest of his life in prison. He cheated the gallows only by confessing that top leaders of the Western Federation of Miners had hired him to assassinate Steunenberg in revenge for his actions in the Coeur d'Alenes six years earlier. Boyce, of course, was no longer associated with the union, but Idaho officials quietly pursued William D. Haywood, the union's secretary-treasurer, Charles Moyer, the union's president, and George Pettibone, a blacklisted Coeur d'Alene miner and now a hardware merchant. With the full support of the governors of the two states involved, Idaho lawmen kidnapped the three men in Denver and rushed them to Boise aboard a special train furnished by the Union Pacific Railroad. Idaho's high-handed extradition by abduction outraged organized labor and civil libertarians and thrust the case into the national spotlight. The United States Supreme Court ruled that although the seizure had been illegal, the three men were now in Idaho's custody and had no legal remedy.

The most sensational trial in Pacific Northwest history opened in Boise in 1907, almost eighteen months after Orchard was arrested. It pitted Idaho's special prosecutor and newly elected U.S. Senator William E. Borah against the famed Chicago attorney Clarence Darrow for the defense. For almost two months local and national attention focused on the proceedings. In the end the jury deliberated twenty hours before acquitting Haywood.

Idaho law required a witness to corroborate Orchard's claim of a union conspiracy, and Stephen M. Adams, the only person who might have done so, retracted a confession he claimed was coerced by Pinkerton detective James McParland. Many people found it difficult to believe Orchard's many sensational claims to bigamy, arson, assassination, and mass murder. After eighteen months in the Ada County jail, Haywood was again a free man. Pettibone was acquitted in January 1908, and Moyer was eventually released without having to stand trial.

This profile of the world of May Arkwright Hutton is not simply a story of luck and misfortune in the Coeur d'Alenes or even a glimpse at the violent underside of mining. It is about one of the many disturbing changes that occurred in the Pacific Northwest during the decades from the 1880s to the 1930s, in this case, the rise of wagework and the attendant exploitation of labor.

During those years, existing laws and public policies often seemed incapable of addressing a growing array of social and economic ills that afflicted workers and the larger society. The juxtaposition of technological progress and grinding poverty and other forms of human misery perplexed the nation's leading thinkers and called forth new political movements and popular crusades. The paradox of progress and poverty together with a host of more specific injustices caused Pacific Northwesterners from various walks of life—agriculture, labor, and the professions—to participate in a series of crusades, some successful and others quixotic and doomed to failure. Collectively, however, these popular battles revealed the many stresses the region experienced during the rapid transition from frontier-agrarian to urban-industrial society.

# CHAPTER 15

# Commonwealth of Toil

*

The "blanket-stiff" now packs his bed
Along the trails of yesteryear—
What path is left for you to tread? . . .
Do you not know the West is dead?
—Ralph Chaplin,
"The West is Dead," *Wobbly* (1948)

*

The stereotypical picture of Oregon pioneers is of land-hungry farmers, but the westbound wagons and ships also brought mechanics and artisans. Some of those new arrivals carried with them the seeds of trade unionism. Printers in Portland organized the local Typographical Society in 1853, and locomotive engineers and longshoremen formed additional unions in the late 1860s. The few unions that predated 1880 were for the most part weak and tenuous, but after completion of the Northern Pacific Railroad, labor's power increased noticeably. Oregon became the first state in the nation to legalize the Labor Day holiday in 1887; and for many years, the percentage of unionized non-agricultural workers was greater in Washington than in any other state. But the story of working people in the Pacific Northwest is more than the history of unions.

Work for wages is today the most common way Pacific Northwesterners earn a living. That was not true before 1880, when most people were self-employed. Early residents sustained themselves by farming or perhaps by

63. Wilhelm Hester posed the officers and crew of the
*Flottbek* with their musical instruments. The date is
1905 and the location is Tacoma. Courtesy San Francisco Maritime National Historical Park, Wilhelm Hester Collection, P51.12,448n.

running a small shop or store, but generally not by selling their labor for
wages. Although wagework began as early as the era of fur companies, it did
not become common until the construction boom of the 1880s. Building
the region's railroads and cities, harvesting its timber and grain, and mining
its coal and metals created a great demand for hired muscle. In many ways
the rise of wagework in the Pacific Northwest mirrored national trends, yet
within the region, the sometimes strained relationship between workers
and their employers also reflected a frontier heritage. In fact, from the 1880s
until the First World War, the Pacific Northwest could accurately be labeled
a wageworkers' frontier.

Conflict between labor and management characterized the wageworkers' frontier, as it did industrialized areas of the East—but with added vol-

atility when frontier ideals of individualism and personal advancement clashing with the dependency inherent in working for wages. Because many unskilled or semiskilled workers headed west expecting to achieve personal success, they easily became disappointed and outraged by anything that prevented them from claiming the rewards promised by promoters of western opportunity. Time after time the clash between unrealistic expectations and harsh reality gave rise to radical crusades, militant unions, and violence. The existence of the wageworkers' frontier perhaps explains why the Pacific Northwest experienced a sometimes troubled transition from rural-agrarian to urban-industrial society. Because dramatic incidents like the Coeur d'Alene mining wars, bloody clashes in Everett and Centralia, and unconventional personalities like May Arkwright Hutton and William D. "Big Bill" Haywood enlivened the years from 1885 to 1919, popular writers have tended to romanticize the troubled time as colorful and exciting, alive with revolutionary fervor. Most workers, however, were not revolutionaries: they wanted only to earn a fair return for their labor.

## LABOR'S NORTHWEST

A key feature of early Pacific Northwest labor was a work force composed predominantly of young single males who depended upon the major extractive industries of the West for jobs. The world of wageworkers exuded youthful vitality, although, in fact, it was quite vulnerable, forever at the mercy of market prices paid for its basic commodities. The population of the Pacific Northwest, a mere 1.5 percent of the national total in 1900, formed too small a market to absorb the region's outpouring of raw materials, and therefore major commercial producers had to depend on distant markets. The resultant boom-and-bust economy heightened workers' sense of dependency, encouraged their mobility, and added to their frustrations.

In some ways, settlements on the wageworkers' frontier resembled factory towns in Pennsylvania or Massachusetts, but with one exception—they were frontier-urban communities, and more important, they were western. This meant that workers in places like the mining towns of the Coeur d'Alenes or lumber towns of Grays Harbor lived in close proximity both in time and place to attitudes and ways of life rooted in the classic American West.

Apparently for many workers, the Pacific Northwest was not simply a fact of geography but a fantasy of mind inspired in part by the millions of promotional pamphlets issued by railroads, immigration bureaus, and real estate speculators. A typical example was a brochure that the Union Pacific Railroad distributed in 1889. Titled *The Wealth and Resources of Oregon and Washington*, it painted a bright future for unemployed workers who would move to either state and promised that "the opportunities for work are so extensive that the wage-earner has never been driven to seek relief or protection in the 'strike' nor the capitalist, to preserve or augment his power, ever resorted to the 'lock-out.'"

That assertion was totally false, as labor-management strife in the Cascade coalfields in the 1880s proved. But workers living in the eastern United States or in Europe would not know that. The pamphleteers were myth-makers, and effective ones, too, because workers planning to move to the Pacific Northwest or already there in the 1880s and 1890s occasionally repeated the belief that the region was a land of exceptional promise. This sense of regional advantage became a tool in the hands of labor organizers, who urged Northwest workers to unionize in order to prevent themselves from being reduced to the downtrodden status of eastern workers.

The physical dimension of the wageworkers' frontier changed as the Pacific Northwest became more urbanized. A map in 1900 would have shown railway lines crossing open spaces to link a series of dots representing mining and lumber camps, smelter and sawmill towns, ranches and orchards. Less easily depicted were the temporary communities of men who harvested grain, fruit, and vegetables or graded new railway lines and then dispersed only to reassemble on other jobs or to winter in the cheap hotels, soup kitchens, bars, socialist clubs, and hiring halls of the region's larger cities. On the map some dots clustered together to represent the mining camps of northern Idaho or British Columbia's Kootenays or the great ranches of the Palouse or the orchards of the Yakima Valley. The dots bore names like Butte, Wallace, Everett, and Medford, and the Burnside district in Portland and Pioneer Square in Seattle, two typical extensions of the wageworkers' frontier into urban centers. Every metropolis of the region had one such district.

The size of the wageworkers' frontier was ever in a state of flux. It expanded as new agricultural lands and timber and mining camps opened, and it contracted when older camps were abandoned with the depletion of natural resources or, as infrequently happened, when one of the raw, socially unstable communities survived and matured. In 1870 the wageworkers' frontier consisted mainly of scattered fish canneries, tidewater sawmills, and woolen and flour mills; it would reach its greatest size after construction of the region's railway network in the 1880s and 1890s, then rapidly fade away following the First World War.

The most noted aspect of the wageworkers' frontier was the mobility and apparent rootlessness of its work force. Certainly the act of moving to the Northwest meant the temporary loss of the stabilizing ties of the old neighborhood and perhaps also of family and church. Hence, because of the transient nature of their employment, some workers found it difficult to forge enduring social relations in the new setting. In all but the most skilled trades, occupational boundaries meant little as job seekers shifted back and forth from the docks or the woods to mining, construction, or harvesting. The boom-and-bust cycles of the region's extractive economy and the seasonal alternations between work and idleness placed a premium on physical mobility and a broad definition of personal job qualifications. Perhaps, too, a mobile lifestyle resulted from a worker's desire to grasp opportunities that were supposedly widespread but for some reason very elusive.

It would be a mistake to assume, however, that all Northwest workers had little skill and floated from job to job. During the 1880s the region became home to at least two categories of wageworkers. One was a stationary group sometimes known as home guards and composed mainly of skilled workers who married, raised families, and put down roots in the community. In another category was the migratory bindle stiff, so named because he carried his worldly possessions on his back in a blanket roll or bindle. Many such men seemed destined by temperament or lack of education or skill to the migratory way of life. There were also thousands of unskilled or semiskilled industrial workers who alternated from one category to the other as prosperity permitted or frequent unemployment demanded.

Coexistence between home guards and bindle stiffs gave a frontier character to work life even in metropolitan areas, where an unusual demographic pattern prevailed. The federal census of 1900 ranked cities with populations of twenty-five thousand or more by percentage of males. Butte, Montana, the self-proclaimed greatest mining camp on earth, ranked third in that category, with a population almost 60 percent male, a figure typical of mining settlements. Far more revealing was the city of Seattle, which ranked first in the United States with a population that was nearly 64 per-

## PRIMARY GAINFUL OCCUPATIONS[a]

|  | 1870 | 1880 | 1890 | 1900 | 1910 | 1920 | 1930 |
|---|---|---|---|---|---|---|---|
| **Miners[b]** | | | | | | | |
| Idaho | 5,579 | 4,708 | 5,200 | 4,089 | 2,971 | 1,898 | 981 |
| Oregon | 3,965 | 3,699 | 2,308 | 3,910 | 2,509 | 1,375 | 930 |
| Washington | 173 | 985 | 3,105 | 6,459 | 8,303 | 6,613 | 3,219 |
| **Loggers and Rafters** | | | | | | | |
| Idaho | 45 | 224 | 373 | 701 | 2,246 | 5,127 | 4,910 |
| Oregon | 232 | 642 | 2,555 | 2,681 | 6,189 | 10,394 | 15,392 |
| Washington | 642 | 998 | 5,947 | 8,290 | 21,949 | 24,424 | 24,931 |
| **Sawmill Workers** | | | | | | | |
| Idaho | 36 | 100 | 237 | 349 | 2,469 | 2,904 | 4,296 |
| Oregon | 145 | 865 | 1,962 | 2,449 | 8,432 | 11,482 | 16,480 |
| Washington | c | 684 | 3,734 | 5,936 | 23,171 | 25,133 | 26,990 |
| **Fishermen and Oystermen** | | | | | | | |
| Idaho | 0 | 6 | 13 | 11 | 15 | 12 | 26 |
| Oregon | 93 | 3,192 | 1,473 | 2,756 | 1,744 | 1,894 | 2,067 |
| Washington | 184 | 613 | 1,202 | 3,225 | 3,711 | 4,959 | 5,569 |
| **Agricultural Laborers** | | | | | | | |
| Idaho | 720 | 593 | 2,862 | 7,814 | 19,588 | 22,024 | 20,421 |
| Oregon | 3,126 | 6,598 | 10,605 | 17,316 | 27,136 | 23,815 | 26,769 |
| Washington | 742 | 3,304 | 8,224 | 17,455 | 34,658 | 28,991 | 34,374 |

[a]Federal census takers used the term "gainful occupations" to encompass all people earning a living from a particular trade or industry. Thus, for example, they made no distinction between fishermen who were owner-operators and those who worked for wages. The above figures represent approximations of the number of wageworkers.

[b]Before the 1900 census, compilers made no distinction between precious metals and coal mining; figures shown here represent both gold and silver miners and coal miners.

[c]The census lists no one in this category, an obvious error.

cent male. By contrast, older settlements like San Francisco and industrial centers in the East recorded male populations of 50 percent or less.

Relatively few women worked for wages prior to the Second World War. Because so much of the region's economic activity centered on natural resource industries dominated by males, it was a rare woman who found a job

## LOGGING CAMPS: TREATMENT OF HORSES AND HUMANS

In the early twentieth century, timber emerged as the largest industry in the Pacific Northwest. Dotting the woods were a rapidly growing number of logging camps, most of them located either on river banks or alongside the tracks of special railroads built by the lumber companies. These camps traditionally closed in November or December and reopened in April or May. As the forest was cut, camps moved to another location.

Loggers who lived in the camps typically worked six days a week and ten hours a day. Many of them customarily wore two-piece, woolen long underwear both winter and summer, though early-day camps rarely provided bathing facilities or laundry tubs. That hardship, however, was only one of many endured by loggers, a fact emphasized in the following testimony by J. G. Brown, president of the International Union of Timber Workers, to the U.S. Commission on Industrial Relations holding hearings in Seattle in August 1914:

*Commissioner O'Connell.* What is the condition comparatively between the horses and human beings as to bunking arrangements?
*Mr. Brown.* Well, the beds are always made for the horses, the other fellows have to make their own beds, if they are made. Usually these men are tired out, and have no chance to, or care or desire to improve their conditions. They just come in and sleep. Nearly all of these camps are infested with bedbugs, some of them have fleas, and some of them are lousy. One camp down on Grays Harbor—the men last summer went out and slept out doors in the woods, rather than tolerate the conditions in the bunk house. They would take their bed and go out and sleep on the ground in the woods. They did that for quite a period of time to get rid of the bed bugs.—*Report of the Commission on Industrial Relations* (1916), 5: 4212

in mining or timber except as a clerk, cook, or laundress. An unknown number of women worked as prostitutes, especially in the predominantly male-oriented world of the wageworkers' frontier. Across the Pacific Northwest a few women found jobs in skilled trades, perhaps operating a Linotype machine, and many more became telephone operators. Women also worked as operatives, running machines in the region's food processing industries. But by far the largest number of wage-earning women held jobs as school teachers and nurses. Even so, the percentage of female and child labor in the Northwest's nonagricultural work force remained significantly lower than in the industrialized parts of the Northeast and South.

As a rule, men on the wageworkers' frontier never labored alongside women. Away from the job, a variety of situations prevailed. Women could be found in any mining camp, though not at first in large numbers; a few

64. Women apple sorters were part of the huge temporary labor force required to process Washington's fruit
crop in 1933. At the height of the season in September,
approximately thirty-five thousand agricultural
workers were required full-time in the fields and orchards around Yakima, Ellensburg, and Wenatchee, in
contrast to late fall and spring, when only about five
hundred workers were needed. Courtesy National Archives, 115-JAI-3152.

arrived as wives, others to manage rooming houses and eating places. The
Bannock (Idaho City) mining district in 1862–63, for example, recorded
only 59 women in a population of 670 people. The women enjoyed great
prestige, and if a mining camp survived to become a town or village, the
number of males and females tended to reach parity as miners got married
and raised families. But in logging camps, which were essentially crude,
makeshift work sites in the woods, there were few females until conditions
changed after the First World War. Some loggers, in fact, regarded a woman
in camp as bad luck.

---

ON THE ROAD AGAIN

"The life of the migratory workers was isolated from that of the stationary workers in the cities. They seldom left the skid row areas of the various cities. They were not welcome 'uptown.' They traveled by freight cars. Their work was hard and laborious. They were strong and hardy, tanned and weather-beaten by summer suns and winter snows. They regarded the city workers as stay-at-home softies— 'scissorbills.' They referred to a wife as 'the ball and chain.' "—Elizabeth Gurley Flynn, *The Rebel Girl*, (1955, rev. ed. 1973), 103

---

The Pacific Northwest remained also a stronghold of white labor. In most locales, blacks were a rarity both on and off the job. One exception was Roslyn, Washington, a coal-mining town in the Cascades seventy miles east of Seattle, where blacks were about 10 percent of the twenty-eight hundred inhabitants in 1900. That statistical anomaly dated from the 1880s and 1890s, when mineowners imported blacks from other regions to serve as strikebreakers in coal towns on both sides of the Cascades. Asians, particularly the Chinese, were the largest racial minority on the wageworkers' frontier, although beginning in the early twentieth century, Mexican and Mexican-American laborers became an increasing presence, primarily in the fields of sugar beets.

Boarding houses and company-owned bunk houses provided temporary homes for the men working in the Northwest's many mining and timber camps. Hotels, some of them large and elegant, appeared in every community worthy of the name, not just to cater to travelers and tourists but also to provide rooms for young families and others who had not yet settled permanently in the community.

### THE RISE OF ORGANIZED LABOR

Organized labor never attracted more than a minority of wageworkers even in Washington, the most pro-union of the three Pacific Northwest states. At the same time, working-class organizations made their presence felt in a variety of ways; they sponsored dozens of protest journals and rallied support for reform legislation in state capitols, among other activities. The influence of organized labor was always most pronounced in western Washington and least effective in agrarian parts of southern Idaho and the rural eastern portions of Washington and Oregon.

The distinguishing features of the wageworkers' frontier—notably the

| PERCENT OF POPULATION IN ECONOMIC FAMILIES IN 1900[a] | |
| --- | --- |
| Wyoming | 15.6 |
| Montana | 15.3 |
| Washington | 13.8 |
| Nevada | 11.6 |
| Arizona | 11.2 |
| California | 11.1 |
| Oregon | 10.1 |
| Colorado | 8.0 |
| Idaho | 7.4 |
| Utah | 3.4 |
| New Mexico | 3.1 |
| United States | 3.4 |

[a]The 1900 Census recognized two types of families: natural and economic. The latter classification included dwellers in hotels, boarding houses, institutions, and construction, timber, mining, and military camps. That is, an economic family was defined as people who lodged together but had no natural or private family relationship.

Source: *Twelfth Census of the United States: 1900; Supplementary Analysis and Derivative Tables* (Washington, D.C.: Government Printing Office, 1906): 376–79

predominance of manual labor and a largely nonfactory work force—were reflected in the character of the Pacific Northwest's labor movement. The peculiar occupational composition of the local work force enabled industry-wide unions to overshadow specialized or craft unions in membership, influence, and public awareness. These conditions gave unions like the radical Industrial Workers of the World (iww) a prominence seldom attained in other parts of the United States. Confronting some of the roughest and most arbitrary working conditions in the nation, unions like the iww exhibited a strain of militancy that was seemingly a natural by-product of the struggle for existence. Even among more conservative unionists, a sense of westernness occasionally put them out of step with their eastern-oriented national leaders, creating friction that lessened union solidarity. The militant radicalism that encouraged workers to challenge the prerogatives and powers of management made violent clashes an ever-present possibility.

Most residents of the Pacific Northwest grew concerned about labor's political influence, labor-related violence, and radicalism only after unions attracted widespread public attention during the 1880s. The first national labor organization to attract a mass following in the region was the Noble and Holy Order of the Knights of Labor, a union that originated in Philadelphia in 1869. An idealistic and reform-minded group, it emphasized the solidarity of all branches of honorable toil—both skilled and unskilled workers, including women and blacks (but excluding Asians, liquor dealers, lawyers, stockbrokers, and professional gamblers). Local assemblies of the Knights combined the functions of a labor union, fraternal lodge, debate and educational society, and political reform group. They supported reading rooms, study groups, and guest lecturers to furnish adult education for workers. The Knights were early advocates of reforms like equal pay for men and women and elimination of child labor.

After the first local assemblies appeared in the Pacific Northwest in the early 1880s, the Knights grew rapidly. But their emphasis on labor solidarity revealed an ugly dimension when the Knights encouraged white workers to boycott businesses that hired Chinese labor. And when a sudden and severe depression followed the completion of the Northern Pacific and Canadian Pacific railroads in the mid-1880s, the Knights spearheaded the crusade to expel Chinese labor.

Acting without the approval of their national leaders, agitators for the Knights in the region recruited a large following on Puget Sound by skillfully interweaving the issue of white unemployment with the region's enduring anti-Chinese prejudice. In all of the region's large cities and in several coal towns in the Cascades, agitators encouraged white labor to regard the Chinese as pawns of corporations that would deny Caucasians jobs and a living wage. The result was the first major outburst of labor-related violence in the Northwest.

The Knights of Labor in Tacoma together with the mayor and leading citizens orchestrated the expulsion of the city's seven hundred Chinese (about one-tenth of Tacoma's population) in November 1885. In much the same way, the Knights expelled Chinese labor from nearby coal towns. But in Seattle the following February, the white community divided on expulsion, and a conservative law-and-order group clashed in the streets with the Knights and their allies. When confrontation left one worker dead and several injured, the territorial governor, Watson C. Squire, declared martial law. In Portland, where more Chinese lived than in all of Washington Territory, the city's powerful business establishment resisted the Knights, and the anti-Chinese crusade failed.

But the agitation and violence focused public attention on organized labor as never before. Here was a new force that frightened residents who idealized the supposed simplicity and self-sufficient individualism of pioneer days. Another consequence was the appearance of the first of several utopian colonies on Puget Sound. A group of Knights disenchanted by the street violence organized the Puget Sound Cooperative Colony near Port Angeles as an alternative to modern industrial society. Still other Knights turned to protest politics, organizing several short-lived third parties that supported the "Chinese Must Go" cause. They helped elect a reform mayor in Seattle in 1886 and a prolabor Democratic governor, Sylvester Pennoyer, in Oregon that same year. Pennoyer rewarded the Knights for their support when he persuaded legislators to make Labor Day a legal holiday.

The return of prosperity in the late 1880s diminished the Knights' appeal to the jobless. In addition, their reputation for radicalism and violence frightened away would-be members and divided the union's national and Northwest leaders. By the early 1890s, many skilled home guard workers had switched their allegiance to various craft unions affiliated with the newly formed (1886) American Federation of Labor.

But the Knights did not disappear at once. During the half decade following anti-Chinese violence on Puget Sound, the Knights led several worker protests in the Cascade coalfields. Their grievances centered on low wages and poor working conditions and led to violent confrontations with management in the late 1880s and early 1890s. Coal companies hired armies of detectives to battle the strikers, but those armies proved so odious that Washington's constitution of 1889 outlawed them. When state officials failed to enforce the ban and the hired guns returned to the coalfields, the Knights organized the Peoples (or Populist) party in 1891. The Knights were also prominent in Populist movements in Oregon and Idaho, and in Spokane and its tributary mining areas, they guided the labor movement until the early twentieth century.

Despite their decline and eventual disappearance, the Knights of Labor cannot be dismissed as inconsequential. They were the region's first major labor organization, and their involvement in anti-Chinese agitation and reform politics left an enduring and paradoxical legacy of race prejudice mixed with high-minded idealism. Those themes influenced the platforms of several subsequent reform organizations. For a full generation, the leaders of the region's union movement identified themselves by their acceptance or rejection of the Knights' basic policies. A legacy was the uneasy coexistence between reform-minded unionism that included nearly all workers and the cautious, craft-oriented unionism of the American Federation of Labor.

65. The Burke, Idaho, Miner's Union Tug of War Team in 1906. Fraternity was a very important element in early-day labor unions. Men and women gathered in union halls to hear debates and lectures. Occasionally the hall was the setting for a prize fight. Courtesy Barnard-Stockbridge Collection, University of Idaho Library, Moscow ID, 8-x242.

As time passed, skilled home guard workers reflected ever more strongly the conservatism of the American Federation of Labor and railway brotherhoods. The region's numerous transient and less skilled industrial workers pursued another tradition, one that animated the several militant and radical unions that arose on the wageworkers' frontier. But no clear line divided the two forms of organized labor, for even home guard workers sometimes manifested attitudes shaped by their earlier experiences on the wageworkers' frontier, which for many had been a waystation to a more stable style of life. Some of those workers promoted industrial unionism within the Amer-

---

SAWMILL LIFE

"Winter or summer, workers contended with noise so loud it prohibited talk, especially inside the saw and planing mills," notes Keith C. Petersen in *Company Town* (1987), a history of Potlatch, Idaho, where local boosters claimed title to the largest white pine sawmill in the world. "Crews became proficient at sign language." In this way they would tell stories, joke, and even swear. A Greek worker recalled that sign language enabled him to make friends before he could speak English. But communication was not infallible: one worker chewed off another's ear in a fight that ensued when he misinterpreted a hand signal comment about his sister.

---

ican Federation of Labor. That leaning was especially pronounced in unions on Puget Sound before and during the First World War, and it irritated the federation's conservative national leadership.

## WOBBLIES

For a brief time in the late 1890s and early 1900s, unions affiliated with the American Federation of Labor clearly predominated in the Northwest, and they virtually abandoned the region's large pool of unskilled and semi-skilled labor as unorganizable. But the ideal of labor solidarity did not die. The first group to pick up the Knights' burden was the Western Federation of Miners. The union that Ed Boyce and his fellow hard-rock miners organized in 1893 continued the tradition of industry-oriented, reform-minded unionism. It also linked the Knights and the most famous of all Northwest labor organizations, the Industrial Workers of the World (whose members were popularly referred to as the Wobblies), which western metal miners helped organize in Chicago in 1905.

The Wobblies represented the most alienated of Northwest laborers—migratory harvest hands, timberworkers, and similar categories of labor—a fact clearly stated in the IWW constitution: "The working class and the employing class have nothing in common." The Wobblies believed that all workers in each major industry should belong to the same union and that together the industrial unions should run society. The IWW gained widespread attention because of the militant radicalism expressed in colorful protest songs like "Dump the Bosses off Your Back" and unorthodox organizing tactics. Wageworkers who cared nothing for the Wobblies' syndicalist ideology might still join them to battle those who exploited labor.

Not long after the jury acquitted him in the 1907 Steunenberg assassination trial, William D. Haywood joined Wobblies seeking to organize workers in the Pacific Northwest. Free speech fights, which erupted in Missoula in 1909 and spread to Spokane, Vancouver, B.C., and about twenty-five other communities before culminating in the Everett massacre of 1916, aided the Wobbly mission.

The Spokane free speech fight popularized the new organizing tactic. At issue were dishonest employment agencies, or sharks, that took the workers' money and directed the job seeker to nonexistent employment. On occasion the agent split fees with foremen after a quick hiring and firing. When Spokane officials refused to redress their grievances, the Wobblies deliberately violated a city ordinance forbidding street-corner speaking. Some IWW members chained themselves to lampposts and read the Declaration of Independence. For five months city police jailed hundreds of Wobbly protesters, despite the fact that nearly every incoming train brought still more of the footloose rebels. Finally, the Wobblies overburdened Spokane's jail facilities and its treasury, and city officials revoked the licenses of nineteen employment agencies. The Washington legislature later passed a law regulating such establishments. Whatever its successes, the Spokane free speech fight gave Wobblies a notoriety they never had before. Their reputation for defiance aroused the deepest anxieties of many Northwesterners and made Wobblies vulnerable to vigilantism and other forms of repressive action.

Although the Wobblies did not limit their activities to the Pacific Northwest, they appeared more at home in the region than elsewhere. At a time when nationally oriented trade unions concentrated their organizing efforts on skilled labor, the Wobblies emphasized the solidarity of all workers— men and women, whites and blacks, and even the Asians who were shunned by the Knights of Labor. The IWW kept membership dues low and ignored political action, which made little sense to workers who seldom remained in one locale long enough to qualify to vote. Moreover, the American political system made it difficult for third-party protest movements to win elections and to get their programs enacted. Wobblies also refused to sign contracts with employers, whom they regarded as mortal enemies. To businessmen, therefore, they appeared to be an utterly unreasonable and undisciplined work force. "Their policy is to demand more and work less until the industry is ruined," a lumber industry journal complained.

The unorthodox tactics of the IWW, its radicalism and contempt for authority, and its members' vulnerability to persecution as community outsiders led to several violent and celebrated clashes with employers and

### THE REBEL GIRL

"When I came to Spokane in December 1909 the all-male committee was somewhat disconcerted to be told that I was pregnant. They decided that I was not to speak on the forbidden streets but confine myself to speaking in the IWW halls, to clubs and organizations willing to give us a hearing, and in nearby places to raise defense funds. I made trips to Seattle, British Columbia, Idaho and Montana. A few months later after five editors of the *Industrial Worker* had been arrested and it was harder for me to travel, I was put in charge of the paper. I felt fine, but my co-workers were disturbed about having me appear in public. In those days pregnant women usually concealed themselves from public view. 'It don't look nice. Besides, Gurley'll have that baby right on the platform if she's not careful!' one fussy old guy protested. One night on my way to the IWW hall, I was arrested, charged with 'conspiracy to incite men to violate the law,' and lodged in the county jail. I was only in jail one night and was released the next day on bail, put up by a prominent club woman.

There had been such an orgy of police brutality in Spokane that my friends back East were greatly concerned. I struck the Spokane authorities a real blow, however, by describing in the next issue of the *Industrial Worker* my overnight experiences in the county jail. The entire edition of the paper was confiscated and suppressed. But the story went all over the country and hundreds of protests poured in. I took my story to the local Women's Club, and they demanded a matron be placed in the jail."— Elizabeth Gurley Flynn, *The Rebel Girl*, 108–9

lawmen. Violence, more than any other characteristic, was popularly attributed to Wobblies. Zane Gray, the author of numerous western novels, portrayed the Wobblies as pro-German saboteurs of eastern Washington's wheat harvest during the First World War in *The Desert of Wheat* (1919). In truth, Wobblies were more often the victims of violence than the perpetrators of it. And it should be recalled that major episodes of labor-related violence in the Northwest antedated the IWW by a full two decades. The region's turbulent labor relations owed far more to the special circumstances of life on the wageworkers' frontier than to any single organization or radical philosophy. Rather than initiate a new and violent era of labor-management relations, the IWW merely elaborated on a tradition of militancy and radicalism that already existed among Northwest wageworkers.

### THE VIOLENT YEARS

Labor-related violence occurred most frequently during the years that began with anti-Chinese agitation in 1885 and ended with a notorious shoot-out

---

THE SPIRIT OF THE IWW

"The nomadic worker of the West embodies the very spirit of the I.W.W. . . . . His anomalous position, half industrial slave, half vagabond adventurer, leaves him infinitely less servile than his fellow worker in the East. Unlike the factory slave of the Atlantic seaboard and the Central States he is most emphatically not 'afraid of his job.' His mobility is amazing. Buoyantly confident of his ability to 'get by' somehow, he promptly shakes the dust of a locality from his feet whenever the board is bad, or the boss too exacting, or the work unduly tiresome, departing for the next job, even if it be 500 miles away. Cost of transportation does not daunt him. 'Freight trains run every day,' and his ingenuity is a match for the vigilance of trainmen and special police. No wife or family cumber him. The workman of the East, oppressed by the fear of want for wife and babies, dares not venture much. He has perforce the tameness of the domesticated animals."—Solidarity, 21 November 1914, as quoted in Howd, "Industrial Relations in the West Coast Lumber Industry," Bulletin of the United States Bureau of Labor Statistics No. 349 (1923), 54

---

between Wobblies and American Legionnaires in Centralia, Washington, in 1919. During no other era did industrial and racial violence influence so many aspects of public life or raise so many troubling questions. A period of mass unemployment or an employer's arbitrary assertion of power usually set the stage for confrontation. When individuals and organizations voiced worker grievances and suggested a course of action—as the Knights of Labor did when they orchestrated removal of the Chinese on Puget Sound—violent clashes with employers or lawmen often took place.

The importance of such episodes rested not only in the number of people killed or the value of property destroyed. By those measures, labor-related violence in the Pacific Northwest was not substantively worse than that which occurred in the industrialized states of the East. Rather, the impact of violence on public life made the episodes important. They spurred political protest movements and legislative attempts to redress worker grievances.

The labor-related violence of the 1880s and 1890s occurred during a time of profound economic change. Unemployed workers could expect no help from government, and no legal authority governed labor-management relations. Employers and workers groped their way along unfamiliar terrain toward the resolution of conflicts. Existing laws were usually the product of rural-agrarian thinking and did little to address the needs of industrial workers. To militant workers confronted by legislative inaction and powerful employers, it sometimes appeared that violence was the only alternative to subservience.

| MAJOR EPISODES OF LABOR-RELATED VIOLENCE, 1885–1919 | | |
|---|---|---|
| | *Lives Lost* | *Property Destroyed* |
| Anti-Chinese agitation, 1885–86 | 4–6 | Tacoma's Chinese quarter later burned |
| Idaho mining war, 1892 | 6 | Idled ore concentrator destroyed in Gem |
| Idaho mining war, 1899 | 2 | $250,000 Bunker Hill concentrator destroyed |
| Everett massacre, 1916 | 12 | minimal |
| Centralia massacre, 1919 | 5 | iww hall vandalized |

Lawmakers and other public officials began to address worker grievances and trim away the once nearly absolute power of employers mainly after 1900. A series of new laws provided for workmen's compensation, safer machinery and workplaces, and payment in money instead of scrip redeemable only at the company store. These measures helped some workers but did not completely eliminate incidents of labor-related violence involving groups (like the iww) still confined to the fringes of society. It was the Wobblies who figured in the Everett massacre of November 1916, the bloodiest single episode of labor-related violence in Pacific Northwest history.

The oppressive tactics of Everett employers clashed with iww stubbornness. The result was tragedy. A free speech fight began when Wobblies intervened in a strike initiated earlier by shingle weavers affiliated with the American Federation of Labor. In response, local deputies beat Wobblies and expelled them from town. Hoping to avoid the lawmen who patrolled the highways and rail lines into Everett, more than two hundred Wobblies sailed north from Seattle on the steamship *Verona* on 5 November 1916. A large force of gun-toting deputies awaited them on the Everett dock. Shots rang out—from where was never proven—and when the firing stopped moments later, five Wobblies and two deputies lay dying. Several panicked Wobblies jumped overboard and apparently drowned; a total of fifty men on both sides were wounded. In the ensuing trial in Seattle of the first of seventy-four Wobblies charged with first-degree murder, the attorney George Vanderveer, the self-described "counsel for the damned," won an acquittal. Everett was the Wobblies' last major free speech fight.

As much as circumstances permitted, workers in the Pacific Northwest actively shaped their lives both on and off the job. More than most resi-

---

FORGOTTEN WORKERS: THE WIVES OF LABORING MEN

"There is one class of laborers who never strike and seldom complain. They get up at five o'clock in the morning and never get back to bed until ten or eleven o'clock at night; they work without ceasing the whole of that time, and receive no other emolument than food and the plainest clothing; they understand something of every branch of economy and labor, from finance to cooking; though harassed by a thousand responsibilities, though driven and worried, though reproached and looked down upon, they never revolt, and they cannot organize for their own protection. Not even sickness releases them from their posts. No sacrifice is deemed too great for them to make, and no incompetency in any branch of their work is excused. No essays or books or poems are written to tribute their steadfastness. They die in the harness and are supplanted as quickly as may be. These are the housekeeping wives of the laboring men."—*West Shore*, October 1886, 307

---

dents, they confronted the unpleasant reality that life in the urban-industrial Northwest was not the same as it had been in pioneer days. Worker responses varied across the region. Some took to the streets in strikes and protests, others organized unions and attended labor lectures; and still others created utopian colonies or participated in one of the several great political crusades that swept across America and the Pacific Northwest between 1890 and 1920. The wageworkers' frontier thus left its mark on the region's history.

In the end it was changing technology, not the repression of organized labor, that did most to close the wageworkers' frontier. During the years between the two world wars, mechanical harvesters and the shipment of wheat to market in bulk rather than in burlap sacks dramatically reduced the need for harvest hands. Steam shovels displaced many of the common laborers who constructed and maintained railway lines and irrigation ditches. Improved living conditions in the logging industry made it possible for the lumberjack to get married and settle down outside the camps. In a number of cases, a logger was able to drive to work in his own automobile. For many workers, "automobility" became the equivalent of upward social mobility.

CHAPTER 16

# Adjustments: Progressivism and World War I

*

Oregon has more fundamental legislation than any other state in the Union excepting only Oklahoma, and Oklahoma is new. Oregon is not new; it is and it long has been corrupt, yet it has enacted laws which enable its people to govern themselves when they want to. How did this happen? How did this state of graft get all her tools for democracy? And, since it has them, why don't her people use them more? The answer to these questions lies buried deep in the character and in the story of W. S. U'Ren (accent the last syllable), the lawgiver.—Lincoln Steffens, "U'Ren, The Law-Giver," *American Magazine* (1908)

*

The turn-of-the-century years that gave rise to the builders of a New Northwest also called forth the talents of adjusters, a generation of reform-minded men and women who would reshape old laws and inherited patterns of thought to fit such complex new realities as urbanization, organized labor, nationwide transportation and communication networks, and expanded governmental responsibilities for the well-being of its citizens.

To many adjusters it seemed that social, political, and moral developments lagged behind the era's impressive financial and technological achievements. Why, they wondered, should unprecedented feats of engineering and dramatic economic growth be accompanied by such debilitating increases in poverty and other forms of human misery? The qualities motivating individuals to seek answers to such questions ranged from sim-

345

ple naiveté and good-natured optimism to moral earnestness and fear of social upheaval. Some adjusters were religious zealots, but relatively few of them were committed revolutionaries.

Adjusters from both farm and labor backgrounds had flocked to the Populist banner during the troubled 1890s, whereas in the opening decades of the twentieth century it was primarily (but not exclusively) members of the growing urban middle class who promoted various "progressive" causes. The spirit of progressivism had both secular and religious roots, especially among evangelical Protestants who sought to revitalize traditional American values in the face of what many people saw as selfish and blind individualism.

There never was a truly unified progressive movement analogous to the Populist party insurgency, and certainly not all people who identified themselves as progressives supported the same causes. Sometimes they even worked at cross-purposes with one another. But regardless of labels or organizational structures or social backgrounds, adjusters of the Progressive Era all wrestled with one or more consequences of a village-based economy that had evolved into a complex nationwide one dominated by large and distant corporations.

For example, progressive reformers responded to dirty and dangerous foods processed in faraway cities by enacting pure food and drug laws on the national level and by funding more intense health inspection at the state and local levels; they sought to curb the abuse of power in high places by enacting direct legislation measures that gave average citizens a greater say in governmental matters. Other Progressive Era concerns ranged from woman suffrage and occupational safety to alcohol consumption and maldistribution of wealth. Some of attempts at public betterment, however, amounted to little more than local spasms of moral indignation that rallied citizens to banish houses of prostitution.

A few of the more utopian minded believed that the relatively unspoiled Pacific Northwest was an excellent setting for a radical reconstitution of American society. As a consequence, the region, and especially western Washington, witnessed the rise of several communitarian ventures and an unusually militant strain of socialist politics. Both the radical political parties and communes eventually failed, and World War I redirected the efforts of adjusters; but the great reform campaigns left an impressive legacy of laws and practices that still influence the daily lives of Pacific Northwesterners.

### THE PROGRESSIVES

Of all the reforms, progressivism remains in many ways the hardest to categorize. It can perhaps best be described as a commitment to the amelioration of a variety of social, economic, political, and moral ills by activists from often different backgrounds. Unlike populism during the 1890s, it attained prominence during a time of general prosperity and never became identified solely with a third party. The primary political vehicle for progressives was the reform wing of the Republican party, but they also found support among some Democratic officeholders. Progressivism had its greatest impact in Oregon and Washington and its least in Idaho.

Northwest politicians who labeled themselves progressive included the former Oregon silverite Jonathan Bourne Jr., who as a reform-minded Republican became a U.S. senator (1907–13). Prominent Democrats among Oregon progressives were George E. Chamberlain, governor (1903–09) and U.S. senator (1909–21); Oswald West, governor (1911–15); and Harry Lane, U.S. senator (1913–17). Idaho's long-serving U.S. senator (1907–40) William E. Borah was squarely in the progressive tradition of such prominent colleagues as Robert M. La Follette of Wisconsin and Hiram Johnson of California, but he did not identify with progressivism at the state level. Borah, however, helped sponsor such Progressive Era measures as the income tax and direct election of senators.

No one from the Pacific Northwest gained greater national recognition as a spokesman for progressive causes than the indefatigable Oregon reformer William S. U'Ren. Because of his prominence, U.S. history texts still occasionally—and incorrectly—refer to him as the governor of Oregon, although his political career was actually limited to a single term in the Oregon legislature (1897–99). It was primarily through his activities as secretary of the People's Power League that he wielded influence during the time of the great reform campaigns. It was sometimes said that Oregon had two legislatures, one at the capitol and "one under W. S. U'Ren's hat."

U'Ren was a religious mystic who cheerfully embraced several unorthodox notions; he fathered the "Oregon System" of political reforms that included a corrupt practices act, presidential primary, direct election of U.S. senators, and the initiative, referendum, and recall, measures widely copied in other states, including Washington and Idaho. His rise to prominence began with involvement in the Populist crusade of the 1890s. Though Oregon Populists won few elections, the legacy of U'Ren, their most outstand-

66. William S. U'Ren (1859–1949), indefatigable reformer and "father of the Oregon System of Direct Legislation." Courtesy Oregon State Historical Society,
Oreg. 4406.

ing spokesman, overshadowed their party's electoral victories in Washington and Idaho and remains a vital part of the region's issue- and personality-oriented political culture.

It was U'Ren and his ally Jonathan Bourne Jr. who in 1899 pressured the Oregon legislature to pass a voter registration bill aimed at permanently eliminating political corruption, and they pushed through initiative and referendum amendments that Oregon voters approved in 1902. Armed with those two weapons and prodded by the People's Power League, Oregon voters enacted a host of other measures designed to clean up politics.

Washington progressives included the leaders of labor and farmer groups like the Washington State Grange, the Farmers' Union, and the State Federation of Labor. Those individuals joined with urban middle-class reformers from the Direct Legislation League to create a Joint Legislative Committee. Beginning in 1907, that committee functioned for a decade as a pressure group marshaling both legislative and voter support for a variety of reform measures.

Washington's Joint Legislative Committee distinguished itself as one of the most influential of several such reform committees that existed in the United States prior to the First World War. It contributed to the enactment of a direct primary law (1907), a model workmen's compensation program (1911), an eight-hour day for women (1911), and constitutional amendments providing for woman suffrage (1910) and direct legislation (1911). Following decades of agitation, Washington voters approved an initiative in 1914 that restricted the sale of alcoholic beverages, a measure in tune with the progressive belief that it was possible to improve society merely by passing laws.

Washington progressives scored their greatest victories during the administration of Marion Hay (1909–13), a small-town merchant and Republican who became governor when his predecessor, Samuel G. Cosgrove, died. But critics questioned Hay's personal commitment to reform because of his prodevelopment stand on the state's natural resources. He also suffered from a drab personality and lacked the political flair that characterized the nation's better known progressive governors and senators.

Washington progressivism is most closely identified with Miles Poindexter, a lawyer and judge from Spokane. Working closely with local businessmen and reformers, he was elected to Congress in 1908, where he distinguished himself as an insurgent Republican. Poindexter ultimately broke with his party leader, President William Howard Taft, because he did not believe that Taft was fully committed to the conservation of natural

resources. Poindexter handily won election to the Senate in 1910 and remained a Republican activist there until the First World War.

The high tide of Northwest progressivism occurred in 1912, when Idaho
joined Oregon and Washington in adding initiative, referendum, and recall
measures to its constitution. But during that year, several reformers in all
three states embarked upon what they later realized was a disastrous detour
into third-party politics. The Progressive or Bull Moose party originated
when former President Theodore Roosevelt stormed out of the Republican
National Convention when it renominated President Taft. Although Roosevelt's Progressive party platform appeared bold and innovative in some
parts of the United States, in the Pacific Northwest its proposals for abolition of child labor and for woman suffrage had already become law.

Progressive party members were chiefly Protestant middle-class Republicans—often professionals in occupation but not party politics—who idolized Roosevelt. Most of them had little in common with Populists except
that both refused to accept the status quo. Roosevelt carried Washington;
Oregon and Idaho went for the Democrat Woodrow Wilson, the ultimate
beneficiary of the Republican split. Apart from placing Wilson in the White
House, the primary accomplishment of the Bull Moose insurgency of 1912
was to draw numerous reformers outside the Republican party into an ill-
conceived protest vehicle that had no future. After Roosevelt's defeat and
his subsequent return to Republican ranks, the seceders realized that in
their third-party misadventure they had abandoned the Republican party to
conservatives who would soon seek to undo past reforms.

The Washington legislature passed a handful of reform measures in 1913,
but by 1915 the political pendulum had swung far to the right, and conservative—even reactionary—Republicans controlled the body. They attempted
to repeal or sabotage by amendment several progressive measures enacted
in years past. Underscoring the conservatives' vengeance was their attack
on Professor J. Allen Smith of the University of Washington, a middle-class
reformer whose book *The Spirit of American Government* (1907) raised
disturbing questions about undemocratic aspects of the United States Constitution. Unable to get at Smith directly, legislators introduced an amendment to a University of Washington appropriations bill proposing to abolish
the political science department of which Smith was then the sole member.
In Idaho, where the rise of the Nonpartisan League frightened conservative
Republicans, the legislature repealed the direct primary law in 1919.

Despite those efforts, an impressive body of reform legislation survived.
During the Progressive Era, all three Pacific Northwest states passed mea-

67. F. Jay Haynes photographed the interior of Madden
and Sargent's Saloon in Coulee City, Washington, in
1891. The era's many saloons were the favorite targets
of temperance reformers who deplored the connection
between alcohol, prostitution, and political corruption.
Courtesy Haynes Foundation Collection, Montana Historical Society, H-2631.

sures providing for direct legislation, workmen's compensation, abolition
of child labor, and restriction of the manufacture and sale of alcoholic beverages. Women gained an eight-hour work day and the right to vote.

### RADICAL ALTERNATIVES

Reformers have sometimes been likened to tree surgeons hacking away at
ugly and misshapen growths while the tree continues to thrust out new
shoots. The more radical adjusters would prefer to uproot the whole dis-
eased tree if necessary. Radical alternatives before the First World War took
many forms, the most prominent being the Socialist Party of America and
the Industrial Workers of the World.

The Socialist Party of America emerged in 1901 from several socialist splinter groups and the wreckage of the Populist movement. Some former middle-of-the-road Populists (those who refused to compromise their principles by joining forces with either of the two major parties) remained committed to reform and sought an alternative in the socialist movement. The new Socialist party and the socialist utopias on Puget Sound benefited from an infusion of the Populist spirit. The state of Washington eventually emerged as one of the movement's strongholds.

Washington also became an arena for conflict between moderate "gas and water" socialists and a much smaller revolutionary faction led by the physician Hermon Titus of Seattle. Members who sought little more than public ownership of utilities waged bitter fights with radicals like Titus, who called for worker ownership of the means of production and distribution.

Compared to the strength of the Democratic and Republican parties, Socialist electoral clout was seldom impressive even in Washington. But voters elected moderate socialists to several positions: city commissioner in Spokane, mayors in Pasco and Edmonds, and members of the Washington legislature. Eugene V. Debs, the party's best-known national figure and perennial candidate for president, received 12 percent of Washington's popular vote in 1912, setting a high-water mark for the region's socialist politics.

If socialism seldom influenced election results, it still had an impact on the region's labor and agricultural movements. C. B. Kegley, a Whitman County Populist who turned Socialist before becoming a Roosevelt Progressive and finally a supporter of the Nonpartisan League, is a good example. A respected leader, Kegley kept the Washington State Grange at the forefront of progressive reform between 1905 and 1917. The U.S. Senator Homer T. Bone, a Democrat from Tacoma and staunch advocate of public power, was once a member of the Socialist party.

### THE WAR TO END ALL WARS: 1917–1918

Above all else, progressivism was rooted in the idealistic belief that better living and working conditions would elevate the human race. That idea fueled many a progressive cause and even helped to inspire American participation in the First World War, a conflict that represented both the culmination of the early twentieth-century reform campaigns and their perversion.

For nearly three years after the Great War erupted in Europe in August 1914, the United States tried to steer a neutral course between the Allies (Great Britain, France, and Russia) and the Central Powers (Germany,

## THE CONTINUING QUEST FOR UTOPIA

The Pacific Northwest has long been a favorite destination for political and religious utopian colonists. Wilhelm Keil viewed the region as a potential utopia when he led a party of Christian communists from Missouri to Willapa Bay on the Washington coast and then to the Willamette Valley in 1855, where they established the Aurora Colony.

During the years of the great crusades, utopians established several socialist communities and one anarchist commune on Puget Sound. Governor John R. Rogers encouraged social experiments and even joined one colony to participate in its insurance benefits. He also wrote a utopian novel called *Looking Forward, or the Story of an American Farm* (1898). Young Jewish refugees fleeing anti-Semitism in Russia established a utopian socialist colony called New Odessa near Roseburg, Oregon, that lasted from 1882 to 1887. Consisting of approximately ninety people, this commune supported itself mainly by selling railroad ties and cords of wood for fuel to Henry Villard's Oregon and California line. In more recent times, "hippies" formed several rural and urban communes during the 1960s. That movement no doubt inspired Ernest Callenbach's 1975 novel, *Ecotopia*, the story of an environmental utopia located in northern California and the Pacific Northwest.

But no utopian experiment attracted more attention in recent years than Rajneeshpuram, a sixty-four-thousand-acre communal settlement established in rural Wasco County, Oregon, in 1981. At its height the Far Eastern–oriented religious commune attracted a population of some 4,000 red-clad disciples, many of them affluent and highly educated professionals. When adherents took over the nearby village of Antelope (which they rechristened Rajneesh City) and bused in hundreds of potential voters from the slums of eastern cities in 1984 in an attempt to outvote longtime Wasco County residents, Oregonians became apprehensive. The $100 million experiment collapsed in 1985 following the arrest and deportation of its spiritual leader, Bhagwan Shree Rajneesh, who had entered the United States illegally from India. At one time the bhagwan possessed ninety-five Rolls Royce automobiles as tokens of affection given to him by his devoted followers.

Austria-Hungary, and Turkey). Because Great Britain's fight was also that of the British Empire, war came to Canada in 1914. A few adventuresome Pacific Northwesterners went to British Columbia to enlist, but for most Americans the call to arms did not come until April 1917 when Congress formally declared war on the Central Powers. An idealistic President Woodrow Wilson promoted United States participation in the war as if it were a crusade, asking Americans to fight not for materialistic or territorial gain but "to end all wars" and "to make the world safe for democracy." Obviously, it did neither.

Democracy took a real beating on the home front. Members of Congress who dared to vote against the declaration of war, such as Oregon's ailing Democratic senator Harry Lane, were vilified and publicly humiliated. Others were soundly defeated at the polls, a fate suffered by the four-term Washington Republican congressman William La Follette when he failed to survive his party's primary in 1918.

Wartime zealotry and a spirit of conformity spread across the Pacific Northwest. A quasi-governmental Council of Defense inaugurated a county-by-county card index in Idaho to flush out "slackers," a term applied to anyone who contributed less than was expected of him or her to the war effort. Special distrust focused on the state's twenty-six thousand German and Austro-Hungarian born residents, and the self-appointed patriots closely monitored their activities. Throughout the Pacific Northwest, Germans had to prove their patriotism by abandoning their native language and culture and buying Liberty bonds. Some communities eliminated German from school curriculums.

Reformers were now denounced as "boat rockers." Radicals and nonconformists who identified with organizations like the Socialist party and the Industrial Workers of the World were singled out for special punishment. Emil Herman, the German-born secretary of the Socialist party in Washington, was arrested and sentenced to ten years in federal prison because someone discovered "disloyal" books and stickers in his office.

Authorities also persecuted members of the Nonpartisan League, an insurgent farm organization that originated among the disgruntled farmers of North Dakota in 1915 and quickly spread to the Pacific Northwest. Its quasi-socialist program called for cooperative buying organizations and publicly owned power companies, railroads, and grain elevators. By resurrecting the old Populist spirit, the league attracted the support of farmers who still nursed grievances against the monopolistic power of "big business." To enact their proposals, league members rejected the third-party alternative of the Populists and sought instead to use direct primaries to elect reformers under Republican and Democratic banners.

Conservative businessmen and politicians in all three Northwest states reacted to the Nonpartisan League with every weapon at their disposal, both fair and foul. With war turning many cherished values and traditions upside down, many a foul weapon not only became fair but also enjoyed the sanction of government. Federal and state agents shadowed league organizers and covertly pried into their private lives.

Vigilantism erupted on occasion. In Walla Walla in June 1918, when the annual convention of the Washington State Grange refused to repudiate the

Nonpartisan League, vigilantes disrupted the gathering and forced nearly five hundred conventioneers to leave town. Many Grangers, ironically, had sons in the military and considered themselves good patriots. Their leaders wired President Wilson a formal protest, but the Justice Department concluded that nothing could be done to punish those who had harassed the grange in Walla Walla.

A favorite weapon used to discredit the Nonpartisan League was to identify it with the much-feared Wobblies, who were accused of being agents of enemy Germany. Few if any groups suffered more harassment during the war than did the Wobblies, hated and feared because of their self-proclaimed willingness to use sabotage, sit-down strikes, slow-ups, and passive resistance to accomplish a revolutionary restructuring of society and economy. Some self-appointed patriotic organizations voiced the dark foreboding that German groups planned to form a secret alliance with the Wobblies to undermine the nation's war effort.

When America entered the war, Wobblies were conducting perhaps their most successful strike in the history of the Pacific Northwest lumber industry. Their protest—which included the classic on-the-job slowdown—cut production to 15 percent of normal and drove the industry to its wits' end. Wobblies were similarly active among itinerant harvest workers as organizers moved from field to field to promote the idea of "Six Dollars a Day or No Work." Although Industrial Workers of the World had only a small impact on the rural Northwest, the mere mention of Wobbly agitation could paralyze farmers with fear and anger. It even became common to attribute forest fires to Wobbly sabotage.

It was to harass and indeed destroy the Industrial Workers of the World that Idaho passed the first criminal syndicalism law in the United States in early 1917. This statute made it illegal for anyone to advocate (as distinct from practice) crime, sabotage, or terrorism as a means to achieve industrial or political change. The repressive measure was a model for similar legislation enacted in other states.

Some Idaho citizens would have taken even more extreme measures but for Governor Moses Alexander, who resisted the near hysteria voiced in parts of the state. Alarmist reports flooded his office, and an increasing number of people urged him to drive out the Wobblies, whom they labeled "the plainclothesmen of the Kaiser." Alexander was wary of industry's alarmist rhetoric, but nonetheless requested that companies of federal troops be sent to Wallace and Lewiston as a precautionary move. More zealous local officials constructed makeshift prison camps called "bull

68. A Spokane newspaper cartoon accurately portrayed
the popular pressure on Governor Moses Alexander
(1853–1932) to use force to suppress the Industrial
Workers of the World. Courtesy Museum of North
Idaho.

pens" in St. Maries, Coeur d'Alene, and Moscow to confine alleged Wobbly troublemakers.

Alexander's restraint required more than the usual amount of political courage because he was not only the nation's first elected Jewish governor, he was also a native of Germany. Born in 1853, young Moses Alexander immigrated to the United States at the age of fourteen. He cast his future with Boise in 1891 when he opened a clothing store there. At the time of his election in 1914 Alexander owned a chain of stores in southern Idaho and

356

eastern Oregon. Reelected in 1916, he was fated to serve as governor during the frenzy of hatred directed against Germany. When Alexander resisted hasty action on the numerous appeals that urged him to short circuit civil liberties, some people accused him of overt disloyalty, and at least one individual demanded an investigation into how much the German Kaiser influenced the Idaho governor.

It was in the strike-troubled lumber industry that Wobblies faced their greatest challenge when the owners gained a powerful new ally in Uncle Sam. The number of strikes in the region's lumber industry soared from 44 in 1916 to 295 in 1917, severely hampering production for war. Because the lumber industry convinced the federal government that spruce, a light strong wood used in aircraft construction, was vital to the war effort, Uncle Sam was in no mood to tolerate a strike. The government's response to the Wobbly slowdown was a two-fisted attack: creation of a military organization, the Spruce Production Division headed by Colonel Brice P. Disque, which put twenty-seven thousand soldiers to work in the lumber camps; and a civilian organization, the Loyal Legion of Loggers and Lumbermen (4-L's), which was essentially an enormous company union. Formed during the summer of 1917, the Loyal Legion gained about one hundred thousand members who signed a patriotic pledge not to strike. Together those two organizations provided spruce and other lumber for the war effort. Membership in the Industrial Workers of the World declined precipitously not only because of the Spruce Production Division and the 4-L's but also because of federal raids and vigilante attacks on its meeting halls and leaders. Ironically, the presence of Uncle Sam's troops in the lumber camps mandated many improvements that Wobblies had long sought, such as the eight-hour day, shower facilities, and clean bunkhouses.

War brought change to the woods and to every main street in the Pacific Northwest. The region's newspapers carried headline stories of the struggle in France and urged citizens to conserve food and fuel and to buy war bonds. Seemingly overnight, shipbuilding ranked second in size only to the lumber industry. Seattle shipbuilders alone employed thirty-five thousand workers, some of them coming from as far away as Idaho and Montana. The Northwest's forty-one boat- and shipyards delivered 141 wooden sailing ships and 156 steel vessels by June 1919.

Small by comparison was the aircraft company founded in Seattle in 1916 by wealthy young lumberman William E. Boeing. Son of a Michigan lumber and minerals baron, Boeing attended Yale but did not graduate before striking out on his own in the timber business. Locating first on Grays

Harbor, Boeing moved to Seattle in 1908 and soon became a prominent member of the city's social elite. Flying became a hobby after he attended an air meet in California two years later. With the help of his friend G. Conrad Westervelt and a small group of shipwrights, carpenters, and seamstresses, Boeing assembled his first aircraft, the "B & W Seaplane," on the shore of Seattle's Lake Union in 1916. This was the humble beginning of Pacific Aero Products Company, the hobby that eventually evolved into Washington's number one industrial employer. The name was changed to the Boeing Airplane Company in 1917, when the firm received federal contracts to build several different types of military planes. When the First World War ended, however, times were so lean that the Boeing Airplane Company kept going only by building speedboats and bedroom furniture, often meeting its payroll by tapping into William E. Boeing's personal finances.

Unlike the neighboring states of Oregon and Washington, Idaho did not develop large-scale industries as a result of World War I. Instead, its forests supplied wood for ship and aircraft construction; its mines provided lead and other vital minerals; and its farms produced food needed to feed the troops and the wool needed to clothe them. Some twenty thousand of its young people served in the military: in the nation at large, one of every twenty-two persons was in military service; in Idaho, where patriotic fervor ran especially high, the ratio was one in eighteen. Approximately 130,000 Pacific Northwesterners served in the armed forces.

Of the many war-induced changes, perhaps none was more profound than conscription, enacted in 1917 both in Canada and the United States. Soon, thousands of draftees from "the orange-groves and oil-fields of California, from the apple-orchards of Oregon, from the lumber-camps of Washington, from the cattle-ranges of Montana, from the ranches of Wyoming, from the mines of Utah and Nevada and Idaho, from the gold-fields of the Yukon" converged on Camp Lewis, Washington, to be forged into the Army's 91st Division.[1] Later nicknamed the "Wild West Division," this unit greatly intrigued Americans who struggled to understand the sudden changes overtaking the Pacific Northwest. One writer in *Sunset, The Pacific Monthly* described the soldiers-in-training at Camp Lewis as members of "the romantic legions of the world's fiction, gathering in from all the fringes of the last frontier . . . river-men, sure-footed, alert-eyed, slow-walking, timber cruisers, loggers, miners, ranch-hands, fishermen . . . and the

1. E. A. Powell, "Making the Makers of Victory: Camp Lewis—the Camp of the Frontier," *Scribner's Magazine* 63 (June 1918): 363.

cowboy . . . stepping straight from the pages of 'The Virginian.' "[2] Of course, not all members of the 91st Division were frontier types—many were from the towns and cities of the Pacific Northwest—yet the frontier image persisted and these soldiers reveled in it. It is curious that despite this image of robust westerners, the Army Surgeon General reported that over five thousand of the initial draftees (about 11 percent) at Camp Lewis were rejected for health reasons, and the percentage of venereal disease cases was the highest of any camp, a fact he attributed to so many draftees being from mining regions of the interior West.

Camp Lewis, located fifteen miles south of Tacoma, became the largest of sixteen military cantonments constructed during the war, with forty-eight thousand troops, and the only one west of the Rocky Mountains. Work began in July 1917; within three months 1,757 buildings and 422 other structures had been completed. Despite the wartime urgency, civilian advisers like Frederick Law Olmsted Jr. applied the principles of city planning to military needs, and Spokane architect Kirtland Cutter designed a main gate of fieldstones and squared logs to resemble an old blockhouse of the type once common in the Pacific Northwest. Camp Lewis, in short, was not only to be functional but also attractive. When the war ended, the base languished for a time, but in 1927 it was upgraded to a fort. Today Fort Lewis still functions as a major military installation.

A few women served in uniform, but most rallied to the Allied cause by participating in a variety of charitable efforts, such as by sewing and knitting garments for the Red Cross to distribute to the needy. Women also engaged in various types of fund-raising and aided in the conservation of vital supplies such as meat, wheat flour, and sugar. One hundred fifty Pocatello women found employment in the Oregon Short Line shops cleaning railroad cars and running lathes, drill presses, and other machines, but work in railroad shops and other areas of heavy industry was not typical of middle-class women, nor was there a long-term breakdown of the distinction between "men's work" and "women's work" as a result of the First World War.

When the Great War finally ended on 11 November 1918, spontaneous celebrations greeted the news. "EXTRA! WAR'S OVER. CITY WILD WITH JOY" screamed a typical banner headline. Hardly had Pacific Northwesterners properly celebrated the Allied victory over Germany and the Central Powers

2. Cyril Arthur Player, "The Frontier Trains for War," *Sunset, The Pacific Monthly* 40 (June 1918): 21–22.

before a perplexing series of new problems and worries contributed to a troubled postwar era. Four years of inadequate diets, carnage in the trenches, and stress opened the door to a new killer, Spanish influenza, that swept across Europe and North America in late 1918 with deadly results. Tanks and bullets had no effect on Spanish influenza. In fact, no one knew how best to combat the new scourge. Some people thought laundering money—literally—might help; others tried staying away from crowds. Thanksgiving festivities had to be canceled in some parts of the region because of bans on public gatherings. Various communities required people to wear gauze masks in public, deferred any type of public meeting, or closed theaters. The pandemic, which subsided in December and then made a brief comeback in early 1919, ultimately took a larger toll of life than the war itself: 500,000 to 700,000 Americans died of influenza, whereas the combat toll was 50,000. The influenza killed between 20 million and 40 million people worldwide.

The world had changed radically since 1914: in war-weary Europe, the conflict toppled dynasties that had ruled Germany, Russia, Austria-Hungary, and Turkey for centuries and enabled Communist revolutionaries (Bolsheviks) to seize power in Russia—later the Soviet Union—in November 1917 and lead revolts in Germany and Hungary. Still more unsettling was the belief that Communism had extended its reach to the United States, perhaps to Seattle where in February 1919 a general strike by sixty thousand organized workers shut down the city for four days.

Mayor Ole Hanson asserted that revolutionaries were responsible for the unprecedented work stoppage. After claiming to crush the strike and thus briefly making himself a local hero—when in fact it expired of its own lack of clearly enunciated goals—he resigned and joined the lecture circuit, taking his message "Americanism versus Bolshevism" to the American people. Sometimes overlooked in all the excitement was the true cause of the Seattle general strike: wages that had failed to keep pace with the wartime inflation. Although Seattle's four-day "revolution" ended without bloodshed, and radicals did not control the strike, it cost organized labor popular support and contributed to the mounting national hysteria known as the great red scare.

The culminating event of the immediate postwar years occurred in Centralia, Washington, on 11 November 1919, where members of the newly formed American Legion staged a parade to celebrate the first anniversary of the end of the Great War. The parade route wound past the Wobbly hall, where some marchers broke ranks and charged toward the building. Shots rang out. Who fired first remains unknown, for both sides were armed, but

360

in a confusing few seconds four Legionnaires fell to the ground, fatally wounded. That night vigilantes terrorized Wobbly prisoners held in the Centralia jail and seized Wesley Everest, a United States Army veteran, and hanged him from a nearby railroad bridge. After a celebrated trial, a court convicted eight Wobblies of second-degree murder and sentenced them to lengthy prison terms. The last of the jailed Wobblies was not released until 1939. No one was ever charged with the murder of Everest.

The spirit of reform so prominent in the early twentieth century largely spent itself during the Great War. The terrible slaughter on the battlefields of Europe disillusioned many progressives who believed that the human race was basically inclined to good conduct. In others, the martial spirit twisted the progressive faith into a caricature of its former self. One-time progressives like Senator Miles Poindexter and Mayor Ole Hanson became reactionaries of the most rabid sort. An excess of patriotic fervor caused Poindexter to charge that the Seattle labor movement was a Communist conspiracy. In 1918 he introduced a bill to make strikes illegal. So drastically did the war change Poindexter that Washington voters dumped him in the 1922 election in favor of Clarence C. Dill of Spokane. Dill was the first Democrat elected to either house of Congress from Washington since it became a state more than three decades earlier.[3]

In Washington the spirit of farmer-labor cooperation that had been so visible since the early days of the Populist movement exhausted itself in the aftermath of the Great War. A newly organized Farmer-Labor party ran better in Washington in the 1920 election than in any other state, in many races finishing well ahead of the Democrats, but not well enough to capture a single statewide election or congressional seat. Two years later in southern Idaho, a local Progressive party captured control of several county governments by expressing the discontent of farmers living on the Snake River plain when their crops died after irrigation projects repeatedly failed to deliver the water they had promised.

None of the post-war producer protest movements endured, and what some hailed as the dawn of a new era was in reality the neo-Populist twi-

3. Dill had earlier served in the House of Representatives but had been defeated for reelection largely as a result of his vote against U.S. entry into the First World War. He was one of the few congressmen able to make a political comeback after having voted against the war.

light of an aging generation of reformers. In early 1920s Oregon, in what was really a perversion of the typical reform campaign, a brief but powerful spasm of Ku Klux Klan–directed hysteria caused voters to attempt to outlaw private and parochial schools.

Prohibition, widely regarded as a key progressive reform, became the law of the nation in January 1920, so stated the Eighteenth Amendment to the Constitution and the Volstead Act. Proponents had long asserted that elimination of the saloon and alcoholic beverages would clean up politics and bring much-needed sobriety and efficiency to the workplace, but like a good many reform measures, prohibition never achieved all that its supporters promised. Its fate—repeal by the Twenty-first Amendment in 1933—proved that no reform meant much unless grounded in popular support and backed by a long-term commitment to enforcement. The level of support for prohibition dropped during the 1920s, and its supporters realized only too late that the achilles heel of any reform law was the willingness of government officials to make it work. The prohibition experience serves, too, as a useful reminder that one person's reform may well be another's poison.

Whatever reservations an observer has about the reform crusades, the sheer variety of ameliorative measures dating from the early twentieth century remains impressive. Certainly the lot of women, children, and industrial workers was substantially better by 1920 than it had been in 1900, and so, too, the general level of public health. During those years, the states of the Pacific Northwest democratized the political process and enlarged the electorate, mandated safer factories and mines, outlawed child labor, limited the hours of work for women, created railroad and other regulatory commissions, and passed a variety of sanitary codes forbidding the sale of tainted milk and other foods. On more than one occasion—as with U'Ren's Oregon System or Washington's Workmen's Compensation Law—Pacific Northwesterners pioneered a course eventually adopted by many other states.

# CHAPTER 17

# Birth of the Modern

*

After the Armistice there was the terrible let-down of realizing that our land was worth less than it had been before the war, that there was nothing to do but to worry over the mortgages. The price of wheat had been arbitrarily fixed, but not the price of labor or of anything else that the farmer used. We could have paid off our mortgages and kept even with our expenses had the law of supply and demand been allowed to operate, as in every other field of business. Millionaires were made by the war, and the American farmer was impoverished.—Annie Pike Greenwood, *We Sagebrush Folks* (1934)

*

Historical trends seldom divide neatly into decades, yet major events of the 1920s seemed to be bracketed by the general malaise that opened the decade and the even more severe economic trouble that closed it. During this decade significant and lasting changes resulting from a growing number of automobiles, the movies, and commercial radio first became fully apparent to Pacific Northwesterners. Finally, and with no public awareness of it, during the twenties the future technology of television had its tentative beginnings in a high school chemistry lab in Rigby, Idaho. In so many ways —especially in terms of new technologies, changing tastes in popular entertainment, increased personal mobility, and the growing impact of the city on rural life—this was the Pacific Northwest's first truly modern decade.

POST-WAR MALAISE

A variety of economic troubles cast long shadows across the lives of Pacific Northwesterners during the 1920s. The high cost of living during the Great War elicited so many comments that newspapers resorted to the abbreviation HCL to save space in columns on inflation. The cost of living continued upward during the first several months of peace, until by 1920 it stood 70 percent higher than in 1913. Other leading economic indicators rose or fell in ways that portended troubled days ahead.

As the region's shipyards, sawmills, and mines scaled back war production, unemployment rose rapidly. In what was the largest cutback in the timber industry until that time, Oregon mills and camps laid off seven thousand men, while in Washington that number was fifteen thousand. Northwesterners soon worried less about the HCL than about labor unrest and agrarian dislocation, especially when the price of wheat dropped from nearly $2.06 a bushel in 1919 to $0.84 in 1921 and brought many farmers to the brink of ruin.

The abrupt turnabouts culminated in a brief but severe depression that jolted the United States in 1921, and although prosperity returned to enrich the lives of many urban dwellers, who fondly recalled the 1920s as the Jazz Age or the Prosperity Decade, the pall of hard times never really lifted from timber towns and agrarian areas. Most Northwest farmers remained mired in economic difficulties that originated during the boom years of the First World War, when government appeals for more food caused them to buy land on credit and expand their capacity to produce far beyond what a peacetime world could consume. The result was a dramatic postwar drop in farm income and land values, with debts and bankruptcies piling up alongside unsold stores of wheat and other commodities.

Hardest hit of the Pacific Northwest states was Idaho, where even in 1929 wheat brought only $1.30 a bushel. The state's all-important potato crop sold for $1.51 cents a bushel in 1919, sank to a low of $0.31 in 1922, and rose only gradually during the rest of the decade, nearly reaching the 1919 price in 1929 before it plummeted to less than $0.25 a bushel in 1932. Because the farm crisis was both national and international in scope, Pacific Northwesterners were helpless to do anything about it on the state level.

The Oregonian Charles L. McNary served in the U.S. Senate from 1917 until his death in 1944, and he was best known for his efforts in behalf of American farmers. The McNary-Haugen bill was formally introduced on Capitol Hill in 1924 and sparked one of the chief ideological debates of the

1920s. The emergency farm relief measure mandated that the federal government promote economic justice for farmers during hard times. Idaho's Senator William E. Borah supported a more radical form of farm relief, but with no more success than McNary, who never got his plan past a presidential veto.[1]

The prolonged agricultural depression accounted for the fact that Idaho was second only to Montana among western states in the number of residents who moved out during the 1920s. Idaho's chief export in the 1920s and 1930s was the bright young men and women seeking jobs elsewhere, perhaps in one of the Northwest's growing cities where the future seemed brighter.

## URBAN GROWTH IN PERSPECTIVE

During the opening years of the twentieth century, the Pacific Northwest experienced rapid population growth, especially in its urban areas. The region's population climbed from approximately 1 million in 1900 to slightly more than 2.5 million in 1920, with an urban increase of 254 percent overshadowing a rural increase of 79 percent. Accounting for at least part of the urban growth were newcomers who moved to the Northwest from other regions and residents who relocated from farm to city within the region.

It has often been said that the United States was born in the country and moved to the city, but that pattern of development has not been so evident in the Pacific Northwest. Idahoans, in fact, initially moved the other way, relocating from early mining camps and agricultural villages onto farms and ranches and seeming to return only reluctantly to an urban environment. In 1900 the state had only two communities of 2,500 or more inhabitants, with Boise topping the list with 5,957 residents. Well into the twentieth century and far longer than either Oregon or Washington, the state of Idaho managed to keep one foot firmly planted in the country while inching the other tentatively toward the city. In 1900 slightly more than 6 percent of all Idahoans lived in urban areas, whereas in 1990 some 57 percent did.

What is remarkable about this shift is that not until 1970 did the federal census record a majority of Idahoans living in urban areas. The nation as a whole crossed that important statistical divide fifty years earlier, in 1920,

1. Borah opposed the McNary-Haugen plan because it taxed farmers in order to dispose of their surplus crops at competitive prices abroad; the Idaho senator favored direct federal relief to distressed agrarians.

CITIES WITH 10,000 OR MORE RESIDENTS

|            | 1910 | 1920 | 1930 | 1940  | 1950  |
|------------|------|------|------|-------|-------|
| Idaho      | 1    | 2    | 2    | 7     | 9     |
| Oregon     | 2    | 4    | 6    | 7     | 11    |
| Washington | 7    | 10   | 15   | 14    | 20    |
| U.S.       | 597  | 752  | 982  | 1,077 | 1,320 |

and the state of Washington even before that, in 1910. Oregon did so in 1930, but only barely, for the next decennial census recorded a temporary drop to 48.8 percent urban.

This measure of urban growth must be used with caution, however, because the federal government defined communities of 2,500 or more residents as urban. Many Pacific Northwesterners, although not living on farms and ranches, were residents of towns too small for the federal bureaucracy to classify as urban. In fact, as recently as 1980, about one-third of all county seats in Washington and Idaho (one-fourth in Oregon) had fewer than 2,500 residents and thus did not qualify as urban. Yet it was to such towns and villages that nearby residents went to transact legal business, take care of banking needs, purchase groceries and other supplies, and catch up on local news.

Pacific Northwesterners in the 1920s could ponder their impressive urban growth of recent decades from an historical perspective; that is, they could look back with a mixture of nostalgia and amazement at a far different world that existed only a few decades earlier when simple patterns of rural life were the norm throughout the region. Indeed, social institutions as basic as marriage had changed dramatically during the previous eighty years. Although pioneer settlers of the 1840s and 1850s married quite young (sometimes in their midteens), that trend was reversed as the nineteenth century progressed, and courtship often lasted for years. Divorce was a rarity among Northwest farm folk, even in marriages in which the couple had not spoken to each other for years.

Mothers and daughters manufactured most family clothing from raw materials close at hand; shirts, underwear, and bedding were all made at home. The whir of the spinning wheel and the click of several pairs of knitting needles were two defining sounds of the rural household economy. With sewing machines unknown on most nineteenth-century farms, boys as well as girls were taught to knit and often to sew. During the overcast

THE URBANIZATION OF THE WEST

| | Total Population (in thousands) | | Urban Population (in percent) | |
|---|---|---|---|---|
| | *1900* | *1990* | *1900* | *1990* |
| Arizona | 123 | 3,487 | 15 | 88 |
| California | 1,485 | 29,760 | 52 | 93 |
| Colorado | 540 | 3,294 | 48 | 82 |
| Idaho | 162 | 1,006 | 6 | 57 |
| Montana | 243 | 799 | 35 | 53 |
| Nevada | 42 | 1,202 | 17 | 88 |
| New Mexico | 195 | 1,515 | 14 | 73 |
| Oregon | 414 | 2,842 | 32 | 71 |
| Utah | 277 | 1,723 | 38 | 87 |
| Washington | 518 | 4,867 | 41 | 76 |
| Wyoming | 93 | 454 | 29 | 65 |
| United States | 75,994 | 248,710 | 40 | 75 |

days of a Northwest winter, there were always shoes and harnesses for a rural man to mend and broken furniture to repair. In fact, the typical Northwest farm was a miniature factory. In this simple economy, the farmer paid no bills for gas, fuel, light, water, phone, garbage, or rent. The only utility expenses might be for coal oil (or kerosene) to light the lamps that supplanted tallow candles after the Civil War.

Daily meals relied heavily on meat processed locally from cattle, hogs, and sheep; the work of butchering and smoking or pickling to preserve meat was no small undertaking for a family that might average ten to twelve hungry people. Wild game also furnished abundant food for rural households. Farmers usually kept a few cows to supply milk, cream, and butter. They raised vegetables of all sorts, and probably the most popular and versatile fruit was the apple, large quantities of which were stored in bins for winter use, dried, or made into apple butter.[2]

Transition from this lost world to modern times of the 1920s happened only slowly at first. Changes were often incremental and their implications little appreciated until later, such as when creameries gradually replaced the household butter churn and dash and barbed wire fences supplanted

2. Adapted from C. Louis Barzee, *Oregon in the Making* (Salem: Statesman Pub. Co., ca. 1936).

wooden ones. Similarly, more and more farmers acquired buggies for plea-sure drives, store-purchased clothing replaced the handmade, and timbered lands receded as fields and orchards expanded. As nearby undeveloped areas shrank, so too did the number of game animals. Finally, as more farm pro-duce was sold on the market, a greater amount of money entered circulation in rural areas. By the late 1890s it was possible for an increasing number of farm men and women to order modern clothes from a catalog and have them delivered from distant supply houses to the nearest railroad station.

By the turn of the century, entirely new definitions of time and space emerged as once-familiar rhythms and patterns of rural life disappeared. Residents of the Pacific Northwest had once reckoned time mainly in terms of the larger rhythms of life, by seasonal changes, sunrise and sunset, and Sunday as the start of a new week. In the 1840s and 1850s emigrants headed their covered wagons west from the valley of the Missouri River in spring when grasses of the Great Plains were lush and green, fattening their draft animals in anticipation of the ordeal ahead; they hoped to reach the Conti-nental Divide at South Pass by midsummer and the Willamette Valley by early fall. As late as July 1863, when the armies of North and South decided the fate of the United States on the battlefields of Gettysburg and Vicks-burg, it still took three weeks or longer for news of the outcome to reach many rural parts of the Pacific Northwest.

Preindustrial societies did not ordinarily require precise measurements of time. Although Pacific Northwest residents eventually added hours to their concept of time, railroad travel and urban life demanded even shorter intervals than that. People now had to learn to think in terms of minutes, a measure that clearly defined the pace of life in an increasingly urban and industrial America.

Spatially, the narrow confines of rural neighborhoods enlarged consider-ably with the extension of passenger train service along the region's growing network of railroad tracks during the 1880s and 1890s, and also with the first telephones. Early rural telephone lines sometimes consisted of little more than a wire strung from tree to tree to connect one farm house to another. A long line stretched three miles, but the telephone's possibilities intrigued both rural and city folk. Over time, an increasing number of older people left their farms to younger hands and moved to an easier life in town. But for many of the young people left behind, farm life became entirely too tame as the pull of the city grew ever stronger.

By the 1920s two primary agents of urbanization and social change were talking motion pictures and radio, which brought a whole new world of news and entertainment even to the region's widely scattered rural commu-

## TENTATIVE BEGINNINGS FOR TELEVISION

Before radio entered its golden age, a fifteen-year-old lad from Rigby, Idaho, designed an electronic device that would alter popular forms of entertainment even more dramatically than radio had. He was Philo T. Farnsworth, who in 1922 showed his high school chemistry teacher his design for a system to transmit pictures electronically: here was the key that would unlock the television age. In 1930 Farnsworth patented the picture-tube electronics. The Radio Corporation of America, which initially experimented with an inferior mechanical system, attempted to patent a competing design, but late in the 1930s a court ruled in Farnsworth's favor. Farnsworth later leased his design to RCA.

nities. The lonely sheepherder on some remote part of the range could now tune to events halfway around the globe. The establishment of commercial radio stations in all three Northwest states in 1921 and 1922 quickly changed the nature of entertainment, further expanding the influence of the metropolis at the expense of rural regions, and fueling the growing American passion to consume. The cosmetics industry set new records during the 1920s, and so, too, did the electrical industry, which powered a host of new consumer products ranging from refrigerators and vacuum cleaners to record players and hair curlers. Yet of all the technological innovations to come of age during the 1920s, none had a more far-reaching influence than the automobile.

### THE TWENTIETH-CENTURY TRANSPORTATION REVOLUTION

When the twentieth century dawned, Pacific Northwesterners still utilized stagecoaches, steamboats, and railroads as their primary means of public conveyance. Perhaps the most innovative transportation technology was the electrically powered railway, which resulted in new trolleys and interurban lines shortly before the turn of the century. By promising cheap and convenient carriage, electric railway lines of all types became quite popular during the first two decades of the twentieth century. The trolley was not merely a public conveyance but also a source of community pride and a symbol of modernity. Every large city had electric trolley lines, as did several smaller ones, including Yakima, Walla Walla, and Lewiston. Trolley companies developed parks and other recreation facilities to increase their excursion business, especially on the weekends.

When the first automobiles appeared in the Pacific Northwest shortly before the turn of the twentieth century, few people regarded them as threats to traditional modes of transportation. Because early automobiles were expensive and virtually inoperable in bad weather, many observers regarded the wheezy and temperamental vehicles as little more than rich men's toys. Then in a historic move in 1913, Henry Ford initiated assembly-line production of his Model-T automobile, dropping its price from $850 in 1909 to a relatively affordable $440 in 1915 (and even less for used models). Output leaped right off the production charts.

The Pacific Northwest's pioneer motorists were an intrepid lot. Among the difficulties they faced were hard-to-find fuel (initially available only at auto dealers and hardware stores), rough roads that caused many flat tires, and lack of good direction signs on intercity roads that in many areas amounted to little more than two ruts across a muddy field. Before the invention of something so basic as antifreeze, year-round operation of automobiles was impossible in colder parts of the Northwest.

Citizens demanded and got more and better roads and highways, especially after Oregon took a fundamental step toward creating a network of good roads in 1919 by becoming the first American state to levy a tax on gasoline. With the rallying cry "Lift Oregon out of the Mud," contractors soon blanketed the state with hundreds of miles of good roads, many of them paved. Washington and Idaho followed the Oregon example by levying gasoline taxes in 1921 and 1923. During the interwar years the region's highway network expanded at a rate never since equaled. During those two decades the mileage of hard-surfaced all-weather roads increased in Idaho and Washington by nearly 300 percent and in Oregon by nearly 250 percent. The Pacific Northwest contained a total of twelve thousand miles of all-weather roads by 1940.

More than anything else it was the expanding road network that encouraged automobile ownership. By the mid-1920s the automobile was no longer popularly regarded as a useless "go-devil," as some farmers had once labeled it. It had become a necessity of life, especially for rural dwellers.

Road building and automobile ownership had a troubling impact on the once almighty railroad industry, which saw its nationwide network of track reach a peak in 1916 and passenger traffic decline sharply during the 1920s. "The rural steam railroad in many instances is an anachronism in communities of homes equipped with steam heating plants, radios, modern plumbing conveniences and telephones, the owners of which have their own automobiles. It is 1875 set down in the midst of 1925," complained one critic.[3]

Trains, moreover, carried people along designated routes—about 250,000

3. *Bus Transportation* 4 (January 1925): 27.

| PEOPLE PER MOTOR VEHICLE | | | | | |
|------------|-------|------|------|------|------|
|            | *1910* | *1920* | *1930* | *1940* | *1950* |
| Idaho      | 700.5 | 8.5  | 3.8  | 3.2  | 2.2  |
| Oregon     | 127.5 | 6.8  | 3.8  | 2.8  | 2.2  |
| Washington | 157.1 | 7.9  | 3.5  | 3.1  | 2.6  |
| U.S.       | 197.2 | 11.5 | 4.6  | 4.1  | 3.1  |

miles of railway line nationwide—at specified times, whereas automobiles could drive off the beaten path or to another town or city at any hour of the day or night. As a result, a majority of commercial travelers, or salesmen, abandoned the passenger train for the automobile during the 1920s, and following them were many other categories of travelers. By the end of the decade, life in the region's once isolated towns and villages no longer centered on the arrival and departure of the daily train or stagecoach. Citizens came and went as they pleased in their own automobiles, and the road map, not the railroad timetable, became their window to the larger world. It was not uncommon for railroad passenger stations less than two decades old to be boarded up or converted to other uses.

Especially hard hit by this transportation revolution were the region's thousand miles of electric interurban lines, none of which had been in existence prior to 1893. Some trolley and interurban lines survived into the 1930s, but most of them succumbed to competition from private automobiles during the 1920s. Some lines, like the Puget Sound Electric that opened between Tacoma and Seattle in 1902, were entirely abandoned, while others, like the Oregon Electric linking Portland and Eugene, survived only by dropping passenger service and hauling freight.

One of America's pioneer bus operators was the Spokane, Portland, and Seattle Railway which in 1924 began substituting buses for steam-powered trains linking Portland, Astoria, and Oregon's north coast. By the end of the decade, nearly every major railroad in the Pacific Northwest had done likewise on lightly patronized branch lines. Innovation was the keynote of early-day bus travel; some companies offered sleeper coaches between the Northwest and California, and some adopted a double-decked design especially suited for enjoying the scenery of the Pacific Northwest. The Greyhound Corporation, a holding company formed in the late 1920s, eventually acquired most bus lines of the Pacific Northwest.

Railroads faced further competition from the airline industry that origi-

OREGON TAKES TO THE AIR

"In those 'early days' of commercial aviation, passengers went through the inconvenience and formality of working themselves into 'monkey suits' before they climbed into the open cockpits of the 'speedy' 90-mile-an-hour planes then adopted for transport use. If mail, baggage or express was carried, it was piled in the lap of the passenger, or he was obliged to literally sit upon it when it was crowded in around his seat.

"Goggles protected the passenger's eyes, but there was nothing at all to protect his face and ears, and often his hands, from the biting effects of rushing air, damp clouds, wind, rain, snow and hail. When the plane landed at the end of its journey, the passenger's face was beet red from the torture he had suffered. His ears were deafened from the roar of the plane's motor and the swish of passing wind. An attendant helped him to wipe away the smudge of oil that flicked back upon his face."—Ray Conway, "Oregon Takes to the Air," *The Oregon Motorist* 16 (May 1934): 10–11

nated in the 1920s. Few people then could have imagined that by the 1950s more people would travel by air than by rail. The first airlines were exceedingly small operations, often consisting of little more than one or two open cockpit planes that carried a passenger or two in addition to the mail. Until better aircraft and navigational aids became available in the late 1920s, none dared fly across the Cascades during winter months. One airline pioneer was the Boeing company of Seattle, which in 1926 inaugurated Boeing Air Transport, a progenitor of United Airlines. The Boeing company secured a federal contract to operate between San Francisco and Chicago carrying mail and two persons per plane on what was then the longest airmail route in the world. In 1933 Boeing built the model 247, an all-metal streamlined two-engine transport. Capable of carrying ten passengers plus a crew of three, it made possible coast-to-coast flight in twenty hours (with seven intermediate stops).

Railroads made no attempt to fight back in any meaningful way until the mid-1930s, when they introduced streamlined passenger trains that featured air-conditioned cars and clean-burning internal-combustion locomotives. The first of those in the Pacific Northwest (and one of the earliest in the United States) was the Union Pacific's innovative City of Portland, which after its introduction in 1935 reduced travel time between Chicago and the Rose City from fifty-eight to forty hours. But nothing short of fuel rationing and the speed limits of thirty-five miles per hour imposed during the Second World War could arrest the downward trend in railroad passenger travel, and then only temporarily.

69. The automobile age in downtown Pullman, Washington, during the 1920s. Courtesy Oregon Historical Society, ORHI 8104.

Trucks, automobiles, all-weather highways, and gasoline-powered tractors and other implements noticeably altered the daily lives of farmers, dramatically reducing their need for casual labor. Motor transportation ended the isolation of the region's farms, ranches, and lumber camps and eliminated what remained of the wageworkers' frontier after the First World War. Many former harvest hands abandoned the life of the hobo, got married, and took their families with them to the job in their own automobiles. In forest industries, too, the home guard logger driving to work in his own car or truck replaced the bindle stiff. Like nothing else, owning a car—even a used one—symbolized admission to the middle class. Organizers for the Industrial Workers of the World deplored the trend and complained that the automobile gave labor a false sense of upward mobility, but their complaint fell on deaf ears.

The transportation revolution of the 1920s changed the face of the Pacific Northwest by ending the isolation of rural dwellers (including those who lived in logging camps) and by encouraging urban dwellers to move to suburban neighborhoods, a trend that became especially noticeable after the Second World War. All-weather roads and automobiles greatly extended the reach of medium- and large-size trading centers, and motorized buses enabled schools to consolidate at the expense of one-room rural facilities.

Thus the county seats and trade centers prospered at the expense of remote villages, many of which simply disappeared. In short, the motor age transformed the Pacific Northwest during the 1920s and 1930s much as the railway age had during the 1880s and 1890s.

## PARADOX POLITICS

While the impact of the automobile on Northwest life was little short of revolutionary, during the years immediately following the First World War, the region's residents often seemed more preoccupied with revolution of another sort, the Communist variety that began in Russia in 1917 and threatened to spread to eastern Europe and even to Portland and Seattle, or so some frightened people believed. That fear, coupled with very real and disturbing changes brought by the First World War, contributed to political turbulence in the early 1920s.

The Republican party dominated politics in all three Pacific Northwest states throughout the decade. Republicans held every elected state and congressional office in Idaho. They also controlled Washington, where Roland H. Hartley, a mean-spirited, antilabor timber baron from Everett, served as governor from 1924 to 1932 and gave the period a rancorous political tone. Democrats enjoyed only modest successes in Oregon and Washington.

Republicans won an impressive string of election victories and maintained overwhelming majorities in all three state legislatures, but too much emphasis on Grand Old Party invincibility obscures important undercurrents of Northwest politics. In agrarian Idaho, which never fully tasted the fruits of prosperity during the 1920s, Republicans benefited at least in part from the Democrats' inability to resolve factional disputes over personalities and programs. On the other hand, especially during the first half of the 1920s, a mood of insurgency complicated life for Northwest Republicans. On the left were the Nonpartisan League and the Progressive party, which frightened Idaho Republicans immediately after the war, and the Farmer-Labor party, which had the same effect on Washington Republicans. The main insurgency on the right was the Ku Klux Klan; it rose to power amidst the burning of crosses and public parades of new initiates in Oregon in the early 1920s.

Oregon, which included a large number of residents whose heritage was that of the Bible Belt, had a tradition of nativism. Together with the wartime mood of distrust and apprehension and the economic chaos caused by runaway inflation followed by a severe depression, it created the circumstances in which the Ku Klux Klan flourished. Discontent in the South after

374

the Civil War gave rise to the original Klan, which faded away after a decade or two. A second Klan arose in 1915 and borrowed ritual and doctrine from its predecessor. But its targets now included not just the blacks singled out for persecution by the original Klan, but also Catholics, Jews, and immigrant groups.

The Klan entered Oregon from California in 1921 by capitalizing on the fears generated by the First World War. Spreading rapidly, it established branches in Portland and a number of outlying communities. By the mid 1920s, its membership was estimated to be between fourteen and twenty thousand, with numerous sympathizers adding to its influence. In 1922, together with Freemasons, Klansmen spearheaded a drive to outlaw private and parochial schools, which they viewed as the primary obstacle in their drive for "Americanism" and national conformity. Such schools were operated by a number of groups, most notably the Roman Catholics. The Klan's weapon was an initiative that if passed by Oregon voters would require all children between the ages of eight and eighteen to attend public schools. The rallying cry of its sponsors was "One Flag! One School! One Language!" Opponents invoked the American tradition of free choice, but that apparently held little appeal; at the polls that fall, Oregonians by a margin of eleven thousand votes made their state the first in America to mandate a monolithic school system.

Walter M. Pierce of Pendleton, a popular Democrat and uncompromising advocate of the public school measure, was elected by the largest vote given a gubernatorial candidate in Oregon up to that time. Though perhaps not a Klansman himself, he enjoyed the Klan's backing in the general election. The new speaker of the Oregon House of Representatives was a Klan-supported Republican with an interesting set of initials: Kaspar K. Kubli.

Opponents of the public school measure subsequently took their case to the federal court in Portland and obtained a temporary injunction, but supporters were confident that the new law would go into effect as scheduled in 1926. They launched a crusade in neighboring Washington, where the Klan had chapters in every major city. A measure identical to Oregon's "Compulsory Education" initiative appeared on the Washington ballot in 1924, but Washingtonians rejected it by sixty thousand votes. Much of the Americanism fervor had ebbed since 1922, and supporters of the initiative received a major setback in mid-1924 when the federal court in Portland declared the Oregon law unconstitutional. A year later, in the case of *Pierce* v. *Society of Sisters,* the United States Supreme Court dealt the Oregon measure a fatal blow. By the late 1920s the Klan would be a spent force.

Much about the Ku Klux Klan movement in the Pacific Northwest made

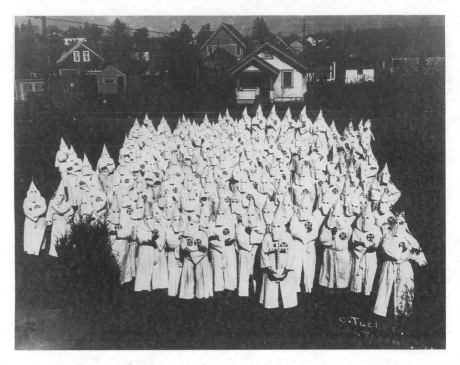

70. A rally of the Ku Klux Klan in South Tacoma about
1923. Courtesy Tacoma Public Library, 029.

it difficult to categorize. From one perspective it embodied the narrow-minded, illiberal spirit that swept across America during the World War I. It appeared to be conservative, even reactionary. But the Klan also embodied some of the region's old-time spirit of populism; angry and frightened citizens joining together to combat a host of, in this case, enemies; imagined Catholics, Jews, foreigners, and radicals substituted for Wall Street bankers and the gold standard of years gone by. In a perverse sort of way, the Klan insurgency tapped the reform spirit of prewar decades.

The seemingly contradictory currents of Oregon politics during the 1920s were mirrored in the public life of the state's Klan-supported governor, Walter M. Pierce. As a politician, Pierce was never easy to classify: he possessed a populist streak that in 1919 caused him to cast the sole vote in the Oregon Senate against a harsh criminal syndicalism bill. Political opponents later charged that he was a radical, a secret member of the Nonpartisan League. Although defeated in his bid to be reelected governor in 1926, Pierce at the age of seventy-two made a comeback in 1932, when the Democratic tidal wave swept him into a seat in Congress. There he remained for ten years, a staunch backer of public power, farm relief, and other New Deal measures.

Oregon voters as a whole manifested similarly contradictory tendencies. Their legislators in 1923 passed the Alien Property Act, which in effect prohibited the state's growing number of Japanese residents from owning and leasing land. Corresponding measures had already been passed by California and Washington and upheld by federal courts. Yet Oregon voters in 1926 finally repealed the constitutional provision barring blacks from the state, and the following year they eliminated restrictions that discriminated against black and Chinese voters. In 1922 the Klan stirred up prejudice against Jews (who constituted approximately 1 percent of the state's population) in an unsuccessful effort to prevent Julius Meier from serving on a Portland commission to study whether to hold a special exposition. Yet eight years later, Meier—co-owner of Portland's Meier and Frank department store—ran for governor as an independent who championed the cause of public power and won with 55 percent of the vote.

Among insurgents of the 1920s, the cause of public power was especially popular. One of the idea's most determined supporters was Homer T. Bone of Washington. Bone jumped from party to party: he was a Socialist in 1912, was elected to the state legislature as a Farmer-Labor candidate in 1922, was a Progressive in 1924, a Republican in the late 1920s, and finally won election to the U.S. Senate in 1932 as a Democrat. But Bone never lost his devotion to public power. For the most part, however, public power remained an idea whose time did not come until Washington lawmakers approved Bone's public utility district bill in 1930, opening the door to statewide public power.

As for the Farmer-Labor insurgency, its time never did arrive. In the 1920 election, the Farmer-Labor party, which succeeded the Nonpartisan League in Washington, ran a respectable campaign. Robert Bridges, an old-time Populist and the Farmer-Labor candidate for governor, ran second to the victorious Republican, Louis Hart. But in the aftermath of the election, Farmer-Labor partisans bickered among themselves, and that infighting, together with growing prosperity in the state's urban areas, reduced the party to insignificance by the 1924 election.

Insurgency on the left took yet another twist when many one time Farmer-Laborites supported Robert M. La Follette, the Wisconsin senator who ran for president as a Progressive in 1924.[4] The La Follette campaign, which called for farm relief measures, public ownership of railroads and

4. In Oregon La Follette ran under the Independent banner.

waterpower, and legal recognition of collective bargaining, threw a genuine scare into the two major parties. La Follette finished second to the victorious Republican candidate, Calvin Coolidge, in all three Pacific Northwest states. In Washington, in fact, he bested the hapless Democrats by nearly a 4-to-1 margin, yet the La Follette campaign represented the last hurrah of left-wing insurgency during the 1920s. In the last half of the decade, Republican dominance of Pacific Northwest politics went all but unchallenged. The only notable exceptions were Senator C. C. Dill and Congressman Sam B. Hill of Washington.

The region's Democratic party, especially in Idaho and Washington, remained in a woebegone condition, weak and generally ineffectual at the polls and badly divided as a result of personality conflicts and the inability of anyone to bring discipline to the motley assortment of disgruntled agrarians, trade unionists, onetime Populists, Nonpartisan Leaguers and all-around political cranks who drifted into its ranks. With a history of defeat at the polls, the Democratic party could not afford to be too choosy.

## BORAH OF IDAHO

Republicans dominated government not only in the Pacific Northwest during the 1920s but also in many other states outside the South. The party elected three presidents—Harding, Coolidge, and Hoover—and controlled Congress. During this era, one of the most prominent Republicans both on Capitol Hill and abroad was Senator William Edgar Borah, the man who represented Idaho in the U.S. Senate from 1907 to 1940.

Borah was an orator without peer and perhaps the best debater in the Senate. He could draw a crowd to the galleries simply by giving notice of his intention to speak. "Borah's up!" was a phrase that could bring a stampede of newsmen from the senate press room, "like firemen answering the alarm." Humorist Will Rogers once quipped that, when Borah left the Senate, the gallery seats could be destroyed.

Even more important, as chairman of the Senate's prestigious Committee on Foreign Relations from 1924 to 1933, Borah played an influential role in national and international affairs, becoming better known abroad than almost any previous Northwest political figure. In some countries he became the best-known living American. Once a European press agency cabled its Washington correspondent: "Never mind Hoover statement, rush comment from Borah."[5]

5. Frank Church, "Borah the Statesman," *Idaho Yesterdays* 9 (summer 1965): 3.

During the interwar years, few public figures better exemplified the Pacific Northwest's tradition of political independence than did Borah. Though he was a life-long Republican, the dictates of his conscience always took precedence over party platforms or labels. Neither an organization man nor an ideologue, he saw himself as a moral force in politics. The Idaho senator continued his independent ways during the 1920s by championing diplomatic recognition of the Soviet Union, a then-unpopular step that President Franklin D. Roosevelt took only in 1933. As chairman of the Foreign Relations Committee, Borah maintained the belief that the United States must follow an independent course in world affairs.

Born in southern Illinois in 1865, he moved west to Boise in 1890, where he gained fame for his role as a prosecutor in the celebrated trial of "Diamondfield" Jack Davis, the alleged hired gun of cattlemen, and later in the case of William D. Haywood, who was accused of plotting the assassination of Governor Frank Steunenberg. Despite his role in the Haywood trial and the probusiness inclination of his party, Borah was not antilabor. In the Senate he demonstrated his independence by representing the cause of labor and vigorously opposing corporate monopoly.

During the First World War, Borah defended civil liberties at a time when the Bill of Rights if put to a popular vote would almost certainly have lost. He supported President Woodrow Wilson's conduct of the war, and that was one reason why the Democratic chief executive privately endorsed the Republican senator's bid for reelection in 1918. But a year later, Borah was involved in the successful fight against Senate ratification of the Treaty of Versailles and U.S. participation in Wilson's beloved League of Nations.

In domestic politics, he worked for measures to aid farmers impoverished by low commodity prices and thus time and again placed himself out of step with Republican party officials on both the national and state levels. He declined to support Herbert Hoover's reelection in 1932 because the president had opposed direct relief to the needy, and thereby Idaho's senior senator earned the title "William the Silent." With characteristic independence, Borah supported some of Roosevelt's New Deal reforms while adamantly opposing others. During the New Deal years he maintained a closer relationship with Roosevelt than perhaps any other Republican senator.

Whatever his apparent inconsistencies and mistakes, and there were many, Idaho voters had an uncommon pride in Borah, who was popularly referred to as "the Lion of Idaho." They remained loyal to Borah, and he to them. A man of amazing energy and drive, he returned to Boise every summer and rented a car and driver to take him around the state to visit his constituents—loggers and university professors alike. Critics charged that

---

LARGER-THAN-LIFE BORAH

The story is told that in the 1930s a farm boy went to Boise. When he returned home he told his father that he had seen the internationally famous Senator William E. Borah shaking hands with people in the Owyhee Hotel.

"Don't be ridiculous," his father scolded. "What would a big man like Borah be doing way out here in Boise, Idaho?"—Frank Church, "Borah the Statesman," *Idaho Yesterdays* 9 (summer 1965): 3

---

Borah was in fact a "spearless leader," a do-nothing type of statesman who substituted oratory for solid accomplishments. Whatever the merit of that argument, Borah "represented a public asset through which Idahoans could be assured that the rest of the nation knew they existed."[6] As senator he often functioned as Idaho's permanent ambassador to the outside world.

Borah's stature as an international celebrity brought more attention to Idaho than the state would have received otherwise, and his lofty profile in the nation's capital helped Borah secure an ample share of New Deal money for Idaho. Such federal aid was especially welcomed during the lean years of the Great Depression, which severely battered all three states of the Pacific Northwest during the 1930s.

6. Robert James Maddox, *William E. Borah and American Foreign Policy* (Baton Rouge: Louisiana State University Press, 1969), xiii.

# CHAPTER 18

# Depression Decade

Yet the program of the New Deal, with all its faulty management, represents the first conscious attempt of the government to utilize for all the people the vast, untapped resources of the frontier. Whatever else Mr. Roosevelt may have done to or for the country, that much he has accomplished in the Columbia River basin. Never again can the natural riches of the hinterlands be left as undeveloped as they were in the years before the New Deal.—Richard L. Neuberger, *Our Promised Land* (1938)

The Great Depression that began on the heels of the stock market crash in the fall of 1929 crippled the Pacific Northwest economy and dominated everyday life for a decade. The lengthy malaise was mitigated only slightly by the fact that most of the region had never really prospered during the 1920s, and thus residents typically had not indulged in the "two-cars-in-every-garage" kind of optimism common in more affluent states.

The Depression dealt the Pacific Northwest's extractive industries a severe blow. About half of Idaho's population in 1930 depended directly on agriculture for a living, about one-tenth relied on manufacturing—mostly timber—and a much smaller portion on mining. Agrarian Idaho had never shared the prosperity of the 1920s, but the disastrous economic decline of the early 1930s made the previous years seem almost prosperous by comparison. The average income of Idahoans plunged by 50 percent between 1929 and 1932. In Oregon the economic collapse brought 90 percent of the timber companies to the verge of bankruptcy, and at least half of the state's

## WE'RE BUSTED FLAT

"With increasing frequency we heard the Pacific Northwest mentioned as a haven for the Dust Bowl refugee. A World War veteran used his bonus money to take his family to Northern Idaho. He wrote back accounts of cheap, cutover land, of abundant rains and beautiful gardens.

"The peak of migration to the Pacific Northwest was reached in 1936. We heard of no migrants coming back, or going elsewhere, once they had reached 'the promised land.' . . . We chose the north end of the Panhandle of Idaho because it offered cheap land, good soil, and abundant moisture. Except for the fact that we would be among strangers, we could be no worse off in this strange land than in our own, and it was imperative that we take the children out of the dust. . . .

"For six days we coaxed the weary, heavy-laden old car along, westward and northward. As mile after mile passed, certain other equipages became familiar to us. Here was an old truck with a Colorado license plate. Under a 'tarp' stretched across the back was an assortment of children, luggage, and household goods. Across one open side flapped a piece of heavy cardboard on which was scrawled:

Idaho, we're busted flat.
Here we come in spite of that;
Not expecting wealth or gain—
Just want our kids to see it rain.

If we passed this outfit during the forenoon, it usually passed us before evening. Twice, when night overtook us, we stopped at the same cabin court. We have wondered about this family many times since. Did they find the land of their dreams?"—Nelle Portrey Davis, *Stump Ranch Pioneer* (1942): 38–39

timberlands were tax delinquent. The Pacific Northwest as a whole experienced mortgage foreclosures, delinquent taxes, and sharply rising unemployment. A sense of desperation led to protests and in some cases to direct action and other forms of self-help by angry farmers and industrial workers. The situation grew so bad in 1932 that arsonists ignited forest fires and then sought to earn money putting them out. The incendiary epidemic became so widespread that the governor of Idaho declared the timber country to be in a state of insurrection, proclaimed martial law, and used national guard troops to bar public access to the forests.

Many of the region's jobless clustered under bridges and wherever else they could find shelter. One of the largest of these encampments was Seattle's Hooverville, a city of shacks fashioned from every conceivable sort of material. It was home to hundreds of men, the Seattle authorities having decreed that no women or children were permitted to live there. A good many of the middle-aged laborers who predominated in this community had once supplied the migratory muscle needed on the wageworkers' frontier.

Adding to the region's unemployment woes was the arrival of two hundred thousand or more refugees from the Dust Bowl of the parched Great Plains—commonly called "Okies " and "Arkies"—who mistakenly hoped to find some relief in the Pacific Northwest. During 1936 alone, an estimated ten thousand farm families fled the northern Great Plains for Washington, Oregon, Idaho, and western Montana. These people headed West, as thousands had done before them, paralleling the route of the Oregon Trail in search of a new life in the fabled promised land of the Pacific Northwest. "Drive out on any of the main highways of our State," observed Idaho's Senator Borah, "and you will see cars, sometimes almost caravans, fleeing from the devastations of the drought." Were it not for the subsistence doles the newcomers received from state and federal governments, many would have starved.

Ironically for Dust Bowl refugees, the Pacific Northwest itself experienced severe drought and dust storms in the early 1930s: the massive tempest of 21 April 1931 began in eastern Washington and blackened the sky from Pullman west to Aberdeen and south to Roseburg with swirling dust. Nineteen thirty-four was the driest year in southern Idaho since record keeping began in 1909.

## A NEW DEAL FOR THE NORTHWEST

A major beneficiary of the malaise of the early 1930s was the Democratic party. In the wake of the Great Depression, voters in all three Northwest states turned to the Democrats. When he ran for president in 1928, Herbert Hoover, a Republican, lost only one county in the three-state region, sparsely populated Fremont on the eastern edge of Idaho. Running for reelection four years later, Hoover, who in the popular mind bore primary responsibility for the hard times, lost all but two counties.[1] The abrupt swing to the Democratic party also benefited state and local candidates.

In the 1930 election, Idaho Democrats chose their first governor since 1917. He was Charles Benjamin ("Cowboy Ben") Ross, a reformer in the populist tradition. Two years later, a discontented Idaho electorate chose its first Democratic U.S. Senator in fourteen years, James P. Pope, and toppled the state's two veteran Republican congressmen, Burton French and Addison Smith, who between them had forty-six years of service on Capitol Hill. The sole Republican officeholder of consequence was Senator Borah, and he now remained aloof from the partisan struggle.

1. In 1932 Hoover carried Bear Lake County, Idaho, and Benton County, Oregon.

It was much the same story throughout the West in 1932. Of four states electing governors, all chose Democrats. Washington voters replaced Wesley L. Jones, a Republican senator since 1909, with the liberal Democrat Homer T. Bone. Capping the Democratic sweep of the West was the victory of Franklin D. Roosevelt, who promised Americans a New Deal. Exactly what that New Deal entailed, neither Roosevelt nor anyone else could say in 1932. This much was certain: after the president-elect took office in March 1933, each day brought dramatic new developments, beginning with his proclamation of a bank holiday to halt the general collapse of the nation's banking system.

Except during the First World War, the federal government had never before been so involved in so many aspects of American life as during the era of Franklin D. Roosevelt and the New Deal. Pacific Northwesterners grew familiar with a host of new abbreviations—CCC, PWA, WPA, AAA, NRA, and many others—each standing for a federal agency charged with implementing part of the president's program. The New Deal's imprint on the Pacific Northwest took many forms, some as awesome as the Grand Coulee Dam—frequently described as "the biggest thing on earth"—and others as mundane as new roads and trails through national forests, concrete sidewalks, picnic shelters, low income housing, wildlife refuges and ranges, highway bridges along the Oregon coast, and post office murals. The WPA constructed ten new courthouses in Idaho. Timberline Lodge, located at the six-thousand-foot level on Oregon's Mount Hood, bore the handprint of New Deal CCC and WPA labor. Dedicated in 1937 by President Roosevelt, the 53-room lodge now ranks as one of the region's most popular tourist attractions.

The Works Progress Administration was one of the largest New Deal agencies, though its projects were usually small in scale and sometimes consisted of little more than leaf raking. The WPA nonetheless constructed several new courthouses in the Pacific Northwest; its artists were responsible for murals in public buildings like post offices and libraries and for traveling exhibits; its actors took federal theater projects even to remote parts of the Pacific Northwest.

Also included in the WPA was the Federal Writers' Project, an unusual program that put unemployed novelists and other writers to work producing a series of state guidebooks. Heading the Idaho project was the state's best known novelist, Vardis Fisher, who crisscrossed the state and wrote most of the book himself. He endured the bureaucratic ignorance of Washington-based editors who on one occasion told him that Grand Teton National Park was located in Idaho and that a natural bridge near Arco did not

71. Timberline Lodge was located about halfway up Oregon's highest peak, Mount Hood, which reached a height of 11,235 feet. Architects specified the use of hand-hewn timbers and handcrafted furnishings, including handwoven draperies, to pay tribute to the region's pioneer heritage. Various carved-wood and wrought-iron designs also captured the Indian spirit. The Works Progress Administration employed about five hundred local artists and craftsmen. Courtesy Oregon Historical Society, ORHI 42785.

exist because they had never heard of it. To the consternation of federal officials in Washington who hoped that a "more important" state would lead the way, Fisher's *Idaho: A Guide in Word and Picture* was the first of the state guides to appear (in early 1937), and it served as a model for others.

A common thread running through many new federal programs was work for the unemployed. The Civilian Conservation Corps put young men to work on reforestation projects. In Idaho alone 163 CCC camps employed nearly twenty thousand men and left a lasting impression on the state's landscape.

Building Bonneville and Grand Coulee dams on the Columbia River cre-

NEW DEAL OUTLAYS PER CAPITA, 1933–1939
(BY REGION AND STATE)

|  | Rank | Allocation in Dollars |
|---|---|---|
| Pacific | 2 | 536 |
| California | 10 | 538 |
| Oregon | 12 | 536 |
| Washington | 13 | 528 |
| Mountain | 1 | 716 |
| Arizona | 4 | 791 |
| Colorado | 14 | 506 |
| Idaho | 5 | 744 |
| Montana | 2 | 986 |
| Nevada | 1 | 1,499 |
| New Mexico | 8 | 690 |
| Utah | 9 | 569 |
| Wyoming | 3 | 897 |

Source: Don C. Reading, "New Deal Activity and the State,
1933–1939," *Journal of Economic History* 33 (1973): 794–95

ated thousands more jobs in Washington and Oregon. Besides creating jobs, the dams were promoted as ways to control flooding and generate electricity. The Columbia River contained 40 percent of the nation's potential for hydroelectric generation. The U.S. Army Corps of Engineers supervised construction of Bonneville Dam forty miles east of Portland, begun in 1933 and placed in service in 1938; the Bureau of Reclamation took charge of Grand Coulee Dam, begun in 1934 and placed in service in late 1941.

Grand Coulee, unlike Bonneville, was also conceived as part of a vast irrigation project. Its twelve massive pumps would lift water from Franklin D. Roosevelt Lake to transform thousands of acres of parched, sagebrush-covered land in central Washington into a garden that boosters hoped in time would support half a million people. The Columbia Basin Project first received water in 1951, and forty years later it remains an evolving network of pumping plants, reservoirs, and canals. As of the early 1990s the project contained six thousand farms on 560,000 irrigated acres producing more than sixty different crops. The ultimate goal was 1.1 million acres of irrigated land, but support for finishing the project waned during the 1970s and 1980s.

72. The WPA offered a class in placer mining in Spokane.
The well-dressed students look as if they could have
been stockbrokers in more prosperous days. Courtesy
National Archives, 69-N-14467.

Columbia River dam projects, like most New Deal projects, were not
without their critics. An Indian chief told the Oregon journalist Richard
Neuberger that the "white man's dams mean no more salmon." He was
partly right, but the situation could have been far worse, because the original design for Bonneville Dam did not include fish ladders and thus would
have blocked all salmon from spawning farther upriver. Only a public out-
cry prevented that tragedy.

When Grand Coulee Dam was finished, it was as tall as a forty-six-story
building and as wide as twelve city blocks. As the largest concrete structure
on earth, it was often described as the Eighth Wonder of the World. Others
called it a white elephant and wonder how the sparsely populated Pacific
Northwest would ever use all the power it generated. The entry of the
United States into World War II only months after the completion of Grand
Coulee Dam silenced the critics, for a host of war-related industries needed
all the power that dams could generate.

BIGGEST THING ON EARTH

Grand Coulee Dam was a structure so immense that journalists struggled to find words to describe its size: "Four ocean liners the size of the giant *Queen Mary* could be placed on the crest of the dam, and still they would not stretch from one end to the other. In bulk Grand Coulee will exceed the twenty next largest dams in the country combined. It will contain enough concrete to build a standard automobile highway from Philadelphia to Seattle and back by way of Los Angeles. Sufficient water will flow through the dam each year to provide New York City's drinking supply for a century. In the twin powerhouses, each more than twice as high as the Leaning Tower of Pisa, so much electricity will be generated that all the switches will have to be thrown far away from the plant by remote control; otherwise the men operating the dam would be instantly electrocuted."—Richard L. Neuberger, *Our Promised Land* (1938): 69–70, 73

CIRCUS POLITICS AND OTHER TRENDS

The political tide that buoyed the political fortunes of Roosevelt and the New Deal also swept into office a number of new Democratic faces at the state and local level. In Washington, the electorate's swing to the Democratic party brought to prominence many of the reform-minded individuals who had found the party a refuge during the lean years of Republican domination. Joining them in the early 1930s was an assortment of idealists, opportunists, and radicals. One commentator, remarking on Washington's "Circus Politics," said: "A smart promoter could now put the entire state under a tent, charge admission, and get it." Among Democrats elected to the legislature in 1932 were three candidates in trouble with the police for statutory offenses, and one of these was actually in jail for the rape of a twelve-year-old girl. The incoming lieutenant governor was Victor Meyers, a former speakeasy orchestra leader who had once run for mayor of Seattle as a joke dressed in the flowing robes of the Mahatma Gandhi and promising "a hostess on every street car." Despite his quirks, Meyers capably ran the state's volatile legislature and was subsequently elected to several terms as secretary of state, serving a total of thirty years in those two offices.

Washington's Democratic governor was Clarence Martin, a conservative banker and wheat miller who espoused stringent economy in government, but within his party were dozens of reformers, each peddling his own specially bottled brand of political cure-all. The most influential of the left-wing pressure groups that operated within the Democratic party was the Wash-

73. Grand Coulee Dam in 1945. Courtesy Library of
Congress.

ington Commonwealth Federation, an organization of liberals, socialists,
and Communists formed in 1935. Claiming thirty thousand members across
the state, it advanced a program advocating production for use, not for profit.
This latest manifestation of the state's radical heritage allegedly prompted
the Democratic national chairman James Farley to quip, "There are forty-
seven states in the Union, and the Soviet of Washington."

Politics in neighboring Oregon and Idaho were sedate by comparison.
Oregon voters chose General Charles H. Martin as governor (1935–39). He
was a conservative Democrat who opposed labor unions, public power, and
the New Deal. The Oregon Commonwealth Federation was less radical
than its counterpart in Washington, but it functioned to marshal support for
New Deal measures in the state legislature and played a role in defeating
Martin's bid for reelection. Idaho's governor Ben Ross promoted various
self-help ideas that clashed with the public welfare plans endorsed by federal New Dealers. Programs of benefit to and popular in Idaho, Ross accepted, but those of little use to the state, he rejected. Roosevelt and Ross
came close to open conflict during the summer of 1933. "Cowboy Ben"

particularly opposed the repeal of Prohibition, which his party favored. Ross was a popular leader, but he made a big mistake in 1936 when he ran for Senate against Borah and was crushed in a landslide.

In 1931 Idaho reinstated the direct primary (which was abandoned twelve years earlier), and Washington took the idea to its extreme by adopting the blanket primary in 1934, becoming the first of only two states (Alaska also) that gave voters complete freedom to choose from among all candidates of all parties in primary elections.

## ORGANIZED LABOR AND DAVE BECK

The 1930s were an especially stormy time of strikes and schism in the house of labor. In 1935 alone, fifty-one thousand Northwest workers went on strike and lost 1.6 million man-hours of work. The Washington National Guard intervened in strikes in Aberdeen and Tacoma. Trouble on the waterfront in 1934 closed West Coast ports for nearly four months, and a strike at the Seattle *Post-Intelligencer* in 1936 ended in recognition of the American Newspaper Guild.

The ranks of organized workers expanded rapidly as a result of federal prolabor legislation, but the nearly uncontrolled growth worsened friction between advocates of craft and industrial unions. When the American Federation of Labor expelled proponents of industrial unionism in 1937, they formed the Congress of Industrial Organizations (CIO) the following year. The labor rivalry became especially bitter in the Pacific Northwest, where the aggressive CIO in some ways embodied both the fiery militancy of the Industrial Workers of the World and the idealism of the Knights of Labor. The CIO's strength in the region lay in the timber and mining industries, in the fish canneries, and on the waterfront. The International Woodworkers of America, formed in 1937, battled for the CIO in the Northwest's woods and mills. The membership of the conservative, craft-oriented AFL was less concentrated, but under the leadership of Dave Beck, a fast-rising star in the Teamsters' Union, it vigorously opposed the CIO and labor radicalism.

Capitalizing on the revolution in motor transport, Beck had moved rapidly through Teamster ranks—from organizing laundry drivers in Seattle to being elected national head of the union (1952–57). In the mid-1930s Beck was easily the Teamsters' most powerful regional leader and the dominant personality in Northwest labor.

Beck's main nemesis in the labor movement was Harry Bridges, an Australian radical based in San Francisco who rose to prominence during the single most important labor disturbance on the West Coast in the 1930s: the great maritime strike of 1934. This dispute erupted when the International Longshoremen's Association challenged the hated "shape-up" whereby the workers who loaded and unloaded cargo ships arrived at the docks early in the morning and waited for company foremen to select a fortunate few for the day's work, often receiving a kickback from the men chosen. When some thirty-five hundred longshoremen quit work in protest, they were joined by members of various marine unions.

Together they tied up ports from Seattle to San Diego for almost four months. Frightened residents came to believe that the strike was a Communist plot and that the ranks of subversives included strike leader Harry Bridges. In San Francisco in July 1934 the dispute erupted into a pitched battle between strikers and police. This in turn led to a three-day general strike that idled 127,000 workers. Shortly after this show of force the walk-out ended, and through arbitration the longshoremen won most of their demands, including an end to the hated shape-up. However, when the forces of Harry Bridges attempted to "march inland" from the docks to protect their flanks by organizing warehousemen, Beck countered with club-swinging squads of hired thugs.

In time, both the strikes and labor's internecine warfare diminished, and Beck even came to be regarded as a respectable citizen of Washington; he served on numerous state boards and committees and was elected in 1946 to the Board of Regents of the University of Washington. Beck was standing at the pinnacle of his career in 1962 when he was convicted of income tax evasion, lost his union post, and spent the next thirty months behind bars at the McNeil Island federal penitentiary.

## POWER PLAYS: THE WIRED NORTHWEST

Apart from the growing muscle of organized labor, few subjects sparked more impassioned debate in the Pacific Northwest during the 1930s than did electric power. At issue was who should generate and distribute it: government- or investor-owned utilities, and at what price?

The Pacific Northwest has historically consumed a prodigious amount of electricity. The seemingly limitless supply of cheap hydropower attracted a heavy user in the aluminum industry, which after the region's first plant opened on the Columbia River in 1940 would supply the lightweight metal so vital to aircraft builders. In more recent decades, household electric bills in Seattle have averaged one-sixth those in New York City and helped to encourage residents to use four times as much electricity as New Yorkers. Largely as a result of the electric pumps and giant sprinklers that water crops on the Snake River plain, Idaho consumes far more electricity per capita than any other state.

Electric power in the Pacific Northwest dates from the early 1880s, about the same time that Thomas Edison opened his municipal lighting system in New York City. The region's first hydroelectric dam was completed in Spokane in 1885 and supplied electricity to illuminate a part of the downtown area. Other early generating systems in Seattle, Portland, and smaller communities powered sawmills, printing presses, elevators, and streetcars. In the booming mining communities of the Wood River Valley, where Idaho's first electric generating facility was installed in 1882, the rate to operate Hailey's first 214 lights was ten cents a day for each all-night lamp, and eight cents for lamps that went off at midnight.

Electric equipment was initially crude and not very reliable. But the technology soon improved and so did the ability to transport power from central generating stations over long distances, a development that made large-scale electric systems possible. The first long-distance transmission of electricity in the world occurred in 1889, when a direct current line was strung from the Willamette Falls at Oregon City to Portland to provide current for streetlights. In the opening years of the twentieth century, the Washington Water Power Company built a long-distance transmission line to electrify the Coeur d'Alene mines and make their year-round operation possible.

Although urban dwellers were first to reap the benefits of electricity, some of the region's rural dwellers were not too far behind. Expansion of the Spokane-based Washington Water Power Company into adjacent rural areas through purchase of small-town systems was typical of what happened around several cities, and the spreading network of power lines gave local operations a degree of reliability they never had before.

Passage of the federal Reclamation Act of 1902 led to the construction of Minidoka Dam, the first federal hydroelectric facility in the Pacific Northwest, between 1907 and 1910; its power pumped Snake River water to transform 50,000 acres of arid land and electrified nearby towns and farms. Some rural electrification projects, primarily on Puget Sound and in southern Idaho, dated from before the First World War, but many other rural areas did not receive electricity until the late 1930s and 1940s. When the New Deal's Rural Electrification Administration was established in 1936 to encourage the wiring of the countryside, 70 percent of the farms in Idaho were still without electric power, 60 percent in Oregon, and 50 percent in Washington. By the early 1950s fewer than three percent of the region's farms were without electricity.

Electrification of the Pacific Northwest was far more than a matter of technology or finance. Electrification became a source of community pride (the Idaho town of Rupert boasted in 1914 that it had the first electrically heated high school in the United States) and an instrument of social change. As Martha Spangler, editor of the *Idaho Clubwoman*, commented in 1910: "With the household appliances of modern time, woman is fast coming into her own. She has more time for study and recreation, she is brighter, happier, more intelligent, and let us add, a more 'chummy' companion for her husband and children." Among the beneficiaries of electrification were farmers' wives, who before electrification cooked on woodburning stoves, washed clothes by hand, heated irons on a stove to press clothes, and stored food in cellars or cisterns to keep it cool. Some farm wives recalled the arrival of electricity with comments like "All I wanted in the world was an electric iron," and "We thought we were in heaven."

Almost from the beginning, public- and investor-owned electric utilities had their proponents. McMinnville, Oregon, inaugurated the first municipally owned electric system in the Pacific Northwest in 1889. Within the next fifteen years, large publicly-owned systems evolved in Tacoma and Seattle. Overseeing the rapid expansion of Seattle City Light was J. D. Ross, later to be the first administrator of the Bonneville Power Administration.

Most of the region's investor-owned electric companies—including Puget Sound Power and Light, Washington Water Power, and Pacific Power and Light—were early acquired by giant holding companies headquartered in the Midwest and East. About fifty separate electric enterprises, for example, were originally located in the area now served by Idaho Power of Boise. When Idaho Power commenced operation in 1916 it was owned by the Electric Bond and Share Company of New York. "Absentee owners" retained control until the 1940s, when the federal government broke up the holding companies.

The battle between public and private power intensified during the 1920s and 1930s as advocates of "people's power" confronted critics who warned of the dangers of "creeping socialism." Both Oregon and Washington passed legislation in the early 1930s to permit formation of public utility districts (people's utility districts in Oregon). These measures allowed rural areas and small towns to acquire and operate their own electric systems. In Idaho, unlike Oregon and Washington, opponents of public power were far more powerful than advocates: in 1937 the legislature turned thumbs down to a proposal that would have allowed the creation of public utility districts throughout the state.

The issue of marketing hydroelectric power generated by the Bonneville and Grand Coulee dams first came before Congress in 1935. Senator James P. Pope of Idaho and Congressman Knute Hill of Washington, two public power Democrats, introduced legislation that would have created a comprehensive Columbia Valley Authority modeled after the Tennessee Valley Authority. It was the first of five unsuccessful attempts to pass such a measure. The Bonneville Power Administration (BPA) created in 1937 was originally seen only as a stopgap measure to market power from Bonneville and Grand Coulee dams until the creation of the Columbia Valley Authority. Now more than fifty years old, the BPA exercises enormous influence as a federal agency that markets wholesale electric power from thirty federal dams to public and private utilities throughout the West. BPA currently supplies nearly half the electricity consumed in the Pacific Northwest.

In 1941 the Bonneville Power Administration hired folk singer–writer Woody Guthrie for a month to compose music for a documentary film celebrating its accomplishments in the Pacific Northwest. During that brief time, Guthrie wrote twenty-six songs and earned $266.66. Best known of the series was "Roll On, Columbia," which the Washington legislature in 1987 designated the state's official folk song.

Battles over electric energy enlivened Northwest politics during the New Deal years and would continue to be fought in the decades that followed. When, for instance, the Idaho town of Arco became in 1955 the world's first community lighted by nuclear-generated electricity, few Northwesterners then could have imagined the controversy that would surround nuclear power plants a quarter-century later, or that dams built to generate electricity would by the 1990s generate impassioned debates over declining populations of wild salmon.

### INTERWAR YEARS IN PERSPECTIVE

Some events of the 1920s and 1930s represented fundamental breaks with the past, whereas others furnished glimpses of the future, and not just in the political arena. During the Depression W. Averell Harriman, the youthful chairman of the board of the Union Pacific Railroad, undertook to develop a ski resort in the western United States. He envisioned a resort that rivaled the best Europe had to offer as well provided a destination that might enhance his railroad's lagging passenger revenues. To that end the Union Pacific hired Count Felix Schaffgotsch, an Austrian ski enthusiast, to search for the prime location. After visits to numerous western sites that he dismissed as too high, too windy, or too remote, Schaffgotsch finally located his ideal place on the slopes above the old Idaho mining town of Ketchum. It had dry-powder snow, spectacular vistas, and all-weather access from the railroad's main line at Shoshone. Upon Schaffgotsch's recommendation, the Union Pacific purchased a 3,888 acre ranch for $39,000.

There a world-class resort called Sun Valley took shape. A massive 220-room lodge was constructed with an unusually high proportion of the lower floors made of dense concrete because of the company's fear of fires. So cleverly was the concrete etched and stained to resemble wood that few guests realized the difference. The lodge opened on 31 December 1936, although the first snow did not fall until more than a week later. *Life* magazine depicted the resort as "society's new western playground." In 1941 Twentieth-Century Fox featured the resort in a feature-length film called *Sun Valley Serenade*. When the Union Pacific Railroad opened the complex it inaugurated a new era for Northwest tourism. The rival Milwaukee Road promoted snow skiing at Snoqualmie Pass in Washington, and the Great Northern did likewise in the mountains of northern Idaho and northwestern Montana. A growing network of all-weather highways made possible the development of numerous other ski areas.

The decade that reshaped the region's tourist industry also dramatically increased the impact of the federal government on the lives of ordinary citizens. New Deal programs institutionalized a vastly enlarged role for the federal government in the region. Planning on both state and regional levels became much more common as New Deal conferences enabled administrators to explain and promote their programs. The Pacific Northwest Regional Planning Commission, a small group of private citizens, began in 1934 to hold annual meetings to study the best uses of the region's resources. But all of these new departures pale when compared to the impact of World War II, the event that more than any other hastened the region's coming of age.

# Part V

# The Pacific Northwest Comes of Age

# Profile: Tom McCall of Oregon

*

The developers said Tom McCall stunted our growth. Well, maybe he did, but we're growing anyway because where we live is so beautiful. Tom preserved the beauty.—quoted in William F. Asbury, "In the Mountains' Shadow," *Amtrak Express* (1984)

*

Thomas Lawson McCall was born in 1913 and died in 1983. Far more than most public officials before him, the controversial Oregon governor confronted the problems of a state and region coming-of-age. He did so with a gusto that made him legendary and his administration one of the best shows in the Pacific Northwest. His resourcefulness and farsightedness at a time when those qualities seemed sadly lacking in the administration of fellow Republican, President Richard M. Nixon, gained McCall a national reputation and frequent mention as a possible presidential candidate in 1976.

New England–born and the grandson of a Massachusetts governor and congressman, McCall spent his childhood on the lingering edge of the frontier in central Oregon's Crooked River country near Prineville. On the family ranch he developed what became a lifelong respect for the environment. As a student at the University of Oregon, he furthered his ambition to become a sportswriter. During his Eugene years he met two of Oregon's future United States senators: Richard Neuberger, a gifted journalism student and campus liberal, and Wayne Morse, dean of the university's law school and later a fiery political maverick known to Oregonians as the Tiger in the Senate. Although McCall did not realize it then, he would someday share the political spotlight with these two men.

Not long after he graduated in 1936 with a degree in journalism, McCall moved to Moscow, Idaho, where he eked out a living covering local news, mainly sporting events at the University of Idaho. As publicity chairman of the Latah County Wildlife Federation, he demonstrated a growing awareness of conservation issues. He also helped to form the Young Republican Club. The five years in Moscow and those that followed in Portland, where McCall worked as a reporter and radio newscaster, added to his political education. During the Second World War, he joined the navy and served in the South Pacific as a correspondent.

After the war, he returned to a broadcasting job in Portland and a growing involvement in Young Republican politics. A pivotal event in his career occurred in 1949 when Governor Douglas McKay, impressed by one of McCall's speeches, invited the young journalist to Salem to serve as his executive secretary. McCall's informal training for governor included two and one-half years with McKay and a term as secretary of state (1965–67), Oregon's second-highest elective office.

When not in government he continued to pursue a career in journalism. Working for KGW-TV in Portland, McCall produced a documentary called "Pollution in Paradise," which described the Willamette River as an "open sewer" clogged with the effluent of Oregon's four largest cities and several pulp and paper mills. The film won a national award as the outstanding documentary for 1962 and stimulated efforts to clean up the Willamette. By 1969, the river had clearly made a comeback. Soon its entire length was clean enough for swimming, boating, and fishing. More important, through the efforts of crusading journalists like McCall, a growing number of Pacific Northwesterners came to realize during the 1960s that pollution was not something that happened only to rivers and lakes east of the Rocky Mountains.

McCall was elected governor of Oregon in 1966, the year that another Republican, Ronald Reagan, was first elected governor of California. Although the two men were members of the same party, they represented its liberal and conservative wings. The blunt-spoken McCall later said of Reagan that he had no experience in government and had run on a simplistic platform composed mainly of conservative shibboleths. McCall's candor sometimes embarrassed associates and got him in trouble with party leaders, but his warm and friendly approach to people was a compensating trait. He was a large and handsome man, at six feet, five inches tall a standout in any crowd—and some would say with an oversized ego to match.

An increasingly important word in the vocabulary of Oregonians during the 1960s was livability, popularized by McCall's predecessor as governor, Mark O. Hatfield, a former professor of political science and dean at Willamette University. McCall soon gave the term added meaning by stressing the need for Oregon to acquire its beach land, and he made a dramatic commitment to clean up the Willamette by appointing himself interim chairman of the State Sanitary Authority. No Oregon governor before him had appointed himself to a state board or commission.

McCall propounded an eleventh commandment, "Thou shalt not Pollute," which he intended to enforce. Working closely with the 1967 legislature, he bragged that he and the lawmakers put together "the greatest bulk of environmental measures, the largest one-whack commitment of any state in history." Critics claimed that he happened along at the right time; nonetheless, by mid-1971 the governor had maneuvered more than one hundred environmental protection measures through the state legislature. The cornerstone, a comprehensive program to curb air and water pollution, established the Department of Environmental Quality in 1969. On a related front, in December 1969 McCall led a successful protest by Pacific Northwesterners against shipment of thirteen thousand tons of army nerve gas from Okinawa to an ordnance depot near Pendleton, Oregon.

McCall served as governor during a particularly volatile time in American history, an era filled with violent protests against the war in Vietnam. On 4 May 1970, Ohio National Guardsmen shot fifteen students during a demonstration at Kent State University, killing four. A nationwide student strike followed, shutting down some twenty-five hundred colleges and universities. President Richard M. Nixon declared a state of emergency and invited the governors to the White House for a meeting to discuss the crisis. Oregon's chief executive declined, pointing out that he was needed at home, where every week many visitors stopped by his office to express their concern about America's faltering course.[1] In keeping with his campaign promise to make this a "citizens' administration," McCall conducted open house in his office for half an hour every day; during his first four months as governor, seventeen thousand constituents came to discuss their concerns.

Not long after Kent State, McCall received word that Oregon was to be the next battleground. That year the American Legion scheduled its national convention in Portland, and the Justice Department reported that fifty thousand young people calling themselves the People's Army Jamboree would come to town at the same time. Some of the group's members

---

1. McCall himself had been a supporter of the war in Vietnam.

74. Thomas Lawson McCall (1913–83), governor of
Oregon from 1967 to 1975. Courtesy Oregon Historical
Society, CN 012693.

openly welcomed a riot. McCall arranged a free rock concert at McIver State
Park thirty-five miles southeast of Portland to defuse the threat. Called
Vortex I, the concert attracted thirty-five thousand people. Although some
concert-goers—much to the dismay of most Oregonians—engaged in nude
bathing and marijuana smoking, the crowd remained peaceful and friendly.

Elsewhere in the United States that week, bombings killed one student and injured four others at the University of Wisconsin, two more died at an army arsenal in Virginia, and a bomb rocked American Legion offices in Seattle. In Portland the toll from the week's unrest was a broken window at Portland State University. McCall described Vortex I as "a great contribution to an understanding between the ages and generations."[2] Evidently a majority of Oregonians approved of McCall's performance, because later that year they reelected him governor with 56 percent of the vote. His Democratic opponent, Robert Straub, suffered an even greater defeat than he had when he ran against McCall four years earlier.

McCall never hesitated to plunge into controversial issues. During the struggle to save the Willamette from pollution, management shut down a Boise Cascade pulp and paper mill at Salem in the face of court action. The plant had been discharging 150,000 gallons of sulfite waste into the river daily. Fearful of losing their jobs, two hundred angry employees confronted McCall on the capitol steps.

"Hitler, Hitler," they chanted.

When explanations bellowed by the governor and his director of the Department of Environmental Quality got across—that workers were being used by their own management—one spokesman shouted back, "Okay, Governor, you lead us and we'll picket our own plant and management."

Eventually, industries and municipalities along the Willamette cleaned up their discharges, at the cost of many millions of dollars. The governor and others sought to implement the concept of a "Greenway" or park extending from Portland to Eugene along the river's banks. But water pollution was not the only environmental problem confronting the Willamette Valley. Grass-seed farmers whose industry centered in the Salem-Eugene area burned their fields each summer in order to produce a multimillion-dollar crop. In 1969 heavy smoke blanketed the freeway and poured into Eugene, creating an environmental crisis. The governor used his emergency police power to stop further burning temporarily and then undertook the difficult task of finding a long-range solution to the problem.

In 1971 McCall uttered his most famous remark to a Junior Chamber of Commerce convention in Portland: "We want you to visit our State of Excitement often," he said. "Come again and again. But, for heaven's sake, don't move here to live." The delegates listened in disbelief. They greeted

2. Unless otherwise noted, the quotations that follow in this chapter are from *Tom McCall, Maverick: An Autobiography with Steve Neal* (Portland: Binford and Mort, 1977).

the comment with a moment of silence followed by a burst of laughter. But McCall was serious; he was committed to livability. As he told a group of visiting businessmen from Los Angeles, "Oregon has not been an over-eager lap-dog to the economic master. Oregon has been wary of smokestacks and suspicious of rattle and bang. Oregon has not camped, cup in hand, at anyone's affluent doorstep. Oregon has wanted industry only when that industry was willing to want what Oregon is."

His statements provoked criticism. An angry California businessman who thought that McCall had originated the slogan Don't Californicate Oregon responded with a counterproposal, Don't Oregonize California. McCall noted, however, that some of his staunchest supporters in the controversy were Californians who had recently moved to Oregon. "They seem to resent bitterly the intrusion of another Californian."

A Eugene artist and greeting-card entrepreneur created a line of "Oregon Ungreeting Cards," one of which read: "Tom Lawson McCall, governor, on behalf of the citizens of the great state of Oregon, cordially invites you to visit. . . . Washington or California or Idaho or Nevada or Afghanistan." A popular bumper sticker read Oregon for Oregonians, and in the same vein a whimsical group, the James G. Blaine Society (named for a onetime presidential candidate from Maine), proposed building a freeway from California to Canada with no off-ramps.

In grappling with the problem of unchecked population sprawl, McCall was a modern pioneer. But he was bucking one of the oldest traditions in the American West, that of real estate promotion and an individual's assumed right to develop his own land, whether that meant carving pristine meadows into "mini-estates" or bulldozing wetlands to build a marina. That was the "Buffalo Hunter mentality," McCall complained, and he cited Lincoln City on the central Oregon coast as "a model of strip city grotesque." In his call for state land-use policy, new subdivision laws, and new standards for planning and zoning by cities and counties, he urged Oregonians to protect their present and future interests from "grasping wastrels of the land. We must respect another truism. Unlimited and unregulated growth leads inexorably to a lowered quality of life."

A major step toward realization of McCall's dream was passage of Oregon senate bill 100 in 1973 to address the problem of disorderly patterns of growth. That measure created the Land Conservation and Development Commission, which had the power to review land-use plans from Oregon's 278 localities and to accept or reject them on the basis of whether they complied with nineteen state land-use goals. Business and labor leaders who feared it would drive up the cost of land and make industries reluctant to locate in Oregon criticized the controversial measure. The measure survived three initiative challenges but faced continued pressure as Oregon's population grew during the 1990s.

Of all the reforms McCall sought during his ten years in elective state office, he took the greatest pride in the passage and implementation of the Oregon bottle bill, the first state measure enacted in the nation to outlaw pull-tab cans and nonreturnable bottles, sources of much highway litter. The new law required consumers to pay cash deposits on all beer and soft-drink containers. Before the legislature approved the bottle bill in 1971, McCall was subjected to the most intense opposition in his public life. For him the issue was larger than merely providing the money necessary to clean up litter along Oregon's streets and highways. It symbolized "the switch society has to make everywhere from profligacy to husbanding diminishing resources. It is a practical first bridge for this most wasteful of all countries to cross, in reducing a lifestyle bordering on opulence to a level of relative affluence." McCall credited the law with reducing the volume of litter by 47 percent during its second year of operation. The neighboring state of Washington, in contrast, was not able to pass a similar litter measure, nor has it duplicated Oregon's tough standards for building nuclear power plants.

With characteristic directness McCall confronted a prolonged energy crisis that began in the spring of 1973. A severe water shortage that threatened the region's supply of hydroelectric power was followed by an Arab embargo on oil shipments to America. The Oregon governor directed thirty-two thousand state employees to minimize their use of office lights, hot water, and air conditioners, and to drive state cars sparingly. He issued an order banning all but the most essential outdoor display lighting, lowered the state's speed limit from seventy to fifty-five miles per hour, and caused a stir when he suggested that schools consider discontinuing night football. The gasoline shortage that fall created long lines at service stations, and there were reports of angry customers menacing station operators with tire irons. Working with dealers statewide, McCall implemented a voluntary plan in January 1974 to sell gasoline on alternate days to motorists with odd- or even-numbered license plates. The Oregon plan was soon adopted in other states as an alternative to ration coupons.

Criticizing gas-guzzling American cars as "Belchfire Eights" and "Gas

Glutton Supremes," the governor switched to a German-made compact car. The attempt to set a good example soon conflicted with the uncomfortable reality of his more-than-six-foot-frame, and he returned to a standard-size car. Even Tom McCall came to realize that he could not implement all of his good intentions.

McCall's unorthodox ways captured the attention of many Americans yearning for an alternative to the sleazy politics and wooden-headed policies of the Watergate era. He was the first Republican governor to call for President Nixon's resignation as a result of the deepening scandal. Discussions of a McCall campaign for president in 1976 appeared in several respected national publications, including *Time* and the *Washington Post*. McCall talked of a "Third Force" alternative to Democratic and Republican parties. Quite in the Pacific Northwest tradition of political independence, he emphasized to eastern Republicans that "for some time, I have enunciated the thesis that issues are more significant than party labels." William S. U'Ren could not have stated the essence of the Oregon System more succinctly. The exact nature of the Third Force eluded definition, as McCall himself acknowledged. "Its genesis," he explained, "was the Oregon Story with the story's emphasis on problem solving in a climate of openness and probity, reverence for nature, and sometimes daring innovation—free from conniving, coercion, and partisan gamesmanship." That was McCall's corollary to the good-government dream of U'Ren.

McCall left the governor's office in January 1975 but declined to run for president the following year, preferring to let Gerald Ford and Jimmy Carter contest that prize while he and his wife temporarily retired to campus life at Oregon State University. After a stint as professor of journalism, McCall produced five television and six radio commentaries a week in addition to a Sunday television show.

An abiding interest in the governor's office caused him to attempt a political comeback in 1978, but Victor Atiyeh defeated him in the Republican primary. Equally unsuccessful was McCall's long battle with cancer that began in 1972 while he was still governor.

Confronting the third of the initiative measures to overturn the land-use planning law, McCall acknowledged in 1982 that it would be his last fight: "You all know that I have terminal cancer, and I have a lot of it. But what many of you might not know is that stress induces its spread and induces its activity. Stress may even bring it on. Yet stress is the fuel of the activist. This activist loves Oregon more than he loves life. I know I can't have both very long, but the tradeoff is all right with me." McCall died three months later, but the land-use protections remained, as did other McCall-era innovations.[3]

During his public life, McCall promoted civil rights and administrative and tax reforms. A commentator in the *New Yorker* observed in 1974 that Oregonians "have laws so progressive that, by comparison, many other states look doddering," and he attributed much of that progress to McCall's policies.[4] But Oregon's activist governor will probably be best remembered for championing environmental causes. He was the region's first prominent public official to make a career out of reminding voters that the Northwest's age of environmental innocence was past. McCall's crusade highlighted the conflicting forces that would shape the Pacific Northwest during the latter half of the twentieth century.

With the state's unemployment rate topping 12 percent in 1982 and Oregon's corporate climate ranked a low thirty-sixth in the continental United States, Governor Victor Atiyeh sought to send a distinctly new message to the world: "Oregon is open for business." Whether Oregon—and the entire Pacific Northwest—can balance economic growth with McCall's vision of environmental quality remains to be seen. The ongoing dilemma was perhaps best expressed in a 1985 *Wall Street Journal* headline that read: "Eugene, Ore., May Be a Great Place to Live, But Not Without a Job."

3. Neal R. Peirce, and Jerry Hagstrom. *The Book of America: Inside Fifty States Today* (New York: Warner Books, 1984), 826.
4. E. J. Kahn Jr., *New Yorker* 50 (25 February 1974): 88–99 passim.

CHAPTER 19

# From World War to Cold War

\*

"What's going to happen," some ask, "when the fighting stops? Can the
Northwest go back to fish, fruit, and sawmills, or have these changes come
to stay?"—Frederick Simpich, "Wartime in the Pacific Northwest,"
*National Geographic Magazine* (1942)

\*

The Second World War brought important and lasting changes to the Pacific
Northwest. Although no region of the United States escaped the impact of
war, few if any experienced a more rapid or intense transformation than the
Pacific Northwest. Wartime social and economic pressures scarcely left a
corner untouched. In what would prove to be a classic understatement, the
Portland *Oregonian* observed on 6 April 1941: "Few persons realize the
magnitude of the national defense efforts in the Pacific Northwest."

Fifty years later a shroud of secrecy still conceals some details of the
war's impact, but what was clearly visible to Pacific Northwesterners in the
early 1940s was the quickened pace of life and the amazing construction
boom that transformed the region's two main centers of war production:
Puget Sound and the Portland-Vancouver area. The wartime transformation
was no less visible in seemingly remote and isolated places like Idaho's Lake
Pend Oreille, where in 1942 Uncle Sam built Camp Farragut; the largest
inland naval base in the world, it had the capacity to handle thirty thousand
recruits at a time in its six self-contained training camps and was for a time
the largest city in Idaho.

In an even more remote corner of the Pacific Northwest—the Targee

National Forest located just west of Yellowstone National Park—the army conducted secret tests of phosgene and other chemical weapons to learn how poison gases might react in battle on similar terrain in Europe. Most improbable of all was the war's dramatic impact on the villages of Hanford and White Bluffs in central Washington. Residents of the bucolic fruit-growing communities were surprised to receive an eviction notice from the federal government in early March 1943 stating that it was purchasing their land and giving them thirty days to leave. The letter provided no explanation. In this summary way the federal government acquired title to the "virtually unhabited" 560-square-mile area and removed fifteen hundred residents. In their place an army of workers built a multimillion-dollar complex of 554 buildings, 386 miles of road, 158 miles of railroad, three massive chemical plants, and the world's first full-sized nuclear reactors. Hanford's purpose was to produce plutonium for the world's first atomic bombs, notably the one called "Fat Man" that devastated Nagasaki in 1945, killing thirty thousand people and injuring sixty thousand. Japan began negotiating a surrender two days later.

Located nearer the Pacific conflict than any other part of the lower forty-eight states, the Pacific Northwest with its several vital war industries feared invasion and air raids. Military and civilian volunteer units patrolled the coast looking for Japanese invaders, antisubmarine nets guarded Puget Sound, and Boeing Airplane Company cleverly camouflaged the roof of its sprawling airplane factories to resemble a residential neighborhood.

The Second World War brought social dislocation, privation, and death. It also created unprecedented prosperity and a rare sense of common national purpose. At no time since then have Americans been so united in the conviction that they were fighting a "good war" to defeat unmitigated evil. Such a belief, reinforced in countless ways by patriotic exhortations and demonstrations, helped Pacific Northwesterners adjust to rationing, high prices, overcrowded streetcars, and news of destruction and death.

### WINNING THE BATTLE FOR PRODUCTION

Even before the United States formally declared war on the Axis nations of Japan, Germany, and Italy in December 1941, the Pacific Northwest experienced the impact of increased production for defense and for aid to friendly nations already at war. The surprise Japanese attack at Pearl Harbor rapidly accelerated that trend. Industries large and small produced ships, barges, aircraft, lumber and various kinds of wood products, metals, food, machin-

ery, clothing, munitions, and armaments. Seattle alone secured war contracts totaling $5.6 billion, ranking it among the nation's top three cities in per capita war orders.

The region's two best-known war industries were the Kaiser shipyards in the Portland-Vancouver area and the Boeing Airplane Company. Boeing had large assembly plants in Seattle and Renton and several smaller subassembly and parts factories located throughout the Pacific Northwest. Before war broke out in Europe in September 1939, it employed about four thousand people and produced military planes for the Army Air Corps and a limited number of commercial aircraft.

One of Boeing's models from the 1930s was the B-17 or Flying Fortress, which Britain's Royal Air Force purchased to strike at the Germans. By mid-1941 nearly ten thousand people worked for Boeing, a number that jumped to twenty thousand in September, and to thirty thousand when the United States officially entered the war a few months later. At the peak of B-17 production, Boeing's Seattle plant rolled out sixteen B-17s every twenty-four hours.

A larger and longer-range Boeing plane, the B-29 Super Fortress, became operational in 1943. On each of its assembly lines in Renton, Boeing was capable of building a B-29 bomber in five days. By mid-1945 six new planes rolled out of the plant each day for a wartime total of 1,119 B-29s, in addition to the nearly 7,000 Boeing B-17s produced in the Seattle plant. At its peak of production in 1944, Boeing employed nearly fifty thousand people in the Seattle area and amassed total sales of more than $600 million, an impressive sum considering that in 1939 the value of all Seattle manufacturing totaled only $70 million.

Vital to the success of the aircraft industry were the region's five new aluminum reduction plants—the first of which Alcoa opened near Vancouver in 1940—and Bonneville and Grand Coulee dams, which supplied the cheap power necessary to convert alumina (aluminum oxide) into ingots of aluminum. Congress provided the Bonneville Power Administration more than $2 billion to increase the generating capacity of the dams sixfold between 1941 and 1945.

75. Only in August 1945, after atomic bombs destroyed Hiroshima and Nagasaki, did most of the nearly fifty thousand people who crowded into the Hanford area at the height of wartime activity learn what the strange complex produced. Courtesy Oregon Historical Society, CN 010921.

In the production of aluminum goods, the Pacific Northwest supplied little more than electricity and reduction facilities. Aluminum originated in the tropics as bauxite ore, and after being refined in the Columbia Valley, it was shipped across North America to be fabricated into semifinished products. Another reminder of the region's continuing status as an economic colony was the fact that, of all the major components in a B-29, Boeing itself fabricated only the spar chord (a support assembly for the wings). Wing tips were manufactured in Cleveland, landing gear in Milwaukee, engine housings in Detroit, and engines in a Dodge factory in Chicago. Puget Sound businesses handled no more than 5 percent of Boeing's subcontracted work.

Even more spectacular than Boeing's accomplishments were those of the three Kaiser shipyards in the Portland-Vancouver area. With the aid of federal subsidies, the aggressive and blunt-spoken industrialist Henry J. Kaiser became the world's foremost shipbuilder. For a time nearly one hundred thousand people worked in the three Kaiser yards, which displaced Pacific Telephone and Telegraph as Portland's biggest employer. Between mid-1941, when his first yard opened on the banks of the Willamette River, and August 1945, Kaiser constructed about fifty "baby flattop" aircraft carriers and several hundred Liberty ships. The shipyards used fast and simplified methods of welding and steel produced in Kaiser plants in Utah and California.

In mid-1942, a Kaiser yard could build a ship in seventy-two days, half the national average. By the war's end, one of Kaiser's Oregon yards launched a ship in a mere ten days. Kaiser facilities in Vancouver and Portland built more vessels than were constructed anywhere else in the United States and compiled a productivity record unmatched among shipyards.

Other war facilities in the Portland-Vancouver area employed from a few hundred to several thousand workers. Subassembly plants for ships and airplanes, and industries manufacturing wartime chemical, aluminum, steel, and other products were also located in Portland. Elsewhere, smaller plants like the Pacific Car and Foundry Company in Renton converted from making logging trucks to Sherman tanks. Eighty-eight ship- and boatyards in Washington—including the navy's big facility at Bremerton—employed a total of 150,000 workers in 1944.

FEATURES OF WARTIME LIFE

War industries and military installations wrought profound population changes in the Pacific Northwest. In the state of Washington were located more than fifty relatively large army and navy bases, with the greatest concentration of military personnel being in the Fort Lewis–Camp Murray–McChord Field area south of Tacoma. The population growth that accompanied the establishment of military bases nearly overwhelmed small communities like Ephrata, Soap Lake, Moses Lake, and Oak Harbor.

In Portland, where Kaiser shipyards employed nearly 70 percent of the city's labor force, job seekers arrived from ranches in Idaho and Montana—even from as far away as New York City—by special Kaiser trains. Five such trains left New York City on a single weekend in late 1942 carrying five thousand workers. Kaiser charged a fare of $75 to be deducted from subsequent paychecks.

The region's population shifts were phenomenal. Between 1940 and 1944, Seattle increased from 368,302 to approximately 530,000 people (650,000 in the greater metropolitan area); Tacoma from 109,408 to 140,000; and Bremerton from 15,134 to 48,000. Portland gained 160,000 new residents, a figure that did not include another 100,000 people in the industrial suburbs of Troutdale, Oregon City, Vanport, and Vancouver. Oregon's population growth during the 1940s nearly equaled its increase for the entire nineteenth century.

Although many war workers came from outside the Pacific Northwest, residents of the region made up the largest percentage of the work force. As a consequence, urban growth represented mainly a redistribution of population within the region. The exodus of people to the boom areas and into the armed forces resulted in stationary or declining populations in agricultural areas east of the Cascades. Except for Camp Farragut and a large naval ordnance plant in Pocatello, Idaho contributed mainly the traditional products of its mines, forests, and fields to the war effort. The state actually lost 15,000 residents between 1940 and 1945. During that same time, the states of Oregon and Washington gained 194,000 and 533,000 new residents respectively.

Seattle doubled its number of manufacturing employees between 1940 and 1942. Nearly half the people initially hired in its war plants were men under twenty-five. The rapid influx of young males without strong community ties was common to all the major cities of the region. Typically, they came from small town or rural areas where, if previously employed, they had been working in one of the region's principal extractive industries—forestry, mining, and fishing. About 10 percent had formerly worked on farms. In addition to the lure of high pay offered by war industries, such jobs were exempt from the draft, at least in the early part of the war.

Married men among the newcomers faced the problem of finding suitable housing for their families or leaving them behind—as Kaiser advised his imported East Coast workers to do. In the late summer of 1941 when the large influx of new residents began, the vacancy rate for housing in Seattle, Tacoma, and Everett dropped to 1 or 2 percent, and rents rose accordingly. Nearly one-third of all Seattle dwellings renting for less than $50 a month suddenly commanded higher rents, a far greater proportion of increases than occurred in any other large city in the United States. That was one reason why inflation in Seattle exceeded that in any comparable city, climbing 74 percent from 1939 to 1947.

Wartime Seattle and Portland also confronted some of the nation's worst housing problems. To alleviate the shortages, shortcuts were taken, few of them satisfactory. Many existing dwellings were hastily divided into apartments; trailer camps were established; obsolete and condemned houses were patched up; and chicken coops, sheds, lodge halls, empty service stations, and offices were converted into dwellings. Even tents were used. People lived in the back seats of cars or took turns sleeping around the clock in "hot beds." The result was overcrowded and substandard facilities— houses without adequate sanitary arrangements—that created considerable dissatisfaction among war workers. In an attempt to relieve the shortage, federally financed housing projects were hastily constructed, such as the Hudson House Dormitory in Vancouver, which accommodated six thousand men in single and double rooms.

The most spectacular effort to address the housing problem was a completely new working-class town built in a lowland area adjacent to the Columbia River just north of Portland. Called Kaiserville and then Vanport, it became one of the world's largest housing projects. In mid-1942, Henry J. Kaiser's son, Edgar, signed a contract with the U.S. Maritime Commission to build a six thousand–unit project. Five thousand construction workers (including two hundred women who pushed wheelbarrows and wielded shovels) literally slapped Vanport together. Units were built on wooden block foundations and had thin fiberboard walls. Vanport received its first tenants in December 1943 and increased almost overnight to thirty-five thousand residents, making it the second-largest community in Oregon.

Housing was only one of many wartime shortages. More physicians, dentists, and hospital facilities were desperately needed in communities experiencing exceptional growth. Many people feared that crowded conditions, substandard housing, inadequate and overloaded sewage and garbage disposal systems, vermin and rodents, and communicable diseases—especially syphilis and gonorrhea—menaced public health. Even so, health care throughout the Pacific Northwest was probably better than in many parts of wartime America, thanks in part to Henry J. Kaiser's establishment of the Northern Permanente Foundation to furnish medical and hospital care to his shipyard workers and their families.

An ordeal often as bad as finding housing or adequate medical care was getting to and from work. On some Seattle streets the traffic flow nearly doubled by late 1941, and when gasoline and tire rationing restricted automobile use in mid-1942, streetcars and buses labored under crushing passenger loads. Everyday shopping posed the challenge of standing in long checkout lines or doing without. The daily discomforts endured by shift workers may have been responsible for the unusually high absentee rates in places like Portland and Vancouver. The annual rate of labor turnover reached 150 percent in 1943. It became so great at Boeing that observers described the company as a "giant turnstile."

Other by-products of massive social dislocation included increased juvenile delinquency, divorce, and prostitution. In Portland, juvenile delinquency rose 30 percent. Prostitutes flocked to industrial centers and nearly surrounded Army and Navy posts. When the Army closed Portland's red light district in 1942, hundreds of prostitutes transferred their activities to rooming houses and beer parlors. Some took industrial jobs and transferred their profession to the holds of unfinished ships. Others among the city's new women taxi drivers were fired for similarly "combining business with business."

The shortage of labor created legitimate jobs for all seekers. The number of lines in the "help wanted" section of the *Seattle Times* jumped from 28,631 during the first nine months of 1940 to 225,515 during the same period in 1943. Employers paid good wages and competed with one another for workers. They used newspapers, billboards, radio, and movies to attract help: "Older Men and Women, We Have a Place for You . . ."; or "Contribute to Victory by Doing Your Share on the Home Front . . ."; or "New and Higher Wage Scale."

At the peak of wartime production, some 46 percent of Boeing's nearly fifty thousand employees were women. In the spring of 1942 approximately 80 percent of the local trainees for aircraft manufacturing jobs were women, many of them wives of military personnel. At the Puget Sound Navy Yard, employment of women in production jobs increased from virtually none in 1941 to 21 percent of the yard's thirty thousand employees in mid-1943. In all the important industrial facilities of the Puget Sound area combined, women formed about one-fourth of the work force. Housewives without

76. Liberty ships under construction in Portland in
early 1942. Courtesy San Francisco Maritime National
Historical Park, George A. Patterson Collection,
P83-103.87n.

any work experience or educational qualifications beyond a few years in grade school earned $200 to $250 a month at Boeing, at the shipyards, or as bus drivers. Day-care centers for the first time became a significant feature of urban life. Although women performed many jobs traditionally done by men, they rarely received the same pay. Their entry into the work force, moreover, was regarded as a temporary wartime expedient by most men— and by many women, too.

Not every woman, of course, became Rosie the Riveter. Those who remained at home contributed to the war effort by raising victory gardens; preparing meals that took into account shortages of meat, sugar, vegetables, and other staples of the American diet; saving tin cans, shortening, and other items for salvage drives; and often raising a family while a husband was away at war.

Organized labor experienced a great influx of new members during the war, but life in the burgeoning union ranks was not harmonious. Industrial workers who had been recruited from rural regions and small towns often regarded unions with apathy or even antagonism and resented paying any dues. The addition of women and blacks to the industrial work force further disrupted several unions. Tensions arose when blacks in the aircraft and shipbuilding industries applied for union membership. At Boeing, the union refused to admit them and thus helped to shape company policy. Boeing never hired a significant number of blacks during the war. Kaiser opposed racial discrimination, but nearly all his employees were members of metal trades unions that had no desire to admit blacks to membership. The Boiler-makers' Union segregated black shipyard workers into auxiliary unions and blocked them from holding skilled jobs. Blacks paid dues but had no vote in union matters, and when the war ended they found that their classification as temporary members gained them no seniority in the scramble for jobs.

High wages in shipyards and factories created an unreal situation for many people who had weathered hard times during the 1930s. Yet even as the prevailing standard of living rose, consumer goods and services became increasingly high priced, rationed, or simply unavailable. During the war, meat, milk, and clothing were all in short supply; overcrowded passenger trains and the rationing of tires and gasoline discouraged vacation travel or even short pleasure trips. People coped in a variety of ways: Idaho fish and game officials used horses and other forms of nonmotorized transport; vacationers stayed close to home; cooks substituted honey for sugar in dessert recipes. Because gasoline rationing in late 1942 made Idaho's Sun Valley virtually inaccessible to tourists, the resort was converted to a navy convalescent center.

People saved part of their newly acquired earnings and spent the rest on the goods and services that were available. As a consequence, retail sales boomed, and new department stores opened. Bulging savings accounts helped to fuel a sustained buying spree when the conflict ended.

### RACE AND RELOCATION

The Second World War noticeably altered the region's racial composition. Between 1941 and 1945 the Pacific Northwest experienced a significant influx of blacks and the forced removal of the Japanese. When the war began, the Seattle and Portland areas each had approximately eight thousand residents of Japanese ancestry. Prevailing anti-Asian prejudice together with the surprise attack on Pearl Harbor created among Pacific Coast residents an almost hysterical fear of Japanese invasion. In the spring of 1942 all persons of Japanese heritage living in western portions of Oregon and Washington—approximately two-thirds of whom were American citi-

During World War II, Oregon was the only U.S. state to be shelled by enemy naval craft, to be bombed by enemy aircraft, and to suffer civilian deaths as a result of enemy action. The latter incident occurred in south-central Oregon near Bly on 5 May 1945, when a Japa- nese balloon bomb killed six people on a church outing. During the final weeks of the war, Japan launched hundreds of incendiary balloon bombs from its home islands in a desperate effort to set U.S. fields and forests afire.

zens—were peremptorily dispatched to inland camps by the Wartime Civil Control Administration.

Federal authorities sent Japanese Americans to inland camps like the Minidoka Relocation Center located on a sixty-eight-thousand-acre desert tract north of Twin Falls, Idaho. The camp was a desolate place, hot and dusty in summer and frigid in winter. Surrounded by barbed wire and armed guards, it served as home for ten thousand people mainly from the Portland and Seattle areas, many of them second- and third-generation Japanese Americans. Anyone with as little as one-sixteenth Japanese blood could be incarcerated. Ironically, the twelve hundred Japanese Americans already living in Idaho were not relocated, and as a result some people at risk in other areas moved voluntarily to Idaho to escape internment.

What they could not escape was prejudice. When, for instance, Idaho firms hired Japanese workers, the Pocatello Central Labor Union protested: "We request all members of organized labor to refrain from patronizing any and all business establishments employing Japs."[1] In the fall of 1942, in what was labeled the Retreat from Moscow, the University of Idaho denied admission to six persons of Japanese descent born in the United States after having initially accepted them as transfers from the University of Washington. Local citizens created such a furor over the acceptance that two of the women were temporarily housed in jail under "protective custody."

Japanese Americans confined to the Minidoka relocation camp sought to fashion an environment as livable as their bleak conditions permitted. They planted "victory gardens" and fielded a first-rate baseball team against players from nearby communities. Many hundreds of internees were allowed outside the camp to work harvesting the crops of the inland Northwest.

1. As quoted in David Glaser, "Migration in Idaho's History," *Idaho Yesterdays* 11 (fall 1967): 29.

Urban dwellers with no agricultural experience went to work in potato and sugar beet fields of the Snake River valley to assist Idaho farmers beset by a severe labor shortage. By October 1945 some twenty-four hundred Japanese Americans worked in the fields of Idaho, northern Utah, eastern Oregon, eastern Washington, and Montana. Supplementing their labor was that of Mexican nationals, Jamaicans, and German prisoners of war.

Legal challenges to the relocation edict, like that mounted by Gordon Hirabayashi, a University of Washington student who refused to leave Seattle, reached the U.S. Supreme Court. But in each case, the high court upheld the constitutionality of the removal order, although one justice commented in *Hirabayashi* v. *United States* (1943) that the curfew order bore "a melancholy resemblance to the treatment accorded members of the Jewish race in Germany and other parts of Europe."[2] In 1987 the Ninth U. S. Circuit Court of Appeals reversed the wartime decisions, and the following year Congress provided $20,000 compensation to every Japanese American who was relocated.

The property of the Japanese was held for them by the United States Alien Property custodian and, in many cases, returned after the war. Some belongings were vandalized, however, and in urban areas, former Japanese dwellings and jobs went to newcomers, many of whom were black. The black population living west of the Mississippi River totaled about 171,000 in 1940; it increased to approximately 620,000 by 1945. During that time the black population of the Pacific Northwest probably doubled, while in urban areas like Portland and Seattle, it increased even more. By early 1945, nearly 7,000–8,000 blacks lived in Seattle where, a reporter noted, "the feeling against them is high. In Portland, where there are 15,000 it is much higher." The number of blacks in Portland actually climbed from 2,000 to 22,000, then declined to 11,000 after the war.

Many blacks moved to the region to take industrial jobs. Of 7,541 nonwhite workers in Portland on 1 September 1944, 7,250 were employed in the shipyards. Other blacks arrived as army and navy personnel. Though the black population in the region remained small compared to that in other parts of the United States—an estimated 14,000 in Washington in 1943—racial hostility caused some smaller communities to exclude blacks from nearly every form of public recreation. Discriminatory signs such as "We Cater to White Trade Only" appeared for the first time in Northwest cities.

2. As quoted in David H. Stratton, ed., *Washington Comes of Age: The State in the National Experience* (Pullman: Washington State University Press, 1992), 21.

77. Howard Clifford photographed the relocation of Japanese Americans in the Puyallup, Washington, evacuation center ("Camp Harmony"). Courtesy Special Collections Division, University of Washington Libraries, UW 526.

Army officials occasionally retaliated by placing such establishments off limits, but some residents found it difficult to understand why the army expected civilians to practice nonsegregation when the military segregated its own eating and recreation facilities. Scuffles between white and black industrial workers flared on occasion in Vancouver, Bremerton, Seattle, and other cities, and the question of admitting blacks to union membership remained controversial.

## THE IMPACT OF WAR

Even while the war continued abroad, planning for postwar America began. "In Seattle everybody has a postwar plan," observed a correspondent for the

---

THE BRACEROS

When the Second World War created a shortage of white itinerant farm workers, the U.S. government imported workers directly from Mexico to the Pacific Northwest. Between 1943 and 1947 more than forty-seven thousand Mexican males or braceros (strong-armed workers) supplied farm labor in Oregon, Washington, and Idaho. Most lived in farm labor camps, subjected to various forms of exploitation and discrimination.

Migrants complained about living conditions: their housing often amounted to little more than tents in the winter and their food was often spoiled or dust covered, as was the case in a mess tent in Wilder, Idaho, where strong winds blasted through the facility and seasoned the food with grit. They endured low incomes, although on one occasion, in June 1944, the braceros at Preston, Idaho, went on strike over poor wages.

Life in the labor camps was at best Spartan because braceros were allowed no families in order to encourage them to return to Mexico after the war. Among the three Northwest states, Idaho developed the most notorious reputation for discrimination. In some agricultural towns, signs in restaurant windows reading "No Mexicans" joined those that warned "No Indians" and "No Negroes."

---

*New Republic.* Pacific Northwesterners dreamed of a new day when the West Coast would escape the essentially colonial economy of the past. Washington's governor, Arthur Langlie, predicted in mid-1944 that "our colonial status as shippers of fruit, timber, and other raw materials will be overcome by facilities set up within our states to produce for vast new markets across the Pacific." Others spoke glibly of the region's expanding array of new manufacturing and service industries and a growing trade with the "unsaturated markets" of the Pacific basin that contained half the world's population. The timber industry envisioned a bright future supplying materials to rebuild the cities of Europe. Yet all but the most optimistic Northwesterners couched their predictions in words like "should" and "must" that betrayed lingering doubts about whether old economic patterns could be broken.

The postwar economic situation in the Pacific Northwest simply did not inspire much confidence. "The unemployment that is going to hit the West Coast when the war ends will be disastrous—unless something is done about it," predicted a writer for *Fortune* in early 1945, and statistics soon underscored that gloomy assessment. After the region's index of business activity reached an all time high in January-February 1945 (in contrast to the national peak in October-November 1943), it dropped sharply in May 1945 with the war's end in Europe. By August employment in the Portland-

Vancouver shipyards had already dropped to sixty-five thousand and would soon drop much farther; payrolls in Portland declined from a mid-1943 peak of $44 million to $18 million in early 1947. Many predicted that Boeing would retain only 10 to 15 percent of its wartime work force. The inevitable cutback in ship and aircraft building seemed certain to create massive unemployment that would place a heavy burden on employment services, public works, and relief agencies.

Moreover, many who had migrated temporarily for jobs or military service now wanted to establish permanent homes in the Pacific Northwest. This resulted in a lasting population increase. By 1947 the region's population had climbed an estimated 25 percent higher than it had been in 1940. Could enough peacetime jobs be found for all takers, and what, if anything, could be done to prevent massive unemployment and concomitant social unrest?

History served as a grim reminder of what happened during a troubled and unplanned conversion from war to peace. After the First World War, employment in Northwest shipyards dropped from thirty thousand workers to a few hundred. People who recalled Seattle's 1919 general strike feared that it would be difficult to avoid similar unrest after the Second World War.

In contrast to the Midwest or East, the Pacific Northwest had converted from peace to war production in a peculiar way: the war superimposed huge new industries on top of an existing extractive economy. There was no reason to believe that war industries would outlive the conflict or that the region's traditional natural resources–based industries could absorb more wage-earners, or even maintain the record levels of wartime output.

Uncertainty also accompanied the postwar return of the Japanese. Residents of the White River and Puyallup valleys of western Washington, where the Japanese had once had extensive agricultural holdings, were vehemently opposed to their return. Among the most frequently stated reasons were that "the Japanese stabbed us in the back at Pearl Harbor"; that "one can never tell what a Jap is thinking"; or that "they want social equality." Several organizations passed resolutions opposing the return of the Japanese. In time, of course, the Japanese did return, and despite the potential for violence, there was no serious trouble.

As it turned out, the Northwest's postwar economic adjustments also proceeded far more smoothly than experts dared to predict. Population growth coupled with a contracting job market failed to produce hard times and social unrest. Unemployment increased immediately after the war, but then it dropped dramatically in 1946. There were many reasons for that pattern: instead of immediately flooding the job market, a number of servicemen discharged in the Northwest exercised their option to attend college under the GI bill, a congressional package of veterans' benefits. Many female war workers, observed one contemporary, were "retiring to their homes." That made room, another added, for the fifteen thousand servicemen who returned to jobs in Spokane.

For others, wartime savings, termination pay, and unemployment compensation discouraged a desperate scramble for jobs. Moreover, savings accumulated during the war enabled a record number of people to purchase cars, new homes, and a comfortable middle-class life in the suburbs, thus buoying up the nation's construction and forest products industries. An inadequate number of houses built during the war coupled with the move to suburbia and an increase in the number of new families kept the Northwest's forest products industry producing at record levels for more than two decades after the war, though at the cost of reducing the region's timber supply. Logging and sawmilling regained their prewar status as Oregon's leading industry as early as 1946. Tourism boomed too. When gasoline rationing ended, tourists withdrew money from their bulging savings accounts, cashed in their war bonds and stamps, and took to the road in record numbers. The number of visitors to Mount Rainier in 1946 broke all previous records.

The Second World War brought dramatic change to the Pacific Northwest, but though some changes endured—perhaps forever in the case of Hanford's atomic waste storage tanks—others proved only temporary. Camp Farragut on Lake Pend Oreille closed permanently in 1946, and eventually forests and fields reclaimed most of the land that is now Farragut State Park. Nature also reclaimed the swampland from which Vanport arose; on Memorial Day 1948 a Columbia River flood left 39 people dead and obliterated the declining settlement.

For all the lasting changes that the Second World War brought to the Pacific Northwest—including the enlargement of Boeing and the development of a regional aluminum industry—the economic well-being of the region remained closely tied to the fate of its forest, mining, fishing, and agricultural industries. Distance from markets, freight rates, and a small population base explain much of the region's enduring economic backwardness. Yet there were also a few Pacific Northwesterners in the immediate postwar years who believed that quality of life should not be sacrificed to rapid and unchecked economic growth. They did not want the City of Roses to become another Pittsburgh, and people who wondered what an industrial future would bring had only to observe how wartime manufacturing had fouled the waters of the Willamette River. In short, the experience of World War II and later the Cold War hastened a confrontation between Pacific Northwesterners and the economic, demographic, and environmental problems that increasingly beset their maturing region.

## COLD WAR NORTHWEST: ANXIETY AND AFFLUENCE

In one sense World War II did not end until decades after 1945. The infusion of federal dollars into the Pacific Northwest economy during the New Deal and World War years continued unabated when Cold War fears of the Soviet Union (ironically, a U.S. ally in World War II) prolonged indefinitely the life of many industries fostered by World War II. As a result, the Pacific Northwest's aircraft factories employed twice as many people immediately after the Second World War as in 1939—some nine thousand at Boeing—and the shipyards three times as many as before the war. "Air power is peace power," declared William M. Allen, president of Boeing in 1947. During the Cold War years his company remained the region's largest manufacturer, meeting military and, later, civilian needs. From the 1940s through the early 1990s, federal investments in science, defense, reclamation, and highways combined to promote industrialization and urbanization of the Pacific Northwest.

A major Cold War legacy, far less publicized at the time than either Boeing or Hanford, was the sprawling nuclear reservation located on a sparsely populated portion of the Snake River plain west of Idaho Falls. It dated from early 1949 when the federal Atomic Energy Commission acquired a total of 870 square miles—an area about three-quarters that of Rhode Island —and invested millions of dollars to build fifty-two nuclear reactors. Most were one-of-a-kind experimental facilities that were subsequently phased out.

Residents of nearby communities welcomed the National Reactor Testing Station, which provided jobs and created a new population mix that included numerous engineers and nuclear research specialists. Their efforts resulted in the nation's first electricity generated from nuclear energy in 1951, and Arco became the first city in the world lighted by the atom in 1955. For more than forty years—from the early 1950s, when the Navy developed the first reactor to power submarines, until the station shut down its test facility in the 1990s—about a thousand students a year trained at the land-locked site to run nuclear submarines. At one time it was even rumored that Admiral Hyman G. Rickover, the visionary "father of the nuclear navy," planned to build a canal from Idaho to the Pacific Ocean. The federal facility also revealed the dark underside of nuclear technology when in January 1961 a technician pulled a control rod too far out of a test reactor core and caused a steam explosion that killed three people. The force of the blast was so great that it pinned one of the victims to the reactor ceiling.

The facility, which became the Idaho National Engineering Laboratory (INEL) in 1974, employed about ten thousand military and civilian personnel and provided almost 5 percent of the state's jobs in the early 1990s. Over the years the facility's scientists considered plans for nuclear powered railway locomotives and aircraft; in more recent years they engaged in research projects involving electric vehicles, lasers, and biotechnology. For fifteen years, in fact, until the money stopped in 1961, a nuclear airplane was the Air Force's $1 billion dream. The plane was never built, and one can only wonder whether it would have ever gotten off the ground (just one of its massive engines weighed 225 tons). More than anything else it was Cold War paranoia and federal money that kept the project, if not the airplane, aloft.

The growing investment of federal dollars in sophisticated military and aerospace technology was especially noticeable on Puget Sound and in the Hanford area, where jerrybuilt but booming Richland gained a look of permanence after 1955 when Congress permitted its residents to purchase the land and buildings. It was during the Cold War years from 1956 to 1963, not during World War II, that the most intense production of nuclear weapons took place at the Hanford site: Richland proudly billed itself as the "Atomic City," and the local high school nicknamed its teams the "Bombers." The mushroom cloud became the school's emblem. In truth, however, no part of the Pacific Northwest lay outside the long shadow cast by the Cold War's horrific emblem of atomic destruction and nuclear fallout.

In the late 1940s and 1950s, the Cold War haunted the imaginations of Pacific Northwesterners even as it took tangible shape in defense-related products such as atomic bombs and long-range aircraft and in the parade of troops shipping out from the docks of Seattle to fight a grim new hot war with Communism in Korea. Closer to home the media was filled with talk of Communist conspiracy. Schools ran atomic-bomb drills along with fire drills, and a Boy Scout "Family Be Prepared Plan" of 1951 admonished people to stockpile food and to keep doors and windows shut during an atomic attack, advice better suited to the dangers of World War II than to the realities of the 1950s.

Early in the decade, the editor of *Galaxy Science Fiction* noted that over

90 percent of all submissions to the magazine discussed atomic or bacteriological warfare, biological degeneration, or mutant children. Among the popular science fiction films of the decade was *Them*, which depicted the power of radioactivity to produce genetic changes resulting in giant, menacing ants. *On the Beach*, produced five years later in 1959, depicted the bleak last days of the human race after a nuclear war.[3]

The globe shrank dramatically and uncomfortably when Americans learned in the early 1950s that Soviet bombers could reach across the North Pacific to deliver a lethal payload of atomic bombs, and no state was located closer to the main Cold War threat than Washington. Defense facilities like Hanford and Boeing would certainly make tempting targets in any enemy attack. The Soviets exploded their first atomic bomb in 1949, far earlier than most people believed was possible, and that same year China fell to the Communists. Fast on the heels of those two ominous events came war in Korea. Even when it ended in stalemate and an armistice agreement in 1953, there was no decrease in anxiety. That same year, less than twelve months after the United States did so, the Soviet Union exploded its own hydrogen bomb.

In October 1953, *Newsweek* quoted Val Peterson, President Eisenhower's civil defense chief, gloomily predicting that "atomic warfare is inevitable and the United States faces the possibility of destruction by bombs, disease carriers, sabotage, and possibly gas." When asked what Americans could do, he advised, "go underground." No wonder that when the first issue of *Playboy* magazine appeared two months later, it promoted voyeurism as "a little diversion from the anxieties of the Atomic age."[4]

Anxiety manifested itself in several ways. There was, of course, considerable concern about a sneak attack by air. After all, the bombing of Pearl Harbor had occurred barely a decade earlier, and its images of sudden death and destruction were seared into the memory of every adult American. In response, some Pacific Northwesterners volunteered for the Ground Observer Corps to scan the sky for Soviet bombers that might invade the United States by flying low and eluding radar detection. In April 1954 Spokane became the first U.S. city to evacuate its downtown area in a civil-defense drill; the exercise optimistically labeled Operation Walkout only

3. James Gilbert, *Another Chance: Postwar America 1945–1985*, 2d ed. (Chicago: Dorsey Press, 1986), 171.
4. *Newsweek* 42 (19 October 1953): 35; Loren Baritz, *The Good Life: The Meaning of Success for the American Middle Class* (New York: Alfred A. Knopf, 1989): 189–90.

revealed the futility of trying to escape atomic destruction. Throughout most of the decade, defense spending amounted to about 10 percent of the Gross National Product and about 50 percent of the federal budget. The Pentagon continued buying Boeing's new generation of global bombers, the B-47s and B-52s. By 1959 Boeing provided one of every two manufacturing jobs in King County; during the 1950s aircraft manufacturing overtook the timber industry as Washington's largest employer.

U.S. military power grew in size and might, but it never seemed large enough to relieve the nation's prevailing anxiety. Always there was some ominous new threat, as in early October 1957 when the Soviet Union successfully launched *Sputnik*, the world's first artificial space satellite. The United States lacked a parallel success. The implication that Soviet intercontinental ballistic missiles could fly high into space to rain nuclear warheads on unsuspecting U.S. cities created new anxieties as well as a sense of national humiliation that found expression in the National Defense Education Act of September 1958, which allotted $877 million in emergency aid to bolster the U.S. educational system. Pressure to build personal fallout shelters increased after *Sputnik*, and the notion of a "missile gap" that threatened U.S. security became an issue in the presidential campaign of 1960.

Even if enemy bombers could not penetrate U.S. defenses, there was still the possibility of a sneak attack by means of internal subversion. Fear of Communist infiltration of the United States became an acute worry during the Cold War years. Hostility to it took a dramatic new turn in 1948 when Spokane Representative Albert Canwell chaired a state legislative committee that heard charges about Washingtonians who were allegedly members of the "Communist conspiracy." Denounced as a witch hunt by some observers, the Canwell investigation anticipated the rise of Senator Joseph R. McCarthy of Wisconsin at the national level, who in the early 1950s was seen either as a great patriot fighting the Communist menace or as a menacing bully bent on destroying civil liberties.

Ironically, Pacific Northwesterners in the 1950s faced possible conflict with the Soviet Union and the threat of atomic annihilation while enjoying a period of prosperity and conspicuous consumption. Anxiety and affluence seemed closely related. A list of the nation's fastest growing industries between 1950 and 1966—ammunition, cathode-ray picture tubes, semiconductors, computers and related equipment, small arms, tufted carpets and rugs, primary nonferrous metals—clearly shows how production for defense kept pace with that for personal consumption. Perhaps it was the sense of uncertainty that the Atomic Age created, especially its intimations of doom, that caused Americans to seek diversion in their newfound prosperity. Perhaps, too, the haunting memory of the Great Depression for the generation that came of age in the 1950s, or their memories of World War II which ended only five years before the new decade began, spurred Pacific Northwesterners to enjoy the years of comparative affluence.

# CHAPTER 20

# Roller-Coaster Years

*

Many Pugetopolitans are now worried about whether, in the process of industrialization, their paradise will be lost. "How can our state grow with grace?" asks Governor Evans. "We have been the beneficiaries of time and space, we have not suffered the silt and smoke of overindustrialization— yet. We have not succeeded in completely obliterating the beauty of our countryside or polluting our waters—yet. But time, which has been on our side, is rapidly running out."—*Time*, 27 May 1966

*

A motorist who drove from Pocatello to Portland and Seattle and then circled back to Spokane and the Coeur d'Alene mining region in 1950 and repeated that trip in 1990 would have sampled most visible changes that occurred in the Pacific Northwest following the Second World War. Not all changes were as dramatic as those from the growth decade of the 1880s or from the two world wars, but they were significant. This three-chapter overview of recent developments in Pacific Northwest history begins by reflecting on major changes such a traveler might have observed.

### THE CHANGING FACE OF THE PACIFIC NORTHWEST

Between 1950 and 1990, two-lane U.S. 30, which once threaded its way west across the Snake River plain and along the south bank of the Columbia River, was supplanted by Interstate 84, a four-lane superhighway that was part of a forty-one thousand–mile national network authorized by Congress in 1956. Before the oil shortage of 1973, a motorist could follow this route across Oregon at the legal speed limit of seventy miles per hour and hardly worry whether an automobile averaged ten miles or twenty miles to a gallon of gasoline. Few American-made cars got more than that, and as late as 1973 regular gasoline seldom cost more than thirty-five cents a gallon. The speed limit in 1990 was sixty-five (after falling to fifty-five for several years),[1] the cars were smaller and often foreign made, and the price of a gallon of gasoline hovered around a dollar.

Billboards that once lined portions of the old route were mostly gone by 1990, as the result of a federal highway beautification program initiated in the mid-1960s. But there were trade-offs, because travelers crossing tedious stretches of the Snake River plain missed the diversion offered by advertisers' wry comments.

The mighty and picturesque falls of the Columbia River at Celilo, east of The Dalles, were gone, too. The falls and a way of life for Indian tribes who had fished there for millennia disappeared in 1957 beneath forty feet of slack water created by The Dalles Dam, one of more than a dozen dams constructed on the Columbia and lower Snake rivers after 1950. The dams impounded water to generate much of the region's electricity and turn arid regions into farmland.

In the 1930s and 1940s dams were widely viewed as good and useful legacies bequeathed to future generations, but by the 1980s many Pacific Northwesterners condemned them because of declining fish runs and the inadequacy of their supposedly limitless supply of electricity. How ironic that the Portland General Electric Company chose to build a large coal-burning power plant near Boardman, Oregon, in the late 1970s, not too many miles from McNary Dam on the Columbia River; and that in 1976 the utility put into operation one of the nation's largest nuclear power plants. Situated on the bank of the Columbia approximately forty miles downstream from Portland, the $240 million Trojan Nuclear Plant represented a significant departure from the region's dependence upon hydropower.

Trojan was one of at least twenty nuclear power plants once projected for the Pacific Northwest. Its location and operation were the subject of controversy and protest from the early 1970s until its permanent closure in 1993, yet the facility generated nothing like the controversy that surrounded the nuclear power debacle of the Washington Public Power Supply System.

1. In 1987 the speed limit was increased from 55 to 65 on rural sections of interstate highways.

### THE WASHINGTON PUBLIC POWER SUPPLY SYSTEM

The wppss debacle is a sad tale of the technological euphoria of the 1960s gone awry. When sixteen public utility districts formed the Washington Public Power Supply System in 1957, it was distinctly a low-budget operation. It successfully built a hydroelectric plant at Packwood Lake in the Washington Cascades and a nuclear plant on the Hanford reservation. From there it plunged headlong into the construction of five nuclear plants and in the process became the largest issuer of tax-free municipal bonds in American history. Several of the region's major private utilities and nearly one hundred public utility districts guaranteed the bonds in exchange for future wppss electricity.

Originally estimated at slightly more than $4 billion, the price tag for the five plants ballooned to some $24 billion before wppss defaulted on the bonds for plants 4 and 5 in 1983. That was enough money in current dollars to build both the Alaska Pipeline and the Panama Canal. By the early 1990s, two of the units had been abandoned (to be later cut up and sold for scrap), two were mothballed as a hedge against future power shortages at a cost of $10 million a year, and only one plant produced electricity—electricity far more expensive than that generated by hydroelectric power. One of the mothballed plants, Satsop near Grays Harbor, was 76 percent completed when construction·halted. (In 1993 a private consortium with ties to the nuclear industry at Hanford proposed completing and operating the two mothballed reactors in order to destroy a portion of the world's plutonium weapons stockpile: the two plants would burn the plutonium to generate electricity).

What went wrong with wppss? First, the projected demand for electricity in the Pacific Northwest actually fell slightly instead of doubling every decade as the experts had originally predicted. The Bonneville Power Administration estimated that the Pacific Northwest would need ten nuclear plants by the year 2000, and it used its considerable influence to back the bonds issued for three wppss facilities.

The financial and technological complexity of the projects apparently overwhelmed the wppss board of directors, a group that was best suited to run a local public utility district. Compounding their problems was the fact that the five plants were to be built according to three different designs by three different contractors and dozens of subcontractors, and no one seemed capable of taking charge. The result was managerial bumbling and labor greed on a monumental scale.

In some ways the nation's largest municipal bond default represented yet another chapter in the Northwest's lengthy saga of popular democracy. Public protests mounted as ratepayers came to realize that, whether or not the plants were ever built, they were legally obligated to holders of wppss bonds. This meant staggering increases in their monthly electric bills. The twenty-five thousand ratepayers of the Mason County Public Utility District, for example, discovered that they owed approximately $200,000 a month for the next thirty-five years. "We are not going to pay the bigwigs on Wall Street," a former mayor of Hoquiam told the Seattle *Post-Intelligencer* in 1981. And they didn't. When the Washington State Supreme Court sided with ratepayers, the losers were those who had purchased wppss bonds thinking they had made a safe investment.

The sole operational power plant of WPPSS (pronounced "whoops") is not easy for casual travelers to spot: it is located on the sprawling Hanford reservation near Richland, Washington, a two-hour detour off the main highway from Pocatello to Portland. Of concern to ratepayers and investors are the four other WPPSS plants that remain unbuilt or in mothballs. The program's financial collapse in 1983 ranks as the largest municipal default in American history and was the subject of lengthy litigation.

The motorist of 1950 and 1990, continuing down the Columbia River would have passed a grandfather among Columbia dams: Bonneville. Over Bonneville's fish ladders pass numerous salmon returning upstream to spawn, though their numbers were far smaller in 1990 than before the river was dammed. The completion of a series of dams on the lower Snake River in 1975 made it possible for towboats and barges passing through Bonneville's locks to continue upriver as far as Lewiston. The Idaho community finally realized a century-old dream when a paved highway (now U.S. 12) was completed up the Clearwater Valley and across Lolo Pass to Missoula in 1962. The route became a funnel for thousands of truckloads of Montana and Dakota grain that annually poured into Lewiston after it became Idaho's only seaport in 1975.

At the height of the dam-building boom of the 1960s, federal outlays for development in eastern Washington topped $100 million, about 10 percent of the federal public works budget for an area with .4 percent of the nation's population, a tribute perhaps to the power of Washington's congressional delegation. Washington, unlike Oregon and Idaho, also received large military installations, such as the Trident submarine base at Bangor on the Olympic Peninsula. One Trident submarine carries enough nuclear warheads to vaporize 240 cities. The base was designed to house ten such submarines.

Not everything along the highway has changed. A traveler entering the Portland metropolitan area in 1990 would have seen a large pulp and paper mill across the river at Camas, Washington. That mill and its predecessors have operated there since the 1880s, and if the wind was blowing from a northerly direction, the motorist would notice a distinct odor. To some people it was the flatulent pungency of rotten eggs; to others it was the smell of jobs. Travelers around the Northwest can still smell those effluents and similar ones at locations scattered from Lewiston to Bellingham to Coos Bay.

The region's pulp and paper industry expanded rapidly following World War II. It represented one way the forest products industry efficiently utilized the region's natural resources. Another tribute to efficiency was clear-cutting, a logging practice that left a bold and unsightly signature across the mountain landscape. Clear-cutting, like nuclear power, has its advocates, but critics have turned both technologies into topics of public debate.

Battles over the fate of the region's natural resources grew more frequent from the 1950s to the 1990s, and while truly monumental ones like the Hells Canyon controversy were won by advocates of recreation and scenic preservation—not hydroelectric power—the struggle continued. In the mid-1980s a major fight erupted over the fate of the scenic Columbia River gorge.

Resistance to Oregon's environmentalists surfaced late in 1971 when industrial and union leaders formed a unique alliance called the Western Environmental Trade Association to fight the "environmental hysteria" they claimed was hurting the state's economy. Continued conflict over wilderness lands raised vexing questions that go to the heart of the Pacific Northwest's identity as a region. So vital are these environmental issues to an understanding of the region's past and future that they form the concluding chapter of this book.

A traveler would also have noted dramatic changes in the region's urban landscape. Seattle's tallest building in 1950 was the twenty-six–story L. C. Smith Tower. By 1990, from a distance the city's skyline resembled a bar graph; now the most prominent profile belongs to the seventy-six–story Columbia Center, the tallest building west of Minneapolis and north of San Francisco.

Seattle hosted its second world's fair in 1962. Called Century 21, it not only provided Seattle a needed economic boost but also bequeathed it the Space Needle, a monorail, and a vastly enhanced civic center. Across the Cascades in Spokane, the 1974 world's fair brought even more dramatic changes by converting an unsightly thirty-eight hundred–acre complex of warehouses and railroad tracks into park and recreation facilities along the Spokane River and revitalizing the city's center. The theme of the Spokane fair, "Progress without Pollution," was in tune with the region's growing environmental consciousness.

Architectural daring rather than size characterized Portland's new downtown buildings, and certainly no city in the Northwest rivaled Portland for architectural excitement. Boise, alas, for a time represented the other extreme. Its downtown renewal program removed many structures but seemed incapable of replacing them with anything other than parking lots.

One critic likened Boise to a doughnut because of its disappearing downtown structures and booming suburbs. During the 1980s, however, Boise made dramatic progress in renovating its remaining historic buildings and refurbishing its downtown by turning vacant lots into a glittering expanse of steel and glass buildings, shops, and urban apartments. The city even received top ranking in the United States as a good place to raise children because of its low crime rate, healthy economy, and abundant parks.

Probably the single most visible change in the urban Northwest since 1950 was suburban sprawl, which one critic blasted as "the jive-plastic commuter tract-home wastelands, the Potemkin village shopping plazas with their vast parking lagoons, the Lego-block hotel complexes, the 'gourmet mansardic' junk-food joints, the Orwellian office 'parks' featuring buildings sheathed in the same reflective glass as the sunglasses worn by chain-gang guards, the particle-board garden apartments rising up in every meadow and cornfield."[2] Some observers feared this kind of sprawl would ultimately extend from Eugene to Portland and forever compromise the natural beauty of the Willamette Valley. Of equal concern was the rise of Pugetopolis, a composite city that may one day stretch north from Olympia to encompass Tacoma, Seattle, and Everett.

Across Lake Washington from Seattle is Bellevue, a former suburb that not long ago was disparaged as "Boeing's bedroom" but which now together with neighboring Redmond forms the heart of the region's computer software industry. Today the Bellevue-Redmond area along with suburban Boston and California's Silicon Valley ranks as a focal point for the nation's computer industry, especially for the sophisticated software that makes computers run. Statewide, Washington's software industry grew from a mere fourteen companies in 1975 to more than five hundred by 1990 (although no more than forty are economically significant); employment in the industry during the same period jumped from eighty-eight to more than seventy-three hundred employees. Microsoft emerged as the behemoth of the new industry, with its chairman William Gates III becoming the world's youngest billionaire.

The Bellevue-Redmond area also constitutes a prime Northwest example of the "exurbia" phenomenon so noticeable all across the United States, the urban trend of the late twentieth century. Both Bellevue and Redmond, like suburban communities in other parts of the Pacific Northwest, began as bedroom communities for nearby central cities, where the jobs were.

2. James Howard Kunstler, *The Geography of Nowhere* (New York: Simon and Schuster, 1993).

78. In December 1939, workers in Seattle assembled the final sections of what was then the world's longest concrete pontoon bridge. When it opened to traffic a few months later, the 6,661-foot-long structure spurred suburban growth on Mercer Island and along the east side of Lake Washington. Courtesy Tacoma Public Library.

Over time that distinction was largely erased by the growth of jobs in the suburbs themselves, thus creating the new category of "exurban" America, or what Joel Garreau has labeled an "Edge City." A prime example of this phenomenon was Redmond, which evolved from a village of 573 residents in 1950 into a city of 35,800 by 1990.

Not all suburban growth came at the expense of the central city. In Portland during the 1970s and 1980s the number of people working downtown actually increased from fifty-nine thousand to ninety-four thousand and the central city evolved from undistinguished and declining to vibrant and growing, bucking the trend toward municipal decay so visible in many U.S. cities. The reason for the renaissance of central Portland partly lies in an efficient and focused mass transit system that makes a trip downtown both convenient and pleasurable for residents of outlying neighborhoods. Portlanders also generally oppose urban sprawl, not wanting to become another

Los Angeles, although sprawl still seems inevitable in outlying areas as separate as Beaverton and Gresham.

A motorist traveling in 1990 from Puget Sound to the Idaho panhandle would have been able to contrast within a day's drive the economic vitality that transformed the Bellevue-Redmond area with the stagnation of the Coeur d'Alene mining region, only one part of the Northwest afflicted with massive unemployment and population decline. Many of the physical changes a person would observe while driving around the Pacific Northwest dated from the last two decades, whereas others were products of World War II and its aftermath.

BABY BOOM AND SUBURBAN SPRAWL

This much is certain: the generation that suffered through the Great Depression and won World War II was not going to let the threat of atomic destruction deter it from settling into the business of raising new families and enjoying its newfound affluence. The baby boom (1946–1965) was itself a response to the general prosperity of the postwar years. During the 1950s, the first full decade of the baby boom phenomenon, some 41 million children were added to the nation's population. That was twice the number of immigrants who streamed into the United States during the first two decades of the twentieth century. New babies promised to sustain the unprecedented prosperity, for as *Life* magazine phrased it, "Kids: Built-In Depression Cure—How 4,000,000 a Year Make Billions in Business."[3]

During the 1950s, Oregon's population increased by more than one-quarter million and Washington's by almost half a million. Even more noteworthy was the fact that in 1960—when there were 1.8 million Oregonians, 2.8 million Washingtonians, and 667,000 Idahoans—almost one third of each state's population was less than fifteen years old. The populations in the three states were becoming not only younger, but—especially in Oregon and Washington—also increasingly urban. During the 1950s, approximately 52,000 Oregonians and 58,000 Washingtonians left the farm. Rural areas of those two states were by no means dead, but they certainly were being reconfigured. In both states the number of acres in farmland actually increased slightly, mainly as a result of newly irrigated land east of the Cascade Mountains, and so too did the average size of farms. By the end of the

3. Loren Baritz, *The Good Life: The Meaning of Success for the American Middle Class* (New York: Alfred A. Knopf, 1989), 195.

1950s about two-thirds of all residents of Oregon and Washington lived in urban areas, and notably in the suburbs. In Idaho these same changes would eventually occur too, but often only two or three decades later than in Oregon and Washington.

During the 1950s white-collar workers for the first time in U.S. history outnumbered blue-collar workers, and suburbs replaced cities and farms as the habitat of the typical American family. Suburbs were not new in the 1950s; some actually dated back to World War II or earlier. Renton provided many wartime jobs for workers who built Boeing aircraft, and even earlier suburbs existed as havens from city unpleasantness for the rich. But after World War II a growing middle class, both blue- and white-collar, spearheaded the exodus to the suburbs.

The pace of suburban growth was dramatic, and perhaps nowhere more so than along the eastern rim of Lake Washington. There the process was formalized with the incorporation of Bellevue in 1953, a rural lakeside retreat of six thousand people; growing rapidly over the next thirty-five years, Bellevue emerged as Washington's fourth largest community with a population of nearly eighty-seven thousand residents in 1990. By then its soaring skyline seemed destined to match Seattle's across the lake. Following on the heels of Bellevue were other booming suburban communities like Lynnwood and Redmond.

With jobs plentiful and wages high, an increasing number of residents spent their earnings to buy new single-family dwellings (veterans could purchase these with no-money-down loans at 4.5 percent interest), which in turn brought prosperity to the Pacific Northwest's vitally important timber industry. Bulldozers outside every one of the largest cities rooted up thousands of acres of grass and timberland to clear the way for suburbia. Some new growth took place at the outskirts of the cities, but much more took place well beyond the city limits where land was cheaper and taxes lower. In fact, downtown areas, by contrast, seemed to languish, in some cases their physical appearance having changed little since the 1920s. During the 1950s many a central city experienced noticeable decay, whereas new suburbs, by contrast, gained the reputation of being good places to raise children: they were clean and uncrowded havens from the noise, dirt, congestion, and sometimes dangerous streets of the central city.

In a world filled with anxiety, more and more Pacific Northwesterners fled to the suburbs and to the comfortable surroundings of newly built and freshly scrubbed neighborhoods. By the end of the 1950s, nearly one-third of the nation's population was suburban, whereas in metropolitan Seattle the suburban population equaled that of the central city for the first time. In Washington more people lived in suburbia by 1960 than either in central cities or rural areas.

Automobile ownership was an integral part of the move to the suburbs. Attached to growing numbers of ranch-style or split-level homes were two-car garages to stable the new cars that were big and loaded with lots of shiny chrome to mirror the general affluence of the 1950s. Enormous tail fins gave some automobiles the look of the space age. The station wagon in particular became the new symbol of suburbia, as mothers drove baby-boom children to school or hauled groceries from the local supermarket.

Arterial highways leading out to suburbia lacked aesthetic appeal because they were invariably lined with a jumbled array of used car lots, drive-in restaurants, real estate offices, dry cleaners, and sprawl-marts. Many new houses were themselves little more than plain, little boxes ("Ticky-Tacky houses"), but a home in the new suburban environment was never a matter of mere shelter. For their proud owners these dwellings represented a step up from the apartments, boarding houses, or military barracks of earlier years. For many, the cost of owning a home in the suburbs was actually less than renting an apartment in the city.

Comedian Bob Hope used kindly humor to describe one popular new form of suburban housing: "The prefabricated houses are really cute. They come in several styles. Some even look like houses." More often, however, the nationwide flight to the suburbs elicited fierce denunciations from numerous self-appointed cultural critics. They blamed suburban life for a host of social ills, from undermining the family to weakening the national character, and described suburbs as synonymous with complacency and conformity. The "pink lampshade in the picture window" became a term of scorn for "middle-brow" culture. Such bitter criticism was surely a sign that a significant social change had taken place.[4]

With the flight to the suburbs came renewed emphasis on religion in American life, although the connection between the two was by no means clear. An increasing number of people professed their belief in God and attended church. "Under God" was added to the nation's Pledge of Allegiance and "In God We Trust" to the dollar bill. A strong faith, like a strong national defense, became a bulwark in the time of Cold War anxiety.

Whether Pacific Northwesterners of the 1950s were fully conscious of it

4. Marty Jezer, *The Dark Ages: Life in the United States 1945–1960* (Boston: South End Press, 1982), 188.

or not, their affluence allowed them to redefine space radically in a variety of ways. Money could buy security, not just in the form of big, shiny cars and single-family suburban dwellings, but also in terms of the larger economic and social environment. When Northgate opened just north of Seattle in 1950, the forty-acre emporium of affluence and consumerism was the world's first regional shopping center. Not only did it contain more than a hundred specialty shops and department stores, it also had a hospital and movie theater, just like any respectable town, which indeed it was. Portland's Lloyd Center reigned briefly after its 1960 opening as the nation's largest shopping center. Both the shopping center and suburbia were manifestations of middle-class desires to redefine space to reflect the triumph of affluence over anxiety: even if individuals could do nothing to deter Soviet bombers, they could find solace by moving to a quiet house in the suburbs and shopping in the friendly space of a shopping mall, all the while driving between the two in the enclosed space of a large and comfortable automobile.

The billions of federal dollars that poured into the Pacific Northwest during the 1950s and 1960s funded massive public works projects like damming the Columbia and Snake rivers: transforming deserts into new Gardens of Eden was then widely regarded as a desirable way to redefine space. Pacific Northwesterners, who enjoyed some of the cheapest electricity in the nation, hastened to adopt a host of new household electrical appliances.

Modern equipment in the home became something of a middle-class fetish during the 1950s, as was the case with the barbecue grill in the backyard. The average middle-class home then contained seven times the equipment it had in the 1920s, although in fact this array of gadgets offered only the illusion of greater personal control over time and environment. The time required for the household chores of cooking or washing dishes decreased, but shopping actually took more time because of the dispersion of suburban stores and shopping centers. Perhaps more than any other room in the house, the kitchen—with all its modern equipment—became a symbol of American affluence in the 1950s. In the famous "kitchen debate," Vice President Richard Nixon, visiting a U.S. exhibit in Moscow, directed the attention of Soviet Premier Nikita Khrushchev to a model of a ranch-style house complete with furniture and appliances as proof of American superiority.

Promising to redefine space in a still larger arena were the new superhighways initiated by Congress in 1956. This network of multilane interstate expressways, as was appropriate to the national thinking of the era, was promoted in the name of national defense. Actually the new roads most benefited those people who had moved to the suburbs, and they created a fitting environment for the gas-guzzling, high-compression, high horse-power, ego-boosting automobile behemoths of the era. When Interstate 5 was finally completed, it connected all the major population centers east of Puget Sound and from Portland south through the Willamette Valley and further aided the development of suburban malls and the flight from the central city.

Even before superhighways were built, Pacific Northwesterners used their automobiles to maintain the region's long-standing love affair with its out-of-doors. People spent their newfound affluence to travel to Mount Rainier, Mount Hood, and Olympic National Park in record numbers. Many recreation-minded residents also headed for the water and for the ski slopes. Vacations for the rich were nothing new, but the combination of paid vaca-tions for the masses, cheap gas, and new highways and cars proved an irre-sistible lure for middle-class travelers in the 1950s and 1960s. The number of suburban and rural motels increased while the number of downtown hotels actually decreased, a reflection perhaps of middle-class opposition to the practice of tipping in large hotels but more likely a product of the diffi-culty of finding parking space downtown. Roadside iconography changed visibly in 1952 when the first Holiday Inn opened on the outskirts of Mem-phis, Tennessee, as three single-story buildings clustered around a swim-ming pool, and again in 1956 when Ray Kroc opened the first of the familiar McDonald's fast-food restaurants in a Chicago suburb.

Finally, redefining space on a global scale was Boeing's luxurious new 707 jetliner, which, it should be noted, was derived from the design of mili-tary jets. The 707 entered commercial service in 1958, and soon nonstop jet service linked Seattle and the Pacific Northwest to cities of the East Coast as well to those of the Far East, thus helping the once isolated region play a pivotal role in expanding trade with Pacific Rim countries. That important relationship was emphasized anew in November 1993 when President Bill Clinton hosted a summit of America's Asian trading partners in Seattle.

### FURTHER ECONOMIC BOOM AND BUST:
### WILL THE CYCLE BE UNBROKEN?

The Cold War Northwest experienced economic downturns, as occurred most severely in the late 1950s, and poverty remained a problem, but pros-perity was most clearly the hallmark of the immediate post–World War II decades. For the first time in history a majority of Americans lived on the comfortable side of the poverty line, and it was widely assumed that even those left behind would eventually share in the general prosperity. The truly impoverished people remained largely invisible, "forgotten Americans," until national policy makers rediscovered them in the 1960s.

During the prosperity decades, the economic health of the Pacific Northwest remained closely linked to extractive industry, although manufacturing and service enterprises grew in importance. These, however, proved no more immune to the familiar boom-and-bust cycles than the region's traditional industries. Boeing was the Pacific Northwest's largest manufacturer and private employer; following one postwar peak in 1968, there were 101,500 people on its Washington payroll, but then the number dropped dramatically, only to rise again. By 1988, Boeing employment had climbed back to 106,670, when it was responsible for one in every six jobs in Washington, before beginning a gradual decline that lasted into the 1990s.

Writing and manufacturing computer software increased in importance during the 1980s and 1990s, and the multibillion-dollar high-tech industry spread to many parts of the Pacific Northwest besides Bellevue and Redmond and included the manufacture of computer hardware as well. Even in Idaho, long the most rural of Northwest states, jobs in electronics climbed from thirty-nine hundred in 1980 to seventy-one hundred in 1984, and despite the cutbacks of mid-decade, reached new highs as the state entered the 1990s. Idaho's largest electronic employer in the late 1980s was Hewlett-Packard which provided almost four thousand jobs in Boise producing laser printers, disk drives, and related equipment. This company launched its operation in the Idaho capital in 1973 with just thirty employees.

While glamorous new "high tech" enterprises fostered the illusion of sustained growth and prosperity, a truly sobering day of reckoning jolted the region's old mainstay, the forest products industry. During the first two decades after World War II, the industry prospered as never before. Eugene, Springfield, and Coos Bay vied for the title of lumber capital of the world. The number of people employed in the woods and mills and the production of lumber topped even the record years of World War II as a result of a building boom in the nation's suburbs.

As late as 1964, 30 percent of the lumber used on the East Coast came from the Pacific Northwest. Oregon remained the nation's leading timber-producing state for nearly five decades after 1937, but its output peaked in 1955 and was followed by a gradual decline that accelerated in the late 1970s and early 1980s when a variety of ills caused mills all over the Pacific Northwest to close.

Among the problems plaguing the industry were antiquated and ineffi-

Cold War tensions, the rise of suburbia, the baby boom, and other even less definable phenomena all played a role in shaping the Pacific Northwest economy since 1945. But that economy also bears the imprint of highly talented individual entrepreneurs, some of whom recall rags-to-riches sagas. There was, for example, young Freddy Grubmeyer, who beginning in Portland in 1908 sold cups of coffee from the back of a horse-drawn wagon to loggers and miners. Eventually he built an empire of retail stores known throughout the Pacific Northwest and Alaska as Fred Meyer.

Floyd Paxton of Yakima invented the Kwik-Lok, a little tab used to seal plastic fruit and bread bags. After the high-school dropout whittled a prototype device out of Plexiglas in 1952, it so impressed the head of Pacific Fruit that he ordered a million of them. In addition to fruit packers and grocery stores, America's baking industry used four billion of the unassuming devices annually. When Paxton became rich, he used a portion of his growing fortune in an unsuccessful bid to enter politics, running four times for Congress as an ultraconservative.

There is also Boise-based Morrison-Knudsen, a billion-dollar multinational corporate giant that has over the years engaged in heavy construction, ship building, steel fabrication, and myriad other activities. It traces its origins to 1912 and the entrepreneurial talents of Harry Winford Morrison, an Illinois farm boy, and Morris Hans Knudsen, a Danish immigrant. Starting with $600 worth of horses, scrapers, and wheelbarrows, their general contracting partnership dug canals during the reclamation and irrigation boom of the early twentieth century and built logging roads and a variety of railroad projects.

Morrison-Knudsen gradually extended its range until in the early 1930s it joined with five other construction firms to build Hoover Dam on the Colorado River, the world's largest construction venture to that time. The Boise firm also participated in the construction of the San Francisco–Oakland Bay Bridge and Grand Coulee Dam. Between 1930 and 1940, in fact, Morrison-Knudsen was a partner in the construction of twenty major dams. World War II and the Cold War required many additional construction projects that called for the talents of Morrison-Knudsen. In 1954, a *Time* magazine cover story acclaimed Harry Morrison as "the man who has done more than anyone else to change the face of the earth."

cient mills, the revival of southern pine forests (which Pacific Northwesterners once dismissed as having the quality of weeds), competition from Canadian imports, a housing slump caused by high interest rates, and a shifting market. Producing for the Japanese market involved a fundamental change in the way the industry did business. Instead of sawed timber, the Japanese purchased shiploads of logs and cut lumber in their own mills. That arrangement cost Northwest jobs.

When the economic downturn of the early 1980s was viewed from a

79. Idaho's "Potato King," John Richard Simplot (b.
1909), had already begun to amass a fortune from the
vegetable when this photograph was taken circa 1940.
Starting in the potato business modestly enough by
renting 160 acres of land near Burley, Simplot's big
boost came when the Second World War created an
enormous demand for dehydrated potatoes, onions, and
other food products needed to feed the troops. Courtesy
Idaho State Historical Society, 77-2.45.

national perspective, it was a recession. But to residents of mill towns like
Potlatch and Coos Bay, which were devastated by an unemployment rate
that occasionally topped 25 percent, the downturn was nothing less than a
great depression that persisted even when the national economy boomed
again in the mid-1980s. Some 60 percent of Oregon loggers lost their jobs: a
total of forty-eight thousand lumber jobs disappeared in the Pacific Northwest. The shutdowns exacted a psychological and social toll measurable in
an increase in family-related problems.

A classic example of the painful transition is Potlatch, Idaho, for almost
eighty years a company town where timber was the lifeblood of the commu-

nity. Beginning in 1905 the Potlatch Lumber Company constructed more than 250 buildings on hills that overlooked the largest white pine sawmill in the world. At one time, two thousand people lived in the bustling community that could boast of an opera house, paved streets, and wooden sidewalks. But the mill closed in 1981 and many sawmill workers left. A way of life ended. The millsite is today a concrete slab in a grassy field. The community survived, however, as a bedroom community for the university towns of Moscow and Pullman, located just across the border in Washington.

The Georgia-Pacific Company's decision to move its headquarters from Portland to Atlanta, Georgia, in 1982 typified the long-term changes that overtook the timber industry. The forest products giant believed that the future looked brighter in the timber belt of the South, where a warm and humid climate supposedly grew trees faster than the cool weather of the Pacific Northwest. Even when the industry revived—as it did in the late 1980s, innovative technology that included computers and lasers enabled modern sawmills to employ far fewer hands than they had only a decade earlier. Such changes forced many workers to make painful and permanent transitions in their life-style. Never again would it be possible to describe the Pacific Northwest as a Sawdust Empire. An era ended when sawmills closed for good in Potlatch, Coeur d'Alene, and other communities.

Mining was another of the region's extractive industries to face an uncertain future. The silver mines of northern Idaho boomed during the late 1970s, when Americans, frightened by an inflation rate that reached 18 percent, rushed to buy gold and silver as a hedge against further erosion of the dollar's buying power. But when the rate of inflation dropped during the 1980s, so did the price of silver.

As late as 1982 Idaho produced 37 percent of the nation's silver, but plunging prices coupled with rising labor costs caused several large companies to close their mines rather than operate them at a loss. When the Bunker Hill Mine and Smelter, Idaho's second largest employer, halted operations in Kellogg in 1981, it idled two thousand workers. Five years earlier, Kellogg had been a bustling community of five thousand, hub of the fifty-mile-long Silver Valley where one-quarter of the twenty thousand residents worked in mining. By the mid-1980s Kellogg's population had fallen below three thousand and fewer than four hundred people remained employed in the valley's mines. For many miners the era was a replay of the Great Depression of the 1930s. Even when silver prices rebounded, technological changes in the mining industry—like those in the lumber industry—permanently eliminated hundreds of jobs. For some, it seemed that if the silver valley had a future it was as a ski resort.

Agriculture, too, experienced change following the Second World War. The waters impounded by Grand Coulee Dam were raised by a complex system of pumps and siphons to irrigate a vast stretch of semiarid land in central Washington. The Columbia Basin Project transformed sagebrush plains into fields of sugar beets, potatoes, and dozens of other crops. An influx of settlers swelled the populations of towns like Moses Lake and Othello. But farmlands of the Columbia Basin Project proved no more immune to changing prices and tastes than those elsewhere. Sugar beet producers suffered a severe blow when soft-drink bottlers responded to rising sugar prices in the mid-1970s by switching to less expensive corn sweeteners. Orchardists planted thousands of acres to Red and Golden Delicious trees only to face severe losses and forced changes when public taste turned to new varieties, like the tart green Granny Smith. Washington production of this popular variety increased tenfold between 1975 and 1985.

For more than a century, wheat had been the mainstay of the region's export economy, yet in the mid-1980s huge piles of unsold grain dotted the landscape of eastern Washington. Exports of wheat to Asia were down 55 percent from those five years earlier. A global glut of wheat severely jolted the Northwest economy, and not just in rural areas. In Spokane, for example, twenty-five to thirty jobs out of every hundred were directly dependent on agriculture. Largely as a result of the malaise in timber, mining, and agriculture, Idaho in the mid-1980s experienced its largest net out-migration in fifteen years, as people looked elsewhere for jobs. From 1980 to 1985, Oregon experienced a total net migration of −1.7 percent, while Washington's growth rate was a minuscule 2.1 percent. That was a far cry from the previous decade when the population of all three states grew at rates that exceeded 20 percent.

Many observers believe that the economic health of the Pacific Northwest now and for years to come will be closely tied to an Asian export economy, the so-called clean industries of electronics and computer software, and tourism, which is predicted to become Oregon's largest industry by the year 2000. It has already emerged as Idaho's largest employer and the state's third-ranked industry in number of dollars generated. By the start of the next century it would probably also rank as Washington's number one industry were it not for the enormous size of Boeing.

During the bust of the 1980s an increasing number of the region's natural resource–based communities turned to tourism for their economic salvation, and the trend continued into the next decade. Riggins, for example, was a timber town on Idaho's Salmon River until its mill burned in 1982, but whitewater rafting and outfitting had emerged as the community's economic mainstay when the decade ended. In 1985 the old mining town of Kellogg began the slow transformation into a tourist-oriented, Bavarian-style ski village (following the example of Leavenworth, Washington), and its population began to rebound a bit. An even more spectacular sign of the times was Duane Hagadone's $60 million Coeur d'Alene Resort, which represented an up-to-date blend of big-city lifestyle with an Idaho setting rich in natural beauty and outdoor attractions. The massive resort became one of the most powerful tourist magnets in northern Idaho.

Even tourism, however, came with strings attached. The Oregon coast, paralleled for most of its length by U.S. 101, was a top tourist attraction, yet an unpicturesque string of pizza parlors, salt-water taffy stands, and rock hound shops detracted from the seashore's natural beauty. The proliferation of such unsightly businesses made some people wonder how benign tourism really was. Locals blamed the ten million tourists who came to Oregon every year, mainly from California, for crowded state parks, litter, and vandalism. Tourism, moreover, tended to generate mainly low-paying service jobs.

As for high tech's economic magic, the industry proved no more immune to swings of the business cycle than traditional resource-based industries. During the early 1970s and again in the early 1980s, Boeing experienced slowdowns that cost thousands of jobs and temporarily dimmed the economic outlook of Seattle and the Puget Sound region. As a result of massive layoffs of sixty-five thousand workers at Boeing, Seattle experienced 13 percent unemployment in 1971, the worst in the United States. In 1970, the Portland area's biggest employer was Tektronix, which kept six thousand workers busy assembling oscilloscopes, but during the slump of the early 1980s it discharged many of its workers. In Idaho during one six-month period in 1985, major electronics companies laid off two thousand people.

These then are the economic changes that in recent years have created the two Pacific Northwests so obvious in the 1990s. One centered on trans-Pacific commerce and high-technology enterprises like Boeing and the expanding electronics and computer software industry; the other remained dependent on traditional natural resources–based industries, but with their future prospects clouded by an expanding array of popular environmental concerns.

GROWING PAINS: SOCIAL AND EDUCATIONAL TRENDS

During the postwar decades, Pacific Northwesterners spent their time and money not only on a variety of outdoor pursuits but also on an important new medium of instruction and entertainment: television. The first commercial stations did not begin broadcasting until the late 1940s in Oregon and Washington and the early 1950s in Idaho. In those early years, television stations were on the air only in the afternoon and evening and the programs were initially available only in major cities.

Completion of a transcontinental microwave relay in 1951 enabled some nine million viewers to watch the first live nationwide television broadcast, the signing of a peace treaty with Japan. Set ownership increased at the rate of roughly four million a year for the decade, to a total of 44 million in 1959. By that year about 90 percent of all U.S. homes had a television set. The new medium seemed ready-made for suburban dwellers, and watching television in the evening became a national pastime. The small screen became a magnet for family togetherness and appeared to fill any void created by suburban life; the TV dinner appeared in 1954.

Pacific Northwesterners during the 1950s joined other Americans in watching live broadcasts of atomic bomb tests in the Nevada desert. Sipping their morning coffee in the comfort of their suburban homes, they could ponder this vision of the apocalypse. The new medium also provided Pacific Northwesterners a living-room seat from which to watch a series of hearings on Capitol Hill involving Communism or crime. For thirty-five days in the spring of 1954 they could weigh the charges and counter-charges of the Army-McCarthy hearings broadcast on live television. In 1957 the televised hearings of the Senate Rackets Committee again brought them disconcerting matters to ponder, this time concerning a series of sordid revelations about organized crime and the Teamsters Union, including questions about one of Washington's own, Dave Beck. The national head of the Teamsters Union, Beck repeatedly invoked the Fifth Amendment against self-incrimination when grilled about misuse of teamster funds. Beck wound up in prison after the federal government convicted him of falsifying his income tax returns and the state did likewise for his misappropriating $1,900 from the sale of a Cadillac owned by the union.

Given the unsavory and unsettling revelations about Communism or crime on live television in the 1950s, it is perhaps not surprising that in the evenings Pacific Northwesterners found solace in the comfortable brand of entertainment offered by *I Love Lucy, Leave It to Beaver, Father Knows Best,* and *Ozzie and Harriet,* four top-rated shows that portrayed middle-class values.

The television set itself consisted of a modest-sized black-and-white screen housed in a large cabinet of polished wood designed to look more like a piece of furniture than a revolutionary new technology. It was a consumer item, but more importantly, it promoted consumption, as happened, for example, when Walt Disney's three one-hour shows on the frontiersman Davy Crockett aired in the mid-1950s to create almost overnight a $300 million business in fake coonskin hats, Davy Crockett dolls, and T-shirts.

Television's impact on the region's newspapers was visible in the changes that occurred after the Second World War. Where once half a dozen papers competed in metropolitan areas, the trend was toward one newspaper—or a morning and evening paper controlled by the same company. Among the important survivors were the Portland *Oregonian,* Eugene *Register-Guard,* Boise *Statesman,* Spokane *Spokesman-Review,* the Seattle *Times* and *Post-Intelligencer,* and the Tacoma *News-Tribune.* Fine papers continue to be published in the region's smaller towns and cities too, but many were acquired by regional or national chains. Sometimes the infusion of outside capital and talent improved a newspaper. But too often the emphasis was on advertising and profits, and the result was editorials so bland as to offend no one—especially the advertisers. The growth of newspaper chains dominated by city dailies, together with the outreach of television, increased the influence of the Northwest's largest metropolitan centers over its rural hinterlands.

Another form of education undergoing change was the region's public school system. In all three states, higher education evolved along similar lines during the decades following the Second World War. Starting in the fall of 1945, veterans aided by federal money swelled the region's college and university population. At the University of Washington, where civilian enrollment dropped from 10,000 to 7,000 during the war, the student population climbed to 16,650 by the fall of 1948. After the veterans graduated, many campuses experienced a slight decline in enrollments. That changed in the mid-1960s when the first members of what became known as the baby boom generation arrived on campus. Enrollments burgeoned as a result of the "baby boomers" and because the unpopular Vietnam War encouraged young men to attend college in order to qualify for student draft deferments.

Despite campus unrest in the late 1960s, the decade may well be viewed as higher education's golden age. Across the region, colleges expanded into universities, and campuses came alive with the construction of new buildings, the inauguration of new departments and majors, and rapid faculty promotion. Several entirely new institutions were founded, especially in the category of two-year community colleges. During the twenty years after Washington created a state system of community colleges in 1967, the number of campuses increased from nineteen to twenty-seven and enrollment climbed from 50,000 to 159,000.

Illustrative of the era's unprecedented expansion was the evolution of Boise State University: founded in 1932 as a private junior college, it developed into a four-year college in 1964, became a state-supported school in 1969, and achieved university status in 1974. Another metropolitan campus, Portland State University, originated as the Vanport Extension Center in 1946 and attained university status in 1969. Of the new public colleges and universities, none was more innovative—or controversial—than the Evergreen State College, which opened in Olympia in 1971. Eschewing a traditional curriculum, it placed great emphasis on individualized courses of study that seemed especially attuned to the "do your own thing" urges of the 1960s and 1970s. Yet by the mid-1980s, the school had acquired a national reputation for academic excellence.

The campus population leveled off in the mid-1970s, shortly before the region's economy slumped, then grew again during the next two decades, although state funding for higher education did not keep pace with needs. As a result, on many campuses the 1980s and 1990s will be remembered as years of academic malaise, of recurrent funding crises and drastic retrenchment, of salaries that failed to keep pace with inflation, and of declining faculty morale. During the euphoric 1960s and early 1970s, it had been politically popular to create new campuses and institutions, but the consequence was diminished financial resources and diluted educational quality for all state schools during the hard times that followed. When the recession of the early 1980s cut state tax revenues and again during the tax revolts of the early 1990s, decreased funding for higher education forced the Pacific Northwest's public universities to eliminate personnel, programs, and in some cases entire departments.

Northwest elementary and secondary schools experienced a similar cycle. The postwar baby boom swelled school populations in the 1950s and 1960s, created crowded classrooms, and forced school boards to construct a number of new facilities, far more than could be fully utilized when the number of school-age children dropped in the late 1970s. The cost of public education continued to climb, even as parents and educators worried about declining standards and the graduation of high school students woefully unprepared in such basics as mathematics and science, English composition, public speaking, and history.

The baby boom and the move to suburbia were only two of the significant population changes to occur in the Pacific Northwest during the post–World War II decades. Census statistics reveal that, while the human face of the Pacific Northwest remained overwhelmingly Caucasian and western European in origin, important racial and ethnic changes were taking place. In 1990, Washington had the region's largest non-Caucasian population, more than 10 percent of the state's total—the fastest-growing segment being Asians. This included a new population of refugees from Southeast Asia.

During the Second World War, black migration to jobs in Seattle's booming war industries made African Americans the city's largest minority, and they remained so until 1990, when the number of Asians surpassed that of blacks. From 1945 to the 1970s, African-American newcomers to Seattle tended to cluster in central city neighborhoods where people shared many problems common to other black urban areas and where growing tensions culminated in a lengthy civil disobedience campaign in the early 1960s and bloody racial confrontations at the end of the decade.

Hispanic Americans of all races formed the region's single largest minority group in the 1990s. Beginning in the late 1940s, the lure of jobs prompted a new wave of Mexican-American emigration from the Southwest, with many workers bringing along their families, in contrast to the male-only bracero labor of the Second World War. Additional emigration north from Mexico permanently changed the region's minority composition. People of Hispanic origin numbered 380,256, or 4.4 percent of the Pacific Northwest's total population by 1990.

Some agricultural communities experienced especially dramatic increases in the number of Hispanic residents since 1980. In Othello, in Washington's Columbia Basin agricultural empire, the growth rate was 58 percent during the 1980s, and Hispanic residents formed a slight majority of the town's population by the early 1990s. Othello was typical of some two dozen Columbia plateau towns that experienced soaring growth of their Hispanic populations between 1980 and 1990 (some by 50 percent and more), so that Hispanics, nearly all of Mexican descent, made up about 10 percent of the population of rural eastern Washington. Most had come for work opportunities. In Othello and similar communities, residents of different races and ethnic backgrounds were forced to work out differences of language and culture, and for a time it seemed that an invisible wall might split such communities, even as differences also arose between Mexican nationals and Mexican Americans.

In the early 1990s, people of Mexican descent made up at least 15 percent of the population in Yakima, Grant, Adams, and Franklin counties, Washington; Malheur and Hood River counties, Oregon; and Minidoka and Owyhee counties, Idaho. Though these were rural counties and though people of Mexican origin were often stereotyped as agricultural workers, an ever-increasing number of Hispanics found employment in white-collar jobs, pursuing careers in education, business, medicine, law, and other professions.

The Pacific Northwest's Native American population in 1990 was 133,749. In Idaho the largest group was the Nez Perce. Except for the loss of a Pend Oreille or Flathead band to Montana in 1854, and the gain of a Delaware band that settled on an island north of New Plymouth in 1924, Idaho's organized tribes of the early 1990s were identical to those of 1800. Today's Northwest Indians pursue a variety of lifestyles. Some Native Americans are urban professionals, although many still live on one of the Pacific Northwest's reservations. In 1986 Idaho's Kootenai tribe, with assistance from hotel magnate Duane Hagadone, opened a forty-eight-room inn in Bonners Ferry. After the facility had been in operation for only a year, Best Western motels named the Kootenai River Inn the best in its worldwide association.

### MORE ABOUT THE ARTS

During the years beginning in the late 1920s, but especially after the Second World War, the Pacific Northwest recorded some notable achievements in the arts. Encouraging Northwest writers was *Frontier*, a college literary journal launched in 1927 at the University of Montana by Harold G. Merriam to offer an outlet for regional writing. Together with *Status Rerum*, it goaded Northwest writers to rise above the region's reputation for literary mediocrity and to seek national prominence and critical acclaim. H. L. Davis's Pulitzer Prize–winning novel *Honey in the Horn* (1935) offered inspiration to Northwest novelists and poets.

Another writer of note was Vardis Fisher, whose thirty-six published books began with *Toilers of the Hills* (1928), a novel that vividly portrayed the trials of pioneers in the dry and lonesome sagebrush country of his native Idaho. Born in poverty in a rural part of the Snake River plain, Fisher graduated magna cum laude with a doctorate in English literature from the

University of Chicago in 1925, taught at various universities, and wrote history as well as fiction. His largely autobiographical *In Tragic Life*, a brooding account of the underside of the frontier experience, was rejected by several eastern publishers; but when it finally appeared in 1932 by a western publisher, it was well received by critics and established Fisher as an important novelist of the 1930s.

Theodore Roethke, who arrived from the Midwest to teach at the University of Washington in 1947, stayed until his death in 1963. He produced brooding and introspective poetry that captured the spirit of the Northwest's environment without trivializing it as so many of the region's early poets and novelists had done. Roethke won the 1954 Pulitzer Prize in poetry and had an enormous influence on the region's writers. Richard Hugo, a native of the Pacific Northwest, took advantage of the GI bill to study creative writing with Roethke at the University of Washington and became his disciple. Hugo reflected on his experiences in the Pacific Northwest in several collections of poems that achieved national visibility.

No Northwest writer reached a larger audience than Ken Kesey, whose 1962 novel *One Flew over the Cuckoo's Nest*, a story of individualism versus authority set in an Oregon mental hospital, was made into a prize-winning film. Kesey's other well-known work, *Sometimes a Great Notion* (1964), which is set on the Oregon coast and details the struggle of an individualistic family of gyppo loggers defying bureaucratic organization and authority, was also made into a movie.

Ivan Doig, a professionally trained historian and novelist living in the Seattle area, won critical acclaim with his first book, *This House of Sky: Landscapes of a Western Mind* (1978), an autobiographical account of his youth in Montana. Among his subsequent works is *English Creek* (1984), the first of a trilogy of novels set in post-frontier Montana. The Oregonian Don Berry wrote two novels, *Trask* (1960) and *Moontrap* (1962), which offered sensitive treatment of a mountain man undergoing social transition.

A distinctive, coherent school of thought was more noticeable among the region's postwar visual artists than among its writers. The term Northwest School was first used in 1947 to describe a group of paintings shown in museums in the East. They included the abstract art of Morris Graves, Mark Tobey, Kenneth Callahan, Guy Anderson, and others who found inspiration in rain- and mist-obscured scenes of the Pacific Northwest. That movement attained its greatest prominence during the 1950s.

Not one of the Pacific Northwest states lavished public money on the arts. In the mid-1980s, Idaho's appropriation for the arts placed it dead last in the United States, behind even Puerto Rico, Guam, and American Samoa. When the national average was 85 cents per capita, Idaho spent 13 cents, Oregon 18 cents, and Washington 43 cents. If state spending for the arts is any reflection of public support, then Northwest artists gave the region far better than it deserved.

During the half-century after World War II numerous trends and events that shaped the contours of life in the contemporary Pacific Northwest generated considerable public debate and political controversy. These conflicts were often resolved in the arena of government. Regardless of political persuasion, most Pacific Northwesterners still have faith in the political process, a fact confirmed by their frequent use of direct legislation and a voter turnout in presidential elections that ranks among the highest in the United States. The following chapter examines the role of political institutions, processes, and leadership in shaping the Pacific Northwest since World War Two.

# CHAPTER 21

# The Politics of Anxiety
# and Affluence

*

"The State of Washington is famous in the nation's capital for its salmon, its stability, and its United States senators. The salmon is matchless, and some of the stability is probably illusory, but the contributions to the political system made by such senators as Henry M. Jackson and Warren G. Magnuson are undisputed. In fairness, the name of Daniel J. Evans, especially as governor, should be added to this equation. The common thread of Jackson's and Evans's political careers is a constructive independence that avoids the extremes of the maverick or of rigid partisanship."—Louis S. Cannon, *Washington Post* political reporter and National Public Radio's *Morning Edition* commentator, Fall 1986 Pettyjohn Lecture

*

During the decade of the 1950s, a majority of voters in all three Pacific Northwest states twice turned to Dwight D. Eisenhower, the popular general who had helped win World War II and who as president of the United States seemed the ideal person to fight the Cold War. He offered comfort during a decade of anxiety: to the *New York Times*, Ike resembled "everybody's grandfather."

It was possible to become too complacent during a time of unpredictable changes, as the world of popular music discovered. Hits of the early 1950s were safe and comfortable ditties like "Lady of Spain," "Doggie in the Window," and "Catch a Falling Star." But when popular music became too predictable, too lifeless, or too sweet for the generation of baby boomers, an increasing number of young people turned to the pounding new sound of rock-'n'-roll. The popular radio-television show, *Your Hit Parade*, born in the Big Band era, died in 1959. It could not capture the appeal of the new rock-'n'-roll music exemplified by Dick Clark's *American Bandstand*, broadcast on national television for the first time in 1957.[1]

Elvis Presley was certainly not the first prominent rock-'n'-roll musician, but beginning with his discovery in 1956 his rise to fame was meteoric. He became the symbol of an age. A recording star who openly exploited sexuality and rebelliousness, Presley touched off the biggest popular music craze since Glenn Miller and Frank Sinatra in the 1940s. In September 1957 Presley leaped onto a stage at Tacoma's Lincoln Bowl and in front of six thousand screaming fans, 80 percent of whom were teenage girls, belted out songs that would make him "The King."

Cold War fears seldom intruded into the lively new world of rock-'n'-roll, but they seemed omnipresent everywhere else in the 1950s, and especially in politics where they took such forms as anti-Communist crusades and more dollars for defense. The states of the Pacific Northwest produced no Red-baiting politician as prominent as Senator Joseph R. McCarthy of Wisconsin. Perhaps only Idaho's Herman Welker, U.S. senator from 1951 to 1957, really fit that mold: his staunch support for McCarthy earned him the nickname Little Joe from Idaho. Some politicians mistakenly believed that stirring popular fears of Communists (or "Reds") was a sure way to win elections, as did Washington's incumbent Republican Senator Harry Cain in 1952. He even invited his friend and fellow "Commie hater" Joe McCarthy to Seattle to campaign for him; Eisenhower carried the state in a Republican landslide, but the party's hapless incumbent senator lost his seat to Henry "Scoop" Jackson, a Democrat. Rejected by the voters, Cain relocated to the nation's capital, where he served three years on the Subversive Activities Control Board.

Despite several cheerless episodes of anti-Communist paranoia, at least it can be noted that state governments and political parties in the Pacific Northwest since 1945 have generally been free of scandal, although a few prominent politicians ruined their careers by scandalous behavior. The region has also been fortunate to escape domination by a single company or industry (unlike neighboring Montana, which was long under the heel of Anaconda Copper), although Washington's close relationship with the state's largest corporation gave rise to the popular joke that, when Boeing

1. James Gilbert, *Another Chance: Postwar America 1945–1985*, 2d ed. (Chicago: Dorsey Press, 1986), 124–27.

sneezes, Washington catches cold. Especially at the state level, politics during the postwar decades remained issue and personality oriented, and some
of the key issues related to education, taxes, natural resources, and the
environment.

## TRENDS: POLITICAL MAINSTREAMS AND BACKWATERS

During the years immediately following the Second World War, Republicans continued to dominate politics in Oregon, as they had for nearly three-
quarters of a century. The journalist Richard Neuberger was one of the
people most responsible for the rebirth of a viable Democratic party: bucking the Eisenhower landslide of 1952, he won a seat in the Oregon Senate,
while his wife, Maurine, won a seat in the House, thus becoming the first
husband-and-wife team in U.S. history ever elected simultaneously to both
chambers of a state legislature. Between them the Neubergers accounted for
15 percent of the entire Democratic membership in the legislature, leading
one observer to quip that for the first time a political party could caucus
in bed.

The party's fortunes began to improve in 1954 when Richard Neuberger,
running as an avowed liberal in what was then a very conservative state,
beat a colorless and reactionary Republican incumbent, Guy Cordon, and
became the first Oregon Democrat in forty years to sit in the U.S. Senate.
Two years later, Democrats gained control of both houses of the state legislature for the first time since 1880, won the governorship, three of four
congressional seats, and a second seat in the U.S. Senate. Clearly a significant realignment had occurred in Oregon politics.

"Until 1954, we had the strains of the conservative Southern Democrat
and the Progressive New England Republicans in Oregon politics," explained Mark O. Hatfield, a long-time Republican senator from Oregon and
former professor of political science. "What happened in that election was
that the Oregon Democratic Party seized the liberal perspective, overturn-
ing the conservative tradition within its own party. That gave progressives
in the Republican party more competition, which turned state politics,
Republican and Democratic, more toward the liberal side."[2] Further boost-
ing Democratic fortunes were the war workers who remained to put down

2. Steve Forrester, "Senator Richard Neuberger: A Man Ahead of His Times," in Win
McCormack and Dick Pintarich, eds., *Great Moments in Oregon History* (Portland: New
Oregon Publishers, 1987), 169.

roots in Oregon, and an influx of liberal-leaning newcomers from the East during the 1960s and 1970s. Neuberger, incidentally, had earlier gained insight into the art of politics during long drives across Idaho with the legendary William E. Borah, whose activities he covered for the *New York Times*.

During the first three decades of the twentieth century, Washington could usually be counted on to elect Republicans. Of the 873 members elected to the state's House of Representatives between 1914 and 1930, only 72 were Democrats, while in the state's Senate, one lone Democrat sat in the upper chamber during the sessions of 1921, 1923, 1927, and 1931. So weak were Democrats during those lean years that on five occasions they were unable to field a full ticket to contest Congressional elections.

The relationship between the two parties changed radically during the early years of the 1930s. Washington's Democrats carried everything before them in the 1932 election, leaving only seven Republicans in the state's House of Representatives and a minority of only twenty-one Republicans in the state's Senate, most of these being holdovers who were gone by 1935. A viable two-party system finally emerged in the 1940s, although Washington voters were committed ticket-splitters. Fifty-four percent of the state's voters supported a Republican for president in 1952, but 56 percent also preferred a Democrat for the U.S. Senate; four years later Eisenhower repeated his triumph by the same margin, yet 55 percent of the voters preferred the Democrat Albert Rosellini as governor. From 1940 to the mid-1990s, Democrats often controlled Washington's two U.S. Senate seats, but Republicans did well in the governor's office, where Arthur Langlie and Dan Evans were each elected to three consecutive four-year terms.

Democrats in Idaho held a U.S. Senate seat during all but six years from 1945 to 1981 and retained the governor's office for more than two decades after 1971, but, paradoxically, Republicans dominated the legislature. In fact, during the century from 1889 to 1989 the Democratic party controlled both houses a total of only ten years, and not once since 1961. The Democratic party fared even worse in Oregon until the realigning election of 1956. Before that time, Republicans had dominated the state legislature without exception since 1880; but from 1957 through at least the early 1990s, Republicans were *never* able to control simultaneously both houses of the Oregon legislature.

In Idaho, clearly the most conservative of Pacific Northwest states in recent years, Democrats generally fared poorly in contests for the House of Representatives. Including the election of 1992, sixteen Republicans have

457

held House seats from Idaho for a total of 117 years, while ten Democrats have served for a total of 52 years. From 1966 until 1984 not a single Democrat was elected from the state's two Congressional districts, and the variety of Republican that Idaho sent to Congress grew increasingly conservative. Next door, from the time of Oregon's admission to the Union in 1859 until 1945, Democrats controlled the state's Congressional seats a mere 35 percent of the time; but during the four decades since the 1956 election that measure of success jumped to 65 percent.

Patterns of voter support for the two major parties during the years after 1945 were fairly consistent in some areas, but changed dramatically in others, primarily as a result of population growth and economic change. In Oregon and Washington, Republicans as a rule did better east of the Cascades, although urban Spokane with its large Roman Catholic population tended to vote Democratic, as did west-side industrial centers with their heavy labor vote. Multnomah County, which included the city of Portland, was important to Democratic successes in state-wide elections in Oregon. The Willamette Valley was once solidly Republican, but beginning in the 1980s its voters have more often than not been found in the Democratic camp, especially on issues labeled social liberalism (such as relate to the environment, children, minorities, and women).

Idaho had its own peculiar voting patterns. For much of the twentieth century, Democrats tended to be the majority party in counties north of the Salmon River, while Republicans were dominant south of that divide, where in recent years three-fifths of the state's population lived. A conspicuous exception to the Republican south was working-class Pocatello. This pattern changed noticeably during the 1980s as organized labor declined both in membership and power in its strongholds of Pocatello, Lewiston, and the Coeur d'Alene mining area (Shoshone County). By 1982, only 16 percent of the state's work force was still unionized, down from 25 percent of non-agricultural workers in the 1950s, and this adversely affected the Democratic vote. Seeming to hasten the declining power of organized labor was enactment of Idaho's first right-to-work law, a controversial measure that survived both a ballot challenge in 1986 and several legal battles.

In the fast-growing and increasingly wealthy resort city of Coeur d'Alene (as distinct from the gritty and declining mining region of the same name) and surrounding Kootenai County, an influx of affluent retirees together with the closure of several sawmills gave Republican fortunes a boost. Also aiding Republicans was the fact that eleven of fourteen counties in the state's southeast corner were at least half Mormon, the large majority of whom usually supported the Grand Old Party. Regardless of party labels, though, Idaho politics tended to be personality oriented, populist, and conservative—especially so when viewed from a national perspective.

Since the election of Franklin D. Roosevelt in 1944, only one Democrat has won a *majority* of Idaho votes cast for president: that happened in 1964 when Lyndon Johnson beat the conservative Republican candidate, Barry Goldwater, by the slimmest of margins (.92%). The Idaho vote was Goldwater's best showing in any non-Southern state except in his native Arizona. Four years later George C. Wallace's right-wing American Independent Party captured 13 percent of the state's vote; and in 1972 John G. Schmitz, presidential candidate of the right-wing American Party, ran better in Idaho than in any other state (winning 9.2 percent of the state's vote). In the three presidential elections of the 1980s, only in Utah did the Republican candidates run better than in Idaho.

It is hard to reconcile the political character of contemporary Idaho with the fact that an ultraliberal Democrat, Glen H. Taylor, represented the state in the U.S. Senate from 1945 to 1951 and ran for vice president of the United States on the left-wing Progressive ticket in 1948, or that from 1956 to 1974 the liberal Democrat Frank Church won four elections to the Senate. The fact is that conservative or liberal, Idahoans are notorious ticket-splitters who take their civic duty seriously. In the elections of 1952, 1956, and 1960, the Gem State ranked first in the nation in terms of voter turnout. Since that time it has remained among the top states. Someone once joked, perhaps unfairly, that three "boxes" defined the Idaho character: the ballot box, the pickup truck box, and the ammunition box.

In any case, voters in all three states have a history of active participation in the political process, either by voting for candidates or supporting various direct legislation measures. From 1902 through 1992, Oregonians used initiative petitions a total of 244 times and referendums 50 times. The popularity of direct legislation throughout the region is one indicator of its weak party system, and so, too, is power of personality in winning elections.

PERSONALITIES: THESPIANS AND STATESMEN

From the end of World War II through the election of 1992, the number of men and women from the Pacific Northwest who served in the House of Representatives and the U.S. Senate was ninety-five; they were divided almost evenly between Democrats and Republicans. Most of those elected to serve on Capitol Hill or in various branches of state government were

MR. JUSTICE DOUGLAS

In a category all by himself among public officials and policy makers from the Pacific Northwest was William O. Douglas, who in 1975 ended his thirty-six-year tenure as a member of the United States Supreme Court. This unabashed liberal from conservative Yakima served on the high court longer than any other person in the nation's history, and was the only member ever from the Pacific Northwest.

Born in Minnesota in 1898, Douglas was the son of a minister who took his family west to California and then to eastern Washington where he died in 1904, leaving his widow to raise the three Douglas children. Young William Orville grew up in Yakima, where he retrained and strengthened his polio-stricken legs by long hikes in the surrounding hills and in the Cascade Mountains. After attending Whitman College in Walla Walla, he returned to Yakima to teach high school before swinging aboard a freight train and either worked or bummed his way east to enter the Columbia University Law School in New York in 1922. Douglas claims to have arrived in Manhattan with six cents in his pocket.

After holding a number of law-related jobs, Douglas became Sterling Professor of Law at Yale University and then a rising star in Franklin D. Roosevelt's New Deal. He served as chairman of the recently formed (1934) Securities and Exchange Commission. In 1939, Roosevelt appointed the Pacific Northwesterner to the high court. Becoming one of the legendary "Nine Old Men" at the youthful age of 40, he distinguished himself as a vigorous defender of the Bill of Rights and of the nation's environment.

Douglas had a passionate love of the out of doors, often returning to the Yakima area to fish and hike with friends in his beloved Cascade mountains. His stands on various public matters did not necessarily make him popular in his hometown, however. When as head of the Securities and Exchange Commission he made national headlines exposing corrupt business practices on Wall Street, the anti–New Deal Yakima *Republic* disclaimed the native son in an editorial headlined, "Yakima Not At Fault." Douglas responded with amusement, carrying a copy of the clipping in his wallet until it became tattered. He was probably the most unpretentious person ever to sit on the nation's highest court: once after Douglas met with railroad workers in the Union Pacific yards at La Grande, Oregon, an old locomotive engineer groused, "He looks and acts a hell of a lot more like my fireman than a Supreme Court Judge."[3] A tireless traveler and prolific writer, Douglas suffered a debilitating stroke in 1974 and died in 1980.

In his *Of Men and Mountains* (1950), Douglas wrote in passionate terms of the land he loved. A typical passage read, "As I walked the ridge that evening I could hear the chinook on the distant ridges before it reached me. Then it touched the sage at my feet and made it sing. It brushed my cheeks warm and soft. It ran its fingers through my hair and rippled away in the darkness. It was a friendly wind, friendly to man throughout time. It was beneficent, carrying rain to the desert. It was soft, bringing warmth to the body. It had almost magical qualities, for it need only lightly touch the snow to melt it."

uncommonly able people. To put the region's political good fortune in perspective, one need only think of the postwar South's sizable crop of racist demagogues or the Midwest's several red-baiting senators.

To be sure, the Pacific Northwest was not immune to corrupt public servants, officeholding non-entities, or outright embarrassments like Republican Idaho Congressman George Hansen, a free-wheeling populist champion of far-right causes. Variously described as a knight-errant and the "Huey Long" of Idaho politics, "George the Dragon Slayer," as Hansen once styled himself, served in the House of Representatives for fourteen years and grabbed many headlines. When he went to the Iranian capital of Teheran in 1979 in an unsuccessful attempt to negotiate for the release of U.S. hostages, President Jimmy Carter complained about his meddling in foreign affairs. A court convicted Hansen of violating a 1978 ethics law for failing to report $333,000 in loans and other transactions and sentenced him to a five-to-fifteen-year prison term. The House reprimanded him in a 354 to 52 vote of censure. More than balancing that unfortunate political record were numerous capable and hard-working elected officials. Both the Democratic and Republican parties could claim notable political leaders, while Oregon's maverick U.S. Senator Wayne Morse was twice elected as a Republican and twice as a Democrat.

It would be unwise, if not impossible, to discuss here all ninety-five Pacific Northwesterners who served on Capitol Hill, or to provide even brief sketches of the region's twenty-eight governors who held office during that same time span, but a few individuals do merit particular attention. Oregon's Tom McCall was one of a trio of exceptionally competent chief executives who included Daniel J. Evans of Washington and Cecil Andrus of Idaho. The two Republicans and the Idaho Democrat got along like brothers. In a reminder that personality and issues commonly took precedence over party labels in the Pacific Northwest politics, McCall endorsed Andrus for reelection at some personal risk in 1974, and Evans did likewise when Andrus ran for governor again in 1986.

During the years from the mid-1950s until 1980, when Democrats controlled the U.S. Senate, the Washingtonians Warren G. Magnuson and Henry M. Jackson formed an exceedingly powerful duo, gaining more seniority than any other senators from the North and more, too, than most of their colleagues from the one-party Democratic South. Both men headed

---

3. Steve Neal, ed., *They Never Go Back to Pocatello: The Selected Essays of Richard Neuberger* (Portland: Oregon Historical Society Press, 1988), 115.

80. (Left to right) Thomas Foley (b. 1929), Henry M. Jackson (1912–1983), and Warren G. Magnuson (1905–1989), three of the biggest names in Washington politics during the middle and late twentieth century. Courtesy University of Washington Archives.

major committees and became noted for aiding their constituents, for looking after the interests of the Pacific Northwest. They believed in an active and compassionate federal government that built dams and maintained a strong national defense.

Both senators were New Deal economic liberals, but Jackson's support for a strong national defense puzzled other liberals (mainly of the social and cultural variety who came to dominate the Democratic party during the 1980s and 1990s) and earned him the reputation of being "hawkish"—a derogatory term in the liberal vocabulary. The former Minnesota senator Eugene McCarthy once laughingly remarked, "You can't get enough security for Henry. If he had his way the sky would be black with supersonic planes, preferably Boeings, of course." Jackson's interests actually ranged far beyond national defense from hydroelectric power to the environment. He helped steer several conservation bills through the Senate, most notably the Wilderness Act of 1964, the Redwoods National Park Act, the Natural Environmental Policy Act of 1969, and the North Cascades National Park Act.

Democrats and Republicans alike respected Jackson as a man of great integrity. At the polls he was unbeatable: he served in Congress from 1941 (the Senate from 1953) until his sudden death in 1983. In the 1970 election he crushed his Republican opponent with an amazing 83.9 percent of the vote. Magnuson served even longer, from 1937 (the Senate from 1944) until the Republican Slade Gorton defeated him in the 1980 election. During his long tenure on Capitol Hill, Magnuson never sought the limelight, preferring instead to build his reputation by attention to detail and his ability to forge agreements that benefited the people of Washington.

Another avowed liberal in the New Deal tradition was Idaho's Frank Church, who was first elected to the Senate in 1956 at the age of thirty-two, thus becoming one of the youngest members ever to sit in that body. In 1962 he became the first and so far only Democratic senator from Idaho ever to win a second term. He went on to serve a total of four terms.

Like William Borah, the long-time Republican senator from Idaho that he most idolized, Church was an impressive orator; but more important, he chaired the Senate's prestigious Committee on Foreign Relations and emerged as a major critic of America's interventionist foreign policy, increasingly clashing with Lyndon Johnson over the president's Vietnam war policies. The egotistical Johnson, who took a dim view of criticism from members of his own party, reportedly responded that Idaho had sent him the dumbest senator. Church would later regret that in 1964 he joined with all but two senators (Oregon's Wayne Morse and Alaska's Ernest Gruening) to support the Gulf of Tonkin Resolution giving the president a free hand in Vietnam. His increasingly outspoken opposition to American participation in the Vietnam War, his support for a treaty phasing out U.S. control over the Panama Canal (he was floor leader for the controversial matter, which passed the Senate by 68 to 32, only one vote more than the required two-thirds majority), and his investigation of Central Intelligence Agency misdeeds all cost Church votes in Idaho and quite probably the 1980 election.

A liberal Democrat for twenty-four years in a state growing increasingly conservative, Church was narrowly defeated in his bid for a fifth term by Republican Congressman Steven D. Symms, whose margin of victory was less than 1 percent of the votes cast. Some commentators maintain that the Reagan landslide helped Symms, especially when President Jimmy Carter conceded defeat while Idaho polls were still open.

When Republicans gained control of the Senate in 1980 for the first time in twenty-five years, Oregon's Mark Hatfield and Robert Packwood assumed roles not unlike those Magnuson and Jackson had played. Joining them after Jackson's death in 1983 was another Republican, Daniel J. Evans, Washington's only three-term governor and a man rated as one of the nation's ten best governors in the twentieth century. From 1965 to 1977, Evans had proved a popular and able chief executive. An engineer by training, he was well suited to deal with matters of administrative reorganization, tax reform, and environmental and social issues. As governor, Evans was regarded as more liberal than many of his Democratic opponents, although during his early years in the Senate he surprised some constituents by sometimes siding with conservatives.

From 1983 until 1987, for the first time in fifty years, Republicans held all six U.S. Senate seats from the Pacific Northwest. That changed with the election of 1986 when Brock Adams, transportation secretary under President Carter, unseated Republican Slade Gorton. Adams had publicly opposed locating a nuclear waste dump at Hanford, while Gorton supported legislation that led to Hanford's being selected one of three finalists, a move vigorously opposed by many Washington voters. In the election, Gorton carried the Tri-Cities (Richland, Kennewick, and Pasco, where the economy largely depended on the nearby Hanford facility) but lost the state to Adams.

Adams was first elected to the House of Representatives in 1964, and he seemed destined for a honored place in Pacific Northwest history, especially as a result of his cabinet service and Senate seat. But in the early 1990s, his once-promising political career self-destructed amid sworn accusations by nine women of sexual misconduct. There was even a lurid tale by a Democratic party activist in Seattle who claimed that Adams drugged and raped her. Ironically, the accused senator had earlier gained recognition as a proponent of women's issues, including strong support for abortion rights and women's health care.

Claims of sexual harassment were not limited to the Democratic side of the aisle, however: only a short time after the Adams scandal, the Oregon Republican Robert Packwood also experienced public humiliation. A sexual-misconduct inquiry by the Senate ethics committee, prompted by allegations from at least twenty-six women, appalled Oregonians and brought an ignominious end to his long political career. Even before the Packwood mess, general voter revulsion against sexual harassment in high places enabled Patty Murray, a Democrat and relative political unknown who billed herself as a "mom in tennis shoes" to win the Senate seat vacated by Adams, who declined to run for reelection in 1992.

464

As for Thomas Slade Gorton III, whom Adams originally defeated in 1986, he managed to shed his reputation for being occasionally cold, aloof, and arrogant, and made a political comeback as a mellower, more middle-of-the-road Republican. He regained one of Washington's Senate seats in the 1988 election, defeating liberal Democratic Congressman Mike Lowry, who in turn waged a successful political comeback of his own in 1992 to win election as the state's governor. Gorton (reelected to a third term in 1994) became one of the few people in U.S. history to return to the upper chamber after a previous defeat, although his political maneuvering over the years earned him the nickname "Slippery Slade" in some circles (mostly Democratic). Chicago-born and Dartmouth- and Columbia-educated, Gorton moved west from the Ivy League campuses to Seattle in 1956 because "Washington was not a place where you and your family had to have been for an extended period of time."[4] As Gorton recognized, Washington's wide-open primary and its issue- and personality-oriented politics created for newcomers perhaps the nation's most accessible political structure.

Confirming that statement was the political career of Dixy Lee Ray, who won the governorship of Washington in 1976, having never before held elective office. Ray was in many ways a pioneer in politics: she was one of the first two women in the United States to be elected governor without benefit of a husband having first served in that office. Holding a doctorate in marine biology from Stanford University, Ray was highly intelligent yet was undiplomatic in her criticism of measures favored by environmentalists. Her outspoken views also earned her the enmity of the press. After a single term as governor, Ray lost her bid for renomination in the Democratic primary.

During the two decades that followed Daniel J. Evans's twelve years as Washington's chief executive, the state was beset by a succession of well-meaning but relatively ineffective governors, both Republican and Democratic. Ray later admitted that she was more a Republican in attitude than a Democrat, an attribute long suspected by many observers, and one that complicated her life as a Democratic governor. Her successor, Republican John Spellman, held the governor's office for one term beginning in 1980. He presented himself to voters as the consummate manager, but Spellman spent much of his four-year term muddling through problems associated with cutting government programs to bring state spending into line with lagging tax revenues.

Booth Gardner, the heir to a big lumber fortune, defeated the luckless

4. "Slade Gorton," *Current Biography* 54 (August 1993): 12–15.

Spellman in 1984 to lead the Democrats back into the governor's mansion. Gardner was a pleasant man who served two terms, but his governing talents were probably overrated. Describing himself as a manager rather than a politician, Gardner talked about reforms but too often failed to use the power of the governor's office to deal effectively with major problems, such as Washington's poorly structured tax system. Gardner had great vision but, in the words of one newspaper critic, also had "non-existent follow-through."

Succeeding Gardner, who declined to run for a third term in 1992, was Mike Lowry, a liberal Democrat, former Congressman, and twice-defeated candidate for Senate. With characteristic energy, Lowry charged into the state's tax mess with all the finesse of a bull in a china shop and thereby helped to trigger voter backlash in the form of two tax limitation initiatives on the ballot in 1993. When voters approved one of the measures, Lowry spoke for chastened public officials when he pledged that his majority Democrats would redouble efforts to streamline state government.

In the same 1986 election that launched the fateful senatorial career of Washington's Brock Adams, two other former cabinet officers of the Carter administration emerged as winners in the region's gubernatorial elections. Former Transportation Secretary Neil Goldschmidt became Oregon's chief executive, and former Interior Secretary Cecil Andrus returned as Idaho's chief executive, having previously served as governor from 1971 to 1977 before resigning to join the cabinet.

Andrus first won the Idaho governorship in 1970 when he broke a twenty-four-year Republican hold on the office that dated back to 1947. Half of those years belonged to Robert E. Smylie, the only man in Idaho history to serve three consecutive four-year terms as governor. Smylie was a personable and energetic man, a progressive in the Republican ranks. In his first eight years, Idaho built more roads than during any previous twenty-four-year period. The state also trebled its budgetary commitments to education, and reform of the school system went forward rapidly: the 1,250 school districts that existed in 1947 were reduced to a more realistic 110 by 1962. Smylie's biggest political liability was backing a sales tax to finance the increased cost and responsibilities of government. The 3 percent tax won voter approval in a referendum, but conservative Don Samuelson blocked Smylie's quest for a fourth term in the Republican primary of 1966.

Samuelson was so pro-development that Cecil Andrus, his opponent in his reelection match in 1970, made protection of the environment a key issue for the first time in an Idaho gubernatorial campaign. Andrus, a former logger from rural Clearwater County, declared, "The most important long-range issue is the protection of our magnificent Idaho environment." Like Tom McCall of Oregon, he defined a key issue that would animate Pacific Northwest politics for years to come.

At the center of the 1970 campaign was the White Clouds Peak controversy. This beautiful alpine area, located twenty-five miles northwest of Sun Valley, was where the American Smelting and Refining Company of New York (ASARCO) wanted to dig a 740-acre open-pit facility to mine molybdenum, a metal used to harden steel for use in high-temperature applications such as the space program required. The mine meant jobs, and also it meant the despoliation of a primitive area one local newspaper called the "crown jewels of Idaho." Governor Samuelson sprang to the defense of the company saying, "The raw materials are here and should be exploited to the fullest possible extent."[5] Here was a classic statement of the user-oriented mentality that had long held sway in Idaho and much of the Pacific Northwest. Yet in 1970 a significant number of Idahoans were no longer persuaded by the traditional arguments. Helped by the environmental issue and the rare ability of the usually fractious Democrats to close ranks, Andrus won.

After cabinet service and time spent in business pursuits, Andrus returned as Idaho's chief executive after the 1986 election. Following a landslide reelection victory four years later, he could claim to have served as governor longer than anyone else in Idaho history (though his tenure was broken into two parts). He presided over a time of tremendous change, when the state's population increased from 740,000 to over a million and nonfarm employment doubled. Andrus proved to be a good politician, reaching out to the people in a folksy and easy-going way, and a savvy administrator, working closely with a Republican-dominated legislature. He was also favored during his second tenure in the governor's mansion by an exceptionally robust economy. Andrus declined to run for reelection in 1994. That year voters chose onion farmer and longtime state legislator Phil Batt as their first Republican governor since 1966.

Historically, several different tactics have led to political success in statewide elections in geographically divided Idaho, and one of the most obvious was to cultivate a flamboyant personal style to gain the attention of voters. Long before Ronald Reagan and other actors first became prominent in politics in the 1960s, Idaho had Glen H. Taylor, the Singing Cowboy. In a

5. Neal R. Peirce, *The Mountain States of America: People, Politics, and Power in the Eight Rocky Mountain States* (New York: Norton, 1972), 151.

scenario typical of his 1930s and 1940s campaigns, he would come to town with his hillbilly band, the Glendora Ranch Gang, play and sing a few songs to attract a crowd, and then preach his message, a program of near socialism and world peace that he toned down as the years went by.

Taylor was a loved and hated man. He ran for office eight times but was elected only once, in 1944, when he won a term in the U.S. Senate. A liberal Democrat, Taylor distinguished himself as a staunch advocate of civil rights and better relations with the Soviet Union. Many people, however, regarded Taylor as nothing more than an opportunist who avidly sought publicity. They cited the time he put on a large Stetson hat and sang and accompanied himself on a guitar on the Capitol steps to call attention to the housing shortage in wartime Washington. To the tune of "Home on the Range" Taylor pleaded:

> Oh, give us a home
> Near the Capitol Dome
> With a yard where the children can play—
> Just one room or two,
> Any old thing will do,
> We can't find a pla-a-ce to stay.

More than anything else, it was his teaming up with former Secretary of Agriculture and Vice President Henry Wallace on the Progressive ticket in 1948 that tainted Taylor as an incorrigible leftist in the eyes of many Idaho voters. The Progressive party, which Communists infiltrated heavily at the national level, attracted only five thousand votes in the Gem State and probably foreshadowed Taylor's rejection in the Democratic primary in 1950. Taylor left the Senate and moved to California to become a manufacturer of wigs called "Taylor Toppers." Replacing him on Capitol Hill was Herman Welker, a conservative Republican defeated after one term by Frank Church.

Steve Symms, a Republican spokesman for right-wing causes who in turn defeated Church twenty-four years later, once appeared at an anti–gun control news conference packing two revolvers. "They can call me a right-wing kook," he declared, "but I'm out there on the fringe with Ronald Reagan." He won reelection in 1986, narrowly beating former Democratic Governor John V. Evans, but Symms retired unbeaten in 1992. In that year's election, a majority of Idaho voters selected Boise's popular young mayor Dirk Kempthorne over Democratic Congressman Richard Stallings to keeping the senate seat in conservative Republican hands. In this way the Republicans retained control of both Senate seats.

Oregon politics was enlivened over the years by several colorful personalities, too. One was Tom McCall; another was Wayne Morse, ever the political maverick and a latter-day gadfly in the tradition of Robert M. La Follete of Morse's native Wisconsin and George Norris of Nebraska, two progressive Republicans of the early twentieth century. Morse, one-time dean of the University of Oregon law school, was first elected to the U.S. Senate in 1944 as a Republican, although one who followed in the progressive tradition. Morse had never before run for political office.

Morse's slogan in the 1944 election was "Principle above Politics," but that lofty principle often translated into idiosyncratic behavior on Capitol Hill. When a Senate vote was unanimous save one, that lone dissenter was usually Morse. A naturally talkative man, he set the all-time Senate record for filibustering: in 1953 he held the floor for twenty-two hours and twenty-six minutes, speaking the entire time himself without even a bathroom break. His aggressiveness on issues he believed in earned him the nickname the Tiger in the Senate; although to some observers, Morse's trimmed mustache, thick black eyebrows, sleek black hair, and dark complexion gave the Tiger a sinister appearance.

As a Democrat, Morse became an early and outspoken critic of his own party's president, Lyndon B. Johnson, and American policy in Vietnam. Of his opposition to the war it was once said: "Wayne Morse didn't come early or late to the peace movement—there was a time when he *was* the peace movement."[6] Attempting to steer a political course between the extremes of left and right, he eventually alienated party colleagues as well as Oregon voters, who in the 1968 election dumped the Tiger in the Senate in favor of Robert Packwood.

Packwood served with Oregon's senior senator, Mark Hatfield, until 1995. Part of their success as Republicans was that they were liberals on many issues dear to the hearts of such traditional Democratic constituencies as organized labor, women's groups, and environmentalists. Packwood's philosophy was once described as "Loophole Liberalism," of using conservative means (such as tax incentives) to achieve liberal social objectives.

By the mid-1990s Hatfield had become the most senior member of the U.S. Senate from the Pacific Northwest. He first entered that body in 1966, having previously served two terms as governor. A veteran of World War II, he was originally elected to the Senate as an opponent of the Vietnam War.

6. Win McCormack, ed., *Profiles of Oregon, 1976–1986* (Portland: New Oregon Publishers, 1986), 96.

81. Mark O. Hatfield (b. 1922), governor of Oregon from
1959 to 1967. He was first elected to the U.S. Senate in
1966. Courtesy Mark O. Hatfield.

A deeply religious man who favored limiting military spending and opposed abortion, he nonetheless received little support from the new religious right.

Another of Oregon's unusual breed of liberal Republicans, Tom McCall, was barred from seeking a third consecutive term as governor in 1974 by the Oregon constitution. Anyone who succeeded the colorful McCall was bound to suffer by comparison. First there was Robert Straub, a Democrat during whose administration Oregon became the first state in the union to ban aerosol spray cans to protect the ozone layer (in 1977). Republicans recaptured the governor's office under Victor Atiyeh, who four years later surrendered it to Neil Goldschmidt, a Democrat and former mayor of Portland who as Carter's Secretary of Transportation was the first Oregonian in more than twenty years to hold a cabinet post. In office, Goldschmidt tended to be a social liberal on issues affecting children, minorities, and women, but after four years in office, the ebullient Democrat declined to run for a second term.

Conspicuously missing from the ranks of Pacific Northwest politicians has been a serious contender for president of the United States. Borah, Church, Jackson, and Morse all threw their hats into the ring, but none survived the primaries.[7] Running for president from a remote state containing 1 percent or less of the nation's population presented formidable obstacles (though Bill Clinton of Arkansas proved in 1992 that it is not impossible).

Also conspicuously missing were women of the Pacific Northwest who held office as governors and U.S. senators and representatives, although that began to change in recent years. Theirs was a saga of incremental political shifts that dates back at least to 1898 in Idaho, when Mary Wright, Hattie Noble, and Clara Campbell became the first women elected to one of the region's state legislatures. Bertha Knight Landes became the first chief executive of any big city in the United States when she was elected mayor of Seattle in 1926, though two years later she lost a campaign for reelection. Landes was both competent and progressive as mayor, but voters were irritated by the taunt, "What's the matter with you folks out there; haven't you got any men in Seattle that you have to have a woman for mayor?"[8]

Twenty years after Landes left office, Dorothy McCullough Lee became

7. Senator Charles McNary of Oregon ran for vice president on the Republican ticket headed by Wendell Willkie in 1940.

8. As quoted in Julia N. Budlong, "What Happened in Seattle," *Nation* 127 (29 August 1928): 197–98.

the first woman elected mayor of Portland. Earlier, she had been elected to the Oregon legislature in 1928 and to the state senate in 1932. Lee began her political career as a conservative Republican who gradually expanded her public agenda to include issues relating to women, children, and education (including backing state kindergartens), and old-age pensions. She was elected mayor of Portland in 1948 as a reformer who promised to clean up a serious crime problem. To newspaper photographers who wanted to record her historic victory with frivolous poses, Lee quipped, "There'll be no cheesecake, boys." She did don an apron for one shot but told onlookers that she was unable to boil water and that her husband did much of the family cooking. When she tried to clean up Portland's seamy side, including slot machine gambling, *Life* magazine called her "Dottie-Do-Good," a name that stuck. Lee survived a recall by people opposed to her anticrime crusade, but lost her bid for reelection in 1952.

When Barbara Roberts was elected governor of Oregon in 1990, she became a charter member of a select group of Northwest women governors that included Dixy Lee Ray of Washington. Oregon's first woman chief executive had previously served two terms as secretary of state and been the first woman House majority leader. Roberts proclaimed herself to be a strong advocate of public education and handicapped rights, but she was fated to serve at a time when voters approved a tax cut initiative that effectively mandated a reduction in all state programs and spending. Roberts, who chose not to run for reelection after a single term, did expand the number of women and minority appointees in Oregon government. Succeeding her was John Kitzhaber, also a Democrat.

Including the results of the 1994 election, nine Northwest women have served as members of Congress—five from Washington, two from Oregon, and two from Idaho; two more served in the U.S. Senate. Idaho Democrat Gracie Pfost was a member of the House of Representatives from 1953 to 1963, a total of five terms, and she is credited with playing a crucial role in the House passage of the Wilderness Act. Her nickname on Capitol Hill was "Hells Belle" because of her fight against private construction of dams in Hells Canyon. Defeated in her bid for a Senate seat, Pfost returned to Washington and took a position with the Federal Home Administration. Jolene Unsoeld, a Democrat, was elected from the southwest corner of Washington by a razor thin margin in 1988, and joining her as a member of the state's congressional delegation after the 1992 election was Jennifer Dunn, a Republican from a Seattle suburban district. Apart from Catherine May, who represented a largely rural district in southeastern Washington from 1959 to

1971, all other Northwest women sent to the House of Representatives were Democrats, though this changed in 1994 with the defeat of Unsoeld by Republican Linda Smith and a win by Republican Helen Chenoweth in Gracie Pfost's former district in Idaho.[9]

Following the unexpected death of Oregon's Senator Richard Neuberger in 1960, his wife, Maurine, completed his term and was elected to a full term of her own (1961–67) where she carried on her husband's unfinished work relating to billboard regulation and the Oregon Dunes park. She later became known for her own fight for smog-control legislation and a bill to convert the United States to the metric system. Only the third woman in U.S. history to serve in the Senate, like her husband she was a political pathbreaker. The second Northwest woman to serve in the Senate was Patty Murray, elected from Washington in 1992.

Another significant change noticeable in Pacific Northwest politics in the 1980s was the loss, at least temporarily, of the region's once legendary seniority and clout on Capitol Hill. The Reagan tide of 1980 helped sweep away the long careers of three powerful Northwest liberals in Congress: Warren G. Magnuson, six-term senator and head of the Appropriations Committee; Frank Church, head of the Foreign Relations Committee; and Oregon's twelve-term representative, Al Ullman, Ways and Means Committee leader. All three lost to conservative Republicans. The sudden death of Henry M. Jackson in 1983 further reduced the region's national political influence. The one conspicuous exception to this trend was the election of Thomas Foley of Spokane as Speaker of the House.

### ISSUES: FROM TAX CUTS TO CLEAR CUTS

No single topic dominated Pacific Northwest politics during the four decades after World War II. Instead, a series of issues competed for public attention. Many, like education, highway construction, public welfare, and taxes arose year after year to bedevil legislators, while others surfaced only briefly and were soon forgotten, leaving posterity to wonder what all the commotion was about.

For a time, primarily in the late 1940s and early 1950s, the Cold War and related fears of Communism were the major issue, especially in Washington, where conservative Republicans gained control of the state legislature

9. The Democrats are Nan Wood Honeyman, who represented northwestern Oregon from 1937 to 1939; Edith Green who represented the same district from 1955 to 1975; Julia Butler Hansen who represented southwestern Washington from 1960 to 1975; and Elizabeth Furse, elected in 1992 to represent northwestern Oregon.

## MR. SPEAKER FOLEY

When Thomas Foley of Spokane became the Speaker of the House of Representatives, he was the first person from the Far West to hold that powerful and prestigious office. As a result, probably no other Pacific Northwesterner, not even Idaho's William Edgar Borah, achieved greater prominence in the national and international political arenas. (Of course, Borah did not have C-Span and CNN to broadcast his every move.)

Foley, who represented Washington's Fifth District for more than thirty years, was first elected to the House of Representatives in 1964, one of sixty-seven new Democratic Congressmen who rode to Washington on President Lyndon Johnson's broad coattails. Henry Jackson persuaded the reluctant Foley to enter the race only hours before the filing deadline. Serving in the House longer than anyone else from Washington, Foley won the respect both of his constituents and colleagues, who chose him House majority whip in 1981, majority leader in 1987, and finally speaker in 1989 following the resignation of his predecessor, Jim Wright of Texas. Over the years the new Speaker developed an intimate knowledge of Capitol Hill power brokers and centers of influence.

A big (6 feet, 4 inches tall) and gregarious man of Irish ancestry, Foley had deep roots in his hometown of Spokane, where his paternal grandfather had once been foreman of the Great Northern Railway's boiler shops. The city's large Roman Catholic population was his original power base in the sprawling district that extended north from the Oregon border to the frontier of southern British Columbia.

Except for Spokane and such smaller cities as Walla Walla and Pullman, the district was largely rural and spanned a seemingly endless expanse of rangeland, wheat fields, and forests. It was also largely conservative, a fact that complicated life for Foley, who was clearly a liberal on many matters.

Foley opposed the death penalty but was pro-choice on abortion, a stance that dismayed the Christian right and probably did not gladden many of his Catholic constituents on whose support he always relied. For many years he opposed gun control, with the result that it was possible to see pickup trucks in his district sporting bumper stickers reading "This family is insured by Smith & Wesson" alongside another that simply said "Tom Foley." Foley bucked the Reagan landslide in 1980 by a narrow margin; yet in 1988 he won almost 80 percent of the vote.

In each of the various House leadership positions he held, including his time as chair of the Agriculture Committee from 1975 and 1980, Foley distinguished himself as a person who preferred consensus to confrontation. Perhaps for that reason, and despite an abundance of political savvy to draw upon, the easy-going Foley in 1992 found himself at the center of a storm of criticism focusing on forty years of lax administration and abuse at the House bank. His support in the House eroded to the point where it threatened his position as speaker. In 1994 disaffected voters replaced one of the most powerful lawmakers on Capitol Hill with Republican newcomer George Nethercutt. Not since 1860 had voters unseated a Speaker of the House.

in the 1946 election. A new Red Scare spilled out of the political arena and onto the campus of the University of Washington. Three professors were fired following a 1948 investigation by an un-American activities committee under the direction of the state representative Albert F. Canwell. Professors circulated an open letter criticizing the firing, but only 103 of a faculty of 700 signed it. Illustrating what would happen on other campuses during the McCarthy era, the University of Washington became the nation's first institution of higher learning to dismiss tenured professors for being members of the Communist party.

In the long run, though, it was probably questions of taxation, resource development, and related concerns over environmental degradation that generated the most debate, with taxes and the environment clearly emerging as defining issues in the 1990s. The debate over taxes gained a high profile in the 1990s because the region's mushrooming population required that state and local revenues be spent for basic services like roads and schools before funds could be raised by expanding the existing tax base; at the same time, many long-time residents were angered that their increasing real estate values translated into higher property taxes.

Controversy over taxes was nothing new: Oregon voters had on several occasions rejected a sales tax, and Washingtonians did the same to an income tax. What was different in the 1990s was the Draconian approach that voters took to tax matters. In Oregon they successfully backed Initiative Measure 5 in 1990, a statewide property tax limitation that capped spending for public schools and government operations. By creating budget shortfalls in 1991 and 1992, it forced deep cuts in state and local services. When in the 1993 election Oregon voters rejected a sales tax measure to replace revenues lost through Measure 5, Governor Barbara Roberts ordered a $200 million cut in the administration of state government, an amount equal to 8 to 10 percent of most budgets. No one could predict where the cycle of cuts would end.

Yet another tax revolt erupted in Washington, where the state's government began the decade of the 1980s as a $3 billion a year enterprise and ended it costing twice as much. As the expense of state government increased, so inevitably did taxes: the sales tax rate climbed from a basic 4.5 cents on the dollar to 6.5 (with more added on by local governments) and the state gasoline tax grew from 12 to 18 cents a gallon. In 1980 there was one state employee for every sixty-two permanent Washington residents; ten years later there was one for every fifty-eight residents. Such statistics were not lost on the tax protesters.

475

The result, following a new round of tax hikes by the legislature in early 1993, was a tax revolt in the form of two initiatives presented to voters in the fall election. The more drastic of the two measures, which would roll back the recent tax and fee hikes approved by the legislature, failed; but Initiative 601 narrowly passed, mandating that future state tax increases be indexed to a combination of population growth and inflation and making such increases more difficult for the legislature to enact.

In Idaho, where a balance of sales and income taxes already existed, backers of an initiative to limit property taxes to 1 percent of assessed value lost in the 1992 election because a powerful coalition of opponents from business and education convinced a majority of voters that passing the One Percent initiative would be the beginning of a downhill slide for Idaho. "Many of us saw the deterioration of California after their initiative [Proposition 13] passed." Proponents of tax cuts vowed to try again, their hopes buoyed no doubt by the success of tax revolts in neighboring states. Regardless of the outcome, the 1990s may well be remembered as the time when angry voters finally forced state governments to streamline and economize the way they delivered public services.

In recent years various other controversies have centered on dams and water resources, on scenic back country (and, eventually, on wilderness lands in general), and on pollution—nuclear waste and heavy metals and acid rain in the some of the region's rivers. An overview of these issues, collectively the Pacific Northwest environment at risk, offers a fitting way to conclude the history of a region where politics, economics, and even the arts are closely linked to the natural setting.

CHAPTER 22

# Environment at Risk

\*

Below Wallace, the valley of the Coeur d'Alene R[iver] is like something out
of Dante's "Inferno." In the days before measures were taken against stream
pollution, the R[iver] overflowed every spring, carrying mine wastes into
the bottoms & destroying all vegetation.—*The American Guide* (1949)

\*

In the Pacific Northwest, as in few other parts of the United States, regional
identity is almost wholly linked to natural setting. The Pacific Northwest
without its mountains, its rugged coastline, its Puget Sound fogs, its vast
interior of sagebrush, rimrock, and big sky is as unthinkable as New England without a Puritan heritage, the South without the Lost Cause, the
Midwest without its agricultural cornucopia, or California without its gold
rush mentality.

In the Pacific Northwest, however, nature long had to perform double
duty. While on one hand she was revered as a source of aesthetic pleasure
and outdoor recreation, on the other she was exploited and abused to provide profits and jobs. Until the twentieth century there was little tension
between these two views of the environment. Nature had so lavished her
favors on the region that few could conceive of her limits—or wanted to.
Wilderness was something to be subdued, and water had a limitless capacity to absorb the effluents of industry. Even in the latter part of the twentieth century, the pioneer's belief in nature's abundance refused to die, despite considerable evidence of nature's limits.

To early settlers of the region, nature assumed heroic proportions. People

477

TIMBER BILLIONS OF THE PACIFIC NORTHWEST: THE VIEW FROM 1923

*Timber!* Two axmen run as they shout the warning; a forest giant snaps its last supporting sinews, moves with majestic grace as the topmost branches soar through the sky, gathers momentum quickly and falls with a swelling roar and crash. Two hundred feet of strait timber. All the years since Columbus are recorded in its concentric rings—its log of life—and the last one measures twenty-four feet! A great historian is dead. But the life of service has just begun. Three more families can have homes.

*Timber!*

On a thousand hills, from a thousand slopes, comes the woodcutter's cry. A battle cry! The nation's great forest reserve is going into action. An industrial army is on the march. From the timberlands of the East, from the pine regions of the South, from the Great Lakes region comes this army of might and men to the virgin forests of the Pacific Northwest. Wartime destruction and peacetime construction both have swelled its ranks. Great sawmills are unlimbered. Hundreds of logging camps are pushing back the forest frontier. Cities with a permanent economic support in lumber are springing up. One hundred and fifty thousand men in camps and mills are producing nearly one-third the nation's lumber cut.— *Timber Billions of the Pacific Northwest* (1923)

used words like *endless, inexhaustible,* and *spectacular* to describe the land and its resources. Trees like the Douglas fir, sometimes 12 feet in diameter at the base and more than 200 feet tall, were incomparably larger than anything pioneers had known in the East; the fertile topsoil of the Willamette Valley was thought to be a dozen feet deep; and year after year the rivers and tidal estuaries yielded their abundance of fish, clams, and other edibles. When the tide was out, the table was set, according to a pioneer saying. Perpetually snow-clad mountains like Hood, Rainier, and Baker awed and inspired their beholders, and their beauty together with a general lack of severe and destructive storms heightened the impression that nature especially favored the Pacific Northwest. "Here are the greatest and most valuable forests on the continent, if not in the world, an apparently inexhaustible supply of timber," observed Ray Stannard Baker in 1903, adding that "one may travel for days through the primeval forests and see not the slightest evidence of men. So dense is the timber that an entire logging crew will work for months on a few acres of land."[1] This was when trees were cut fifteen feet from the ground to save a little sawing, although a single stump contained a thousand board feet or more of the best possible timber, and

1. Ray Stannard Baker, "The Great Northwest," *Century Magazine* 65 (March 1903): 656.

steam donkey fires were fed clear logs. Nothing but the best timber went to market.

And so loggers felled the trees—letting daylight into the swamp they called it—with wasteful methods and a misplaced confidence that the region's forests were without end; farmers worried little about conserving the topsoil; fishermen assumed there would always be another big catch; and industries dumped wastes into the Willamette River and Puget Sound, certain that they could always dispose of more. A day of reckoning inevitably arrived, and with it the loss of jobs, diminished yields, and bankruptcies. In a region so heavily dependent upon the bounties of nature, abuse and exhaustion of natural resources raised searching questions about long-term economic adjustments and about the future of the region itself. Coming face to face with nature's limitations—a confrontation especially traumatic in the forest products industry in recent years—produced unease and something of an identity crisis in a region where economic well-being had long been rooted in nature's largesse. This brief examination of an environment at risk reveals a region standing at a major crossroads in its history.

## A CHANGING LANDSCAPE

Humans have left their mark on the landscape since they first arrived in the Pacific Northwest. Indians occasionally set fire to the forest and thereby altered small portions of their surroundings. But the Indian impress was for the most part subtle and nearly invisible compared to the impact of whites —settlers and non-resident exploiters. Whites not only surveyed the land and laid out their farms and towns in more or less artificial geometric patterns, but they also hastened depletion of natural resources, a characteristic first observed in the maritime fur trade. But that first encounter with nature's limits meant little to a region blessed with so many other resources to exploit.

In the late 1870s commercial fishermen on the lower Columbia noticed diminished catches, and during that decade Oregon took its first halting steps toward conservation. Industry simply shifted its attention to the waters of Puget Sound and continued its profligate ways. The idea that Americans should conserve their abundant natural resources simply had little appeal until the early twentieth century, and even then it remained unpopular in the developing Northwest.

The battle between development and conservation—and later preservation—would be waged on many fronts during the twentieth century. A popular general concern for the environment is relatively recent, however.

479

82. An abandoned farm fifteen miles south of Boardman, Oregon. Badly overgrazed land was subject to
wind erosion. Courtesy Oregon State University Archives, P89:251.

Before the 1970s, environmental concerns tended to be restricted to protection of a single natural resource so as to preserve profits and livelihoods.
Later, pollution came to be viewed as a threat to public health or recreational activities like swimming and sport fishing. Attention then focused
on a particular lake or river. Only since the 1970s has a significant portion of
the public viewed environmental matters philosophically or in terms of
comprehensive biological systems and processes. Indicative of changing
attitudes was the Washington legislature's creation of the Department of
Ecology in 1970 and its passage a year later of the state's comprehensive
Environmental Policy Act. Oregon's Department of Environmental Quality
dates from 1969.

One of the earliest cases of environmental concern expressed as a need to
protect jobs and profits occurred in the 1920s, when people realized that
there were limits to Puget Sound's magnificent water resources, a concern

raised first by the growing number of sulfite-process pulp mills along its shores. The problem was not so much the stench in the air as it was the pulp liquor that flowed untreated into Puget Sound. The waters of the sound had long absorbed the organic wastes of fish canneries without difficulty, although residents sometimes complained about the smell, but not even crabs and barnacles could survive in waters laden with pulp liquor.

The prospects of a paper mill in Shelton alarmed commercial oyster growers, who raised the shellfish in beds protected by networks of dikes. In June 1926 they appealed to the state supervisor of fisheries for protection from harmful effluents, but officials did nothing, for oyster growing was a small-scale enterprise with no great influence in Olympia. The yield of the beds declined, and the industry's fear of pollution—primarily a simple matter of economics—proved well founded.

The need to conserve a declining resource for economic reasons also prompted commercial salmon fishermen and cannery operators to address environmental issues. Here was an industry that at one time ranked second only to timber in importance. But the Northwest salmon pack peaked between 1910 and 1919 and declined afterwards. In an effort to halt the downward trend, commercial fishermen and an influential legion of sportfishermen joined forces in the 1920s against destructive practices on Puget Sound. Their primary concern was a proliferation of fish traps. These became illegal in Oregon in 1927 and in Washington five years later.

The law failed to address the fact that net-fishing boats powered by internal-combustion engines were simply too efficient to insure the industry's long-term survival. Craft of that type first appeared on Puget Sound shortly before the First World War, and their numbers increased after the Second World War. Technological advances such as hydraulic-powered winches first employed in the mid-1950s to work a salmon seine net made them still more efficient. Fishing periods had to be shortened to avoid complete depletion of the fish, but short seasons made it difficult for commercial fishermen to earn a living, much less a profit. Clear-cutting along stream banks exposed spawning grounds to the sun's heat, warming the water, and killing salmon fry, which are sensitive to variations in temperature. Removing the riparian vegetation also diminished the insect populations, a source of food needed to sustain the fish population. Some logging practices literally buried the streams in which fish spawned.

In their fight for survival, commercial fishermen eventually turned against their former allies, the sportfishermen, although both groups opposed the pulp mills that continued to dump whatever they liked into Puget

---

### THE BOLDT DECISION

To non-Indian commercial fishermen, the Boldt decision of 1974 (*United States* v. *Washington*) compounded the problems besetting their declining industry. In a 254-page decision that drew heavily on the region's history and anthropology, federal judge George Boldt ruled that treaty Indians of Puget Sound were entitled to half of all fish that passed, or normally would pass, by the "usual and accustomed grounds and stations" and that could be caught without endangering the runs.

Indians had long contended that treaties signed in 1854 and 1855 with Isaac I. Stevens guaranteed them the right to continue fishing at all their traditional locations regardless of state laws. To emphasize their concern, In-

dians staged "fish-ins" during the early 1970s. Those acts of civil disobedience were similar to the "freedom rides" that blacks staged in the South in the early 1960s, and both forms of protest occasionally resulted in violence.

To Indians, the Boldt decision represented vindication. To white fishermen, it meant that they were suddenly competing for half as many fish and that Indians now had the other half to themselves. Even after the United States Supreme Court upheld Boldt's decision in 1979, the issue remained a sensitive and potentially explosive blend of economics and race. Boldt was burned in effigy, vilified, and accused of having an Indian mistress; he also received several death threats.

---

Sound. More than anything else, the mills became regional symbols of pollution. The movement that oystermen had initiated in a limited way during the 1920s was taken up by sport fishermen, and in 1945 a bill passed the Washington legislature establishing the state's first independent pollution control board. It was a landmark, but at first the board lacked enough power to be effective, and certainly not all the sound's pollution was caused by pulp and paper mills.

In the mid-1950s, concern about pollution and public health caused residents of the Seattle area to do something about the sewage dumped into Lake Washington. After a lengthy battle, proponents of a big pipeline linking communities around the lake to a treatment plant won a crucial bond vote. The METRO project represented one of the earliest commitments to fight pollution made by any major metropolitan area in the United States. Within a decade Lake Washington was nearly as clean as it once had been.

But Puget Sound remained an object of environmental concern. A federal government report indicated as early as 1951 that the Sound was the sixth most polluted area in the United States. But attempts to control the discharge of pulp liquor by requiring the industry to use evaporating ponds raised community hackles in Port Angeles, Bellingham, and other communities that depended on the manufacture of pulp and paper and feared that pollution control measures would cause the mills to close.

Concern mounted in 1969 when a company announced that it planned to lay an oil pipeline under Puget Sound. The Northern Tier project was part of a scheme to transport Alaskan oil to the Midwest. Arriving by supertanker at Port Angeles on the Olympic Peninsula, oil would flow east from that point by pipeline. Opponents ranging from Indian tribes to the Sierra Club feared that if the underwater line ever sprang a leak, the resulting spill would create a monumental disaster, killing wildlife and perhaps permanently fouling one of the state's great natural attractions. Although Washington's Democratic governor, Dixy Lee Ray, favored the project, another and far more powerful Democrat, Senator Warren G. Magnuson, did not. Responding to a rising chorus of complaints from environmentalists, he promoted legislation that effectively killed the project.

Even without the pipeline, Puget Sound faced a severe pollution problem. The Washington legislature in 1985 formulated a long-term clean-up plan and provided preliminary funding through a tobacco tax. The cleanup of Puget Sound could ultimately cost from $4 billion to $14 billion, more money than it took to build the Alaska pipeline.

The Oregon equivalent of the cleanup of Lake Washington centered on the Willamette River, where the battle cry was sounded by conservation groups that described the river as a "stinking, slimy mess" and by Tom McCall's award-winning documentary "Pollution in Paradise." Even Idaho, despite the vastness of its virtually uninhabited backcountry, grappled with major pollution problems. For decades the south fork of the Coeur d'Alene River transported a dangerous load of zinc, cadmium, and lead from numerous mine tailings to the muddy bottom of seemingly pristine Lake Coeur d'Alene.

The lead level in the Coeur d'Alene River delta in the mid-1980s ranged from one thousand to eight thousand parts per million; a normal range was fifteen to twenty parts per million background count. That was perhaps the highest lead level recorded in United States waters. Over the years, high mountain streams leached through mine wastes and kept depositing toxic sediments along the downstream banks. As early as 1932 an investigator recommended construction of settling ponds to deal with the problem, but not until 1968 when mining firms were subjected to heavy pressure from state and federal governments did they take that step. A study conducted for the U.S. Geological Survey in 1992 characterized the bottom of Lake Coeur d'Alene as the world's most heavy metal–contaminated site.

Of no less concern to many people was the polluted air that drifted above the Coeur d'Alene River and the Silver Valley during the decades from the opening of a large smelter at Kellogg in 1917 until it closed in 1981. The

83. Concerns about polluted rivers in the Pacific Northwest had been voiced on various occasions well before
the heightened public consciousness of the 1960s and
1970s. On November 6, 1938, Portland's mayor Joseph
Carson joined with students demonstrating for a Clean
River measure with a band and placards. Courtesy
Oregon Historical Society, CN 001253.

highest levels of sulfur dioxide gas recorded in the United States made the
soil so acidic that it could not support plant life, and the forest and mountain landscape around one of the world's chief sources of silver and lead
became almost lunaresque in its bleakness. In addition, along Interstate 90
outside Kellogg arose a jet-black mountain composed of millions of tons of
smelter tailings. Until the late 1980s, unknowing city officials spread this
sand-like waste on icy winter streets, leaving a residue of toxic heavy metals to run off into yards, puddles, and storm sewers.

Gulf Resources, which owned the massive Bunker Hill smelter complex,
knew as early as 1972 about the health hazards of lead emitted from its
smelter stacks. At that time it relocated salaried employees from areas
downwind of its smelter stacks and razed their houses. But court records
show that Gulf Resources never warned its wageworkers that they and their

families were at risk. In 1981, soon after settling a multimillion-dollar lawsuit involving the lead-poisoned children of two employees, Gulf closed its mine and smelter complex, putting twenty-two hundred Bunker Hill employees out of work. Gulf sold the property a year later, not long before the federal Environmental Protection Agency placed the twenty-one square miles of the Silver Valley on its Superfund National Priority List to be cleaned up by dollars from federal sources and from mining companies and their insurers. That was little comfort to the parents of school children in Kellogg who recorded abnormally high levels of lead in their blood. Only in the early 1990s was it revealed that the Gulf USA Corporation had shifted $160 million in assets (the bulk of which had been pledged to clean up the Bunker Hill Superfund site) mainly to commercial real estate ventures in New Zealand. In 1993 the company filed for bankruptcy, thus adding the pensions of retirees to the endangered category, and possibly leaving Idaho taxpayers to pay the bill for the pollution mess.

Mining, metal-processing, and pulp mill wastes from Montana increasingly fouled the waters of another northern Idaho river, the Clark Fork, which flows into Lake Pend Oreille. Cleanup will necessarily require cooperation between the two states or federal intervention.

Water and more recently air pollution were two of the Northwest's most talked about environmental problems because they most directly affected the region's largest urban centers, but problems with the land proved serious, too, though many residents remained unaware of them. To pioneers, no natural resource seemed more abundant than land. But how land could be abused and exhausted under the impact of agricultural technology could clearly be seen in the fertile Palouse country of eastern Washington and northern Idaho.

Before the rolling hills of the Palouse became synonymous with the highest wheat yields per acre in the United States, they formed a bunchgrass-covered rangeland favored by sheep and cattle raisers. Toward the latter part of the nineteenth century, new barbed wire fences marked the boundaries of an ever-increasing amount of land devoted to wheat. But with sodbusting came the new problems of the rapid spread of alien weeds and soil erosion.

When it rained, silt-laden water coursed down the steep hillsides and turned the once sparkling Palouse River into a sluggish, dirty stream; after 1910 dust storms became frequent. Despite the warnings of experts, as long as the fertile land produced good crops, farmers did little to stop the soil loss. The historian and agribusinessman Alexander C. McGregor estimated that one small conservation district in Whitman County annually lost the equivalent of a 148-mile-long train of gondola cars filled with silt. A scientist observed in 1973 that the worst soil erosion in the United States was in the Palouse country. There were no easy solutions, however, because alternative methods of farming such as minimum tillage only increased the need for herbicides to kill the weeds not removed by plowing and disking. Moreover, potentially dangerous levels of nitrates from fertilizer began appearing in private wells in the early 1990s, affecting the quality of drinking water in the Palouse country.

Land abuse was not just a matter of soil erosion but also of lack of vision and poor planning. At the time Washington's constitution was written in 1889, the public owned the state's tidelands. But the 1889–90 legislature authorized their sale to private individuals. When the practice was halted in 1971, some 60 percent of Washington's noncoastal tidelands were in private hands.

Public planning designed to prevent private abuse of the land took a different turn in Oregon. As early as 1899 Clatsop County declared its beaches to be a public highway. Governor Oswald West declared that Oregon beaches were public highways in 1911, and two years later the state extended the right of public access to all its beaches. The enactment of senate bill 100 in 1973 called for all cities and counties to adopt comprehensive planning to meet state standards known as Statewide Planning Goals.

ENDANGERED SPECIES: "IF IT'S HOOTIN', I'M SHOOTIN'"

Two natural resources above all others served as potent symbols of regional identity, and both were at the center of stormy controversies that erupted in the late 1980s and early 1990s and extended from remote corners of the Pacific Northwest all the way to the White House and Capitol Hill. These two natural resources were trees and salmon.

Tall trees, loggers, and sawmills are so much a part of the region's identity that it is impossible to imagine the Pacific Northwest without them. In a region where trees stood nearly as high as the Washington Monument, were often taller than the Statue of Liberty, and were sometimes so large that whole families lived in the stumps, trees are woven into literature, history, and leisure. They are also an integral part of the economy and the built environment. Salmon was an equally powerful regional symbol: its single-minded drive to leap rapids and small waterfalls to return home to spawn connoted endurance and vigor, and it epitomized the region's wildness. Salmon not only buoyed the regional economy but also sustained

Native Americans from earliest times and figured prominently in their religious and cultural lives. Both salmon and trees (or more accurately, the region's remaining old-growth forests) were thrust into the public spotlight as a result of the federal Endangered Species Act of 1973.

As early as the 1930s, depletion of the region's timber supply had a profound and unsettling impact on some Pacific Northwesterners who began to question the prevailing conviction that there would always be more trees to cut. For years the philosophy of "cut and run" had led to tremendous waste, social dislocation, and community instability as one district after another was logged, but what to do with the newly denuded land seemed to be the most pressing concern.

If it was federal land, the matter was left to Uncle Sam. Logged-off land in private hands might be sold to stump farmers, who attempted to coax a meager living from the thin soil, or it might simply be abandoned to avoid tax liabilities. Another possibility was reforestation. The Weyerhaeuser Timber Company in 1941 initiated the development of tree farms. The dream was to reforest logged-off land so as to produce a sustained yield, but many smaller businesses did not have the financial strength or vision necessary to operate a successful reforestation program. After all, a company needed a source of income until new growth timber matured some thirty or forty years later. Sustained yield remained an elusive goal, especially when companies might refocus their attention on maturing stands of second growth timber in the South.

During the 1980s popular concern shifted from logging trees and sustained yields to the even more complex matter of logging whole forests and thereby endangering species, specifically the northern spotted owl. This shy creature, standing barely a foot tall and weighing no more than 22 ounces, would figure so prominently in the ranging controversy over the region's forest resources that in June 1990 it was featured on the cover of *Time* magazine. The spotted owl, however, was really only a symbol of a larger issue. Because the United States does not have an "Endangered Ecosystem Act," environmentalists seized upon the endangered status of this rare, seldom-seen bird in an effort to save its habitat, the dwindling old-growth forests located in western Washington and Oregon and northern California. In other words, the bird became a surrogate for a much larger issue, and a legal device enabling environmentalists to force consideration of old-growth forests.

Many would argue that the old-growth forests constituted a national treasure, not unlike Yellowstone National Park or the Grand Canyon.

Across the nation, less than 10 percent of these forests remained uncut. Perhaps it is important to emphasize here that these forests are not just stands of trees, but large and interdependent communities of wildlife, filtering sponges for clean water, and green lungs that breathe out oxygen. The forest industry had long emphasized that wood was "America's Renewable Resource," but no tree farm had the biodiversity of a mossy old-growth forest, which like an oil reserve or an extinct species was gone forever when it disappeared.

During the early 1980s, when recession hobbled the Northwest timber industry, some communities witnessed an odd new form of polarization as management and labor joined forces against environmentalists, the more militant of whom opposed all forms of logging. Particularly in old-growth forests, environmental zealots engaged in guerrilla warfare by driving large metal spikes into tree trunks. This form of sabotage had the potential to maim a logger using a chainsaw or shatter a high-speed bandsaw and spray shards of steel across a mill.

The so-called spotted owl controversy first sent shivers through the region's timber industry in 1989 when it sparked a series of lawsuits that halted logging of owl habitat in old-growth forests. When the federal Fish and Wildlife Service officially declared the owl a threatened species in June 1990, citing excessive logging as a threat to its survival and thereby triggering legal mechanisms that could drastically curtail logging on federal lands, emotions boiled over. Bumper stickers proclaimed the battle lines: "I Like Spotted Owls—Fried" versus "Save an Owl, Educate a Logger."

In many ways the controversy that swirled about the twenty-five hundred pairs of northern spotted owls merely hastened an inevitable day of reckoning, forcing people to consider the long-term consequences of logging. In the late 1980s, a logger could fell a six-hundred-year-old Douglas fir in fifteen minutes, and enough old-growth trees were removed from the Pacific Northwest each year to fill a convoy of trucks twenty thousand miles long. Many sawmills would have inevitably closed for lack of logs even had there been no owl. The Pacific Northwest timber industry was simply running out of suitable places to cut. With old-growth forests disappearing from private lands and extensive stands of second-growth timber not yet ready to harvest, Pacific Northwest members of Congress pressured the Forest Service to make more timber available during the 1980s, although federal forests could not support the heightened level of cutting without sustaining severe environmental degradation.

When Seattle federal judge William Dwyer first froze most timber sales in the spring of 1991 to protect spotted owl habitat, outrage and alarm erupted in timber towns of western Washington. On the Olympic peninsula, annual timber harvests plunged to just 14 percent of their 1970s peak because of court decisions involving the spotted owls.

Critics complained that the Endangered Species Act was never intended to serve as a tool for radical environmental groups to use against timber workers. John Krogh, a rancher and president of the Washington Cattlemen's Association, warned in mid-1992 that the Endangered Species Act "is being used as an effective tool to stop economic growth, by preservationist groups who are intent on destroying the livelihoods of millions of Americans."[2] People like Krogh proposed to make the act more responsive to economic considerations when it came up for renewal before Congress.

In many Pacific Northwest towns, logging was not just an industry; it was the only industry. In such communities signs proclaiming "This Family Supported By Timber Dollars" appeared in the windows of homes to emphasize the obvious economic relationship. Equally important, the loss of timber jobs had a "multiplier effect" in one-industry towns, causing the loss of tax dollars needed to support police, firefighters, libraries, and schools. At the same time, unemployment contributed to increased child abuse, mental instability, and crime. Even rumors of mill closures contributed to free-floating anxiety and plummeting morale among loggers and sawmill workers. Their common fear was, "Will it be me?" In many cases it was, for in the Pacific Northwest between 1990 and 1993 a total of 132 sawmills and plywood mills closed.

Worsening the problem of supply for timber towns was the increasing number of raw logs shipped from the Pacific Northwest to Asian sawmills. Japan, Korea, and Taiwan, rather than local economies, got the jobs. Federal law banned the export of raw logs from federal land, but Pacific Northwest companies could process federal timber even as they shipped raw logs from their own timberlands abroad. Thus even as mills were closing and towns dying for lack of timber, private companies were sending much of their own unprocessed timber overseas. In 1988, 3.7 billion board feet of raw logs were exported from Oregon and Washington, a quarter of the total cut for those two states. "It is a paradox . . . to have a dwindling supply of logs for mills in the Northwest, and at the same time you can go out to Port Angeles and see logs stacked to the sky, as far as the eye can see, destined for mills and jobs in Japan," observed Interior Secretary Bruce Babbitt in March 1993.[3]

The controversy over the future of Northwest forests became so encom-

2. *Spokesman-Review*, 14 June 1992, sec. A, p. 15.
3. *Spokesman-Review*, 23 March 1993, sec. B, p. 2.

passing that in April 1993 President Bill Clinton convened a much bally-hooed "Forest Summit" in Portland, Oregon, where he optimistically promised to end the gridlock. The nation's chief executive even ordered his cabinet to resolve the forest controversy within 60 days by finding a "balanced solution," although Clinton admitted that it would be difficult to make both the industry and the environmentalists happy.

The following summer, the Clinton administration proposed a plan that would sharply reduce logging on federal land in the old-growth timber area at the heart of the controversy. It predicted that nine thousand jobs would be lost as a result, but industry sources pegged the number at closer to eighty-five thousand when related jobs were included, and predicted a series of devastated timber towns. Loggers, who saw the issue as owls versus jobs, protested the Clinton compromise by tossing empty caskets on a flaming pyre and sending a funeral wreath to the White House (the Clinton administration did propose a $1.2 billion aid package to help timber communities diversify their economies), while conservationists opposed *any* additional logging in the remaining old growth forests. More than ever the Pacific Northwest seemed divided into two polarized groups, each in its own way equally enamored of trees.

Loggers, no less than environmentalists, saw themselves as caring deeply about trees and the environment because of their jobs. But in addition to the old-growth timber woes, they also endured the highest fatality rate among Oregon occupations. More than two thousand loggers were killed in Oregon between 1945 and 1990, twice the number of Oregonians who died in the Vietnam War. The most dangerous job was timber falling, where about one in a hundred workers died each year; one in six loggers suffered a debilitating injury each year.[4]

Part of the problem faced by Pacific Northwest loggers was that their numbers were dwindling. Oregon was the most timber-dependent state in 1992, but while it gained 219,000 jobs overall during the past decade, it lost another 25,400 lumber and wood products jobs mainly through mill automation and greater log exports. As of the early 1990s the timber industry provided only about 5 percent of all Oregon jobs. The region's politicians could not ignore the reality that, although loggers were losing their clout, a growing number of voters hated to look at denuded mountainsides and supported the environmentalists. It was equally clear that the Pacific Northwest was not experiencing just another cycle of boom-and-bust in its

4. *Oregonian* (Portland), 29 November 1990, 16.

timber regions but a historic and long-term restructuring of its economy (and perhaps its attitudes).

In any case, between October 1992 and March 1993 lumber prices nearly doubled, sending American homebuilders into near panic and causing them to join with the timber industry to blame the crisis on environmentalists. The United States Wildlife Federation responded that wood prices were high in part because 8 percent of the nation's timber harvest was exported in 1992.

The debate over dwindling salmon runs occurred almost simultaneously with the spotted owl controversy and was an equally defining moment in the region's history. In fact, the two debates over endangered species were in many ways interconnected. The old-growth forest habitat of the spotted owl was also home to spawning Pacific salmon and some three hundred other threatened species. The endangered fish, like the spotted owl, functioned as a symbol of a much larger issue. Yet controversy over spotted owls paled next to the battle over the future of Pacific salmon, protection of which could have profound consequences for users of the vast Columbia River system, including shippers, fishermen, electric ratepayers, and farmers. If endangered runs of salmon are lost, an estimated sixty thousand jobs will vanish in fishing and related industries.

At one time it was believed that hatcheries would solve the problem of declining salmon runs, but during the last fifty years, even with hatcheries pumping millions of fish into the Columbia River system, salmon runs continued to decline dramatically. Some people looked upon the problem of salmon recovery as solved once and for all by the 1980 Northwest Power Act, which mandated that a four-state Northwest Power Planning Council bring back the remaining salmon population. The historic level of 16 million wild salmon was impossible to attain because whole river drainages have been blocked by dam building since the mid-1930s, but the council set a goal to increase their numbers from 2.5 million to 5 million. Twelve years later the total salmon population had increased by only a few hundred thousand, while the number of wild fish had dropped to about half a million fish. Wild salmon that spawn in streams, as distinct from hatchery-raised fish, are critical to survival of the species. The Northwest Power Planning Council seemed incapable of addressing the fact that dams were responsible for more than 90 percent of all human-caused salmon mortality.

The ultimate solution to the problem would inevitably involve painful choices: lowering water levels behind Columbia and lower Snake River dams could flush the young fish to sea more quickly, but this would halt barge traffic for months at a time. The Grand Coulee Dam has become a symbol of what ails the fish, but that dam alone produces about the same amount of electricity as six nuclear power plants, which are not popular in the Pacific Northwest. Saving endangered salmon runs could also mean closing public campsites near spawning grounds, forcing cattle off grazing lands, and pitting Idaho against its downstream neighbors, Oregon and Washington.

Biologists in 1989 believed the Idaho sockeye would soon join the hundred or so other genetically distinct runs of wild salmon (including steelhead) that have vanished since dams were built on the Columbia River drainage system. Decades ago the seagoing sockeye flourished. In 1881 one gold miner snagged more than 500 of the four-pound sockeyes in a single day; he fed these to dozens of prospectors in the jagged Sawtooth mountains of central Idaho. But in the fall of 1991, four sockeye salmon returned the 900 miles from the Pacific Ocean to spawn in Idaho's Redfish Lake, a lake named for the sockeye which turn bright red when spawning. That year, the Snake River sockeye was added to the nation's endangered species list. In the fall of 1992, only one fish returned, and scientists believed that the lone sockeye salmon swimming in a concrete tank at the state fishery near Redfish Lake was Idaho's last wild sockeye salmon.

Leading the drive to protect dwindling salmon runs was Idaho's governor Cecil D. Andrus, former Secretary of the Interior, a conservationist, and strong backer of the Endangered Species Act. He threatened legal action to increase water flow on the Columbia and Snake River system by diverting more from irrigation, hydroelectric power, and river transport to meet the needs of anadromous fish. After the 1993 Forest Summit in Portland, Andrus met separately with President Clinton to press the fight to save Idaho's dwindling salmon runs.

In Idaho, there was plenty of pristine salmon habitat: the eight major dams on the Snake and Columbia Rivers were killing the state's endangered and threatened runs, complained Andrus in the fall of 1993. He blasted one salmon recovery plan proposed by a team of scientists for lacking a sense of urgency: he called them "academicians who order salmon in a restaurant and don't know what it is in the river." Their solution—which called for barging or trucking fish around dams—ignored the fact that after twenty years that approach had already left runs in a debilitated condition. Andrus joined with Washington governor Mike Lowry, Oregon's Barbara Roberts, and Montana's Marc Racicot to urge President Clinton to appoint a "salmon czar" to coordinate the work of federal agencies on this critical matter.

Meanwhile, a downriver group of aluminum producers threatened to sue

It is ironic that Cecil Andrus began his long political career as a logger from timber-dependent Clearwater County. He waged his first campaign for governor in 1970 only after the Democratic nominee died in an accident. In a public address given in 1979 when he was Secretary of the Interior, Andrus observed:

"When I was growing up here in the Northwest, we lived in the midst of a great, relatively undeveloped area. De facto wilderness was abundant. Pressures of growth were the farthest things from our minds.

"Even twenty years ago when I was a young man struggling to support my family in what I called the 'slab, sliver, and knothole business,' we had little realization of the stresses we were starting to put on the land, or of the severe stresses about to close in on us. Regretfully, I can recall skidding logs down streambeds—because that was the easiest way to move them—and because those of us in logging in those good old days simply did not know any better. We were too engrossed in the everyday effort of earning a living to consider the long-term damage our activity might cause to fish and wildlife, to the streams, river and watershed, to the forests, and to the land itself. We thought, as our parents and grandparents and earlier generations had thought, that the natural resources of this continent were inexhaustible."— Cecil D. Andrus, address at the University of Idaho, 27 April 1979

Idaho for diverting Snake River water for irrigation in violation of the Endangered Species Act. Andrus denounced their claim as the downstream industrialists' "long-awaited Idaho water grab." He warned that "if they get their way, the water that helps raise Idaho crops and sustains our economy will be siphoned off to keep them from having to do anything to change the way they do business."[5]

Along the coast of Oregon, once-thriving sport and commercial fishing industries seemed doomed because salmon were also in trouble in coastal streams all along the Pacific. The year 1992 was rated the worst commercial fishing season to date. The bad news seemed worse because during the 1980s the U.S. government spent about a billion dollars in the Pacific Northwest to rebuild salmon runs and other wildlife affected by federal hydroelectric dams. Equally discouraging was the fact that the region's watersheds and rivers were declining toward such biotic impoverishment that the condition could become in large part irreversible. In April 1992, conservation group American Rivers placed the Columbia and Snake River system at the top of its list of the twenty-five most endangered rivers in the United

5. *Spokesman-Review*, 21 October 1993, sec. B, p. 5; *Lewiston Tribune*, 20 October 1993, sec. A, p. 5.

States because of the hydroelectric dams that caused a massive decline in the river's population of sockeye salmon.

Livability was a quality often attributed to Pacific Northwest towns and cities during the 1970s. But whether cities of the next generation remain livable remains to be seen. Portland, which had taken great pride in its ranking as the nation's most livable city in 1975, slipped to eighth place in 1981 and to sixty-third place in 1985. Uncertainties cloud the future of the region's outdoor recreation facilities, too.

The Pacific Northwest's environment remains vulnerable on two fronts. One is thoughtless development and the other is pollution. Development is not simply a matter of filling in wetlands to create a golf course or a condominium complex. It also means the transformation of prime agricultural land into look-alike suburban housing tracts and other tasteless outgrowths of metropolitan America. And it means damming scenic canyons to control floods or produce electricity.

One of the monumental political battles in the Pacific Northwest since the Second World War has centered on damming up the Snake River's scenic Hells Canyon. The controversy began in 1950 and ultimately ended up in the U.S. Supreme Court. It pitted proponents of private power against backers of public power and both of them against proponents of preservation, an issue that arose in the mid-1960s and gradually won the day. Environmental concerns helped turn a local issue into a national one.

In 1964 the Federal Power Commission granted a license to the Pacific Northwest Power Company—a consortium of privately owned utilities—to construct High Mountain Sheep Dam on the middle Snake River. People interested in public power development appealed to the U.S. Supreme Court. Years of debate followed. In a landmark ruling written in 1967 by ardent conservationist William O. Douglas, the Supreme Court ordered the Federal Power Commission to hold more hearings "on the subject of whether any dam should be built at all, not just which one." A year later, Idaho Senators Frank Church and Len B. Jordan agreed to a ten-year moratorium on dam building. Although members of different parties, the two worked together once again in 1968 to thwart an effort by Oregon's Senator Robert Packwood to lift the ban.

The outcome of the delay was the 650,000-acre Hells Canyon National Recreation area, created in 1975 despite a last-minute effort by Congressmen George Hansen and Steve Symms of Idaho to turn the canyon over to private power companies. Nonetheless, Idaho Power completed a massive dam at the southern end of the natural wonder in 1968, and for at least another decade developers dreamed of building at least one more dam across the Snake River north of the protected area. Efforts to further protect the Hells Canyon area as a national park have been blocked by those who fear an excessive concentration of people or the disruption of hunting, power-boating, and logging in the area.

Although the 130-mile-long canyon is remote and difficult to reach, it has remained contested terrain for many diverse interests, such as happened in the early 1990s when unregulated powerboaters were pitted against floaters (rafters and kayackers). A suggestion by the Forest Service to limit each group to alternate weeks on the river brought cries of foul from both sides. The Northwest Powerboat Association argued in one promotional brochure that, while the Snake River was designated wild for thirty-one miles, "a wild river is not the same as wilderness. Motors are not banned; the world 'soli-tude' doesn't appear in the act [whereby Congress created the Hells Canyon National Recreation Area in 1975]. None of the Snake River corridor is wilderness." To this argument, some preservationists responded by likening jetboaters to "Hell's Angels in the Sistine Chapel" and concluded that the only way to protect the scenic gorge was to designate it a national park.

A similar battle in the 1980s centered on a ninety-mile-long section of the Columbia River gorge between The Dalles and Portland. Opponents of a national scenic area feared that communities hemmed in by the preserve would become ghost towns; they preferred development to aesthetics. Late in 1986 President Ronald Reagan signed a bill creating the Columbia River Gorge Scenic Area, its 277,000 acres to be managed by the U.S. Forest Ser-vice.

Besides the Columbia Gorge Scenic Area, the Pacific Northwest today includes six national parks, national monuments like the Oregon Caves and Idaho's Craters of the Moon, national recreation areas like Hells Canyon on the Oregon-Idaho border and Oregon Dunes on the coast, more than 6.5 million acres of wilderness land, and numerous Forest Service camp-grounds. After Mount St. Helens National Volcanic Monument opened in 1983, it became an increasingly popular tourist attraction. Oregon led the way in creation of state parks, with Idaho a very distant third, although, ironically, Idaho created the region's first true state park in 1911 at Lake Chatcolet (now Heyburn State Park).[6]

Setting aside state and federal land as parks and recreation areas was

6. Washington obtained its first state park in 1915 and Oregon its first in 1920.

often justified in economic terms—either the land was worthless, lacking minerals and timber, or the action was a way to generate tourist dollars. But what about wilderness lands? For many people, that question posed another, whether it is better to log or mine the backcountry for the sake of jobs and profits or to preserve the region's remaining wilderness areas for their own special qualities. Critics charge that locking-up so much land is elitist and economically indefensible. During the 1980s few topics produced more heated public debates, especially in Idaho, than what to do with wilderness lands.

"For nearly as long as I can remember, wilderness has been a political hot potato," Idaho Senator Steve Symms reported to his constituents in late 1889. Indeed, the wilderness controversy has a lengthy history. America's first designated wild land areas were set aside in 1924. By the end of the 1950s, it became obvious in the face of a housing boom that some of the Forest Service's dwindling wild lands would have to be reserved. In the 1960s, Idaho Senator Frank Church, who sought a middle ground between developers and preservationists, was viewed as standing up for the environment in a state where in years past "conservation" had been a dirty word and few people objected to any type of timber cutting because that meant jobs. Leader of the successful fight to pass the Wilderness Act of 1964, he emphasized that "without wilderness, the world is a cage."

The Wilderness Act originally protected about nine million acres of forest land in the West previously classified as wild or wilderness, and in so doing it precipitated a lengthy debate on how much additional land to include in those areas. Environmental groups and timber and mining interests locked horns for a protracted fight. The issue engendered such strong emotions that opponents hanged Church in effigy during hearings on Idaho's Gospel Hump Wilderness.

Idaho Congressman (later Senator) Larry Craig proposed in the summer of 1986 to build a two-lane paved highway into the heart of the 2.3 million–acre Frank Church River of No Return Wilderness so as to make it more accessible to tourists. To lovers of wilderness, Craig's trial balloon made about as much sense as crushing Plymouth Rock and distributing the pieces to the fifty states to make history more accessible to schoolchildren. Environmentalists responded that the nation needs wild country even if most people only drive to the edge for a quick look. Recent evidence indicated that wilderness land actually benefited local economies by attracting new residents who enjoy a small-town or rural lifestyle.

When the Wild and Scenic Rivers Act was passed in October 1968, Oregon's Rogue and Idaho's Middle Fork of the Clearwater and Middle Fork of the Salmon rivers were among the original eight waterways protected. The act was envisioned as a way to keep dams from destroying the region's best whitewater rivers. Its original purpose was mainly to protect visual beauty, but in time its range of concerns expanded to include the restoration and protection of fish and other wildlife populations. One hundred forty-four portions of rivers have been added to the Wild and Scenic Rivers system since 1968, a total of ten thousand miles of protected waterways, but that figure still represents less than one percent of the total river network of the nation.

Not entirely removed from controversies about pristine rivers and wilderness lands were some of the region's ongoing battles over pollution. There were fears, for example, that Wild and Scenic Rivers like the Salmon, which cuts through the rugged Frank Church River of No Return Wilderness, could be loved to death because of their popularity, with beaches littered with beer cans, broken bottles, and fire rings. Outhouses were being phased out along the Salmon in the early 1990s and floaters were expected to carry out all their wastes. Some struggles with pollution have been won, but others, potentially more severe, remain to bedevil future generations of Pacific Northwesterners. These run the gamut from destructive oil spills on Puget Sound to chemical dumps leaching into the ground water. Yet none of these problems will endure longer than that of improper disposal of nuclear waste at the region's nuclear reservations.

In May 1986, Washington's Hanford site gained the dubious distinction of being selected one of three semifinalists to become the nation's sole dump site for high-level nuclear waste. Except for residents of nearby Richland, Kennewick, and Pasco who anticipated the possibility of new jobs, most Washingtonians were dismayed at the prospect of becoming the nation's nuclear garbage can. The state's Democratic governor and Republican attorney general joined hands to mount a court challenge to the federal decision.

Why the concern? Since the Second World War, Washingtonians had generally accepted Hanford's nuclear presence without protest or undue worry. In early 1986—only weeks before a disaster at the Chernobyl nuclear power facility in the Soviet Union caused heavy loss of life and heightened global fears of the atom—some thirty-nine thousand pages of declassified federal documents disclosed that the Hanford reservation was anything but a good neighbor.

The once-secret documents revealed that on several occasions beginning in the mid-1940s, several thousand tons of pollutants, including radioactive arsenic, iodine, manganese, and other heavy metals, had been released into the atmosphere, the ground water, and the Columbia River—685,000 curies of iodine 131 gas from 1944 to 1947, or thousands of times more than the 15 to 24 curies released by the Three Mile Island accident in Pennsylvania in 1979. Scientists calculated that infants living near Hanford during these emissions and drinking milk from cows grazing on contaminated grass may have ingested radiation equal to nearly 35,000 chest X-rays.[7]

"Green Run," an off-site release of 4,000 curies in December 1949 that was part of a Cold War military experiment to evaluate how radiation would spread when using uncooled fuel containing high amounts of iodine 131, extended a radioactive plume hundreds of miles from Spokane to Klamath Falls, Oregon. The public was not notified. One more morbid statistic from the 1940s: there was a 160 percent increase in infant mortality in three downwind counties at a time when the rest of Oregon and Washington recorded a decrease.

Over a forty-year period, billions of gallons of radioactive cooling water containing six hundred pounds of plutonium and hundreds of thousands of pounds of uranium was simply dumped onto the soil. Plutonium, a man-made element that is one of humanity's most toxic substances, causes lung cancer if inhaled. Other waste, which was poured into septic tank–like cribs, ponds, and ditches, contained 3.2 million curies of radiation, and still more was stored in 177 huge steel tanks, some 67 of which were reported to leak. Having the biggest potential for disaster was tank 101-SY, which held more than a million gallons of nuclear waste and every hundred days or so burped hydrogen gas that could cause an explosion and fire to spread plutonium across a wide area. When something similar happened in 1957 in the Soviet Union, it scattered intense radioactivity across an area the size of Rhode Island and killed hundreds of people. In late 1993, the U.S. Department of Energy announced that the Hanford site still contained more than eleven metric tons of plutonium.

In the fall of 1986, even before the full extent of the Hanford mess was revealed, Washington voters approved a referendum opposing imported nuclear waste by a lopsided 86 percent. With this measure the state hoped to send Congress the message that it did not want to be the nation's first high-

7. In addition to radioactive discharges, during a two-year period in the mid-1980s, a plutonium plant at Hanford spewed some twenty tons of the carcinogen carbon tetrachloride into the air of eastern Washington.

Certainly the oddest and perhaps the most ghoulish nuclear-related facility in the Pacific Northwest, if not in the world, is a former Spokane motel that preserves the remains of 20,000 people exposed to radiation at United States nuclear facilities, laboratories, and industrial sites. Here are bones from Marie Curie, the French scientist who discovered radium and various organs from eleven thousand women, some as young as 13, who once painted glow-in-the-dark radium on watch dials and later died of bone cancer. Rows of cardboard boxes marked only with case numbers hold dried bones or organs dissolved in acid, while industrial freezers preserve body parts from nuclear workers. There is a dissecting room awaiting the next corpse.

Called the National Human Radiobiological Tissue Repository, this collection of remains was assembled in Spokane in 1992 as part of a $1 million grant to Washington State University from the U.S. Department of Energy. The purpose of the collection is to aid scientists studying the impact of radiation on humans.—*Spokesman-Review* (Spokane), 8 August 1993

level nuclear depository. Even Washington's agricultural industry feared that a high-level nuclear waste dump could stigmatize Washington farm products because of public concern about radiation contamination—even though the products were not tainted. Russell Jim, a tribal spokesman for the Yakima Nation which borders the Hanford reservation, said of the referendum, "This is the first time in history that the state of Washington and the Yakima Nation have ever been on the same side."

Late in 1987 Congress chose Nevada as the depository site. It would have been a terrible irony if the Pacific Northwest, a region long famed for its special environmental qualities, had become home to all the high-level nuclear waste generated in the East. In more recent years, Hanford's "downwinders" sued the federal government, which claimed no one was harmed by its radioactive releases. As of mid-1992, the cost of the government's legal bills totaled $39 million and the case had yet to go to trial.

A similar nuclear mess prevails in Idaho, where some people fear that the Idaho National Engineering Laboratory produced and stored nuclear wastes that could permanently foul the Snake River Plain aquifer, an underground body of water the size of Lake Erie and source of 25 percent of the state's drinking water. Their concerns were not unfounded: declassified government documents reveal that between 1957 and 1963 there were intentional leaks of six million curies of radioactive gas into the atmosphere, more by far than the known releases at Hanford.

Most of INEL's nuclear waste is stored in thousands of barrels, crates, and

84.–85.–86. Three signs of the times: When the author first moved to the Pacific Northwest in 1969, several large signs stood alongside highways near the Hanford Reservation to warn motorists of possible radiation danger. Such warnings have since been removed, but because of the large amount of volatile radioactive waste stored in underground tanks, the danger may be no less real today. In the early 1990s the town of Arco, Idaho, still proudly proclaimed its historic role in development of atomic energy, while a sign posted at the border of nearby Blaine county took a much dimmer view of Idaho's nuclear heritage. Photos by the author.

boxes, or in pools containing spent fuel elements from nuclear reactors, a volume of material large enough to pave a radioactive highway ten feet wide and a foot deep across the entire width of southern Idaho. But there is more: in the mid-1990s about twenty-two thousand metric tons of highly radioactive spent-fuel rods were stored at nuclear power plants across the United States and their final destination could be INEL. Already one 140-acre landfill is home to 75 percent of all buried transuranic waste in the United States. Various isotopes of plutonium have been detected about one hundred feet below the ground at one storage site. The *New York Times* called the area "one of the most contaminated sites in the weapons industry." Late in 1988, Governor Cecil Andrus halted shipment of more nuclear wastes to the Idaho site and thereby called national attention to a new protective attitude in the state.

It was estimated in late 1993 that to clean up the nuclear waste at Hanford alone would take forty years and cost billions of dollars, creating the largest and most expensive public works project in American history. The cost of constructing a new plant at Hanford to convert radioactive liquids into glass logs was by itself $1.5 billion. Not surprisingly, in the early 1990s the work of cleaning up the Hanford nuclear site caused employment in nearby Richland to climb to its highest level in forty years. Some observers feared that the massive clean-up project would become a black hole for taxpayer dollars and give the country little to show for its money.

Yet one additional grim legacy of the Cold War was Oregon's Umatilla Army Depot and its huge stockpile of nerve gas. By the late 1980s when Congress mandated destruction of the lethal agents, some bombs stored in the huge steel-and-concrete "igloos" were approaching forty years old and leaking.

In the 1980s and 1990s, like a century earlier, natural resources and the environment remained the underlying concerns in many political controversies around the Pacific Northwest. A century ago the main question was how to develop nature's abundance, and in the 1990s many people still see the development of natural resources as the key to the region's future prosperity. But there was also a rising chorus of dissenters who wondered if the region needed another dam or a facility for processing nuclear waste if that meant further damage to the environment.

By the early 1990s the physical changes that occurred during the last hundred years were obvious. The wonder is that despite various forms of environmental degradation, the Pacific Northwest still managed to preserve many desirable qualities, including its physical beauty, the pleasant ambiance of small-town life, and the work ethic. Ironically, these were the very qualities that threatened to flood the region with newcomers in search of the good life and thus further stress its natural resources.

# Epilogue:
# Redefining the Pacific Northwest

*

"Compared to my own bulging, booming state of Arizona, the future of Idaho looks clean, bright, free, and hopeful. Maybe I'll move."—Edward Abbey, *The National Geographic Traveler* (July/August 1989), 96

*

Is it still appropriate to describe the Pacific Northwest as an American hinterland? In what way, if any, does the region remain remote from the nation's centers of population and influence? How and when did the region's historical identification with nature cease being a liability—the mark of a cultural backwater—and become an asset luring a growing number of new residents, including many at the forefront of their professions?

There was a time in the not-too-distant past when, to many people outside the Pacific Northwest, the region projected a rather unrefined image—even Seattle, its largest city. In the 1937 movie *Stage Door*, Lucille Ball, portraying an aspiring actor, complains to a friend, "Am I supposed to apologize for being born in Seattle?" Played by Eve Arden, her friend sarcastically comments, "I thought the people out there lived in trees," to which Ball replies, "Only in the summertime; in the winter they live in burrows." Probably not until the 1950s and 1960s would the Pacific Northwest cease being viewed by most outsiders as an artistic backwater content with a largely derivative cultural life and begin to develop its own distinctively regional style of painting and literature.[1]

1. Tim Appelo, "Culture in the Northwest Takes Center Stage," *Alaska Airlines Magazine* (July 1991): 30–34, 70ff.

87. Night at "Century 21." The 1962 world's fair bequeathed two of the modern symbols of Seattle: the
monorail and the futuristic Space Needle. Courtesy
Special Collections Division, University of Washington
Libraries, Neg. UW 856.

The natural setting that once contributed so much to the region's backwoods image became an asset when Pacific Northwest locations gained favor with film directors. The region's scenery figured prominently in the television series *Twin Peaks* and *Northern Exposure*—the latter program ostensibly set in the fictional town of Cicely, Alaska, but actually filmed in Roslyn, Washington. Located eighty miles east of Seattle, Roslyn was a typical natural resource–based community when its last coal mines closed in the early 1950s, but discovery by creators of the CBS television series in the spring of 1990 transformed Roslyn into a popular stop for tourists attracted to the community's rustic charms. The work of fabricating tourist attractions out of declining natural resource–based towns was not confined to Roslyn. Leavenworth and Winthrop, Washington; Sisters, Oregon; and Kellogg, Idaho, are all examples of places that sought to project the ambiance of a movie set, their urban motifs being either the old West or old Bavaria.

Far longer than either Oregon or Washington, Idaho had a image problem. It was the "riddle of the Rockies" to many out-of-state commentators, perhaps the least known and most puzzling of all American states. During the 1980s the national news media typically ignored Idaho except for activities of Richard Butler and his Aryan Nations followers, some of whom engaged in overt violence and criminal activities to further their cause. Attracted from California to the Gem State in the mid-1970s because of its isolation and homogenous population, Butler built a fortress compound at Hayden Lake complete with school, guard post, and living quarters. As head of the Church of Jesus Christ (Christian) he expounded a white-supremacist gospel. Despite all the media attention given to Butler and his followers, their annual "Aryan Congress" at Hayden Lake typically drew more reporters and protesters than participants.[2]

Too often obscured by the glare of unfavorable publicity was the fact that less than ten miles from Butler's compound was booming Coeur d'Alene, fast becoming a world-class resort city. Farther north was the trendsetter community of Sandpoint, which held an annual music festival that attracted nationally recognized artists. In his 1982 best seller, *Megatrends*, John Naisbitt predicted that Sandpoint would become the next Aspen, a reference to the glittery Colorado ski resort community.

2. It became increasingly clear that hate groups were not confined to the woods of northern Idaho. Some surfaced in the region's largest cities. In fact, a study by the Klan watch in late 1992 counted ten different hate groups in Oregon, eight in Washington, and only two in Idaho.

In *Megatrends* Naisbitt also classified Washington as one of America's five bellwether states. Along with California, Colorado, Connecticut, and Florida, it was a state "in which most social invention occurs in this country." Naisbitt noted that Washington was one of the first states to elect a woman governor in her own right and that Seattle was the first place in the nation to outlaw mandatory retirement laws. He might have added that in the 1970 election, Washington became the first state in which a majority of voters favored legalized abortion. Such trend-setting behavior hardly seems characteristic of a hinterland.

As the United States faced a future that was increasingly linked to Asia, Seattle, Tacoma, and Portland were transformed from backdoors of the continent into strategic gateways to the Pacific Rim and its bright economic future. In the 1990s, Pacific Northwest ports had the advantage of being one day's sailing time closer to the Far East than competing California ports. Export trade, however, was not really new to the region: Ray Stannard Baker noted a great fleet of foreign vessels loading grain in Portland in 1901 and observed that there were "seventy-seven British vessels, two Danish, one Dutch, eleven French, thirty-four German, two Italian, and one Norwegian, and their cargoes went to nearly every part of the world."[3] But it was the sheer volume and variety of the export trade that had become critical to the regional economy by the mid-1980s. In the late 1993 vote on the North American Free Trade Agreement, the only member of Washington's congressional delegation to vote against the measure was Jolene Unsoeld, who feared an outmigration of jobs from the state. Other Democrats, as well as the Republicans who represented Washington, were apparently swayed by reports such as the one that claimed the state's trade with Mexico during the past five years had grown by 600 percent and now supported forty-two hundred jobs.

It was indisputable that Washington's international trade topped $33 billion in 1985, with airplanes being the state's chief export, followed by

---

3. Ray Stannard Baker, "The Great Northwest," *Century Magazine* 65 (March 1903): 658.

---

88. Downtown Portland as photographed in the fall of 1991: natural objects juxtaposed with tall buildings created a visually arresting effect on city streets. Photo by the author.

grain, logs, aluminum, and fish. Eight years later it ranked among the most trade-dependent states in the nation because of exports of aircraft from Boeing and computer programs from Microsoft, with Japan far outranking neighboring Canada as Washington's main trading partner. Japan alone accounted for 50 percent of Oregon's total trade dollars in the mid-1980s; Korea and Taiwan ranked a distant second and third. Some observers now speak of the old Pacific Northwest as Japan's new opportunity-rich Pacific North*east*.

Over time the entire Pacific Northwest, not just the coastal ports, became oriented toward exports destined mainly for Asian consumers, as when Columbia River barges in Umatilla, Oregon, take on large containers of frozen French fries destined for transshipment in Portland to buyers in Hong Kong. In 1989, when grain growers in Oregon, Washington, Idaho, and Montana planted 10.8 million acres of wheat (a typical year's amount and about one-sixth the U.S. total), more than half the crop was exported to China, Japan, Russia, Korea, and Egypt.

Evidence of the region's having shed its old hinterland status abounds. Even a casual reading of computer magazines reveals how great an impact the programmers of Bellevue and Redmond have on future generations of computer software. The University of Washington ranks among the nation's top public universities in the amount of federal research and development money received. An observer need spend only a few hours at the Seattle-Tacoma International Airport ("Seatac") to realize how the sprawling complex of runways and terminals functions as a hub for an expanding network of commuter airlines that link once-remote communities in the Pacific Northwest to major carriers and the world beyond, making it possible to fly from places like Pullman and Pasco to New York and Washington DC in a matter of hours. Any farm or ranch with a satellite television receiver gains instant awareness of events around the world.

Yet, if it is no longer appropriate to describe the entire region as an American hinterland, it is undeniable that many parts the Pacific Northwest do retain hinterland characteristics. The juxtaposition of metropolitan trendsetter and hinterland is, in fact, the defining quality of life in the modern Northwest. The accessibility of the hinterland from metropolitan centers remains the *key* feature of what residents regard as a desirable life style. It is appropriate that two of the nation's best-known manufacturers and marketers of outdoor wear—Eddie Bauer and REI—originated and are still headquartered in Seattle.

The juxtaposition of trendsetter and hinterland is apparent in a myriad of

89. Barge traffic on the Columbia River below Bonneville Dam in October 1992. Photo by the author.

different ways across the Pacific Northwest. Even as I type these words in
Moscow, Idaho, using the most up-to-date version of Microsoft Word, I
glance south across a rolling landscape of wheat and barley that stretches as
far as the horizon. From my hilltop office I see an occasional barn and
storage bin, but mostly the country is empty. Although farm equipment is
modern, some of the seasonal rhythms of ranch life in the Palouse country
have scarcely changed during the past century. Yet within eight miles of my
home are two public universities conducting state-of-the-art research in
many fields.

I also recall the nights spent camped with a class on the Lewis and Clark
trail in the Bitterroot Mountains. At dusk when the stars first came out and
only the profiles of the mountains were still visible, we saw almost exactly
what Lewis and Clark saw nearly two hundred years ago. The closest telephone and gas station were fifty miles away.

When an anthropology professor from Washington State University proposed to use sophisticated equipment to search the mountains of southeastern Washington for a "Sasquatch," a legendary Northwest creature also
known as "Big Foot," that somehow managed to elude humans in that re-

mote region, many people scoffed. Yet, whether the venture is credible or not, anyone who has tramped through remote canyons in the Blue Mountains, the Cascades, or the Olympics can understand the feeling that in some remote part of the region an unsolved mystery of nature may still await the persistent searcher. In this regard, it is worth recalling that the mountainous interior of the Olympic Peninsula was first entered by white explorers only in 1890, well after their counterparts had penetrated into the heart of Africa.

The juxtaposition between hinterland and trendsetter is observable when killer whales breach within sight of Seattle's tall buildings. It occurs when new vineyards rise from the sagebrush-covered hills of southeastern Washington. Wine is one of the Pacific Northwest's newest industries, and wineries are located in all three states. During the 1980s, the wineries of Washington have grown from a handful to nearly seventy, and vintners bragged that they produced more premium wine than any other state except California.

Obviously, some parts of the Pacific Northwest will long remain hinterlands in the thinking of metropolitan Pacific Northwesterners, and of many Easterners too. For urban dwellers on Puget Sound, a trip to Pullman to attend a conference at Washington State University on the state's eastern edge is a venture into the hinterland. The entire state of Idaho remains a hinterland in the minds of many Americans, and an article of Idaho folklore is the person who when back East introduces himself as being from Idaho, and is met with the misinformed response, "Yes, but back here we pronounce it Ohio."

Not without reason did Idaho recently sell itself as The Great Getaway. The Frank Church River of No Return Wilderness is the largest in the lower forty-eight states. Capitalizing on nature's abundance, Idaho lures tourists from the city to dude ranches, whitewater rafting, and mountain trails, and an increasing number of people are electing to stay on as residents.

POPULATION GROWTH:
"HORDES RIDE MIGRATIONAL TIDE NORTH"

Even in Idaho the hinterland is not what it used to be. Just north of my Moscow home is a large tract of land that just a year or two ago was a rolling wheatfield but is now divided into city streets and boxy apartments and condominium blocks without any redeeming aesthetic value. Probably the same thing will occur in the near future to spoil my pastoral view to the south. This sort of transformation is occurring even more rapidly in places like Boise, Nampa, and Coeur d'Alene. *USA Today* called booming Boise one of the six cities to watch during the 1990s, but why? Boise—where a trout stream is located five minutes from the state capitol and downtown high-rise buildings—has more Fortune 500 companies than any other city its size in America. In the early 1990s Boise received numerous inquiries from more businesses interested in relocating to the area. One can only wonder, however, if the Boise-Nampa-Caldwell area will become the next Phoenix or Los Angeles, two bywords for decentralized urban growth.

Around all the larger cities of the Pacific Northwest, suburban sprawl continued to swallow the farmland that once reached their doorsteps. Ranking high on a 1993 list prepared by the American Farmland Trust of the dozen most threatened agricultural regions in the United States were both the Puget Sound lowlands and the Willamette Valley.

Despite its Fortune 500 giants and its high-tech upstarts, much of Idaho will retain a close relationship with nature for the foreseeable future. The accessibility of mountain slopes and pristine rivers from metropolitan centers will likely remain the key feature of what residents regard as a desirable lifestyle; of the state's 53 million acres, only about one-third of one percent are urban. Put another way, counties with fewer than two persons per square mile, the traditional definition of "frontier," in the 1990s still account for 44 percent of the land area of Idaho and 27 percent of the land area of Oregon (see Appendix Table 10).

One of the biggest problems the entire region faces today is that its back-to-nature image resonates positively with a growing number of Americans, but explosive population growth will inevitably destroy the very qualities that make the region so attractive. In fact, a key development in the late twentieth-century Pacific Northwest was the flood of newcomers. According to the 1990 census, more than half of the 2.6 million residents of metropolitan Seattle were born outside the state. Early in the century a majority of newcomers to the region arrived from the Midwest, primarily Minnesota, the Dakotas, and Wisconsin. A trend noticeable in the 1980s and 1990s was the influx of foreign-born, primarily of Asians, to Seattle and other parts of western Washington. In fact, the 1990 census revealed that 40 percent of the Seattle area's eighty thousand foreign born arrived during the previous decade.

By far the most commented upon population trend of the 1990s was the large number of new residents arriving from California. During the decade from 1975 to 1985, Idaho watched a tide of young people flow out of the state in search of jobs, but in 1987 that population visibly flowed the other way, making Idaho a bright spot in the otherwise dreary national economic picture. In the early 1990s Idaho was producing jobs faster than any other state, and much of that was because people had discovered a desirable quality of life in the northern Rocky Mountains. But the boom has not been without its problems.

Newcomers to the Northwest were lured by a combination of such things as less crime, lighter traffic, uncongested surroundings, a slower pace of life, and fresh air. Outdoor recreation opportunity, which often topped the list of reasons given by people relocating to Oregon, Washington, or Idaho, was followed by scenery, lower housing prices, and friendly people. Front-page newspaper stories with headlines reading "Hordes Ride Migrational Tide North" told tales of people who were glad to leave California's regulations and high taxes.[4]

One study found that out-of-staters moving to the region in 1990 consisted mainly of the yuppie burnouts, professionals, retirees, and the desperates who said, "We just really wanted out of Southern California." Other former Californians explained their move north with the words, "There's still hope up here."

The state of Washington was for a time the number one destination for ex-Californians, but it was at the county and local levels that the population shifts were most visible. Middle-class Californians headed to the Pacific Northwest, often in search of cozy towns and rural retreats, their hunger for the good life in suburban California replaced by yearning for the good life in Pacific Northwest towns close to open land.

When newcomers chose to congregate in once lightly populated and relatively unspoiled places—like the Port Angeles–Sequim area of Washington; or Bend and Ashland, Oregon; or Coeur d'Alene, Idaho—their collective impact contributed to increased grumbling among the people already in residence. They feared that the Northwest dream could turn into a California-style nightmare equated with traffic jams, spiraling population growth, and rising housing prices in dense subdivisions like those the newcomers left behind: "Californians have ruined California, and now they're coming up here," grumbled novelist Tom Robbins, a nineteen-year resident of La-Conner, Washington (pop. 633).[5]

So great was the 1980s influx to Oregon that from April 1985 to April 1990 an average of 220 new people arrived each day, the result being that 20

4. *Spokesman-Review*, 7 September 1993.
5. *USA Today*, 25 July 1989.

90. This sign along Highway 97 in Terrebonne, Oregon, in September 1993 expressed the resentment of a growing number of Pacific Northwesterners toward excessive population growth, in this case in the Bend area. Photo by the author.

to 35 percent of all Oregonians in the early 1990s had resided in the state less than ten years. "It's no wonder that we're seeing such a reaction among some of the state's old-timers," observed University of Oregon law dean Dave Frohnmayer in 1993. Drivers with California plates reported dirty looks and rude catcalls. When Oregonians in a recent survey were asked to finish the sentence, "My biggest fear for Oregon is . . . ," the number one answer was overpopulation; number two was "becoming like California." In truth, noted Frohnmayer, some of the newcomers were from Washington and many were foreigners, and most newcomers tended to mirror traditional Oregon concerns.[6]

Rapid growth nonetheless bred resentment because it was also expensive, requiring that taxpayers fund enlarged budgets for health and welfare, fire and police protection, and for an expanding infrastructure of roads and schools. These costs, plus construction of palatial new homes based on

6. *Oregonian*, 12 September 1993, sec. D, pp. 1, 4.

California dollars, sent property tax rates soaring and contributed to tax revolts in all three Pacific Northwest states in the 1990s. The typical California émigré was easy to resent, observed demographer Jim Hebert: "He or she is 43 years old, earns more than $50,000 a year, and can pay cash for a huge house after selling a bungalow on California's superheated housing market."[7] One fear in Coeur d'Alene, Idaho, was that affluent newcomers would use their money to destroy the city's ambiance by erecting high-rise buildings along the scenic waterfront.

For a time, California bashing became a favorite pastime in many parts of the Pacific Northwest. "You're unwanted if the word California appears on your résumé," complained one disgruntled new arrival.[8] Newspapers occasionally printed stories about people who returned to California after feeling unwelcomed in the Pacific Northwest.

Besides the wave of newcomers from California, there were significant relocations of populations from one part of the Pacific Northwest to another during 1980s and 1990s. Some people moved from growing metropolitan centers on Puget Sound or the Willamette River to smaller interior cities like Spokane and Boise. The federal census also revealed that during the 1980s many downtown neighborhoods continued to lose population, while nearby suburbs experienced dramatic gains of 25 percent or more. The trend was for the poor to remain behind in the cities while the rich got out of town.

Something similar happened in rural communities, where people with money moved away (presumably to the suburbs) and left the poor behind. Between 1910 and 1990, for example, Washington's Whitman County lost about a third of its permanent residents. In nearby Columbia and Garfield counties, the outmigration was even more dramatic, with losses of 43 and 46 percent respectively. In some rural areas, whole towns dried up and disappeared. Yet by the early 1990s, some small towns were experiencing growth for the first time in decades. Twenty of twenty-six farm towns with fewer than a thousand residents in Spokane, Whitman, and Lincoln counties lost residents during the 1980s, but during the 1990s all but tiny La-Mont increased their populations, some by 10 percent or more. The newcomers tended to be people who no longer wanted to live in big cities.

Some pilgrims to the Pacific Northwest during the 1980s and 1990s were New Age prophets of doom, bringing followers with them in search of so-

---

7. *Idahonian* (Moscow), 20 and 21 January 1990.
8. *Register-Guard* (Eugene), 4 February 1990, sec. A, p. 4.

PACIFIC NORTHWEST RELIGIOUS COMPOSITION

(IN PERCENT)

| | Bap- tist | Cath- olic | Jew- ish | Lu- theran | Meth- odist | Mor- mon | Presby- terian | Unaffil- iated |
|---|---|---|---|---|---|---|---|---|
| Idaho | 3.9 | 11.5 | — | 5.8 | 2.0 | 30.5 | 4.1 | 11.9 |
| Oregon | 8.7 | 15.3 | 0.4 | 4.9 | 4.2 | 2.4 | 6.7 | 17.2 |
| Washington | 7.2 | 19.0 | 0.4 | 6.2 | 4.6 | 1.9 | 7.8 | 14.0 |
| United States | 19.4 | 26.2 | 1.8 | 8.0 | 2.8 | 1.4 | 5.2 | 7.5 |

Source: 1991 poll by the Graduate School of the City University of New York

lace in a world that seemed to be spinning dangerously out of control. People making this type of odyssey often claimed that mainstream American society left them socially alienated and spiritually unfulfilled. Their arrival underscored the curious religious composition of the Pacific Northwest in the late twentieth century, where Washington, in fact, ranked among the most unchurched states in the nation. Some observers have even spoken of an Unchurched Belt extending from California to Alaska as the West Coast counterpoint to the South's Bible Belt. In a 1985 Oregon survey, only 53 percent of the respondents said they belonged to any church or synagogue, compared to 68 percent nationwide, but 96 percent expressed belief in a supreme being. The Unchurched Belt may account for recent successes of new religious movements on the West Coast.

## ECONOMIC REALIGNMENTS

Occurring simultaneously with the various population shifts was a historic reorientation of the Pacific Northwest economy away from extractive industry to a growing number of tourist and leisure-time businesses. The Hood River area, long famous for fruit and more recently as a mecca for windsurfers in the Columbia Gorge, billed itself as the "Sailboarding Capital of the World" in the early 1990s. The fruit orchards were still there, but the community's image had certainly changed.

An even more graphic illustration of historic realignments in the Pacific Northwest economy occurred in January 1993 when several thousand onlookers, some bearing video cameras, gathered to watch as explosive charges leveled what was once the world's tallest smokestack, in Ruston,

Washington, near Tacoma. The 562-foot landmark had vented sulfur dioxide and other noxious fumes downwind from ASARCO's large copper smelting facility, which was also dismantled. The sprawling complex, which specialized in foreign ores with a high arsenic content and once accounted for a third of the world's arsenic production, had provided jobs for an average of 1,250 people until it closed in 1985. At that time the stack was spewing two hundred tons of sulfur dioxide into the air each day; the 97-acre site was later declared a federal Superfund site because of arsenic and lead contamination. Like the Kellogg area of northern Idaho, it had also at one time been part of the Bunker Hill and Sullivan complex.

Dramatic changes of another sort continued to affect the region's once-almighty timber industry. Beginning in the fall of 1987, the export market in logs boomed. During the following year alone, more than 3.6 billion board feet of raw logs were shipped out of Oregon and Washington, many of them headed for Japan's sixteen thousand sawmills. South Korea and China also bought Northwest logs. Prices soared, fueling an export frenzy. About three-quarters of the timber harvested in 1988 from Oregon's state forests went overseas, where they brought sellers a premium price about 40 percent higher than logs sold domestically.

Weyerhaeuser, based near Tacoma, Washington, the biggest timber company in the Pacific Northwest with 2.7 million acres of land in Washington and Oregon, exported about 40 percent of its regional harvest in the early 1990s. Yet, in one notable case, Weyerhaeuser closed an aging mill at North Bend, Oregon, and converted a nearby cedar mill into its "mill of the '90s" to provide metric-dimension lumber to Japanese home builders.

Lumber was still Oregon's number one manufacturing industry in the early 1990s, but the timber famine that resulted from log exports and the spotted owl controversy threatened the future of many timber towns. This was unusual because previous periods of economic bust were typically caused by rising mortgage rates or dips in the housing market. In 1991, only 56,100 people worked in logging and sawmilling in Oregon, down from the 70,500 employed during boom times only four years earlier. During the 1980s, the membership of the Coos Bay local of the International Woodworkers of America dropped from 3,500 to 500. In March 1989, for the first time in 130 years, not a single sawmill operated in Coos Bay. This time fewer and fewer families waited around for logging to rebound or for mills to reopen. Those who could moved away in search of a more stable life for themselves and their families. It was much the same story in Washington and Idaho.

91. An awesome display of nature's fury reduced to tourist kitsch, Mount St. Helens is recalled thirteen ycars later (1993) in a roadside museum along Washington Highway 504. Photo by the author.

Unfortunately, the region's shift toward greater reliance on tourist dollars was not without its economic and social underside either. An increasing number of service jobs in the tourist industry, which often paid near-minimum wages, had to be balanced against a decreasing number of jobs in industries like logging and mining, where the pay was much higher. In an affluent tourist community like Sun Valley, Idaho, which evolved in recent years from a winter sports mecca to a year-round resort, many service workers could not afford the skyrocketing price of local real estate and had to drive to work from homes located as far away as Twin Falls, seventy miles distant. In southeastern Idaho, service workers commuted to the pricey environs of Jackson, Wyoming, from more affordable housing as far away as Idaho Falls, nearly ninety milcs distant. Some people also made the commute to escape the hoards of tourists who overflowed Jackson's streets in summer and the ski bums who crowded its bars in winter.

The story of how tourism seemed to create a permanent underclass of minimum wage workers was not mentioned in the glittery brochures that advertised the Sun Valley area's groomed ski slopes, polo clubs, "delicious dining and Nightlife," and upscale shopping boutiques. And that is not the only problem: the manicured lawns and expensive homes crowded onto elk winter habitat and blocked deer migration routes. In truth, much of Idaho's Wood River Valley was becoming a upscale suburb of Los Angeles; its residents just had a longer commute.

Among the new resorts is Skamania Lodge in the Columbia River Gorge, but large-scale resort developments increasingly meet stiff opposition from local citizens. The proposed 4,000-acre-plus Valbois resort near McCall, Idaho, would have dwarfed Sun Valley, provided an impressive complex of mountain and lake recreation, and created more than two thousand jobs. Aroused citizens, however, feared its impact on local highways and water resources, and they did not welcome the social change that would inevitably result if the area became another haven for the California rich, like Sun Valley or Jackson.

Like the upscale resort complexes, the new wineries booming around the Pacific Northwest consciously sought to project an aura of elegance. Like tourism, however, the wine business had a dark underside that few people within the industry liked to ponder. Long hours, low pay, and marginal housing was the norm in Washington vineyards for agricultural laborers, many of whom were impoverished migrants from Mexico, who produced grapes for Chateau St. Michelle, Columbia Crest, and other well-known wineries. The right to a union contract is guaranteed to farm laborers in the neighboring states of California, Oregon, and Idaho, but not in Washington as of 1993, where an estimated 150,000 farm laborers worked, primarily east of the Cascades, to harvest the state's fruits and vegetables and tend its fields.

Among the most controversial new economic developments were gambling casinos operated by Native Americans. For a number of years, Indians all over the Pacific Northwest utilized their separate-nation status to sell goods and services on reservations that were banned elsewhere. Typically this meant open-air stands that sold tax-free cigarettes or high-powered fireworks ("Boom City" and "Safe and Insane Fireworks" were the names of two such businesses). The Indian Gaming Regulatory Act passed by Congress in 1988 allowed Native Americans to expand the scope of their enterprises by operating casinos in states where such gambling was already allowed, even if only for charitable purposes. Such casinos created thousands of jobs in poverty-stricken areas and offered tribes their first real chance at economic self-sufficiency. Washington's Tulalips have built retirement homes for their elders and the Lummis have started youth sports programs

92. Larry EchoHawk (b. 1948). When he was inaugurated Idaho's attorney general in 1991, he was among the first Native Americans to be elected to a statewide constitutional office in the United States. The Wyoming-born EchoHawk is a member of the Pawnee Tribe. "My family is the realization of the American dream," he stated on the eve of his inauguration. Courtesy Larry EchoHawk.

using income from their low-stakes casino operations, but the gambling has also been the subject of much criticism.

In the 1992 election, Idaho voters overwhelmingly supported a constitutional amendment that prevented Native Americans in the state from launching casino-style games on their reservations under provisions of the 1988 law. Idaho's Attorney General Larry EchoHawk, himself a Pawnee, warned that while gambling could raise a lot of money quickly, it was no panacea for the tribes: "Emphasis should be on education and giving reservation youth a hunger for learning, not on get-rich-quick schemes."[9]

Despite several troubling aspects of its economy, the Pacific Northwest in the late 1980s was the nation's business hot spot, seemingly able to defy the recession that gripped the rest of the nation. During the recession of the early 1980s, the Northwest had suffered longer than the rest of the nation, but about 1987 the region came roaring back. Especially amazing was the newfound economic vitality and appeal of Idaho, Montana, and other states of the interior West, which only a few years before had been dismissed in a *Newsweek* cover story as a troubled American outback. In the early 1990s, Idaho ranked top in the nation in terms of employment and personal income growth.

*Forbes* business magazine profiled Idaho and its neighboring states in the Rocky Mountains, noting: "For better or worse, satellites, fax machines, telephone lines and cellular service have removed these states from their splendid isolation and tied them to the rest of the country and the world. Add Federal Express, and anyone with some imagination can earn a living in even the remotest locations."[10]. A fall 1993 *Time* cover story called "Boom Time in the Rockies" reported: "On the strength of current migration trends, some experts believe the region may even be on the way to becoming a magnetic pole of a New West, replacing California as the ultimate, mythmaking destination, tantalizing the daydreams of restless souls itching to pick up and move."[11]

### FUTURE SHOCK?

During these boom years, the supercharged pace of real estate development across the Pacific Northwest transformed many a once-pristine meadow

9. *Spokesman-Review*, 4 April 1993, sec. B, p. 3.
10. *Forbes*, 21 December 1992, 114.
11. *Time*, (6 September 1993): 22.

and forest glade into recreation estates and tract housing. In several places, surging urban growth threatened wetlands and other natural preserves so crucial to the regional identity.

Even so, it is the continuing juxtaposition of hinterland and trendsetter that will likely shape the course of public debate in the Pacific Northwest into the twenty-first century. Although agriculture, mining, and timber will still be the backbone of the region's rural economy, tourism will become increasingly important. There is even talk of timber communities transforming themselves into tourist centers where visitors would come to spend money to see the old-growth forests.

With the increased emphasis on tourism will come the realization that some river canyons may be more valuable for their wild waters than as hydroelectric reservoirs, timber more valuable as shade for hikers and campers than as two-by-fours, and mountains more important for their scenic beauty or as objects to be climbed than as repositories of ore. Legislatures and courts will probably have to resolve the inevitable conflict between metropolitan dwellers who regard the nonagricultural hinterland as a recreational escape and those who wish to use it for its natural resources.

One such fight erupted in the early 1990s when Battle Mountain Gold of Houston, Texas, proposed to build Washington's biggest cyanide-leach gold mine in the Okanogan highlands. Foes worried about environmental damage, including pollution from toxic cyanide, from the giant hole the company proposed to dig in Buckhorn Mountain, about 180 miles northwest of Spokane. Mine supporters saw jobs and economic development as vital in the remote region: "God put these resources here for us to use. It's disturbing to see the alternative life-stylers, the newcomers, come in and want to change our way of life. I'm live and let live, and we really need those jobs."[12]

"Our natural environment is critical to our way of life," maintained Oregon governor Barbara Roberts.[13] But in the name of jobs will legislators and other public officials permit logging or mining of lands better set aside as a wilderness heritage for future generations of Pacific Northwesterners more likely to spend their working lives in offices than in the fields, forests, or mines? It is worth noting that the Pacific Northwest already has more teachers than loggers, and more white-collar professionals than commercial fishermen. The influx of new arrivals, especially the "lifestyle refugees" from California, could have an impact on politics in the Northwest, espe-

12. *Spokesman-Review*, 5 September 1993, sec. A, p. 10.
13. *USA Today*, 12 August 1991, 1.

cially in Idaho, long a Republican party stronghold: many people have relocated to the Pacific Northwest because of a love of its environment, not because of any desire to protect jobs in traditional industries, and thus they may give its politics a "greener" tint.

A sense of the region's past will help the present generation to understand better the kind of Pacific Northwest that evolved in recent years when the modern metropolis intersected with a hinterland rich in beauty and natural resources. The region's future looks to be as exciting as its past.

# The Pacific Northwest:
# A Statistical Portrait

## TABLE I: AREA
### (IN SQUARE MILES)

|  | Land Only | Total | Rank among States |
|---|---|---|---|
| Idaho | 82,751 | 83,574 | 14th |
| Oregon | 96,002 | 96,093 | 9th |
| Washington | 66,581 | 70,637 | 18th |
| Combined | 245,334 | 251,304 |  |

Note: The Pacific Northwest constitutes 8 percent of the total area of the contigous United States.

### For Comparison:

|  | Land Only | Total | Rank among States |
|---|---|---|---|
| Alaska | 570,374 | 615,230 | 1st |
| Texas | 261,914 | 267,277 | 2d |
| California | 155,973 | 158,869 | 3d |
| Montana | 145,556 | 147,046 | 4th |
| Delaware | 1,955 | 2,397 | 49th |
| Rhode Island | 1,045 | 1,231 | 50th |
| British Columbia |  | 358,971 |  |
| France |  | 220,668 |  |
| Germany |  | 137,838 |  |
| Switzerland |  | 15,941 |  |

## TABLE 2: COASTLINE AND SHORELINE
### (IN MILES)

|  | Coastline | Shoreline |
|---|---|---|
| Oregon | 296 | 1,410 |
| Washington | 157 | 3,026 |
| *For Comparison:* | | |
| California | 840 | 3,427 |
| Alaska | 5,580 | 31,383 |
| Atlantic and Gulf coasts (U.S.) | 3,700 | 45,814 |

## TABLE 3: RIVERS

|  | Average Discharge at Mouth (Cubic Feet per Second) | Length (Miles) | Drainage Area (Square Miles) |
|---|---|---|---|
| Columbia | 262,000 | 1,243 | 258,000 |
| Snake | 50,000 | 1,038 | 109,000 |
| Willamette | 35,660 | 270 | 11,200 |
| Pend Oreille | 29,900 | 490 | 25,820 |
| Deschutes | 5,800 | 250 | 10,500 |
| John Day | 2,000 | 281 | 7,580 |
| Fraser | 128,000 | 850 | 89,900 |
| *For Comparison:* | | | |
| Mississippi/Missouri | 640,000 | 3,710 | 1,247,300 |
| Amazon | 7,000,000 | 4,000 | 2,722,000 |
| Nile | 100,000 | 4,145 | 1,107,227 |

## TABLE 4: STATE POPULATIONS, 1990

|  | Number | Rank among States |
|---|---|---|
| Idaho | 1,006,749 | 42nd |
| Oregon | 2,842,321 | 29th |
| Washington | 4,866,602 | 18th |
| Total | 8,715,672 | |
| *For comparison:* | | |
| California | 29,760,021 | 1st |
| Wyoming | 453,588 | 50th |
| United States | 248,709,873 | |

Note: Los Angeles County, California, has a population of 8,863,052, approximately equal that of the Pacific Northwest. The population of the *city* of San Diego is 1,110,554, or slightly more than that of Idaho.

## TABLE 5: POPULATION DENSITY, 1990

|  | People per Square Mile of Land Area | Rank among States |
|---|---|---|
| Idaho | 12.2 | 44th |
| Oregon | 29.6 | 40th |
| Washington | 73.1 | 28th |
| *For Comparison:* | | |
| Alaska | 1.0 | 50th |
| New Jersey | 1,042 | 1st |
| California | 190.8 | 12th |
| United States | 70.3 | |

Note: If the Pacific Northwest were as densely populated as New Jersey, it would contain more residents than the entire United States currently does.

## TABLE 6: POPULATION CHANGE, 1980–1990

|  | Percent | Rank among States |
|---|---|---|
| Idaho | +6.7 | 23rd |
| Oregon | +7.9 | 21st |
| Washington | +17.9 | 10th |
| *For Comparison:* | | |
| Nevada | +50.1 | 1st |
| West Virginia | −8.0 | 50th |

## TABLE 7: POPULATION IN METROPOLITAN AREAS, 1990

|  | Percent | Rank among States |
|---|---|---|
| Idaho | 20.4 | 50th |
| Oregon | 68.5 | 22d |
| Washington | 81.7 | 12th |
| *For Comparison:* | | |
| New Jersey | 100.0 | 1st |
| California | 95.7 | 2d |
| United States | 77.6 | |

## TABLE 8: CITY AND SUBURBS
### PERCENTAGE DISTRIBUTION OF STATE'S TOTAL URBAN POPULATION

|  | 1980 | | | 1990 | | |
|---|---|---|---|---|---|---|
|  | Central Place | Urban Fringe | Other Urban Areas | Central Place | Urban Fringe | Other Urban Areas |
| Idaho | 29 | 8 | 63 | 37 | 11 | 52 |
| Oregon | 34 | 37 | 29 | 37 | 33 | 30 |
| Washington | 37 | 49 | 14 | 36 | 51 | 13 |

TABLE 9: THE PACIFIC NORTHWEST'S LARGEST COMMUNITIES
POPULATIONS AND RANKING WITHIN STATES

| Rank | City | 1900 | City | 1990 | Percent Change, 1980–1990 |
|------|------|------|------|------|---------------------------|
| | | | *Idaho* | | |
| 1st | Boise | 5,967 | Boise | 125,738 | +22.7 |
| 2nd | Pocatello | 4,046 | Pocatello | 46,080 | −0.6 |
| 3rd | Moscow | 2,484 | Idaho Falls | 43,929 | +11.0 |
| 4th | Lewiston | 2,425 | Nampa | 28,365 | +13.0 |
| 5th | Wallace | 2,265 | Lewiston | 28,082 | +0.3 |
| | | | *Oregon* | | |
| 1st | Portland | 90,426 | Portland | 437,319 | +19.3 |
| 2nd | Astoria | 8,381 | Eugene | 112,669 | +7.0 |
| 3rd | Baker City | 6,663 | Salem | 107,786 | +21.0 |
| 4th | Pendleton | 4,406 | Gresham | 68,235 | +107.0 |
| 5th | Salem | 4,258 | Beaverton | 53,310 | +74.0 |
| | | | *Washington* | | |
| 1st | Seattle | 80,671 | Seattle | 512,259 | +4.5 |
| 2nd | Tacoma | 37,714 | Spokane | 177,196 | +3.4 |
| 3rd | Spokane | 36,848 | Tacoma | 176,664 | +11.5 |
| 4th | Walla Walla | 10,049 | Bellevue | 86,874 | +17.6 |
| 5th | Everett | 7,838 | Everett | 69,961 | +29.0 |

TABLE 10: THE LINGERING FRONTIER, 1990

COUNTIES WITH FEWER THAN TWO PERSONS PER SQUARE MILE,
THE TRADITIONAL CENSUS MEASURE OF A FRONTIER

| County | Land Area (Square Miles) | People per Square Mile |
|---|---|---|
| *Idaho* | | |
| Boise | 1,901 | 1.8 |
| Butte | 2,236 | 1.3 |
| Camas | 1,071 | 0.7 |
| Clark | 1,763 | 0.4 |
| Custer | 4,927 | 0.8 |
| Idaho | 8,497 | 1.6 |
| Lemhi | 4,564 | 1.5 |
| Owyhee | 7,643 | 1.1 |
| Valley | 3,670 | 1.7 |
| *Oregon* | | |
| Gilliam | 1,223 | 1.4 |
| Grant | 4,525 | 1.7 |
| Harney | 10,228 | 0.7 |
| Lake | 8,356 | 0.9 |
| Wheeler | 1,713 | 0.8 |

*Note:* Counties with fewer than two persons per square mile account for 44 percent of the land area of Idaho and 27 percent of the land area of Oregon. Ferry County has the lowest population density in Washington, with 2.9 people per square mile of land.

TABLE II: RACIAL AND ETHNIC COMPOSITION OF THE PACIFIC NORTHWEST, 1990

|  | *White* | |
| --- | :---: | :---: |
| *State* | *Percent of Population* | *Rank among 50 States* |
| Idaho | 92.2 | 7th |
| Oregon | 90.8 | 12th |
| Washington | 86.7 | 22nd |

For Comparison:

| | | |
| --- | :---: | :---: |
| Hawaii | 33.4 | 50th |
| Vermont | 98.6 | 1st |
| California | 69.0 | 47th |
| United States | 80.3 | |

Hispanic

| | | |
| --- | :---: | :---: |
| Idaho | 5.3 | 14th |
| Oregon | 4.0 | 19th |
| Washington | 4.4 | 18th |

For Comparison:

| | | |
| --- | :---: | :---: |
| West Virginia | 0.5 | 50th |
| New Mexico | 38.2 | 1st |
| California | 25.8 | 2d |
| United States | 9.0 | |

African American

| | | |
| --- | :---: | :---: |
| Idaho | 0.3 | 49th |
| Oregon | 1.6 | 41st |
| Washington | 3.1 | 35th |

For Comparison:

| | | |
| --- | :---: | :---: |
| Montana | 0.3 | 50th |
| Mississippi | 35.6 | 1st |
| California | 7.4 | 24th |
| United States | 12.1 | |

*Asian*

| | | |
|---|---|---|
| Idaho | 0.9 | 30th |
| Oregon | 2.4 | 11th |
| Washington | 4.3 | 3rd |

*For Comparison:*

| | | |
|---|---|---|
| West Virginia | 0.4 | 50th |
| Hawaii | 61.8 | 1st |
| California | 9.6 | 2nd |
| United States | 2.9 | |

*Native American*
*(Including Eskimo and Aleut)*

| | | |
|---|---|---|
| Idaho | 1.4 | 12th |
| Oregon | 1.4 | 13th |
| Washington | 1.7 | 9th |

*For Comparison:*

| | | |
|---|---|---|
| Pennsylvania | 0.1 | 50th |
| Alaska | 15.6 | 1st |
| California | 0.8 | 18th |
| United States | 0.8 | |

TABLE 12: COMPARATIVE SOCIAL STATISTICS

| | Median Income in 1992 (in dollars) | Poverty Rate in 1992 (Percent) | Population without Health Insurance 1990–1992 (Percent) |
|---|---|---|---|
| Idaho | 27,784 | 15.0 | 16.4 |
| Oregon | 32,114 | 11.3 | 13.3 |
| Washington | 34,064 | 11.0 | 10.7 |

*For Comparison:*

| | | | |
|---|---|---|---|
| California | 35,173 | 15.8 | 19.0 |
| Mississippi | 20,585 | 24.5 | 19.3 |
| West Virginia | 20,301 | 22.3 | 15.0 |

# Suggestions for Further Reading

The following bibliography seeks to guide readers to my major sources and suggests where to pursue further study of specific topics. This list is by no means inclusive of books and articles on a subject.

### CHAPTER 1: A SENSE OF PLACE

Attebery, Louie W., ed. *Idaho Folklife: Homesteads to Headstones*. Salt Lake City: University of Utah Press, 1985.

Austin, Judith. "Desert, Sagebrush, and the Pacific Northwest." In *Regionalism and the Pacific Northwest*, edited by William G. Robbins, Robert J. Frank, Richard E. Ross. Corvallis: Oregon State University Press, 1983.

Bingham, Edwin R., and Glen A. Love, eds. *Northwest Perspectives: Essays on the Culture of the Pacific Northwest*. Seattle: University of Washington Press, 1979.

Blair, Karen J., ed. *Women in Pacific Northwest History: An Anthology*. Seattle: University of Washington Press, 1988.

Booth, Brian, ed. *Wildmen, Wobblies and Whistle Punks: Stewart Holbrook's Lowbrow Northwest*. Corvallis: Oregon State University Press, 1992.

Brewster, David, and David M. Buerge. *Washingtonians: A Biographical Portrait of the State*. Seattle: Sasquatch Books, 1988.

Brown, Richard Maxwell. "Rainfall and History: Perspectives on the Pacific Northwest." In *Experiences in a Promised Land: Essays in Pacific Northwest History*, edited by G. Thomas Edwards and Carlos A. Schwantes. Seattle: University of Washington Press, 1986.

Cantwell, Robert. *The Hidden Northwest*. Philadelphia: J. B. Lippincott, 1972.

Clark, Norman H. *Washington: A Bicentennial History*. New York: W. W. Norton, 1976.

*The Compact Atlas of Idaho*. Moscow: University of Idaho, 1983.

Dicken, Samuel N., and Emily F. Dicken. *Oregon Divided: A Regional Geography*. Portland: Oregon Historical Society, 1982.

Dodds, Gordon B. *The American Northwest: A History of Oregon and Washington*. Arlington Heights IL: Forum Press, 1986.

———. *Oregon: A Bicentennial History*. New York: W. W. Norton, 1977.

Egan, Timothy. *The Good Rain: Across Time and Terrain in the Pacific Northwest*. New York: Alfred A. Knopf, 1990.

Ficken, Robert E., and Charles P. LeWarne. *Washington: A Centennial History*. Seattle: University of Washington Press, 1989.

Jackson, Philip L., and A. Jon Kimerling, eds. *Atlas of the Pacific Northwest*. 8th ed. Corvallis: Oregon State University Press, 1993.

Johansen, Dorothy O., and Charles M. Gates. *Empire of the Columbia: A History of the Pacific Northwest*. 2d ed. New York: Harper and Row, 1967.

Lang, William L., ed. *Centennial West: Essays on the Northern Tier States*. Seattle: University of Washington Press, 1991.

Loy, William G., Stuart Allan, and Clyde P. Patton. *Atlas of Oregon*. Eugene: University of Oregon, 1976.

Nash, Tom, and Twilo Schofield. *The Well-Traveled Casket: A Collection of Oregon Folklife*. Salt Lake City: University of Utah Press, 1992.

*Oregon Historical Quarterly* 93 (fall 1992). Theme issue devoted to the Columbia River in Pacific Northwest history.

Palmer, Tim. *The Snake River: Window to the West*. Washington DC: Island Press, 1991.

Peirce, Neal R. *The Mountain States of America: People, Politics, and Power in the Eight Rocky Mountain States*. New York: W. W. Norton, 1972.

———. *The Pacific States of America: People, Politics, and Power in the Five Pacific Basin States*. New York: W. W. Norton, 1972.

Peterson, F. Ross. *Idaho: A Bicentennial History*. New York: W. W. Norton, 1976.

Pomeroy, Earl. *The Pacific Slope: A History of California, Oregon, Washington, Idaho, Utah, and Nevada*. New York: Alfred A. Knopf, 1968.

Schwantes, Carlos A. *In Mountain Shadows: A History of Idaho*. Lincoln: University of Nebraska Press, 1991.

Schwantes, Carlos, Katherine Morrissey, David Nicandri, and Susan Strasser, eds. *Washington: Images of a State's Heritage*. Spokane: Melior Publications, 1988.

Stratton, David H., ed. *Washington Comes of Age: The State in the National Experience*. Pullman: Washington State University Press, 1992.

Tisdale, Sallie. *Stepping Westward: The Long Search for Home in the Pacific Northwest*. New York: Henry Holt and Company, 1991.

Warren, Sidney. *Farthest Frontier: The Pacific Northwest*. 1949. Reprint, Port Washington NY: Kennikat Press, 1970.

Winks, Robin. "Regionalism in Comparative Perspective." In *Regionalism and the Pacific Northwest*, edited by William G. Robbins, Robert J. Frank, Richard E. Ross. Corvallis: Oregon State University Press, 1983.

### PROFILE: THE THIRD VOYAGE OF CAPTAIN JAMES COOK

Beaglehole, J. C. *The Life of Captain James Cook*. Stanford: Stanford University Press, 1974.

Conner, Daniel, and Lorraine Miller. *Master Mariner: Capt. James Cook and the Peoples of the Pacific*. Seattle: University of Washington Press, 1978.

Cook, James. *The Journals of Captain James Cook on his Voyages of Discovery*. 3 vols. Edited by J. C. Beaglehole. Cambridge: Hakluyt Society, 1955–69.

Fisher, Robin, and Hugh Johnson, eds. *Captain James Cook and His Times*. Seattle: University of Washington Press, 1979.

Gough, Barry M. *Distant Dominion: Britain and the Northwest Coast of North America*. Vancouver: University of British Columbia Press, 1980.

Hough, Richard. *The Last Voyage of Captain James Cook*. New York: William Morrow, 1979.

Pethick, Derek. *First Approaches to the Northwest Coast*. Vancouver: J. J. Douglas, 1976.

Villiers, Alan. *Captain James Cook*. New York: Charles Scribner's Sons, 1967.

Withey, Lynne. *Voyages of Discovery: Captain Cook and the Exploration of the Pacific*. New York: William Morrow, 1987.

### CHAPTER 2: THE FIRST PACIFIC NORTHWESTERNERS

Cole, Douglas. *Captured Heritage: The Scramble for Northwest Coast Artifacts*. Seattle: University of Washington Press, 1985.

Drucker, Philip. *Indians of the Northwest Coast*. New York: McGraw-Hill, 1955.

Holm, Bill. *Northwest Coast Indian Art: An Analysis of Form*. Seattle: University of Washington Press, 1965.

Kirk, Ruth. *Tradition and Change on the Northwest Coast: The Makah, Nuu-chah-nulth, Southern Kwakiutl and Nuxalk*. Seattle: University of Washington Press, 1986.

Kirk, Ruth, with Richard D. Daugherty. *Exploring Washington Archaeology*. Seattle: University of Washington Press, 1978.

McFeat, Tom, ed. *Indians of the North Pacific Coast*. Seattle: University of Washington Press, 1967.

Madsen, Brigham. *The Bannock of Idaho*. Caldwell: Caxton Press, 1958.

Miller, Christopher L. *Prophetic Worlds: Indians and Whites on the Columbia Plateau*. New Brunswick NJ: Rutgers University Press, 1985.

Ramsey, Jarold, ed. *Coyote Was Going There: Indian Literature of the Oregon Country*. Seattle: University of Washington Press, 1977.

Ruby, Robert H., and John A. Brown. *A Guide to the Indian Tribes of the Pacific Northwest*. Norman: University of Oklahoma Press, 1986.

Stern, Theodore. *The Klamath Tribe: A People and Their Reservation*. Seattle: University of Washington Press, 1966.

Walker, Deward E., Jr. *Indians of Idaho*. Moscow: University Press of Idaho, 1978.

——. *Myths of Idaho Indians*. Moscow: University Press of Idaho, 1980.

Zucker, Jeff, Kay Hummel, and Bob Høgfoss. *Oregon Indians: Culture, History and Current Affairs; An Atlas and Introduction*. Portland: Oregon Historical Society, 1983.

CHAPTER 3: ENCOUNTERS WITH A DISTANT LAND

Anderson, Bern. *Surveyor of the Sea: The Life and Voyages of Captain George Vancouver*. Seattle: University of Washington Press, 1960.

Beals, Herbert K., trans. *Juan Pérez on the Northwest Coast: Six Documents of His Expedition in 1774*. Portland: Oregon Historical Society, 1989.

Cook, Warren. *Flood Tide of Empire: Spain and the Pacific Northwest, 1543–1819*. New Haven: Yale University Press, 1973.

Cutter, Donald C. *Malaspina and Galiano: Spanish Voyages to the Northwest Coast, 1791 and 1792*. Seattle: University of Washington Press, 1991.

Engstrand, Iris H. W. *Spanish Scientists in the New World: The Eighteenth-Century Expeditions.* Seattle: University of Washington Press, 1981. Especially pp. 44–75 on the Malaspina expedition.

Fisher, Raymond H. *Bering's Voyages: Whither and Why.* Seattle: University of Washington Press, 1977.

Fisher, Robin. *Vancouver's Voyage: Charting the Northwest Coast, 1791–1795.* Seattle: University of Washington Press, 1992.

Gamboa, Erasma. "Washington's Mexican Heritage: A View into the Spanish Explorations, 1774–1792." *Columbia* 3 (fall 1989): 40–45.

Gibson, James R. *Otter Skins, Boston Ships, and China Goods: The Maritime Fur Trade of the Northwest Coast, 1785–1841.* Seattle: University of Washington Press, 1992.

Glover, Richard, ed. *David Thompson's Narrative, 1784–1812.* Toronto: Champlain Society, 1962.

Gough, Barry M. *The Northwest Coast: British Navigation, Trade, and Discoveries to 1812.* Vancouver: University of British Columbia Press, 1992.

Henry, John Frazier. *Early Maritime Artists of the Pacific Northwest Coast, 1741–1841.* Seattle: University of Washington Press, 1984.

Howay, Frederic W., ed. *Voyages of the "Columbia" to the Northwest Coast, 1787–1790 and 1790–1793.* Portland: Oregon Historical Society, 1990.

Lamb, W. Kaye, ed. *The Journals and Letters of Sir Alexander Mackenzie.* Cambridge: Hakluyt Society, 1970.

——. *The Voyage of George Vancouver, 1791–1795.* 4 vols; Cambridge: Hakluyt Society, 1984.

Lower, J. Arthur. *Ocean of Destiny: A Concise History of the North Pacific, 1500–1978.* Vancouver: University of British Columbia Press, 1978.

Nokes, J. Richard. *Columbia's River: The Voyages of Robert Gray, 1787–1793.* Tacoma: Washington State Historical Society, 1991.

Pethick, Derek. *First Approaches to the Northwest Coast.* Vancouver: J. J. Douglas, 1976.

——. *The Nootka Connection: Europe and the Northwest Coast, 1790–1795.* Vancouver: Douglas and McIntyre, 1980.

Ronda, James P. "Calculating Ouragon." *Oregon Historical Quarterly* 94 (summer/fall 1993): 121–40. Perceptions of the early Oregon country.

Smith, Barbara Sweetland, and Redmond J. Barnett. *Russian America: The Forgotten Frontier.* Tacoma: Washington State Historical Society, 1990.

Vaughan, Thomas. *Soft Gold: The Fur Trade and Cultural Exchange on the Northwest Coast of America.* Portland: Oregon Historical Society, 1982.

Williams, Jacqueline. "Sailor's Scourge: The Battle Against Scurvy in the Pacific Northwest." *Columbia* 6 (spring 1992): 9–12.


CHAPTER 4: CONTINENTAL DREAMS AND FUR EMPIRES

Allen, John Logan. *Passage through the Garden: Lewis and Clark and the Image of the American Northwest*. Urbana: University of Illinois Press, 1975.

Chittenden, Hiram Martin. *The American Fur Trade of the Far West*. 2 vols. 1935. Reprint, Lincoln: University of Nebraska Press, 1986.

Cline, Gloria Griffen. *Peter Skene Ogden and the Hudson's Bay Company*. Norman: University of Oklahoma Press, 1974.

DeVoto, Bernard, ed. *The Journals of Lewis and Clark*. Boston: Houghton Mifflin, 1953.

Duncan, Janice K. *Minority without a Champion: Kanakas on the Pacific Coast, 1788–1850*. Portland: Oregon Historical Society, 1972.

Franchère, Gabriel. *A Voyage to the Northwest Coast of America*. 1854. Reprint, New York: Citadel, 1968.

Galbraith, John S. *The Hudson's Bay Company as an Imperial Factor, 1821–1869*. Berkeley: University of California Press, 1957.

Goetzmann, William H. *Exploration and Empire: The Explorer and Scientist in the Winning of the American West*. New York: Alfred A. Knopf, 1966.

——. *New Lands, New Men: America and the Second Great Age of Discovery*. New York: Viking, 1986.

Hussey, John A. "The Women of Fort Vancouver." *Oregon Historical Quarterly* 92 (fall 1991): 265–308.

Irving, Washington. *Astoria; or Anecdotes of an Enterprise beyond the Rocky Mountains*. Edited by Richard Wilworth Rust. Boston: Twayne Publishing, 1976.

Jackson, Donald, ed. *Letters of the Lewis and Clark Expedition with Related Documents, 1783–1854*. 2d ed. Urbana: University of Illinois Press, 1978.

——. *Thomas Jefferson and the Stony Mountains: Exploring the West from Monticello*. Urbana: University of Illinois Press, 1981.

Jones, Robert F., ed. *Astorian Adventure: The Journal of Alfred Seton, 1811–1815*. New York: Fordam University Press, 1993.

Lavender, David. *The Way to the Western Sea: Lewis and Clark Across the Continent*. New York: Harper and Row, 1988.

Mackenzie, Alexander. *Voyages from Montreal on the River St. Laurence, through the Continent of North America, to the Frozen and Pacific Oceans: In the Years 1789 and 1793.* 1801. Reprint, New York: Citadel, 1967.

Merk, Frederick, ed. *Fur Trade and Empire: George Simpson's Journal.* rev. ed. Cambridge: Harvard University Press, 1968.

Moulton, Gary E., ed. *The Journals of the Lewis and Clark Expedition.* 9 vols. to date. Lincoln: University of Nebraska Press, 1983–.

Rich, E. E. *The History of the Hudson's Bay Company, 1670–1870.* 2 vols. London: Hudson's Bay Record Society, 1958–59.

Ronda, James P. *Astoria and Empire.* Lincoln: University of Nebraska Press, 1990.

——. *Lewis and Clark among the Indians.* Lincoln: University of Nebraska Press, 1984.

Ross, Alexander. *Adventures of the First Settlers on the Oregon or Columbia River, 1810–1813.* 1849. Reprint, Lincoln: University of Nebraska Press, 1986.

Townsend, John Kirk. *Across the Rockies to the Columbia.* 1839. Abridged reprint, Lincoln: University of Nebraska Press, 1978. Originally publishes as *Narrative of a Journey Across the Rocky Mountains to the Columbia River.*

## PROFILE: THE WHITMAN TRAGEDY

Drury, Clifford M. *Marcus and Narcissa Whitman and the Opening of Old Oregon.* 2 vols. Glendale CA: Arthur H. Clark, 1973.

*Idaho Yesterdays* 31 (spring/summer 1987): 2–116. Special issue devoted entirely to the missionary era of Pacific Northwest history.

Jeffrey, Julie Roy. *Converting the West: A Biography of Narcissa Whitman.* Norman: University of Oklahoma Press, 1991.

Ruby, Robert H., and John A. Brown. *The Cayuse Indians: Imperial Tribesmen of Old Oregon.* Norman: University of Oklahoma Press, 1972.

Thompson, Erwin N. *Shallow Grave at Waiilatpu: The Sagers' West.* Portland: Oregon Historical Society, 1973.

Whitman, Narcissa Prentiss. *My Journal, 1836.* Edited by Lawrence Dodd. Fairfield WA: Ye Galleon Press, 1982.

## CHAPTER 5: BOUND FOR THE PROMISED LAND

Bright, Verne. "The Folklore and History of the 'Oregon Fever.'" *Oregon Historical Quarterly* 52 (December 1951): 241–53.

Carriker, Robert C. *Father Peter John De Smet: Jesuit in the West.* Norman: University of Oklahoma Press, 1995.

Clark, Malcolm, Jr. *Eden Seekers: The Settlement of Oregon, 1818–1862.* Boston: Houghton Mifflin, 1981.

Drury, Clifford M. *Nine Years with the Spokane Indians: The Diary, 1838–1848, of Elkanah Walker.* Glendale, CA: Arthur H. Clark, 1976.

Faragher, John Mack. *Women and Men on the Overland Trail.* New Haven: Yale University Press, 1979.

Horner, Patricia V. "Mary Richardson Walker: The Shattered Dreams of a Missionary Woman." *Montana, the Magazine of Western History* 32 (summer 1982): 20–31. Issue devoted to nineteenth-century women on the frontier.

Johansen, Dorothy O. "A Working Hypothesis for the Study of Migrations." *Pacific Historical Review* 36 (February 1967): 1–12. Examines why westering emigrants selected either Oregon or California as destinations.

Loewenberg, Robert J. *Equality on the Oregon Frontier: Jason Lee and the Methodist Mission, 1834–43.* Seattle: University of Washington Press, 1976.

Merriam, Paul. "Riding the Wind: Cape Horn Passage to Oregon, 1840s and 1850s." *Oregon Historical Quarterly* 77 (March 1976): 37–60.

Nash, John J. "The Salmon River Mission of 1855." *Idaho Yesterdays* 11 (spring 1967): 22–31.

Newsom, David. *The Western Observer, 1805–1882.* Portland: Oregon Historical Society, 1972.

Peterson, Jacqueline. *Sacred Encounters: Father DeSmet and the Indians of the Rocky Mountain West.* Norman: University of Oklahoma Press, 1993.

Prucha, Francis Paul. "Two Roads to Conversion: Protestant and Catholic Missionaries in the Pacific Northwest." *Pacific Northwest Quarterly* 79 (October 1988): 130–37.

Unruh, John D., Jr. *The Plains Across: The Overland Emigrants and the Trans-Mississippi West, 1840–1860.* Urbana: University of Illinois Press, 1979.

Warre, H. J. *Overland to Oregon in 1845: Impressions of a Journey across North America.* Edited by Madeline Major-Fregeau. Ottawa: Public Archives of Canada, 1976.

*Wilderness Kingdom: Indian Life in the Rocky Mountains: 1840–1847: The Journals and Paintings of Nicholas Point, S.J.* Translated by Joseph P. Donnelly. New York: Holt, Rinehart and Winston, 1967.

CHAPTER 6: OREGON COUNTRY

Boag, Peter G. *Environment and Experience: Settlement Culture in Nineteenth-Century Oregon.* Berkeley: University of California Press, 1992.

Bordwell, Constance. "Delay and Wreck of the Peacock: An Episode in the Wilkes Expedition." *Oregon Historical Quarterly* 92 (summer 1991): 117–98.

Bowen, William A. *The Willamette Valley: Migration and Settlement on the Oregon Frontier.* Seattle: University of Washington Press, 1978.

Carey, Charles H. *General History of Oregon.* 1922. Reprint, Portland: Binfords & Mort, 1971. Provides a detailed study of Oregon's territorial years.

Graebner, Norman A. *Empire on the Pacific: A Study in American Continental Expansion.* New York: Ronald Press, 1955.

Hendrickson, James E. *Joe Lane of Oregon: Machine Politics and the Sectional Crisis, 1849–1861.* New Haven: Yale University Press, 1967.

Hussey, John A. *Champoeg: Place of Transition; A Disputed History.* Portland: Oregon Historical Society, 1967.

Johnson, David Alan. *Founding the Far West: California, Oregon, and Nevada, 1840–1890.* Berkeley: University of California Press, 1992.

Merk, Frederick. *The Oregon Question: Essays in Anglo-American Diplomacy and Politics.* Cambridge: Harvard University Press, 1967.

Murray, Keith A. *The Pig War.* Tacoma: Washington State Historical Society, 1968.

O'Donnell, Terence. *An Arrow in the Earth: General Joel Palmer and the Indians of Oregon.* Portland: Oregon Historical Society Press, 1991.

Throckmorton, Arthur L. *Oregon Argonauts: Merchant Adventurers on the Western Frontier.* Portland: Oregon Historical Society, 1961.


CHAPTER 7: GROWING PAINS

Arrington, Leonard J., and Davis Bitton. *The Mormon Experience: A History of the Latter-day Saints.* New York: Alfred A. Knopf, 1979.

Bensell, Royal A. *All Quiet on the Yamhill: The Civil War in Oregon; The Journal of Corporal Royal A. Bensell, Company D, Fourth California Infantry.* Edited by Gunther Barth. Eugene: University of Oregon Books, 1959.

DeLorme, Roland L. "Westward the Bureaucrats: Government Officials on the Washington and Oregon Frontiers." *Arizona and the West* 22 (autumn 1980): 223–36.

——. "Crime and Punishment in the Pacific Northwest Territories: A Bibliographic Essay." *Pacific Northwest Quarterly* 76 (April 1985): 42–51.

Edwards, G. Thomas. "Holding the Far West for the Union: The Army in 1861." *Civil War History* 14 (December 1968): 307–24.

Johannsen, Robert W. *Frontier Politics and the Sectional Conflict: The Pacific Northwest on the Eve of the Civil War*. Seattle: University of Washington Press, 1955.

Josephy, Alvin M., Jr. *The Civil War in the American West*. New York: Alfred A. Knopf, 1991.

Limbaugh, Ronald H. *Rocky Mountain Carpetbaggers: Idaho's Territorial Governors, 1863–1890*. Moscow: University Press of Idaho, 1982.

Hilleary, William M. *A Webfoot Volunteer: The Diary of William M. Hilleary, 1864–1866*. Edited by Robert B. Nelson and Preston E. Onstad. Corvallis: Oregon State University Press, 1965. Firsthand account of military life in the Pacific Northwest during the Civil War.

McClelland, John, Jr. "Almost Columbia, Triumphantly Washington." *Columbia* 2 (summer 1988): 3–11.

Richards, Kent D. *Isaac I. Stevens: Young Man in a Hurry*. Provo: Brigham Young University Press, 1979.

Swan, James G. *The Northwest Coast, or, Three Years' Residence in Washington Territory*. 1857. Reprint, New York: Harper and Row, 1969.

Wells, Merle W. *Gold Camps and Silver Cities: Nineteenth Century Mining in Central and Southern Idaho*. Moscow: Idaho Department of Lands/Bureau of Mines and Geology, 1983.

Wells, Merle. "Walla Walla's Vision of a Greater Washington." *Idaho Yesterdays* 10 (fall 1966): 20–32.

CHAPTER 8: HOLES IN THE SOCIAL FABRIC

Beckham, Stephen Dow. *Requiem for a People: The Rogue Indians and the Frontiersmen*. Norman: University of Oklahoma Press, 1971.

Beeton, Beverly, and G. Thomas Edwards. "Susan B. Anthony's Woman Suffrage Crusade in the American West." *Journal of the West* 21 (April 1982): 5–15.

Brown, Mark H. *The Flight of the Nez Perce*. New York: G. P. Putnam's Sons, 1967.

Burns, Robert Ignatius. *The Jesuits and the Indian Wars of the Northwest*. New Haven: Yale University Press, 1966.

Edwards, G. Thomas. *Sowing Good Seeds: The Northwest Suffrage Campaigns of Susan B. Anthony*. Portland: Oregon Historical Society Press, 1990.

Fahey, John. "The Nevada Bloomer Case." *Columbia* 2 (summer 1988): 42–45.

Fisher, Robin. "Indian Warfare and Two Frontiers: A Comparison of British Columbia and Washington Territory during the Early Years of Settlement." *Pacific Historical Review* 50 (February 1981): 31–51.

Gay, E. Jane. *With the Nez Perces: Alice Fletcher in the Field, 1889–92*. Lincoln: University of Nebraska Press, 1981.

Gibbs, Granville H. "Mormonism in Idaho Politics, 1880–1890." *Utah Historical Quarterly* 21 (October 1953): 285–305.

Josephy, Alvin M. *The Nez Perce Indians and the Opening of the Northwest*. New Haven: Yale University Press, 1965.

Lavender, David. *Let Me Be Free: The Nez Perce Tragedy*. New York: HarperCollins, 1992.

McLagan, Elizabeth. *A Peculiar Paradise: A History of Blacks in Oregon, 1788–1940*. Portland: Georgian Press, 1980.

Madsen, Brigham D. *The Shoshoni Frontier and the Bear River Massacre*. Salt Lake City: University of Utah Press, 1985.

Mark, Joan. *A Stranger in Her Native Land: Alice Fletcher and the American Indians*. Lincoln: University of Nebraska Press, 1988.

Moynihan, Ruth Barnes. *Rebel for Rights: Abigail Scott Duniway*. New Haven: Yale University Press, 1983.

Murray, Keith A. *The Modocs and Their War*. Norman: University of Oklahoma Press, 1971.

Schlicke, Carl P. *General George Wright: Guardian of the Pacific Coast*. Norman: University of Oklahoma Press, 1988.

Stern, Theodore. *The Klamath Tribe: A People and Their Reservation*. Seattle: University of Washington Press, 1965.

Stratton, David H. "The Snake River Massacre of Chinese Miners, 1887." In *A Taste of the West: Essays in Honor of Robert G. Athearn*, edited by Duane A. Smith. Boulder CO: Pruett Publishing, 1983.

Taylor, Quintard. "The Emergence of Black Communities in the Pacific Northwest, 1865–1910." *Journal of Negro History* 64 (fall 1979): 342–54.

Trafzer, Clifford E., and Richard D. Scheuerman. *Renegade Tribe: The Palouse Indians and the Invasion of the Inland Pacific Northwest*. Pullman: Washington State University Press, 1986.

Wells, Merle W. *Anti-Mormonism in Idaho, 1872–92*. Provo: Brigham Young University Press, 1978.

White, Sid, and W. E. Solberg, eds. *Peoples of Washington: Perspectives on Cultural Diversity.* Pullman: Washington State University Press, 1989.

Wilfong, Cheryl. *Following the Nez Perce Trail: A Guide to the Nee-Me-Poo National Historic Trail with Eyewitness Accounts.* Corvallis: Oregon State University Press, 1990.

Wunder, John. "The Courts and the Chinese in Frontier Idaho." *Idaho Yesterdays* 25 (spring 1981): 23–32.

Wynne, Robert Edward. *Reaction to the Chinese in the Pacific Northwest and British Columbia, 1850–1910.* New York: Arno Press, 1978.

PROFILE: HENRY VILLARD AND THE LAST SPIKE

Grinnell, George Bird. "Building the Northern Pacific." *Idaho Yesterdays* 16 (winter 1972–73): 10–13. First-person account from 1882.

Hedges, James B. *Henry Villard and the Railways of the Northwest.* New Haven: Yale University Press, 1930.

Nolan, Edward W. "Not without Labor and Expense: The Villard–Northern Pacific Excursion, 1883." *Montana, the Magazine of Western History* 33 (summer 1983). 2–11.

——. *Northern Pacific Views: The Railroad Photography of F. Jay Haynes, 1876–1905.* Helena: Montana Historical Society Press, 1983.

Seckinger, Katherine Villard, ed. "The Great Railroad Celebration, 1883: A Narrative by Francis Jackson Garrison." *Montana, the Magazine of Western History* 33 (summer 1983): 12–23.

Smalley, Eugene V. *History of the Northern Pacific Railroad.* New York: G. P. Putnam's Sons, 1883.

CHAPTER 9: METROPOLITAN CORRIDORS

Athearn, Robert G. *Union Pacific Country.* Chicago: Rand McNally, 1971.

Fahey, John. *Inland Empire: D. C. Corbin and Spokane.* Seattle: University of Washington Press, 1965.

——, *The Inland Empire: Unfolding Years, 1879–1929.* Seattle: University of Washington Press, 1986. Especially the chapter titled "The Railroads: Beneficent, Malignant, Fickle."

Hidy, Ralph W., Muriel E. Hidy, and Roy V. Scott, with Don L. Hofsommer. *The Great Northern Railway: A History.* Boston: Harvard Business School Press, 1988.

Hofsommer, Don L. *The Southern Pacific, 1901–1985.* College Station: Texas A&M University Press, 1986.

Jackson, W. Turrentine. *Wells Fargo and Co. in Idaho Territory*. Boise: Idaho State Historical Society, 1984.

Johansen, Dorothy. "The Oregon Steam Navigation Company: An Example of Capitalism on the Frontier." *Pacific Historical Review* 10 (June 1941): 179–88.

Lewty, Peter J. *To the Columbia Gateway: The Oregon Railway and the Northern Pacific, 1879–1884*. Pullman: Washington State University Press, 1987.

Martin, Albro. *James J. Hill and the Opening of the Northwest*. New York: Oxford University Press, 1976.

Meinig, D. W. *The Great Columbia Plain: A Historical Geography, 1805–1910*. Seattle: University of Washington Press, 1968. Especially chapter 9, "Strategy: Settlers and Railroads, 1870–90."

Mills, Randall V. *Stern-Wheelers up Columbia: A Century of Steamboating in the Oregon Country*. 1947. Reprint, Lincoln: University of Nebraska Press, 1977.

Nicandri, David L. "The Romantic Northwest of the Army Engineers." *Columbia* 12 (winter 1989): 38–45.

Richards, Kent D. "The Young Napoleons." *Columbia* 3 (winter 1989/90): 21–28. Isaac I. Stevens, George B. McClellan, and the Cascade Mountains Route.

Runte, Alfred. *Trains of Discovery: Western Railroads and the National Parks*. Rev. ed. Niwot, CO: Roberts Rinehart, 1990.

Schwantes, Carlos A. *Railroad Signatures Across the Pacific Northwest*. Seattle: University of Washington Press, 1993.

Stilgoe, John R. *Metropolitan Corridor: Railroads and the American Scene*. New Haven: Yale University Press, 1983.

Strahorn, Carrie Adell. *Fifteen Thousand Miles by Stage*. 1911. Reprint, Lincoln: University of Nebraska Press, 1988.

Weinstein, Robert A. *Tall Ships on Puget Sound: The Marine Photographs of Wilhelm Hester*. Seattle: University of Washington Press, 1978.

Winther, Oscar Osburn. *The Old Oregon Country: A History of Frontier Trade, Transportation, and Travel*. 1950. Reprint, Lincoln: University of Nebraska Press, 1969.

CHAPTER 10: THE STUMPS OF ENTERPRISE

Attebery, Louie W. *Sheep May Safely Graze: A Personal Essay on Tradition and a Contemporary Sheep Ranch*. Moscow: University of Idaho Press, 1992.

Britton, Diane F. *The Iron and Steel Industry in the Far West: Irondale, Washington*. Niwot: University Press of Colorado, 1991.

Carstensen, Vernon. "Distant Markets: The Early Days." *Portage* (autumn 1983): 4–9. Issue devoted to international trade in Washington State.

Coman, Edwin T., Jr., and Helen M. Gibbs. *Time, Tide and Timber: A Century of Pope and Talbot*. Stanford: Stanford University Press, 1959.

Cox, Thomas R. *Mills and Markets: A History of the Pacific Coast Lumber Industry to 1900*. Seattle: University of Washington Press, 1974.

Dodds, Gordon B. *The Salmon King of Oregon: R. D. Hume and the Pacific Fisheries*. Chapel Hill: University of North Carolina Press, 1959.

Ficken, Robert E. *The Forested Land: A History of Lumbering in Western Washington*. Seattle: University of Washington Press, 1987.

Gibson, James R. *Farming the Frontier: The Agricultural Opening of the Oregon Country, 1786–1846*. Seattle: University of Washington Press, 1961.

Greever, William S. *Bonanza West: The Story of the Western Mining Rushes, 1848–1900*. 1963. Reprint, Moscow: University of Idaho Press, 1986.

Grover, David H. *Diamondfield Jack: A Study in Frontier Justice*. Reno: University of Nevada Press, 1968.

Hidy, Ralph W., Frank Ernest Hill, and Allan Nevins. *Timber and Men: The Weyerhaeuser Story*. New York: Macmillan, 1963.

McGregor, Alexander Campbell. *Counting Sheep: From Open Range to Agribusiness on the Columbia Plateau*. Seattle: University of Washington Press, 1982.

Meinig, D. W. *The Great Columbia Plain: A Historical Geography, 1805–1910*. Seattle: University of Washington Press, 1968.

Morgan, Murray. *The Last Wilderness*. New York: Viking Press, 1955.

———. *The Mill on the Boot: The Story of the St. Paul and Tacoma Lumber Company*. Seattle: University of Washington Press, 1982.

Netboy, Anthony. *The Columbia River Salmon and Steelhead Trout: Their Fight for Survival*. Seattle: University of Washington Press, 1980.

Oliphant, J. Orin. *On the Cattle Ranges of the Oregon Country*. Seattle: University of Washington Press, 1968.

Ostler, Jeffrey. "The Origins of the Central Oregon Range War of 1904." *Pacific Northwest Quarterly* 79 (January 1988): 2–9.

Robbins, William G. *American Forestry: A History of National, State, and Private Cooperation*. Lincoln: University of Nebraska Press, 1985.

———. " 'At the End of the Cracked Whip': The Northern West, 1880–1920." *Montana, the Magazine of Western History* 38 (autumn 1988): 2–11.

Seufert, Francis. *Wheels of Fortune.* Edited by Thomas Vaughan. Portland: Oregon Historical Society, 1980. The story of the Seufert Brothers salmon packing company on the Columbia River.

Shepherd, James F. "The Development of Wheat Production in the Pacific Northwest." *Agricultural History* 49 (January 1975): 258–71.

Simpson, Peter K. *The Community of Cattlemen: Social History of the Cattle Industry in Southeastern Oregon, 1869–1912.* Moscow: University of Idaho Press, 1987.

Trimble, William J. *The Mining Advance into the Inland Empire.* Madison: University of Wisconsin, 1914.

Twining, Charles E. *Phil Weyerhaeuser: Lumberman.* Seattle: University of Washington Press, 1985.

Webb, Robert Lloyd. *On the Northwest: Commercial Whaling in the Pacific Northwest, 1790–1967.* Vancouver: University of British Columbia Press, 1988.

Young, James A., and B. Abbott Sparks. *Cattle in the Cold Desert.* Logan: Utah State University Press, 1985.

CHAPTER 11: A QUICKENING PACE OF LIFE:
IMMIGRATION AND URBAN GROWTH

Abbott, Carl. *The Metropolitan Frontier: Cities in the Modern American West.* Tucson: University of Arizona Press, 1993.

——. *Portland: Planning, Politics, and Growth in a Twentieth-Century City.* Lincoln: University of Nebraska Press, 1983.

Brown, Arthur J. "The Promotion of Emigration to Washington, 1854–1909." *Pacific Northwest Quarterly* 36 (January 1945): 3–17.

Clark, Norman H. *Mill Town: A Social History of Everett, Washington, from Its Earliest Beginnings on the Shores of Puget Sound to the Tragic and Infamous Event Known as the Everett Massacre.* Seattle: University of Washington Press, 1970.

Cox, Thomas R. *The Park Builders: A History of State Parks in the Pacific Northwest.* Seattle: University of Washington Press, 1988.

Dahlie, Jorgen. "Old World Paths in the New: Scandinavians Find a Familiar Home in Washington." *Pacific Northwest Quarterly* 61 (April 1970): 65–71.

Edwards, G. Thomas. "Walla Walla: Gateway to the Pacific Northwest Interior." *Montana, the Magazine of Western History* 40 (summer 1990): 29–43.

Etulain, Richard W., ed. *Basques of the Pacific Northwest*. Pocatello: Idaho State University Press, 1991.

Fargo, Lucile F. *Spokane Story*. New York: Columbia University Press, 1950.

Gamboa, Erasmo. "Mexican Mule Packers and Oregon's Second Regiment Mounted Volunteers, 1855–1856." *Oregon Historical Quarterly* 92 (spring 1991): 41–59.

———. "Washington's Mexican Heritage." *Columbia* 3 (fall 1989): 40–45.

MacColl, E. Kimbark. *The Shaping of a City: Business and Politics in Portland, Oregon, 1885 to 1915*. Portland: Georgian Press, 1976.

MacDonald, Norbert. *Distant Neighbors: A Comparative History of Seattle and Vancouver*. Lincoln: University of Nebraska Press, 1987.

Merriam, Paul G. "Urban Elite in the Far West: Portland, Oregon, 1870–1890." *Arizona and the West* 18 (spring 1976): 41–52.

Morgan, Murray. *Puget's Sound: A Narrative of Early Tacoma and the Southern Sound*. Seattle: University of Washington Press, 1979.

———. *Skid Road: An Informal Portrait of Seattle*. Seattle: University of Washington Press, 1982.

Nicandri, David L. *Italians in Washington State: Emigration, 1853–1924*. [Tacoma]: Washington State American Revolution Bicentennial Commission, 1978. Other books in this series study Washington's Chinese, German, Gypsy, Indian, Scots, and Yugoslav populations.

Petersen, Keith C. *Company Town: Potlatch, Idaho, and the Potlatch Lumber Company*. Pullman: Washington State University Press, 1987.

Renk, Nancy F. "Off to the Lakes: Vacationing in North Idaho During the Railroad Era, 1885–1915." *Idaho Yesterdays* 34 (summer 1990): 2–15.

Reps, John W. *Panoramas of Promise: Pacific Northwest Cities and Towns on Nineteenth-Century Lithographs*. Pullman: Washington State University Press, 1984.

Robbins, William G. *Hard Times in Paradise: Coos Bay, Oregon*. Seattle: University of Washington Press, 1988.

Sale, Roger. *Seattle, Past to Present*. Seattle: University of Washington Press, 1976.

Scott, Mary Katsilometes. "The Greek Community in Pocatello, 1890–1941." *Idaho Yesterdays* 28 (fall 1984): 29–36.

Stratton, David H., ed. *Spokane and the Inland Empire: An Interior Pacific Northwest Anthology*. Pullman: Washington State University Press, 1991.

Toll, William. *The Making of an Ethnic Middle Class: Portland Jewry over Four Generations*. Albany: State University of New York Press, 1982.

Taylor, Quintard. "Blacks and Asians in a White City: Japanese Americans and African Americans in Seattle, 1890–1940." *Western Historical Quarterly* 22 (November 1991): 401–29.

Warnock, James. "Entrepreneurs and Progressives: Baseball in the Northwest, 1900–1901." *Pacific Northwest Quarterly* 82 (July 1991): 92–100.

Weinstein, Robert A. *Grays Harbor, 1885–1913.* New York: Viking Press, 1978.

Wells, Merle. *Boise: An Illustrated History.* Woodland Hills CA: Windsor Publications, 1982.

CHAPTER 12: A TIME OF TESTING:
OMNIBUS STATES AND THE EXCESSES OF THE 1890S

Beckett, Paul L. *From Wilderness to Enabling Act: The Evolution of a State of Washington.* Pullman: Washington State University Press, 1968.

Berton, Pierre. *The Klondike Fever: The Life and Death of the Last Great Gold Rush.* New York: Alfred A. Knopf, 1982.

Colson, Dennis C. *Idaho's Constitution: The Tie that Binds.* Moscow: University of Idaho Press, 1991.

Gaboury, William J. *Dissention in the Rockies: A History of Idaho Populism.* New York: Garland Publishing, 1988.

Griffiths, David B. *Populism in the Western United States, 1890–1900;* 2 vols. Lewiston NY: Edwin Mellen Press, 1992.

Hicks, John D. *The Constitutions of the Northwest States.* Lincoln: University of Nebraska Studies, 23 (January/April 1923): 5–152.

Hunt, William R. "Goldfield Gateway." *Columbia* 4 (winter 1990/91): 36–41. On the evolution of the connection between Seattle and Alaska.

Hynding, Alan. *The Public Life of Eugene Semple: Promoter and Politician of the Pacific Northwest.* Seattle: University of Washington Press, 1973.

Limbaugh, Ronald H. *Rocky Mountain Carpetbaggers: Idaho's Territorial Governors, 1863–1890.* Moscow: University Press of Idaho, 1982.

Murray, Keith A. "Statehood for Washington." *Columbia* 2 (winter 1989): 30–35.

Richards, Kent D. "Insurrection, Agitation, and Riots: Police Power and Washington Statehood." *Montana, the Magazine of Western History* 37 (August 1987): 2–21.

Sims, Robert C., and Hope A. Benedict. *Idaho's Governors: Historical Essays on Their Administrations.* Boise: Boise State University, 1992.

Wells, Merle. "Idaho's Season of Political Distress: An Unusual Path to

Statehood." *Montana, the Magazine of Western History* 37 (autumn 1987): 58–67.

——. "The Long Wait for Statehood." *Columbia* 2 (fall 1988): 18–23.

——. "Politics in the Panhandle: Opposition to the Admission of Washington and North Idaho, 1886–1888." *Pacific Northwest Quarterly* 46 (July 1955): 79–89.

CHAPTER 13: REMOVING THE ROUGH EDGES

Bailey, Margaret Jewett. *The Grains; or, Passages in the Life of Ruth Rover with Occasional Pictures of Oregon, Natural and Moral*. 1854. Reprint, Corvallis: Oregon State University Press, 1985.

Bingham, Edwin R., and Glen A. Love, eds. *Northwest Perspectives: Essays on the Culture of the Pacific Northwest*. Seattle: University of Washington Press, 1979.

Bingham, Edwin R. "Pacific Northwest Writing: Reaching For Identity." In *Regionalism and the Pacific Northwest*, edited by William G. Robbins, Robert J. Frank, and Richard E. Ross. Corvallis: Oregon State University Press, 1983.

Davis, H. L. *H. L. Davis: Collected Essays and Short Stories*. 1959. Reprint, Moscow: University of Idaho Press, 1985.

Etulain, Richard. "Novelists of the Northwest: Opportunities for Research." *Idaho Yesterdays* 17 (summer 1973): 24–32. Includes bibliography.

Foote, Mary Hallock. *A Victorian Gentlewoman in the Far West: The Reminiscences of Mary Hallock Foote*. Edited by Rodman Paul. San Marino: Huntington Library, 1972.

Gates, Charles M. *The First Century at the University of Washington, 1861–1961*. Seattle: University of Washington Press, 1961.

Knight, Oliver. "The *Owyhee Avalanche*: The Frontier Newspaper as a Catalyst in Social Change." *Pacific Northwest Quarterly* 58 (April 1967): 74–81.

Nash, Lee. "Harvey Scott's 'Cure for Drones': An Oregon Alternative to Public High Schools." *Pacific Northwest Quarterly* 64 (April 1973): 70–79.

Robbins, William G. "The Historian as Literary Craftsman: The West of Ivan Doig." *Pacific Northwest Quarterly* 78 (October 1987): 134–40.

Simonson, Harold P. "Pacific Northwest Literature: Its Coming of Age." *Pacific Northwest Quarterly* 71 (October 1980): 146–151.

Strelow, Michael, ed. *An Anthology of Northwest Writing: 1900–1950*. Eugene: Northwest Review Books, 1979. Contains a copy of *Status Rerum*, of which Stevens and Davis printed only two hundred.

Warren, Sidney. *Farthest Frontier: The Pacific Northwest*. New York: Macmillan, 1949. Emphasizes high and low culture in the region.

Woodward, Tim. *Tiger on the Road*. Caldwell: Caxton Printers, 1989. A biography of Vardis Fisher.

Wyman, Mark. "Frontier Journalism." *Idaho Yesterdays* 17 (spring 1973): 30–36.

## CHAPTER 14: ENVISIONING A NEW NORTHWEST

Abbott, Carl. *The Great Extravaganza: Portland and the Lewis and Clark Exposition*. Portland: Oregon Historical Society, 1981.

——. "Longview: The Career of a Washington Model City." *Columbia* 4 (summer 1990): 14–20.

Allen, Barbara. *Homesteading the High Desert*. Salt Lake City: University of Utah Press, 1987. Study of homesteading in south-central Oregon in the early twentieth century.

Bosker, Gideon, and Lena Lencek. *Frozen Music: A History of Portland Architecture*. Portland: The Press of the Oregon Historical Society, 1985.

Coate, Charles. "Federal-Local Relationships on the Boise and Minidoka Projects, 1904–1926." *Idaho Yesterdays* 25 (summer 1981): 2–9.

Dunbar, Robert. *Forging New Rights in Western Waters*. Lincoln: University of Nebraska Press, 1983.

Engeman, Richard H. "The 'Seattle Spirit' Meets *The Alaskan*: A Story of Business, Boosterism, and the Arts." *Pacific Northwest Quarterly* 81 (April 1990): 54–66.

Fahl, Ronald H. "S. C. Lancaster and the Columbia River Highway: Engineer as Conservationist." *Oregon Historical Quarterly* 74 (June 1973): 104–44.

Findlay, John M. "Closing the Frontier in Washington: Edmond S. Meany and Frederick Jackson Turner." *Pacific Northwest Quarterly* 82 (April 1991): 59–70.

Garfield, Leonard. "At Home in Washington." *Columbia* 4 (spring 1990): 36–45.

Greenwood, Annie Pike. *We Sagebrush Folks*. 1934. Reprint, Moscow: University of Idaho Press, 1988. Firsthand account of irrigated farming in southern Idaho.

Hart, Arthur A. *Camera Eye on Idaho: Pioneer Photography, 1863–1913.* Caldwell ID: Caxton Printers, 1990.

*Idaho Yesterdays* 30 (spring/summer 1986). Special issue devoted to irrigation in Idaho.

Knight, Oliver. "Robert E. Strahorn, Propagandist for the West." *Pacific Northwest Quarterly* 59 (January 1968): 33–45.

Lovin, Hugh. "Water, Arid Land, and Visions of Advancement on the Snake River Plain." *Idaho Yesterdays* 35 (spring 1991): 3–18.

John M. McClelland. *Longview: The Remarkable Beginnings of a Modern Western City.* Portland: Binfords and Mort, 1949.

Neil, J. Meredith. *Saints and Odd Fellows: A Bicentennial Sample of Idaho Architecture.* Boise: Boise Gallery of Art Association, 1976.

Rydell, Robert. "Visions of Empire: International Expositions in Portland and Seattle, 1905–1909." *Pacific Historical Review* 52 (February 1983): 37–66.

Toedtemeier, Terry. "Oregon Photography: The First Fifty Years." *Oregon Historical Quarterly* 94 (spring 1993): 36–40.

Washington State Office of Archaeology and Historic Preservation. *Built in Washington: 12,000 Years of Pacific Northwest Archaeological Sites and Historic Buildings.* Pullman: Washington State University Press, 1989.

Woodbridge, Sally B., and Roger Montgomery. *A Guide to Architecture in Washington State.* Seattle: University of Washington Press, 1980.

Wright, Patricia, and Lisa B. Reitzes, *Tourtellotte & Hummel of Idaho: The Standard Practice of Architecture.* Logan: Utah State University Press, 1987.

## PROFILE: THE WORLD OF MAY ARKWRIGHT HUTTON

Conlin, Joseph R. "The Haywood Case: An Enduring Riddle." *Pacific Northwest Quarterly* 59 (January 1968): 23–32.

Fahey, John. *The Days of the Hercules.* Moscow: University Press of Idaho, 1978.

Hart, Patricia, and Ivar Nelson. *Mining Town: The Photographic Record of T. N. Barnard and Nellie Stockbridge from the Coeur d'Alenes.* Seattle: University of Washington Press, 1984.

Montgomery, James W. *Liberated Woman: A Life of May Arkwright Hutton.* Fairfield WA: Ye Galleon Press, 1985. Includes a reprint of May Arkwright Hutton's *The Coeur d'Alenes; or, A Tale of the Modern Inquisition in Idaho* (1900).

Siringo, Charles A. *A Cowboy Detective: A True Story of Twenty-Two Years with a World Famous Detective Agency.* 1912. Reprint, Lincoln: University of Nebraska Press, 1988.

Smith, Robert Wayne. *The Coeur d'Alene Mining War of 1892: A Case Study of an Industrial Dispute.* 1961. Reprint, Gloucester MA: Peter Smith, 1968.


CHAPTER 15: COMMONWEALTH OF TOIL

Aiken, Katherine G. " 'It May be Too Soon to Crow': Bunker Hill and Sullivan Company's Efforts to Defeat the Miners' Union, 1890–1900." *Western Historical Quarterly* 24 (August 1993): 309–31.

Alborn, Denise M. "Crimping and Shanghaiing on the Columbia River." *Oregon Historical Quarterly* 93 (fall 1992): 262–91.

Brown, Richard Maxwell. *No Duty the Retreat: Violence and Values in American History and Society.* New York: Oxford University Press, 1991.

Broyles, Glen J. "The Spokane Free Speech Fight, 1909–1910: A Study in IWW Tactics." *Labor History* 19 (spring 1978): 238–52.

Chaplin, Ralph. *Wobbly: The Rough-and-Tumble Story of an American Radical.* Chicago: University of Chicago Press, 1948.

Dembo, Jonathan. *Unions and Politics in Washington State 1885–1935.* New York: Garland Publishing, 1983.

Laurie, Clayton D. "The United States Army and the Labor Radicals of the Coeur d'Alenes: Federal Military Intervention in the Mining Wars of 1892–1899." *Idaho Yesterdays* 37 (summer 1993): 12–29.

LeWarne, Charles Pierce. "The Aberdeen, Washington, Free Speech Fight of 1911–1912." *Pacific Northwest Quarterly* 66 (January 1975): 1–12.

Phipps, Stanley S. *From Bull Pen to Bargaining Table: The Tumultuous Struggle of the Coeur D'Alenes Miners for the Right to Organize, 1887–1942.* New York: Garland Publishing, 1988.

Prouty, Andrew Mason. *More Deadly than War! Pacific Coast Logging, 1827–1981.* New York: Garland Publishing, 1985. Detailed study of work and its hazards in the lumber industry.

Robbins, William G. "Labor in the Pacific Slope Timber Industry: A Twentieth-Century Perspective." *Journal of the West* 25 (April 1986): 8–13.

Schwantes, Carlos A. *Hard Traveling: A Portrait of Work Life in the New Northwest.* Lincoln: University of Nebraska Press, 1994.

——. "The History of Pacific Northwest Labor History." *Idaho Yesterdays* 28 (winter 1985): 23–35.

Stone, Harry W. "Beginning of Labor Movement in the Pacific Northwest." *Oregon Historical Quarterly* 47 (June 1946): 155–64.

Tyler, Robert L. *Rebels of the Woods: The I.W.W. in the Pacific Northwest.* Eugene: University of Oregon Books, 1967.

Williams, William J. "Bloody Sunday Revisited." *Pacific Northwest Quarterly* 71 (April 1980): 50–62. Eyewitness account of the Everett massacre.

Wollner, Craig. *The City Builders: One Hundred Years of Union Carpentry in Portland, Oregon, 1883–1983.* Portland: Oregon Historical Society Press, 1990.

CHAPTER 16: ADJUSTMENTS

Allen, Howard. *Poindexter of Washington: A Study in Progressive Politics.* Carbondale: Southern Illinois University Press, 1981.

Arrington, Leonard J. "The Influenza Epidemic of 1918–1919 in Southern Idaho." *Idaho Yesterdays* 33 (fall 1988): 19–29.

Berner, Richard C. *Seattle 1900–1920: From Boomtown, Urban Turbulence, to Restoration.* Seattle: Charles Press, 1991.

Boylan, Bernard L. "Camp Lewis: Promotion and Construction." *Pacific Northwest Quarterly* 58 (October 1967): 188–95.

Clark, Norman H. *The Dry Years: Prohibition and Social Change in Washington.* Seattle: University of Washington Press, 1965.

Copeland, Tom. *The Centralia Tragedy of 1919: Elmer Smith and the Wobblies.* Seattle: University of Washington Press, 1993.

Friedheim, Robert L. *The Seattle General Strike.* Seattle: University of Washington Press, 1964.

Gaboury, William J. *Dissention in the Rockies: A History of Idaho Populism.* New York: Garland Publishing, 1988.

Graff, Leo W., Jr. *The Senatorial Career of Fred T. DuBois of Idaho, 1890–1907.* New York: Garland Publishing, 1988.

Gunns, Albert F. *Civil Liberties in Crisis: The Pacific Northwest, 1917–1940.* New York: Garland Publishing, 1983.

LeWarne, Charles Pierce. *Utopias on Puget Sound, 1885–1915.* Seattle: University of Washington Press, 1975.

Lovin, Hugh T. "The Red Scare in Idaho, 1916–1918." *Idaho Yesterdays* 17 (fall 1973): 2–13.

McClelland, John M., Jr. *Wobbly War: The Centralia Story.* Tacoma: Washington State Historical Society, 1987.

McClintock, Thomas C. "Seth Lewelling, William S. U'Ren and the Birth of the Oregon Progressive Movement." *Oregon Historical Quarterly* 68 (June 1967): 197–220.

*Oregon Historical Quarterly* 92 (winter 1991/92). Theme issue on various aspects of the Aurora colony.

Rockafellar, Nancy. " 'In Gauze We Trust': Public Health and Spanish Influenza on the Home Front, Seattle, 1918–1919." *Pacific Northwest Quarterly* 77 (July 1986): 104–13.

Ruckman, JoAnn. " 'Knit, Knit, and then Knit': The Women of Pocatello and the War Effort of 1917–1918." *Idaho Yesterdays* 26 (spring 1982): 26–36.

Schwantes, Carlos A. *Radical Heritage: Labor, Socialism, and Reform in Washington and British Columbia, 1885–1917.* Seattle: University of Washington Press, 1979.

Sharbach, Sarah E. "A Woman Acting Alone: Louise Olivereau and the First World War." *Pacific Northwest Quarterly* 78 (January–April 1987): 32–40. Story of a Seattle woman's opposition to the First World War.

Sims, Robert C. "Idaho's Criminal Syndicalism Act: One State's Response to Radical Labor." *Labor History* 15 (fall 1974): 511–29.

Soden, Dale E. "Billy Sunday in Spokane: Revivalism and Social Control" *Pacific Northwest Quarterly* 79 (January 1988): 10–17.

Tripp, Joseph F. "An Instance of Labor and Business Cooperation: Workmen's Compensation in Washington State (1911)." *Labor History* 17 (fall 1976): 530–50.

Woodward, Robert C. "William S. U'Ren, A Progressive Era Personality." *Idaho Yesterdays* 4 (summer 1960): 4–10.

Woolley, Ivan M. "The 1918 'Spanish Influenza' Pandemic in Oregon." *Oregon Historical Quarterly* 64 (September 1963): 246–58.

CHAPTER 17: BIRTH OF THE MODERN

Ashby, Leroy. *The Spearless Leader: Senator Borah and the Progressive Movement in the 1920s.* Urbana: University of Illinois Press, 1972.

Barrett, Gwynn, and Leonard Arrington. "The 1921 Depression: Its Impact on Idaho." *Idaho Yesterdays* 15 (summer 1971): 10–15.

Burton, Robert E. *Democrats of Oregon: The Pattern of Minority Politics, 1900–1956.* Eugene: University of Oregon Books, 1970.

Dembo, Jonathan. "Dave Beck and the Transportation Revolution in the Pacific Northwest, 1917–41." In *Experiences in a Promised Land: Essays in Pacific Northwest History*, edited by G. Thomas Edwards and Carlos A. Schwantes. Seattle: University of Washington Press, 1986.

Horowitz, David. "The Klansman as Outsider: Ethnocultural Solidarity and Antielitism in the Oregon Ku Klux Klan of the 1920s." *Pacific Northwest Quarterly* 80 (January 1989): 12–20.

Johnson, Claudius O. B*orah of Idaho*. 1936. Reprint, Seattle: University of Washington Press, 1967.

LaLande, Jeff. "Beneath the Hooded Robe: Newspapermen, Local Politics, and the Ku Klux Klan in Jackson County, Oregon, 1921–1923." *Pacific Northwest Quarterly* 83 (April 1992): 42–52.

Lovin, Hugh. "The Nonpartisan League and Progressive Renascence in Idaho, 1919–1924." *Idaho Yesterdays* 32 (fall 1988): 2–15.

Neal, Steve. *McNary of Oregon: A Political Biography*. Portland: Western Imprints, 1985.

Pierce, Walter M. *Oregon Cattleman, Governor, Congressman: Memoirs and Times of Walter M. Pierce*. Edited by Arthur H. Bone. Portland: Oregon Historical Society, 1981.

Toy, Eckard V. "The Ku Klux Klan in Oregon." In *Experiences in a Promised Land: Essays in Pacific Northwest History*, edited by G. Thomas Edwards and Carlos A. Schwantes. Seattle: University of Washington Press, 1986.

CHAPTER 18: DEPRESSION DECADE

Arrington, Leonard J. "Idaho and the Great Depression." *Idaho Yesterdays* 13 (summer 1969): 2–8.

Austin, Judith. "The CCC in Idaho." *Idaho Yesterdays* 27 (fall 1983): 13–17.

Berner, Richard C. *Seattle 1921–1940: From Boom to Bust*. Seattle: Charles Press, 1992.

Dembo, Jonathan. "The Pacific Northwest Lumber Industry during the Great Depression." *Journal of the West* 24 (October 1985): 51–62.

Freidel, Frank. "Franklin D. Roosevelt in the Northwest: Informal Glimpses." *Pacific Northwest Quarterly* 76 (October 1985): 122–31.

Lowitt, Richard. *The New Deal and the West*. Bloomington: Indiana University Press, 1984.

McKinley, Charles. *Uncle Sam in the Pacific Northwest: Federal Management of Natural Resources in the Columbia River Valley*. Berkeley: University of California Press, 1952.

Malone, Michael P. *C. Ben Ross and the New Deal in Idaho*. Seattle: University of Washington Press, 1970.

Mullins, William H. *The Depression and the Urban West Coast, 1929–1933: Los Angeles, San Francisco, Seattle, and Portland*. Bloomington: Indiana University Press, 1991.

Neuberger, Richard. *Our Promised Land*. New York: Macmillan, 1938.

Pitzer, Paul C. *Grand Coulee: Harnessing a Dream*. Pullman: Washington State University Press, 1994.

Taber, Ronald W. "Vardis Fisher and the 'Idaho Guide': Preserving the Culture for the New Deal." *Pacific Northwest Quarterly* 59 (April 1968): 68–76.

Tollefson, Gene. *BPA and the Struggle for Power at Cost*. Portland: Bonneville Power Administration, 1987.


PROFILE: TOM MCCALL OF OREGON

McCall, Tom. *Tom McCall: Maverick; An Autobiography with Steve Neal*. Portland: Binford and Mort, 1977.

McCormack, Win. "Eulogy to Tom McCall." In *Profiles of Oregon, 1976–1986*, edited by Win McCormack. Portland: New Oregon Publishers, 1986.

Peirce, Neal R. *The Pacific States of America: People, Politics, and Power in the Five Pacific Basin States*. New York: W. W. Norton, 1972. Chapter on Oregon titled "For God's Sake, Don't Move Here."

Peirce, Neal R., and Jerry Hagstrom. *The Book of America: Inside Fifty States Today*. New York: Warner Books, 1984. Chapter on Oregon titled "Fearing Growth, Seeking Growth."

"Tom (Lawson) McCall." *Current Biography* (1974): 252–54.

Walth, Brent. *Fire at Eden's Gate: Tom McCall and the Oregon Story*. Portland: Oregon Historical Society Press, 1994.


CHAPTER 19: FROM WORLD WAR TO COLD WAR

Abbott, Carl. "Planning for the Home Front in Seattle and Portland, 1940–45." In *The Martial Metropolis: U. S. Cities in War and Peace*, edited by Roger Lotchin. New York: Praeger, 1984.

Daniels, Roger. *Asian America: Chinese and Japanese in the United States since 1850*. Seattle: University of Washington Press, 1988. Especially chapter 6, "Asian Americans and World War II."

———. *Concentration Camps USA: Japanese Americans and World War II*. New York: Holt, Rinehart and Winston, 1972.

Droker, Howard A. "Seattle Race Relations during the Second World War." *Pacific Northwest Quarterly* 67 (October 1976): 163–74.

Gamboa, Erasmo. *Mexican Labor and World War II: Braceros in the Pacific Northwest, 1942–1947*. Austin: University of Texas Press, 1990.

Gerber, Michele Stenehjem. *On the Home Front: The Cold War Legacy of the Hanford Nuclear Site.* Lincoln: University of Nebraska Press, 1992.

McConaghy, Lorraine. "Wartime Boomtown: Kirkland, Washington, a Small Town during World War II." *Pacific Northwest Quarterly* 80 (April 1989): 42–51.

Maben, Manly. *Vanport.* Portland: Oregon Historical Society Press, 1987.

Nash, Gerald. *The American West Transformed: The Impact of the Second World War.* Bloomington: Indiana University Press, 1985.

Ourada, Patricia K. "Reluctant Servants: Conscientious Objectors in Idaho during World War II." *Idaho Yesterdays* 31 (winter 1988): 2–14.

Sanger, S. L. *Hanford and the Bomb: An Oral History of World War II.* Seattle: Living History Press, 1989.

Schwantes, Carlos A., ed. *The Pacific Northwest in World War II.* Manhattan KS: Sunflower University Press, 1986. Essays on World War II in the Pacific Northwest and Alaska.

Serling, Robert J. *Legend and Legacy: The Story of Boeing and Its People.* New York: St. Martin's Press, 1992.

Simpich, Frederick, Sr. "Wartime in the Pacific Northwest." *National Geographic Magazine* 82 (October 1942): 421–64.

Sims, Robert C. " 'A Fearless, Patriotic, Clean-Cut Stand': Idaho's Governor Clark and Japanese-American Relocation in World War II." *Pacific Northwest Quarterly* 70 (April 1979): 75–81.

Taylor, Quintard. "The Great Migration: The Afro-American Communities of Seattle and Portland during the 1940s." *Arizona and the West* 23 (summer 1981): 109–26.

Webber, Bert. *Retaliation: Japanese Attacks and Allied Countermeasures on the Pacific Coast in World War II.* Corvallis: Oregon State University Press, 1975.

Woodward, William, ed. *Military Influences on Washington History: Proceedings of a Conference.* Tacoma: Washington Army National Guard, 1984. Covers all facets of Washington's military history.

CHAPTER 20: ROLLER-COASTER YEARS

Abbott, Carl. "Regional City and Network City: Portland and Seattle in the Twentieth Century." *Western Historical Quarterly* 23 (August 1992): 293–319.

Chasan, Daniel Jack. *The Fall of the House of WPPSS.* Seattle: Sasquatch Publishing, 1985.

Cumming, William. *Sketchbook: A Memoir of the 1930s and the Northwest School.* Seattle: University of Washington Press, 1984. A memoir treatment of Morris Graves, Mark Tobey, Guy Anderson, Kenneth Callahan, and others.

Dodds, Gordon B., and Craig E. Wollner. *The Silicon Forest: High Tech in the Portland Area, 1945–1986.* Portland: Oregon Historical Society Press, 1990.

Findlay, John M. *Magic Lands: Western Cityscapes and American Culture after 1940.* Berkeley: University of California Press, 1992. Especially chapter 5 on Seattle's World Fair of 1962.

Gamboa, Erasmo. "Mexican Migration into Washington State: A History, 1940–1950." *Pacific Northwest Quarterly* 72 (July 1981): 121–31.

[Norwood, Gus]. *Columbia River Power for the People: A History of the Policies of the Bonneville Power Administration.* Portland: Bonneville Power Administration, 1981.

Pitzer, Paul C. "A 'Farm-in-a-Day': The Publicity Stunt and the Celebrations that Initiated the Columbia Basin Project." *Pacific Northwest Quarterly* 82 (January 1991): 2–7.

Pope, Daniel. "Seduced and Abandoned." *Columbia* 5 (fall 1991): 12–20. Utilities and the wpss nuclear plants 4 and 5.

Robbins, William G. "Lumber Production and Community Stability: A View from the Pacific Northwest." *Journal of Forest History* 31 (October 1987): 187–96.

Sanders, Jane. *Cold War on the Campus: Academic Freedom at the University of Washington, 1946–64.* Seattle: University of Washington Press, 1979.

Slatta, Richard W., and Maxine P. Atkinson. "The 'Spanish Origin' Population of Oregon and Washington: A Demographic Profile, 1980." *Pacific Northwest Quarterly* 75 (July 1984): 108–16.

CHAPTER 21: THE POLITICS OF ANXIETY AND AFFLUENCE

Ashby, LeRoy. "Frank Church Goes to the Senate: The Idaho Election of 1956." *Pacific Northwest Quarterly* 78 (January/April 1987): 17–31.

Ashby, LeRoy, and Rod Gramer. *Fighting the Odds: The Life of Senator Frank Church.* Pullman: Washington State University Press, 1994.

Burton, Robert E. *Democrats of Oregon: The Pattern of Minority Politics, 1900–1956.* Eugene: University of Oregon Books, 1970.

Church, F. Forrester. *Father and Son: A Personal Biography of Senator Frank Church of Idaho by His Son.* Boston: Faber and Faber, 1985.

Eells, Robert, and Bartell Nyberg. *Lonely Walk: The Life of Senator Mark Hatfield.* Portland: Multnomah Press, 1979.

Hagstrom, Jerry. *Beyond Reagan: The New Landscape of American Politics.* New York: W. W. Norton, 1988.

Neal, Steve, ed. *They Never Go Back to Pocatello: The Selected Essays of Richard Neuberger.* Portland: Oregon Historical Society Press, 1988.

Neuberger, Richard L. *Adventures in Politics: We Go to the Legislature.* New York: Oxford University Press, 1954.

Newbill, James G. "William O. Douglas: Of a Man and His Mountains." *Pacific Northwest Quarterly* 79 (July 1988): 90–97.

Ognibene, Peter J. *Scoop: The Life and Politics of Henry M. Jackson.* New York: Stein and Day, 1975.

Peterson, F. Ross. *Prophet without Honor: Glen Taylor and the Fight for American Liberalism.* Lexington: University of Kentucky Press, 1974.

Pitzer, Paul C. "Dorothy McCullough Lee: The Successes and Failures of 'Dottie-Do-Good.'" *Oregon Historical Quarterly* 91 (summer 1990): 5–42.

Prochnau, William W., and Richard W. Larsen. *A Certain Democrat: Senator Henry M. Jackson, A Political Biography.* Englewood Cliffs NJ: Prentice Hall, 1972.

Smith, A. Robert. *The Tiger in the Senate: The Biography of Wayne Morse.* New York: Doubleday, 1962.

Stapilus, Randy. *Paradox Politics: People and Power in Idaho.* Boise: Ridenbaugh Press, 1988.

CHAPTER 22: ENVIRONMENT AT RISK

Abbott, Carl, and Deborah Howe. "The Politics of Land-Use Law in Oregon: Senate Bill 100, Twenty Years After." *Oregon Historical Quarterly* 94 (spring 1993): 4–35.

Ashworth, William. *Hells Canyon.* New York: Hawthorn Books, 1977. Legislative and political history of the Hells Canyon controversy.

Barker, Rocky. *Saving All the Parts: Reconciling Economics and the Endangered Species Act.* Washington DC: Island Press, 1993.

Casner, Nicholas A. "Toxic River: Politics and Coeur d'Alene Mining Pollution in the 1930s." *Idaho Yesterdays* 35 (fall 1991): 2–19.

Chasan, Daniel Jack. *The Water Link: A History of Puget Sound as a Resource.* Seattle: University of Washington, 1981.

Dietrich, William. *The Final Forest: The Battle for the Last Great Trees of the Pacific Northwest.* New York: Simon and Schuster, 1992.

Lien, Carsten. *Olympic Battleground: The Power Politics of Timber Preservation.* San Francisco: Sierra Club Books, 1991.

Loeb, Paul. *Nuclear Culture: Living and Working in the World's Largest Atomic Complex.* Philadelphia: New Society Publishers, 1986. Account of Richland, Washington, and the Hanford Nuclear Reservation.

Pyle, Robert Michael. *Wintergreen: Rambles in a Ravaged Land.* New York: Charles Scribner's Sons, 1986. Reflections on the environment of the Willapa Hills area of southwestern Washington.

Rabe, Fred, and David C. Flaherty. *The River of Green and Gold.* Moscow: Idaho Research Foundation, 1974. Environmental history of the Coeur d'Alene River.

Runte, Alfred. "Burlington Northern and the Legacy of Mount Saint Helens." *Pacific Northwest Quarterly* 74 (July 1983): 116–23.

Seideman, David. *Showdown at Opal Creek: The Battle for America's Last Wilderness.* New York: Carroll & Graf, 1993. Logging controversies in the modern Pacific Northwest.

White, Richard. *Land Use, Environment, and Social Change: The Shaping of Island County, Washington.* Seattle: University of Washington Press, 1980. This is a model environmental history.

——. *The Organic Machine: The Remaking of the Columbia River.* New York: Hill and Wang, 1995.

EPILOGUE: REDEFINING THE PACIFIC NORTHWEST

Ajo, James A. *The Politics of Righteousness: Idaho Christian Patriotism.* Seattle: University of Washington Press, 1990.

Duncan, Dayton. *Miles from Nowhere: Tales From America's Contemporary Frontier.* New York: Viking Penguin, 1993.

Robbins, William G., Robert J. Frank, and Richard E. Ross, eds. *Regionalism and the Pacific Northwest.* Corvallis: Oregon State University Press, 1983. Perceptive essays on recent trends in Pacific Northwest regionalism by Richard Maxwell Brown, John M. McClelland Jr., David Sarasohn, and Richard White.

# INDEX